Psychiatric Rehabilitation

Psychiatric Rehabilitation

Third Edition

Carlos W. Pratt
Kenneth J. Gill
Nora M. Barrett
Melissa M. Roberts

*Department of Psychiatric
Rehabilitation & Counseling Professions
School of Health Related Professions
Rutgers - The State University of New Jersey*

AMSTERDAM • BOSTON • HEIDELBERG • LONDON
NEW YORK • OXFORD • PARIS • SAN DIEGO
SAN FRANCISCO • SINGAPORE • SYDNEY • TOKYO

Academic Press is an imprint of Elsevier

Academic Press is an imprint of Elsevier
32 Jamestown Road, London NW1 7BY, UK
225 Wyman Street, Waltham, MA 02451, USA
525 B Street, Suite 1800, San Diego, CA 92101-4495, USA

Notice

No responsibility is assumed by the publisher for any injury and/or damage to persons or property as a matter of products liability, negligence or otherwise, or from any use or operation of any methods, products, instructions or ideas contained in the material herein.

Because of rapid advances in the medical sciences, in particular, independent verification of diagnoses and drug dosages should be made

British Library Cataloguing-in-Publication Data
A catalogue record for this book is available from the British Library.

Library of Congress Cataloging-in-Publication Data
A catalog record for this book is available from the Library of Congress.

ISBN : 978-0-12-387002-5

For information on all Academic Press publications
visit our website at elsevierdirect.com

Typeset by TNQ Books and Journals Pvt Ltd.
www.tnq.co.in

Printed and bound in United States of America

13 14 15 16 17   10 9 8 7 6 5 4 3 2 1

Working together
to grow libraries in
developing countries

www.elsevier.com • www.bookaid.org

Dedication

This book is dedicated to people with psychiatric disabilities and to the psychiatric rehabilitation providers who strive to improve the quality of their lives and promote their recovery.

Contents

Foreword

As you will discover in this text, the field of psychiatric rehabilitation (PsyR) has seen many changes since 1975, when the International Association of Psychosocial Rehabilitation Services (IAPSRS, now USPRA) was established. Indeed, many significant changes have occurred since 1999, when the first edition of this book was published. For new practitioners, and students planning to enter this exciting field, an understanding of history helps give a context for services offered today. Throughout this text, you will find descriptions of how we got where we are today and of the key players who helped get us here.

Although I was not present at the "birth" of IAPSRS, my work in the mental health field parallels the trajectory of PsyR. Sometimes, I feel a bit like Forrest Gump (being in the right place at the right time). I was fortunate to have had early exposure to ideas and people who sparked and then affirmed my commitment to the principles of choice and voice (self-determination and empowerment). Because of that early exposure, I was driven to find and nurture a community of like-minded thinkers and, ultimately, was spared the challenge of unlearning, as the concepts of recovery and rehabilitation have been more widely accepted.

The ideas that influenced me came from skeptics and radicals like R. D. Laing and Thomas Szasz, who doubted and denied the existence of "mental illness," and from well-known counseling theorists like Rollo May and Carl Rogers, who advocated for understanding the unique perspective of each individual service user. From philosophers like Alan Watts and Ludwig Wittgenstein, and from fiction, including the works of Aldous Huxley, I developed a sense that we each live within our own experience. For people who get diagnosed with a psychiatric disorder, some experiences can be difficult and frightening, making it difficult to manage from day to day. While I never fully subscribed to the idea that mental illnesses are a myth, I have retained the belief that it is not possible to understand the "illness" without understanding the person. The PsyR principles of individualizing services, active involvement of the service user, and a focus on strengths became important to me long before I had heard of PsyR.

With key PsyR values as my foundation, it was a good fit when I learned about social skills teaching through my college internship in 1973, and about the importance of environment when I volunteered, and was later employed, at the Syracuse Psychopathic Hospital, which relocated to become Hutchings Psychiatric Center—an award-winning re-envisioning of an inpatient facility. Moving people from a large and impersonal ward to an attractive and "normal-looking" setting (with small living rooms and kitchenettes on multiple floors) was significant and provided respect and dignity to the people who stayed there.

When I moved to Boston, I met Isaiah Uliss and Judi Chamberlin—visionaries both, and powerful advocates. Chamberlin was tireless in her fight for human rights within the mental health system, and continued fighting for dignity in care even when she was in hospice in her final months. Uliss, a former organizer for the Teamsters, was largely responsible for opening USPRA membership to people who had a psychiatric condition. His lapel button said "speak loudly," which was both practical advice (he was hard-of-hearing) and a metaphor for advocacy. They taught me that "recovery is real" long before I ever heard the phrase.

Over my first years in the mental health field, I was lucky to learn early on to really listen to people using my services, rather than to categorize, label, and objectify them. I consider myself fortunate to have learned this before I was taught otherwise in professional training settings. From many people, both service users and service providers, I heard the same message—change in the mental health system was both needed and possible.

As described in this text, change has occurred. Public inpatient facilities may still seem to be too numerous, too full, and too often either benignly unhelpful or outright harmful. Yet, even there, change has occurred for the better. When I applied for a job in 1975 at a public institution, I was told that the men on one unit were taken into the courtyard in warm weather, stripped from the waist down, and hosed off—it saved time. A few years later, when some units in that institution closed, I met a man who had lived there since childhood, yet whose primary disability was a hearing impairment. He was successful living on his own, and, within months of discharge, he had started his own business mowing lawns and doing odd jobs. That institution is now gone, along with many others, and positive changes are happening in many of the inpatient facilities that remain.

"Work promotes recovery" is an assumption of PsyR that was present as an idealistic vision in the early days, but is now proven and well accepted by experts, although implementation lags behind knowledge in many locales. Clubhouses, which were the foundation of IAPSRS, expect contributions from all members to work inside the club, and now support growing numbers of workers outside the club. Supported employment and its close relative supported education bring hope and opportunity to many who, in spite of regulatory disincentives, take on competitive jobs. A new emphasis on financial literacy and asset development is a sign that many people in recovery are now working and can benefit from support in managing their paychecks.

Psychotropic medications have been around for a long time now (Thorazine, often cited as the first, is about as old as I am). They have contributed to symptom control, benefiting many. In the mid-1970s, work was under way on testing a new generation of medication, and I worked on an inpatient unit where a drug trial was being conducted. I saw psychosis clear completely for a young man who had been alert and active, although psychotic, on a steady dose of 1000 mg of Thorazine, only to see him laid low from a physical illness that, in retrospect, must have been agranulocytosis. This raised my suspicion that the medications brought dangers along with benefits, which was confirmed first by conversations with many people taking medications and, later, by research. The recent work of Robert Whitaker, admittedly controversial, has raised further questions about the value and best use of medications.

One clear danger of medications for psychosis is weight gain and, often, metabolic syndrome—a big contributor to the shortened lifespan of people being treated for a serious mental illness. Peggy Swarbrick and colleagues are raising awareness of the need to prevent and, if possible, reverse many of the dangerous physical conditions that coexist with psychiatric disorders. A national effort to improve physical health, combined with recent changes in the health care system (and more to come), hold promise for helping people regain the physical capacity for an active life, making it easier to work, to live independently, and to participate in the community.

PsyR recognizes that a person-centered and person-driven rehabilitation process bases interventions on each individual's uniquely meaningful goals. In my work at the Boston University Center for Psychiatric Rehabilitation, I developed a deeper understanding of both the "person-centered" and the "rehabilitation" parts of PsyR. In teaching a "technology" for helping people achieve their goals, I became increasingly aware that PsyR is as much a philosophy as a practice. Learning PsyR can be a transformative experience for practitioners, as they set aside the urgency to fix what they see as "the problem" and become more like a catalyst that stimulates growth, following the person's own timeline, building on strengths, and bolstering the person's own efforts.

Of course, there's still a lot to do. More change is needed. Most significant, perhaps, is the need to reduce the time lag between discovering what works and actually doing it. When it takes 10, 20, or even 30 years to get to the point where the field begins to implement what works, there are too many individuals who are unnecessarily losing decades of their lives to discomfort, distress, and despair. Better training, using more effective and efficient methods, and taking advantage of new instructional technologies are key to closing the knowledge gap. This text, which summarizes the history and current practice of PsyR, certainly helps to get the word out.

Granted, systems change is like turning a battleship—you can't do it quickly. But practice change can be swift, if each practitioner takes responsibility for learning and sharing new ideas. Recognizing that the only constant is change, practitioners, service teams, and programs can challenge themselves to improve daily. Of course, all levels of the system are overtaxed—burdened by too much to do and too few people to do it. Funding restrictions are a reality and a barrier to change. But making small changes costs little or nothing—such as asking, "If you were working, what sort of work would interest you?" instead of asking, "Do you want to work?" or, more commonly, neglecting the topic of employment altogether.

I am honored to be invited, again, to write the foreword for this third edition of *Psychiatric Rehabilitation*. I am fortunate to know the authors, and count it as another piece of luck in my professional development that I have had the chance to collaborate with them. As I mentioned in the second edition (and can't think how to improve what I said then), I appreciate both their personal and professional qualities. They are active drivers of change within the field, and have invested much time and effort in improving the quality of the PsyR workforce—through their academic programs, through training in the field, and through their commitment to raising standards through certification of practitioners.

The need for a third edition so soon is evidence of the changes occurring in the field. A text such as this one—well organized and accessible to the wide variety of students and practitioners in the field—will go a long way toward helping to prepare the workforce needed to do the jobs of tomorrow. As Forrest Gump would say, "Life is like a box of chocolates; you never know what you're going to get." I can't predict exactly what the mental health system will look like in 2024, on the 50th birthday of IAPSRS. I hope for continued positive developments in integrating general healthcare and behavioral healthcare. I hope that these changes will result in longer lives for people using publicly funded mental health services and that those lives will be enriched with meaning and purpose. I hope for a sense of belonging so that people with psychiatric conditions feel part of society, as participants and contributors who are surrounded by a circle of support. I hope for a continued sense of pride within the community of PsyR practitioners, who recognize that they are part of a vision of change and hold the power to make that change happen.

Patricia B. Nemec
Warner, New Hampshire
January 2013

Acknowledgments

The field has made significant advances since the publication of the first edition of *Psychiatric Rehabilitation* in 1999. We hope this third edition reflects much of this progress. Certainly any oversights in that regard are entirely our own. We continue to be grateful to our friends and colleagues who have contributed their time, effort and support to this project: Joe Birkmann, Joni Dolce, Patti Holland, Bill Burns-Lynch, Lia Lewis, Joe Marrone, Deelip Mhaske, Michelle Mullen, Ann Murphy, Pat Nemec, Phyllis Solomon, and Margaret (Peggy) Swarbrick. We must also acknowledge the patience of our editors at Academic Press, Elsevier, Nikki Levy, Barbara Makinster and Caroline Johnson. Finally, we are grateful for the patience of our families and friends who have made allowances for our absences and distractions.

Understanding the Nature of Severe Mental Illness

1

The Experience of Mental Illness
An Introduction to Psychiatric Rehabilitation

Our researchers asked people: What do you want in order to recover? What do you need? And interestingly enough they said things like, a job, relationships...decent place to live ... back to school. All the things that anybody needs to live a good life.
William Anthony

CHAPTER OUTLINE

Psychiatric Rehabilitation. http://dx.doi.org/10.1016/B978-0-12-387002-5.00001-9

Chapter 1 begins with the story of Paul, a young man who faces a severe mental illness, schizophrenia. After reading about Paul you will cover basic definitions of severe mental illness, disability, and stigma. Most importantly, this chapter introduces you to the field of psychiatric rehabilitation, an evolving set of services designed to foster the community integration, improved quality of life, and recovery of persons with severe mental illness. The final section of the chapter discusses how psychiatric rehabilitation knowledge is developed, the identification of evidence-based practices, and the sources of that knowledge for professionals and students.

This chapter will provide answers to the following questions:

1. *What are some of the symptoms and problems that might afflict a young person stricken with a severe mental illness?*
2. *What are severe mental illnesses and how are they defined?*
3. *What is psychiatric rehabilitation?*
4. *How and when did the practice of psychiatric rehabilitation begin?*
5. *What is the state of psychiatric rehabilitation today?*

Introduction

Psychiatric rehabilitation, sometimes referred to as "psychosocial rehabilitation," is a set of strategies and techniques designed to meet the needs of persons with psychiatric disabilities. A true understanding of psychiatric rehabilitation (PsyR) begins with an awareness of and sensitivity to the personal lived experience of serious mental illnesses.

Unlike diseases with predictable symptoms and outcomes, the experience and consequences of mental illness vary considerably from person to person. This is true even for individuals diagnosed with exactly the same condition. Consider two persons, both with a diagnosis of schizophrenia, undifferentiated type. One individual may be experiencing auditory hallucinations (hearing voices), while the other person is plagued by paranoid ideas and experiences but no auditory hallucinations. The history or course of mental illness may also differ from person to person. One person may experience frequent relapses, and another after many years may have had only one short relapse. In addition, each person adjusts and responds to his or her illness differently. One may be severely disabled throughout the course of his or her life, while the other may cope well and overcome the disability. Interestingly, the connection between having less-troubling symptoms or fewer relapses and long-term disability from the disease is not as straightforward as one might expect.

The Story of Paul

Like any person's story, Paul's is unique. At the same time, in many respects, Paul's story resembles many similar situations that unfold every year throughout our country and around the world. Each of us has ideas and attitudes about mental illness that we get from personal experience, from the media, or from speaking with others. Some of these ideas are accurate. Others are half-truths and myths. Some are just plain wrong. As you read about Paul's experience, consider the attitudes and ideas you have about mental illness. Also, consider the following questions:

1. Why did Paul become ill when he did? Were there any events or situations that might have led to Paul's illness?
2. What kinds of things did Paul experience as he became ill? Did the disease itself cause all these things?
3. Could Paul's illness have been predicted or even avoided?
4. How did Paul's family handle the situation, and should they have done some things differently?
5. Are there any clues to how Paul will respond to treatment?

Paul began to realize something was wrong when he realized that he would sit through an entire class and not seem to remember anything that was discussed. It wasn't anything wrong with his memory; he had just been distracted and not paying attention. In fact, anything would become a distraction. A crack in the blackboard or the inflection of a particular word would seem as important to him as what the professor was saying. Even in his favorite class, Macroeconomics, with a professor he really liked, he couldn't keep his attention on the material. Nineteen years old, a college freshman, and living away from home for the first time in his life, Paul found school was becoming a nightmare. An A–/B+ student in high school, now halfway through his first college semester, Paul was losing his ability to concentrate. He strained to listen and take good notes, but his thoughts were confused. He could not seem to maintain his focus. Instead, he would hear a particular word, his thoughts would go off on a tangent, and he would miss the focus of the lecture. After class, he would struggle to summarize the main points, but nothing seemed to stand out; everything seemed to be of equal importance. At first Paul felt frustrated and confused, but as his inability to focus continued, his anxiety increased and he began to feel frightened.

In his suburban middle class high school, Paul's friends were mostly college-bound students: not nerds, but not the most popular students, either. With a moderately high IQ, Paul could usually get above average grades by paying attention in class and cramming for his finals. His dream, which he didn't share with anyone but his closest friend, was to become a successful entrepreneur. He spent hours reading about business successes like Steve Jobs, Michael Dell, and Bill Gates and describing how successful companies like Facebook were created, developed, and managed. He dreamed of one day developing and becoming the CEO of his own company. For Paul, the business environment seemed to offer opportunities for creativity and self-expression. While not interested in the personal contact necessary for a sales career, Paul was attracted to the problem solving and planning required of a successful executive.

Paul's neighbor Nancy was his love interest during high school. Like Paul, Nancy was on the quiet side and they got along well together. Paul and Nancy would ride bikes, go to the movies, play computer games, and study together. They were best friends and talked about getting serious. Paul viewed it as a tragedy when she moved out-of-state with her family the summer after their sophomore year. At first they wrote to each other weekly, but the connection grew weak, and after about six months they hardly corresponded at all.

Paul enjoyed playing soccer during his junior and senior years in high school. Tall for his age with a slight build, he was a good runner and played center forward, mostly on offense but sometimes on defense as well. Although not a star player, Paul played a good steady game, made friends with his teammates, and enjoyed the camaraderie the sport offered.

Paul also enjoyed browsing various sites on the Internet, particularly Facebook. He and his friends spent a lot of time sharing pictures and commenting on each other's Facebook statuses. Paul's best friend Kevin was also a soccer player and interested in business as a possible career. He and Paul shared many hours together discussing soccer and sharing Web sites and books that had to do with entrepreneurs and business successes. For fun, they set up imaginary investment portfolios and competed to see who earned the most (imaginary) money. As they grew closer, Paul felt safe confiding in Kevin. They often talked about their hopes and dreams for the future and their pet likes and dislikes. Although they weren't considered popular, Paul and Kevin were liked by most of their high school peers. Kevin was really serious about his studies. His family didn't have much money, so he was working toward getting scholarships to pay for school. He planned to be a math and computer science major in college, and his motivation to get the grades he needed to pursue his goal rubbed off on Paul.

Childhood had been a happy time for Paul. As the oldest child in his family he always got plenty of attention and love from his parents and a lot of encouragement. Paul really enjoyed spending time with the family. He thought of his family as an ongoing source of friendship, love, fun, and support. Paul's father worked as a personnel manager for a large manufacturing company. He liked his job, loved his family, and usually had a kind word for everyone. Paul's mom worked as a medical technician at the local laboratory. She was proud of this job because it required technical skill. She also liked it because she could schedule her own hours to make time for her family if she was needed at home. It was no secret that her family came first. Paul's sister, Alice, was a junior in high school and his younger brother, Ted, was in the eighth grade.

Going away to college had seemed like a great adventure to Paul. During orientation, he met his future roommate, Ira, who came from out of state. A psychology major, Ira shared Paul's interest in surfing the Internet and using Facebook. An instant friendship emerged. At first, as classes started, Ira had the same positive effect on Paul's study habits as had his friend Kevin. Ira, like his mother whom he looked up to, wanted to pursue a PhD in psychology. Being very organized, he set aside time each evening for study and it was very easy for Paul to fall into the same schedule. Ira and Paul joked about becoming too nerdy, but Paul was secretly glad that he had a studious roommate who helped him by setting a good example. He was doing well in school, getting good grades, and being recognized by his professors for his effort.

About halfway through the semester, Paul began to realize that things were changing. Several weeks after he noticed he was having trouble focusing on lectures, Paul found himself feeling both suspicious toward and angry with Ira. Whenever Ira said something to him, Paul would become suspicious of what he meant or what he "might be up to." He felt that Ira was only being friendly with him in order to take control of their relationship. He began to refuse to speak with Ira so that he would not feel like he was being manipulated. But keeping distant only made him feel rejected and angry, and he blamed that on Ira as well. He found that no matter how much he wanted to mend their relationship, he was not really able to be friendly with Ira. When he tried to communicate, he felt manipulated and controlled. When he withdrew, he felt angry and rejected.

At the same time, he noticed that he was beginning to have trouble relating to his professors. He felt they were manipulating him as well. Studying every night had given Paul a real edge in his classes, and early on his professors thought of him as one of the brighter students. Now, after an excellent start, his apparent total reversal came as a surprise to his professors. Several of them asked to speak with Paul after class, asking if everything was all right. Paul denied any problems while wondering why they were singling him out, since he still had a good average. Paul decided that he was being held to a stricter standard than the other students and that the school was closely observing him. After several of these inquiries, Paul found it harder and harder to get to class. His inability to concentrate made it seem pointless anyway. Instead, he cut his classes regularly and spent most of his time alone in his dorm room, playing computer games and "de-friending" people on Facebook. Finally, with failing grades in every class, Paul left for home before finals.

His parents were worried and confused by Paul's behavior. Telephone conversations with Paul had alerted them that something was wrong, but left them puzzled. Paul talked about isolation, people manipulating and controlling him, and being "observed" by the school. Their first thought was that Paul was using drugs. They knew Paul had experimented with marijuana in high school, but that had not seemed to be a problem at the time. When they asked Paul about drugs, he adamantly denied it and showed none of the telltale signs. When he got home, it was obvious to his parents that something else was wrong. Both parents were very upset, and after long discussion they decided to ask Paul to see Dr. Williams, the family doctor. Paul had always liked Doc Williams, and he was clearly fond of Paul. Ashamed of his poor performance at school and confused by his own thoughts and feelings, he agreed to see him the following week.

Home in a safe place and feeling less suspicious, Paul was able to tell Dr. Williams everything that had been happening to him. As he conveyed his story, he felt that much of what he told the doctor made no sense. Why had he mistrusted his new friend? Why wasn't he able to concentrate in class? Why had he started cutting classes? All the behaviors, thoughts, and feelings he reported seemed strange, as if they had happened to someone else. Dr. Williams listened to Paul's story and reassured him that it was not uncommon for students going away to college for the first time to have an anxiety reaction. He suggested that Paul see a colleague of his with special training to work with these types of problems, a psychiatrist named Dr. Kline.

During the week he had to wait before his appointment with Dr. Kline, Paul started to become withdrawn and suspicious of his family. During evening meals, he heard a voice telling him that he wasn't his mother's child. His parents tried to hide their own anxiety by accepting Paul's odd behavior. When he saw Dr. Kline, he was so suspicious that he had trouble relating his story. Dr. Kline suggested that, in addition to some medication, Paul might consider signing himself into a hospital for a period of observation and treatment. He assured Paul that this was the best course of action and that he would be able to leave if he ever changed his mind. Feeling very distrustful, Paul refused the hospital as well as the medication Dr. Kline prescribed. Paul stayed home throughout that winter and into the spring. He became progressively more withdrawn and uncommunicative. Most of the time, he stayed in his room, listening to music. During June, Paul told his mom that Dr. Kline was giving him orders by broadcasting thoughts to him telepathically. As these symptoms increased, Paul became agitated and threatening. Finally, at Dr. Williams's suggestion, his parents took him to a local private psychiatric hospital, where he stayed for two weeks.

After two weeks in the hospital, Paul felt like he wasn't ready to be discharged. He was still hearing voices, feeling withdrawn, and on a high dose of injectable medication, but the nurses assured him that living at home and going to the community mental health center would be much better for him. Paul visited the mental health center before he was discharged. A staff person conducted a clinical intake interview and gave him a tour of the mental health center. There, Paul could attend individual or group therapy, see a psychiatrist for his medication, and get help finding a job, getting back to school, or accomplishing other goals. People there seemed friendly and the programs looked interesting, but he still wasn't sure because many of the people were older and "looked sick" to him. His parents were both hopeful and concerned about Paul's return. At the suggestion of the hospital social worker, they told Paul that if he were going to live at home he would have to agree to attend the community mental health center.

His first week at home was difficult. He still wasn't sure what was wrong with him. His doctors at the hospital had been vague about his condition. When he thought about being mentally ill, he became really scared, tried to think about something else, or decided he was just suffering from stress. While he and the mental health center case manager he was assigned to filled out his initial treatment plan, the staff person told him that his diagnosis was schizophrenia.

Paul wasn't exactly sure what that meant, but at the same time, it was what he had dreaded all along. He felt fear growing in the pit of his stomach. His old life was over; he felt that the staff person was telling him that he was insane.

Discussion of Paul's Story

Paul's story raises a number of important issues about mental illness that you will learn more about as you read this book. Many of these issues remain controversial. Throughout this text you will see that, depending on training and orientation, theorists, researchers, and mental health professionals often have very different answers to these questions.

One important issue involves questions of **etiology**, or the cause(s) of such illnesses. What caused Paul's illness? Could someone have predicted that Paul would become ill by observing his development, and could the illness have been prevented? Partly because there is still a great deal we do not know about the etiology of the major mental illnesses, this is an area of controversy and sometimes heated debate. Some professionals believe that aspects of Paul's personal history, environment, and family life may help us to understand the cause of his illness. Others feel that these issues have little or no bearing on the disease because its cause is essentially biological rather than environmental. Most importantly, the different etiological beliefs held by professionals, family members, and people like Paul lead to specific treatment strategies.

Another important issue that is raised is the question of **prognosis**, the probable course or outcome of the disease. Will he recover with medication and treatment? Or will he become progressively more confused, alienated, and withdrawn over time? Can the prognosis of such a disease even be established? While there is increasing agreement among professionals on the prognosis of these diseases given correct medication and services, there is still great variability between people with the same illness. The final and most important issue remains: What is the best way to help Paul and other people like him? As you will see, there are many aspects to the care of mental illness. **Treatment** is usually considered to be any action designed to cure a disease or reduce its symptoms. **Rehabilitation**, on the other hand, is usually defined as any action intended to reduce the negative effects of the disease on the person's everyday life.

To help explain this difference, let's look at a stroke victim who has lost her ability to walk. A doctor might prescribe anticoagulants, blood pressure medication, change in diet, and regular exercise to help reduce the probability of future strokes. These prescriptions would be considered treatment. The doctor might also prescribe physical therapy to help return the patient to the highest level of physical mobility possible after the deficits caused by the stroke. This therapy, aimed at returning the patient to normal or near normal functioning, would be considered rehabilitation. Finally, a rehabilitation professional making a home visit might recommend that a ramp be built to the front door, that doorknobs be changed to levers, and that the bathroom be fitted with hand bars. These modifications to the patient's environment would also be considered part of the rehabilitation process.

The differences between treatment and rehabilitation seem clear for the stroke patient. But for the person with mental illness, like Paul, the difference between treatment and rehabilitation is not always clear. Indeed, some professionals believe that it is a mistake to make a distinction between the treatment of mental illness and a process of rehabilitation. In fact, some researchers have found evidence that the rehabilitation process itself has a direct and positive effect on the disease (e.g., Siu, Tsang, & Bond, 2010). Most PsyR professionals believe that treatment and rehabilitation are complementary processes.

The importance of the differences and similarities between treatment and rehabilitation will become evident as you move through this text. This issue is vital when considering questions like: "Who provides treatment? Who provides rehabilitation? What is the role of the psychiatric rehabilitation practitioner? What kinds of services should be provided?"

This textbook will provide you with answers to many of these questions. Real people like Paul and his loved ones are dependent on the answers. You will also learn about new, challenging, and complicated issues that address the best ways to help persons with severe mental illness.

The Serious Mental Illnesses

Serious mental illnesses, like the one that struck Paul, afflict many people in our society and around the world. In the United States in 2008, approximately 4.5 percent of the population had a serious mental illness (SMI) according to the National Institute of Mental Health (NIMH). NIMH defines SMI as "a mental, behavioral, or emotional disorder (excluding developmental and substance abuse disorders) … resulting in serious functioning impairment, which substantially interferes with or limits one or more major life activities" (http://www.nimh.nih.gov/statistics/SMI_AASR.shtml). The population of the United States in 2008 was estimated at 304 million, which translates to 13,680,000 persons with SMI that year if these estimates are correct.

The President's New Freedom Commission on Mental Health 2003 report put the estimate somewhat higher, at 5 to 7 percent of adults with SMI in the United States or 15 to 20 million persons (President's New Freedom Commission for Mental Health, 2003).

For society as a whole, schizophrenia, which strikes an estimated 1 percent of the population, is by far the most devastating and the most feared mental illness. In addition, there are several other mental illnesses that cause untold suffering and disability. The *Diagnostic and Statistical Manual of Mental Disorders* (DSM-IV-TR, Fourth Edition, Text Revision, American Psychiatric Association, 2000) recognizes recurring depressive disorders, bipolar and unipolar disorders (commonly known as manic-depressive disorders), schizoaffective disorder, and organic brain syndromes, among others, as serious mental illnesses that can become long term, cause psychosis, and lead to psychiatric disability.

Today there is increasing awareness that people who experience severe mental illness often suffer from other serious maladies as well. These "dually diagnosed" individuals may be coping with co-occurring substance abuse problems, developmental disabilities, severe learning disabilities, PTSD (post-traumatic stress disorder), and chronic physical illnesses at the same time they are struggling with their mental illness. As you might imagine, the problems raised when someone is suffering from more than one disorder at the same time can be very difficult to address. Which disorder should be treated first? Does the treatment of one disorder negatively affect the treatment of another disorder? Which disorder is causing the symptoms that are present? Special programs for people who are dually diagnosed that are staffed by professionals cross-trained to address multiple problems are increasing around the country. The issue of co-occurring disorders, mental illnesses, and addictions is covered in depth in Chapter 9.

The Symptoms of Mental Illness

Mental illnesses may present a wide variety of symptoms. One way to understand the symptoms of severe mental illnesses is to classify them as either positive symptoms or negative symptoms. **Positive symptoms** refer to what is *added* (i.e., what is present but should not be) to the individual because of the disease. The faulty interpretation of reality due to incorrect sensory perceptions (**hallucinations**) or thoughts (**delusions**) are good examples of positive symptoms. **Negative symptoms** refer to things that the individual has *lost* or that are missing because of the disease. Social withdrawal and an inability to experience pleasure, **anhedonia**, are typical examples of the kinds of negative symptoms someone with severe mental illness might experience. Many persons experiencing these symptoms of **psychosis** are diagnosed with schizophrenia or a bipolar disorder (manic depression). Chapters 2 and 3 will cover the causes, symptoms, and treatments of mental illnesses in more depth.

The Cause(s) of the Major Mental Illnesses

The pathological processes that cause these conditions are still poorly understood. Nevertheless, there is consensus that these conditions have a strong biological component (Mueser & Gingerich, 2006; Torrey, 2006). With the development of increasingly sophisticated soft tissue and metabolic imaging techniques such as CAT, PET, and MRI scans, researchers have been able to demonstrate actual changes in brain tissue and brain functioning corresponding with psychotic episodes (Torrey, 2006; Andreasen, 1984). At the same time, researchers have looked at the contribution of genetics, by comparing individuals whose parents have schizophrenia with those whose parents do not have schizophrenia (Marcus et al., 1987) and studying identical and fraternal twins when one of the twins has the disorder (e.g., Torrey, 1994). These studies provide strong evidence that genetics play an important role when someone is stricken with a major mental illness. Despite these advances, the cause(s) of major mental illness are not known. Chapters 2 and 3 will cover the symptoms, diagnosis, probable causes, probable courses, and outcomes of these illnesses in more detail.

Psychiatric Disability

Without effective rehabilitation, a major mental illness can disable a person for life. Most often striking during the late teens and early twenties, major life disruptions like the one Paul experienced are very common. When school, work, and family are disrupted, the individual cannot acquire the skills needed to cope with the demands of modern life. Without these skills, which many take for granted, the individual cannot function successfully.

These conditions tend to be long lasting as well as severe, and they often disrupt and stunt normal intellectual, social, and vocational development or lead to

CONTROVERSIAL ISSUE
Schizophrenia, or a Less Stigmatizing Label

Since Swiss Psychiatrist Bleuler coined the term "schizophrenia" in 1911 and distinguished it from dementia praecox, the term has been widely used in psychiatry. The DSM-IV-TR (and its earlier editions) have consistently used the term "schizophrenia," modifying it with disease categories like paranoid, catatonic, undifferentiated, etc. Today, literally millions of persons in the United States and around the world carry a diagnostic label of schizophrenia.

The term "schizophrenia" is widely used by the media and entertainment industries, where it is portrayed as the very essence of major mental illness. The paranoid schizophrenic label used by the media conjures up images of wild-eyed homicidal maniacs who kill and maim for no apparent reason.

The term "schizophrenia" is also used to denote apparent contradictions in people, organizations, or polices. A scandal during the Reagan administration dubbed the "Iran-Contra affair" was frequently referred to as "schizophrenic." The policy consisted of selling arms to our enemies (Iran, which had just held American embassy personnel hostage) in order to raise clandestine funds to support our allies (the Contra Guerrillas in Nicaragua). This misuse of the term also reinforces the common misconception that schizophrenia is a form of multiple personality disorder, which it is not.

The clear abuse of the term and increased understanding of these illnesses has prompted debate about the continued use of "schizophrenia" as a diagnostic label. Jerry Dincin—who served for many years as the Executive Director of Thresholds, a large psychiatric rehabilitation agency in Chicago—once argued that the diagnostic label "schizophrenia" should be changed to "neurotransmitter/stress syndrome" (Dincin, 1990). This new diagnostic label captures both the biological basis (**neurotransmitter**) and the environmental vulnerability (stress) aspects of the major mental illnesses. But more importantly, "neurotransmitter/stress syndrome," or a similar term, does not necessarily carry the stigma and negative connotation of a label like schizophrenia. Dincin used an analogy from the developmental disabilities field to make his point. The terms "morons," "idiots," and "imbeciles" of 50 years ago (when they were used as diagnostic labels by professionals) have been replaced by terms with much less negative impact (Dincin, 1990). More recently, the term "mental retardation" has been replaced by "intellectual disability" (http://www.aamr.org/content_96.cfm?navID=20). The probable relationship of neurotransmitters to major mental illness will be discussed in more depth in Chapter 2.

In Japan in 2002, they actually did change the diagnostic label of schizophrenia from "seishin bunretsu byo" (literally: mind splitting disease) to "togo shitcho sho" (i.e., integration disorder) (Sato, 2006). The new term "integration disorder" conveyed the implication that treatment and recovery were possible and was rapidly adopted by providers and consumers. Interestingly, one measure of the success of this change was that the proportion of patients who were correctly informed of their diagnosis nearly doubled after the change in terms.

One might also consider the US media's response to such a change. Popular culture would still need a label for "madness" since individuals with these labels supply the motivating force for many real and fictional stories of crime and violence. Could a label like "neurotransmitter/stress syndrome" become the stigmatized label of the future?

In the 20 years since Dincin's proposal there is some evidence that the general public is becoming more knowledgeable about mental illness and that the level of stigma may be receding. This might be an opportune time for a change in diagnostic labels.

conditions in which acquired skills are lost due to disuse. This lack of ability, whether skills were never acquired or were acquired and subsequently lost, is the hallmark of psychiatric **disability**. While psychiatric symptoms can often be controlled by medication and therapies, disability secondary to the illness often persists. The analogy of a physical trauma may help to clarify this issue. A person who loses the use of his legs because of an automobile accident becomes disabled because he lost skills like walking and running. The damage from the accident persists long after the initial injury or is permanent.

Some PsyR theorists such as William Anthony and Robert Liberman (e.g., Anthony & Liberman, 1986) cite evidence that the degree of psychiatric disability is related to the individual's **premorbid** skill level. The term "premorbid" refers to the period before the individual became ill. In this case, it refers to what the individual's skill levels were before the illness. In addition, Anthony and Liberman infer that higher skill levels can reduce the intensity of psychiatric illness. We will cover the contributions of these theorists in a later chapter.

Disability is an important medical and social concept. The Americans with Disabilities Act of 1990 and amended in 2008, which is discussed in Chapter 10, defines disability as a substantial limitation in a major life activity (Lawn & Meyerson, from Liberman et al., 1993). Another important medical body, the World Health Organization (http://www.who.int/en/), defines "disability" as an inability to participate or perform at a socially desirable level in activities such as self-care, social relationships, work, and situationally appropriate behavior.

Most importantly for Americans, the Social Security Administration defines disability as the inability to engage in any substantial gainful activity (SGA) by reason of any medically determinable physical or mental impairment(s) which can be expected to result in death or which has lasted or can be expected to last for a continuous period of not less than 12 months (http://www.ssa.gov/disability/professionals/bluebook/12.00-MentalDisorders-Adult.htm).

The Stigma of Major Mental Illness

When someone has a major mental illness the diagnosis itself can cause serious problems. As Hall, Andrews, and Goldstein (1985) point out, "Schizophrenia is ... a sentence as well as a diagnosis." The person who has the diagnostic label of schizophrenia carries a powerful stigma to which other people may react with fear and rejection. Because the symptoms of these diseases can affect how a person thinks, feels, behaves, and communicates, the effects of the disease are often apparent to other people. Unlike cold symptoms like coughing, sneezing, or running a fever, psychiatric symptoms are often not attributed to a disease. Because they are so little understood, some persons even attribute psychiatric symptoms to supernatural, spiritual, or demonic causes.

E. Fuller Torrey, M.D., a psychiatrist who treats, researches, and writes on schizophrenia, believes that persons experiencing schizophrenia are treated like the lepers of the 20th century (Torrey, 2006). The term "stigma" originally referred to the ancient practice of physically marking (scarring) villains so that others would know that they were criminals and would be on their guard. Many persons today react in the same way when they meet a person they perceive to be mentally ill.

Peoples' reaction to stigma refers to what Coleman (1986) called "the dilemma of difference." Most people generally accept that individuals are different in many ways. When some differences are deemed unacceptable, those with undesirable characteristics or differences may be stigmatized. What a given society chooses to stigmatize is somewhat arbitrary. In the past, some societies considered persons who today might be diagnosed with schizophrenia as higher beings who were specially gifted and able to commune with God. Saint Francis of Assisi was known to speak with the animals, which was considered proof of his saintly nature. Today, our first reaction might be to consider such behavior as evidence of a psychotic process.

Much of the stigma around mental illness has its roots in ignorance and fear. This is not surprising, since until very recently there was little scientific evidence to support any theory explaining serious mental illness. Some scholars even questioned the very existence of mental illness. In his writing, Thomas Szasz (2010) suggested that mental illness is simply a learned behavior which, for some people, is a realistic reaction to modern society. Today, as we are beginning to get a clearer understanding of mental illness, we can begin to combat the stigma left by centuries of ignorance and fear.

One of the most insidious forms of stigma, labeled self-stigma, occurs when a person with a mental illness internalizes the negative image the stigma conveys to others. Patrick Corrigan and his colleagues (Corrigan, Larson, & Rusch, 2009) describe a three-step process of self-stigma: "Awareness of the stereotype, agreement with it, and applying it to one's self" (p. 75). Further, they assert that self-stigma results in lowered self-esteem and self-efficacy, resulting in a syndrome they label "Why try."

Yet another insidious form of stigma involves the attitudes of professionals toward persons with psychiatric disabilities. While most professionals would strongly deny having stigmatizing or prejudicial attitudes toward the people they service, negative attitudes about individuals' chances for employment, a productive life, and recovery suggest otherwise. One of the advantages, among others, of including peer providers (persons with the lived experience of mental illness) in PsyR treatment teams is the reduction of professional stigma (see Chapter 13).

The stigma surrounding mental illness can be eliminated. The ignorance that has surrounded mental illness since the beginning of history is being lifted by sharing research findings with the public. While we fear cancer and have compassion for those who are stricken, medical science has increased our understanding of the disease and reduced the stigma cancer patients once experienced. Recent progress in the treatment of AIDS is helping to reduce the stigma associated with that condition. In the same way, future citizens educated about mental illness may fear the disease but not the person.

In addition to knowledge about the disease, contact with individuals who successfully cope with it can eradicate the stigma it carries. Actual contact with persons who have these serious mental illnesses has been shown to decrease stigma under many circumstances (Spagnolo, Murphy, & Librera, 2008; Corrigan et al., 2003).

The community treatment of mental illness also has the potential of reducing stigma. Treating persons experiencing serious mental illness in the community means that at one time or another everyone may come in contact with them. As most psychiatric rehabilitation staff will tell you, persons with mental illness are no different from anyone else, except for their disease. Keeping these persons in institutions adds to the stigma surrounding the disease. Accepting them into the community helps to eliminate stigma because living and working in the community highlights their basic humanity, not their disability.

What Does the Term "Psychiatric Rehabilitation" Mean?

In the helping professions, the term "rehabilitate" means to restore to an optimal state of constructive activity. Of course, what is "optimal" is relative to the individual. An individual's "optimal" level of constructive activity depends on several factors. How well a person functions depends on how severe his or her illness is at the time, the severity of the disability, the abilities he or she still possesses, the outside supports that are available, and what some theorists call the "stage of recovery." Stage of recovery refers to the individual's level of progress in his or her ability to cope with the disease and disability and his or her self-image as a functioning person. The concept of recovery will be dealt with in some depth in Chapter 4.

Psychiatric rehabilitation (PsyR) refers to efforts to restore persons with psychiatric disabilities to optimal states of constructive activity. The degree of disability a person experiences is often variable. Some persons who have a serious mental illness may be disabled in many aspects of their lives. Other persons may be disabled in only one area, such as employment while functioning well in other life domains.

There are a number of definitions of PsyR reflecting a range of philosophical and technical differences among practitioners (Rutman, 1994; Hughes, 1994; Anthony, 1979; Anthony & Liberman, 1986; USPRA, 2007). Ruth Hughes (1994), former Executive Director of IAPSRS (International Association of Psychosocial Rehabilitation Services)—now USPRA—provided an excellent definition that most PsyR practitioners can agree with:

> *The goal of psychiatric rehabilitation is to enable individuals to compensate for, or eliminate the functional deficits, interpersonal barriers and environmental barriers created by the disability, and to restore ability for independent living, socialization and effective life management.*
>
> *IAPSRS,* An Introduction to PsyR, *p. 11*

In 1992, the *Psychosocial Rehabilitation Journal* asked its readers to submit definitions of PsyR. The following definition of PsyR, which received an Honorable Mention in the contest, captures both the humanity and the hope inherent in the rehabilitation process:

> *Psychosocial rehabilitation means that a person who before was afraid to go into a store to order an ice cream soda can now be an ice cream store manager.*
>
> Martha Green (Rutman, 1994)

The definition adopted by USPRA in 2007 is:

> *Psychiatric rehabilitation promotes recovery, full community integration and improved quality of life for persons who have been diagnosed with any mental health condition that seriously impairs functioning. Psychiatric rehabilitation services are collaborative, person-directed, and individualized, and an essential element of the human services spectrum and should be evidence-based. They focus on helping individuals develop skills and access resources needed to increase their capacity to be successful and satisfied in the living, working, learning and social environments of their choice.*

The Emergence of Psychiatric Rehabilitation

Practitioners of PsyR are united in believing that persons who have a serious mental illness can achieve greater independence and a better quality of life with the help of psychiatric rehabilitation services. This assumption, that persons with psychiatric disabilities can successfully participate in rehabilitation, is in marked contrast to the beliefs of many mental health professionals in the past. Until the late 1970s and early 1980s, the conventional wisdom about severe mental illness was that it took an insidious downward course with little or no hope of recovery. Prior to 1987, the DSM-III (*Diagnostic and Statistical Manual of Mental Disorders*, Third Edition) published by the American Psychiatric Association stated that the most common course of schizophrenia consisted of acute episodes followed by "increasing residual impairments" (p. 185). In contrast to this pessimistic view, many studies have demonstrated that, even for those with severe psychiatric disability once labeled as "back ward" patients, the long-term prognosis is positive (DeSisto, Harding, McCormack, Ashikaga, & Brooks, 1995a & b; Harding, Brooks, Ashikaga, Strauss, & Breier, 1987a & b; Harrow & Jobe, 2007).

Another positive development is the work researchers, practitioners, and consumers of PsyR services are doing to develop the concept of **recovery** from psychiatric disability. Even though some of the disabilities and residual symptoms may be lifelong, the field of PsyR is learning what it means to "recover" from serious mental illness (Anthony, 2000; Anthony, 1993; Deegan, 1988; Roe, Rudnick, & Gill, 2007; Onken, Craig, Ridgway, Ralph, & Cook, 2007). As already mentioned, the concept of recovery will be discussed in greater detail in Chapter 4.

Deinstitutionalization

The emergence of PsyR as a unique enterprise can be directly traced to the **deinstitutionalization** movement that began in the 1960s and early 1970s. Between 1960 and 2006, approximately 90 percent of the persons in long-term state psychiatric institutions were discharged into the community (Torrey, 2006). Looking at it another way, psychiatric hospital censuses went from 339 persons per 100,000 person population to 21 persons per 100,000 person population by 1998 (Lamb & Bachrach, 2001).

When the policy of deinstitutionalization began, literally thousands of patients who had been institutionalized for much of their adult lives were discharged into the community for treatment. Given their traditional mental health training, many, if not most, of the community mental health staff were unprepared for this challenge (Stern & Minkoff, 1979; Farkas, Cohen, & Nemec, 1988). In many areas of the United States, persons who were deinstitutionalized were deemed by practitioners to be "inappropriate" for the community services available at that time. This assessment was made despite the fact that the major impetus for the nationwide federal funding of community mental health centers begun in 1963 was community-based care for this population. Staff trained to provide individual psychotherapy for persons with supposed psychodynamic problems tended to classify these people as not being good "treatment cases." Marianne Farkas, of the Center for Psychiatric Rehabilitation, Boston University, found that this newly deinstitutionalized population had "low patient status" because they were not highly verbal and did not demonstrate high rates of treatment success (1988). As a result, many persons with serious mental illness were relegated to programs staffed by less educated persons with nontraditional academic degrees and by paraprofessionals (persons without academic credentials).

Torrey (2006) asserts that only about 5 percent of the 789 federally funded community mental health centers (CMHCs) accepted the challenge of providing appropriate services to the deinstitutionalized population. The majority of the centers focused their efforts on providing counseling, psychotherapy, and consultation and education in the broader area of mental illness. Mostly because CMHC staff members were ill-equipped to deal with them, persons with severe mental illness became increasingly isolated and remained underserved in the community.

The academic preparation of mental health professionals was very slow to adjust to the needs of the deinstitutionalization movement. This poor academic response was caused by a lack of recognition of the plight of this population as well as a lack of awareness of the treatment strategies necessary to aide them. A review of introductory undergraduate psychology textbooks carried out as late as 1992 revealed that lobotomy (an outdated type of brain surgery) was written about more than psychiatric rehabilitation (Halter, Bond, & De Graaf-Kaser, 1992). None of the 28 Introductory Psychology textbooks reviewed mentioned common PsyR approaches such as the Clubhouse Model (e.g., Fountain House, Horizon House, etc.), the National Institute of Mental Health's Community Support System, or social skills training. In addition, hospital treatment was given much more coverage than community treatment at a time when hospital stays were being reduced and large psychiatric hospitals were being closed.

In addition to the textbooks, in many cases undergraduate curricula have remained focused on the more traditional psychodynamic, cognitive, and behavioral treatment models. Graduate education curricula have often sidestepped the issue of treating persons with major mental illness by stating that this population is not appropriate for the treatment strategies they are training their students to use (e.g., psychotherapy).

There have been efforts in recent years to update the education of all professionals who provide treatment to individuals living with severe mental illnesses. The Annapolis Coalition on the Behavioral Health Workforce, formed in 2000 with support from SAMHSA (Substance Abuse and Mental Health Services Administration), brought together stakeholders to create a plan to bring the competencies for behavioral health providers into the 21st century (Hoge & Morris, 2002). A 2007 report for SAMHSA pictured a behavioral health workforce in crisis with, for example, disconnects between how professionals are trained and what they need to carry out their professional roles in the field (Hoge, Morris, Daniels, Leighton, & Adams, 2007).

Despite growing scientific evidence that the major mental illnesses have a strong biological component, some applied graduate programs have maintained their focus on psychodynamic approaches emphasizing individual therapy aimed at uncovering past trauma. There has been evidence for some time that this type of intense, interpersonal treatment can be harmful for persons with major mental illness (see, e.g., Linn, Caffey, Klett, Hogarty, & Lamb, 1979). The neglect of the proper care for persons with these illnesses is especially troubling given the emphasis many of the helping professions place on championing the needy and downtrodden. Persons diagnosed with major mental illness constitute one of the most rejected, stigmatized, disadvantaged, and needy groups in our nation.

Today, a growing number of academic programs are devoted to psychiatric rehabilitation education at all academic levels. Special issues of the journals *Psychiatric Rehabilitation Skills* (Gill, 2001), *Rehabilitation Education* (Nemec, Spaniol & Dell Orto, 2001), and the *American Journal of Psychiatric Rehabilitation* (Pratt, 2005) have been devoted to progress in psychiatric rehabilitation education and credentialing. In addition, a nationwide consortium of psychiatric rehabilitation educators meets annually to discuss PsyR education issues (Gill & Barrett, 2009; Barrett, MacDonald-Wilson, & Nemec, 2005).

Besides the mental illnesses themselves, community staff of the 1960s and 1970s had to face an additional problem when providing services to this newly deinstitutionalized population. Not surprisingly, spending years in an institutional setting like a large psychiatric hospital caused many of the patients to become **institutionalized**. This institutionalization syndrome caused functional deficits, atypical or inappropriate behavior, and extreme dependency in long-term patients (Lehrman, 1961; Schmieding, 1968; Ridgeway & Zipple, 1990). This syndrome often combined with an individual's mental illness, increasing the level of psychiatric disability. Awareness of the debilitating effects of long-term institutionalization brought about increased emphasis on the community mental health principle of *least restrictive treatment environment*. This principle holds that every individual should be provided treatment in an environment that provides as much freedom as possible. For example, consider a patient who might equally benefit from hospitalization or a community treatment program. The patient should be treated in the community program because it is a less restrictive treatment environment and less likely to promote "institutional" behavior. The individual in the community program is also more likely to retain skills and have the opportunity to be part of the community.

The 1990 Americans with Disabilities Act (ADA) strongly supports the concept of deinstitutionalization. One part of the act, the "integration regulation," requires a "public entity [to] administer ... programs ... in the most integrated setting appropriate to the needs of qualified individuals with disabilities" (28 CFR § 35.130(d)). A Supreme Court decision, Olmstead versus L.C. and E.W. (1999), upheld this interpretation of the ADA and is currently being used to help deinstitutionalize individuals with disabilities around the nation.

Psychiatric Rehabilitation Terminology and Language

Each profession has its own peculiar jargon of words, names, and sayings. Psychiatric rehabilitation is no different. The language we use can reflect our attitudes and prejudices. The words we use to describe others may also designate whether we consider them to be like us or different from us. When we label people, we relegate them to a particular category. Some categories can be innocuous ("She's a Packer's fan"), some negative ("He's an ex-con"), and some may frighten ("He's an AIDS victim"). As the labels help determine how we feel about someone, they tend to determine how we will react to that person in the future. This issue is particularly important for persons with mental illness.

Since the deinstitutionalization movement and the advent of community treatment, the labels given to persons who experience serious mental illness have taken on some very specific meanings. When these persons are hospitalized, they are known as "patients" since they are in a medical environment. This term usually connotes dependency. After discharge, if they attend a Clubhouse-type day program, they are often known as "members." The "member" label conveys the philosophy of egalitarianism, sharing, and inclusion espoused by Clubhouse programs. Conversely, if they attend a more traditional community mental health center they are probably known as "clients" or "consumers." This labels them as recipients of the center's services. Persons living in residential facilities, whether operated for profit or by a publicly funded community mental health facility, are usually known as "residents."

Some persons unhappy with existing labels began calling themselves "consumers" (meaning consumers of mental health services). Other persons have labeled themselves "survivors." For some, the "survivor" label represents the fact that they have been able to exist with a terrifying illness. For others, the label denotes their displeasure with the services they have been provided, indicating that they have "survived" the system and their treatment. Today, increasing numbers of persons who are living with a serious mental illness are working in psychiatric rehabilitation settings and providing services to others who have a serious mental illness (see Chapter 13). These individuals are known as peer providers (Swarbrick, Schmidt, & Gill, 2010) and, less frequently, as consumer providers (or "prosumers," to list some of the current labels). How persons with mental illness label themselves or how a professional labels them can carry a great deal of meaning about their status and the kinds of services they are receiving and expect to receive.

In the mid-1990s, a survey of 300 persons receiving mental health services found that "client" was the term most preferred (48 percent), followed by "patient" (20 percent), and "consumer" (8 percent). The remainder of those surveyed (24 percent) responded "other" or "don't care" (Mueser, Glynn, Corrigan, & Baber, 1996). No doubt, a similar survey conducted today would find different results.

Person-first Language

Consumer groups and PsyR professionals concerned with combating the negative effects of stigma have emphasized the need for person-first language. For example, rather than calling someone a schizophrenic, which is calling them their disease, using person-first language, the individual would be called a person who has schizophrenia. This may seem a subtle difference but it is very important for the person being so labeled.

The statement in Box 1.1 was put out by the Center for Community Change through Housing and Support formerly at the University of Vermont.

BOX 1.1   CHOOSING WORDS WITH DIGNITY

The words we choose to use to portray people with mental illness reflect our attitudes and beliefs about the value, dignity, and worth of people with disabilities. Our words influence the public perception and acceptance of people with disabilities. People with disabilities are person-first and foremost, who also happen to have a disability, or a different set of abilities.

Progressive mental health systems use, at all times, descriptive words that emphasize the person's worth and abilities, not the disabling condition. They understand that people may have a disorder or disability but the people are not the disability. They also recognize that people are diminished when they are described by diagnosis (e.g., "schizophrenic," "paranoid," "borderline"), by slang (e.g., "psychos," "schizos"), and by phrases that negatively categorize them (e.g., "the mentally ill," "the chronically mentally ill," "young chronics," "retarded," "dually diagnosed"). Medical terms such as "patient" are not used in these systems to refer to people who are not in medical settings, because they are inconsistent with rehabilitation and community support philosophy.

USPRA, the United States Psychiatric Rehabilitation Association (2003) proposed use of the term "people in recovery," in an attempt to reflect the fact that many, if not all, persons living with serious mental illnesses are engaged in an active process of recovery. This term reflects "person-first" thinking but actually begs the question of whether all people with mental illness are recovering or not. While everyone has the potential for recovery, assuming that everyone is currently in recovery may trivialize the process.

It should be the written and public policy of all systems and agencies working with people with disabilities not to use labels like "the seriously mentally ill" or use terms like "he is

(Continued)

> **BOX 1.1   CHOOSING WORDS WITH DIGNITY—Continued**
>
> a bipolar." It should be the policy of all programs to consult with consumers and ex-patients in their states to identify a phrase or phrases that are respectful of individual dignity and reflect the preferences of the majority of individuals. Some phrases with general growing acceptance are "people with psychiatric disabilities," "ex-patients," or "consumers." All current and future documents should reflect this policy.

Developing Psychiatric Rehabilitation Knowledge

Early practitioners of psychiatric rehabilitation learned much of their trade by experience through a trial and error process. The typical community-based mental health center was originally designed for persons with less severe conditions. When the national policy of deinstitutionalization began, community-based staff and services were confronted with a large group of individuals being released from psychiatric institutions who responded poorly to existing treatment modalities, medications, and services. It was soon apparent that neither the existing community services nor the types of services previously offered in the psychiatric hospitals were helping this new group adapt to the community environment. In response, many of the community mental health staff assigned to work with this population began devising new strategies and services to meet their needs. These pioneer staff struggled to develop treatment philosophies consistent with the needs of persons with persistent mental illness living in the community. They often had to design entirely new programs for this population. Without recourse to references or handbooks, using emerging concepts like least restrictive treatment environment, client involvement, and **normalization** as guidelines, innovative programs and services were created. These new services were evaluated by their success or failure. Of course, many of these innovative program models failed or were later discarded as better models were developed.

Some successful models already existed in places like Fountain House in New York City and Horizon House in Philadelphia. These successful programs, which we will cover in greater depth in Chapter 7, served as models for the services that were being developed in communities around the country.

Since very little if any formal education about psychiatric rehabilitation existed at the time, programs tended to hire bright, young, motivated individuals and teach them psychiatric rehabilitation on the job as it was practiced at that setting. Much of what was known was handed down from supervisor to supervisee, and the staff from individual programs tended to share the same ideas and philosophy. Knowledge was also picked up at yearly conferences of emerging PsyR professional associations, or from journal articles on PsyR that appeared infrequently in publications dedicated to other disciplines.

The process of developing new programs and services based on emerging philosophical concepts made psychiatric rehabilitation an exciting and very creative profession in the 1970s and 1980s. Without models or reference points, program staff members were free to create programs in many forms, and they did. Psychiatric rehabilitation services today cover a wide range of styles, types, and philosophies. This wealth of program types and designs has provided excellent opportunities for testing and refining PsyR theories and practices. Like other evolving fields, PsyR periodically experiences a "shaking out" of some of these ideas as new knowledge is acquired and agreement is reached on which are the most effective (producing positive results) and efficient (producing results economically). Ideally, the more effective and efficient strategies are retained while the others are discarded or defunded. The identification of some psychiatric rehabilitation strategies as Evidence-Based Practices (EBP), which will be covered extensively in this text, is ushering in just such a "shaking out."

Psychiatric Rehabilitation: A Science or an Art?

Brainstorming sessions, sometimes with staff and consumers combined, to develop creative strategies for achieving PsyR goals and objectives are a far cry from the systematic precision required for scientific research. Creating new programs and strategies can be an art and some of the creations are ingenious. One example is using fellow consumers of services as job coaches to help other consumers learn and keep regular jobs in the community. Another is helping consumers learn about their illnesses by participating in discussion groups where they read and discuss research literature from PsyR journals, such as the *Psychiatric Rehabilitation Journal* and the *American Journal of Psychiatric Rehabilitation.*

The developments of strategies like these are often serendipitous. New strategies and techniques are also developed by improving on the ideas of others. A previous executive director of a very large rehabilitation agency known for developing innovative programming once stated that he really is not that intelligent, he mainly "steals" or adopts other people's ideas and then improves on them. Of course, we can judge the intelligence of this strategy by observing the effectiveness of the programs he developed.

Many of these creative solutions work, as the staff and consumers who utilize them will attest. But what is it about these strategies that work and what should another PsyR program do to insure that the same strategies will work for them? Many of the solutions that appear to be effective to staff and consumers alike in fact are not. A common mistake, for example, is crediting a new strategy with rehabilitation gains when the improvement is actually caused by what is known as a "Hawthorne Effect." You may have heard about the experiments at the Hawthorne plant of the Western Electric Company in Cicero, Illinois, during the 1930s. In one experiment, researchers found that no matter how they manipulated the lighting intensity in the work rooms (higher, lower, or no change), production went up. After much consideration, they concluded that instead of responding to the intensity of the lighting, the workers were responding to being studied by the researchers. In the case of PsyR, a Hawthorne Effect implies that the consumers' improvements or gains may actually be caused by the attention they are getting in trying the new strategy, not because of the strategy itself. This might also be the case with staff members who strive harder when they are enthusiastic about a new program and convey their optimism to the consumers they are working with.

Is PsyR a science, an art, or some combination of both? The three goals of any scientific inquiry are (a) description—what is the process or phenomenon under study? (b) explanation—how does it work? and (c) prediction—what will happen in the future? These principles can be applied to severe mental illness. Therefore, we would like to (a) describe the effects of severe mental illness; (b) explain why mental illness has these effects; and (c) predict the course and outcome of these illnesses. The same set of principles can be applied to PsyR interventions. We need to (a) describe a PsyR intervention; (b) explain how the intervention will work; and (c) predict what the outcome of the intervention will be. Many dedicated PsyR practitioners believe that approaching the task from this technical-scientific perspective will produce the best results for persons with psychiatric disabilities. In fact, it is just this formulation that is behind the advent of evidence-based practices (Gill & Pratt, 2005).

Scientific research is designed to produce knowledge. Scientific PsyR knowledge is developed through rigorous systematic research based on the scientific method of observation, description, control, and replication. For PsyR this means that, in general, if we apply the same treatment to the same population under the same conditions we expect to get approximately the same results. In order to foster this type of scientific knowledge, several research centers focusing specifically on PsyR and the community treatment of persons with severe mental illness have received public funding. Notable among these research centers are the Dartmouth Psychiatric Research Center, the Center for Psychiatric Rehabilitation at the Illinois Institute of Technology, and Thresholds, Chicago, Illinois. Also receiving funding are the National Institute for Disability and Rehabilitation Research (NIDRR) funds Rehabilitation Research and Training Centers (RRTCs) at Boston University, Temple University, and University of Illinois at Chicago to develop and disseminate new PsyR knowledge. Many of these RRTCs deal with aspects of the rehabilitation of severe mental illness. These research centers strive to increase our knowledge of how to provide effective services for persons with severe mental illnesses.

Evidence-based Practices

From its earliest beginnings, psychiatric rehabilitation has sought, usually by trial and error, to develop effective services for persons with severe mental illness. This process has led to the existence of a large number of essentially idiosyncratic services, some of which are effective and some of which are not. The adoption of an evidence-based practice (EBP) approach is addressing this problem. The EBP process employs controlled clinical trials to identify effective services and define the critical elements that produce positive outcomes.

The Implementing Evidence-based Practice Project

As the PsyR research and knowledge base grew, it became clear that some practices and strategies were superior to others at producing desired outcomes for persons. This situation has been clearly demonstrated by the recommendations of the Schizophrenia Patient Outcomes Research Team (PORT) project (Lehman & Steinwachs, 1998; Lehman et al., 2004; Dixon et al., 2010. The PORT studies, which periodically make recommendations for the treatment of schizophrenia, have also found that in many cases individuals with schizophrenia are not provided with proper treatment and services. Additionally, there is increasing recognition by researchers and administrators that service providers and programs are slow to adopt research findings to usual practice, creating a long time lag between new research findings and utilizing those findings in the field.

To address this issue, in 1998 the Robert Wood Johnson Foundation sponsored a meeting of researchers, clinicians, administrators, consumers, and family members to begin the process of identifying evidence-based practices for PsyR. This group, dubbed the Implementing Evidence-Based Practices Project, was charged with identifying interventions that were backed up by reliable research results. Through an extensive review of the research literature, this group was able to identify six potential evidence-based practices.

SAMHSA (Substance Abuse and Mental Health Services Administration) developed an evidence-based practice KIT (KIT = knowledge informing transformation) for each of the six initial evidence-based practices. These KITs provide implementation instructions for each of the major stakeholder groups involved (consumers, practitioners, family members, program leaders, and mental health authorities). Materials and resources necessary for implementation, evaluation, and assessment were also included. KITs also provide scales, called "fidelity scales," to measure how well the actual services are provided.

These KITs are available to mental health services free of charge from SAMHSA.

Identifying an Evidence-based Practice

There are a number of important steps that must be carried out to establish an EBP. Most EBPs started from a service innovation. Such innovations (e.g., assertive community treatment (Chapter 8) and supported employment (Chapter 10)) typically begin as trial and error efforts of dedicated professionals trying to improve services. After an innovation shows promise, the next step is to carefully and objectively define the service including explaining just how the service is performed, who performs it, for how long, etc. The definition of the service becomes the service model, which will subsequently be field-tested.

The service model of a potential EBP must be studied using multiple **controlled clinical trials**. This type of research, which typically involves random assignment of participants to experimental and control groups, has the advantage of allowing researchers to make causal inferences between the variables under study. For example, a researcher may determine that a specific educational strategy helps consumers learn about their illness or that a specific medication reduces a specific category of symptoms. In addition, controlled clinical trials greatly reduce the possible effects of bias on the

BOX 1.2   ROBERT DRAKE

Robert E. Drake, MD, PhD, is the Andrew Thomson Professor of Psychiatry and Community and Family Medicine at Dartmouth Medical School. He is also the Director of the New Hampshire-Dartmouth Psychiatric Research Center. Dr. Drake has been a long-term contributor to the psychiatric rehabilitation knowledge base through his work developing and evaluating innovative community programs for persons with severe mental disorders. He is one of the recognized leaders in the development of evidence-based practices for PsyR. He is well known for his work in Integrated Dual Disorders Treatment (substance use disorder and severe mental illness), Supported Employment Services, and Assertive Community Treatment, among other things. Dr. Drake's many books and over 500 papers cover diverse aspects of adjustment and quality of life among persons with severe mental disorders and those in their support systems. Educated at Princeton, Duke, and Harvard Universities, he has worked for many years as a clinician in community mental health centers. Dr. Drake is a sought-after speaker in the United States and internationally regarding his work on improving services for people with severe mental illness.

results. A good example of bias reduction in research is the use of "blind" evaluators. In an experiment comparing, for example, consumer quality of life in different housing situations, the "blind" evaluator would not know which experimental condition (e.g., experimental group or control group), in this case which housing type, was represented by the consumers she was evaluating. In this way, the evaluator is protected from unconsciously biasing the evaluations and hence the research results. Evaluators might also be blind to the hypothesis being studied or the exact form of the research design.

The evidence to support an EBP must be reliable and objective. Of course, we have just stressed that controlled clinical trials are designed to produce reliable, objective evidence, if it is present. Still, the reliability of data and the objectivity of data can and should be independently assessed. In addition, such research needs to be repeated in different settings, by different researchers, and produce similar corroborating results. This replicability is one of the hallmarks of science.

If the model for the EBP, refined by the research results, proves to consistently produce specific desirable outcomes for persons with severe mental illness its elements are converted into a **fidelity scale**. Think of this fidelity scale as a blueprint for how the service should be provided as well as a rating scale determining how close a service comes to replicating the model. The fidelity scale of an EBP is used to determine how well other programs are providing the same service. In short, how much fidelity to the EBP model do they demonstrate? Research findings suggest that services with higher fidelity to an effective program model produce better outcomes (e.g., Bond, 2004). Figure 1.1 outlines the major elements necessary for establishing an evidence-based practice.

Current Evidence-based Practices

SAMHSA has made implementation KITs available for eight evidence-based practices for addressing serious mental illness. In addition to background information, each KIT contains a detailed description of the EBP, a fidelity scale for assessing how well the EBP is

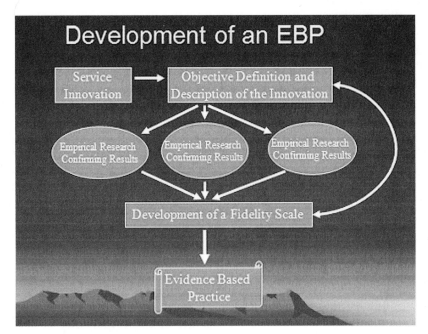

FIGURE 1.1 Schematic of the development of an evidence-based practice.

carried out, and instruments for assessing outcomes. KITs are available for download from the SAMHSA Web site. The current evidence-based practices with implementation KITs are:

(1) Assertive Community Treatment (ACT)
(2) Supported Employment (SE)
(3) Illness Management and Recovery (IMR)
(4) Family Psychoeducation
(5) Integrated Treatment for Co-occurring Disorders
(6) MedTEAM (medication treatment, evaluation, and management)
(7) Consumer-operated Services
(8) Permanent Supported Housing

KITs for these practices can be found at (http://store.samhsa.gov/list/series?name=Evidence-Based-Practices-KITs).

Three of these EBPs (ACT, SE, and Family Psychoeducation) have a very strong evidence base. Specifically, multiple controlled clinical trials of the EBPs above have been shown, among other things, to produce:

• Symptom improvement
• Less hospital utilization
• Fewer, shorter, and less severe relapses
• Higher rates of competitive employment
• Improved quality of life
• Increased community involvement

Medication has been shown to reduce symptoms, hospitalization utilization, and number of relapses.

Scientific Literature and Meetings

Starting from a small group of psychiatrists, psychologists, social workers, and other professionals working and publishing in related areas, PsyR research has come into its own during the last four decades. The first regular issue of *Schizophrenia Bulletin*, a quarterly journal of the National Institute of Mental Health, was published in 1974 and is now available online through the Oxford Press. This journal is dedicated to facilitating "the dissemination and exchange of information about schizophrenia." In 1977, the International Association of Psychosocial Rehabilitation Services (IAPSRS) and the Boston University Center for Psychiatric Rehabilitation launched the *Psychosocial Rehabilitation Journal*, today called the *Psychiatric Rehabilitation Journal*. This quarterly journal has been the primary source for PsyR research, evaluation, and ideas. *Psychiatric Rehabilitation Skills*, today called the *American Journal of Psychiatric Rehabilitation*, published by the Illinois Institute of Technology and the University of Medicine and Dentistry of New Jersey, is dedicated to publishing PsyR research from around the world.

Several other journals regularly carry PsyR research and evaluation reports, including *Psychiatric Services*, an American Psychiatric Association journal, and *Community Mental Health Journal*, the journal of the American Association of Community Psychiatrists. Articles about PsyR also appear in journals from the fields of psychology, psychiatry, social work, vocational rehabilitation, and other disciplines.

International, national, and local PsyR conferences are excellent places for discussing PsyR research, evaluation, and ideas. Initially, these conferences provided the opportunity for PsyR professionals to get together with others doing the same work to share ideas. Today's conferences may include consumers and family members and take in a broad spectrum of issues and interests. USPRA (United States Psychiatric Rehabilitation Association, formerly IAPSRS), which holds a yearly conference at a major city in the United States, has chapter organizations in over 30 states. These state organizations also sponsor conferences, meetings, and institutes on special topics. The World Association for Psychosocial Rehabilitation (WAPR) sponsors a worldwide congress of PsyR professionals approximately every two to three years at an international city. WAPR congresses are genuine multilingual, multicultural events with presentations by PsyR professionals representing countries from the Americas, Europe, Asia, Africa, and Australia.

These worldwide conferences help to emphasize the global nature and impact of severe mental illness. The plight of persons experiencing serious mental illness in third world countries is especially troubling. According to the World Health Organization (2011):

> *Mental, neurological, and substance use disorders are common in all regions of the world, affecting every community and age group across all income countries. While 14 percent of the global burden of disease is attributed to these disorders, most of the people affected—75 percent in many low-income countries—do not have access to the treatment they need. (http://www.who.int/mental_health/mhgap/en/index.html)*

At the 1989 Congress of the World Association for Psychosocial Rehabilitation, Dr. Vijay Nagaswami of the Schizophrenia Research Foundation, Madras, India, stated that "In developing countries … the mentally ill continue to languish and can be considered lucky if they receive even medication." Unfortunately, scant progress has been made to improve this situation. The international PsyR movement is actively promoting the sharing of knowledge and ideas to meet this challenge.

Standards for Psychiatric Rehabilitation Professionals and Programs

USPRA (previously IAPSRS), the oldest and largest organization of psychiatric rehabilitation professionals in the United States, has taken the initiative in establishing PsyR as a profession. This effort includes the establishment of a national test-based professional certification for PsyR professionals, the CPRP (Certified Psychiatric Rehabilitation Practitioner). IAPSRS first outlined a Code of Ethics for PsyR professionals in 1996, which was updated in 2001, and is currently being updated again by the CPRP Commission for approval by the USPRA Board. At the same time, many PsyR agencies and services are accredited through the Council on the Accreditation of Rehabilitation Facilities (CARF) and the Council on Accreditation (COA).

As in other professions such as medicine, the law, and public school teaching, official recognition of one's professional status requires being licensed by the state where the professional provides services. In order to be licensable by states, a profession needs to have very clear guidelines spelling out who practitioners are, what special knowledge they have, what services they provide, and their professional standards and ethics. In short, guidelines must define who is qualified to provide what types of services to the public.

The Certified Psychiatric Rehabilitation Practitioner (CPRP)

Defining the professional role of the psychiatric rehabilitation practitioner has advanced significantly over the last decade. In 2000–2001, IAPSRS sponsored a role delineation study (Columbia Assessment Services, 2001), which was updated in 2007. The seven broad domains that were identified are described in Box 1.3.

BOX 1.3   USPRA, THE KNOWLEDGE AND SKILLS OF PSYCHIATRIC REHABILITATION

As a first step toward professional certification and licensing, in 1996, the International Association of Psychosocial Rehabilitation Services, now the United States Psychiatric Rehabilitation Association (USPRA), established the national Registry for Psychiatric Rehabilitation Professionals. In 2001, the registry was replaced with a test-based certification program, establishing a new credential, the Certified Psychiatric Rehabilitation Practitioner (CPRP) administered by the USPRA Commission on the Certification of Psychiatric Rehabilitation. This exam is based on input from more than 500 subject matter experts—psychiatric rehabilitation practitioners from the United States and Canada. They defined the role of the psychiatric rehabilitation practitioner, identifying the knowledge and skills that are most important and most frequently used to deliver competent services. More than 90 tasks were identified, which were grouped into seven domains (IAPSRS, 2001). As is required in order to keep the certification exam current, subsequent role delineation studies were conducted and the exam blueprint was revised accordingly (USPRA, 2007, 2013). Currently, the seven domains of psychiatric rehabilitation practice are:

1. **Interpersonal Competencies**—this domain focuses on establishing collaborative relationships with persons with psychiatric disabilities, which is integral to the delivery of effective PsyR services. It also addresses the importance of having the knowledge and skills needed to instill hope regarding persons' potential for recovery. Group facilitation competencies are also addressed in this domain of practice.
2. **Professional Role Competencies**—CPRPs should have the knowledge and skills needed to provide evidence-based and emerging best practices, which are addressed in detail later in this book. They also need to conduct themselves in an ethical manner, as specified in the

---

(Continued)

BOX 1.3   USPRA, THE KNOWLEDGE AND SKILLS OF PSYCHIATRIC REHABILITATION—Continued

USPRA Code of Ethics. Other areas of practice covered in this domain include skill in helping people make informed choices, knowledge of relevant laws and regulations, ability to facilitate activities in natural settings, and utilization of advocacy and conflict resolution techniques.

3. **Community Integration**—knowing and accessing the resources and services the community offers that can promote the recovery and quality of life of those served by PsyR service recipients is essential. For example, a CPRP must be able to make linkages to entitlement and benefit programs, legal and advocacy resources, alternative supports (such as self-help groups), and natural supports. Sometimes they also need to develop community resources if gaps exist in the community support system.

4. **Assessment, Planning, and Outcomes**—rehabilitation or recovery planning is critical to the practice of PsyR and is discussed in detail in Chapter 5. Helping individuals define and refine their goals and develop the plans to achieve these goals is critical. Identifying personal strengths and personal interests and assessing readiness for rehabilitation as well as conducting specialized functional and environmental assessments are included in this practice domain.

5. **Strategies for Facilitating Recovery**—this domain addresses the types of interventions that a CPRP must be able to provide to help facilitate recovery. These strategies include skills in teaching, environmental modification, motivational enhancement, outreach, crisis de-escalation, problem solving, and other interventions.

6. **Systems Competencies**—understanding the various components of mental health systems, including government agencies and regulations, the network of relevant service providers, and the role of advocacy organizations is an important area of PsyR practice. CPRPs should be able to navigate these systems and collaborate with stakeholders to participate in systems-level advocacy.

7. **Supporting Health and Wellness**—Health and wellness in all its dimensions are important aspects of rehabilitation and recovery. The CPRP must support individuals in developing the knowledge, skills, and attitudes to attain and sustain a wellness lifestyle. This may involve assistance in accessing specialized services as well as devising strategies for improving various dimensions of wellness (Chapter 6).

Source: USPRA, 2007, 2013.

This role delineation report was used to develop the test questions contained in the Certified Psychiatric Rehabilitation Practitioner (CPRP) examination. This standardized exam, which serves as a demonstration of competence, is combined with an assessment of level of education, amount of experience, and professional references to designate an individual a Certified Psychiatric Rehabilitation Practitioner. The certification program, now overseen by the Certification Commission for Psychiatric Rehabilitation, is a major development in the definition of PsyR professionals. The written test is now used on an international basis to evaluate PsyR knowledge. Since 2002, it has been regularly offered in the United States and Canada. It has also been offered in Singapore.

At the time of this writing, there are approximately 2400 CPRPs worldwide, 2200 of whom are in the United States. Fifteen US states have recognized the CPRP through some form of legislation as identifying individuals qualified to deliver these services in their state. Several states are considering a license based on this credential.

Summary

Being diagnosed with a serious mental illness can be a devastating experience affecting a person's entire life. Particularly because they tend to strike during the late teen or early adult years, these diseases often cause severe disabilities. An additional major source of distress is the stigma attached to these diseases, which often results in prejudice, discrimination, and reduced opportunities to live, work, and socialize in the community. Increased knowledge and education are helping to reduce stigma, but there is still a long way to go in this respect. Despite the extreme personal and societal costs of these conditions, we are still unclear as to their cause. With the advent of modern research methods, it has become clear that these conditions are biologically based.

Psychiatric rehabilitation encompasses the community treatment and rehabilitation of persons with severe mental illness. Psychiatric rehabilitation in its present form began in response to the deinstitutionalization movement in the late 1960s. Initially through trial and error, and later through systematic clinical research, services are increasingly becoming more refined. Psychiatric rehabilitation has emerged as a unique discipline with its own body of research, journals and publications, and professional organizations and conferences. The major US organization, USPRA, is actively working toward the professionalization of PsyR personnel and practices.

Class Exercise
Addressing the stigma of serious mental illness

1. What are some specific ways that stigma can negatively affect the lives of people who have a serious mental illness? Think about how stigma affects the attitudes of community members and mental health providers and the effect of self-stigma. If possible, give specific examples that you have witnessed.
2. Identify specific strategies for reducing the stigma associated with severe mental illness. Doing a Web search on combating stigma and reporting on what you find is one way you can contribute to this discussion.

Symptoms and Etiology of Serious Mental Illness

All illnesses have some heredity contribution. It's been said that genetics loads the gun and environment pulls the trigger.
Francis Collins, Human Genome Project

CHAPTER OUTLINE

Psychiatric Rehabilitation. http://dx.doi.org/10.1016/B978-0-12-387002-5.00002-0

People with a variety of serious mental illnesses can benefit from psychiatric rehabilitation (PsyR) services. The most common diagnoses in PsyR programs are from the schizophrenia and mood disorder categories. The symptoms of these illnesses can be catastrophic in their impact, threatening the integrity of the person's thoughts, feelings, and sense of self. Today, we under-stand that these illnesses are primarily brain disorders that have severe physiological, psycho-logical, and social consequences. The causes of these illnesses seem related to an interaction of hereditary factors, other biological influences, and the environment. Being vulnerable to these disorders appears to be genetic; that is, inherited. This genetic vulnerability apparently interacts with environmental and developmental factors, both biological and psychological, to provoke the onset of these disorders. This chapter and the next include brief vignettes about individuals with mental illnesses. All are factually based, but readers should keep in mind that they represent only a brief interval in that person's life and only one aspect of the life of a person with a severe mental illness. In other words, all individuals have characteristics, abilities, interests, and ex-periences that make them unique. A person who is utilizing mental health services should never be viewed simply as having an illness.

This chapter will answer the following questions:

1. What are the most common symptoms of the severe mental illnesses?
*2. What are the current scientific theories about the **etiologies** (causes) of these conditions?*
3. What is the relationship of stress to severe mental illnesses?

Introduction

The goal of PsyR is to help individuals recover from the catastrophe of serious mental illnesses. The disabling nature of these disorders results from their severity and persis-tence. PsyR programs serve people with a variety of disorders, primarily individuals recovering from psychoses, as discussed in Chapter 1. In a study of 13 PsyR programs, 65 percent of the individuals served had schizophrenic disorders, 25 percent had mood disorders (bipolar disorder, major depression, etc.), and 10 percent had a variety of other conditions (Arns, 1998). Therefore, this chapter will focus primarily on schizo-phrenia, with some attention to serious mood disorders, bipolar disorder, and major depression.

Symptoms

Symptoms are literally signs or indicators of an illness or disease. They are also a cause of suffering for the individual with the disease. According to the traditional medical model, observing symptoms, or patterns of simultaneously occurring symptoms, leads to the diagnosis of the underlying disorder. An example is a young child who has the sniffles, is cranky, tugs at his or her ear, and has a fever. The doctor examines the middle and inner ear and sees that it is red. All of these are symptoms or indicators of the illness commonly known as ear infection. The earache, while a symptom of an infection, is also causing pain for the child. The treatment is usually to provide antibiotics to stop the bacterial infection, which also relieves the child's symptoms and pain.

The symptoms of mental illness, as discussed in Chapter 1, involve the senses, emotions, and **cognition** (thinking). These symptoms shape how the person perceives, thinks about, and reacts to the world around him or her. Besides indicating a serious illness, like the child's earache, these symptoms can become a preoccupying and consuming experience in the person's life. In the case of the earache, with treatment, the situation is temporary and specific. With serious mental illnesses, the severity and the persistence of symptoms may be disruptive to the person's functioning at home, school, work, and in the community in general and require lengthy and complex intervention.

Persistence of Symptoms over Time

One of the most devastating features of mental illness is that psychiatric symptoms often reoccur and persist, in one form or another. For some, symptoms can persist for their entire life. This persistence of symptoms led to the term **chronic** mental illnesses and labeling individuals whose symptoms persisted "chronics." Fortunately, with the emergence of people first language (e.g., "a person with schizophrenia" rather than "a schizophrenic"), and increased awareness of the possibility of recovery, the term, which implied "low functioning" and "hopeless," has fallen out of use. The overall negative associations with this label turned out to be not only inaccurate but also very harmful (Harding, Zubin, & Strauss, 1992). Chapter 3 discusses evidence of the inaccuracy of the "chronic" label.

Nevertheless, the fact that psychiatric symptoms may persist, despite treatment, is one of the most important PsyR challenges. In short, how can we help persons recover and live meaningful, productive lives despite the continuing presence of psychiatric symptoms?

The Symptoms of Schizophrenia

Schizophrenia, arguably among the most disabling of mental illnesses, is the most common disorder of persons who utilize PsyR services (Arns, 1998). Diagnosing schizophrenia is difficult and takes time, in part because the symptoms are varied and numerous and must be present for a specific length of time. As yet, there is no single definitive sign that indicates schizophrenia is present. Other serious disorders must be

---

BOX 2.1   THE FIFTH EDITION OF THE DSM (DSM-V)

DSM-V, appearing in 2013, is the fifth full edition of the American Psychiatric Association's *Diagnostic and Statistical Manual of Mental Disorders*, the first major revision in over 20 years. According to its developers, its virtues include a greater awareness of cultural, gender, and most importantly, developmental issues (Kupfer, Juhl, & Regier, 2013). It has also been made to be more compatible with the *International Classification of Disorders*, Eleventh Edition (ICD-11), and has other changes that will make it useful to both psychiatrists and other physicians, in that the new DSM will more closely resemble the diagnostic systems for other medical disorders (Kupfer, Kuhl, & Regier, 2013). Over a period of six years, 400 international experts contributed to its development. Yet, it is embroiled in controversy. Its critics include the chairs of previous DSM task forces (Allen, 2012). The task force's activities have been described as fairly secretive and not as open to peer review (i.e., the review of other researchers and clinicians) as in the past. There are a number of possibly well-founded accusations that it is "medicalizing" or "pathologizing" conditions in order to justify insurance reimbursement and pharmacological treatment, instead of focusing primarily on existing research. One change, for example, may make it more likely for people who are experiencing normal grief after a death to be diagnosed as depressed. In addition, compared to the earlier editions of DSM-III, DSM-IV, and DSM-IV-TR, there is less inter-rater agreement on the diagnoses. For better or worse, it will likely become the official manual of diagnostic nomenclature in May 2013.

---

ruled out first. For example, many drug reactions look strikingly like schizophrenia during the acute phases of the illness; hence the term "psychedelic drug," which refers to a class of drugs that causes psychotic-like symptoms. Unlike the symptoms of schizophrenia, these drug-induced conditions are short lived and have a very different impact on the individual.

The symptoms of severe mental illness are not transient experiences. In the case of schizophrenia, an individual's most serious symptoms may last from several days to many years, waxing and waning in intensity. While there are some subtle physiological signs, they are not diagnostic in themselves.

Positive and Negative Symptoms

According to the official manual of the American Psychiatric Association (APA, 2000), *Diagnostic and Statistical Manual of Mental Disorders*, Fourth Edition, text revision (DSM-IV-TR), the characteristic symptoms of schizophrenia can be categorized into two broad groups: **positive symptoms** and **negative symptoms**. (A fifth edition is appearing in 2013; see Box 2.1 for more information.) The positive symptoms appear to reflect an excess or distortion of normal functions, whereas the negative symptoms appear to reflect a diminution or loss of normal functions (APA, 2000, p. 299). It is important to note that negative symptoms are considered much more difficult to treat and are often much more disabling than positive symptoms. Positive and negative symptoms are described and illustrated in the following paragraphs; they are also summarized in Box 2.2.

BOX 2.2   POSITIVE AND NEGATIVE SYMPTOMS OF SCHIZOPHRENIA

The positive symptoms of schizophrenia include distortions or exaggerations of:

1. Thinking and ideas (delusions)
2. Perception and sensations (hallucinations and illusions)
3. Language and communication (disorganized or bizarre speech)
4. Behavioral self-control (grossly disorganized or catatonic behavior)

Negative symptoms include losses or deficits in:

1. The range and intensity of emotional expression (flat affect)
2. The fluency and productivity of thought and speech (alogia)
3. The initiation of goal-directed behavior (avolition)

We will consider negative symptoms first. Clearly, all of the symptoms of schizophrenia are "negative" in the sense that they are harmful. However, this class of symptoms is referred to as "negative" because it is characterized by the absence or loss of something that is normally present. For example, **avolition** and **anhedonia** are common negative symptoms. In these terms, "a" is similar to "anti" and literally means "not." Thus, avolition is the lack of willpower or motivation. Anhedonia means "not in pursuit of pleasure," and the term refers to an inability to experience pleasure. Both are common negative symptoms experienced by people recovering from psychotic disorders. Many mental health professionals mistake these symptoms as simply a choice not to be motivated. Consider the experience of Pete, a newly hired psychiatric rehabilitation staff person:

> *I went to the rooms throughout the program and then to the work units, but it was all the same. Most of the time, it seemed members of the program were sitting around, doing nothing, staring into space. Some of the staff persons were really good at engaging the members, but the members had a hard time sustaining activity. People seemed to move slowly; they were slow to smile. I thought to myself, why are these people so negative and down, so unwilling to do anything?*

In contrast, positive symptoms, such as hallucinations, delusions, and most thought disorders, are, in a sense, more blatant signs of a mental illness. They are known as positive symptoms because they are added to the individual's experience as a result of the disease. For example, when someone with schizophrenia or another mental illness hears voices it is defined as a positive symptom, because these auditory hallucinations are something added by the disease.

Sometimes people who have serious mental illnesses appear distracted; they mumble or talk to themselves, are bewildered, or are "in their own world." These behaviors are often secondary to positive symptoms, such as auditory hallucinations or other internal stimuli, which are described in detail later in this chapter.

Delusions

Among the most common positive symptoms of psychosis (defined in Chapter 1) are delusions; bizarre beliefs or ideas that the person cannot be "talked out of." A common type of delusion is the feeling that one's actions are under the control of others. Consider this example:

> *Sal was a bright man who formerly worked as a teacher. Since developing schizophrenia, he thought that two individuals were controlling his actions, "Marlboro Man" and "Frank." These were not their real names, he said, but code names or aliases. They were real people, cousins of Sal's, but Sal thought they were controlling his life, intervening to make him fail, talking to his students (when he still had students), and talking to his employers, who would then fire him. Sal thought "Marlboro Man" and "Frank" caused his other symptoms, polluted his water, and contaminated his bathroom. Once, Sal started teaching at a day program, helping his fellow consumers learn Spanish. When the students had normal difficulties, making mistakes, confusing pronunciation, etc., Sal gave up. In explanation, he said, "It's no use, it's Marlboro Man and Frank interfering again." In the early phases of Sal's illness he talked about the two men, but in the active phase he was totally preoccupied with them. Even when he was relatively well, they were always in his thoughts.*

Another category of delusions, grandiose delusions, involves believing one has great worth, power, knowledge, a special identity, or a special relationship with God or a famous person. Typical grandiose delusions include believing one is God or Jesus Christ. Other typical delusions involve believing oneself to be especially famous, beautiful, or influential.

> *Louise, a plain-looking person, average in many ways, arrived at her day program one day saying, and believing, that she was a famous designer of clothes and that a new perfume had been named after her.*

Other types of delusions might include believing there are evil or negative forces targeting one's self or a loved one. Examples include believing the Mafia is harassing you or that the CIA or FBI has you under surveillance. These delusions can also take the form of ideas of reference, in which an individual believes special messages are being sent to him by the radio, television, computer, smartphone, or even in an everyday remark.

> *Carol, a middle-aged woman with schizophrenia, had not been hospitalized for many years. She was concerned because she thought television programs were sending her special messages and she knew this was a bad sign. She wished to reassure her caseworker (and herself) that she was not getting ill. She called her caseworker on the phone and said she had something to tell her. Carol's comment was, "Don't worry, I won't let the TV bother me."*

The impact of delusions on an individual's behavior can be extreme, with the individual taking specific actions in response to a belief. Uncontrolled emotional responses, such as inappropriate laughter and crying, occasionally occur. Delusions may occur by themselves or simultaneously with the next major symptom we will discuss: hallucinations.

Hallucinations

Hallucinations are incorrect sensory information that the individual experiences as real. The individual must deal with heightened internal stimulation (often in the form of a hallucination) or exaggerated experiences of external stimuli (illusions). Some people experience visual, olfactory, or tactile hallucinations, but the most common hallucinations, which are usually the worst during the active phase of illness, are auditory in nature. Poor concentration and attention span seem to be a natural outgrowth of these sensory experiences. As will be discussed, there may be other reasons for distractibility, including various types of thought disorders.

Auditory hallucinations may include a variety of experiences, such as a voice that keeps a running commentary on one's actions or thoughts or multiple voices conversing with each other. These hallucinations can take the form of:

- Voices speaking one's thoughts aloud; as one man said, "I have very loud thoughts."
- Two or more voices arguing; as one woman said:

  I heard the voices of the staff here at the program yelling at each other. It started as two voices, later more voices were added, including yours. Later, it was like eighteen voices or something like that. It was so overwhelming I stayed in bed and never got out.

- Voices commenting on or narrating one's actions; for example, consider Ralph's predicament:

  Ralph did not like walking around his neighborhood. It was pleasant and safe enough, except he could not stand the chatter of his neighbors. He could hear their voices as he passed their homes. Wherever he lived it was always similar, voices saying what he happened to be doing at the time.

- A voice or voices telling or ordering the individual to do a specific thing. These hallucinations, called *command hallucinations,* can have dangerous consequences. A woman, who had jumped from a bridge into the river, later reported that voices had been telling her to jump for several days before she complied.

Thought Disorders

In addition to delusions and hallucinations, individuals may experience thought disorders, which are symptoms associated with cognition or thinking (i.e., the processing of information). In schizophrenia, the cognitive symptoms are quite prominent and include thought disorders, thought broadcasting, thought insertion, and racing thoughts. Consider the story of Betty, who experienced thought broadcasting:

> *For years, I could never understand why people acted certain ways, especially why they never responded to me when I sent them messages. Then I went to a group in which I learned that not everybody thought in the way I did. For a long time, I believed people could hear my thoughts. I could hear theirs. At first, I didn't believe that people could not hear my thoughts, because as far as I'm concerned I still hear others' thoughts.*

Other individuals complain of very intrusive thoughts being put into their heads (thought insertion) or not being under their control:

> *Elise believed that her parents and doctors conspired against her by arranging to have a surgical procedure performed on her while she was asleep. She thought the procedure involved the insertion of "metal patterns" in her brain that controlled many of her thoughts and actions. This delusional system provided an explanation for Elise who experienced some of her thoughts as being intrusive and inconsistent with her thinking prior to the onset of her illness.*

Other people experience racing thoughts, such as Tommy, who stated:

> *My thinking is all messed up; it moves really fast and makes me nervous because I can't keep up with it.*

The Experience of Symptoms

Sometimes it is difficult to tell specifically which symptoms someone is suffering from. At the same time, it is apparent that the person is currently experiencing one type of psychotic symptom or another.

> *In a meeting with her doctor, Andrea said she was no longer taking her medicine. When her doctor asked why, Andrea responded, "Because God told me not to take it." The doctor tried several different ways to persuade Andrea to take her medicine, including saying to her "God helps those who help themselves," but Andrea just kept repeating, "God told me not to take it." Almost exasperated, the doctor said, "Andrea, God told me to tell you to take the medicine." The doctor was startled when Andrea said, "OK."*

Was this evidence of a grandiose or religious delusion, that God was sending direct messages, or was it an auditory hallucination? After all, if you were hearing a disembodied voice, where would you think it was coming from? It should also be noted that this is a relatively rare example of effective communication within the delusional system of a person who is actively psychotic. The doctor did not challenge the person's beliefs, but communicated based upon them; rarely is such a workable resolution reached so quickly.

Early in the onset of the disorder, it can be difficult to determine whether someone is even experiencing symptoms. Sometimes symptoms are difficult to distinguish from the norms of behavior or attitudes within one's social niche and where one lives. Consider these comments from Pete, the brother of Mike who has been diagnosed with a serious mental illness. It turns out Mike's attitudes and beliefs were not so distinguishable from those of his neighbors and family:

Frankly, it was hard to tell at first. Mike was suspicious growing up, we all were, it's that kind of neighborhood; in fact, that was the safest way to be. We always had, what's the nice way to say it … minorities here. In recent years, a lot of immigrants, people speaking other languages, different foods, taking over the businesses, store signs in foreign languages. Then 9/11 happened, and we found out some of the hijackers lived in a neighborhood like ours. Afterwards, Mike, and a lot of people, were worried about terrorists, al-Qaeda, the whole bit. Then, he was suspicious of the guys working at the gas stations, with the turbans; I think they are called Sikhs. Where it crossed the line into his illness, I don't know, but soon he was completely preoccupied with these people, terrorism, that he was being watched, that an attack was going to happen again, etc. It was not that unusual here to think like that. Are people like him racists, prejudiced? Maybe, but I don't blame anyone who thinks that way given the world we live in. Anyway, Mike spoke like that. He would be watching the cable news all day and night; my mother would make him turn it off. Then he started surfing the Web all night reading about plots and conspiracies. I told him, "Enough already, you're making yourself nuts, shut it down!" I've since learned that his extra suspiciousness, even the sleepless nights, were actually part of his illness, not the cause of it. Who knew?

It was difficult to distinguish Mike's beliefs as different from his neighbors'. His brother thought his suspiciousness was reasonable. Someone else might think he was just intolerant of the new ethnic groups in his city.

Even people very familiar with psychiatric illnesses do not always recognize its symptoms as they are emerging or reemerging. Consider what friends of Jan had to say about the time period just preceding a relapse:

I don't know how I missed it. She had been calling me a lot. But that wasn't out of the ordinary; she usually "chews my ear off." The conversations were usually one-sided, she was never a great listener, but a little worse than usual. I lost my patience with her and said, "Stop calling me, I talk to you more than I talk to my own family!" I ran into her at a social event; she stuck to me like glue, criticizing other people she met there, literally "in my face" the whole time. I tried to ignore her, and then I had to leave. Another friend tried to give her a ride home from the party. Jan said, "No one is taking me seriously; none of you really care about me." Her friend said, "I told her to get out of the car. I felt so bad later. In a week, she was in the hospital;

I felt terrible. Look, I have the same issues myself; I've been in the hospital. I try to be sympathetic, but I didn't see it coming."

In this instance, Jan's demeanor or behavior change was only a matter of degree, an exaggeration of her usual personality and tendencies. People who knew her reacted to it as if it were expected of her. Complicating the picture, Jan's relapses were not always similar. Sometimes she withdrew rather than become very demanding of attention just before her illness. Another friend of Jan's said on a different occasion:

Oh, I saw it coming this time. How? She totally withdrew. Never picked up the phone, didn't bother anyone, no one heard from her. That's how I knew it was trouble.

This friend describes an abrupt change in Jan's personal style. Are Jan's friends just "rationalizing" or justifying the signs of an onset of renewed symptoms? That's one possible explanation. Another possible explanation is that there is something to their descriptions, and the changes in onset they have seen are signs of the complex course of Jan's illness.

The effect of symptoms on a person's behavior can vary markedly, with younger individuals at higher risk for acting in response to both hallucinations and delusions.

Rachel, a meek and mild, middle-aged woman, who has suffered from schizophrenia for most of her life, recalled how she lost the custody of her children more than 10 years ago because she responded to a delusion. She thought her crying infant son had been sent by the devil, so she threw him out of the window. Fortunately, he survived, but she lost custody of all three of her children. Since that time, she not has committed any violent acts. Over the years, she has developed a good, but generally long-distance, relationship with her children. She has held several jobs and has some close friends. In retrospect, she could not believe what she had done, particularly since she rarely acts in response to her symptoms now. Today, she occasionally feels hostile, angry, or a bit suspicious, but she knows that this is often a sign that she needs some assistance, so she picks up the phone and calls her case manager or a friend.

Rachel's experience provides an extreme example of a bizarre and violent act committed in response to a hallucination or delusion. While such an event is quite dramatic, it is also rare.

Some individuals have adapted to their symptoms quite well and while they certainly would prefer not to have them, they experience a relatively peaceful coexistence with them.

When it was Catherine's turn to speak about the experience of auditory hallucinations at a psychoeducation group, this generally cantankerous 70-year-old said with a grin, "Yeah, sure, I hear voices, but what the hell? I argue with them, put them in their place, and that's the end of it. I don't let them bother me."

While experiencing severe symptoms, the self-regulation of one's behavior becomes more difficult, as was evident in Rachel's experience. Often, however, along with the psychotic symptoms, the individual will have some self-awareness, as Catherine's comments indicate. Consider this vignette:

> *Andrew had not been doing well lately. He hid from the outreach workers when they came to his home. One day, he became convinced that his voices would stop if he jumped in the river and "washed them away." Andrew went down to the polluted river in his city and jumped in. In the water, he felt his nostrils fill with water and realized he was drowning. He swam to safety. Sopping wet, he walked to the local mental health center and asked for help.*

Although his behavior seemed very bizarre and dangerous, Andrew was not totally out of touch with reality and had some awareness of his actions. Perhaps, like Catherine, he might be able to develop a proactive stance toward his symptoms and self-regulate his behavioral responses accordingly in the future.

Were Andrew's actions in response to a delusional belief? Did voices tell him to jump in the river? Or was it a thought disorder, an example of concrete thinking, the "washing away" idea, taken too literally? Andrew's own description of his experience was not clear enough to ascertain what symptoms prompted his behavior. It is unclear. Behavior is often the result of an array of symptoms rather than a response to one symptom. Most critically, Andrew and his helpers recognized that he was in the acute or active phase of the illness and that his behavior had become unpredictable.

Many people who are relatively unfamiliar with severe mental illnesses presume that all persons with disorders such as schizophrenia are very disabled and need close supervision at all times. On the contrary, many individuals who experience severe psychotic symptoms, such as hallucinations or delusions, still manage to care for themselves and others. Many maintain their own homes, hold jobs, or attend school despite their symptomatology. This is discussed in detail throughout this text.

Lack of Awareness of One's Own Symptoms as a Symptom

Although not explicitly included as one of the symptoms of schizophrenia or other severe mental illnesses, a lack of awareness of the symptoms themselves by the persons with the disorder seems to be a common characteristic of the illness. This is especially evident during the acute phase of the disorder. Individuals seem unaware of the fact that their symptoms are, in fact, symptoms of an illness. It seems that the disordered brain, attempting to make sense of its own state, interprets its disordered functioning as normal. Xavier Amador (Amador, 2007) investigated this phenomenon at length.

Borrowing a term from neurology, Amador has studied ***anosognosia*** (not knowing you do not know). Sometimes mistaken for denial or lack of insight, an individual experiencing anosognosia confabulates or makes up explanations that apparently make sense to him or her, but seem absurd to others. An extreme example is a person who has been blinded due to a brain injury, who seems apparently unaware of the fact that he or she is blind and explains his or her difficulties by saying the lighting is bad, furniture has been moved, and so forth.

An example of an individual with schizophrenia's lack of awareness comes from earlier in our chapter. You will recall Andrea, who believed God was speaking to her. She was not aware of the fact that these were auditory hallucinations. In fact, Andrea believed she was not sick at all and did not require intervention. Andrea's physician did not try to contradict her beliefs, or label them as denial, but employed an intervention that was consistent with her frame of reference and her reality at the moment.

Even Dr. Amador, a psychologist, who reports he has a mental illness himself, and who has a family member affected by mental illness, was unaware of his own depression for a time. A colleague who was learning how to administer a scale to measure depression asked him to complete it so he could practice scoring it. The colleague, after scoring the form, spoke to Dr. Amador and pointed out that he might be depressed.

The title of Amador's book on this subject sums it up: *I Am Not Sick, I Do Not Need Help* (Amador, 2007). The book suggests that many people with mental illness, instead of being in irrational denial of their illnesses, are simply reporting what they perceive and believe. Logically, they conclude there is no evidence of illness and thus no need to pursue help. This could be a large contributing factor to the high rate of medication non-adherence among persons with serious mental illness (discussed further in Chapter 3). Why take medication if you believe you are not sick? Traditionally, this has been referred to as lack of insight, but Amador prefers the term "anosognosia," literally, not knowing what you do not know.

Recovered individuals commonly report recognizing this lack of awareness or not knowing what they do not know. That is, when not acutely ill, they report that during the acute stages of their illness, they were, in fact, unaware they were sick. Equally startling is that sometimes, having recovered from a relapse, the individual who previously acknowledged the presence of illness, once again loses awareness of the fact that he or she has a mental illness.

> *Jerry, when well, could describe the antecedents of his illness, the various symptoms: the restlessness and the desire to wander aimlessly. He knew these were indicators of a relapse coming soon. Yet, the next couple of times Jerry relapsed, while others could see it coming, he could not. Eventually, he did learn that when he started to wander, an early warning sign for him, he should seek help. However, Jerry still did not directly connect his "wandering" to his psychiatric illness or its symptoms. He did associate it with "upcoming trouble," but did not see it as part of a psychiatric illness when he was in the midst of experiencing this problem.*

Amador strongly suggests that direct confrontation is rarely a useful approach. Rather, it is better to communicate that you understand the person's frame of reference, in order to build rapport. Then, when the opportunity arises, gently raise doubt about inconsistencies the individual might be experiencing. This is the beginning of the often gradual process of motivating the individual to see things differently, want changes in his or her own life, and pursue active treatment.

Phases of Schizophrenia

The duration (see Box 2.3, Criterion C) of an episode of schizophrenia must persist for at least six months for an accurate diagnosis to be made (APA, 2000). The symptoms a person experiences during an episode may vary considerably depending on which "phase" of the illness is present.

The **prodromal phase** (before the full syndrome) is a period of deterioration in functioning and increase of symptoms, both positive and negative. In "The Story of Paul," from Chapter 1, Paul's inability to focus on college lectures, his suspicious feelings about his roommate and professors, and his increasingly withdrawn behavior were all indicative of the prodromal phase of schizophrenia.

The **acute** or **active phase** is the period with the most severe and extreme symptoms. Positive symptoms are most prominent during this phase. In "The Story of Paul," hearing voices, increased suspicion and withdrawal, and the belief that his doctor was giving him orders by broadcasting thoughts to him telepathically occurred during the active phase of Paul's illness.

During the **residual phase**, symptoms become milder. Both positive and negative symptoms decrease, but negative symptoms are more likely to persist. Paul's story left off when he was most likely nearing the end of the active phase of the schizophrenic episode. In a few months, as Paul entered the residual phase of the illness, while he still might have been withdrawn and felt mistrustful, his auditory hallucinations would likely have decreased in frequency and intensity.

How the Phases of Schizophrenia Affect a Person's Life

To experience the phases of schizophrenia only once would be very disruptive to one's life. Unfortunately, many individuals experience this dreaded sequence of phases repeatedly, resulting in numerous and unpredictable disruptions to their lives. Persistent negative symptoms during long residual phases with occasional bursts of positive symptoms may dominate the person's existence, making it difficult to concentrate or focus, even on simple day-to-day tasks. Functional deficits associated with the disorder interfere with goal-directed behavior involving one's career and lifestyle. Thus, a large proportion of the people living with schizophrenia are chronically unemployed, have not finished their education, do not reside in their own homes, are unmarried, and are estranged from their relatives. Later in this book, we will address how the interventions of psychiatric rehabilitation can help these individuals to cope more effectively, regain control over their lives, and successfully achieve goals such as employment and independent living.

BOX 2.3   DIAGNOSTIC CRITERIA FOR SCHIZOPHRENIA

A. Characteristic symptoms: Two (or more) of the following, each present for a significant portion of time during a one-month period (or less if successfully treated):

(1) Delusions (i.e., bizarre beliefs or ideas)
(2) Hallucinations (usually auditory, i.e., "hearing voices")
(3) Disorganized speech (e.g., frequent derailment or incoherence)
(4) Grossly disorganized or catatonic behavior
(5) Negative symptoms (i.e., flat affect, alogia, or avolition)

Note: Only one Criterion A symptom is required if delusions are bizarre or hallucinations consist of a voice keeping up a running commentary on the person's behavior or thoughts, or two or more voices conversing with each other.

B. Social/occupational dysfunction: For a significant portion of the time, since the onset of the disturbance, one or more major areas of functioning such as work, interpersonal relations, or self-care are markedly below the level achieved prior to the onset (or when onset is in childhood or adolescence, failure to achieve expected level of interpersonal, academic, or occupational achievement).

C. Duration: Continuous signs of the disturbance persist for at least six months. This six-month period must include at least one month of symptoms (or less if successfully treated) that meet Criterion A (i.e., active phase symptoms) and may include periods of prodromal or residual symptoms. During these prodromal or residual periods, the signs of the disturbance may be manifested by only negative symptoms or two or more symptoms listed in Criterion A present in an attenuated form (e.g., odd beliefs or unusual perceptual experiences).

   [Additional criteria caution the diagnosing clinician to rule out other physical and psychiatric disorders as well as considering the presence of preexisting developmental disorders of childhood].

Excerpted from DSM-IV-TR (APA, 2000, p. 312).

Mood Disorders

More common than schizophrenia, mood disorders are estimated to affect from 5 to 20 percent of the general population. However, compared to schizophrenia, mood disorders affect a smaller proportion (about 25 percent) of persons served in PsyR programs (Arns, 1998). This is probably because mood disorders cover a wide spectrum of symptoms and functional deficits. Some individuals experience relatively mild or moderate symptoms that do not have a significant negative effect on their day-to-day functioning and therefore do not require PsyR services. Others have occasional bouts of mood swings intermixed with long periods of good mental health. It is not uncommon for people with other serious mental illnesses to experience mood disorders as well.

   The most serious mood disorders are episodic, recurrent, and cause significant functional deficits. Three types of episodes are associated with mood disorders (APA,

2000). Keep in mind that not every individual with a mood disorder necessarily experiences each type of episode.

Depressive episodes are characterized by extreme sadness or emptiness lasting most of the day, every day, for a period of two weeks or longer. **Manic episodes** are marked by an elevated mood, in which the person feels excessively "up" or "high," and occasionally excessively irritable, for a period of a week or more. In a **mixed episode**, a person meets the criteria for both types of episodes, cycling through depressive and manic phases of the illness. When an individual experiences one or more recurrent episodes of depression, he or she may be diagnosed with major depression, recurrent (APA, 2000). Individuals who experience more than one instance of two out of the three types of episodes may have what is known as **bipolar disorder**, formerly called manic depression. Both major depression and bipolar disorder may or may not have some of the psychotic features described earlier, such as hallucinations and delusions.

Most people know what it is like to be "down in the dumps" for a day or two. Some have had longer bouts of feeling sad, perhaps accompanied by insomnia or a change in appetite. By contrast, consider the following:

> *Marian has a mid-management position in a large company. She generally enjoys her work, but she has not made it in to the office for almost three weeks. She cannot rouse herself in the mornings. When she finally does get up, close to noon, she has trouble getting anything done, even a load of laundry. It seems to take an eternity to get herself out of bed, walk to the kitchen, and make a cup of coffee. She feels sadder than she can remember, except perhaps when her father died four years ago. But this seems worse, because at least after her father's death friends could distract her and she could forget her sorrow for brief periods. Her current sadness has a different quality, like she is at the bottom of a pit, with no hope of getting out, or ever feeling happy again. She finds herself crying for hours at a time, but she cannot figure out why she is weeping. Marian knows she needs help, but cannot motivate herself to even make a phone call.*

Marian is experiencing a major depressive episode. While some of her symptoms may have been experienced by many people not diagnosed with a severe mental illness, Marian's symptoms are more severe and of longer duration. In fact, she is experiencing a severe and persistent mental illness that can be extremely disabling. The criteria for making this diagnosis are outlined in Box 2.4.

The symptoms of a manic episode are almost literally the opposite of those of a depressive episode. They are outlined in Box 2.5. Consider the experiences of Mark, a fairly average, married, middle-aged man, who recalls his earlier manic episodes with a mixture of amusement, embarrassment, and regret.

> *It is pretty wild being in that state; there is even some fun, if you don't get into too much trouble. You have a great feeling of self-confidence. You don't so much*

as feel that you are the president, but feel you have pull with him. I'd always get my hands on a really big, fancy car, which I would rent or even buy. I would head for another state, spending wildly until my credit cards got cut off. Somehow, I would have a pretty girl on my arm, at least some of the time. The stuff I did! I can't believe my wife didn't divorce me. She almost did, more than once, even though she was coming to realize that, bizarrely enough, all this was due to an illness.

BOX 2.4   CRITERIA FOR MAJOR DEPRESSIVE EPISODE

A. Five or more of the following symptoms have been present during the same two-week period and represent a change from previous functioning; at least one of the symptoms is either (1) depressed mood or (2) loss of interest or pleasure.

  Note: Do not include symptoms that are clearly due to a general medical condition, or mood-incongruent delusions or hallucinations.

(1) Depressed mood most of the day, nearly every day, as indicated by either subjective report (e.g., feels sad or empty) or observation made by others (e.g., appears tearful). *Note:* In children or adolescents, can be irritable mood.

(2) Markedly diminished interest or pleasure in all, or almost all, activities most of the day, nearly every day (as indicated by either subjective account or observation made by others).

(3) Significant weight loss when not dieting or weight gain (e.g., a change of more than 5 percent of body weight in a month) or decrease in appetite nearly every day. *Note:* In children, considerable failure to make expected weight gains.

(4) Insomnia or hypersomnia [excessive sleep] nearly every day.

(5) Psychomotor agitation [excessive movement] or retardation [slowed movement] nearly every day (observable by others, not merely subjective feelings of restlessness or being slowed down).

(6) Fatigue or loss of energy nearly every day.

(7) Feelings of worthlessness or excessive or inappropriate guilt (which may be delusional) nearly every day (not merely self-reproach or guilt about being sick).

(8) Diminished ability to think or concentrate, or indecisiveness nearly every day (either by subjective account or observed by others).

(9) Recurrent thoughts of death (not just fear of dying), recurrent suicidal ideation without a specific plan, or a suicide attempt, or a specific plan for committing suicide.

B. The symptoms do not meet the criteria for a mixed episode.

C. The symptoms cause clinically significant distress or impairment of social, occupational, or other important areas of functioning.

  [Criteria D and E caution clinicians to rule out substance use, other medical conditions, and simple bereavement].

Excerpted from DSM-IV-TR (APA, 2000, p. 356).

BOX 2.5   CRITERIA FOR MANIC EPISODE

A. A distinct period of abnormally and persistently elevated mood lasting at least one week (or any duration if hospitalization is necessary).

B. During the period of mood disturbance, three (or more) of the following symptoms have persisted (four if the mood is only irritable) and have been present to a significant degree:

(1) Inflated self-esteem or grandiosity.

(2) Decreased need for sleep (e.g., feels rested after only three hours of sleep).

(3) More talkative than usual or pressure to keep talking.

(4) Flight of ideas or subjective experience that thoughts are racing.

(5) Distractibility (i.e., attention too easily drawn to unimportant or irrelevant external stimuli).

(6) Increase in goal-directed activity (either socially, at work or school, or sexually) or psychomotor agitation [extreme restlessness].

(7) Excessive involvement in pleasurable activities that have a high potential for painful consequences (e.g., engaging in unrestrained buying sprees, sexual indiscretions, or foolish business investments).

C. The symptoms do not meet criteria for a mixed episode.

D. The mood disturbance is sufficiently severe to cause marked impairment in occupational functioning, usual social activities, or relationships with others, to necessitate hospitalization to prevent harm to self or others, or the presence of psychotic features.

E. The symptoms are not due to the direct physiological effects of substance use (e.g., a drug of abuse, a medication, or other treatment) or a general medical condition (e.g., hyperthyroidism).

Excerpted from DSM-IV-TR (APA, 2000, p. 362).

Another individual, Robert, with a history of manic phases put it this way:

I would set out, say, to hitchhike to Hawaii. Yeah, hitch rides, leave the East Coast, and ignore the fact that the Pacific Ocean was in the way, even if I got across the country. Of course, I had to hitchhike, I had already cracked up my car, left my job, stopped paying my mortgage, lost my condo. But I would have big plans for myself.

Both men also described very dark periods. Robert said:

I'd get so I would lose my confidence, not get out of bed, not shower for weeks or change my clothes. The mornings were the worst. Nighttime was not so good either. I'd be in bed, not asleep, not wanting to get up.

Mark noticed a cycle or pattern that was seasonal.

It got so I dreaded the fall, the short days before winter set in. Even on medication, I still feel the changes in myself according to the time of year.

Of course, what is so remarkable are the extremes in symptoms within the same individuals; the two opposite poles, thus the term *bipolar disorder*.

Many individuals only experience depressive episodes, such as Marian, described earlier, or Ann, who reported:

In a way, everything stopped. I didn't take care of anything, anybody, my husband, my kids, no one, not even myself. I mostly did nothing. I thought a lot about death, even suicide, but I did not even have the energy to do anything about it.

While individuals in manic phases are at risk for harming themselves or others, through their impulsive and sometimes dangerous behavior, people in depressive phases are at greater risk for suicide.

Una had made many attempts on her life, so many it was not taken very seriously. These attempts were called "gestures." But she knew for certain she wanted to die. During her last depressive episode, as she was getting better, she started to make plans. She was tired of it all and of all the medications that never really gave her relief. This time she succeeded in slitting both her arms and bleeding to death before she could be found.

A growing concern of people with bipolar disorder is so-called rapid cycling, in which folks change episodes very quickly, sharply changing in mood and staying in an episode only briefly. That is, they quickly change episodes from depressed to manic or mixed, or vice versa. Perhaps a related phenomenon, there are growing number of mixed episodes in which an individual has features of both a manic and depressed episode at the same time.

Rhonda's family has become used to her "mood swings" over the years, but now they think they are worse than ever, that is, more abrupt than ever. Formerly, she had clear "manic" phases and depressed phases that lasted weeks and even months at a time; but now she can go from crying to laughing in no time, and after several days can change phases, which interferes in her life, makes her difficult to live with, and is actually making for more trips to the emergency room. Rhonda is fairly faithful in her adherence to her psychotropic medication regimen. Why? In her words, "it has helped me so much." Her doctor, who has been reading the latest research, is considering the hypothesis that the rapid changes formerly not seen in Rhonda may be adaptations of her brain to the medications. That is, changes in the neurotransmitters due to the medicines may be causing these rapid changes in affect and behavior.

How are Schizophrenia and Mood Disorders Different?

While schizophrenia is characterized by its psychotic symptoms, and a mood disorder is characterized by its emotional or affective symptoms, the distinction between the two diagnostic categories is not always so clear. For example, both Robert and Mark who were diagnosed with bipolar disorders experienced grandiose delusions. They said their thoughts raced quickly, and Mark said that at times he heard voices. These psychotic symptoms are sometimes mistaken for being associated with schizophrenia. Consider what happened to Dave:

> *Dave had racing thoughts, imagined he was a Mafiosi and, at other times, a saint. He spoke quickly and incoherently. At times he would suddenly become sullen and withdrawn. He was treated with antipsychotic medication for many years, without much improvement and with many side effects. He died in the state hospital. Later on, when his daughter was diagnosed with bipolar disorder, manic type, it occurred to the other members of the family that their father might have been incorrectly diagnosed as having schizophrenia and, therefore, improperly treated all those years.*

Many individuals exhibit the symptoms of both schizophrenic and mood disorders. Their diagnosis does not fit neatly into either category. Consider the story of Tara:

> *Tara's mental health workers believed she had schizophrenia because when she became ill she heard voices, had mixed-up thoughts, paced constantly, and believed aliens controlled her. When not sick, she was often cheerful and vivacious. Recently, she sounded sort of hopeless and said, "I can't do anything." Her caseworker was so used to hearing so many clients say that, she barely noticed. Then, Tara began to stop her usual social and volunteer activities. Her personal hygiene became very poor. She stared off into space, and basically stopped talking.*

Does Tara really have schizophrenia? Does she have another type of psychosis? Is she someone who has schizophrenia, but now is also experiencing a depressive episode? Are these the signs of a catatonic episode, perhaps the most bizarre form of schizophrenia, in which movement stops altogether?

Tara's flat affect (the lack of expression of emotions), her withdrawal, and her poor concentration are indicative of a variety of illnesses (see DSM-IV-TR; APA, 2000). Too often, mental health professionals, including psychiatrists, jump to conclusions about a person's diagnosis. The risks associated with an incorrect diagnosis are great, because the choice of psychotropic medication is, in large part, based on the diagnosis. The wrong medications are not only unhelpful; they can be directly harmful because of side effects and the potential aggravation of other symptoms. For example, antidepressant medication can increase symptoms of psychosis and antipsychotic medication can bring on depressive symptoms. Issues about medications will be discussed further in Chapter 3.

The symptoms of mood disorders and schizophrenia resemble each other and in some cases may even be identical. Indeed, many individuals meet the criteria for both schizophrenic and mood disorders at different times throughout their lives or, occasionally, even at the same time. Individuals who have the symptoms of schizophrenia and also meet the criteria for one of the major mood disorders are classified as having **schizoaffective disorder**, which has two subtypes: bipolar and depressed (APA, 2000).

Relevance to Psychiatric Rehabilitation

This introduction to psychiatric symptomatology is intended to help the reader grasp the highly disruptive nature of these disorders. The symptoms of these disorders are far more serious than the ups and downs of everyday life. They are also not transient like the effects of drugs or alcohol. The impact of these symptoms can be all encompassing, causing extreme distress and disrupting the living, working, and learning of individuals who experience them. It is important for PsyR professionals to have a clear understanding of what consumers face every day. Hopefully, some understanding of the nature of symptoms allows us to feel empathy for someone struggling with a severe mood or thought disorder.

Professionals who have knowledge of symptoms can also help consumers learn about, monitor, and cope with the phases of their illness. In addition, this knowledge is sometimes useful in helping individuals communicate with their psychiatrist. However, it is important to understand that most PsyR interventions do not directly address the symptoms of these illnesses; rather, they address the impairments caused by the disruptiveness, severity, and persistence of the symptoms. PsyR professionals emphasize and build on the healthier features of the person: his or her strengths and interests. Unfortunately, many professionals have a tendency to overemphasize symptoms, sometimes even missing alternative and simpler explanations. For example, social withdrawal is a common behavioral symptom of persons with severe and persistent mental illness. The extreme, of course, is the individual who does not speak at all or does not seek the company of others, like Eva, described next. Is Eva withdrawn because of her illness?

> *Eva spoke rarely, if at all, uttering occasional words in a thick Italian accent. Her psychiatrists and caseworkers must have written a thousand times in her chart "socially withdrawn." One day, a thought occurred to her caseworker. The caseworker went to another member of the program who spoke Italian and asked him to talk to Eva. When he did, Eva's face brightened immediately. She then produced long, coherent sentences in Italian. The consumer-translator said, "She speaks Italian, definitely a southern dialect, but I understand her, although she murders a beautiful language."*

Clearly, her social withdrawal was not the symptom that the staff members had assumed it to be. Similarly, there is a tendency for some mental health professionals not only to overemphasize symptoms but also to dwell on crises and bizarre behavior, perhaps because they make for juicy "war stories." The strengths and personal interests of consumers are sometimes overlooked due to this bias by professionals.

> *Leonard was a young, lanky fellow who wore a leather jacket and talked to himself in a combination of tough street language and apparent gibberish, which was referred to as a thought disorder and even described as a "word salad": a jumble of apparently incoherent words, sentences, phrases, and ideas. It was difficult to communicate with Leonard or engage him in activities. Sometimes, he would try to speak to people. One day, all he would say was, "Obama, John Boehner, US Senate," and the like. Because*

of his incoherent speech, all of this was attributed, by a staff person, to delusions of grandeur mixed with a good dose of thought disorder. She assumed that Leonard believed he spoke to or knew these political leaders. However, one day, this staff person asked Leonard to talk more slowly, repeat himself, and so forth. The staff person soon found out that Leonard was quite a history and politics buff. His facts were accurate and he did not believe he was talking with famous politicians; he was just talking about them.

The PsyR practitioner working with Leonard had found an interest around which to engage him, and perhaps a strength on which to build. In subsequent chapters, we will explore how PsyR helps consumers utilize their strengths to overcome functional deficits and ultimately achieve their goals.

The description of dire symptoms in this chapter might lead one to conclude that the outlook is hopeless, but this is far from the case. Indeed, many of the individuals described above who experienced serious problems have continued to struggle with their disorders and achieve successful lives. Chapter 3 will address the long-term outcomes of these conditions.

Dual Diagnosis and Co-occurring Disorders

The term **dual diagnosis** refers to the presence of two coexisting conditions. The two dual diagnoses most often encountered in PsyR services are mental illness and substance abuse (i.e., drug or alcohol) and mental illness and developmental disability. Increasingly, the presence of both mental illness and substance use disorder is referred to as **co-occurring disorders** (see Chapter 9). In both cases, the presence of a dual diagnosis has historically been a complicating factor in receiving adequate and appropriate services. Mental health providers often knew little about substance abuse or developmental disability and may have either declined to provide services to someone with a dual diagnosis or provided mental health services without addressing the coexisting disorder. Similarly, substance abuse service providers and developmental disability service providers often either addressed only the issues with which they were familiar or declined to provide services altogether. Recently, the presence of coexisting conditions and the ways in which those conditions affect each other have received greater attention.

Mental Illness and Developmental Disability

The term **developmental disability** encompasses a number of conditions including cognitive disability, intellectual disability, autism, cerebral palsy, epilepsy, brain injury, and spina bifida. A developmental disability is a severe, disabling condition that arises in infancy or childhood, persists indefinitely, and may cause serious problems in language, learning, mobility, and the capacity for independent living (New Jersey Developmental Disabilities Council, 1997/1998, p. 1). People with a developmental or intellectual disability are diagnosed with a psychiatric diagnosis at a higher rate than the general population (Holt, Hardy, & Bouras, 2011).

Since the mid-1800s, when the first segregated schools were developed for children classified as having mental retardation (the preferred term is now "intellectual disability"), most people with severe developmental disabilities were institutionalized for their entire lives. The first segregated schools were designed to be small, personal, individualized, and temporary, offering services designed to develop the skills necessary for success in the community. Segregated schools quickly became large institutions designed to "protect" society from children with retardation who might grow up to be depraved and dangerous adults (Mauch, 1991, p. 3). In a further attempt to "protect" society, the eugenics movement, begun at the turn of the twentieth century, encouraged the sterilization of people with developmental disabilities.

During the 1950s, parents of people with developmental disabilities began to demand a greater focus on educational and developmental approaches to services. The idea of institutions as the only service option was rejected, and some parents began to keep their developmentally disabled children at home. Parental organizations such as the Association for Retarded Children (ARC) emerged. ARC, which later changed its name to the Association for Retarded Citizens and more recently became simply the Arc (Roberts, 1996), became a strong advocate for family members. During the 1960s and 1970s, litigation and advocacy led to the establishment of rights for people with developmental disabilities, such as public education and services in the least restricted environment (Mauch, 1991). The work of many people such as Wolfensberger, who articulated the principle of normalization (discussed in Chapter 4), and Marc Gold, who demonstrated that people with the most severe cognitive disabilities could learn complex skills, fueled the growing dissatisfaction with institutional care. These new ideas about the rights and abilities of people with disabilities ultimately led to the development of supported employment (discussed in Chapter 10) and other community-based supports for people with developmental disabilities. During the last few decades, we have seen the downsizing and closing of state institutions as more and more people with developmental disabilities are being supported in their efforts to live, learn, work, and socialize in the community (Torrey et al., 1993).

Incidence of Mental Illness and Developmental Disability

Studies of people with developmental disabilities living in the community suggest that the full range of mental illnesses has been identified among this population (Torrey et al., 1993) and that 20 to 35 percent experience a coexisting mental illness (Parsons, May, & Menolascino, 1984; Torrey, Mueser, McHugo, & Drake, 1993; Torrey, 1993; Holt, Hardy, & Bouras, 2011). However, Parsons and colleagues caution that these studies include many children under the age of 12 and, therefore, should not be considered a true reflection of incidence among adults. Szymanski et al. (1998) reported an incidence rate for schizophrenia, other psychotic disorders, and mood disorders among people with developmental disabilities that is similar to that found in the general public. They further reported that the incidence of personality disorders, among people with developmental disabilities, appears to be higher than usual, but suggested that this may be "related to maladaptive personality traits resulting from negative social experiences" (p. 14). However, there does appear to be a higher incidence of so-called behavioral challenges among persons with intellectual disabilities, and sometimes these result in a mis-diagnosis of psychiatric illness (Holt, Hardy, & Bouras, 2011).

Diagnosing mental illness in a person with an intellectual or developmental disability can be difficult. The diagnostic process includes self-report of thoughts, feelings, and symptoms. For individuals with significant communication impairments, this may be difficult, if not impossible. Often, in these situations, a diagnosis is based on reported behavior, such as an increase in aggression, self-injury, tearfulness, and withdrawal. These same behaviors can also be indications of physical illness, psychological stress, or dissatisfaction (Stark et al., 1984; Torrey et al., 1993). The great potential for misdiagnosis and possibly the unnecessary or incorrect use of medication is a concern for people with disabilities, their families, and advocates.

Individuals with both developmental disabilities and mental illness have great difficulty receiving adequate services. Similar to the situation with mental illness and substance abuse (to be discussed in Chapter 9), available services are often provided by different systems and funded by different sources. Programs designed for mental illness often consider individuals with a dual diagnosis to have intellectual disabilities as the primary diagnosis, and programs designed for developmental disorders often consider persons with a dual diagnosis to have a mental illness as the primary diagnosis. PsyR practitioners have to make an effort to work across programs, with people from different disciplines and programs. This problem is receiving new attention in the United States and in some ways is becoming more pronounced. With the new wave of dein-stitutionalization associated with the implementation of the Supreme Court decision *L.C. v. Olmstead* (described in Chapter 12), many long-term care facilities are seeking community placements for some of the remaining people institutionalized. These are disproportionately persons with both an intellectual disability and a mental illness. They often have other conditions or challenges as well (see Chapter 15).

Mental Illness and Substance Abuse

The dual diagnosis of mental illness and substance abuse refers to the presence of a severe psychiatric disorder and abuse of or dependence on alcohol or drugs. This dual diagnosis is referred to in a number of ways, for example, co-occurring disorders, dually diagnosed, dually disordered, MICA (mentally ill chemical abuser), MISA (mentally ill substance abuser), or CAMI (chemical abuse and mental illness) (US Department of Health and Human Services, 1995).

Incidence of Mental Illness and Substance Abuse

Individuals with both a mental illness and a substance-related disorder appear to make up a large proportion of the overall population of people with severe mental illnesses.

Studies indicate that between 17 and 63 percent of individuals diagnosed with a serious mental illness also abuse substances (Drake, McLaughlin, Pepper, & Minkoff, 1991; Sciacca & Thompson, 1996). The best epidemiological study on this, in terms of thoroughness and methodology, was the epidemiological catchment area study. It found the co-occurrence of substance abuse among people with schizophrenia to be about 50 percent in the United States (Regier et al., 1990). Unfortunately, this study was published over 20 years ago with data from the 1980s. Drake and colleagues (1991) suggest that the factors contributing to this high incidence are deinstitutionalization and a reflection of societal norms. In short, because people who have a mental illness now spend more time in the community than in hospitals, they have increased access to drugs and alcohol.

Further complicating this phenomenon, the group of people identified as having a dual diagnosis is not homogeneous. Individuals who have both a mental illness and a substance abuse problem differ from each other in psychiatric diagnosis and severity, type, and level of substance abuse and in extent of the impact either disability has on life functioning (Weiss, Mirin, & Frances, 1992). Luke, Mowbray, Klump, Herman and Boots-Miller (1996) identified seven clusters of individuals by examining the type and level of substance abuse and the impact on medical needs, employment, legal involvement, family/social problems, psychiatric problems, and others. This topic is covered in more detail in Chapter 9, which is devoted exclusively to PsyR interventions addressing co-occurring serious mental illnesses and addictions.

Etiology

What is the origin of the strange symptoms described in this chapter? Why are some people affected by severe mental illnesses such as schizophrenia? What is the source of the vulnerability for these disorders? Is the root cause of these devastating illnesses biological in nature rather than psychological or **psychodynamic** (i.e., theoretically rooted in past events and the unconscious)? Interestingly, much of the progress in this area is attributed to the development of high-speed computers that have made high-definition medical imaging possible.

Physiological Evidence of the Disease Process in the Brain

Many persons with schizophrenia and their families attribute the illness to psychological stress alone, a conclusion that is inconsistent with research. The available evidence suggests that both genetic and prenatal factors can influence vulnerability to this illness. These factors combined with subsequent processes, including brain development and exposure to stressful events, can trigger the onset of what is known as a major mental illness. The same might be said for mental illnesses in general.

The evidence is overwhelming that schizophrenia and similar conditions are due to changes in the structure and functioning of the brain (Buchanan & Carpenter, 1997; Walker, Kestler, Bollini, & Hochman, 2004). Today, very sophisticated neuroimaging techniques, such as magnetic resonance imaging (MRI), computerized axial tomography (CAT) scans, positron emission tomography (PET) scans, and single-proton emission computed tomography (SPECT) can provide a view of living, working brains. Developed with the help of high-speed computers, MRI and CAT scans provide pictures of the brain's structure, whereas PET scans provide snapshots of its functioning. PET and SPECT scans can be specific enough in clarity to note activity between and within cells at the molecular level (Thompson, Urban, & Abi-Dhargam, 2009).

Using these various type of brain scans, the living brains of people with serious mental illnesses have been compared both over time and with other individuals of the same age and sex without mental illness. Based on these comparisons, it has become increasingly clear that the brains of people who have a serious mental illness have a somewhat different **neuroanatomy** and different neural functioning than those of people without major psychiatric disorders (Buchanan & Carpenter, 1997; Thompson, Urban, & Abi-Dhargam, 2009).

An MRI scan provides images of the tissue, structure, and spaces (ventricles and sulci) in the brain. In the MRI scans shown in Figure 2.1, the lighter gray areas are the brain tissue cells, or neurons, and the darker gray areas are the ventricles. The ventricles are large fluid-filled enclosures and the sulci are the spaces or folds in the brain's cortex.

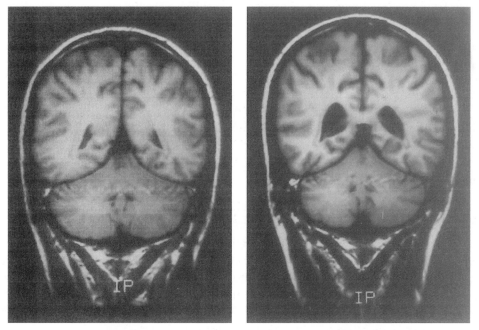

Well twin   Affected twin

FIGURE 2.1 MRI scans of 28-year-old identical twins discordant for schizophrenia, showing enlarged cerebral ventricles in the affected twin. *(Courtesy of Dr. E. Fuller Torrey and Dr. Daniel Weinberger, Clinical Brain Disorders Branch, National Institute of Mental Health.)*

These are part of the normal anatomy or structure of the brain. Normally, ventricles and sulci become enlarged as part of the aging process. In the MRI scans pictured in Figure 2.1, note that the person with schizophrenia, on the right, has less brain tissue and enlarged ventricles compared to the peer of the same age, on the left.

People diagnosed with schizophrenia, compared to others their own age, often have larger spaces in their brain in the form of enlarged ventricles (spaces within the brain) and sulci (folds in the cortex of the brain), indicating they have less brain tissue (Gur & Pearlson, 1993). MRI and CAT scans have consistently found that these spaces are enlarged in the brains of people with schizophrenia (Heckers, 1997). Based on this evidence, it appears that some people with schizophrenia have suffered a type of physical dementia (e.g., enlarged ventricles), perhaps as early as adolescence or young adulthood.

The brains of people with schizophrenia and other serious mental illnesses have other significant structural differences when compared to people of the same age and sex, and they even differ from those of their family. Individuals with bipolar disorder, like people with schizophrenia, have reduced overall brain volume and reduced frontal lobes (Arnone et al., 2009). People with bipolar disorder sometimes have an enlarged amygdala, a structure involved in emotion that is sometimes smaller in people with schizophrenia (Arnone et al., 2009).

Other brain structures differ as well; the **hippocampus** is typically smaller in people with schizophrenia compared to others of the same age and gender (Schulze et al., 2003). The reductions in the size of the hippocampus occur during the first psychotic episode. In addition, there are differences in the frontal and temporal lobe regions of the brains of people with schizophrenia. Parts of the temporal and frontal lobes have less volume and are smaller than they should be (Conklin & Iacono 2002; Kurachi, 2003a, 2003b). Many of the problems people with schizophrenia experience, such as problems with auditory (hearing) processing in the form of hallucinations, understanding concepts and abstract ideas, and other cognitive or thinking problems are associated with these regions of the brain.

The Story of Dara

Besides demonstrating an important point about the physiological basis of severe mental illness, Dara's experience (described ahead) provides a good illustration of the importance of educating consumers and their families. As you read the following story, consider what the family should have known and what effect their not knowing had on their attitude about Dara's chances for recovery.

Dara is a 54-year-old married woman with two children, who has been ill for more than 25 years. Dara is a graduate of a two-year college and worked as an accounting clerk in an insurance agency. Suddenly, for no apparent reason, she stopped going to work. Then, one day, she jumped out into traffic. Fortunately, she was rescued by a police officer. When she was asked why she had jumped out into traffic, she said that voices had been telling her to do this for several hours and she had finally given in. Once in the traffic, she became frightened and yelled for help. At the hospital, she said the president of the United States intervened to save her and had personally sent the police officer.

Upon admission, the doctor ordered a CAT scan to rule out a dementia, such as early-onset Alzheimer's disease, that might have contributed to her seemingly bizarre behavior. He reported to Dara's family that she had enlarged spaces (ventricles) in her brain. Already Dara's son, who was upset enough about her latest "episode," as they called it, said, "Oh my God, what could be worse, more bad news about Mom!" Later, the family learned, it was the same bad news they had already been living with for many years. Like many people with schizophrenia, she had significant changes in the structure of her brain, perhaps for most of her adult life.

Measures of Brain Activity

PET scans provide colored pictures of the brain's activity, by measuring where the brain is metabolizing glucose (sugar). More use of glucose is indicative of more nerve cell activity. Figure 2.2 provides some examples of PET scans. The brighter areas indicate more brain activity and the darker areas indicate less activity. During tasks requiring a great deal of concentration, the areas of the brain known as the frontal lobes typically become very active. Figure 2.2 compares the frontal lobe of a person with schizophrenia, on the right, with a person without schizophrenia, of the same age, on the left. Both are working on the same task, yet the person with schizophrenia, as indicated by the darker frontal lobe area, has far less activity in that area than the other individual.

Cerebral blood flow studies measure brain activity by tracing where the brain is using blood and oxygen. These studies have found results similar to those from the PET scan

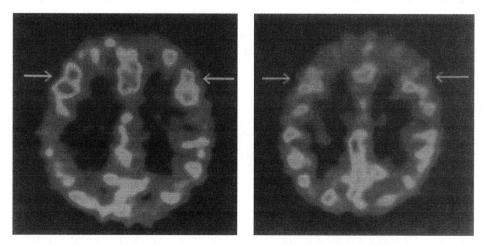

Well twin   Affected twin

FIGURE 2.2 PET scan study of 31-year-old identical twins discordant for schizophrenia. The well twin on the left shows evidence of more cerebral blood flow in the area of the frontal lobe (arrows). The twin with schizophrenia has less cerebral blood flow to the frontal lobe and is thus "hypofrontal." *(Courtesy of Dr. E. Fuller Torrey and Dr. Daniel Weinberger, Clinical Brain Disorders Branch, National Institute of Mental Health.)*

studies (Buschbaum & Haier, 1987), with less blood flow and less electrical activity evidence in certain areas. Once again, the frontal lobes were found to be underactive. The cerebral blood flow studies have also shown that other areas, such as the temporal and parietal lobes, are receiving more blood and oxygen, compared to people without schizophrenia, indicating overactivity in these areas. This overactivity may account for the experience of hallucinations, delusions, and the excessive internal stimulation reported by people with psychoses.

Neurotransmitters

The PET scan and cerebral blood flow studies imply that it is not just the structure of the brain that is different in people with mental illness, but its neural functioning, or the activity of the neurons (brain cells), which are disordered. The brain is an electrochemical organ, and neurotransmitters are literally the chemical messengers of the brain. Neurotransmitters ensure the proper functioning of the brain's electrical circuitry, which underlies all of our behavior and thoughts. Even the simplest actions and thoughts are the result of the functioning of many neurons in many different areas and systems of the brain, working in collaboration to produce complex patterns of activity. One brain cell communicates with many other brain cells through the activity of one or more neurotransmitters. Indeed, neurotransmitters regulate all of this complex electrochemical interaction. Numerous neurotransmitters are at work in the brain. Each neurotransmitter is implicated in many different behaviors or functions. The simplest of behaviors can involve numerous neurotransmitters. Some of the major neurotransmitters are as follows:

- **Dopamine** Involved in all sorts of behavior, especially the regulation of movement, hearing, and perhaps planning.
- **Norepinephrine** Also known as adrenalin, it is involved with the circulatory system and the heart, but also with sleep, appetite, and sexual behavior.
- **Serotonin** Involved in sleep, impulse control, regulation of body temperature, and other functions.
- **GABA** (gamma-aminobutyric acid) Believed to be involved in anxiety.
- **Acetylcholine** Involved in movement and also muscles, learning and memory, and normal intellectual functioning.
- **Glutamen** Involved in cognition, memory, and learning.

Neurotransmitters and Mental Illness

As mentioned previously, a variety of studies have shown that the frontal lobes are underactive in persons with schizophrenia (e.g., Buschbaum & Haier, 1987; Thompson, Urban, & Abi-Dhargam, 2009). The frontal cortex and structures (subcortical areas) are rich in the neurotransmitter dopamine. There has been speculation for more than 40 years that dopamine is central to the cause of schizophrenia. The dopamine theory continues to garner evidence, with disordered dopamine function associated with the frontal lobes, temporal lobes, and additional subcortical (below the cortex) areas. In addition, dopamine problems are most likely related to a variety of contributing causes including pregnancy and obstetric complications, stress and trauma, drug use (cannabis), increased dopamine activity before it is released by neurons, and, of course, genetic vulnerabilities (Kendler & Schaffner, 2011). These factors may converge neurochemically to cause psychosis. It is also clear that the medications used to treat schizophrenia have their main effect upon the dopamine system, as discussed in Chapter 3.

Considering the behavioral functions that are mediated by the frontal lobes, under-activity in this area is likely to result in lack of energy, poor attention and concentration, poor emotional control, flat affect, and restlessness. These problems correspond closely to the negative symptoms of schizophrenia described earlier in this chapter.

As mentioned previously, imaging techniques such as PET and SPECT are precise enough now to examine brains at the molecular level to see what is happening in the pathways of the brain and the spaces between neurons known as synapses (Thompson, Urban, & Abi-Dhargam, 2009). Using these imaging techniques, it has been confirmed that dopamine and the receptor sites for dopamine on neurons are involved with schizophrenia (Thompson et al., 2009).

Yet, the dopamine hypothesis has proven to be an over-simplification. The systems of at least four and maybe five neurotransmitters seem to be involved in schizophrenia: dopamine, glutamen, neureglin, GABA, and possibly serotonin (Chen et al., 2012; Steele et al., 2012). Neurotransmitters are also clearly involved in bipolar disorder and major depression. Serotonin and norepinephrine appear to be involved in mood disorders, particularly major depression, with the possibility of glutamen and GABA being involved as well (Belmaker & Agam, 2008). This combination would account for the changes in sleep, appetite, and drive seen in individuals with these illnesses.

The Role of Genetic Factors

What causes the changes in neuroanatomy and neurotransmitter functioning just described? The evidence suggests that, to a large degree, these changes are inherited. For quite some time, based on simple observations of familial incidence of mental ill-nesses, many experts, including Sigmund Freud, hypothesized that schizophrenia and the other severe mental illnesses were genetic in origin. There is no doubt that the risk of developing schizophrenia is greatly increased if one's biological (or "blood") relatives have the illness. Numerous studies have found that even if you have never had any contact with your biological relative who is affected by schizophrenia, and have never shared the same environment, you have an elevated chance of developing this disease (Kendler & Deihl, 1993).

Risk among Biological Relatives

The genetic component of these illnesses is illustrated by examining changes in the probability of developing these conditions. In the general population, for persons who do not have relatives with these conditions, the risk for schizophrenia ranges from about one-half of 1 percent to 1 percent, or one or two out of 200. If one parent or sibling has the disorder, the risk is ten times larger, jumping to 5 to 10 percent (Torrey, 2006), or 10 to 20 out of 200. If both parents have the disorder, the probability of developing the illness can be nearly 50 percent. Research has demonstrated that these risk increases are independent of environmental factors (Kety et al., 1994).

The exact etiology of schizophrenia has remained one of the major mysteries surrounding this disease. In the past, much of this debate pitted environmental and hereditary factors against each other. Based on a unique environmental characteristic, the Israeli high-risk study (Marcus et al., 1987) attempted to help solve this problem. Many Israeli settlements, particularly in formerly unpopulated areas such as the Negev Desert, were built on the kibbutz model. One characteristic of a kibbutz is that all the children are raised together by child care workers, rather than being raised in the family. This means that for the children raised in a kibbutz, the environment is shared and basically similar. Thus, from a research perspective, it can be assumed that many environmental factors that might contribute to schizophrenia would also be held constant in the kibbutz. To investigate this phenomenon (among others), researchers identified 100 Israeli children: 50 children from the kibbutz and 50 children from the city where they were brought up in traditional nuclear families. Half of the children from the kibbutz (25) and half of the children from the city (25) had one or both parents with a diagnosis of schizophrenia. The other children had parents who were apparently free from mental illness. These children were studied over a 30-year period. Researchers periodically assessed these individuals' neurobiological signs, social adjustment, home life (parenting), and, ultimately, their mental health. One striking finding of this study was that *all* the children who went on to develop either schizophrenia or severe mental illness had a parent diagnosed with a mental illness. Additionally, whether the child was raised by the biological parent with mental illness or the kibbutz, the probability of the child's developing the disorder did not change. This suggested that development of these diseases was not solely based on environmental factors. Similarly, genetic studies in Europe have confirmed this finding (Kety et al., 1994; Kendler, Gruenberg, & Kinney, 1994). The Israeli high-risk study provides one example from the body of compelling evidence that genetics plays a strong role in the etiology of schizophrenia.

Figure 2.3 illustrates in a "tree" or pyramid the nature of the risk factors that are associated with 9 out of 100 individuals ultimately diagnosed with schizophrenia or a related disorder, sometimes called the "schizophrenic spectrum." *Yes* indicates the presence of the risk factor, *No* indicates the absence of the risk factor. The top of the diagram starts with 50 persons who have a parent with schizophrenia and 50 who do not; the bottom row shows the 9 persons who ultimately developed the disorder. Of the 9 who developed the disorder, note that all are in the branch that had a genetic relative with the disorder, but they also experienced other risk factors as well. In fact, they all had at least two of the following three risk factors: early neurobehavioral signs, poor parenting, and

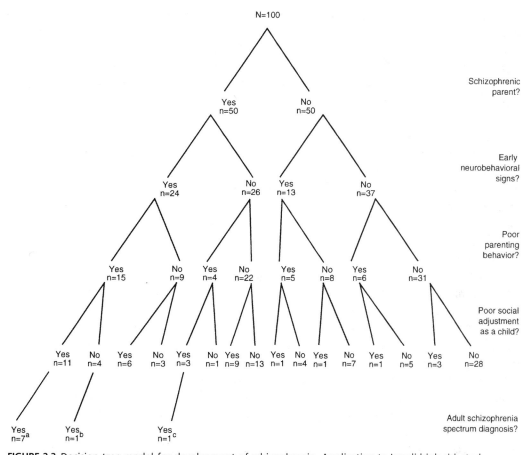

FIGURE 2.3 Decision tree model for development of schizophrenia. Application to Israeli high-risk study data. Breakdown case marked "a" = 1 residual-type schizophrenia, 3 paranoid schizophrenia, 2 schizoid personality disorders, and 1 mixed spectrum disorder. Breakdown case marked "b" = 1 residual-type schizophrenia. Breakdown case marked "c" = 1 schizoid personality disorder with dysthymic disorder. *(From Marcus et al., 1987.)*

poor social adjustment. This illustrates that genetic factors, while necessary, were probably not sufficient to develop the disorder.

When one of a pair of fraternal twins has schizophrenia, the concordance, or probability that the other twin will develop the disease, is similar to the rate for any siblings: 5 to 10 percent. For identical twins, with identical genetic heritage, the concordance rate jumps to 40 to 50 percent (Torrey, 2006). These figures show that while genetics plays a key factor in the etiology of schizophrenia, genetics alone is not a sufficient cause of the disease. If people simply inherited the disorder genetically, the concordance rate between monozygotic identical twins would be 100 percent, since they have identical gene sets. Therefore, some subsequent combination or interaction of developmental or environmental factors must account for one twin having schizophrenia while the other does not.

Heritability of Serious Mental Illness

From many sources, such as those described, it is now clear that the etiology of serious mental illness is primarily inherited. The heritability index of schizophrenia is approximately 81 percent, for bipolar disorder it is 85 percent, for major depression it is much less at about 37 percent, and for anxiety disorder, about 26 percent (Bienvenu, Davydow, & Kendler, 2011). Shared environmental factors, both biological and psychosocial, in the etiology of schizophrenia are estimated to be 11 to 19 percent (Bienvenu, Davydow, & Kendler, 2011). This heritability index does not represent the percentage of one's children that will develop the disorder. Heritability is estimated from the similarities observed in people (in this case, shared psychiatric diagnosis) based on their level of genetic similarity. These percentages were derived from studies known as meta-analyses, the statistical combining of results from studies on the same topic with similar methods. For mental illness, it includes twin studies, adoption studies, and other studies of the prevalence of a disorder based upon the biological or genetic similarity of individuals.

The specific genetics of serious mental illness have been widely studied and yet remain elusive. The quest to find a specific "schizophrenia" gene suggests that no such gene exists. Studies have identified suspicious genes that were later unconfirmed or not found in subsequent studies, which often found new suspicious genes, and so forth. This is further complicated by the fact that genes interact with each other, signaling each other on and off. The **genome** is every gene of the individual on each of his or her 46 chromosomes. With the mapping of the human genome completed, theoretically, an understanding of the specific proteins and their components that make up brain cells (neurons), their cellular structures such as receptor sites, and the neurotransmitters and related enzymes can be identified. This knowledge will help to refine pharmacological and other treatments in the future (Collins, 2010).

A puzzling fact is that disorders such as schizophrenia that clearly have some genetic component do not die out. Despite the fact that people with these disorders tend on average to have many fewer children than the general population, the incidence of these diseases remains roughly constant. Recent findings may be shedding light on why these disorders live on. During reproduction and early fetal development, the cells of the body and the chromosomes replicate or copy themselves. When this replicating takes place, sometimes mistakes are made, and parts of the chromosome that should have been copied are deleted or parts are duplicated twice rather than once. This results in genes being either missing or present when they should not be. These processes, respectively called "microdeletion" and "microduplication," have been associated with several diseases including schizophrenia, bipolar disorder, and depression (Lee, Woon, Teo, & Sim, 2012). Both of these types of genetic anomalies are known as copy number variants (CNVs). For schizophrenia, it appears that:

(1) A certain pattern of genes may be associated with these disorders.
(2) Specific microdeletions must take place before the disorder will emerge in an individual.
(3) There may be additional genetic mutations that take place soon after conception.

Some mutations do not involve deletions nor extra copies. Sometimes they involve a "substitution" of a part of a single gene component, a nucleotide. Thus, another possibility is that the disease is rooted in a set of genetic anomalies known as *single nucleotide polymorphisms* (SNPs). A grouping of nucleotides is responsible for the development of a protein or an enzyme. Sometimes one of the nucleotides has been substituted for another. This phenomenon, known as SNPs, is described in Box 2.6 by the National Institute of Mental Health.

The mapping of the genome and improved technology has helped to foster the development of better techniques to identify inherited genetic anomalies that may cause mental illness. Currently under way are genomewide association (GWA) studies, which compare the entire genomes from one group of individuals to the entire genomes of the individuals from another group (Collins, 2010). You can imagine that in order to find any patterns in a statistically reliable manner, very large samples of individuals are needed.

These GWA studies offer new promise in the understanding of the etiology of schizophrenia, bipolar disorder, and major depression. GWA studies are under way regarding each of these disorders, comparing persons with the diagnosis to other persons without them. In order to garner sufficient statistical power, sometimes results from several separate studies with hundreds or thousands of individual genetic profiles are included (Baum et al., 2008; Lee, Woon, Teo, & Sim, 2011; Wray et al., 2012). These studies often look at 5000 to 500,000 SNPs potentially related to these disorders. These GWA studies should help identify the genetic anomalies associated with specific parts of the

---

BOX 2.6   WHAT ARE SINGLE NUCLEOTIDE POLYMORPHISMS (SNPs)?

Single nucleotide polymorphisms, frequently called SNPs (pronounced "snips"), are the most common type of genetic variation. Each SNP represents a difference in a single DNA building block, called a "nucleotide." For example, an SNP may replace the nucleotide cytosine (C) with the nucleotide thymine (T) in a certain stretch of DNA. SNPs occur normally throughout a person's DNA. They occur once in every 300 nucleotides on average, which means there are roughly ten million SNPs in the human genome. Most commonly, these variations are found in the DNA between genes. They can act as biological markers, helping scientists locate genes that are associated with disease. When SNPs occur within a gene or in a regulatory region near a gene, they may play a more direct role in disease by affecting the gene's function.

Most SNPs have no effect on health or development; however, some have proven to be very important in the study of human health. Researchers have found SNPs that help predict an individual's response to certain drugs, susceptibility to environmental factors such as toxins, and risk of developing particular diseases. SNPs can also be used to track the inheritance of disease genes within families. Future studies will work to identify SNPs associated with complex diseases such as heart disease, diabetes, cancer, and mental illness.

Adapted from National Institute of Health Genetics Home Reference (http://ghr.nlm.nih.gov/glossary (2013)).

brain, cellular structures, neurotransmitters, hormones, and other bodily systems which may be involved with this disorder. At the time of this writing, numerous specific genes on specific chromosomes, pairs of matched genes, and irregularly sequenced genes have been identified as being associated with schizophrenia, bipolar disorder, and, with less promising results, for depression (Baum et al., 2008; Lee, Woon, Teo, & Sim, 2011; Wray et al., 2012). What is a particularly interesting fact is that often what is seen as one disease actually may have numerous and diverse origins genetically. In addition, multiple anomalies on genes may be necessary for a disorder to emerge (Baum et al., 2008).

The Role of Paternal Age

For thirty years we have known that schizophrenia and autism are associated with the age of the biological father as well as the genetic inheritance. Specifically, on average, people with these disorders tend to have older fathers. Recently, this mechanism has been explained by *de novo* mutations, literally meaning "new" mutations, carried, in this case, by sperm cells (Carey, 2012; Hubert, Szoke, Leboyer, & Schurhoff, 2011). As Callaway (2012) explained:

> *Fathers passed on nearly four times as many new mutations as mothers: on average, 55 versus 14. The father's age also accounted for nearly all of the variation in the number of new mutations in a child's genome, with the number of new mutations being passed on rising exponentially with paternal age. A 36-year-old will pass on twice as many mutations to his child as a man of twenty, and a 70-year-old eight times as many. (Callaway, 2012, p. 439)*

Most of these *de novo* mutations are harmless or have no known effect. Rarely, a mutation will have a positive adaptive effect, but some will have the effect of being associated with susceptibility to an illness or disease. A few of these have now been associated with schizophrenia and autism (Hubert et al., 2011). GWA studies are a quickly evolving area being explored by different international teams of researchers. Annually, many reports appear on this subject. Anything committed to paper, such as in this text, may soon be out of date.

Fetal Development and Early Infancy

Events that occur *in utero* (in the womb before birth) seem to be another factor that contributes to the development of schizophrenia. The importance of fetal development in the prenatal environment is highlighted by other findings from twin studies. When twins develop in the same chorion, that is, the same sac in their mother's womb, the concordance rate for schizophrenia is higher than when they develop in separate chorions. Birth during the winter months, maternal infections during the second trimester of pregnancy (a time of extensive brain development), lower birth weights, and complications in the delivery of the child are all associated with a higher incidence or likelihood of developing schizophrenia among those at genetic risk (Cannon, Jones, & Murray, 2002; Torrey, 2001).

Biological factors affect the risk of developing schizophrenia or other severe mental illnesses among people at genetic risk. Their genetic heritage may make the brain more vulnerable to viruses during fetal development or infancy. Obstetric delivery problems such as temporary deprivation of oxygen may be another of these potentially harmful events. All of these are referred to as "insults" to the fetus or infant. These insults, in turn, may lead to abnormal development of brain structure or tissue, altering how the person's brain structure and brain chemistry evolves. Four groups of complications are consistently associated with the development of schizophrenia:

(1) Complications of pregnancy: bleeding, diabetes, rhesus (Rh) factor incompatibility
(2) Abnormal fetal growth and development: low birth weight, congenital malformations, reduced head circumference
(3) Complications of delivery: asphyxia, emergency cesarean section
(4) Maternal inflections

However, the degree to which any of these factors explains the incidence of schizophrenia is relatively small (Cannon et al., 2002). Among the general population, these complications, which are rather common, double the chance of developing schizophrenia, from

---

CONTROVERSIAL ISSUE
The chronological and geographical incidence of schizophrenia

The prevalence rate of schizophrenia is affected by what month people are born in and where they live. These differences may provide a clue to the cause(s) of schizophrenia. Researchers who believe that infectious agents in the environment, such as viruses, are implicated in schizophrenia have pointed to these differences as possible evidence for their theories (Brown, 2012). People born in the winter or early spring have a higher likelihood of developing schizophrenia than persons born during other seasons (Torrey, 2006; Walker, Kestler, Bollini, & Hochman, 2004). This is true regardless of the hemisphere where the individual is born. These seasonal variations, which are probably not due to chance, may relate to diet, climate, risk for infections, or other seasonal changes. Ireland has long been known to have an inordinately high rate of schizophrenia. Some reports found that Ireland had a higher rate of persons hospitalized for schizophrenia than any other country in the world (Torrey, 2006). Torrey, who has studied schizophrenia in Ireland, reported that there were large differences in the prevalence of the disease even among different regions in the country, with the highest rate in its western regions. By contrast, countries such as Ghana and Botswana in Africa and New Guinea and Taiwan in the Pacific have very low rates of the disease. At the same time, schizophrenia is also known to be more prevalent in urban areas, among immigrants, and among ethnic minorities (van Os & Kapur, 2009). Yet, western Ireland is primarily a rural place. How can we account for these differences in rates? Some of the answer may involve how persons with schizophrenia are identified and counted in different settings. Another explanation may deal with genetic heritage interacting with specific environments.

about 1 to 2 percent. Thus, most people who experience these complications do not develop schizophrenia; however, for those at genetic risk, they may be particularly significant.

A leading contributing factor associated with the later development of schizophrenia and other major mental illness is maternal infections during or even prior to pregnancy (Brown & Derkits, 2010). Infections due to rubella, influenza, toxoplasmosis (from cats), or genital or reproductive system infections all increase the risk of schizophrenia and other serious mental illnesses among persons at genetic risk for these disorders (Brown & Derkits, 2010; Brown, 2012).

The Role of Stress

Psychosocial and environmental stress may play a part in brain development and brain chemistry. Responses to environmental and psychosocial stress always lead to changes in the brain's chemical messengers, the neurotransmitters. However, in individuals who are already vulnerable for genetic or developmental reasons, abnormal changes in neurotransmitter functioning may take place or normal changes may provoke a different sort of biological reaction. This is the basic premise of the **diathesis stress model** (see Figure 2.4), which proposes that a biologically vulnerable person, when exposed to a stress or trigger, then develops the disease (Anthony & Liberman, 1986).

Adoption studies have supported the diathesis stress model of etiology. Studying adopted people diagnosed with schizophrenia who had a biological parent with schizophrenia but were raised in an adopted family, the rate of psychoses and other severe disorders was significantly higher than in other adopted people (Walker, Kestler, Bollini, & Hochman, 2004). This confirms the contribution of genetics to the disease. Additionally, in disruptive family environments an elevated rate of schizophrenia was found that was not seen among adoptees at genetic risk reared in healthy family

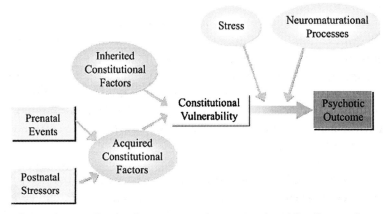

FIGURE 2.4 Stress factors that contribute to the expression of a genetic vulnerability (from Walker, Kestler, Bollini, & Hochman, 2004). *(Reprinted Courtesy of Annual Review of Psychology.)*

environments. This suggests that stress may have played a role in the increased incidence of the disease.

While the onset of schizophrenia is clearly related to the complex biological and environmental factors described above, episodes of the illness can be triggered by various stressors, many of which may appear to be normal in their intensity, but which can lead to the catastrophic symptoms reviewed earlier. Stressors that have the potential to bring on an acute episode include personal losses such as deaths and separations, developmental transitions, and important life events such as marriage, graduation, and moving. Physical illness, injury, substance abuse, and other physiological factors such as sleep deprivation have also been associated with the onset of psychiatric symptoms. "Even in the absence of a time-limited stressor, vulnerable individuals can succumb to ambient levels of challenge, tension, or conflict in their environment ..." (Anthony & Liberman, 1986, pp. 6–7).

The role of stress in the onset of major depression also appears to be a significant but not a sufficient cause of onset (Belmaker & Agam, 2008). The onset of an episode is typically preceded by a serious personal loss of a loved one, a job, a home, or a personal catastrophe. However, although stress has been established as a fairly strong contributing factor, it does not account for why some individuals respond to loss by experiencing a brief period of sadness and hopelessness and others develop a severe condition. The most obvious example comes from examining responses to the death of a loved one. Most individuals have a period of what is known as uncomplicated bereavement. That is, their mood is depressed, they feel hopeless, they may even want to die for a time, are unable to sleep, or lack appetite. Many people experience this for a period of weeks or even months, without its markedly affecting their social or occupational functioning. In sharp contrast, individuals suffering from major depression may experience a full-blown episode of depression that severely disrupts their normal functioning, as described in Box 2.4.

The interaction of life stresses, genetic factors, and the brain's functioning is not fully understood. As discussed elsewhere in this chapter, genetic factors play a major role, but developmental factors that are biological and psychological also influence brain development and chemistry. One involves the role of neurotrophins, which are the hormone-like growth factors that help neurons to grow, arrange themselves properly, and develop synaptic connections with other neurons. People with schizophrenia have an abnormally low level of neurotrophins. One major neurotrophin, brain-derived neurotrophic factor (BDNF), has been found to be significantly lower in people with schizophrenia, major depression, and bipolar disorder (Pirildar, Gonul, Taneli, & Akdeniz, 2004). Lower levels of BDNF are particularly pronounced during acute episodes of mania and depression among individuals with both bipolar disorder and those with major depression (Cunha et al., 2006; Fernandes et al., 2011). These abnormal levels lead to abnormal neuronal development and abnormal development of both the dendrites (branches of brain cells) and synapses (small spaces where different brain cells meet). At the same time, lower levels of BDNF have not been found among people with less serious forms of depression (Cunha et al., 2006).

A history of traumatic experiences has also been found to be associated with reduced BDNF among persons with bipolar disorder compared to those with bipolar disorder who do not have a traumatic history. Specific environmental, psychosocial stressors are associated with the low BDNF levels among persons with bipolar disorder: for example, having been abused as a child. It appears that a genetic anomaly associated with already reduced BDNF and an individual having been abused as a child together make it more likely that one will develop bipolar disorder (Liu, 2010).

Another theory is based on understanding normal physiological stress responses that involve the release of substances known as glucocorticoids (Belmaker & Agam, 2008; Van Winkel, Stefans, & Myen-Germys, 2008). Either because of specific experiences, a series of life events, or a genetic predisposition, some individuals' response to stress is unduly prolonged. Glucocorticoids are known to interact with the hypothalamus-pituitary-adrenal axis (HPA). The hypothalamus is a brain structure associated with many human appetites and drives. It is directly connected to a very important gland, the pituitary, which, in turn, acts upon the adrenal gland found on top of the kidney. High levels of glucocorticoids and prolonged responses to stress have been found among some people who have a serious mental illness. This prolonged stress reaction may lead to the experience of escalating symptoms, relapses, and the deterioration of certain brain structures. Among people with depression, the glucocorticoid named cortisol is sometimes increased among those with severe symptoms. The size of the pituitary and adrenal gland is increased among people with depression, and corticotropin-releasing hormone (CRH) levels in the cerebrospinal fluid of the individual as well as in the limbic region of the brain are elevated. Often, the hippocampus is decreased in size as are the numbers of neurons and glia cells (fat cells around neurons). These changes are due to elevated cortisol levels or to reduced brain-derived neurotrophic factor. In animal studies, the prolonged release of glucocorticoids is associated with the development of a smaller hippocampus, a problem specifically found in schizophrenia and depression (Belmaker & Agam, 2008; Van Winkel, Stefans, & Myen-Germys, 2008).

The Stress/Vulnerability/Coping/Competence Model

The stress/vulnerability/coping/competence model was proposed by two individuals who are well known in PsyR, William A. Anthony and Robert Paul Liberman (1986). An elaboration of the diathesis stress model described earlier, the stress/vulnerability/coping/competence model provides both a theory about the cause of severe mental illness and an explanatory framework for the impact that PsyR and treatment interventions can have on the symptoms and functional level of people who have psychiatric disabilities. The model proposes the following: individuals inherit or otherwise acquire a vulnerability (sometimes referred to as "diathesis") to major mental illnesses such as schizophrenia, major depression, or bipolar disorder. This vulnerability can result in abnormal development of brain structures and processes or an unusual type of stress reaction. As stated earlier, various biological stressors, including maternal infections during pregnancy (Brown, 2012) and psychosocial stressors such as child abuse, have been linked to serious mental illness (Thompson et al., 2009). Geographic displacement, long-term discrimination, and chronic stress have also been linked to serious mental illness (van Os & Kapur, 2009). Fortunately, a number of protective factors can either prevent the onset of an acute episode of illness or lessen the impact of symptoms. These factors include coping skills, supportive resources, competence in relevant life activities, and psychotropic medications. According to this model, the severity and outcome of these disorders have a lot to do with whether or not these protective factors are in place when a stressful event occurs. If an individual does not have adequate coping skills or does not acquire resources or supports that enhance coping, he or she remains very vulnerable to the influence of future stressors and more vulnerable to frequent or prolonged relapses. Conversely, a person with well-developed coping skills and a reliable support system is likely to experience fewer acute episodes of mental illness, as well as episodes that are less severe and shorter in duration. Consider the following vignette:

> *Cheryl has been coping with schizophrenia for ten years. For the last two years, she has been relatively stable, experiencing some negative symptoms, but very few positive symptoms. She sees a psychiatrist once a month who prescribes a relatively low dose of antipsychotic medication for her. Sometimes Cheryl forgets to take her medication, or chooses to skip her morning dose because it makes her drowsy. She used to attend a peer support group regularly, but has gradually lost touch with the group. Cheryl has a part-time clerical job that she likes. She is not particularly close to friends or family, and when not at her job she prefers to keep to herself. Cheryl was doing well at her job until her supervisor, whom she liked and trusted, left to take another position. About a week later, she began to hear disturbing voices. She also had difficulty sleeping and could not concentrate on her filing duties at work. She missed some days at work and was occasionally late. Her new supervisor criticized her performance and questioned her recent tardiness and absenteeism. Unable to face an increasingly stressful work environment, Cheryl quit her job.*

While Cheryl's job history suggests that she had some coping skills and a certain level of vocational competence, she lacked the problem-solving skills and support system she needed to help her cope with a major change at work. The fact that she was not taking her medication regularly at the time she was exposed to psychosocial stress may also have affected her vulnerability to psychosis and the distressing results.

An important role of PsyR is to aid the individual in the development of coping skills and competence (Anthony & Liberman, 1986). By enhancing coping ability and competence in social and vocational environments, the vulnerability to stress is reduced. Psychotropic medications are also an important protective factor, and PsyR practitioners can play an important role in helping consumers obtain the information and skills they need to utilize medications appropriately. For individuals who have mastered coping skills, future stressors that everyone faces will be much less devastating.

Obsolete Etiological Theories

The scientific community has made progress in its understanding of the etiology of the major mental illnesses. Yet, the public is still exposed to a number of discredited or obsolete theories about what causes major mental illness. Harding and Zahniser (1994) describe the familial role in etiology as one of the great myths about schizophrenia. While a dysfunctional family environment is clearly unpleasant, often stressful, and may be associated with some psychiatric disorders, it apparently is not the primary cause of severe and persistent mental illness.

One discredited theory traced the cause of schizophrenia to "schizophrenogenic" mothers. Supposedly, these mothers caused schizophrenia by giving "mixed messages" that many parents send, for example, simultaneously encouraging independence and engendering dependence (Lidz, 1992). Empirical research has provided no support for this theory or other theories that focus on parentally induced intrapsychic conflict, yet some professionals and members of the general public still subscribe to them.

These theories are not only erroneous but are potentially very harmful. Adherents to these theories have blamed family members for the illness of their loved ones. This, in turn, fostered guilt and animosity among family members, making for tense, counterproductive relationships among consumers and their family members and among family members and professionals (Torrey, 2006). This disservice to consumers and their families is also being perpetuated by some educators, who persist in training mental health professionals in these discredited theories, despite the lack of evidence for them (Harding, Zubin, & Strauss, 1992).

Summary of Etiology of Schizophrenia

Considering all available evidence on the etiology of schizophrenia, experts have reached the conclusion that both genetic (inherited) and prenatal (before birth) factors can give rise to a vulnerability to schizophrenia (Walker, Kestler, Bollini, & Hochman, 2004; van Os & Kapur, 2009). The subsequent processes, which affect the development of neurons in the brain, especially those that occur during adolescence and exposure to stressful events, can trigger the behavioral expression of this vulnerability. The etiology of schizophrenia involves the interaction among vulnerabilities within the brain and environmental factors. The illness does not emerge from a single defect in a specific brain region but rather from the dysfunction of different neuronal circuits in multiple brain regions. The brain's maturational processes play a critical role. As discussed earlier, genetic factors play a large role. The risk increases as the father's age at the time of conception increases or if one's biological mother has experienced a serious infection during pregnancy. Some environmental factors do come into play as well. To some extent, urban ethnic minorities are at higher risk, as are immigrants who are not living in their native country. Cannabis (marijuana) use also somewhat increases the likelihood of developing the disorder among those with a genetic vulnerability (van Os & Kapur, 2009). Therefore, schizophrenia is probably "not a single disease entity ... it has multiple etiological factors and pathophysiological mechanisms, but common phenotypic features" (Nasrallah, Tandon, & Keshavan, 2011), p. 317). Different genetic and environmental factors cause similar but not identical problems in brain structure and functioning that result in the expression of similar patterns of symptoms that are given the label "schizophrenia."

Summary

Individuals who are served in psychiatric rehabilitation programs have various psychiatric diagnoses including schizophrenia, schizoaffective disorder, bipolar disorder, and recurrent major depressive disorder among others. Details of the criteria of these diagnoses will be reported in the American Psychiatric Association's DSM-V manual (APA, 2013), which had not yet been released at the time this book was written. Criteria from the previous edition of DSM are included above. These disorders are long term and characterized by episodes of acute illness followed by periods of residual symptoms and remission. In the acute phases of these disorders and occasionally at other times, the resulting symptoms have serious behavioral manifestations and often come to preoccupy the sensory and cognitive experience of the individual.

Most people receiving PsyR services have experienced psychotic symptoms, such as hallucinations, delusions, and thought disorders, which are very severe and disruptive to daily life. The preponderance of evidence is that these major mental illnesses are biological brain disorders associated with changes in the structure and function of the brain. Studies of the structure of the brain through MRIs and CAT scans as well as studies of the functioning of the brain using PET scans and cerebral blood flow analysis confirm this hypothesis. Indeed, the National Alliance on Mental Illness has established a nationwide public relations campaign to replace the term "mental illness" with the term "brain disorder."

Genetic studies, twin studies, and epidemiological investigations all suggest that the vulnerability to schizophrenia and other severe mental illnesses is inherited. Stresses, including biological/physical risk factors and psychosocial/environmental events, contribute to further harm in already vulnerable individuals. This combination of biological influences, environmental factors, and psychosocial stressors apparently changes the structure and functioning of the brain, which results in symptoms such as hallucinations, delusions, and other serious difficulties. These symptoms have severe cognitive (thinking), psychological, and social consequences for the individual. Chapter 3 will focus on the persistence of these disorders, addressing their treatment, course, and outcome. It will discuss the positive impact of medication, rehabilitation, and other psychosocial interventions, as well as the varied outcomes for persons with these disorders.

■ ■ ■ ━━━━━━━━━━━━━━━━━━━━━━━━━━━━━━━━━━━

Class Exercises

The experience of a severe mental illness raises many questions in the minds of people with the illness. Loved ones share these concerns. At times, mental health professionals have been less than forthcoming or honest in their responses to questions. This has often led to misunderstandings and a lack of trust. Sometimes, it has led to the development of very serious misconceptions and misinformation about mental illness. Consider how you might respond in the following circumstances.

Scenario 1

A person who is served by the PsyR program that you work in has approached you, telling you that he does not have schizophrenia, because he has only one personality. You say that multiple personalities is not what schizophrenia is all about and try to leave it at that. But he persists by asking you, "Then what is schizophrenia?" How do you respond?

Scenario 2

The mother of another person served by the program you work for approaches you by asking why her daughter should take medication. She says, "After twenty years, they have told me she has a *mental* disease, but they want her to take pills, I think to sedate her up. Pills! They can only help if you have a problem with the body, but her problem is with her mind!" How would you help to clarify matters here?

Scenario 3

Another person served by the PsyR program and his family believe that the reason he has mental illness is from a curse. They say, "An evil eye was put on him, a spell put upon him by an evil spirit." The family's beliefs are not unusual in their culture. How can you address this issue?

Scenario 4

Another individual that you are working with has obvious symptoms of a psychiatric illness. He believes he shares responsibility for the terrorist attack that occurred in New York in 2001, that he had indications it would happen and did not prevent it. He also thinks that coconspirators in the plot are now after him, have him under surveillance, and send him cryptic e-mails with veiled threats. The individual was a child at the time and clearly has no connection to the incident. When someone tried to explain that these ideas were delusions, he responded, "That's what they want you to think, that I'm paranoid crazy." He doesn't think he is ill and does not want treatment. How might you reach out to this individual?

Scenario 5

You get into a discussion with some of your colleagues about the origins of serious mental illness. They all take different viewpoints. One says, "It's their own fault, if people took better care of themselves, they would never get these illnesses." A second says, "It's all inherited, nothing can be done, just keep them on their medicine." You believe each of these viewpoints to be misinformed; how would you respond to each statement?

━━━━━━━━━━━━━━━━━━━━━━━━━━━━━━━ ■ ■ ■

3

Course, Treatment, and Outcome of Severe Mental Illnesses

Healing is a matter of time, but it is sometimes also a matter of opportunity.
Hippocrates

CHAPTER OUTLINE

Psychiatric Rehabilitation. http://dx.doi.org/10.1016/B978-0-12-387002-5.00003-2

An individual's experience of mental illness can be several weeks to many decades in duration. The course of the illness is often characterized by a significant risk of relapse and may include persistent symptoms. Psychiatric treatments, both pharmacological and psychosocial in nature, are intended to positively impact the course of mental illness by controlling, eliminating, and reducing symptoms, as well as reducing the length, frequency, and severity of relapses. They are also intended to help individuals regain functioning or develop strategies to compensate for lost functioning. For schizophrenia and mood disorders, psychotropic medications are often the primary treatment. These medications, when properly prescribed and taken by the individual, may result in a less virulent course of the illness. Although many individuals experience a great deal of relief, the outcome isn't often a cure. Responsiveness to treatment may vary widely for individuals with the same diagnosis. There is also wide heterogeneity of outcomes, ranging from those who deteriorate over time to individuals who have no symptoms at all and no relapses. In fact, some research suggests that about one out of four people recover completely from these disorders.

While these disorders require biological treatments, they also require psychosocial interventions such as support and rehabilitation to promote the best possible outcomes. Longitudinal studies that tracked persons with severe mental illness for more than 30 years have found that most people who receive psychosocial interventions cope better, have decreasing symptoms, and function better in the community. Even those who are coping well may suffer occasional relapses. Still, relapses do not preclude positive outcomes such as achieving living, learning, and working goals. In addition to the heterogeneity of outcomes among individuals, there is a multiplicity of outcomes for each individual. That is, over the course of many years of dealing with mental illness, the same individual may experience negative outcomes (e.g., persistence of symptoms and relapses) and positive outcomes (e.g., remission of symptoms and achievement of independent living goals).

This chapter will answer the following questions:

1. *Does the functioning of people with severe mental illness deteriorate or improve over the long term?*
2. *What are the probable short-term and long-term outcomes for persons diagnosed with schizophrenia and mood disorders?*
3. *If these illnesses are caused by biological factors, why are psychosocial treatments effective?*
4. *Can support and rehabilitation impact the course of severe mental illness and bring about positive outcomes?*

Introduction

To understand the course, treatment, and outcome of severe mental illness, you should consider the interrelatedness of these three areas. The **course** of an illness is its natural history, that is, the sequence of events throughout the length of the illness. For persons with severe mental illness, this course can be lifelong and marked by a risk of recurrence of severe symptoms. However, this is not always the case. **Treatment** is defined as any action designed to cure a disease or reduce its symptoms. Treatments are intended to alter the course of these illnesses in a positive manner by reducing the intensity of symptoms and the frequency of **relapses**. If treatments succeed, they are said to have good **outcomes**. Outcomes can refer to specific results, the end of a specific course of treatment, or the end result of the course of an entire illness. The term "outcome" can also refer to the long-term consequences of having a severe mental illness on the life of a person with the disorder.

In general, the course or natural history of severe mental illness is uncertain. It is clear, however, that the longer a psychosis goes untreated, the more difficult its course and the more negative the long-term outcomes (Bottlender et al., 2003). As just mentioned, risk of relapse, which is the recurrence of acute phases after periods of remission or lack of symptoms, is a prominent characteristic of severe mental illnesses. Combined with relapse are disruptions in functioning and independent living.

Relapse can lead to the loss of homes and jobs, educational disruption, and familial discord. But the most serious harm of a relapse may be to the individual's personal health. Each additional relapse may contribute to a further disordering of brain structure and functioning (Torrey, 2006). The costs to the individual incurred from a chronic and recurrent course of mental illness is staggering. Keck and McElroy (1998) cite a US Public Health Service study that projected the devastation of bipolar disorder on an individual's life. As an example, consider a woman who at the age of 25 has the onset of bipolar disorder. She can expect a 9-year reduction in life expectancy based on a 25 percent chance of attempting suicide and poorer overall health. In the remaining 40 or so years of her life, she can expect 12 years of overt or acute illness and 14 years of reduced productivity (vocationally, scholastically, and as a parent).

The personal damage of schizophrenia may be even more severe. Wiersma, Nienhuis, Slooff, and Giel (1998) conducted a 15-year **longitudinal study** of 82 people with schizophrenia living in the Netherlands. Their findings revealed a pattern of chronicity and relapses consistent with other studies cited later in this chapter; 67 percent of the individuals had at least one relapse. An additional negative finding was that after each relapse, 16 percent of these subjects (11 percent of the entire cohort) did not fully recover from the episode. Even more disturbing, 10 percent of the individuals committed suicide during the 15-year period.

The Wiersma, Nienhuis, Slooff, and Giel (1998) study highlighted the increased risks associated with each additional relapse. That is, with each relapse the individual has a higher likelihood of suicide and of having persistent symptoms that do not remit (i.e., improve). Nevertheless, while 21 percent of the people in this study had very negative outcomes, almost 80 percent experienced some significant form of recovery. Still, their findings demonstrate the need for an effective relapse prevention program as part of all PsyR services.

In a subsequent study, Wiersma and colleagues (2000) examined social deficits (e.g., lack of relatedness, withdrawal, etc.) among 349 persons with schizophrenia in several European countries. At the 15-year follow-up, individuals with schizophrenia still had persistent social deficits. Nevertheless, the majority lived in normal settings with their family, a partner, or alone, as opposed to a residential program or hospital. While the severity of social disability decreased overall, the social disability of those in the hospital or in shelters and residences supervised by staff did not decrease. The severity of an individual's disability in social functioning at the beginning of the study was predictive of the level of social disability 15 years later.

Course

Short-term Course of These Diseases

What is the likely short-term prognosis for someone with a severe mental illness? For some, accurate diagnosis and effective treatment take place rapidly. But for others, this process can be difficult, making the time it takes to receive effective treatment extremely lengthy. Certainly, for most persons who develop schizophrenia, the initial phase before effective treatment has begun can be the most devastating and the most frightening. As you will see, determining how to treat these diseases is a complicated process. In addition, during the initial stages of the disease the individual is often very unstable, that is, symptoms and their severity change quickly, making an accurate diagnosis even more difficult (Chen, Swann, & Johnson, 1998; Wiersma, Nienhuis, Slooff, & Giel, 1998). For example, many people who are initially diagnosed with a mood disorder will later be diagnosed with schizophrenia. At the same time, those diagnosed with schizoaffective disorder are most likely to have their diagnosis changed at a subsequent psychiatric evaluation (Chen, Swann, & Johnson 1998; Marneros, Tottig, Wenzel, & Brieger, 2004; Wiersma, Nienhuis, Slooff, & Giel, 1998). Many people diagnosed with depression are later found to have bipolar disorder (Angst, 2004). In most cases, effective treatment cannot be provided until an accurate diagnosis is made.

The short-term course of these diseases is stormy for several other reasons. Most persons are diagnosed with these conditions during their late teens or early twenties, a time of life when most people feel almost invulnerable to disease. For many of these young people, the most common response to a diagnosis of mental illness, especially if a remission of symptoms is obtained through medication, is denial (Fox, 2004a). Active denial of a potentially lifelong, debilitating mental illness is in many ways a natural life-affirming response. Unfortunately, it may lead to non-adherence with medication regimens and severe relapse.

Another cause of denial is anosognosia, discussed in Chapter 2. This is the lack of awareness that the symptoms of the illness are in fact symptoms. Whatever the cause, for many persons it takes many cycles of relapse, remission, denial, medication non-adherence, and relapse again before they accept the reality of their condition. It is important for practitioners to be sensitive to the fact that anosognosia, especially in the early stages of severe mental illness, is common and should be expected. At the same time, practitioners should avoid interpreting non-adherence with medication regimens and services as abnormal or intentionally antagonistic.

The Experience of Hospitalization

For some with severe mental illness, the first significant treatment experience is hospitalization. There are important reasons why this is often the preferred initial treatment. In the hospital, the person can be observed to ensure that he or she is not a danger to self or others. The hospital is also the best place to try out different medications to reduce psychotic symptoms. Many medications have side effects that range from mildly annoying to highly dangerous that can also be uncomfortable and frightening. Side effects are often treated by changing medications or adding medicines designed specifically to treat them.

Despite the fact that hospitalization is sometimes required to stabilize symptoms and determine the most effective medication regimen, from the patient's point of view it can be a frightening, dehumanizing experience. On the typical psychiatric ward, locked doors, limited visiting hours, and restricted use of telephones leave people feeling cut off from the outside world. Some individuals are hospitalized against their will. For some, the experience of hospitalization itself is traumatic: for example, when a person is physically restrained or is forced to spend time in a "quiet room." Inpatient hospital treatment and its alternatives are discussed in detail in Chapter 15.

After being discharged from the hospital, what is the likelihood of rehospitalization? One of the most illustrative articles on this topic was published by Anthony, Cohen, and Vitalo (1978). By comparing the reported **recidivism** (rehospitalization) rates from the studies available at the time (see Table 3.1), the authors demonstrated that the probability of relapse in the short term (1 to 5 years) is very high. An examination of Table 3.1 reveals that as the follow-up period increases from 3 months to 5 and 10 years, the corresponding cumulative rate of recidivism also increases from 10 to 15 percent, to as high as about 75 percent.

While relapse rates have improved since then, they still remain high (e.g., Pitschel-Walz, Leucht, Bauml, Kissling & Engel, 2001). For example, the one-year relapse rates have decreased from a range of 20 to 40 percent to a range of 15 to 23 percent for individuals being treated with antipsychotic medication (Leucht, Barnes, Kissling, Engel, Correll, & Kane, 2003). Improved services help. Klinkenberg and Calsyn (1996) found that those individuals receiving aftercare (post-hospital care) and assertive community treatment (see Chapter 8) and medication experienced lower rates of rehospitalization.

Clearly, if you have been hospitalized because of a serious mental illness, the chance you will need rehospitalization at some point in time is high. This high risk of relapse is true of schizophrenia, schizoaffective disorder, major depression, and bipolar disorder.

Long-term Course of These Diseases

Traditionally, the long-term prognosis for a person with a severe mental illness such as schizophrenia was considered bleak. However, numerous studies have challenged this negative prognosis, giving hope to many. The Vermont study conducted by Harding and her colleagues (1987a, 1987b) focused directly on individuals who might be expected to

Table 3.1 Recidivism Rates by Follow-up Periods

Follow-up Period	Recidivism (%)	Authors
3 months	10	Ellsworth et al. (1971)
	15	Orlinsky and D'Elia (1964)
	16	Johnston and McNeal (1965)[c]
	11 to 22[b]	Moos, Shelton, and Petty (1973)
6 months	14	Angrist et al. (1961)[c]
	27	Johnston and McNeal (1965)
	30	Orlinsky and D'Elia (1964)
	33	Friedman, von Mering, and Hinko (1966)
	33	Miller and Willer (1976)
	35	Morgan (1966)[c]
	40	Fairweather et al. (1960)
9 months	29	Lorei (1964)[c]
6 to 13 months[a]	33	Franklin, Kittredge, and Thrasher (1975)
7 to 10 months[a]	39	Cumming and Markson (1975)
1 year	35	Pishkin and Bradshaw (1960)[c]
	36	Wolkon, Karmen, and Tanaka (1966)
	37	Johnston and McNeal (1965)
	37	Michaux et al. (1969)[c]
	37	Katkin et al. (1975)
	38	Williams and Walker (1961)
	38	Freeman and Simmons (1963)
	39	Lorei (1967)
	40	Miller (1966)
	40	Miller (1967)
	41	Schooler et al. (1967)[c]
	42	Bloom and Lang (1970)
	46	Orlinsky and D'Elia (1964)
	48	Savino and Schlamp (1968)
	50	Friedman, von Mering, and Hinko (1966)
1 to 2 years	20	Lewinsohn (1967)[c]
15 months	45	Wilder, Levin, and Zwerling (1966)
18 months	46	Wolkon, Karmen, and Tanaka (1971)
2 years	51	Johnston and McNeal (1965)
	55	Wolkon, Karmen, and Tanaka (1971)
	55	Katkin et al. (1975)
	75	Mendel (1966)[c]
2½ years	60	Wolkon, Karmen, and Tanaka (1971)
3 years	56	Johnston and McNeal (1965)
	64	Sherman et al. (1964)[c]
	65	Olshansky (1968)
5 years	67	Friedman, von Mering, and Hinko (1966)
	70	Freyhan (1964)
	70	Miller (1966)
	75	Miller (1967)
10 years	77	Gurel (1970)

Based on Anthony, Cohen, and Vitalo (1978).

[a]Length of follow-up period not the same for every patient in the study.

[b]Data were presented for individual hospital wards.

[c]Recidivism percentages for these studies were excerpted from a review by Clum (1975).

have the worst prognosis. Starting in the 1950s, Vermont was one of the first states to begin deinstitutionalizing its psychiatric hospital population. This study examined a group of 269 patients who had been discharged from "the back wards" of Vermont's State Psychiatric Hospital 32 years before. The researchers spent a good deal of time locating people and interviewing family members and others who knew the subjects. Look at Tables 3.1 and 3.2. At 10 years post-discharge, 70 percent of the study participants were still out of the hospital, although many required treatment and social supports. At 30 years post-discharge, 50 to 66 percent were recovered or improved. Table 3.2 provides additional detail on the functional level of the study's subjects. As you can see, many of them attained valued social roles and utilized natural supports within the community. By comparing Figures 3.1 and 3.2 at 10 and 30 years, respectively, we can see that the long-term prognosis for schizophrenia is generally positive and appears to improve slightly with time. At both 10 and 30 years, 75 percent of people with schizophrenia are in a recovered, recovering, or improved category. It appears that between 10 and 30 years, an additional 10 percent improved to the point where they no longer required extensive support and became relatively independent.

In an Illinois study, Harrow and his colleagues (Harrow & Jobe, 2007; Harrow, Jobe, & Faull, 2012) tracked people from their first episode of psychosis through the next 20 years. They found that after both 15 and 20 years a large proportion of individuals with schizophrenia and other serious mental illnesses improve markedly and some recover completely. They followed 139 people beginning in young adulthood. Seventy people had schizophrenia and sixty-nine were diagnosed with mood disorders. They were assessed in their first acute phase of the illness and then periodically six times afterward over two decades. The assessments included symptoms, social functioning, personality attributes, attitudes variables, **cognition** (thinking), and treatment. Beginning at 4 to 5 years after the initial episode of illness, 30 to 40 percent of those with schizophrenia were no longer taking antipsychotic medication. Furthermore, the individuals who were not taking antipsychotic medication were less likely to be symptomatic and experienced fewer

Table 3.2   Results from the Strauss-Carpentar Levels of Function Scale for the 168 Subjects of the Vermont Study Who Were Alive and Interviewed[a]

Area of Functioning	N	%
Not in hospital in past year	140	83
Met with friends every week or two	111	66
Had one or more moderately to very close friends	128	76
Employed in past year[b]	79	47
Displayed slight or no symptoms	121	72
Able to meet basic needs	133	79
Led moderate to very full life	128	76
Slight or no impairment in overall function	92	55

[a]Reprinted with permission from Harding et al. (1987a).
[b]Quality of work could not be rated; issues of confidentiality prevented visits to subjects' work sites.

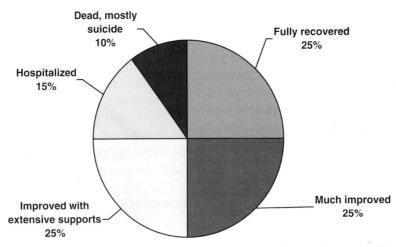

FIGURE 3.1 Outcomes 10 years after discharge from back wards. *(Based on Harding et al., 1987a, 1987b.)*

symptoms. Perhaps most importantly, they relapsed less frequently. As a group, they also had more favorable risk and protective factors before the onset of their illness. Harrow concludes, "They may be a self-selected group with better internal resources and greater resiliency" (p. 406). Indeed, this group did have better **pre-morbid** adjustment (pre-illness functioning) than others, including more developmental achievements, less anxiety, and better cognitive skills.

In addition to the studies conducted in Vermont and Illinois, other methodologically sound studies in both the United States and Europe, involving more than 1300 individuals diagnosed with schizophrenia, have found that 46 to 68 percent of them either improved

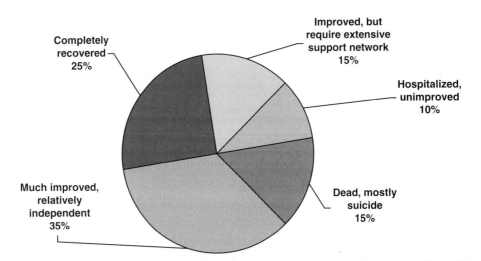

FIGURE 3.2 Outcomes 30 years after discharge from back wards. *(Based on Harding et al., 1987a, 1987b.)*

or recovered significantly over periods of time ranging from 23 to 37 years (Harding, Zubin, & Strauss, 1992). In summary, all these studies suggest that after 20 to 30 years, approximately one in four people diagnosed with schizophrenia are completely recovered (i.e., symptom free), few individuals are hospitalized, few require extensive support networks, and a larger proportion are functioning more independently. Thus, one of the basic values of PsyR, optimism that everyone has the capacity to recover, learn, and grow, which is discussed in detail in Chapter 4, actually has a scientific basis.

While for most people the long-term prognosis for schizophrenia is hopeful, all people with schizophrenia face a number of challenges, including cognitive deficits. Cognitive processes include such functions as thinking and processing information. Deficits in these areas include problems sustaining attention, so-called executive functions (e.g., the ability to plan ahead), and verbal memory. These deficits are likely to be a function of the abnormal structure and function of specific areas of the brain, including the hippocampus and parts of the frontal lobes as discussed in Chapter 2. Some of these cognitive deficits respond to treatment and improve, but others do not and can significantly interfere with community functioning. Dickinson and Coursey (2002) found that cognitive functions are strong predictors of how well people with schizophrenia cope with their illness. For example, "processing" speed and working memory are important cognitive functions associated with both social and vocational outcomes. Harrow et al. (2007, 2012) replicated the finding that better pre-morbid functioning in this area was predictive of better outcomes; before the onset of their illness, these individuals were more independent and had achieved more goals.

Course of Mood Disorders

What is the evidence on the course of mood disorders? Some studies suggest that for a sub-population of individuals the course of chronic or recurrent mood disorders may worsen over time (Kessing, 1998; Colman & Ataullahjan, 2010; Colman & Ataullahjan, Senthilselvan, & Patten, 2011). In terms of major depression, there are at least six different patterns or courses, but it looks like 40 to 50 percent of people with depression recover without repeated episodes, while 50 to 60 percent have repeated episodes. Daily smoking, low feelings of mastery, feeling life circumstances are beyond one's control, and earlier repeated episodes of depression are predictive of recurrence (Colman & Ataullahjan, 2010; Colman et al., 2011).

Outcomes studies of two to five years' duration have found that for individuals with bipolar disorder, recurrent episodes lead to deterioration in both social and vocational functioning (Keck & McElroy, 1998). This observation may seem unexpected to some mental health professionals. Generally speaking, between acute episodes of mood disorders, there is a greater remission of symptoms than is typically found in schizophrenic disorders (APA, 1994). That is, the person with a mood disorder is likely to be symptom free between acute episodes. Interestingly, this does not necessarily imply that the course of a mood disorder is less serious or less virulent. Kessing and his colleagues (1998) found that the number and frequency of episodes of increased symptomatology for persons with mood disorders increase with age. This is in contrast to schizophrenia, where the number and frequency of episodes generally decrease with age.

In one study, for 20 years Kessing and his colleagues followed all individuals admitted for psychiatric care in Denmark diagnosed with an affective disorder. During this time, more than 20,000 first-admission patients had been discharged with a diagnosis of major depression or bipolar disorder. The results indicated that the rate of recurrence increases with the number of previous episodes regardless of gender, age, and type of disorder. This suggests that, for some, the course of these disorders is progressive or worsening despite treatment. In short, an increasing number of relapses predicts an acceleration of relapses for the future (Kessing, 1998). Kennedy, Abbott, and Paykel (2003) followed seventy individuals to ascertain whether the course of depression had improved, given recent developments in pharmacological and psychosocial treatments. Individuals with a history of severe recurrent depression originally recruited in 1990 to 1992 were reassessed after 8 to 11 years. The great majority (92 percent) of the participants recovered during follow-up. Nevertheless, two-thirds suffered a recurrence of symptoms at some point and one out of six (17 percent) suffered from an episode of chronic depression of at least 2 years' duration. Generally, social functioning at follow-up was good and there were high levels of participation in pharmacological and psychosocial treatments. Greater severity of illness was the most consistent predictor of poor outcome.

Individuals with bipolar disorder have a rougher time of it. In a 15-year longitudinal study, compared to people with major depression, people with bipolar disorder were less likely to have good overall functioning, work functioning, and social functioning (Goldberg & Harrow, 2011). Only 35 percent of persons with bipolar disorder had good overall long-term functioning, compared to 73 percent of people with major depression (Goldberg & Harrow, 2011).

The Role of Rehabilitation Services

The results from the Vermont study (Harding et al., 1987a, 1987b), which looked at the long-term outcome of schizophrenia, greatly encouraged the PsyR community. Regardless of how symptomatic individuals are, there is hope that at some future date they will be able to function independently in the community with reduced symptoms and little or no support. Some of the researchers from the Vermont study investigated whether these positive outcomes were the result of the disease process or of the services that people receive.

Vermont had a comprehensive rehabilitation system, with many elements comparable to today's supported employment and supported living initiatives (see Chapters 10 and 12). A neighboring state, Maine, adopted a more traditional approach for the treatment of its deinstitutionalized population, consisting of traditional inpatient treatment and aftercare. Using the same strategy that had been employed in the original Vermont study, DeSisto, Harding, McCormick, Ashikaga, and Brooks (1995a, 1995b) compared 180 deinstitutionalized patients from Vermont with 119 similar patients from Maine. The results were very clear. Individuals from Vermont were more productive, less symptomatic, and had better community adjustment and higher levels of functioning.

In both states, the symptomatology and functioning of persons with these illnesses improved over the long term. However, in Maine, these improvements took much longer. Sometimes, it took ten years longer for people from Maine to achieve the same gains that the Vermonters had attained. Because of this time lag, people in Maine required more mental health services. The authors concluded that these differences were probably the result of Vermont's efforts at community PsyR. In short, better services produced better outcomes for people with psychiatric disabilities.

Treatment

As mentioned above, treatment seeks to cure a disease or reduce its symptoms. Treatment for serious mental illnesses can be broken into two broad categories: biological (somatic) and psychosocial. The biological or somatic category usually refers to medications but also to electroconvulsive therapy. The psychosocial category refers to efforts to reduce symptoms and improve functioning by employing interventions that influence social or psychological factors.

Biological (Somatic) Treatments

One of the primary approaches in the treatment of severe mental illness is to use pharmacological agents to treat acute episodes of psychotic and/or mood symptoms (Lehman & Steinwachs, 1998; Leucht et al., 2003; Walker, Kestler, Bollini, & Hochman, 2004). For schizophrenia and other mental illnesses that involve psychoses, antipsychotic medications are typically used as the first-line treatment to reduce or eliminate psychotic symptoms (Lehman & Steinwachs, 1998; Mueser, Torrey, Lynde, Singer, & Drake, 2003). For acute episodes of major depression, the current treatment of choice is antidepressant medications, such as Tofranil and Prozac. For bipolar disorder, the treatment of choice is a mood stabilizer, lithium (Keck & McElroy, 1998). Antidepressants and mood stabilizers are also used for long-term management of these disorders, although the evidence on their long-term usefulness is less clear.

Efficacy of Antipsychotic Medication

Antipsychotic medications have been used to treat illnesses such as schizophrenia since the early 1950s. Some of the most common early medications that were developed (and are still in use today) include chlorpromazine (the brand name is Thorazine), fluphenazine (Prolixin), and haloperidol (Haldol). Today these are often referred to as traditional, typical, or first-generation antipsychotic medications.

A large body of evidence supports the efficacy of antipsychotic medication in the treatment of schizophrenia, with hundreds of well-controlled studies showing that 50 to 85 percent of persons will experience reductions in hallucinations, delusions, thought disorders, and bizarre behavior (Lehman & Steinwachs, 1998; Dixon et al., 2010). Nevertheless, many trials of antipsychotic medication are unsuccessful (Lieberman & Lewis, 2008).

Those who experience symptom relief with an antipsychotic medication are typically prescribed the medication for at least a year after the acute symptoms have been reduced (Lehman & Steinwachs, 1998; Dixon et al., 2010). The purpose of this long-term treatment is to reduce the risk of relapse or the worsening of positive symptoms. Medications are used in the **acute phase** of an illness to reduce symptoms, in the **residual phase** to keep symptoms from recurring, and sometimes even in the **prodromal phase** to avert relapse. In the case of most serious mental illnesses, medications are also used during periods of remission. Summarizing studies that looked at the outcomes of more than 2300 patients with schizophrenia, Hogarty (1993) found that medication alone could reduce the rate of relapse from 67 to 39 percent in the first year. After the first year, by continuing antipsychotic medication, relapse rates were reduced from 65 percent annually to only 15 percent annually (Hogarty, 1993). This has been confirmed in a review article of 30 well-controlled studies that found using antipsychotic medication reduced the annual relapse rate (Leucht et al., 2003).

When individuals do relapse, many mental health professionals attribute it to suspected medication non-adherence (Gray et al., 2002). However, as Hogarty (1993) has pointed out, even patients whose adherence was known because they received long-acting intramuscular injections of a medication such as fluphenazine or haloperidol (also known as decanoate or depot medications) had approximately the same relatively high rate of relapse. Subsequent research has found the injectable medication is actually somewhat more effective at reducing symptoms (Adams, Fenton, Quraishi, & David, 2001).

Atypical or Second-generation Antipsychotic Medication

Many of the antipsychotics prescribed today are part of a heterogeneous group of medications that are commonly referred to as the "atypical" or second-generation antipsychotics. The second-generation antipsychotics differ somewhat from one another in terms of the neurotransmitter receptors that they occupy, such as different types of dopamine and serotonin receptors. However, they all act as dopamine antagonists to some extent (see Chapter 2). Commonly prescribed medicines include Risperdal (risperidone), Zyprexa (olanzapine), Seroquel (quetiapine), and Geodon (ziprasidone). By the first decade of the new millennium, the second-generation antipsychotics had become the first line of defense in the treatment of schizophrenia and other psychotic disorders (Walker et al., 2004). The advisability of this practice has since been called into question due to the expense, side effects profile, and relative ineffectiveness as reported in two major studies (CATIE and CUTLASS; Lewis & Lieberman, 2008).

The first atypical antipsychotic medication developed was clozapine (brand name Clozaril). It was developed in the 1950s, but was not widely used in the United States until the 1990s. Clozapine has been shown to be highly effective for treatment-resistant schizophrenia, helping people whom the first-generation antipsychotic medications did not. However, because of its potentially serious side effects, including agranulocytosis, a rare immune system problem, and the requirement for frequent blood monitoring, clozapine's use is generally confined to individuals whose psychotic symptoms have not responded to one or more antipsychotic medications (Alphs & Anand, 1999; Naheed & Green, 2001).

Which Are Better, First- or Second-generation Medications?

A major multisite study of 1500 individuals, Clinical Antipsychotic Trials of Intervention Effectiveness (CATIE) was reported on in numerous papers (Lieberman et al., 2005; Rosenheck et al., 2006; Swartz et al., 2007). CATIE compared several of the second-generation drugs to an older drug, perphenazine (brand name Trilafon). After 18 months, the majority of persons receiving each of the new drugs had discontinued treatment. The authors speculated that these dropout rates were mostly related to side effects and concluded that the newer drugs offered no advantage over the more traditional drugs in the trial.

Equally important was the Cost Utility of the Latest Antipsychotic Drugs in Schizophrenia Study (CUTLASS). Both the CATIE and CUTLASS studies—funded by government agencies in the United States and the United Kingdom, as opposed to pharmaceutical companies that make the drugs—have found that the second-generation medications fail as frequently as or more often than the first-generation medications (Lewis & Lieberman, 2008).

Reasons Medications Fail

Psychotropic medications must be tried for a sufficient length of time and under supervision to correctly determine their effectiveness. Initially, both traditional and second-generation antipsychotic medications fail about two-thirds of the time, requiring a change in treatment strategy. A psychiatrist may determine that a particular medication is ineffective because symptoms do not improve, side effects are intolerable, or relapse occurs (Leucht et al., 2003). A systematic approach to the evaluation and characterization of treatment resistance is very important (Conley & Buchanan, 1997). With the introduction of many new drugs, individuals are more likely to be prescribed a variety of psychotropic medications if the first one tried does not work well. Prescribers facing the decision of when to change from one medication to another must clearly understand the appropriate length of a trial and what target symptoms respond to a particular medication in order to maximize the response in persons with treatment-resistant symptoms.

The medication challenges for both the physician and the individual usually revolve around a number of questions. First, which psychotropic medication will be most effective? Second, what dosage is needed to be effective, while at the same time not putting the person at unnecessary risk for side effects? Third, how does one cope with the long-term need to take pills regularly, possibly accompanied by frequent blood tests required for certain medications such as clozapine and lithium. Further complicating matters, even if the right medication is prescribed, there is always some risk of symptom exacerbation and relapse.

Additional reasons why people with severe mental illness have a poor response to various psychotropic medications include:

- Partial adherence by the individual with the treatment regimen
- Inappropriate dosing or length of trial (most medications require four to six weeks to determine efficacy)
- True resistance of the disorder to the medication
- Simply using the wrong medication to try to bring about a therapeutic effect (based on Conley & Buchanan, 1997)

Medication Side Effects

Side effects of psychotropic medication are particularly important. They can be very severe and harmful to the individual. Some common side effects are increased appetite, hormonal difficulties (e.g., failing to menstruate), motor difficulties (e.g., shuffling gate), muscular problems (e.g., stiffness), dryness of mouth, blurred vision, impotence, low blood pressure, seizures, and immune system reactions.

Antipsychotic medication, because it affects the functioning of the neurotransmitter dopamine (discussed in Chapter 2), interferes significantly with motor functions. Some patients, regardless of age, develop the symptoms, but not the actual disease, of Parkinson's disease: resting tremors, poor control of their own movements, and shuffling movements. Another side effect that may occur from use of these medications is **tardive dyskinesia**, which involves an uncontrollable twisting or writhing movement of the mouth and limbs. Unlike some of the other side effects, tardive dyskinesia is usually not reversible once it appears. As if it were not enough to endure the symptoms and behaviors associated with psychosis, the involuntary movements of tardive dyskinesia can make someone appear bizarre to others, which increases stigma. Also common are "extra-pyramidal" syndromes (i.e., movement disorders), including dystonic reactions (sudden onset of sustained intense muscle contraction), and akathisia (restlessness) (Allison & Casey, 2001; Bradford, Stroup, & Lieberman, 2002; Kane, 2003).

A number of studies have found that the mean weight gain for those treated with one of the second-generation antipsychotic medications is significantly more than for those treated with the older antipsychotic medications (Lewis & Lieberman, 2008). Weight gain is not only unpleasant for the individual but can also lead to medical consequences such as diabetes (Allison & Casey, 2001). Weight gain is in turn associated with metabolic syndrome, diabetes, hypertension, and coronary artery disease, all of which are associated with early risk of death, often referred to as increased risk of mortality. Indeed, the manufacturer of Zyprexa, Eli Lilly & Co, settled a class-action lawsuit against them regarding this potentially deadly side effect. Thus, the most serious and distressing side effect of antipsychotic medications is the increased risk of premature mortality. There is little doubt that persons with serious mental illness, many of whom have gained significant weight and have experienced all the effects of obesity, are dying younger (Parks et al., 2006). This topic of the negative impact of weight gain will be dealt with in more detail in Chapter 6.

Pharmacological Treatment of Bipolar Disorder and Mania

Lithium is a mood stabilizer used as a treatment for bipolar disorder in the United States since 1970, and in other countries even earlier. It is an effective medication for both the treatment of acute mania and the prevention of the recurrence of both manic and depressive symptoms in bipolar disorders (Keck & McElroy, 1998). At least 12 studies have shown that lithium reduces the symptoms of acute mania. Like antipsychotic medications, mood stabilizers work by influencing neurotransmitter activity in the brain. Numerous well-controlled studies involving hundreds of patients have demonstrated that lithium prevents recurrent affective episodes of both depressed and manic types (Belmaker, 2004; Keck & McElroy, 1998). Studies suggest that lithium is the best medication for preventing manic episodes (e.g., Popovic, Reinares, Amann, Salamero, & Vieta, 2011). The prevention of future episodes, while an important goal in itself, has the additional benefit of perhaps reducing the likelihood of increased frequency of episodes and more rapid cycling (Cusin, Serretti, Lattuada, Mandelli, & Smeraldi, 2000). Rapid cycling refers to the experience of quick changes between brief episodes of mania and depression. It is also important to note that a significant number of individuals do not respond well to lithium maintenance therapy. Poor medication adherence, in large part due to lithium's side effects, has interfered with its effective use.

The effective treatment of mania needs to anticipate the future course of the illness (Licht, 1998). Lithium is still considered the best mood-stabilizing substance, although it may be insufficient in mixed episodes and severe mania (Licht, 1998). For those who do not respond to lithium, other medications, including carbamazepine and valproate, are available. Carbamazepine is an anticonvulsive medication that is also used to treat seizure disorders. Valproate is preferred for acute episodes—in particular, for mixed episodes. Because the mood stabilizers work slowly, sometimes antipsychotic medications are also used to treat severe mania, particularly during the acute phase, to decrease potentially dangerous behavior (Belmaker, 2004). However, in general, antipsychotics should not be prolonged into the maintenance phase of bipolar disorder. Not surprisingly, persons living with bipolar disorder are also prescribed antidepressants (which are discussed ahead) for the relief of their depressive episodes (Keck & McElroy, 1998). Unfortunately, persons who also suffer manic episodes can have a manic state induced by the use of antidepressants (Belmaker, 2004). Recently, there have been reports of first "manic" episodes among persons taking antidepressants, as well as the experience of rapid cycling. There is some well-founded speculation that both these phenomena might be due to medication side effects (Whitaker, 2010).

Freeman and Stoll (1998) report that polypharmacy (i.e., the use of multiple medications) is common in the treatment of "refractory bipolar disorder," a term used to describe conditions that do not respond readily to a single medication. The interactions of such combinations can be useful but are also complicated and potentially dangerous. The safest and most efficacious mood stabilizer combinations appear to be the mixtures of anticonvulsants, particularly valproate and lithium.

Lithium reduces the likelihood of relapse of both manic and depressive episodes but does not eliminate it. Silverstone, McPherson, Hunt, and Romans (1998) examined the effectiveness of lithium in preventing recurrent episodes of bipolar disorder over a two-year period following hospital discharge. Results showed that, overall, 67 percent had a relapse. While a major reason for this may have been poor medication adherence by study participants, it is clear that in many cases this drug was not effective. Maj, Pirozzi, Magliano, and Bartoli (1998) collected information on 402 people using lithium as a maintenance treatment to prevent relapse. Five years after starting treatment, of those still taking lithium, 38 percent had experienced at least one recurrent episode of the disorder, while 23 percent experienced no recurrent episodes. Those who had discontinued their lithium at follow-up had poorer outcomes than those still taking lithium.

Pharmacological Treatment of Major Depressive Disorders

For depressive disorders, controversy remains regarding whether medication or psychosocial interventions are more effective in bringing symptom relief (Friedman et al., 2004; Nemeroff & Schatzberg, 1998). Nevertheless, there is little question that those treated with antidepressants will have a more favorable course than those who do not take these medications (Angst, 1998).

The treatments of choice for the relief of major depressive disorders are the drugs known as "selective serotonin reuptake inhibitors," such as Prozac (Nemeroff & Schatzberg, 1998). This class of drugs is named for the nature of the effect they have on the neurotransmitter serotonin. Next most commonly used are the tricyclic antidepressants such as Tofranil (imipramine), which are named for their chemical structure of three molecular circles. A third group of drugs, monoamine oxidase (MAO) inhibitors, although effective, are rarely used. Typically, it takes at least three to six weeks to determine whether an antidepressant is effective. Tricyclic antidepressants, at full dose, have been found to be effective in reducing the recurrence of major depressive symptoms or episodes (Frank, Kupfer, & Perel, 1990, 1993).

Viguera, Balderissini, and Friedberg (1998) note that the benefits of long-term antidepressant treatment in major depression and the risks of discontinuing medication are now well established. Reviewing 27 studies, with more than 3000 patients with depressive symptoms, they compared the course and outcome of the illness between patients whose antidepressants were discontinued and those with continued treatment. Those who had continued treatment showed much lower relapse rates (2 versus 6 percent per month) and a lower 12-month relapse risk (20 versus 45 percent). Contrary to prediction, gradual discontinuation (dose-tapering or use of long-acting agents) did not yield lower relapse rates. As mentioned earlier, the number of previous depressive episodes—particularly three or more prior episodes, which was considered a chronic course—was strongly associated with higher relapse risk after discontinuation of antidepressants. Nevertheless, even those with multiple episodes were likely to respond well to medication.

Future Possibilities

Studies demonstrate that while medication helps many people cope with severe mental illness, prescription guidelines are hardly an exact science. Many people suffer for years without finding an effective medication regimen with tolerable side effects. With a better understanding of the human genome (the entire human genetic profile), the potential exists to tailor medication to an individual's genetic profile. The emerging fields of pharmacogenomics and pharmacogenetics are seeking to uncover the genetic basis of differences in medication therapeutic response and side effects (Walker et al., 2004). The goal is to eventually individualize therapy based on a person's genetic makeup (Basile, Masellis, Potkin, & Kennedy, 2002; Collins, 2010).

Unfortunately, a large proportion of individuals with severe mental illness still receive inadequate care, while only a small number are served well (Lehman & Steinwachs, 1998; President's New Freedom Commission on Mental Health, 2003; Satcher, 2000).

Medication Adherence

Many individuals with long-term disorders are prescribed medication regimens to follow. For persons with severe mental illness, the rate of non-adherence for medication regimens has been estimated to be about 50 percent (Gray, Wykes, & Gournay, 2002). While this percentage sounds high, it may be no higher than the rates of non-adherence for all disorders and all medical conditions. As such, non-adherence is a potentially preventable cause of the serious consequences of relapse (Gray, Wykes, & Gournay, 2002). Note that the problems that many individuals have sticking to a prescribed schedule and dose of psychotropic medications is also referred to as "medication non-compliance," but many PsyR experts now prefer the term "non-adherence" to avoid the connotation of submission and disempowerment that the term "compliance" conveys.

As mentioned earlier, injectable medications are sometimes used for individuals who do not want to take pills or cannot remember to take them regularly. But an aversion to oral medications and an inability to remember are only two of the reasons that individuals struggle with medication non-adherence; an unwillingness to be reminded repeatedly of one's illness, serious side effects, and insufficient therapeutic effects also contribute to medication non-adherence (Swarbrick & Roe, 2011). Ironically, feeling better or improving is also a cause of non-adherence, because in the face of improved or eliminated symptoms, stopping the medication seems a logical step (Fox, 2004).

Another factor consistently associated with decreased medication adherence is substance abuse (Heyscue, Levin, & Merrick, 1998). Some individuals discontinue medication when drinking alcohol or abusing substances. Some individuals also may be "self-medicating" with both legal prescription drugs and illicit drugs on a dosage and schedule they choose. This is discussed in more detail in Chapter 9, which addresses co-occurring disorders.

Many mental health practitioners stress the relationship between medication non-adherence and the aggravation of symptoms and potential relapse in an effort to promote medication adherence. For some staff members, it becomes a preoccupation that can lead to blaming individuals for their own relapses, assuming medication non-adherence was the cause. These practitioners do not always realize that the issue of medication adherence is a sensitive and emotional one. Many consumers have experienced or know of medications being misused as "chemical restraints." In other words, individuals were given high dosages of medication to obtain a sedative effect intended to control psychotic symptoms and behavior very quickly. People taking psychotropic medications and experiencing troubling and even dangerous side effects are often reluctant to discuss these matters with their doctors. They may not have the confidence to confront, disagree with, or even question a physician or other professionals. Some may not even know they are "allowed to," having no experience working collaboratively with a psychiatrist. Sometimes, in one's role as a patient, it is just easier to say, "I'm fine," and not bring up troubling concerns. Some may even lie about their side effects in an effort to avoid hospitalization. See Box 3.1 for another perspective on the medication non-adherence issue, written by a mental health professional living with a mental illness.

How, then, can the right medication be prescribed at the right dosage in a manner that maximizes therapeutic effects, reduces side effects, and informs consumers about the choices they actually have? Can communication about these issues be improved, so that consumers can exercise informed choice and self-determination over their medication? Would better communication regarding symptoms and side effects empower doctors as well, by helping them to be better informed on these issues? Kim Mueser and colleagues (2003b) discuss two related solutions to these problems called "collaborative psychopharmacology" and "illness management and recovery services." Both are based on the same premise as a chain store's advertisement slogan, "An educated consumer is our best customer."

Collaborative Psychopharmacology

Collaboration means laboring or working together. Collaborative psychopharmacology involves consumers working with their psychiatrists and other professionals to determine the right medications to use according to current guidelines. Although medications are clearly effective, research has also found that many psychiatrists do not follow the appropriate dosage ranges or take into account the time course for therapeutic response and dosage adjustment, also known as **titration** (Lehman & Steinwachs, 1998). Similarly, guidelines on the identification and management of side effects and methods for the treatment of refractory symptoms are frequently not followed by psychiatrists (Lehman & Steinwachs, 1998).

Because of the complexity of pharmacological treatment for severe mental illness, as well as the rapid evolution in the field as new medications are developed, a recent trend

BOX 3.1   WHEN THE SYSTEM WORKS AGAINST MEDICATION ADHERENCE

Between 2004 and 2005, while serving as the Vice-Chairman on the Governor's Task Force on Mental Health, I had extreme difficulty seeing a psychiatrist. I was in my 25th year as a service recipient in the public mental health system, working full-time, and took the day off to keep a psychiatrist appointment. Checking my cell phone message, I found, "Your appointment is cancelled today because the psychiatrist can no longer take your health insurance. You will be rescheduled with another staff psychiatrist." I went to the agency anyway. After meeting with a person of "authority," I was permitted to see the psychiatrist and informed that I would be billed as if I were uninsured, although that didn't happen.

The psychiatrist saw me and I got the prescriptions. About three months later, I went to see the new psychiatrist who accepted my insurance. We know psychiatrists are stretched thin and see many people; therefore, few get quality service. I suspect the previous psychiatrist probably wasn't supposed to see me even before that last visit, and I had been seeing that psychiatrist for years. Nevertheless, when I tried to meet with the new psychiatrist after handing over my co-pay, I was informed that the psychiatrist was dealing with a crisis. I had taken the day off, and a receptionist could not give me a time when the psychiatrist would be available, i.e., 15 minutes, 30 minutes, or an hour? The expectation was that I would sit and wait. I refused and asked for the prescription to be called in. The response was, "We don't do that." I left and the psychiatrist called me. I made my case and the psychiatrist reluctantly conceded and called in my prescriptions. Three months later, for my next appointment, the same thing happened except the psychiatrist and agency refused to call in my prescriptions: "We don't do that," and really meant it this time.

While I didn't get my medication, the agency was timely in mailing me a termination letter as if I were "non-compliant." The letter failed to state I had paid my co-pay and that the psychiatrist was unavailable. Searching elsewhere and in complete distress, I was referred to a psychiatrist at a community mental health center, but was told I must "commit" to seeing a therapist at the agency. I hadn't seen a therapist in three years. I now feared I was going to lose my job, my career path, and my social standing in the community. I was tired and not going to beg anymore for medication, and I'd end up in a state hospital or criminal justice system. Finally, I got assistance from a friend who referred me to a yet another psychiatrist. I've been seeing that psychiatrist without scheduling and appointment problems since 2006. I believe medication is only a small aspect of one's recovery. My recovery is participating in valued social roles beyond the problems associated with medication adherence. Ironically, these events occurred when the taskforce I was co-chairing was debating Involuntary Outpatient Commitment, which would compel some people to seek the treatment I could not get voluntarily. It is now New Jersey law even though it was strongly opposed by advocates and psychiatric rehabilitation professionals. (http://www.dbsanewjersey.org/conference/2010/IOC_DBSA_2010.pps)

George H. Brice, Jr., M.S.W.,
UMDNJ-SCHOOL OF HEALTH RELATED PROFESSIONS

Note: This account was first presented as part of VocationalVoices.com, the Integrated Employment Institute's blog that can be found at: http://vocationalvoice.com/welcome/.

has been to establish **algorithms** for prescribing medications based on research (Miller et al., 2004; Trivedi et al., 2004). Algorithms are step-by-step instructions to proceed with certain actions based on specific conditions and responses to previous steps. Many of these recommendations require adding expert clinical consensus to the scientific evidence. Implementation procedures for collaborative pharmacological treatment have been developed that include a standard approach to documenting and monitoring symptoms and side effects, guidelines for systematically making decisions about medications, and attempts to engage consumers in decision making about medication-related decisions.

Related to collaborative psychopharmacology, **shared decision making** (Drake, Deegan, & Rapp, 2010) stresses the importance of individuals being informed about medication and other issues and taking part in the decision-making process. Individuals need to be empowered to communicate clearly with their doctors and may need training and support to do so effectively. While often not offered to persons with severe mental illness, shared decision making is closer to the norm for many people seeking medical advice. Finally, when it comes to medications shared decision making represents a practical position between a medication regimen imposed without consultation and consumer choice.

Illness Management and Recovery

Educating individuals with mental illness about their disease and its treatment is central to effective collaborative psychopharmacology and shared decision making. **Illness management and recovery** (IMR), sometimes called wellness management and recovery, is an evidence-based practice designed to provide the knowledge and skills necessary to work effectively with professionals, minimize the effects of the mental illness, and pursue personally meaningful goals. IMR consists of a variety of methods to help individuals deal more effectively with their disorder.

Role of Psychoeducation in Illness Self-management

IMR psychoeducation provides individuals with basic information about diagnoses, symptoms, medications, medication side effects, treatment options, the role that stress can play, and prodromal symptoms that signal a relapse. Psychoeducation is often provided in groups, although it can be provided in a one-to-one format. Groups can last approximately 6 to 18 sessions. To maximize the effectiveness of a psychoeducation intervention, practitioners should do the following:

- Provide it to consumers who are asking for information about their illness.
- Tailor the content so that consumers clearly understand the information.
- Enhance didactic presentations with handouts, articles, videos, and structured small-group discussions.
- Avoid overloading consumers with too much information in a single session.
- Show consumers how the information is relevant to their goals.

The research done on psychoeducation suggests that it increases consumers' knowledge but has little or no impact on behavior. For example, it has not been shown to be an effective way to increase medication adherence. Therefore, psychoeducation groups alone are not a particularly effective intervention for helping to manage the illness and achieve desired outcomes such as reduced symptoms, fewer hospitalizations, and improved quality of life (Mueser et al., 2002). However, if psychoeducation is combined with or incorporated into other illness self-management strategies, such as the cognitive behavioral interventions described later, other positive outcomes might be realized.

BOX 3.2   EVIDENCE-BASED PRACTICE
Illness Management and Recovery

The goal of IMR is to give the individual the knowledge and skills needed to effectively cope with aspects of the illness. These knowledge and skills include:

(1) Understanding recovery and the importance of establishing a recovery goal(s)
(2) Understanding the illness, including symptoms, possible course, and probable long- and short-term outcomes
(3) Understanding the prescribed medications and the possible side effects that may occur
(4) Developing strategies to help ensure medication adherence
(5) Learning how to identify relapse early warning signs and how to respond to these
(6) Developing effective coping skills to effectively deal with persistent symptoms
(7) Developing social support systems

These goals are accomplished using four different strategies that have been found effective in clinical trials: psychoeducation, behavioral tailoring, relapse prevention training, and coping skills training.

CRITICAL INGREDIENTS OF ILLNESS MANAGEMENT AND RECOVERY

- Establishing a recovery goal(s)
- Psychoeducation about illness, medications, and so forth
- Behavioral tailoring for medication regimen adherence
- Relapse prevention training, including warning sign recognition
- Teaching coping strategies for persistent symptoms
- Building social support systems

OUTCOMES OF ILLNESS MANAGEMENT AND RECOVERY

- Improved self-report and clinician ratings of coping and self-management
- Reduced symptoms
- Significant improvement in knowledge about illness, medications, and side effects
- Significant progress toward personal goals
- Increased hope
- Fewer hospitalizations, reduced use of emergency rooms
- Improved social support

Staff Competencies Required for Effective IMR

The staff competencies necessary to provide effective IMR training go well beyond what would be considered the typical PsyR staff training. To provide effective IMR, a staff member should have a fair knowledge of mental illness, have good coping skills, and be proficient at motivational interviewing and cognitive behavioral techniques. In addition to being good educators and trainers, staff members need to understand the IMR training strategy, recovery, and effective goal setting. Given this wide array of knowledge and skills, IMR training is often more effectively provided by a staff team than by an individual staff member. Also, individuals in recovery are probably capable of participating in the delivery of illness management interventions. Mueser et al. (2002) commented: "Research on peer-based illness self-management programs may inform professional-based services and lead to collaborative efforts" (p. 1282). Two more recent studies on peer-based illness self-management programs support Mueser's assertion (Pratt et al., 2011; Garber et al., 2013).

IMR is being adapted for many locations and populations, with successful application in the United States, Australia, the Netherlands, Israel, Pakistan, and Japan reported in the literature. There are freestanding IMR programs, or it can be incorporated into a variety of treatment settings such as assertive community treatment (ACT) teams (Salyers et al., 2009) and inpatient settings (Bartholomew & Zechner, 2013). There are some controlled studies showing modest effects (Roe et al., 2011; Levitt et al., 2009; Pratt et al., 2011).

To reflect a strengths-based view, practitioners in New York and Chicago have renamed IMR to wellness management and recovery (Rychener, Salyers, Labriola, & Little, 2009) or wellness self-management (WSM; Salerno et al., 2011). In WSM, the entire curriculum is presented in a workbook that belongs to the participants. A physical health chapter is included, as are self-directed action steps and a specific group facilitation format (Salerno et al., 2011).

CONTROVERSIAL ISSUE
Symptom Relief by Psychotropic Medications: But at What Cost?

In *Anatomy of an Epidemic*, journalist Robert Whitaker (2010) argues that psychotropic medications, instead of being wonder drugs or magic bullets, may actually be contributing to the increased prevalence and chronicity of some disorders. For example, he cites evidence that the course of depression may be lengthened by the use of antidepressants. While effective for symptom relief in a relatively short time frame (weeks) compared to psychotherapy approaches (months), persons seem to require these medications over the long term. In the past, most depressive disorders were relatively time limited with a fair amount of spontaneous remission. Today, there is evidence the course of depression is lengthened by the use of antidepressants, which are then needed for the long run. He cites other disturbing evidence: for example, a significant number of people have their first manic episode while on an antidepressant. Additionally, Whitaker cites evidences that psychotropic medications may cause the growing phenomenon of "rapid cycling" (i.e., abrupt changes from manic to depressive episodes or vice versa), and the increased prevalence of mixed episodes.

(Continued)

CONTROVERSIAL ISSUE
Symptom Relief by Psychotropic Medications: But at What Cost?—(Continued)

Whitaker says similar phenomena may be at work in illnesses such as schizophrenia, citing evidence of changes in brain anatomy due to medication. Ho and colleagues (2011) conducted a long-term study of factors contributing to the decreased brain volume and enlarged spaces (ventricles) within the brains of people with schizophrenia. Results reaffirmed that decreased brain volume was associated with earlier disease onset, increased symptom severity, and the persistence of symptoms. In addition, they found that decreased brain volume was associated with higher doses of antipsychotic medication. Clearly, the use of psychotropic medications may not be uniformly positive. What is the cause of these problems? What are the implications for the people served by psychiatric rehabilitation practitioners?

The brain is among the most adaptive organs of the body. Psychotropic medications change the functioning of the brain and its neurotransmitter systems. The brain adapts and makes changes in response to the medicines. In combination with these medicines, some of these changes prove maladaptive. It has been known for some time that after taking antipsychotics, which block dopamine receptors, people appeared to grow more dopamine receptors. This change can lead to increased symptomatology.

The obvious "takeaway" is that while psychotropic medications are very effective regarding immediate symptom reduction, the long-term side effects are significant. Hearing this news, some people with serious mental illness understandably do not want to take these medicines.

How should PsyR practitioners address these serious concerns? To start, they can keep the lines of communication open and encourage people who take these medicines to have a dialogue with their physician or other prescriber. In some situations, they might prepare consumers to talk to their prescriber by helping them articulate questions and concerns in advance. They should also make sure that consumers know that abruptly stopping these medicines is a bad alternative because it could cause abrupt maladaptations by the brain. People with mental illness and their physicians need to work together to find the optimal, lowest doses, or if they wish to discontinue the medicines, to follow a tapering, gradual reduction protocol. At the same time, PsyR practitioners can encourage participation in psychosocial alternatives, such as cognitive-behavioral approaches (to be described in Chapter 5).

Psychosocial Treatments

In addition to pharmacological treatments, the other broad category of treatment for severe mental illnesses is psychosocial treatment. **Psychosocial treatments** are approaches that attempt to effect change through the manipulation of social or psychological factors. Specific models that employ psychosocial strategies include, for example, some types of day programs, assertive community treatment, supported employment, and family psychoeducation. These approaches are described in detail in subsequent chapters of this book, Chapters 5 through 15. Also, the various forms of psychotherapies are psychosocial interventions.

The most effective impact on the course of severe mental illness is achieved through a combination of biological and psychosocial interventions (Craighead et al., 1998;

Harding et al., 1992; Hogarty, 1993). Based on the available evidence, the right combination of these two treatment categories results in the lowest possible rates of relapse. The conventional wisdom is that pharmacological interventions are a necessary prerequisite for any psychosocial interventions to be effective. Others consider this to be a myth, believing that psychosocial interventions can be effective regardless of the use of psychotropic medication (Harding & Zahniser, 1994).

Medication and Psychosocial Treatment of Major Depression

Depression can be a chronic disorder with a high risk of relapse requiring active treatment with a combination of medication and psychotherapy. Identifying which individuals would benefit from psychosocial as compared to pharmacological approaches and developing an understanding of the mechanisms of action of these therapies remain major challenges (Scott & Watkins, 2004). In the treatment of major depression, behavioral therapy, cognitive-behavioral therapy, marital therapy, and interpersonal therapy have all been found to reduce depressive symptoms (Craighead et al., 1998a). While some of these approaches are briefly described in Chapter 5, a complete discussion of these treatments is outside the scope of this book.

Treated depressive disorders definitely have a better course than those that remain untreated (Angst, 1998). Interventions using behavior therapy, cognitive-behavioral therapy, and interpersonal therapy have all brought about significant reductions in depressive symptoms. In 12 out of 15 studies, cognitive-behavioral therapy significantly lowered the relapse or recurrence rate for depression (de Almeida & Neto, 2003). These treatments have also been found to be successful in maintaining the gains of the therapy. Arnow and Constantino (2003) found that with long-term major depression, combined treatment has demonstrated superiority over either medication or psychotherapy alone. Similarly, reviewing the literature, Friedman et al. (2004) found that combined treatment is associated with improvements over medication alone. Adding psychotherapy to antidepressant medication may be particularly effective among severely depressed patients. Further, adding cognitive-behavioral therapy to medication may be particularly important in preventing relapse, particularly among individuals discontinuing their medication (Friedman et al., 2004).

Some Ineffective Treatments

Some strategies have deservedly received a bad name for their ineffectiveness or actual harm in treating people. There were efforts to treat people with schizophrenia without antipsychotic medication (available since the 1950s) and with only psychotherapies, such as traditional insight-oriented individual and group therapy. These resulted in very poor outcomes for the treatment recipients (Hogarty, 1993; Lehman & Steinwachs, 1998).

Insight-oriented, psychodynamic therapies can be defined as those that use interpretation of unconscious material and focus on therapeutic transference. In the treatment of serious mental illnesses of all types, this form of psychotherapy has been found to be generally ineffective and sometimes harmful. The consensus is that these therapies should no longer be used to treat schizophrenia (Lehman & Steinwachs, 1998), bipolar disorder (Keck & McElroy, 1998), or major depression (Craighead et al., 1998a). On the other hand, supportive individual counseling can be a helpful component of treatment (Hogarty, 1993). Effective individual counseling with people who have severe mental illnesses generally focuses on support, the person's present life situation, and problem solving, rather than past experiences.

Psychodynamic therapy is not the only treatment approach that may have a negative impact. Therapeutic settings that seem very positive might actually promote relapse in some individuals with schizophrenia, especially if they are very high in intensity and expectations (Hogarty, 1993). For example, programs that combine intensive group therapy with a short length of stay are associated with more hospitalization and longer relapses (Linn, Caffey, Klett, Hogarty, & Lamb, 1979).

Maria's Story

Maria is a new PsyR worker just learning "the ropes." As you read about what happens to Maria and the consumer she is working with, think about how the situation might have been avoided. Also, consider who was really responsible for the problem. (Hint: There was more than one way to avoid this problem and more than one person responsible.)

Maria always knew that she wanted to work with people. During high school she volunteered at a geriatric home on weekends, reading to some of the residents or helping them with activities such as shopping for personal items or just keeping them company. She majored in psychology at the small liberal arts college she attended. Most of the courses she took covered basic psychological theory, research methods, and statistics. Her dream was someday to get her PhD and provide psychotherapy in her own private practice. During college, she volunteered at a private psychiatric hospital working with the activity therapist. She liked working with the patients. Maria could relate well because many of the patients were her age. She found it very interesting to talk with them about their symptoms.

During her senior year, she applied to several doctoral programs in clinical psychology. One of her psychology professors told her that it was harder to get into a clinical psychology program than to get into medical school. She wasn't even contacted for an interview. After graduation, Maria went home and searched for a job where she could use her psychology degree. After looking all summer, she ended up working as a clerk in a local bookstore. One day, a friend of her mother told Maria about a program for people with severe mental illnesses that was looking for people with BA degrees to provide support services. Maria applied, and on the strength of her previous experience and education, she got her first PsyR job. She was really excited.

After a week-long orientation to the program, she was assigned to work with Mark. Mark had a master's degree in rehabilitation counseling and more than four years of experience working in the program. Mark and Maria were responsible for a caseload of 11 clients. Maria quickly got to know these individuals and the tasks she had to perform as their case manager. After only a few months, she and Mark decided that she would be the primary case manager for John and Helen, two clients with whom she had developed a close relationship. Maria felt that she was really starting to grow as a professional.

When it came to her role as case manager, Maria made sure that she covered all the bases. She genuinely liked John and Helen, and she also wanted to prove to Mark that she could do a good job. She reviewed their individualized recovery plans with them and helped them to establish rehabilitation goals. Best of all, they were achieving these goals, and sometimes faster than scheduled. One day, Helen was absent on a day when she had an important meeting. That afternoon, Maria called her boarding home, but they said Helen was out; they thought she had gone to the program. The next day, Helen was absent again. Maria called the boarding home right away and they said that she had left that morning at her regularly scheduled time; they assumed she had gone to the program. Maria became very worried and went to tell Mark what was happening. The police brought Helen in that afternoon. They had found her acting strangely in the park, and when they had asked if she needed any help she started screaming and ran away. Helen was hospitalized that evening.

When Helen returned to the program, Maria asked her what had happened. Why had she stopped going to the program when she was doing so well? Helen said she knew that she was making real progress with Maria's help. One day she began hearing voices and she became unable to sleep at night. She remembered that Maria had said that if she took her medication and worked on her recovery plan she would get better, but at the same time she knew she was getting sick. She knew how much effort Maria put into helping her and what a caring person she was. She felt like she was letting Maria down. Maybe Maria would be very disappointed in her or even very angry. When she got too sick to control her symptoms, she would go to the park rather than let Maria see her that way after all the work she had done.

Understanding Course, Treatment, and Outcome: What Is Not Known Can Hurt!

Knowledge of the facts of the course and outcome of severe mental illnesses is essential for effective PsyR services. Practitioners who are unfamiliar with the findings regarding the probability of relapses, especially that relapse is still likely even with treatment adherence, may set inordinately high expectations for service recipients and themselves. Many well-meaning, enthusiastic staff lack education about severe mental illnesses. As illustrated in Maria's story, some of these individuals inform consumers that strict adherence to their recovery plans and taking their medication as prescribed will prevent relapse. When relapse occurs despite having closely followed the plan, both the individual and the PsyR practitioner may feel they have failed, blaming themselves rather than the disease itself. For consumers, this might result in hiding, denying symptoms, or dropping out of treatment and feeling they were misled. For the PsyR practitioner, this can produce frustration, a sense of failure, and eventually "burnout." Individuals and practitioners need to know that these illnesses do flare up, requiring medication changes, more intense treatment, support, and sometimes hospitalization. Indeed, most are well aware of this, but do not necessarily attribute relapse to the illness itself.

When periodic relapse is seen as a function of the type of illness rather than a personal failure, the chances of a timely intervention are greatly increased. Prompt intervention can sometimes avert severe relapse or shorten its duration. Probably the most important benefit of this knowledge is that relapse is no longer seen as a failure on anyone's part.

Inordinately low expectations, for example, believing that the probability of relapse precludes other positive outcomes, is just as harmful. Deegan (1992) described a vicious cycle of disempowerment. She observed that practitioners' expectations of inevitable consumer incompetence leads to learned helplessness on the part of the individuals served. In other words, low or negative expectations on the part of service providers promote feelings of powerlessness among mental health service recipients. Feeling they are unable to affect their own lives, some individuals have learned to become helpless and inadvertently fulfill the practitioner's expectation of incompetence. This can result in lack of practitioner support for consumers' educational aspirations, vocational goals, or independent living goals.

Conversely, believing positive outcomes are possible often results in the successful pursuit of a higher quality of life. There is evidence that successful PsyR may positively impact symptomatology. For example, it was found that successful vocational rehabilitation actually resulted in lower symptomatology, suggesting that rehabilitation itself may positively affect the course of the illness (DeSisto et al., 1995a, b; Bond et al., 2001; Lysaker & Bell, 1995). Other examples of the positive impact of psychiatric rehabilitation interventions on the course of mental illness appear throughout this text.

Summary

The symptoms of serious mental illness can be very difficult to live with. They can dominate a person's experience, sometimes disturbing a person's thoughts and feelings. They are also harmful to the self-esteem and hopefulness of the individual and may even put the person at risk for suicide. Functional deficits are also associated with these illnesses, specifically in self-care, employment, home making, educational achievements, and independent living. Because of these illnesses, individuals sometimes do not acquire important life skills or are unable to practice the skills they mastered previously.

There are no uniform outcomes for these disorders. Many people with depression or bipolar disorder and some people with schizophrenia will have only one or two episodes and never relapse again. Alternatively, most people with a chronic or recurrent depression, bipolar disorder, or schizophrenia will have a variety of positive and negative outcomes over the course of their lifetime. For persons with schizophrenia, on average the short-term course of the disease is marked by a high probability of relapse. Contrary to previous assumptions, the 20- to 30-year outcomes for schizophrenia are more positive, with one in four persons totally recovered and three out of four persons recovered, greatly improved, or improved. Awareness of these possible outcomes is essential for consumers, their families, and their service providers. Such knowledge will help avoid alienation and learned helplessness on the part of consumers, burnout and pessimism on the part of the staff, and unrealistic expectations by family members.

Individuals with these disorders are often prone to relapse, the risk of which is reduced, but not eliminated, by medication. All of these conditions are treated with powerful psychotropic medications that in addition to their therapeutic effects have numerous side effects. Because of side effects, the limited efficacy of these medicines, and many other reasons, many consumers find it difficult to adhere to their medication regimens. A collaborative approach and clear communication between the consumer and his or her psychiatrist are important aspects of providing effective treatment for these disorders.

In addition to biological or somatic treatments, such as medications, psychosocial interventions are also needed. The symptoms of depression seem to be particularly helped by approaches such as cognitive-behavioral therapies. The symptoms of schizophrenia and bipolar disorders are not helped by insight-oriented psychotherapy; however, supportive counseling may help individuals cope with symptoms and related problems. Cognitive-behavioral techniques, psychoeducation, and illness management strategies such as the evidence-based IMR training are also helpful interventions.

The deficits or impairments in functioning caused by these illnesses are best addressed by PsyR. Psychiatric rehabilitation can eliminate or reduce the impairment the person experiences in his or her living, learning, working, or social environments. In addition, it can help the individual pursue his or her personal goals, achieve these goals, and maintain these gains.

■ ■ ■ ▬▬▬▬▬▬▬▬▬▬▬▬▬▬▬▬▬▬▬▬▬▬▬▬▬▬▬▬▬▬▬▬

Class Exercise

Misconception, Truth, or a Little of Both?

The word *myth* is often taken to mean misconception. Yet many myths, rather than being complete fictions, have a grain of truth. There are numerous myths about severe mental illness. Consider the list of statements below. Do you consider each of them to be a myth? Are they complete misconceptions? Do they have any grains of truth?

Decide how to answer these questions based on the scientific evidence presented in the first three chapters of this textbook.

- "Once a person with schizophrenia, always a person with schizophrenia."
- "All people with schizophrenia are alike."
- "Rehabilitation can only happen when someone is completely stable."
- "Psychotherapy is a waste of time for people with severe mental illness."
- "People with severe mental illness must be on medication for the rest of their lives."
- "People with mental illness can only do low-level jobs." (You may want to check Chapter 10 before guessing on this one.)
- "Families cause mental illness." (See Chapters 2 and 14.)

▬▬▬▬▬▬▬▬▬▬▬▬▬▬▬▬▬▬▬▬▬▬▬▬▬▬▬▬▬▬▬▬ ■ ■ ■

Psychiatric Rehabilitation
Principles and Methodology

4

The Goals, Values, and Guiding Principles of Psychiatric Rehabilitation

I want people to know that growth happens and recovery happens and it's never too late. There's always hope out there.
Lyn Legere (*Shadow Voices*, 2005)

CHAPTER OUTLINE

Psychiatric Rehabilitation. http://dx.doi.org/10.1016/B978-0-12-387002-5.00004-4

This chapter reviews the goals, values, and guiding principles of psychiatric rehabilitation (PsyR). Psychiatric rehabilitation is an evolving discipline, so the approaches and strategies used constantly undergo adjustment and change as the field matures and the methods become more refined. These differences are reflected by the wide scope of PsyR practice currently in use. Despite the diversity of practice, you will see that there is agreement about the goals and values of PsyR. This agreement is clearly demonstrated by the similarity among the many formulations of PsyR principles that have been suggested by different groups and authors.

This chapter will answer the following questions:

1. *How does the concept of recovery inform the goals, values, and philosophy of PsyR?*
2. *What are the goals of PsyR?*
3. *What are the defining values held by PsyR professionals?*
4. *What are the guiding principles that inform state-of-the-art PsyR practice today?*
5. *What are the ethics of PsyR?*

Introduction

This chapter deals with the shared philosophy of PsyR practitioners as reflected in the services they provide. These concepts contribute to making PsyR a unique discipline. A relatively young field, PsyR is actively defining itself by amending its principles as we gain a better understanding of the supports and services needed by persons with psychiatric disabilities. PsyR is one specialty in the broader field of rehabilitation, to which it owes much of its philosophical base.

The Concept of Recovery

Over the last few decades, the concept of **recovery** has become the cornerstone of PsyR philosophy. Recovery represents optimism about the future. For many medical conditions, it implies a cure. Because the challenges faced by persons living with a severe mental illness are sometimes life-long, many advocates and scholars believed it was necessary to adopt a new conception of recovery that could coexist with the ongoing experience of the illness and its symptoms. This view of recovery is partly based on models of rehabilitation and recovery from physical disability and from substance use disorders, as well as on the lived experiences of persons living with severe mental illnesses (Anthony, 1993; Davidson & Strauss, 1992; Deegan, 1988; Jacobson, 2001; Onken, Ridgway, Dornan, & Ralph, 2002; Ridgway, 2001; Onken, Craig, Ridgway, Ralph & Cook, 2007; Slade, Amering, & Oades, 2008; Smith, 2000).

Nationally known consumer advocate, Patricia Deegan, PhD, and William Anthony, PhD, the founding director of the Center for Psychiatric Rehabilitation at Boston University, were early proponents of a recovery vision (Deegan, 1988; Anthony, 1993). Their ideas lay the groundwork for this continually evolving concept. In an early paper on recovery Deegan stated, "The need is to meet the challenge of the disability and to reestablish a new and valued sense of integrity and purpose within and beyond the limits of the disability" (1988, p. 11). Deegan also pointed out that helping someone achieve this kind of fundamental change in self-concept is an important aspect of the PsyR practitioner's work. A few years later, Anthony offered this definition of recovery, which is still widely cited today:

> *Recovery is … a deeply personal, unique process of changing one's attitudes, values, feelings, goals skills, and/or roles. It is a way of living a satisfying, hopeful, and contributing life, even with the limitations caused by illness. Recovery involves the development of new meaning and purpose in one's life as one grows beyond the catastrophic effects of mental illness. (1993, p. 15)*

The emphasis on change highlights several other key aspects of the recovery process. For example, Deegan (1988) stresses that one of the most important ideas is that recovery and rehabilitation are not linear processes. As people strive to adapt to profound changes in their lives, they naturally experience setbacks and temporary failures. Recovery is a journey that involves the exploration of new ideas and opportunities, while dealing with the possibility of failure, disappointment, and relapse. By this logic, PsyR programs that do not make realistic allowances for setbacks do a disservice to the people they serve.

Another corollary of the recovery concept is that each person's road to recovery is unique. Because recovery is based on developing a new self-image, we might assume that there may be as many roads to recovery as there are people. The uniqueness of each person's recovery process has a direct bearing on PsyR services. Effective programs respect diversity and provide many individualized rehabilitation services. "One size fits all" services may be easier and more economical to operate, but, especially in the long run, they are inherently less effective at helping persons recover.

The concept of recovery is supported by the progress made in PsyR and related mental health disciplines since the early days of deinstitutionalization. This progress is illustrated in some of the classic articles in the literature, such as the landmark longitudinal studies on the outcome of schizophrenia (e.g., Harding, Brooks, Ashikaga, Strauss, & Breier, 1987; described in Chapter 3) and a paper that debunked many of the myths about schizophrenia and mental illness that cause stigmatizing attitudes toward people living with severe mental illnesses (e.g., Harding & Zahniser, 1994). In addition, the development of evidence-based practices, such as supported employment (described in Chapter 10), that reliably produce positive outcomes for consumers and help them to find meaning and purpose in their lives supports the idea that recovery from serious mental illness is possible.

The Ongoing Study of Recovery

In the 25 years since Deegan and Anthony began exploring the concept of recovery from serious mental illness, there has been an explosion of scholarly writing and research on the topic. Some scholars and researchers have focused their efforts on better defining the concept, while others have addressed the challenges involved in trying to measure recovery to determine how recovery can be encouraged, helped, or enhanced. There is also a growing body of work focused on the characteristics of recovery-oriented mental health systems.

One of the key themes in the recovery literature is a duality of perspectives on this complex, multidimensional concept. Several authors make a distinction between what has been referred to as clinical, objective, and outcome-oriented recovery and recovery that is personal, subjective, and process-oriented (Drapalski et al., 2012; Onken et al., 2007; Rodgers, Norell, Roll, & Dyck, 2007; Roe, Mashiach-Eizenberg, & Lysaker, 2011; Slade et al., 2008). Clinical recovery is defined by reduction of symptoms, functional improvements, and achievement of specific outcomes such as stable employment or independent living. Scholars who focus on this conception of recovery are interested in researching and measuring recovery using quantifiable methods to measure recovery outcomes (e.g., Andresen et al., 2010; Corrigan & Phelan, 2004; Lieberman et al., 2008; Mausbach, Moore, Bowie, Cardenas, & Patterson, 2009). Such efforts have the potential to inform best practices in PsyR and related mental health disciplines. Some scholars have even suggested that we no longer look at recovery as a global concept, but instead focus on specific domains such as recovery of cognitive functioning, vocational functioning, or quality of life. An advantage of this view is that it helps consumers and providers target current treatment/rehabilitation service needs. For example, a person who has achieved significant recovery in the domains of symptomatology and cognitive functioning can now focus primarily on goals related to recovery of vocational functioning (Lieberman et al., 2008).

Scholars and researchers who have focused on personal recovery view it as a subjective concept and highlight each individual's unique quest to find meaning and purpose in a life that has been altered by a mental illness. Unlike the clinical perspective that highlights symptom stability, personal recovery can occur even while a person is still experiencing significant symptoms. This perspective builds on the initial work done by Deegan (1988) and Anthony (1992).

Much of the exploration of the subjective and personal nature of the recovery process makes use of qualitative research methods to gather information on common themes in recovery journeys. These studies can help us gain a better understanding of the lived experience of recovery (Davidson, 2003). In an early account of the common experiences of recovery, Davidson and Strauss (1992) asked 66 participants who had been hospitalized and then followed for two to three years after discharge to describe their recovery process. Participants discussed the evolving sense of self as an important part of recovery. In another study, Davidson (1992) asked individuals to identify the elements that helped them with recovery. Acceptance of the illness, feeling in control, and support from others were identified as three important elements. Davidson and colleagues also conducted a multinational qualitative study that identified several themes in the participants' recovery stories, including the social nature of the recovery process and the person's own role in developing a new identity and a sense of control (Davidson et al., 2005; Mezzina et al., 2006). Another project completed by Smith (2000) obtained 10 narratives from people who have psychiatric illnesses and attended a consumer-run mental health program. Important parts of the recovery process appear to include medication management, needing to be in control of the illness, support from others, and having meaningful activities. In another study, supportive relationships, meaningful activities, and both traditional and alternative treatments were found to be important resources for the participants' recovery (Mancini, Hardiman, & Lawson, 2005). Onken and colleagues (2002) organized focus groups of mental health consumer leaders to examine recovery. They developed a definition of recovery that included the following elements: having hope, understanding and acceptance of the illness, developing a new sense of self, and the value of supports. They found that individuals attributed recovery to a diverse range of factors influencing their own journeys.

One study examined identity-related themes in 45 first-person accounts written by people with a serious mental illness from two highly regarded journals, *Schizophrenia Bulletin* and *Psychiatric Services* (Wisdom, Bruce, Saedi, Weis, & Green, 2008). They found that major challenges faced by the writers included a lost sense of self and the struggle to deal with dual identities—the real "authentic self" and the "ill self," experienced during acute episodes. The authors concluded that managing these identity challenges is an important part of the recovery process. Earlier, Jacobson (2001) reviewed 30 published recovery narratives and found that important recovery themes were focusing on the role of the self, support from others, the influence of the mental health system, and how the individual views the origin of the illness. Ridgway (2001) reviewed four published narratives and found the components of recovery to consist of experiencing a reawakening, having hope, accepting the illness, and the importance of support from others.

The first systematic review of the qualitative studies of personal recovery formed a narrative synthesis of 97 papers published in 13 countries (Leamy, Bird, Boutillier, Williams, & Slade, 2011). The authors categorized their findings in three areas: characteristics of the recovery journey, recovery processes, and recovery stages. The identified dimensions of the recovery journey included its uniqueness, its non-linearity, and its ability to take place without the illness being cured. The recovery processes included aspects of connectedness, such as relationships with significant others and peer support; hope and optimism about the future; redefining one's identity; and finding meaning in life and empowerment. Again, these findings provide support for the early definitions of recovery put forth by Anthony (1992) and Deegan (1998).

The third aspect of recovery that Leamy and her colleagues (2011) addressed in their literature review were stages of recovery. This is not surprising, since recovery is a dynamic process that often takes place over a long period of time. Most of the stages or phases that have been identified include common themes such as moving from denial or indifference to acceptance, acquiring hope, gaining a sense of control, and eventually working toward personally meaningful goals (Andresen, Oades, & Caputi, 2003; Andresen, Caputi, & Oades, 2006, 2010; Baxter, & Diehl, 1998; Leamy et al., 2011; Rodgers et al., 2007; Young & Ensing, 1999).

A stage model that has been developed in Australia is outlined in Table 4.1 (Andresen, Oades, & Caputi, 2003; Andresen, Caputi, & Oades 2006, 2010; Copic, Deane, Crowe, & Oades, 2011). This model resembles the **transtheoretical model of behavior change** developed by DiClemente and Prochaska (1998), which is presented later in Chapter 9.

Studies that have made use of quantitative methods in examining the personal and subjective aspects of the recovery process have also been conducted. Corrigan and Phelan (2008) examined the relationship between objective and subjective measures of social support and recovery. They used the Recovery Assessment Scale (Corrigan, Giffort, Rashid, Leary, & Okeke, 1999) to measure some of the personal aspects of the recovery process and an expanded version of the Brief Psychiatric Rating Scale as a measure of clinical recovery (Ventura, Green, Shaner, & Liberman, 1993). They also used the Social Network Scale (Stein, Rappaport, & Seidman, 1995) to assess the nature of participants' support systems. They found that those with a more robust social network scored higher on the Recovery Assessment Scale but did not find an association between clinical status and individuals' social support systems.

Lloyd, King, and Moore (2010) looked to see if there was an association between the personal experience of recovery and objective, observable measures of recovery. They also used the Recovery Assessment Scale (Corrigan et al., 1999), as well as two other scales that have been used to assess subjective aspects of recovery such as empowerment: the Empowerment Scale (Rogers et al., 1997) and the Community Integration Measure (McColl, Davies, Carlson, Johnston, & Minnes, 2001). In addition, the Camberwell

Table 4.1 Five-Stage Model of Recovery

Stage	Characteristics
Moratorium	Denial, confusion, hopelessness
Awareness	Hope, recognition of potential for change
Preparation	Work begins, recognition of strengths, connections
Rebuilding	Hard work, responsibility, tenacity
Growth	Increased self-confidence, resilience, optimism

(Andresen, Caputi, and Oades, 2006, 2010).

Assessment of Need Short Appraisal Schedule, or CANSAS (Andresen, Caputi, & Oades, 2000), was administered to measure objective aspects of the subjects' treatment needs. The researchers found strong correlations between the three scales used to measure subjective aspects of recovery. They also found some correlations between subjective and objective measures, for example, persons who were employed had higher recovery and empowerment scores. They concluded that "the measurement of subjective dimensions of recovery such as empowerment has validity in evaluation of global recovery for people with severe mental illness" (Lloyd, King, & Moore, 2010, p. 220).

Recently, another instrument to measure subjective aspects of the recovery process, the Maryland Assessment of Recovery, was developed and field tested (Drapalski et al., 2012). This 67-item scale includes domains identified in the Substance Abuse and Mental Health Service Administration (SAMHSA) consensus statement on recovery (see Box 4.1) and appears to be a practical instrument for future research efforts.

BOX 4.1   THE 10 FUNDAMENTAL COMPONENTS OF RECOVERY

1. **Self-direction** Consumers lead, control, exercise choice over, and determine their own path of recovery.
2. **Individualized and Person-centered** There are multiple pathways to recovery based on an individual's unique strengths and resiliencies, as well as his or her needs, preferences, experiences (including past trauma), and cultural background.
3. **Empowerment** Consumers have the authority to choose from a range of options and to participate in all decisions—including the allocation of resources—that will affect their lives.
4. **Holistic** Recovery encompasses an individual's whole life, including mind, body, spirit, and community.
5. **Non-linear** Recovery is not a step-by-step process, but one based on continual growth, occasional setbacks, and learning from experience.
6. **Strengths-based** Recovery focuses on valuing and building on the multiple capacities, resiliencies, talents, coping abilities, and inherent worth of individuals.
7. **Peer Support** Mutual support—including the sharing of experiential knowledge and skills and social learning—plays an invaluable role in recovery.
8. **Respect** Community, systems, and societal acceptance and appreciation of consumers—including protecting their rights and eliminating discrimination and stigma—are crucial in achieving recovery.
9. **Responsibility** Consumers have a personal responsibility for their own self-care and journeys of recovery.
10. **Hope** Recovery provides the essential and motivating message of a better future, that people can and do overcome the barriers and obstacles that confront them.

(SAMHSA, 2006).

Whether looking at recovery outcomes or the recovery process, it is important to clarify exactly what an individual is recovering from. While one aspect of recovery is certainly learning to cope with illness-related symptoms and functional deficits, for many the greater challenge is recovering from the effects of stigmatizing attitudes, lost educational and vocational opportunities, and poverty (Onken et al., 2007). These challenging experiences take their toll on a person's self-esteem, making it difficult to develop a positive new self-concept and find meaning and purpose in one's life. It is also important to note that the dual recovery perspectives are not mutually exclusive. For example, one person may describe her recovery process as a long and arduous journey characterized by multiple relapses, very gradual acceptance of mental illness, development of a strong connection to a peer support group, and eventually finding meaning and purpose in a new role as a peer provider (see Chapter 13 for more on peer providers). But her recovery can also be described in terms of outcomes, such as fewer hospitalizations, symptom reduction, increased levels of social support, and stable employment.

Recovery-oriented Mental Health Systems

Another key theme in the recovery literature is the characteristics of mental health systems that promote recovery from mental illness. This began with William Anthony's proclamation that recovery should be the guiding vision for mental health service systems in the 1990s and beyond (Anthony, 1993). While today this may not seem like a radical idea, at the time most mental health providers were still oriented toward the medical model, focusing primarily on symptom reduction and harboring low expectations about the long-term functioning of persons living with serious mental illnesses. Efforts to provide rehabilitation-oriented services were certainly present, but most system planners and funders did not see them as a priority. Ten years later, recovery orientation got a substantial boost when the President's New Freedom Commission, a national task force charged with addressing the mental health crisis in the United States, published their report (2003). The New Freedom Commission's report declared that recovery from serious mental illness was possible and should be the primary goal of our mental health systems. While this message did not come as a surprise to many consumers, PsyR providers, and other advocates, it provided an important impetus for psychiatrists and other more traditional service providers to consider the implications of a recovery orientation (Rodgers et al., 2007). In 2006, under the auspices of the SAMHSA, more than 100 mental health service consumers, treatment and rehabilitation providers, family members, researchers, and other advocates were brought together to develop a consensus statement on recovery from mental illness. The result of their work included the identification of 10 fundamental components of recovery, which are outlined in Box 4.1.

The SAMHSA consensus statement was intended to not only create a common vision of recovery for consumers, providers, and family members, but also to guide policy makers and health care finance regulations. SAMHSA also funded a Recovery to Practice

Project, developed to promote a focus on recovery-oriented mental health care among psychiatrists, psychologists, social workers, psychiatric nurses, and peer providers. The goal of this project, which was still in progress as this book was being written, is to develop and disseminate discipline specific training materials through partnerships with US national professional associations. The Recovery to Practice Project has also developed a growing resource bank of materials on recovery and recovery-oriented practice. This information can be found on their Web site, http://www.samhsa.gov/recoverytopractice.

Other efforts to translate the concept of recovery into practical approaches for service providers have been described in the literature. A qualitative analysis of literature that offered guidance on transformation to a recovery orientation was conducted (Boutillier, Bird, Davidson, Williams, & Slade, 2011). Thirty documents from six countries were reviewed, and four domains of practice were identified: promoting citizenship, organizational commitment to a recovery orientation, supporting personally defined recovery, and working relationships/partnerships between practitioners and service users. Another report described a number of key strategies for organizational commitment to system transformation, including establishing a vision, persistent leadership, and consumer inclusion and involvement in the change process (Olmos-Gallo, Starks, Lusczakoski, Huff, & Mock, 2012).

In the United States, both the New Freedom Commission and SAMHSA reports did result in efforts by many states to develop recovery-oriented system transformation plans. While this national- and state-level public policy shift from systems with a narrow focus on treatment of symptoms and crisis intervention to systems that strive to help people live meaningful lives in their communities is certainly welcome, we still have a long way to go to realize the transformation envisioned by the SAMHSA consensus group. The transformation of mental health care systems is a complex process that is often slowed down by resistance to change, government bureaucracy, and lack of resources.

In conclusion, from the PsyR perspective, recovery is an individualized process of learning to live successfully with a serious mental illness. For many people, this involves reformulating one's self-concept, establishing new life aspirations, and becoming a valued and contributing member of the community. Recovery embodies the optimism and hope that underlie the entire PsyR enterprise.

The Goals, Values, and Guiding Principles of Psychiatric Rehabilitation

Goals represent desired states or objectives to strive for and achieve. Goals are usually identified based on their relationship or presumed relationship with values. For example, if we value free expression, we might work hard to achieve the goal of defeating a bill that we believe would stifle free speech on the Internet. Goals are more specific than values. Goals can usually be arrived at by different paths. For example, the goal of an improved quality of life might be achieved in a different manner for each person.

Values are deeply held beliefs that may inform specific behaviors, attitudes, and ideas. An individual's values tend to be stable over time. Because they are deeply held, a person may not articulate or question his or her own values. For example, individuals who value the free expression of ideas may not even be aware of that value until they find themselves coming to the defense of someone who is prevented from expressing his or her opinion at a meeting or gathering. Even then, they may not consider why they felt so strongly about what had just taken place.

Principles, in contrast to goals, are more specific statements specifically designed to promulgate values and goals by providing guidelines for addressing specific situations or behaviors as they arise. As an example, consider the community mental health principle of least restrictive treatment environment. This widely held principle states that an individual should always receive treatment in the most autonomous (i.e., least restrictive) setting or environment that is possible but still effective. This means, for example, that no one should be treated in a psychiatric hospital if there is a community-based program available where he or she can receive equally effective treatment. We can see that this principle is designed to promote goals such as the **community integration** of persons with disabilities, as well as foster the value of respect for the dignity and worth of each human being. Box 4.2 provides a preview of the values, goals, and guiding principles of PsyR that are discussed in the following sections.

The Goals of Psychiatric Rehabilitation

As we stated earlier, the goals of PsyR are what programs and services strive for in their work with persons who have psychiatric disabilities. In that sense, goals provide guidelines for the development and provision of services and go hand in hand with PsyR values. The combination of goals and values helps determine the guiding principles. Our review of several efforts to identify these principles suggests that there is agreement on the three goals of PsyR described below (Anthony et al., 2002; Anthony & Nemec, 1983; Cnaan, Blankertz, Messinger, & Gardner, 1988, 1989, 1990; Corrigan, 2003; Corrigan et al., 2008; International Association of Psychosocial Rehabilitation Services [IAPSRS], 1996; United States Psychiatric Rehabilitation Association [USPRA] 2009).

Recovery

Recovery is the defining goal of PsyR. It embodies both the hope and the challenge of the PsyR enterprise. Because the recovery process is unique for each person, the guidelines for achieving this goal may vary. You will see that some of the values and guiding principles described in this chapter are designed to promote the idea that each individual must follow his or her own path to recovery. In other words, it is something that the individual must achieve, rather than something that we can do *for* or *to* someone. Achieving this goal presents the PsyR practitioner with an important challenge. The practitioner has to help and encourage the individual to do something that the individual

---

BOX 4.2   THE GOALS, VALUES, AND GUIDING PRINCIPLES OF PSYCHIATRIC REHABILITATION

GOALS (3)

1. Recovery
2. Community integration
3. Quality of life

VALUES (6)

1. Self-determination and empowerment
2. Dignity and worth of every individual
3. Optimism that everyone has the capacity to recover, learn, and grow
4. Wellness
5. Cultural diversity
6. Promotion of valued social roles and normalized environments

GUIDING PRINCIPLES (12)

1. Person-centered approach
2. Partnership between service provider and service user
3. Partnership with family members and significant others
4. Utilization of peer support
5. Utilization of natural supports
6. Strengths focus
7. Focus on work and career development
8. Assessments related to person-chosen goals and environments
9. Emphasis on goal-related skills training, resource development, and environmental modifications
10. Integration of treatment and rehabilitation services
11. Ongoing, accessible, and coordinated services
12. Empirical orientation

---

has to accomplish on his or her own. Specific methods for meeting this challenge will be addressed in Chapter 5.

Community Integration

This goal is the most consistently stated goal of PsyR services both nationally and worldwide (e.g., Cnaan, Blankertz, Messinger, & Gardner, 1988, 1989; Corrigan et al., 2008; IAPSRS, 1996; USPRA, 2009). In large part, it focuses on helping individuals live independently in communities of their choice. For most people, residing in one's own home instead of in an institution or a supervised residential program is a critically important goal. It is also a civil right that is sometimes denied to persons with disabilities who are confined to institutions or other restrictive living environments for much longer than they should be. The 1999 US Supreme Court decision *L.C. v. Olmstead* brought attention to the rights of people living with disabilities and has led to increased efforts to deinstitutionalize individuals who are able to safely reside in the community (Bazelon Center for Mental Health Law, 1999). But **community integration** encompasses much more than where a person lives. People living with psychiatric disabilities should also have opportunities to work, attend school, socialize, and otherwise participate in their communities, just like everyone else. In recent years, Mark Salzer and his colleagues at the Temple University Collaborative on Community Inclusion of Individuals with Psychiatric Disabilities have brought attention to other important aspects of community integration, including leisure and recreation, spirituality, parenting, citizenship, and civic engagement (Baron, 2007; Salzer, 2006). Resources that outline strategies for promoting community inclusion can be found on their Web site (http://tucollaborative.org/). The goal of community integration is in many ways inseparable from the goal of recovery. In fact, it has been referred to as "the external, concrete manifestation (viewable to the outside world) of the recovery experience" (Bond et al., 2004, p. 571).

Community integration has been described in the literature as a concept with three interrelated domains: physical integration, social integration, and psychological integration (Wong & Solomon, 2002). Physical integration entails residing in the community and utilizing its resources. To illustrate this aspect of the concept, think about all of the places where you are physically present in a typical week: your apartment, a college campus, your workplace, the YMCA, the local shopping mall, restaurants, etc. Social integration means interacting with a variety of people in one's community. Again, think about all of the people you relate to on a regular basis, including family members, close friends, neighbors, classmates, work colleagues, members of your religious congregation, acquaintances at your gym, etc. In the early days of deinstitutionalization, many ex-patients had limited relationships and interacted primarily with mental health providers and other mental health consumers. Today, for some people, this is still the case, but PsyR practitioners strive to help individuals have many opportunities for meaningful interaction with non-disabled members of the person's community. Social integration also implies that people have social support systems that meet their needs and relationships that are characterized by reciprocity rather than dependence (Wong & Solomon, 2002). Psychological integration refers to perceived community membership or a sense of belonging. To appreciate the importance of this third level of community integration, think about a time when you were a new member of a community, such as your first few weeks at college. In new situations, we may be physically present and interacting socially with people around us, but we may still feel uncomfortable and out of place. Once we begin to make friends and feel more familiar with a new environment, we are more likely to experience the sense of satisfaction and well-being that comes with being part of a community.

PsyR practitioners should strive to help individuals become well integrated in their communities in all of the domains described above. Developing and implementing models of service that promote community integration is a critical aspect of the PsyR field. A good deal of criticism has been directed at antiquated service delivery models, such as group homes or sheltered workshops, that effectively keep individuals segregated from regular community life. Fortunately, in many mental health systems, these models are being replaced by evidence-based and promising practices that have been demonstrated to produce outcomes consistent with the goal of community integration (Bond et al., 2004). These models, such as supported employment, supported education, and supported housing, will be explored in Part 3 of this book, Chapters 10 to 12.

Quality of Life

The third overall goal of the PsyR enterprise focuses on helping all individuals living with serious mental illness experience the highest possible **quality of life**. The concept of quality of life refers to the individual's subjective sense of well-being in various life domains, for example, how the individual feels about his or her living arrangement (Becker, Diamond, & Sainfort, 1993). While quality of life is also sometimes measured objectively, for example, by looking at annual income, most researchers in this area conclude that quality of life is primarily a person-centered construct and that an individual's subjective report of satisfaction or dissatisfaction with his or her life is much more important than an observer's report of objective measures (Basu, 2004). Various instruments for measuring the quality of life of individuals living with serious mental illness have been developed and address life domains such as occupational activities, psychological well-being, physical health, social relations, and economics (Lehman, 1983, 1988, 1996; Becker et al., 1993).

Poverty has a negative impact on quality of life for many individuals living with mental illness. PsyR programs that help people obtain employment and earn a living wage or find decent and affordable housing are particularly good examples of services that are consistent with the goal of helping people to achieve the highest possible quality of life. In recent years, many PsyR programs have also begun to pay particular attention to the life domain of physical health. As will be explored later in the book (see Chapter 6), many individuals living with serious mental illnesses are also living with serious, sometimes life-threatening, physical illnesses and have considerably shorter life expectancies when compared to the general population (Brown, 1997; Hutchinson et al., 2006). Physical symptoms such as low energy, reduced mobility, and chronic pain can significantly reduce a person's quality of life. PsyR programs that promote physical health and wellness are an essential element of mental health systems.

For the PsyR practitioner, quality of life should always be an important goal regardless of the stage of the illness the person is experiencing. The presence of symptoms should not detract from the importance of helping an individual acquire the things that help ensure a reasonable quality of life, such as social support, companionship, employment, recreation, food, shelter, clothing, and an active sex life.

As you can see, the three goals of PsyR are very much interrelated. For example, efforts to enhance an individual's quality of life, such as securing a comfortable apartment in a safe neighborhood, also results in greater community integration and may be a prominent step in the person's recovery journey.

The Values of Psychiatric Rehabilitation

The values that underlie most, if not all, PsyR services relate directly to the goals that PsyR tries to achieve. Values are general attitudes that influence the professional's behavior in many ways. In fact, PsyR practitioners may hold these values without articulating them since they are embedded in the designs of the programs they work in and the service strategies they carry out. As you review the following six PsyR values, consider how they relate to the three overall goals of PsyR.

Self-determination and Empowerment

Everyone should have the right of self-determination, including participation in all decisions that affect their lives. In PsyR programs, this value is often referred to as **empowerment**. Community psychologist Julian Rappaport (1987) characterized the term "empowerment" as conveying ". . . both a psychological sense of personal control or influence and a concern with actual social influence, political power, and legal rights" (p. 121).

While everyone uses the term, there is still a good deal of debate about how to exactly define empowerment, as it relates to PsyR practice. One way of defining something is to formulate a working definition of it so that it can be measured. With input from several consumer groups around the country, Rogers, Chamberlin, Ellison, and Crean (1997) developed a scale designed to measure empowerment. They suggest that empowerment is made up of three elements. The first element is self-esteem/self-efficacy, which can be thought of as optimism and a sense of control over the future. The second element involves possessing actual power. They suggest the final element of empowerment is righteous anger and community activism. It is important to recognize that these elements of empowerment describe characteristics of empowered people. The Empowerment Scale has since been tested for construct validity and used in a number of studies (Rogers, Ralph, & Salzer, 2010).

Similar to the concept of recovery, empowerment is something that must come from within the individual, rather than something done to or for an individual. However, a variety of innovative service delivery strategies have been developed that foster empowerment. For example, the peer-delivered service approaches explored in Chapter 13 have been shown to promote empowerment among service users (Rogers et al., 2007).

Some strategies that promote empowerment focus on resources that help individuals make informed choices about their lives and the services they receive, for example, providing consumers with access to current information about psychiatric diagnosis and treatment. An early study in this area by Warner, Taylor, Powers, and Hyman (1989) found that shared knowledge about psychiatric diagnosis helps reduce psychiatric disability.

Similarly, Pratt and Gill (1990; Gill & Pratt, 1993) developed empowerment and involve-ment strategies for day treatment services that included sharing knowledge, power, and economic resources with consumers. Today, **Illness Management and Recovery (IMR)** and **shared decision making** are used to promote meaningful involvement in treatment goal setting, treatment choices, and active participation in one's own care (for more on these PsyR strategies, see Chapters 3 and 5).

PsyR providers who value self-determination and empowerment believe that unless there is a threat of imminent danger, persons who have psychiatric disabilities should be allowed to make decisions about their own lives. This holds true even if the decision could lead to a negative outcome. Another way of expressing this idea is that all people should have the right to take risks in their lives. Many well-intentioned practitioners struggle with consistently applying this value. They encourage consumers to make decisions, but also want them to play it safe and avoid any actions that could lead to a failure or setback. While it is important to be sure that people understand the potential consequences of their decisions and behaviors, it is ultimately the consumer's choice. For example, a person may feel ready to take on a full-time job, while staff members believe the person should take a less stressful part-time position. Sometimes, options that seem risky work out better than expected, whereas at other times the setback predicted by staff does occur. In either case, people should be empowered to direct their own lives and have experiences that will help them learn about their potential as well as their limitations.

Dignity and Worth of Every Individual

PsyR practitioners believe that every human being has worth, regardless of his or her degree of disability and should be treated with dignity and respect. This core value un-derlies every aspect of PsyR practice. People are in no way lessened as human beings by their illness. If asked, most people would personally endorse this position. Despite these socially correct declarations, the stigma attached to serious mental illnesses engenders prejudice and discrimination, which suggests that in reality this is not a widely held value in our society.

A lack of dignity or worth is conveyed in various ways; some are obvious and others subtle. Consider a setting where the service recipients are addressed by their first names, but the staff members are only addressed by their titles or surnames. The message in such behavior is very clear; the service recipients have low status while the staff members have high status. This same message may be conveyed in other ways as well, for example, when different rules apply to program staff and service recipients regarding use of program areas (e.g., conference rooms where only staff are allowed to congregate, separate bathrooms for service recipients and staff, etc.). While individual situations like these are subtle, if numerous such situations exist together, they convey a clear message that persons who receive services have less worth than the persons who staff the program.

It is important to note that the concept of staff-only bathrooms and lunchrooms is common in many settings and is not intended to carry a negative message. Most people address their own physician by the title "Doctor," while the doctor uses the patient's first name. Nevertheless, for persons who have a mental illness, an accumulation of these situations combined with societal stigma conveys a strong message that they are less valued by society. Wolf Wolfensberger's (1983) efforts to develop surveys and scales to identify these dignity-reducing situations are important simply because they are often subtle and unintended and may be essentially invisible to the staff.

Optimism That Everyone Has the Capacity to Recover, Learn, and Grow

Optimism regarding the improvement and eventual recovery of persons living with serious mental illness is a critical element of all PsyR services. Every person, regardless of his or her symptoms or functional deficits, has the capacity to benefit from services. Real optimism on the part of service providers generalizes to the service recipients. Of course, the ultimate optimistic stance is represented by the concept of recovery described earlier in the chapter. At the same time, providers who lack optimism regarding the potential of consumers may be hard-pressed to maintain the requisite level of motivation to effectively carry out their functions. Worse, even the most symptomatic individuals are aware of when a practitioner believes that they will not achieve their goals. Research has demonstrated that the opinions of others is a key factor in shaping self-efficacy (Bandura, 1986; Lent, Brown, & Hackett, 1994), so conveying optimism is more important than practitioners may realize.

The practical effects of a lack of optimism were often exemplified by the inadequate and inappropriate treatment provided to persons with the most severe mental illnesses by the traditionally trained staff of many community mental health centers (Torrey, 2006). Based on their training, these staff were often pessimistic about the long-term prognosis of persons who they believed lacked appropriate ego functioning and the insight to benefit from treatment. Because of the pervasive belief that these persons could not improve, treatment resources were often allocated to programs providing services for persons with less severe conditions who could benefit from more psychodynamically oriented treatments. Persons experiencing severe and persistent mental illness, labeled "chronics," were often treated by the least trained staff, given minimal psychiatric time, and given minimal levels of supplies, space, and support staff.

Another important aspect of this value is the belief that all people, regardless of their level of disability, can benefit from PsyR interventions such as skill training and education. The presence of a mental illness does not preclude someone's ability to learn and grow. The example ahead, while dated, shows how an individual's characteristics are, in fact, often strengths. Consider what happened to William, who had been attending a PsyR day program for a few years after spending the previous 13 years in a psychiatric hospital.

William, who was always neat and well groomed, was almost entirely non-communicative. One thing that he did communicate was a desire to work. Previous attempts at getting William to be more outgoing had all ended in failure. While he did not speak often, William did seem to like to be around people.

Reviewing past failures, a new support worker hit on an idea. If William could learn to use a few phrases and operate the equipment, he could work as an elevator operator, a job for which some openings existed. William responded very positively to this idea. He learned to greet people and ask them what floor they wanted. He also learned to operate the elevator, paying particular attention to the doors and to whether it stopped evenly with the floor at each level. The staff were amazed that William could learn these things after years of being almost a recluse. William held that job for many years, rarely saying more than "Good morning!," "What floor?," and "Watch your step!"

Wellness

While individuals who utilize PsyR programs initially gain access due to a psychiatric diagnosis, PsyR services should be holistic and help individuals make improvements in multiple life domains, including physical health and wellness. As mentioned previously, many individuals that utilize PsyR services also have been diagnosed with chronic physical illnesses such as diabetes and hypertension. While the staff of PsyR programs may not include physicians and other primary care providers, these programs should address wellness goals and help individuals gain access to primary care services and related resources such as nutritional and exercise programs. Some PsyR programs demonstrate the value they place on wellness by creating a culture where both service providers and service recipients work together on wellness goals such as weight loss and regular exercise. This is a good example of the many ways that PsyR staff use role modeling as an intervention. However, in this example, staff members can also reap the benefits of a healthier lifestyle. The value of wellness and its importance to the PsyR field will be explored in much greater detail in Chapter 6.

Cultural Diversity

Since severe mental illness knows no cultural or ethnic boundaries, effective PsyR services are sensitive to and respectful of the cultural and ethnic differences of each individual. While one may think that mental health providers would be well prepared to provide services to diverse populations, this is not always the case. Inequalities, based on race and ethnicity, have been reported in terms of access, quality of care, satisfaction with services, and outcomes (Alegria, Canino, & Rios, 2002; Barrio et al., 2003; Stanhope et al., 2008). Lack of attention to cultural differences may cause professionals to make incorrect judgments about the persons they serve. For example, consider a practitioner who mistakes an Asian man's reluctance to make direct eye contact as social withdrawal and a negative symptom of schizophrenia, when in fact making direct eye contact with a relative stranger is considered rude and aggressive behavior in his culture. Another common mistake is to impose one's own values on a consumer, for example, a practitioner who encourages a single Latina woman to assert her independence and move out of her parental home, not realizing that she and her family all believe that she should only move away when she gets married. In order to avoid such mistakes and provide services that are both recovery-oriented and culturally relevant, PsyR practitioners must learn about the cultural identities of each person they serve.

It is important to note that a person's cultural identity encompasses much more than race and nationality. "Religious affiliation, language, physical size, gender, sexual orientation, age, disability (both physical and mental), political orientation, socioeconomic status, occupational status, and geographical location are but a few of the faces of diversity" (Campinha-Bacote, 2003). It is also essential to understand the concept of intra-cultural variation, which means that there is not only a great deal of variation in mores, values, and traditions across cultures, but also substantial diversity in these areas within a cultural group (Campinha-Bacote, 2003). Appreciation of intra-cultural variation helps PsyR practitioners avoid the tendency to stereotype individuals based on newly acquired knowledge about a cultural group. Instead, they should remember that the best way to learn about the cultural backgrounds of individual consumers is to respectfully ask them to describe their own cultural identity.

PsyR practitioners also need to be sensitive to the fact that many of the individuals they serve are not only faced with societal stigma toward their mental illness but also prejudice and discrimination based on their cultural backgrounds. Consider the many barriers faced by this man:

> Jamal, who has been diagnosed with both schizophrenia and a substance abuse disorder, describes himself as a gay African-American. He has been unemployed for several years and is at risk of becoming homeless because of a longstanding feud with a landlord who doesn't want to renew his lease. Jamal tells his support worker, "Sometimes I just want to give up because everywhere I look I see hatred in people's eyes. My landlord hates me because he thinks I'm crazy and is afraid I might do something like burn down his house. I can't get hired in this town because I'm black. The lady in the welfare office treats me like a piece of dirt. Even my own family and the people I have known all my life at church look at me differently since I came out."

Recognizing the barriers posed by discrimination and the effects of stigmatizing and prejudicial attitudes helps us stay mindful of the importance of respectful communication and behavior. But PsyR practitioners need to do more than provide empathetic responses; they also need to advocate on both individual and system-wide levels, for example, helping a person fight the discriminating actions of a landlord or potential employer by accessing information about relevant laws and equal opportunity practices, as well as referring consumers to legal aid organizations.

The goal of becoming **culturally competent** has been described as both aspirational and a life-long learning experience (Campinha-Bacote, 2003; USPRA, 2008b). We can never know everything about every culture. But since the task of PsyR is essentially reintegration with the consumer's community of choice, it is the responsibility of the PsyR provider to be sensitive to the particular beliefs, mores, and customs of the community in question. This may mean providing services in the predominant language of the communities they serve, or forging connections with neighborhood cultural groups. For more guidance in this area, review the principles of multicultural psychiatric rehabilitation services that were developed by the United States Psychiatric Rehabilitation Association (USPRA) in order to clearly define the concept of culturally competent practice (USPRA, 2008a, 2008b). They are presented in Box 4.3.

Valued Social Roles and Normalized Environments

Sometimes this value is described as simply wanting to help people live as "normal" a life as possible. But what constitutes a "normal" behavior in multicultural societies? Wolf Wolfensberger, a psychologist whose work was primarily with people who had developmental disabilities, coined the term **normalization** and described it as the promotion of valued social roles (Wolfensberger, 1983). Worker, student, parent, and neighbor are positive social roles that are valued in our society. Psychiatric patient and group home resident are examples of social roles that are devalued. PsyR services are designed to assist people in taking on and succeeding in valued social roles.

Normalized services are appropriate to the person's age, sex, culture, and so forth. For example, in a PsyR program you would not speak to the adults as if they were children or ask them to do finger paintings and then display their work on the wall. Instead, PsyR staff should provide interventions such as goal planning or skill development in ways that normalize the experience. Making statements such as "We all have dreams and goals that we envision for our future" or "In order to succeed in college it's important to have strong organizational skills; I remember that I really struggled to develop them when I was a freshman in college!" highlights similarities in the human experience. Such an approach may help persons who have been labeled "abnormal" in the past believe that a valued social role is within their reach.

Environments where consumers of PsyR services live, work, learn, and socialize should also be normalized. For example, in normalized residential settings consumers live in decent, safe neighborhoods; have access to transportation, shopping, and other community resources; interact with neighbors; and participate in community activities. In contrast, locked institutional settings and group homes in socially isolated locations are inconsistent with this important value.

Guiding Principles of Psychiatric Rehabilitation

The guiding principles of psychiatric rehabilitation comprise a set of rules that can be applied to specific situations in order to achieve the goals and reflect the values of the field. In a sense, they constitute rules of thumb that PsyR practitioners can refer to when faced with important decisions. The principles are important tools for providing day-to-day guidance in clinical situations and for systematizing the practice of PsyR.

Although the higher order values and goals are widely shared by PsyR practitioners, there are still some questions about the application of specific principles. These differences are reflected in the formulations of PsyR principles that have been put forward

BOX 4.3 USPRA PRINCIPLES OF MULTICULTURAL PSYCHIATRIC REHABILITATION SERVICES

Principle 1 Psychiatric rehabilitation practitioners recognize that culture is central, not peripheral, to recovery, as culture is the context that shapes and defines all human activity.

Principle 2 Psychiatric rehabilitation practitioners study, understand, accept, and appreciate their own cultures as a basis for relating to the cultures of others.

Principle 3 Psychiatric rehabilitation practitioners engage in the development of ongoing cultural competency, in order to increase their awareness and knowledge and to develop the skills necessary for appropriate, effective cross-cultural interventions.

Principle 4 Psychiatric rehabilitation practitioners recognize that thought patterns and behaviors are influenced by a person's worldview, ethnicity, and culture, of which there are many. Each worldview is valid and influences how people perceive and define problems, perceive and judge the nature of help given, choose goals, and develop or support alternative solutions to identified problems.

Principle 5 Psychiatric rehabilitation practitioners recognize that discrimination and oppression exist within society; these take many forms, and are often based on perceived differences in color, physical characteristics, language, ethnicity, gender, gender identity, sexual orientation, class, disability, age, and/or religion. Psychiatric rehabilitation practitioners play an active role and are responsible for mitigating the effects of discrimination associated with these barriers and must advocate not only for access to opportunities and resources but also for the elimination of all barriers that promote prejudice and discrimination.

Principle 6 Practitioners apply the strengths/wellness approach to all cultures.

Principle 7 Psychiatric rehabilitation practitioners show respect toward others by accepting cultural values and beliefs that emphasize process or product as well as harmony or achievement. They demonstrate that respect by appreciating cultural preferences that value relationships and interdependence, in addition to individuality and independence.

Principle 8 Psychiatric rehabilitation practitioners accept that solutions to any problem are to be sought within individuals, their families (however they define them), and their cultures. The person using psychiatric rehabilitation services and his/her family are sources of expanding the practitioner's knowledge about that culture, how to interpret behaviors, and how to integrate these cultural perspectives into a rehabilitation/recovery plan. Alternatives identified by service providers are offered as supplementary or educational, rather than compulsory.

Principle 9 Psychiatric rehabilitation practitioners provide interventions that are culturally syntonic and accommodate culturally determined strengths, needs, beliefs, values, traditions, and behaviors.

Principle 10 Psychiatric rehabilitation practitioners are responsible for actively promoting positive inter-group relations, particularly between the people who attend their programs and the larger community.

(Approved by the USPRA Board, 2008).

in the discipline's short history (Anthony et al., 2002; Anthony & Nemec, 1983; Cnaan et al., 1988, 1989, 1990; Corrigan et al., 2008; IAPSRS, 1996; USPRA, 2009). Research methods that have been used to identify the common principles of PsyR are described in Box 4.4.

Rather than outright disagreement on these principles, professionals in different settings often prioritize principles differently. This reprioritization is often a response to real differences that exist between settings or unique situations. For example, in order to justify billing criteria, in some treatment settings staff are required to focus on the consumers' symptoms and deficits when writing clinical notes, rather than on their strengths. As you will see, this emphasis on symptoms and deficits violates the principle of focusing on an individual's strengths. Regardless, for these practitioners, a refusal to comply with billing requirements might jeopardize the existence of PsyR services in general. In this paradoxical case, the best response might be to avoid emphasizing strengths when writing chart notes but still emphasize strengths in actual practice. As you review the 12 guiding PsyR principles discussed next, consider how they relate to the goals and values of PsyR.

BOX 4.4   RESEARCHING THE PRINCIPLES OF PSYCHOSOCIAL REHABILITATION

In an important set of studies, Cnaan and his colleagues (1988, 1989, 1990) addressed the lack of clarity around the definition of "psychosocial rehabilitation" (PSR). (Note: in this case PSR and PsyR are different terms for the same set of practices.) They believed that the lack of agreement on the definition of PSR causes several problems. Lack of a clear definition tends to render any term, such as PSR, meaningless, since anything might be termed or labeled PSR. This all-inclusiveness also hinders the development of an agreed-on body of knowledge that represents PSR. Finally, because there is little agreement as to what constitutes PSR, there is no way to evaluate a program regarding how well it is carrying out PSR. In response to these issues, Cnaan and his colleagues attempted to identify, clarify, and confirm some of the definitional issues surrounding PSR.

In two initial studies (Cnaan et al., 1988, 1989), they identified 15 principles derived from the PSR and PsyR literature. Then, in a third study (Cnaan et al., 1990), the research team translated each principle into two or three specific PSR activities or practices. The presence of these practices indicated that the corresponding principle was adhered to. In other words, if an activity was deemed important in a particular PSR setting, they assumed that the principle that the activity represented was supported.

From this work, a survey instrument composed of activities and practices representing the 15 principles was created. Next, using a Delphi method (i.e., asking the experts in the field for their opinions), the researchers identified a large group of PsyR experts from (1) authors of PsyR research literature, (2) the board of directors of IAPSRS (now USPRA), and (3) recent presenters at IAPSRS conferences. Seventy-two of these experts responded to the survey consisting of items about the importance of different activities PSR practitioners perform (that were presumed to relate to the 15 principles). Results from a factor analysis revealed support for 13 of the original 15 principles.

Person-centered Approach

PsyR services should be person-centered rather than practitioner-centered or program-centered. Applying this principle means that goal formulation strategies, assessments, rehabilitation interventions, and any other services provided respond to the individual needs and desires of each person served in a PsyR program. In contrast, some service providers have a traditional medical model orientation, which is practitioner-centered and assumes that the clinician should dictate the discharge plan and prescribe the treatment. Each of us has a unique set of preferences, values, and aspirations and many of us lose motivation if told that we should choose a different direction. So goals that are selected for the consumer by the practitioner or anyone else are often meaningless and are rarely achieved.

A program-centered or one-size-fits-all approach is also inconsistent with PsyR principles and values. For example, in the early days of deinstitutionalization, transitional group homes were the most common residential service model. Individuals were discharged from psychiatric institutions to a supervised home to live with several other ex-patients. Everyone's service plan was similar, something like, "Prevent rehospitalization and transition to independent living within 18 months." Everyone was expected to do the same chores and attend the same day treatment program five days a week. As you will see in Chapter 12, this residential approach is not consistent with the preferences of most individuals and is also not particularly effective in in promoting true community integration.

Because it allows each person to identify meaningful goals and access supports and services that are consistent with needs and preferences, an individualized and person-centered approach to the provision of PsyR services is a very important element of the recovery process. Because some PsyR services are carried out in groups, strict adherence to this principle can be challenging. Notice how the following supported employment (SE) program is designed to ensure individualization of services and how the curriculum is adjusted depending on the needs of members:

> *The SE program at Shore House offers a six-week Vocational Exploration group. The curriculum for this group includes a review of each member's past experiences, including identification of their occupational values, skills, interests, and preferences. The final step for each group member is the development of a vocational goal. A new member, Arthur, wants to get a job and believes he will need the support of the job coach to secure and maintain employment. After several meetings, the job coach is satisfied that Arthur knows what kind of job he wants. Rather than spend six weeks in the group to gain information he already has, Arthur will begin working with the job coach immediately on job development.*

Partnership Between Service Provider and Service User

To assist a person with the rehabilitation and recovery process, the PsyR practitioner first needs to establish a positive connection with the person that is characterized by mutual respect and trust. It may take considerable time and effort to build such a working relationship. Once established, the relationships between PsyR practitioners and the people they serve are true partnerships (Fox, 2000, 2004a, b; Rapp & Goscha, 2006). In other words, both parties, the consumer and the provider, work together with a common purpose—to help the person achieve his or her goals and move forward in the recovery journey.

> *Larry, who has been a consumer of mental health services for many years, has had some negative experiences in his past relationship with staff members. He doesn't feel that they always understand his point of view and has sometimes felt that they pressure him to sign treatment plans and attend groups that don't pertain to his needs. He is skeptical when he meets Nicole, who introduces herself as his new counselor. What could this young woman possibly know about his life and his dreams? Nicole takes the time to get to know Larry. She encourages him to talk about himself and his interests. She puts in considerable time and effort to help him resolve an ongoing problem he has been having with his landlord. After several months, Larry begins to think that Nicole really is concerned about him. When they begin discussing his rehabilitation goals and recovery plan, he is pleased that she encourages him to do most of the talking about his goals. She does offer helpful suggestions, but never tries to talk him into doing something that he's not interested in pursuing.*

One task in this partnership is choosing the best treatment and rehabilitation options, which should be done using a **shared decision-making** approach. When making these important choices, the perspectives of both partners are viewed as valuable and essential to the work. Practitioners bring specialized knowledge, skills, and resource access to the relationship; consumers bring their experiences and a unique understanding of their own needs and preferences. The goal is to reach consensus on the best course of action. A good example of shared decision making involves use of decision aids to assist consumers in learning more about psychiatric medications. Decision aids can be provided in various formats such as consumer-friendly written materials, videos, or computer-based tools (Adams & Drake, 2006; O'Connor et al., 2009; SAMHSA, 2008). After utilizing a decision aid, a person can then have a more informed discussion with his or her psychiatrist in order to make a mutual decision about a medication regimen. Shared decision making was introduced previously in Chapter 3.

Partnership with Family Members and Significant Others

Families are, in many cases, the most important and stable support system for persons living with a serious mental illness. Like most of us, consumers may live with or have frequent contact with family members. Some live with parents and/or siblings, others with spouses and/or children. Extended family members may also be present in a consumer's home. Still other consumers live with significant others, who the consumer may identify as part of their primary support system. At a consumer's request, all of these individuals can become partners in a person's recovery process and should be considered as important resources by PsyR practitioners. However, it is important to note that in the United States and elsewhere health care privacy laws require that a consumer has provided written authorization before staff members can communicate with family members (and significant others) or include them in their rehabilitation efforts.

There are a number of ways to involve family members in PsyR practice. One example is the family psychoeducation model, which provides the family with current information about psychiatric diagnoses and treatment and then offers them ongoing multiple family support groups. This approach achieves important outcomes for the consumer as well as the family and is recognized as an evidence-based practice (McFarlane, Dixon, Lukens, & Lucksted, 2003). Family psychoeducation and other family intervention approaches are described in more depth in Chapter 14. Family members can play other important roles in the PsyR field, such as contributing their ideas about service needs and advocating for more research studies and stronger service systems. Many PsyR agencies have family members, together with consumers, on advisory and governing boards of directors.

Utilization of Peer Support

For many individuals living with a mental illness, other people facing similar challenges are an important source of hope and support. The idea that peer support is an important component of community support systems was introduced to mental health professionals in the 1970s (Turner, 1977). As described in Chapter 13, peer support has gradually achieved greater acceptance and is now offered in a variety of ways. For example, some individuals attend self-help groups such as those offered throughout the United States by the Depression and Bi-polar Support Alliance (DBSA, http://www.dbsalliance.org). Others regularly attend peer-run support programs, as illustrated by Keisha's experience:

> Keisha is a 35-year-old woman who was has been a recipient of mental health services since she was first hospitalized at age 19. She has attended many outpatient programs over the years, including day treatment programs (described in Chapter 7). She currently sees a psychiatrist once a month, but she credits the friends she has made at a local self-help center for helping her stay out of the hospital and focused on her recovery goals. The self-help center, located in an office building in her neighborhood, is open four days a week from 4:00–8:00 p.m. and on Saturday afternoons. Keisha usually stops by two or three times a week to socialize, share a meal, or sometimes to see a guest speaker talk about topics such as staying fit or the college application process. The self-help center receives a modest state grant and is facilitated by two individuals who are also mental health consumers. Keisha likes that the atmosphere is informal, friendly, and accepting. She says, "Sometimes I go just to hang out with people who accept me, but other times I really need to talk about a problem. I can always find someone who understands because they know what it's like to be in my shoes."

Another form of peer support is the inclusion of individuals who have the lived experience of mental illness on PsyR staff teams. As explored in Chapter 13, PsyR service providers, who have also been consumers of PsyR services, can make very effective practitioners with some unique strengths. Each of these forms of peer support can be helpful at various points in a person's recovery, so it is important that PsyR practitioners help individuals access the type of peer support that they want and need.

Utilization of Natural Supports

Natural supports are the types of supports that we all use when we need help or companionship. They include persons and other resources that are naturally present in our living, working, learning, or social environments. Asking a family member for a ride to work, borrowing notes from a classmate, asking a coworker to cover when you are not feeling well, and asking a rabbi for advice about a troubled marriage are all examples of utilizing natural supports. One of the reasons that PsyR practitioners strive to help consumers become better integrated into their communities is that they want to help them gradually utilize more natural supports and fewer professional supports. In other words, become less dependent on professional services that often emphasize illness and disability. The use of naturally occurring resources is well illustrated by Rapp and Goscha (2006), who describe a program developed at a rural mental health center, which had very limited resources but produced very positive outcomes:

> They had no group homes, so they worked with landlords. They had no "group room," so they used a local fast food restaurant. They had no vocational program, so they worked with employers. They had no drop-in center, so they worked with churches and ministers. (p. 179)

The work of PsyR programs such as supported employment, supported education, and supported housing (see Chapters 10, 11, and 12) that emphasize the goal of community integration and the value of promoting valued social roles reflects this principle. Keeping in mind that becoming less dependent does not necessarily mean completely independent, consider the following situation in which this principle is being applied:

> After many years of being unemployed due to her psychiatric disability, Rosanna is excited when she starts a full-time job as an administrative assistant for a medical supply company. She has excellent clerical skills and quickly learns the required tasks. While the atmosphere in her office is friendly, she struggles at first to make friends with her coworkers. Prior to working, she attended a clubhouse program five days a week for almost two years and she misses the effortless camaraderie she had with some of the other clubhouse members, who were also living with serious mental illness. She talks about feeling shy and lonely during her weekly meetings with her job coach. Together they develop strategies, such as offering to help out a coworker who seems stressed and budgeting her money so she can join coworkers for restaurant lunches at least once a week. Gradually, she feels more

comfortable at work and happily reports to her job coach that she has been invited to attend a baby shower for a coworker. In the meantime, Rosanna continues to attend a weekend social group at the clubhouse. She likes seeing friends there and sharing stories with others who have recently started working. It also gives her an opportunity to check in with a favorite staff member who had helped Rosanna gain the self-confidence needed to get back to work. Rosanna feels fortunate to remain connected to the clubhouse but also feels hopeful about her growing social life at the office and beyond.

Strengths Focus

PsyR services and practitioners recognize and build on an individual's strengths rather than focusing on his or her weaknesses or deficits. This can be a difficult task for both consumer and practitioner. Consumers who have a long history of psychiatric hospitalizations are accustomed to professionals focusing on their symptoms and problems. When first asked "What are your strengths?" they are often at a loss. Initially, practitioners may also have difficulty seeing beyond symptoms and social deficits such as extreme withdrawal. However, PsyR programs typically allow consumers and practitioners to develop relationships around work and recreational activities. These experiences encourage practitioners to relate to consumers as they would to a colleague or friend, and to focus on what a consumer can do and likes to do. Perhaps this principle is best illustrated by the following professional descriptions of the same individual:

Joan is a psychiatric nurse who sees Peter once a month in a medication maintenance group. In a chart note, she describes Peter as appearing depressed and withdrawn with poor eye contact and constricted affect. Phil is a vocational rehabilitation counselor who is working with Peter in a supported employment program. His chart note, written on the same day as Joan's, describes Peter as a diligent worker who completes assigned tasks and communicates effectively with his supervisor. Both descriptions may be accurate and are appropriate to the professional's function. Joan's note may assist the psychiatrist in making a helpful medication adjustment, whereas Phil's PsyR assessment helps him determine that Peter's vocational rehabilitation goals are being achieved.

This emphasis on consumer strengths has been championed by the work of Charles Rapp and his colleagues at the University of Kansas School of Social Welfare. Their strengths model is a recovery-oriented approach that closely parallels what we are calling psychiatric rehabilitation. A strengths-based approach includes an assessment of four categories of a person's strengths: personal attributes, talents and skills, environmental strengths, and interests and aspirations. However, this approach is much more than the identification of strengths on an assessment tool. The practitioner consistently provides a "can do" focus and helps the person develop a meaningful life in the community, while gradually reducing reliance on traditional mental health services that tend to emphasize deficits and limitations (Rapp & Goscha, 2006). More information on this model is provided in Chapter 8.

Focus on Work and Career Development

Work is an important aspect of life and should be available to everyone. Joe Marrone, a nationally known vocational services advocate, believes that not working is not really a viable choice: "I Think You Should Work, That's What I Think" is the title of one of his presentations and he points out the true drawbacks of not working, including poverty and isolation (Marrone & Golowka, 2000). In other words, all adults, with or without disabilities, should work. PsyR practitioners do not question the ability of someone to work, but rather assist the individual to acquire the skills, resources, and supports necessary for success. PsyR practitioners know that it is the absence of skills rather than the presence of mental illness that create barriers to successful living.

A good example of this principle is Carl's story in Chapter 10, which covers employment services. Even though Carl had failed repeatedly at his attempts to work, the program continued to support him in pursuing his goal. Rather than focusing on the failures, the job coach focused on his strengths, skills, and interests and explored the supports that might help him to succeed. Maintaining a consistent focus on a vocational goal eventually leads to vocational success.

The PsyR practitioner also needs to keep in mind that for many consumers vocational rehabilitation efforts should focus on helping people not only obtain employment but develop meaningful careers. Sometimes that means first helping someone return to college to complete a bachelor's degree or enroll in a graduate studies program in his or her chosen profession. Notice that this principle is very much in line with the overall PsyR goals of recovery and improved quality of life. The recovery process is about helping individuals find meaning and purpose in life, which for many of us is related to our careers. Also, achieving an acceptable level of quality in some life domains requires that one has a reasonable income. While obtaining a part-time job earning minimum wage may be an initial employment goal for some consumers, it will not help a person rise out of poverty.

Assessments Related to Person-chosen Goals and Environments

As you will learn when reading the next chapter, mental health practitioners conduct various types of assessments in order to match their interventions to a person's needs. PsyR providers emphasize use of assessments that focus on the particular skills and resources a person needs in order to achieve a chosen rehabilitation goal. These are sometimes referred to as **situational assessments** because they focus on what is needed to function successfully in the environments (i.e., situations) of the person's choice. This is in contrast to doing a **global assessment** unrelated to specific goals. For example, consumers attending a vocational readiness group may have markedly different employment goals. Sarah wants to get a job as a retail salesperson, while Tony would like to pursue work as a laboratory technician. Doing a general assessment of work readiness skills (e.g., ability to follow directions and complete assigned tasks) is not the best way to predict what they will need to succeed in their chosen jobs. The best way to assess their ability to meet the requirements of their chosen career is to observe them completing relevant tasks in these very different environments. It is likely that focusing on interpersonal skills will be crucial for success for Sarah. The ability to carry out precise measurements and record results will be important for Tony's chosen line of work.

Goal-related Skills Training, Resource Development, and Environmental Modifications

PsyR services and providers should be capable of helping individuals acquire the skills and resources necessary to achieve their goals and thus function successfully in the environments of their choice. To illustrate this principle, let's continue with the theme of helping people obtain desired employment. Skills training often encompasses much more than the specific skills one needs to work on a job. We are often unaware of the skills we employ to negotiate everyday situations. Consider the set of skills that need to be mastered just to get through a job interview:

> *Tim tells Nancy, his job coach, that he has an upcoming interview for a job as a computer technician. Nancy suggests they do an initial role play, which reveals that Tim speaks very softly and struggles to make eye contact. Nancy then works with Tim to list the social skills required to make a good impression on an interview, including speaking clearly and making eye contact. She then demonstrates the use of the skills and asks Tim to try another role play. Additional feedback and practice help Tim to use the skills effectively and perform well on the job interview.*

PsyR services and providers also need to help people with disabilities access or negotiate the resources and environmental modifications necessary to function successfully in the environments of their choice. Resources can be monetary, goods, or other entitlements. Examples include a discounted fare bus pass, a rental assistance voucher, or donated clothing suitable for a job interview. Resources also include people, such as the job coach described previously or a family member to provide transportation. Environmental modifications for persons with disabilities can also take many forms. For someone in a wheelchair, providing a ramp into a building is an important modification. For someone with mental illness, a change in working hours to accommodate a public transportation schedule might be a very important modification. Chapter 5 will provide additional information about skills training, resource development, and reasonable accommodations. These intervention strategies are part of what makes the PsyR practitioner's role unique.

Integration of Treatment and Rehabilitation Services

This means that PsyR services and practitioners do not separate the treatment and rehabilitation processes. Rather, the consumer is viewed as a complex individual, taking into account all the aspects of his or her life impacted by these processes. The term "treatment" usually refers to symptom relief, while "rehabilitation" usually refers to overcoming barriers and the pursuit of goals. A modern understanding of PsyR views these as complementary endeavors, although historically medical and rehabilitation professionals have not always seen them as such.

Consider the issue of an essential component of the treatment of serious mental illnesses, taking psychotropic medication. A regimen of psychotropic medication is prescribed by a physician for relief (treatment) of psychotic symptoms. What is the role of rehabilitation in this intervention? On the face of it, one might say it is a simple issue of patient compliance or noncompliance with physician recommendations. However, consumers need knowledge and skills to make informed choices about medication options and to adhere to a medication regimen. In addition, they need to monitor their symptoms and side effects in order to communicate this information to their doctor. This is where rehabilitation can be of assistance to treatment. An individual's ability to monitor and share appropriate information about symptoms, medications, and side effects can be improved through interventions such as psychoeducation groups (e.g., Colom et al., 2009; Pekkala & Merinder, 2002; Pratt & Gill, 1990). Explicit training can be implemented to teach or increase these skills, such as instructional curricula developed as part of the IMR approach (see Chapter 3 for more on this evidence-based practice). Another important point to consider is that rehabilitation goals may be hampered if treatment efforts are unsuccessful. Conversely, successful treatment should promote rehabilitation goals. Thus, treatment and rehabilitation are complementary and inter-dependent efforts.

Ongoing, Accessible, and Coordinated Services

PsyR services should be unlimited with respect to time (e.g., there should not be a prescribed time length for services). They should be easily accessible and be coordinated to ensure availability and avoid duplication. As discussed in Chapter 2 and elsewhere in this book, not everyone experiences mental illness in the same way. Nor do the resulting service and support needs remain consistent over time. PsyR programs must be designed to accommodate the varied and changing needs of individuals who may require different levels of services during different phases of their illness. For example:

Alberto is discharged from a psychiatric hospital and referred to an Assertive Community Treatment (ACT) team that helps him find his own efficiency apartment. While Alberto is happy to be back in the community and living on his own for the first time in many years, he is also worried about his ability to adjust to his new apartment and neighborhood. Initially, he needs substantial help with many tasks such as cooking, cleaning, using public transportation, and remembering when to take his medications. So, during the first few months, a member of the ACT team visits Alberto every morning. They help him plan his day, remind him to take his medication, and spend time teaching him independent living skills. As time passes and Alberto adjusts to his new life, the team begins to cut back on the frequency of visits. A year later, he has gained confidence in his ability to live independently and manage his illness. Since he needs much less assistance, a team member now stops in about once a week to check in and provide supportive counseling. The team still has the capacity to visit each day if Alberto's needs should change, and Alberto likes knowing that the ACT team is just a phone call away (see Chapter 8 for more on the ACT model).

Coordination of services is also a crucial aspect of successful community integration. Consumers may be involved with several different PsyR or mental health agencies at the same time or may need to be referred to different service providers as their needs change over time. Case management services (see Chapter 8) are one effective strategy for accomplishing this coordination. Consider the problem of service coordination described in the following example:

Laura is a quiet and somewhat passive young woman who seeks to please both her family and the various practitioners who work with her. She sees a psychiatrist once a month at a community mental health center where she and her family are also involved in a family psychoeducation and support group. Currently, the group facilitator is encouraging Laura and her family to work toward their stated goal of Laura returning to college. Meanwhile, the clubhouse program that Laura attends three times a week is in the process of placing her in a full-time position through their supported employment program. Laura is ambivalent about her future and becoming increasingly anxious about working toward conflicting goals. Clearly the lack of service coordination described above can interfere with successful rehabilitation. Even more important, more work needs to be done to help Laura clearly determine what she wants. Such situations can result in a waste of professional resources and can set up consumers for failure.

Empirical Orientation

Psychiatric rehabilitation has an empirical orientation informed by the scientific method. When developing intervention strategies and designing new programs, PsyR service providers should be guided by the best available evidence on the subject. Interventions that have been tested rigorously in multiple studies are preferred. Throughout this book, the importance of making evidence-based practices available to consumers is emphasized because these models have consistently produced positive outcomes such as fewer hospitalizations or higher rates of employment. Also highlighted are service models for which there is some evidence base, but additional research studies are needed to demonstrate that they consistently produce desired outcomes. These are often referred to as "promising practices."

An empirical orientation is also important to ensure that existing PsyR programs continue to provide high-quality services. Thus PsyR providers design program evaluation and quality improvement initiatives to continuously measure the impact and outcomes of their services on both an individual and a system-wide level. Continued evaluation and assessment are very important, for instance, to identify changes in the needs of the population that programs are designed to serve. These population changes are much more common than might be imagined. One example is the increase over the last several decades in the number of persons who have both a serious mental illness and a substance abuse problem. Most of the people discharged during the early days of deinstitutionalization (the 1960s and early 1970s) were not dually diagnosed with a substance abuse disorder. Long periods of hospitalization may have reduced the possibility of substance abuse for many of these people. So, when early community-based programs were developed, there was not much of a need for addiction-related services. Later on, when the length of hospital stays decreased and the community-based programs began serving a younger population, professionals became aware of increasing numbers of individuals with co-occurring substance abuse problems (Caton, 1981; Drake & Wallach, 2000; Pepper, Ryglewicz, & Kirshner, 1981). PsyR agencies that employed program evaluation strategies and regularly monitored their outcomes were the first to identify this change in their target population and began to design new services to meet their needs.

At the case management level, keeping good notes and records, seen as a burden by most staff members, is an important aspect of an empirical orientation. Keeping good records helps insure that previous service strategies that led to success or failure are identified. This knowledge is helpful for devising effective future plans for the individual. Knowing what works and what doesn't helps the individual achieve his or her goal as rapidly as possible with the least amount of wasted effort.

Psychiatric Rehabilitation Ethics

A code of ethics is an intellectual framework that is consistent with the principles and values of a profession. It helps us analyze and make decisions when faced with moral choices. All professions (e.g., medicine, law, and psychology) have a specific code of ethics.

An important step in the evolution of PsyR from a service provision approach to a distinct profession was the development and adoption in 1996 of a Code of Ethics for Psychiatric Rehabilitation Practitioners by IAPSRS (now called USPRA). The code of Ethics was revised in 2001 and again in 2012. The current USPRA code has three sections. The first section outlines fundamental principles which, according to the document, "are aspirational in nature" and should "provide an overall framework for guidance in practice." This section addresses the ethical behavior and integrity of practitioners, the importance of promoting freedom of choice for PsyR service users, justice (e.g., insuring fairness, responsibility, and transparency), and respect for diversity and culture.

The second section is fundamental standards, which describes how the practice of PsyR should be guided by important ethical principles. These include competence of the PsyR practitioner, informed consent (which emphasizes confidentiality), the need for advocacy (e.g., promoting social justice), and propriety (i.e., professional conduct of practitioners). The final section of the code offers more specific guidelines for the principles and standards outlined in the first two sections. This third part of the USPRA Code of Ethics highlights some challenging areas of practice that may produce ethical dilemmas. These include multiple roles and relationships, rights protection, the importance of competent and ethical supervision, and guidelines for terminating relationships with service users.

Thus, the USPRA Code of Ethics addresses issues that often arise in day-to-day practice such as confidentiality, relationship boundaries with consumers, and consumers' right to make decisions about the services they receive, including the right to refuse services. What an ethical code cannot do, however, is provide definitive answers for all situations that have ethical implications. Sometimes, the guidelines are very clear; the USPRA code clearly states that it is unethical for a practitioner to have a sexual relationship with a client. It also cautions practitioners not to otherwise exploit their relationships with consumers. So it would be inappropriate for a practitioner who had a side business selling health care products to solicit sales to consumers.

Otherwise, there is a great deal of controversy in the PsyR field about what are the appropriate limits of relationships between practitioners and consumers. Sometimes, practitioners are faced with difficult ethical dilemmas—for example, relationship boundaries between consumers and PsyR practitioners. Many PsyR programs emphasize reduced professional boundaries and staff members are generally encouraged to develop friendly and informal relationships with consumers. Some PsyR programs do not discourage the development of outside friendships with consumers, as long as the relationship is in the best interest of the consumer. But some agencies have strict policies forbidding staff to socialize with consumers outside of the program environment. Thus, in certain social situations PsyR providers have to make difficult decisions. Is it appropriate to take a consumer out to lunch to celebrate a birthday or achievement of a goal? Should one accept a Christmas gift from a consumer? Is it acceptable to attend a consumer's wedding reception?

Practitioners need to be aware of possible ethical dilemmas in their everyday activities. Familiarity with the USPRA Code of Ethics is a good starting point. First of all, it can help practitioners recognize when they are grappling with an issue that has ethical implications. Second, it assists them in determining whether or not a considered solution is consistent with PsyR standards for ethical behavior. Practitioners also need to be aware of specific agency policies and state laws that may apply to practice issues such as client confidentiality. Finally, good practitioners who recognize that they are on the horns of an ethical dilemma seek out supervision and/or team discussion of the situation in order to reach the best possible solution.

CONTROVERSIAL ISSUE
Is Court-ordered Outpatient Treatment a Good Idea or an Unacceptable Violation of PsyR Principles and Values?

A key value held by PsyR providers is an individual's right to self-determination. In fact, the USPRA Code of Ethics requires that practitioners make every effort to support the maximum self-determination of each person. In many ways, this value is supported by the law. Since the 1960s, the civil rights of persons living with serious mental illness have been strengthened. For example, in most of the United States, a person can only be committed involuntarily to a psychiatric hospital if he or she clearly presents an imminent danger to self or to others. In addition, the 1999 *L.C. v. Olmstead* US Supreme Court decision supported the right of people who have disabilities to live in the least restrictive treatment environment. These laws and the rising costs of hospital-based care have accelerated the deinstitutionalization movement. While short-term hospital stays for acute psychiatric episodes are still common, large state-run psychiatric institutions continue to downsize or close. Thus, it is becoming increasingly rare for persons diagnosed with serious mental illness to be hospitalized for any length of time.

The logical outcome of reducing hospital beds is a shift to community-based treatment and the development of additional resources, particularly affordable housing. Some mental health systems are making good progress in this direction and, as was described earlier, are also shifting to a recovery orientation that promotes self-determination and empowerment. But do the available community-based service models meet the needs of everyone living with a serious mental illness? Are individuals experiencing acute psychiatric symptoms able to make decisions that support their own health and well-being? Is too much choice sometimes a bad thing? The answers to these questions are complex and have sparked a number of debates. One of these debates has centered on the issue of involuntary outpatient treatment.

As mentioned previously, in the United States, a person who has a psychiatric diagnosis can be involuntarily hospitalized if he or she shows evidence of dangerousness. Inpatient commitment laws and, in fact, the very definition of dangerousness varies by state. Typically, a trained clinician evaluates a person who is exhibiting acute symptoms, and if the person is deemed to be suicidal, likely to cause physical harm to other people or property, or (in some cases) likely to experience harm due to a gross inability to care for oneself, the clinician recommends hospitalization, which is then mandated by the court.

Many states also have commitment laws that allow a person to be involuntarily committed to an outpatient treatment setting. Again, the specifics of these statutes vary, but typically a person is under an involuntary outpatient commitment (IOC) court order because of a past history of dangerousness and the likelihood that he or she will once again become dangerous if treatment, such as psychotropic medication, is not accepted. Once a person is under an IOC order, he or she must agree to a prescribed treatment plan. Noncompliance typically results in a return court appearance and possibly hospitalization. What follows are the two sides of the IOC debate. While reading about these viewpoints, think about which side is most consistent with your personal opinion. Also consider the debate from the perspective of various stakeholders: consumers who want to direct their own recovery process, concerned family members, mental health providers, and community members.

(Continued)

INVOLUNTARY OUTPATIENT TREATMENT IS SOMETIMES NEEDED AND CAN ULTIMATELY CONTRIBUTE TO RECOVERY

Sometimes, individuals experiencing symptoms of serious mental illnesses such as schizophrenia or bipolar disorder lack insight into their mental health status. Family members and others observe increasingly disturbing behavior, but the person may insist that everything is fine. As discussed in Chapter 2, persistent lack of awareness of the presence of psychiatric symptoms has been called **anosognosia** (Amador, 2007). Those that support IOC laws believe that when individuals deny the presence of a mental illness, they lack the ability to make informed decisions about the need for treatment and thus should be mandated to receive **assisted outpatient treatment**, a term that implies a combination of a court order and access to an enhanced package of treatment services (Phelan et al., 2010). Advocates in favor of IOC point out that persons who experience untreated symptoms of psychosis are at increased risk for becoming homeless, incarcerated, or engaging in violent behavior (Munetz & Frese, 2001; Treatment Advocacy Center, 2012). They also point to a handful of research studies showing evidence that IOC produces some positive outcomes such as reduced psychiatric hospitalizations and decreased incidents of violence (e.g., Swartz et al., 2001; Treatment Advocacy Center, 2012).

Notable proponents of assisted outpatient treatment include E. Fuller Torrey, a psychiatrist and author of books such as *Surviving Schizophrenia* (2006) and *In Out of the Shadows: Confronting America's Mental Illness Crisis* (1997). He is one of the founders of the Treatment Advocacy Center, an organization that has worked diligently to enact IOC legislation, which now exists in some form in 44 states (Treatment Advocacy Center, 2012). Torrey points out that IOC is needed because in many situations the dangerousness standard is set too high, for example, a judge ruling that living on the street and eating your own feces does not constitute a threat to the individual or others. He quotes a psychiatrist, Donald Trefert, commenting on a case where a judge found that a man was within his rights to refuse psychiatric treatment:

> The liberty to be naked in a padded cell in a county jail, hallucinating and tormented, without treatment that ought to be given is not liberty, it is another form of imprisonment— imprisonment for the crime of being ill. (Torrey, 1997, p. 143)

The National Alliance on Mental Illness (NAMI), an advocacy organization founded by concerned family members, also supports court-ordered IOC, although only as a last resort (NAMI, 1995). They have taken this stance at the urging of families who have been devastated by an inability to get help for a loved one. This perspective is poignantly illustrated in a New York Times Magazine exposé written by a woman whose father is diagnosed with bipolar disorder. His increasingly bizarre behavior, threats of violence toward her mother, and refusal to accept treatment create a crisis in the context of a mental health and legal system that does not view him as dangerous enough to be hospitalized. Building frustration and fear eventually force the family to take out a restraining order and eventually incarcerate him in order to get him treatment (Interlandi, 2012).

Some consumers have also supported IOC laws, writing about the utility and necessity of involuntary treatment in helping them begin the recovery process (e.g., Fox, 2001; Munetz & Frese, 2001; Munetz, Galon, & Frese, 2003). They point out that unremitting symptoms cloud judgment and are barriers to recovery, and they credit court-ordered treatment with helping them lead successful lives. In the words of Valerie Fox:

> *"I believe the person should be committed on an outpatient basis to be able to live in society …. A state of schizophrenia is one without reason. I don't think it is fair to the person who may never again know reality if left in this state of schizophrenia, nor do I think it is humane or responsible to society. (Fox, 2001, p. 178)*

INVOLUNTARY OUTPATIENT TREATMENT IS INCONSISTENT WITH PSYR VALUES

While acute episodes of serious mental illness coupled with refusal to accept treatment clearly create significant challenges for both consumers and families, IOC and the corresponding assisted outpatient treatment approach are in conflict with PsyR values and principles, such as self-determination, empowerment, and the person-centered approach. Forced treatment is also counterproductive to rehabilitation and recovery efforts because it does not allow individuals to regain control over their lives or develop a sense of personal effectiveness, which are essential aspects of these processes (Diamond, 1995). Another principle of PsyR that is inconsistent with court-ordered treatment is the partnership between service provider and service user. This relationship, which is the bedrock of the PsyR approach, is built on trust and shared decision making pertaining to treatment and rehabilitation goals and interventions. How can such a relationship be sustained if the power is held by the treatment provider and the threat to report instances of treatment noncompliance to the judge is ever present?

The United States Psychiatric Rehabilitation Association (UPSRA) as well as its state chapters and affiliates, such as the New Jersey Psychiatric Rehabilitation Association (NJPRA) and the New York Association of Psychiatric Rehabilitation Services (NYAPRS), have adamantly opposed IOC laws (NJPRA, 2008; NYAPRS, 2005; USPRA, Committee for Persons in Recovery, 2007). Mental Health America, which is the oldest and largest national mental health advocacy organization in the United States, has also taken a position against IOC (Mental Health America, 2010). They oppose IOC due to the values conflicts mentioned earlier, but also because of civil rights issues. According to a USPRA position paper developed by a committee of individuals who identify themselves as persons in recovery, "IOC fundamentally violates the constitutional right to privacy and due process among individuals in recovery from psychiatric disabilities" (USPRA, Committee for Persons in Recovery, 2007). This group and NYAPRS have also highlighted the observation that court-ordered treatment laws, such as Kendra's Law in New York, have been disproportionally applied to people of color and thus represent a form of discrimination (NYAPRS, 2005; Rosenthal, 2008; USPRA, Committee for Persons in Recovery, 2007). The issue of coercing individuals to take psychotropic medications that may cause very serious side effects is also a major reason for opposition to IOC. The growing understanding that these medications sometimes cause more harm than good is covered in more depth in Chapter 3.

(Continued)

CONTROVERSIAL ISSUE
Is Court-ordered Outpatient Treatment a Good Idea or an Unacceptable Violation of PsyR Principles and Values?—(Continued)

Those who oppose IOC laws also believe that untreated mental illness can lead to negative outcomes such as homelessness, incarceration, victimization, and violence, but they view the situation as the failure of our mental health systems to engage consumers and provide access to comprehensive services, rather than as evidence of a need for coercive methods. They also view the research done on the outcomes of assisted outpatient treatment as inconclusive at best. The most scholarly analyses of scientific evidence for IOC, conducted by the Cochrane Collaborative (Kisely et al., 2005), concluded that when compared to standard community-based care there was little evidence that court-ordered treatment was more effective in improving key outcomes such as use of mental health services, social functioning, or quality of life. They did concede that IOC has some effect, but its size is very small. One statistical measure used to gauge the efficacy of IOC is the number of individuals who must be served to avoid one undesirable outcome. They found that it takes 85 IOC orders to prevent one hospitalization and 238 IOC orders to prevent one arrest. The authors concluded that "it is difficult to conceive of another group in society that would be subject to measures that curtail the freedom of 85 people to avoid one admission to hospital or of 238 to avoid one arrest" (Kisely, Campbell, & Preston, 2005, p. 1). This statement is provocative when one thinks about other persons in our society who may be at risk for hospitalization or incarceration. Do we force treatment on persons who have uncontrolled diabetes and are refusing to follow their doctor's treatment plan, despite the life-threatening consequences of their decision? Do we force gang members to get counseling to prevent them from committing crimes and being sent to prison?

So it appears that individuals living with psychiatric disabilities have better outcomes when they have access to better services, and being forced to accept the services does not significantly improve outcomes. Thus, the real issue is finding ways to better engage individuals who have a serious but untreated mental illness. One strategy is to utilize early intervention teams that provide assertive outreach to consumers who are reluctant to seek treatment. Such teams should first use specialized engagement strategies such as Amador's (2007) LEAP method that emphasizes *listening* to the person's concerns, *empathizing* with his or her perspective, *agreeing* on mutually acceptable goals, and forming a *partnership*. The ability to offer psychoeducation to consumers and family members and to respond to crises around the clock are also critical aspects of a PsyR-oriented early intervention approach.

The Future of Psychiatric Rehabilitation Thought and Practice

It should be clear that some values, goals, and principles were derived from humanistic ideals that seemed "right" to practitioners at the time. Other ideas were borrowed from more established fields such as psychiatry, psychology, rehabilitation, and social work. Regardless of the source of these values, goals, and principles, their continued use will be based on their (1) utility as guides to effective rehabilitation and (2) ability to withstand testing through empirical research and evaluation. No one should be surprised if some of the concepts put forth in this chapter are modified or even discarded over time. Consider, for example, how attitudes about hospitalization have evolved over time. During the period before deinstitutionalization, a person diagnosed with a major mental illness who experienced continuous psychotic symptoms had a very good chance of spending most of his or her life in a psychiatric institution. With deinstitutionalization, the goal was to get people out of the institutions and into the community. Some practitioners embraced this policy with such fervor that one might have suspected that the community itself was a therapeutic agent. Once in the community, the primary goal changed to the prevention of rehospitalization. Many practitioners considered any client who did not require rehospitalization a success. Today, as our understanding of these illnesses has matured, we have adopted the goals of recovery, community integration, and quality of life. In this new conception, hospitalization, if it is necessary, is seen as a manifestation of the illness and treated as a minor setback. PsyR services are often focused on helping people return to work or college. A decade from now will we be discussing additional goals as our knowledge base and attitudes continue to evolve? If so, we should not be surprised. Each of these changes should reflect a better understanding of persons living with mental illness and the conditions themselves. These changes usually represent progress.

Summary

The entire PsyR enterprise is driven by the belief that persons living with serious mental illnesses can recover. Recovery in PsyR does *not* imply the absence of disease. It means that individuals can enjoy meaningful and purposeful lives, even while coping with ongoing symptoms. The primary goals of PsyR are to achieve recovery, maximum community integration, and the highest possible quality of life. These goals are supported by values that include self-determination, respect for human dignity, and cultural diversity, optimism that all people have the capacity for growth, and an emphasis on promoting wellness and the attainment of valued social roles. PsyR goals and values are actualized in practice by following specific guiding principles. USPRA, the national professional organization, has established a code of ethics to help guide the field. These goals, values, and guidelines may change as the field advances and new knowledge is created.

■ ■ ■ ━━━

Class Exercise
Applying the Goals, Values, and Principles of Psychiatric Rehabilitation
Directions: Read the vignettes below and then answer the related questions.

Scenario #1
Eric is a 29-year-old man with a history of many psychiatric hospitalizations. He has been referred to a number of outpatient treatment and rehabilitation programs in the past but has been difficult to engage. Eric's symptoms typically include restlessness, confusion, and paranoia,

and while he seems to respond well to antipsychotic medications, he frequently refuses to take them. Following a hospital discharge, Eric returns home to live with his mother and is assigned to an assertive community treatment program, in which a team of staff provides services for Eric at his home. Eric is reluctant to talk with the team members when they visit and more often than not, despite pleas from his mother, refuses to take medication. The team decides to implement the following plan: Eric's mother, who is the payee for his monthly disability check, will give him a weekly allowance of spending money if he complies with the following conditions: (1) taking his medication as prescribed twice a day and (2) talking with the team members when they visit. Each time Eric refuses to take a dosage or talk to the staff, his mother will deduct a specific amount of money. The staff's rationale is that coercion is necessary to both prevent exacerbation of symptoms and to establish a relationship with Eric. Eric resents the plan, but needs money for cigarettes, so he goes along with it.

Questions

1. From the team's point of view, how can their plan help Eric achieve the PsyR goals of recovery, community integration, and a better quality of life?
2. From Eric's point of view, what are the negative implications of the team's plan? Can the plan interfere with the achievement of the PsyR goals mentioned above?
3. Is the plan consistent with PsyR values such as self-determination?
4. If the answer to Question 3 is "no", can you suggest a plan that would be helpful to Eric and be more consistent with PsyR values?

Scenario #2

Phan is a 58-year-old Vietnamese male who came to the United States with several family members in 1975. For many years, he lived in a community in Louisiana that had a large Vietnamese population. There he met and married a woman who was also from Vietnam; they had three children, who are now adults. Two years ago, he and his wife moved to San Diego, California, for a business opportunity. Phan had difficulty adjusting to the move and also experienced marital problems, which caused Phan's wife to leave him and move in with a friend. Phan then began experiencing symptoms of depression and anxiety, for which he was eventually hospitalized. After discharge, he is referred to a PsyR program. Phan speaks Vietnamese fluently and has some command of English. He has no biological family in San Diego and has been socially isolated since his wife's departure. He reports difficulty concentrating and sleeping, with frequent "flashbacks" to his life in Vietnam prior to his immigration to the United States.

Questions

1. How could Phan's culture play a role in his recovery?
2. Can you identify some culturally competent PsyR interventions that would help Phan in his recovery?

Psychiatric Rehabilitation Methods

You are never too old to set another goal or to dream a new dream.
C. S. Lewis

CHAPTER OUTLINE

Psychiatric Rehabilitation. http://dx.doi.org/10.1016/B978-0-12-387002-5.00005-6

This chapter will outline the basic strategies involved in the rehabilitation of persons living with serious mental illnesses. In the past, most mental health professionals believed that symptoms should be ameliorated and long-term stability achieved before rehabilitation could begin. Many individuals who struggled with the cyclical nature of their illness were therefore never seen as ready to work toward rehabilitation goals such as employment or independent living. Today, as evidenced by the fact that many persons with serious mental illnesses lead full and productive lives, there is general agreement that rehabilitation should begin as soon as possible. There is also a growing body of evidence that there are many social, vocational, emotional, and psychological benefits to the rehabilitation process. Many of the interventions commonly used by psychiatric rehabilitation providers are based on the theory and practice of related professions such as physical therapy, occupational therapy, psychology, counseling, and social work.

This chapter will answer the following questions:

1. *What are the elements of the psychiatric rehabilitation process?*
2. *What is the role of the practitioner in the psychiatric rehabilitation process?*
3. *What is the role of the consumer in the psychiatric rehabilitation process?*
4. *Why is skill development such an important intervention? What is the best way to teach someone a new skill?*
5. *What role do resources, supports, and environmental modifications play in the rehabilitation process?*
6. *What other interventions do psychiatric rehabilitation practitioners commonly use?*

Introduction

The rehabilitation of persons with physical disabilities provides an apt and instructive model or analogy for understanding the rehabilitation process of persons with psychiatric disabilities (Anthony, Cohen, Farkas, & Gagne, 2002; Deegan, 1988). An obvious benefit of this comparison is that rehabilitation from physical injury or disease is a relatively common and acceptable phenomenon in modern society. Sports figures recovering from injuries sustained on the playing field and aging public figures recovering from heart attacks or strokes are frequent subjects of media coverage. In addition, as medicine improves, life expectancy increases, making it more likely that a family member, friend, or acquaintance will develop a physical disability. Like a person living with a physical disability, an individual who has a disability due to a severe mental illness may experience difficulty with aspects of everyday life that require learning or relearning skills, environmental modifications, and other types of professional support.

Inspired by methods used in the rehabilitation of individuals living with physical disabilities, William Anthony and his colleagues at the Center for Psychiatric Rehabilitation at Boston University began developing a "technology" or systematic strategy for the rehabilitation of persons with psychiatric disabilities in the 1970s. They combined knowledge from areas such as psychology, occupational therapy, and rehabilitation counseling, as well as formulating and field-testing strategies based on scientific evidence. In addition, they put a great deal of effort into training practitioners in their PsyR technology, both at

Boston University and through consulting on a national and international basis. At times, their efforts have been met with resistance by mental health practitioners due to misunderstandings about how their techniques worked, as well as perceived threats to cherished beliefs and philosophies such as an adherence to psychodynamic principles. Today, it is generally recognized, by any objective assessment, that the Center's contribution to the successful rehabilitation of persons living with severe mental illness has been incalculable.

Many others have also made important contributions in the area of PsyR methods. For example, Robert Paul Liberman and his colleagues at UCLA have been strong proponents of a skills training approach for some time (Kopelowicz, Liberman, & Zarate, 2006; Liberman, DeRisi, & Mueser, 1989; Liberman et al., 1985; Liberman et al., 1993). PsyR practice also relies on counseling techniques developed by psychotherapy giants such as Carl Rogers and Aaron Beck. The motivational interviewing techniques developed by William Miller and Stephen Rollnick (2002) have also been incorporated into the methods used by current PsyR practitioners. Robert Drake and his colleagues at the Dartmouth Psychiatric Research Center have taken a leading role in the movement toward evidence-based practices in psychiatric rehabilitation, which are described throughout this book (Drake et al., 2000). Still, the work done at Boston University to develop and disseminate strategies for helping individuals move forward in their recovery by pursuing their chosen goals continues to provide the basic framework for the day-to-day practice of PsyR.

The psychiatric rehabilitation process is often preceded by a thorough assessment of an individual's readiness to participate in rehabilitation activities. Next, the person chooses an overall rehabilitation goal related to increased success and satisfaction in a living, learning, working, or social environment and is assisted in the identification of critical skills and resources needed for goal achievement. Using the information from these assessments, a rehabilitation plan that outlines and prioritizes very specific goals and objectives is formulated. Finally, the strategies to accomplish each goal or objective are identified. The Center for Psychiatric Rehabilitation characterizes the steps in the psychiatric rehabilitation process as the diagnostic phase, the planning phase, and the intervention phase (Anthony, Cohen, Farkas, & Gagne, 2002; Anthony & Farkas, 2009). The rehabilitation process has also been described as a choose, get, keep approach; with the help of the PsyR practitioner, the consumer chooses a personally meaningful goal, works toward getting it, and obtains supports needed to keep it (Anthony & Faraks, 2009; Farkas & Anthony, 2010). After examining the connection between PsyR methods and some key PsyR principles and values, we will cover each of the PsyR phases in more detail.

Hallmarks of the Psychiatric Rehabilitation Process

Directed by the Consumer

As you learned in Chapter 4, psychiatric rehabilitation is essentially carried out through a partnership between a person living with mental illness and a PsyR practitioner; it is

---

BOX 5.1   WILLIAM A. ANTHONY

William Anthony is probably the psychiatric rehabilitation professional with the greatest name recognition. In more than 40 years of work in the field, he has received numerous awards including a Distinguished Service Award from the president of the United States (1992) and a Distinguished Service Award from the National Alliance on Mental Illness (NAMI). He has also appeared on *Nightline* with Ted Koppel. Dr. Anthony has published more than 100 articles and more than a dozen books on psychiatric rehabilitation. He was the director of the Center for Psychiatric Rehabilitation at Boston University's Sargent College of Health and Rehabilitation Sciences from its inception in 1979 until his retirement in 2011. Dr. Anthony was also the coeditor of the *Psychiatric Rehabilitation Journal* for many years.

To paraphrase both Laurie Flynn, the former executive director of NAMI, and his presidential award:

> *Dr. Anthony's efforts have challenged ideas that have limited the potential of persons with mental illness. The innovative programs created through his leadership offer hope and opportunity by promoting the dignity, equality, independence, and employment of people with disabilities.*

"a service that must be done *with* a person, never *to* a person" (Cohen & Mynks, 1993). Like most partnerships, both the service recipient and the provider should be involved in making decisions, but the preferences of the person receiving the services should drive the rehabilitation process. This is markedly different from the traditional approach to medical problems where the doctor is unquestionably the primary director of the treatment plan. The PsyR approach is essentially a **person-centered** or **person-directed** process (Adams & Grieder, 2005; Substance Abuse and Mental Health Service Administration, 2006; United States Psychiatric Rehabilitation Association, 2009).

There are also a number of practical reasons why persons using PsyR services should be involved in every aspect of the rehabilitation process, from choosing rehabilitation goals to choosing, developing, and implementing strategies that foster goal achievement. Goals that are set by the practitioner without real input from the consumer, even with the very best intentions, are not likely to be motivating. This may even be true in cases where a practitioner selects the same goal the consumer would have if given the chance. The very act of its selection signifies ownership of a goal and helps to motivate a person to work toward its accomplishment. Consumer involvement in the assessment, planning, and intervention phases of the rehabilitation process is also critical for success. Important information may be missed if the PsyR practitioner makes decisions and launches plans without the consumer's input. For example, a person who likes animals and has some clerical and medical education might not be a good candidate for working in a veterinary hospital if he or she is highly allergic to cats.

The most important reason for maximum consumer involvement in the PsyR process is that it fosters recovery. One of the major challenges faced by persons living with serious mental illness is recovering from the effects of being in the role of psychiatric patient—a role that often strips individuals of their right to self-determination (O'Connell, 2011). For many people, being provided with opportunities to make meaningful choices about their own lives, with support and encouragement from PsyR practitioners, is an important part of their recovery journey. Recovery, after all, is the ultimate goal of the PsyR process (see Chapter 4).

Environments of Choice

Unlike a medical evaluation, which assesses a person's overall health, PsyR assessments are targeted toward consumers' environments of choice. In short, they focus on what will enable the person to be successful and satisfied in the specific environments where he or she chooses to live, work, learn, and socialize (Anthony et al., 2002). By targeting specific environments, the rehabilitation task is made both more relevant and more manageable. Only the skills and resources necessary for success in the environments of choice are developed. Symptoms or negative behaviors that are not problematic in the environments of choice may not be given high priority. This strategy represents a clear difference from the emphasis of some pre-vocational training efforts that have attempted to help consumers become vocationally ready in all areas without regard to the specific characteristics of a particular job.

Rather than just focusing on the individual and his or her disability, PsyR practitioners conduct an assessment of the requirements and characteristics of the environment and may attempt to modify these as part of the overall plan. In a work environment, such modifications might consist of flex hours, more frequent breaks, or a workspace with reduced distractions. The importance of environmental assessment and modification was highlighted by the 1990 Americans with Disabilities Act, which calls for "reasonable accommodations" to assist individuals with disabilities on the job. These reasonable accommodations often take the form of environmental modifications or policy adjustments that help the person to perform effectively at his or her job.

Valued Social Roles

This concept, which is addressed in Chapter 4 when describing PsyR values, is another way to focus on the specific aspects of a person's life that may be targeted during the rehabilitation process. So, in addition to focusing on consumer-chosen living, learning, working, and social environments, the PsyR practitioner helps people to assume specific roles in those environments that are valued by the community. For example, an individual who has resided for the past decade in a state psychiatric hospital or a supervised group home wants to move to his or her own apartment. The PsyR practitioner would assist this person in obtaining the skills and resources needed to successfully adapt to the new living environment. But the person might also want to learn how to be a good neighbor so that he or she is accepted by others in the community. "Good neighbor" is a valued social role that will promote community acceptance. In contrast, "former psychiatric patient" is a devalued role that may increase social isolation. Successful achievement of a goal may thus involve the ability to adapt well to both a new environment and a new role.

The Psychiatric Rehabilitation Process

Phase I: Rehabilitation Diagnosis

The PsyR process begins with the diagnostic phase. When we think about a diagnosis, we might picture a doctor observing symptoms and conducting medical tests. These might lead to the conclusion that a person has a particular physical illness such as diabetes or a psychiatric disorder such as schizophrenia. While they understand that an accurate psychiatric diagnosis is needed for a clinician to prescribe the most effective medications and/or psychotherapy, PsyR practitioners are not particularly focused on clinical assessment of symptoms or diagnostic labels. Instead, they want to gather information about the particular living, learning, working, or social environment in which a person wishes to function. They also want to determine what skills and resources are needed to function effectively in that chosen environment. Thus, identifying an overall rehabilitation goal and conducting both a functional assessment and a resource assessment are the main components of a **psychiatric rehabilitation diagnosis**.

For some individuals, a rehabilitation diagnosis cannot be established until they are ready to identify a meaningful goal and commit to working towards goal achievement. Thus, a readiness assessment and engaging in activities that promote readiness may also be necessary components of the diagnostic phase.

Psychiatric Rehabilitation Readiness

Psychiatric rehabilitation readiness refers to an individual's desire and motivation to engage in the rehabilitation process. Without such desire or motivation, an individual will not act to achieve a goal. Some degree of readiness is, therefore, a necessary element for rehabilitation success. This focus on readiness is in sharp contrast to much of medical and psychological practice. When a treatment is seen as superior for a particular condition, it is often prescribed immediately without offering the patient any alternatives, since in many cases the doctor's view is that there are no realistic alternatives. In the case of psychiatric rehabilitation, the success of the process is dependent on the readiness of the individual to utilize rehabilitation services.

Why would an individual be reluctant to choose and pursue a goal to improve his or her situation in life? A number of factors impede readiness to pursue goals for persons with, and those without, a psychiatric disability. For example, important factors working against many individuals pursuing an employment goal are a lack of knowledge about their own abilities, unfamiliarity with characteristics of various work environments, and a lack of awareness of the supports that are available. Consider the early stages of anyone's career path. Many people do not know enough about their own likes and dislikes, about the kinds of jobs that might be available, and about the kinds of skills that are required for these jobs. For example, how many of your friends know about PsyR, the kinds of skills required, and what a PsyR professional would do all day? A lack of knowledge of who we are and what is possible can narrow anyone's choices and reduce motivation to pursue career goals. For many people with psychiatric disabilities these barriers are compounded by factors such as ongoing symptoms, functional deficits, poverty, and very low self-esteem.

Sometimes, when several of these negative factors are combined in one individual, the level of readiness for psychiatric rehabilitation is very low. Some PsyR candidates have experienced numerous and repeated failures in their attempts to improve their lives. In addition to the impediments mentioned above, these failures may come about because of ineffective services provided by poorly trained or overworked staff or from setting goals that a person is not ready to pursue. After several failures, an individual might be tempted to avoid getting his or her hopes up and just accept his or her lot in life. Other individuals become habituated to the role of "psychiatric patient." They may be fearful of change or simply believe that a positive life change is no longer a possibility.

Assessing Readiness

Several researchers (Roberts & Pratt, 2007; Cohen, Farkas, & Cohen, 1992; Cohen & Forbess, 1992; Cohen & Mynks, 1993) have stressed the importance of readiness assessment in the PsyR process. The goal of this type of assessment is to evaluate the individual's readiness for entering the PsyR process with a good chance of success. A readiness assessment is not simply a practitioner concluding that an individual is not ready to pursue a particular goal. In fact, the judgments of professionals in this regard are often very inaccurate. Experts at the Boston University Center of Psychiatric Rehabilitation (Anthony & Farkas, 2009; Cohen, Farkas, & Cohen, 1992) have recommended that a readiness assessment look at five distinct factors:

- **Need for change**—This asks, does the individual perceive a need for change? Or conversely, how dissatisfied is the individual with his or her current situation? This includes the influence of environmental issues such as how successful the individual is in his or her current environment and whether or not the environment is forcing a change (e.g., being evicted from an apartment).
- **Commitment to change**—This assesses the person's belief that change is (1) necessary, (2) positive, (3) possible, and (4) will be supported. Has the person taken

concrete steps or actions to pursue change? Can the person see himself or herself making the change, or does the individual believe someone else or the circumstances have to change?

- **Environmental awareness**—This assesses the person's knowledge, including previous experiences, about the chosen environment in which he or she plans to operate.
- **Self-awareness**—This assesses the individual's knowledge about himself or herself, for example, his or her likes and dislikes, personal values, and strengths and weaknesses.
- **Closeness to practitioner**—This evaluates the relationship with the PsyR practitioner on dimensions such as trust. A strong partnership is an important ingredient for an effective rehabilitation process.

A person with high scores on each of these five dimensions is considered ready for rehabilitation and, more importantly, has a very good chance of successfully achieving a chosen goal. If, on the other hand, a person has low scores on one or more of these dimensions, services need to be targeted toward improving those areas. Valid and reliable measures of rehabilitation readiness are available to PsyR practitioners (Roberts & Pratt, 2007, 2010).

Building Readiness

A lack of readiness does not imply that a person cannot benefit from PsyR services. Instead, an assessment of low readiness should guide individualized services designed to increase readiness and prepare the individual for the pursuit of goals. Readiness activities should be matched with one or more of the five aspects of readiness reviewed above. For example, a person may not be sure if making a change in his or her life is needed. Activities focused on exploring goals and clarifying values may help such a person realize that changing a living, learning, working, or social environment would improve his or her quality of life. If the person does not believe that he or she is capable of achieving an important life goal, activities that build self-confidence and help secure support for goal achievement may be in order. Lack of environmental and/or self-awareness is not unusual for persons with psychiatric disabilities, who may have been leading marginalized lives for many years. PsyR practitioners can address these readiness deficits by helping the person find opportunities to try out relevant environments and roles; for example, visiting a college campus, talking to college students and professors, observing a lecture while taking notes, and talking to an admissions counselor about possible academic majors may help a person realize that enrolling as a student at the local community college is a realistic possibility.

If the fifth area of rehabilitation readiness, closeness to the practitioner, is lacking, there are many things a PsyR practitioner can do to build an effective partnership. In fact, utilizing engagement strategies is usually the initial focus of a practitioner's work with any newly assigned service user. In the related fields of counseling and psychotherapy a number of personal attributes have been found to contribute positively to the development of a therapeutic alliance. It is important for practitioners to be perceived as respectful, honest, trustworthy, interested, flexible, friendly, warm, open, and confident in their ability to help (Ackerman & Hilsenroth, 2003). The counseling technique of active listening is a particularly important aspect of relationship building (Carkhuff, 2009; Chase et al., 2011). Rapp and Goscha (2006) emphasize the importance of hope-inducing behaviors, such as pointing out a person's strengths and abilities. Other strategic engagement strategies for building effective relationships include demonstrating empathy, monitoring how the relationship is perceived by the service user, providing positive feedback, taking the time to achieve goal consensus and adapting to the other person's preferences (Nemec, 2008; Norcross, 2002). Paying attention to cultural issues is also an important aspect of building effective rehabilitation partnerships (see Chapter 4). Sometimes, particularly when an individual is resisting engagement because of negative past experiences with mental health service providers, the PsyR practitioner needs to be patient and careful not to rush the engagement process. Making statements such as "I'm interested in learning more about you whenever you feel ready to share" lets the person know that he or she is in control of the pace of the relationship. Providing concrete assistance such as driving a person to a medical appointment or helping a person to acquire food stamps can also help forge a positive relationship. As you can see, assessing and building readiness are important aspects of a PsyR provider's work. A lack of attention to the readiness issue may be at the root of some poor PsyR service outcomes.

Choosing a Goal

If a person is ready for rehabilitation, the next step in the diagnostic process is choosing an overall rehabilitation goal. Sometimes the focus of the goal is clear from the onset. For example, at their very first meeting, a person may tell the PsyR practitioner, "I am here because I really want to go back to college and complete my degree in political science. Can you help me do that?" However, for many people choosing an overall rehabilitation goal is not that simple. The PsyR practitioner may first need to learn more about a person's values, interests, and aspirations. Also important is asking about satisfaction with, and ability to function in, current living, learning, working, and social environments. If a person is dissatisfied with more than one environment, he or she may need help with prioritizing which one to focus on first. It should be noted that some goals involve taking on a new role in a new environment, while other goals are focused on achieving greater success and satisfaction in a current role and environment.

Another aspect of setting this goal is looking at choices available for a particular type of environment, as illustrated in the following example:

Phil is a 30-year-old man who has been living with his sister since being discharged from the hospital. Phil is dissatisfied with his current living environment and decides that his most important goal is finding a new place to live. After doing some research, he and his PsyR practitioner determine that there are several housing options that may be available in his community: a studio apartment, a two-bedroom apartment with a roommate, and a shared house with several roommates that is operated by a PsyR agency. In order to decide which type of living arrangement he wants to pursue, Phil and his PsyR practitioner will gather information about each of these options such as rent and utility costs, exact locations, and access to public transportation. They will also examine the personal criteria (Anthony & Farkas, 2009) that are most valued by Phil. Is minimizing expenses most important? Does he prefer to live with others or alone? What kind of neighborhood is he looking for? The job of the PsyR practitioner is to help organize this information in a way that will help Phil determine the living environment that is the best match with his most important personal criteria (Anthony & Farkas, 2009, Farkas & Anthony, 2010).

Once chosen, overall rehabilitation goals should be stated very clearly. They should designate a specific environment and also set a time frame, usually within a 6- to 24-month period. They should also be stated in the first person (Anthony & Farkas, 2009; MacDonald-Wilson, Nemec, Anthony, & Cohen, 2001). For example, "I intend to move to a studio apartment in Middleville within the next year," or "I will enroll at Somerset County College by September, 2014." Time frames can always be altered if the person is still working on steps toward the goal, but very specific overall rehabilitation goals help consumers and practitioners to visualize outcomes and identify the steps needed to get there.

Functional Assessment

Once an overall rehabilitation goal has been established, the PsyR practitioner and the consumer need to determine the skills and supports that the person will need to be successful and satisfied in his or her chosen environment. The concept of the PsyR-oriented **functional assessment** is an example of the PsyR principle of "assessments related to person-chosen goals and environments" (see Chapter 4) as it specifically addresses the **critical skills** that the person and practitioner determine are essential for the person's success in the particular setting and role that has been chosen. These skills need to be described in behavioral terms that allow for an objective evaluation of how well the person performs them and the necessary level of performance needed for success in the living, learning, working, or social environment.

It is important to understand the difference between a PsyR functional assessment that looks only at the critical skills needed for an individual to achieve success and satisfaction in a particular environment and a global assessment of functioning that looks more generally at a person's ability to perform a category of skills in any environment. For example, think about cooking skills. A global assessment of functioning in this area may include a long list of meal preparation skills, including following a recipe, chopping vegetables, and operating a stove, oven, and microwave in various ways. But the types of cooking skills a person actually needs vary a great deal depending on the specific home environment, the preferences of the cook, and the available resources, such as a spouse who does most of the cooking.

Once all the critical skills required for success in a particular environment are listed, an assessment of the person's ability to perform each skill can take place. At this stage, the

PsyR practitioner and the consumer determine which critical skills a person already has and which need to be developed. Skill strengths are behaviors that the consumer does well, meaning at or above the required level. Skill deficits are behaviors that need either improvement or require learning and practicing a new skill. An assessment that identifies critical skill strengths and critical skill deficits illustrates how well the consumer can currently function in his or her environment of choice.

Because an important principle of PsyR is having a "strengths focus" (see Chapter 4) instead of emphasizing deficits, the PsyR practitioner should focus first on a person's skill strengths. Charles Rapp and his colleagues have made important contributions highlighting the importance of focusing on a person's strengths rather than weaknesses or disability (Rapp & Goscha, 2006). Many people make positive changes in their lives when they feel strong enough to accomplish the change. Focusing on one's strengths helps provide a sense that change is possible and will be successful. A person's areas of strength often identify where that person will perform well and can be an important clue to the type of setting where a person will find enjoyment and success. Finally, strengths are what a person has to offer on a job or in any environment. As Pat Nemec, a well-known PsyR educator, points out, when a person has excellent "people skills" (a strength), but is also "disorganized" (a deficit), training and support can reduce the disorganization more easily than if the "people skills" were poor; "crabbiness," for example, cannot be changed very easily.

After the PsyR practitioner has assisted the person in examining critical skill strengths, the critical skill deficits (i.e., areas where the person's performance does not match the required level) are identified for further assessment and future intervention. For example, Jane, who currently volunteers as a receptionist at her self-help center, wants to be a receptionist in a law office. Her skill strengths are the ability to use a clear and pleasant telephone voice and to convey a polite and professional manner when answering the phone and greeting visitors. To be successful, she also needs to accurately record messages listing who the call was for, the caller's name and number, the time of the call, and the reason the person called. A review of her work as a volunteer receptionist indicates that of the 20 or so messages Jane takes on her two-hour shift, at least 25 percent omit some of the needed information. For her new job, Jane will have to be able to always take messages without omitting the required information.

Resource Assessment

Resources are persons, places, things, or activities that a person either has or needs to support achievement of his or her chosen rehabilitation goal (Anthony, Cohen, Farkas, & Gagne, 2002). Very few of us are able to succeed in life without supports or resources. For example, in order to complete a college degree program a student may rely on the support and encouragement of family, classmates, and certain professors (persons). He or she may also require a dormitory room and a quiet area in which to study (places), as well as a computer for writing and researching (thing) and monetary resources for tuition and books (things). Some college students may benefit from attending a weekly study group (activity). Some resources relate directly to the specific environment the person wants to succeed in, such as classmates in a study group, whereas others are important supports that relate to the needs of the individual, such as a parent who sends care packages.

A **resource assessment** that identifies critical resources is usually done in conjunction with a functional assessment of critical skills. Once all of the needed resources are listed, an assessment is made of which ones are already available and which ones need to be accessed or developed. One way to distinguish between a functional assessment and a resource assessment has been nicely articulated by PsyR experts at the Boston University Center for Psychiatric Rehabilitation. When working with a person to establish a PsyR diagnosis, a functional assessment is "evaluating what he or she can or cannot *do* to be successful and satisfied in relation to the [person's overall rehabilitation] goal." A resource assessment is "evaluating what he or she does or does not *have* to be successful and satisfied in relation to the [overall rehabilitation] goal" (Anthony & Farkas, 2009, p. 20).

To summarize, a PsyR diagnosis consists of an overall rehabilitation goal combined with functional and resource assessments. For some individuals a readiness assessment and activities to promote rehabilitation readiness are part of the diagnostic phase. As you can imagine, a rehabilitation diagnosis takes time and is not usually done in a single session; in fact, it may take a number of weeks to complete. The process can be carried out in several ways. Most typically, it is done through individual meetings between the PsyR practitioner and the service recipient. Some programs employ group meetings where several individuals work together with a staff person or a team of PsyR professionals to determine and build readiness, arrive at rehabilitation goals, and conduct PsyR assessments.

Phase II: The Rehabilitation Plan

Traditional mental health providers establish treatment plans that identify the desired outcomes of treatment and the specific interventions such as medication or psycho-therapy that will be used to achieve them. A rehabilitation plan differs from a treatment plan in that it is driven by the consumer-chosen overall rehabilitation goal and is completely focused on the specific skills and resources that need to be developed or improved in order to function successfully in the desired role and environment. It should be noted that in some PsyR or community mental health programs, a treatment plan and rehabilitation plan may be combined into a comprehensive and individualized service plan. More recently, these have sometimes been called "recovery plans," to emphasize a recovery orientation (Davidson et al., 2007).

The rehabilitation plan should identify the overall rehabilitation goal that has been set. It should also list some of the critical skill and resource deficits identified in the functional and rehabilitation assessments. This ensures that the rehabilitation process maintains continuity from the diagnostic phase to the planning phase. While some individuals may need to learn or practice many skills and acquire a number of resources to reach the overall rehabilitation goal, it is usually a good idea to begin by working on just a few skills or resources.

The next step in creating a rehabilitation plan is to identify some short-term objectives that are related to skill or resource development. When behavioral objectives are described in quantifiable ways, they are clear to everyone concerned, particularly the consumer, and can be easily interpreted. So it is important that the objectives written in a rehabilitation plan are specific, measurable, and time delineated. For example, Jane may be maintaining a rate of 75 percent accuracy in her weekly message taking. An objective might be that Jane will improve her accuracy to a rate of 95 percent per week. By giving the objective a time frame, for example, two months, Jane and her PsyR practitioner will be able to objectively evaluate her progress. For another person, who needs to practice the social skill of starting conversations in order to achieve a goal, a short-term objective on the rehabilitation plan may be "For the next month I will start at least one conversation each day while doing errands in my neighborhood."

An important aspect of the rehabilitation plan is that these goals and objectives are prioritized by the consumer. Obviously, some skills need to be acquired before other skills. For example, someone who wants to do word processing should acquire some ability at keyboarding before he or she attempts to learn the intricacies of a word processing program. Another important aspect of this prioritization process is how it is experienced by the consumer. Everyone likes and needs to experience some success from their efforts. For persons who have gone through many previous failures, starting with the most difficult task first might not be the best strategy. Instead, it might be more motivating to start with a task that can provide some success in the short term and build up to the more difficult tasks. Unlike more traditional treatment planning approaches, decisions about this kind of motivational issue are the responsibility of the PsyR professional and the consumer working as partners in the rehabilitation process.

To summarize the second phase of the psychiatric rehabilitation process, the rehabilitation plan is essentially an integration of (1) the decisions the person has made about what environments he or she wishes to operate in, (2) the functional and resource assessments, and (3) knowledge about the individual and the best path to take to achieve specific objectives that will lead to goal achievement.

Phase III: Rehabilitation Interventions

The third phase of the psychiatric rehabilitation process is the intervention phase, in which the consumer and PsyR provider identify and employ specific intervention strategies to support achievement of the objectives identified on the rehabilitation plan. This information is also recorded on a consumer's rehabilitation plan. The primary categories of rehabilitation interventions are the development of skills and the development of supports or resources (Anthony et al., 2002; Nemec, McNamara, & Walsh, 1992). Some additional intervention approaches that support the PsyR process are **environmental modifications** and specialized counseling techniques such as **motivational interviewing** and **cognitive-behavioral therapy** (CBT). Each of these approaches will be described in this chapter.

When choosing the best intervention approach, it is important for the PsyR practitioner to clearly understand a person's needs. Let's get back to the example of Jane, who wants to become a receptionist. A critical skill deficit was her ability to accurately convey phone messages. Before we can determine how a PsyR practitioner can help Jane convey these messages, we need to determine why she is omitting information. It could be, for example, that Jane has a slight hearing problem. Or it may be that Jane doesn't know what information is most important to include in a message. Perhaps she is distracted by either having to field several calls at the same time or by other people speaking to her when she is trying to record a message. Whatever the case, Jane's message-taking ability is unlikely to improve without identifying the reason for the skill deficit. Once understood, appropriate intervention can be chosen. If Jane isn't sure what information should be included, skills training can help. If she has a hearing problem, a resource will have to be acquired, in this case an audiologist. If distractions are the problem, an environmental modification is a possible solution.

Skill Acquisition and Development

As you can see from the preceding examples, a skill is the ability to successfully perform a behavior at a certain level in a specific context. Acquiring and developing skills involves teaching and refining specific behaviors so that they can be performed both correctly and frequently enough for success in the individual's environment of choice (Nemec, McNamara, & Walsh, 1992). Effective skills teaching is much more involved than the kinds of didactic lectures usually experienced by high school and college students. This is particularly true when persons have been discouraged by repeated failures or when they have to simultaneously cope with other issues such as psychiatric symptoms. Before exploring the skills development models that are commonly used in PsyR, it is important to understand that they are based on classic theories of human behavior you may have been introduced to in a psychology class.

Behavioral Strategies

One of the basic ways we teach skills is through the application of behavioral strategies. Popularized by B. F. Skinner, **behaviorism** has often been accused of being an essentially inhuman or insensitive approach to education. In reality, some form of behaviorism underlies almost every teaching strategy or style.

A basic principle of behaviorism is that by using rewards and punishments we attempt to reinforce behaviors or extinguish them. We accomplish this by using either positive or negative rewards or positive or negative punishments. In this case, think of positive or negative as implying adding something or taking something away, respectively—for example, the same way you think of positive (something added) or negative (something lost or taken away) symptoms of schizophrenia. Behavior can be encouraged using positive rewards. For example, if you complete an extra credit project, you will receive a higher grade. A behavior can also be reinforced using negative rewards. For example, if you complete an extra credit project, you will not have to take the final exam. A positive punishment means that something negative is added. For example, if you do not do well on this test, you will have to write an additional paper. A negative punishment means that something positive is taken away. For example, if you do not do well on this test, you will not be allowed to go on the class trip.

This theme of reward and punishment is a common element in education. One point that behaviorists have stressed is that reward is almost always preferable to punishment. Even though both strategies may be equally effective at either encouraging or extinguishing a particular behavior, the use of punishment often causes unwanted negative effects. People do not like to be punished and often feel resentment toward the person or source of their punishment. This resentment often expresses itself in other negative behaviors that can cause unexpected problems. Rewards are more likely to affect behavior when they are granted correctly. You may have noticed that you are less interested in playing a game when you know you will always win. When games are difficult to succeed at, we consider them a challenge and work harder for the reward of winning.

Rewards are very important in the context of rehabilitation. When staff members are uneducated about the importance of rewards, they often give rewards too freely in an effort to encourage a consumer or to be liked. For example, when a reward such as praise is given too freely or given at times when criticism is more appropriate, it loses its value. Rewards need to be given out after careful evaluation to ensure that they are timely and appropriate. People feel rewards are meaningful when they believe they represent real achievement. When handled carefully, providing rewards can be an important form of communication about a person's progress and can reinforce positive behavior and promote skill development.

Modeling

One of the most important and most common ways people learn is through **modeling**. Much of our understanding of this powerful teaching strategy comes from Albert Bandura's (1977) **social learning theory**, which postulates that we learn social behaviors mostly through observational learning. For example, children learn aggressive behaviors by observing aggressive role models, as shown in Bandura's well-known Bobo doll experiment (Bandura, Ross, & Ross, 1961). Everyone has used modeling at one time or another to shape his or her behavior. Consider a time when you were entering a new environment: a new school, a new club, or some other place where you were not exactly sure how to behave, dress, or speak. Your probable response to this situation was to observe others to see how they were acting, how they dressed, who they spoke with, and so on. After observing for a time, you probably began to feel more confident about how to behave in the new environment and you might have modeled your behavior on the behavior you had observed.

At the core of many PsyR approaches, modeling is a powerful tool for providing both hope and specific strategies to achieve goals. The staff members of effective PsyR services, for example, act as role models for those who are receiving their services. Since people are more likely to model the behavior of people they perceive as similar to themselves, many

PsyR professionals strive to reduce the barriers between themselves and the individuals they are assisting. For example, staff members may dress less formally and share in everyday functions and chores as a means of emphasizing their similarities. Modeling is also one reason that peer support is an effective PsyR strategy. Individuals who have achieved a positive self-image despite their mental illness can serve as role models and provide clear evidence that recovery is possible.

Skills Training and Direct Skills Teaching

Several approaches for teaching skills to persons living with severe mental illnesses have been developed since the 1970s. A major proponent for a PsyR skills teaching approach has been the Center for Psychiatric Rehabilitation at Boston University. They call the technology they devised **direct skills teaching** (DST). Like all aspects of the PsyR process, DST is an intervention that is both highly individualized and person-centered (Farkas & Anthony, 2010; Nemec et al., 1992). The focus is on helping consumers learn or enhance skills that they choose to learn in order to function effectively in the environments of their choice. There are no prepackaged modules for DST; practitioners create specific lesson plans for each person they are assisting, taking into account the learning style of the individual as well as the aspects of the skill that are most relevant to the particular person. The **ROPES method** is used to ensure that each lesson plan *reviews* what the person already knows, provides an *overview* of the rationale for using the skills, *presents* a demonstration of skill use, utilizes an *exercise* for practice of the skill, and *summarizes* what has been learned. While there are a number of techniques used in the DST method, the emphasis is on combining the telling, showing (or modeling), and doing aspects of skills teaching (Nemec et al., 1992). **Skills programming** is also an important component of the DST approach (Nemec et al., 1992). Once a new skill is learned, the PsyR practitioner assists the individual in developing a program of skill use that includes real-world practice opportunities in settings that are relevant to the person's Overall Rehabilitation Goal (ORG). The PsyR practitioner also identifies any barriers to successful skill use and develops strategies for overcoming the barriers. This important aspect of the DST process is illustrated in the following example:

> *Joseph's ORG is to obtain his associate's degree at a nearby community college. One of the critical skills needed is to take the bus from home to school. After helping him learn to navigate the local public transportation system, Lawanda, his PsyR practitioner, helps him to schedule some real-world practice opportunities. After the first solo practice run, Joseph tells Lawanda he doesn't think he can take the bus because the experience exacerbated both his anxiety and auditory hallucinations. Lawanda helps him to consider some symptom management strategies and Joseph agrees to try again, this time bringing along his MP3 player because listening to music has helped him manage these symptoms in the past. The following week, Joseph reports to Lawanda that he successfully traveled from home to the college and feels more confident that he can do it on a regular basis.*

The University of California at Los Angeles (UCLA) Center for Research on the Treatment and Rehabilitation of Psychosis led by Robert Paul Liberman also developed an intervention approach focused on skills development. The UCLA group has simply titled their strategy **skills training**. Liberman's group put a great deal of effort into the development of modules for teaching specific categories of skills such as social skills and independent living skills (Liberman et al., 1993). Alan Bellack and his colleagues also made a notable contribution to the dissemination of the skills training model by developing detailed manuals for social skills training that are used by many PsyR practitioners (Bellack, Meuser, Gingerich, & Agresta, 2004). Social skills are an important component of social competence; helping people acquire and improve them through social skills training can help them assume valued social roles such as friend, neighbor, and employee. Social skills also help people to build interpersonal supports that can be critical for coping with life stressors. Thus, they have been identified as a protective factor that may help prevent relapse (Kopelowicz, Liberman, & Zarate, 2006).

Box 5.2 describes the ten steps used in the social skills training process. Note that it is often most effective to do social skills training in small groups, which allows for more modeling and practice opportunities.

BOX 5.2   STEPS OF THE SOCIAL SKILLS TRAINING PROCESS

1. *Establish a rationale for the skill.* (For example, when teaching the skill of starting a conversation, ask the group members to describe situations in their lives where using the skill would be beneficial.)
2. *Discuss the steps of the skill.* (Providing handouts or other visual media that outline the skill steps is recommended.)
3. *Model the skill in a role play and review the role play with the members.*
4. *Engage a group member in a role play using the same situation.*
5. *Provide positive feedback.* (Also ask group members to provide feedback on what the person did well.)
6. *Provide corrective feedback.* (Also ask group members to provide feedback on steps the person struggled with.)
7. *Engage the group member in another role play using the same situation.*
8. *Provide additional feedback.* (Always start with the positive, and then offer corrective feedback if needed.)
9. *Engage other group members in role plays and provide feedback, as in steps four through eight.*
10. *Assign homework that will be reviewed at the beginning of the next session.* (Homework should encourage practice of the skill in the natural environments where the members need to use the skill to achieve stated goals.)

Adapted from Bellack et al., p. 49 (2004).

One benefit of the skills training approach is the availability of manuals and modules that allow for easy replication. Practitioners do not need extensive training or competency in lesson planning to use this approach. The drawback is that the available skills training modules will not meet the individualized needs of every consumer. However, it is possible to customize skills training materials to make them more relevant to the needs of individual consumers. For example, skill steps can be added or modified and new practice scenarios can be developed. It is particularly important to modify social skills training curricula to match them to the cultural norms of an individual (Bellack et al., 2004).

Strategies That Promote Skill Acquisition

An important cognitive strategy for effective skill acquisition and maintenance is establishing a rationale for the skill with the individual (Bellack et al., 2004). In other words, the issue of why it is worth the effort to learn a particular skill needs to be addressed so that the individual is motivated to acquire that skill. As you can see from Box 5.2, this is the very first step in the social skills training process. Individuals may not grasp the relationship between a particular skill, for example, socially appropriate communication, and a vocational goal, such as becoming a secretary/receptionist. Thus, clarification of the need for the skill and how it is related to an individual's goal is a necessary responsibility of the PsyR practitioner.

The concept of **skill generalization** also needs to be considered to ensure the success of the rehabilitation process. Skill generalization refers to the fact that behavior (or skill performance) is situation-specific. In simple terms, just because a person performs a skill in one environment does not mean that he or she can or will perform the same skill in a different environment. This problem has been one of the main drawbacks of many facility-based programs that teach individuals skills in artificial settings and then hope that they will be able to apply them in the real world. For example, a person who demonstrates successful acquisition of some independent living skills (e.g., cooking or budgeting) in a supervised group home may not adequately perform these same skills when living independently. It is important to note that this failure to generalize skills to other environments or settings appears to be a common human failing rather than a characteristic of individuals with mental illness; consider the college student who has learned to do his laundry at home, but when confronted with the laundry room in his dormitory, has no idea how to proceed. This problem relates to the paradigm switch from "train and place" strategies to "place and train" strategies that characterizes supported services. For example, supported housing programs teach individuals independent living skills in their homes and communities, the very places that they need to use them.

PsyR practitioners should also use individualized reinforcement strategies to reward the use of newly learned skills. These strategies may include praise from the person teaching the skill; teaching persons in the consumer's natural environment, for example, family members, to encourage and reward skill use; teaching consumers how to both evaluate and reward themselves; and helping the person to identify intrinsic sources of motivation, such as feeling proud (Anthony et al., 2002).

Skill maintenance is another important consideration for successful rehabilitation. A few skills training sessions may not be sufficient to ensure that a person learns a new behavior and continues to use it over time. As addressed above in the description of the DST skills programming component, the practitioner should help the person find ongoing opportunities to practice relevant skills, assist the individual in identifying challenges encountered when using the skill, and develop a plan to address any problems that emerge. Periodic reassessment of skill performance may also be needed to maintain effective skill use.

The concept of skill maintenance does not apply only to newly learned skills. You have probably noticed that when you do not perform a complex or difficult task for some time, your performance level goes down. You might have experienced this if you used to be a fast typist, a good chess player, or a low handicap golfer or performed any task in which higher levels of practice are necessary to maintain peak performance. A common saying describing this effect is "use it or lose it." Often it is just as important that people maintain the skills they already have as it is to acquire new ones. When individuals with psychiatric disabilities spend long periods of time in institutions, outpatient day programs, or group homes they often become dependent on the staff to do things for them and leave with fewer skills than when they entered. PsyR programs should emphasize strengths and identify and highlight the skills and abilities that individuals possess. Awareness that these skills must be reinforced through regular practice will help to ensure that they are not lost. Lastly, most people take pride in the things they do well. Maintaining skills as a source of pride for individuals is an important element in the PsyR process. The fact that a person can do some things well gives one confidence that, with some time and effort, she or he will be able to do other things equally well.

Cognitive Remediation

Some persons living with serious mental illnesses, particularly those diagnosed with schizophrenia, have impairments that affect cognitive functions such as information processing, sustaining attention, short-term memory, and problem solving (Bellack et al., 2004; Medalia & Choi, 2009). **Cognitive remediation** strategies, sometimes referred to as "cognitive rehabilitation," are behavioral interventions that help improve cognitive functioning through the use of repetitive exercises and positive reinforcers, such as praise and/or tokens for participation and increased attention span. Cognitive remediation interventions can be done either with an individual or in small groups. Sometimes the exercises or drills are done using specialized computer programs (Kopelwicz et al., 2006; Medalia & Choi, 2009). Cognitive remediation can be used to improve overall cognitive functioning or to help individuals participate more actively in treatment settings, but in PsyR it is used to help individuals improve the areas of cognitive functioning needed for the achievement of their chosen goals (Medalia & Choi, 2009). The outcomes of cognitive remediation programs have been studied, and while it does not yet have a solid evidence base, it was identified as an "emerging area of interest" by the Schizophrenia Patient Outcomes Research Team (PORT) (Dixon et al., 2010).

Cognitive remediation has been combined effectively with social skills training to help consumers who have cognitive deficits learn, retain, and apply social skills in real-life settings (Kopelwicz, Liberman, & Zarate, 2006). Using this sort of combination of PsyR interventions is a good example of a key PsyR principle: using a person-centered approach, which requires the individualization of interventions.

Andrea is a PsyR practitioner who runs a social skills training group in a PsyR program. Lisa is a group member recovering from repeated episodes of severe depression, characterized by social isolation. She is attending the group because she wants to interact effectively with coworkers at her new job. Lisa is able to easily remember and demonstrate the skill steps needed to start conversations, but she needs regular coaching from Andrea to help her stay motivated to practice the skill at work on a regular basis. Dupree wants to improve his social skills so that he can get along better with family members. He is recovering from schizophrenia and struggles with a short attention span and memory impairment. To assist Dupree, Andrea utilizes cognitive remediation strategies. She provides Dupree with verbal praise when he is able to stay focused for progressively longer periods of time during the group. After each group, she helps him to consolidate his learning by using a computer program to review skill steps and correctly apply them in social scenarios.

Resources and Supports

An important area of the PsyR intervention phase is the development and coordination of resources and supports. As mentioned earlier in the chapter, resources, which are also referred to as supports in the PsyR literature (Farkas & Anthony, 2010), are persons, places, things, or activities that a person either has or needs to support achievement of the chosen overall rehabilitation goal (Anthony et al., 2002). Like everyone else, individuals who have psychiatric disabilities benefit from a connection to natural supports such as family, friends, and coworkers, and helping people utilize these natural supports is one of the key principles of PsyR (see Chapter 4). However, they may also need access to a number of professional supports and government-funded entitlements to move forward in their recovery.

As mentioned in the previous description of the planning phase of PsyR, a rehabilitation plan should identify the specific resources and supports that a person needs to achieve his or her ORG but does not currently have. The rehabilitation plan should also specify action steps for developing needed resources. Resources can be used in situations where a person is unable to develop a skill or when doing so would take too long. For example, instead of learning the skills of job acquisition, someone might want to rely on a job coach to make contact with potential employers. In this example, the PsyR provider's resource development intervention might be to make a referral to a supported employment program (see Chapter 10).

BOX 5.3   SOCIAL SKILLS TRAINING IS AN EVIDENCE-BASED INTERVENTION

Skills training, and particularly the social skills training (SST) approach described in this chapter, is a widely studied PsyR intervention. The Schizophrenia Patient Outcomes Research Team (PORT), which is introduced in Chapter 1 and cited throughout this book, included skills training as one of eight recommended psychosocial treatments in their most recent scholarly paper (Dixon et al., 2010). They concluded that there is ample evidence that skills training interventions that are structured and utilize behavior techniques are effective ways to teach persons with serious mental illnesses interpersonal and activity of daily living (ADL) skills. There is also some evidence that individuals are able to retain skills over time, although more studies need to be done on retention. It was also noted that some strategies, particularly those that stress practice in real world settings, appear to be more effective than others in supporting the generalization of skills use. There is also evidence that skills training curricula can be adapted to produce positive outcomes in specific settings such as the workplace, as well as with specific populations, such as those with co-occurring psychiatric and substance abuse disorders (Dixon et al., 2010). These intervention strategies will be addressed in more depth in Chapters 9 and 10.

Kurtz and Mueser (2008) identified and analyzed the results of 22 randomized controlled trial trials of SST with individuals diagnosed with schizophrenia. Their study was a **meta-analysis** that sought to determine the effect that SST had on research study participants. A **meta-analysis** is a study that combines the findings of previous studies, statistically combining the effects of all studies to determine an average effect. In terms of the specific outcomes of SST, they found that SST has the strongest effect on mastery of the specific skills taught in the SST program. SST also has a moderate effect on both performance-based measures of social and independent living skills and overall psychosocial functioning. SST also has a moderate (but still statistically significant) impact on reduction of negative symptoms such as blunted affect and avolition, which are associated with poor psychosocial functioning. See Chapter 2 for more about negative symptoms of schizophrenia.

To help individuals access the resources and supports identified in their rehabilitation plans, PsyR practitioners need to be knowledgeable about what is available in their communities. Examples of resources include public entitlements that provide financial assistance to meet living expenses. A PsyR practitioner might assist someone in applying for Social Security benefits, rental assistance, a prescription plan to purchase medications at reduced rates, or other publicly funded entitlement programs. A resource might also be something that improves someone's ability to function in a particular setting, such as a bus schedule or a watch that can beep when it is time to take medication. Resources that support the rehabilitation process are often people. Besides the job coach mentioned previously, a peer counselor at a drop-in center, a yoga instructor at the YMCA, and a friend who provides transportation to the program are all good examples of resources that a PsyR practitioner might help a consumer locate. Of course, the PsyR practitioner who helps a person identify and work toward a chosen goal may be the most important resource of all.

Later in this book we will look at specific models of PsyR, such as supported employment, supported education, and supported housing (see Chapters 10, 11, and 12) that are designed to help people achieve goals in specific environments. PsyR practitioners who have expertise in a particular model are well acquainted with the specific types of resources and supports relevant to their work. For example, a practitioner working in a supported education program should know about financial aid opportunities and student services that are available on local college campuses.

In addition to knowing where and how to locate resources, PsyR practitioners also need to have strong interpersonal and organizational skills to effectively link consumers to needed resources, to monitor resource acquisition, and (in some instances) to advocate for resources. Consider Rafael's situation described ahead and note the importance of collaborating with the people who control needed resources.

Rafael has a long history of psychiatric hospitalizations and has been homeless for several months. Jose is a psychiatric rehabilitation practitioner who works for a homeless outreach program. After spending several weeks getting to know Rafael, he helps him move into a temporary shelter, but he is also committed to helping Rafael achieve his goal of obtaining his own apartment. In order to achieve this goal, Rafael will need a number of resources such as a monthly disability benefit check for his living expenses and a housing voucher to help cover rent and food stamps. Rafael has no idea how to access these resources, but Jose has experience helping consumers acquire them. Rafael also has some social and organizational skill deficits that are barriers to successful resource acquisition. In addition, English is his second language and he sometimes struggles to communicate, particularly in unfamiliar situations. So Rafael needs much more than just resource linkage. Jose accompanies Rafael to the Social Security Administration (SSA) Office. It is crowded with multiple lines of people waiting for services. Rafael feels overwhelmed and anxious, but Jose reassures him, saying in Spanish, "Don't worry. I will help you each step of the way." Jose locates the correct line and while they are waiting he coaches Rafael on what to say to the SSA official. When they finally get to the front of the line, Rafael begins explaining his situation and asks to apply for disability benefits. The SSA official quickly cuts him off and begins to rapidly ask him questions. Rafael becomes anxious and turns to Jose with an expression of panic on his face. Jose steps in and introduces himself as Rafael's advocate. He politely asks the SSA official if she can speak more slowly and ask one question at a time, but is rebuffed when the woman states, "Can't you see how busy I am! If he can't understand English he will just have to come back another time when a Spanish-speaking worker is available." Although annoyed, Jose maintains his composure and tells her that he understands how busy she is and he would be happy to help Rafael answer her questions. They are able to complete the interview and obtain what is needed to continue with the application process. Jose later helps Rafael complete the complicated application and gather the needed documents. Jose also accompanies Rafael to the rental assistance and food stamps office, working closely with Rafael to get through the cumbersome process of applying for all of the benefits he will need. He also works with Rafael to monitor the progress of his applications, which requires several follow-up phone calls and office visits. Several months later, Rafael receives his first disability check; a few weeks after that, he obtains a housing voucher. Jose helps him look for an apartment in a neighborhood that

Rafael likes because of its proximity to family members. From previous efforts to assist clients with housing, Jose has developed a positive working relationship the manager of a rental office of a nice apartment complex. He greets her warmly, introduces Rafael, and helps him fill out yet another application. About six months after his initial visit from Jose, Rafael is thrilled to move into his own apartment.

Modifications of Environments and Resources

Sometimes a needed resource is not available in the community, or a change in a particular environment is needed to support a person's success. In these situations a PsyR practitioner may need to develop new resources or advocate for an environmental modification (Anthony & Farkas, 2010). This type of PsyR intervention can be quite challenging since it may require creativity, problem-solving techniques, and/or persistent advocacy efforts. Some examples of developing new resources are establishing a mentoring program in conjunction with a religious congregation to help persons with psychiatric disabilities find opportunities to socialize and volunteer in their communities; working with a community college to establish a support group for students recovering from mental illness; or working with a cosmetology school to provide free beauty services to members of a PsyR program who want to improve their appearance.

In terms of environmental modifications, to help a person succeed in a working or learning environment, a PsyR practitioner may need to help identify and request **reasonable accommodations**. Examples include a later start to the work day to accommodate a person who has difficulty getting to the office early in the morning because of medication side effects; an office space location that has reduced distractions; and additional time to complete a college exam. Since passage of the Americans with Disabilities Act (ADA) in 1990, reasonable environmental modifications are the law. Some of the more visible results of this law are handicapped parking spaces, cutouts on curbs, and building ramps for wheelchairs. The ADA is explained in more detail in Chapter 10 on employment.

The Story of Paul (Continued from Chapter 1)

We first met Paul in Chapter 1. As you may recall, after a brief psychiatric hospitalization Paul was referred to a community mental health center where he learned he was diagnosed with schizophrenia. The following segment of Paul's story begins with his initial meeting with a PsyR practitioner and follows his progress as he takes the first steps in his recovery journey. As you read the story, notice how it illustrates the phases of the PsyR process described earlier and look for the specific strategies that the PsyR practitioner uses to develop a partnership with Paul and help him achieve his goals.

After an intake interview and the completion of an initial treatment plan at the community mental health center, Paul was referred to Ruth, a PsyR practitioner. Paul was nervous about what would happen at their first meeting. While he understood that the medication he started taking in the hospital was helping him to focus and feel less suspicious of people, he was skeptical about being referred for rehabilitation services and wondered how Ruth could help him. After brief introductions, Ruth invited Paul to have a seat and then chose a seat for herself across from him rather than behind her desk. She said, "Tell me about yourself and what you would like to do with your life." Paul was reluctant at first to tell her much, but he noticed that she was listening very carefully and seemed genuinely interested in his story. Ruth encouraged him to continue talking, and he soon found himself describing his terrible experience at college and disclosing his fears about having schizophrenia. Finally, Paul said, "I can't believe my life is over. I don't want to spend the rest of my life living with my parents and being a psychiatric patient." "Good," said Ruth, "then let's talk about where you do want to be. You and I have some important and exciting work to do. We have to figure out what you want your life to look like, what your goals are, and how to reach those goals."

During the meetings that followed, Paul and Ruth talked about all areas of his life. Paul decided that he was happy living with his parents for now. They got along pretty well and he couldn't afford to pay rent anyway. They seemed happy to have him there, even though they worried a lot about him and he wished they wouldn't. His social life was dismal. He'd pretty much alienated everyone he knew when he was "getting sick"; he wished that he could repair some of these relationships or perhaps make some new friends. Most important to Paul, though, was school. He wanted to get his life back on track, and he believed that he needed to get a college degree in order to pursue his career goals. Ruth and Paul agreed that going back to school was the priority and decided that his overall rehabilitation goal would be to resume college classes in September.

Paul felt hopeful and scared at the same time. His goal of graduating with a degree in business had seemed out of reach a few months ago. Paul wondered if he was kidding himself. He imagined his professors seeing him back in class after he'd failed the first time and remembered the hurtful things he'd said to his friends. But Paul trusted Ruth. When he told her about these concerns, she didn't dismiss them or accept them as evidence that he couldn't go to school. Instead she talked about making sure Paul had the supports and resources he would need to succeed in college.

Paul and Ruth listed the critical skills needed to achieve his goal. Naturally, he'd have to meet all the requirements of the courses, so he would need to be able to focus on oral presentations and written materials, study for exams, and write coherent papers. Although Paul used to excel at these academic skills, he was concerned because both his concentration and stamina were diminished because of the illness and the medication. He'd also have to get some kind of transportation to school because he wouldn't be living on campus this time, and he'd have to learn to manage the symptoms he was still experiencing: hearing voices and feeling withdrawn.

With Ruth's encouragement, Paul contacted the registrar at the college he'd been attending. He found out that he'd withdrawn from some classes and failed others. In any case, he'd have to start over. He decided to take one course, and he and Ruth agreed it should be Introduction to Marketing, since this was an important area of interest and he'd be more likely to do well.

With two months left until the start of the semester, Ruth helped him to contact the student services office and complete the paperwork needed to make him eligible for disability accommodations. Paul requested permission to audiotape the class lectures. This way he could listen to the tapes to help organize his notes. A few weeks before the course started, he was able to obtain the reading assignments for the semester to help him plan his study schedule. He knew that his problems concentrating meant he'd have to start early because he'd need lots of breaks. Ruth also taught Paul how to use the public transportation system. To practice, Paul took the bus to the school a few times to help him feel less anxious about the trip. Finally, Ruth helped Paul set up a schedule that included study time, relaxation time, and meetings with her for support and problem solving.

Paul's parents were skeptical about his plan to return to school. They were convinced that the stress of school was what had "pushed him over the edge." However, with Ruth's help, Paul was able to tell them how important school was for him and how important their support would be to his success. Paul's parents agreed to support his plan as long as they could figure out what to do if Paul got sick again. Paul, his parents, and Ruth made a list of things that would indicate that he was experiencing another episode of his illness and the things people could do to help.

Paul and Ruth had a meeting scheduled the day the midterm grades were posted. Paul arrived looking worried. "You look like your grade wasn't what you'd hoped for," Ruth offered. Paul looked surprised. "Oh, no," he chuckled, "I got a 'B'! It's just that, well, some of the guys in my class invited me out to sort of celebrate, you know. It means I'd have to cut our meeting short." "Go!" Ruth laughed. "Go and have fun! I'll see you next week. Call me if anything comes up before then. Oh, and by the way, Paul, good work!"

Counseling Techniques That Support the Rehabilitation Process

In addition to teaching people skills, helping them access resources and supports, and working to develop new resources and modify environments if needed, effective PsyR practitioners are able to incorporate a variety of counseling techniques into their work. The counseling approaches that PsyR practitioners draw from include client-centered therapy, motivational interviewing (MI), and cognitive-behavioral therapy CBT. In addition, many PsyR practitioners need to be skilled facilitators of support groups and structured activity groups. These techniques are important for engaging consumers, developing therapeutic alliances, and increasing motivation to make the changes needed to achieve rehabilitation and recovery goals.

CLIENT-CENTERED THERAPY

Client-centered therapy, sometimes referred to as person-centered therapy, was introduced by Carl Rogers in the 1940s. It was a substantial departure from the traditional psychoanalytic therapies of that time. Rogers initially called his approach non-directive therapy and proposed that the therapist's role was not to direct or instruct the client but to assist the person in understanding his or her own experience of the world and promote positive change through a trustworthy relationship (Brammer, Shostrom, &

Abrego, 1989; Krech, Crutchfield, & Livson, 1969). To accomplish this, the therapist has to hold the person in positive regard. In other words, the therapist has to respect and empathize with the client.

The basic tenets of client-centered therapy are highly compatible with PsyR and have influenced the field. Client-centered therapy is based on the belief that people will engage in activities leading to positive growth and development if given the opportunity (Krech, Crutchfield, & Livson, 1969). This belief is consistent with the PsyR value of optimism that everyone has the capacity to recover, learn, and grow. Client-centered therapy asserts that the opportunity for growth exists within relationships that offer empathy, positive regard, and genuineness (Brammer, Shostrom, & Abrego, 1989). In PsyR, we know that the quality of the person-practitioner relationship is crucial to recovery and rehabilitation. Here, too, the relationship is an egalitarian one, based on empathy, positive regard, and acceptance.

Client-centered therapy focuses on the person's perception of his or her present circumstances and assists the person in identifying his or her own answers to problems or barriers (Brammer, Shostrom, & Abrego, 1989). PsyR practice also focuses on the individual's current aspirations, concerns, and challenges rather than on rehashing past experiences. An important technique used in client-centered therapy is reflecting back the thoughts, feelings, and experiences that the client has communicated. This technique demonstrates empathy, helps clarify issues that are personally important to the person, and keeps the focus on particular issues that the client wants to work on. PsyR practitioners also use techniques inspired by Rogers, usually called reflective responding or active listening (Carkhuff, 2009). Finally, client-centered therapy places the major responsibility for successful change on the client (Krech, Crutchfield, & Livson, 1969). In PsyR, we also emphasize the value of self-determination in helping individuals achieve personal life goals.

The work of counseling psychologist Robert Carkhuff, author of *The Art of Helping*, now in its 9th edition (2009), has been a great help to many PsyR professionals. Carkhuff's writings help to simplify the helping process of client-centered counseling techniques into comprehensible steps that are easily understood by PsyR practitioners who may not be licensed counselors or therapists. An example is the skill of physical attending that enables the practitioner to use a set of specific nonverbal techniques, such as facing the person squarely, leaning forward slightly, and making eye contact to convey empathy (Carkhuff, 2009).

MOTIVATIONAL INTERVIEWING

Often individuals living with a serious mental illness want to achieve their goals but struggle with the challenging process of making major changes in their lives. The challenge of mustering the motivation needed to make life changes is something most of us can relate to. Think about how difficult it is to achieve a typical New Year's resolution such as to quit smoking, start an exercise regimen, or curtail sugary snacks. **Motivational interviewing** (MI) is a counseling approach designed to help people develop the motivation to make such changes. MI is a person-centered approach that helps individuals explore and eventually resolve their ambivalence about changing their behavior (Miller and Rollnick, 2002). Like Roger's client-centered approach, MI relies on the practitioner's ability to experience and express empathy for individuals. Using MI, the practitioner helps the individual to clarify goals while understanding the conflict between their present behavior and what they seek. While MI can be used to assist with any sort of change, in PsyR it is frequently employed working with individuals with a substance abuse disorder. The strategy of using MI with co-occurring disorders is described in greater detail in Chapter 9.

COGNITIVE-BEHAVIOR THERAPY

In the 1960s, Aaron Beck developed a psychotherapy approach he called "cognitive therapy," which today is more commonly known as **cognitive-behavior therapy**, or **CBT**. This approach emphasizes the impact that our thoughts and perceptions have on our feelings and behaviors. To provide a simple example, if a person has a negative self-image and has thoughts such as "I'm worthless; I'll never be able to accomplish anything," he or she will probably feel sad and hopeless and will experience difficulty achieving personal goals. Beck theorized that individuals living with depression typically developed a very negative view of themselves and the world around them and that many of their thoughts were inaccurate or exaggerated. For example, a woman believes that she is basically unlovable and that no one really cares for her, when in fact she has friends and family members who do care for her and view her as being kind, thoughtful, and generous. Beck postulated that changing these negative thought patterns or cognitions, which he called "automatic thoughts," to a more positive outlook would reduce symptoms of depression and improve psychosocial functioning. By the late 1970s, he had developed and tested a number of effective techniques and had authored books that described his use of cognitive therapy to treat depression and anxiety disorders. In the ensuing years, many mental health practitioners and researchers have built on Beck's work and developed a variety of CBT approaches (Beck Institute for Cognitive Behavior Therapy, 2013; Tai & Turkington, 2009).

CBT is typically a short-term therapy approach. The therapist and the client work together to identify specific problems and they establish a goal for each session: for example, a client wants to reduce the distorted automatic thoughts she typically has when going out to socialize with friends. The therapist teaches the client specific techniques for reducing automatic thoughts during the session and assigns homework for the client to do between sessions, such as practicing CBT techniques in specific situations (Beck Institute for Cognitive Behavior Therapy, 2013; Tai & Turkington, 2009). Some common techniques used in CBT are described as follows:

- **Socratic questioning**—Asking logical questions to determine whether or not a hypothesis is accurate. For example, "What exactly do your classmates do that make you think they don't like you?" Eventually the person can learn to ask him- or herself these questions.
- **Reality testing**—Assigning a client a specific homework assignment, such as examining the evidence for and against a client's delusional belief that radio talk show hosts are communicating directly to him.

- **Mindfulness**—Use of meditation exercises that help individuals focus on the present moment rather than on troubling automatic thoughts. For example, intentionally pausing to notice sights, sounds, and smells in the environment (Tai & Turkington, 2009; Wright et al., 2009).

While CBT techniques were initially developed and used to treat depression and anxiety disorders, they have since been used effectively to help people with other psychiatric diagnoses, such as schizophrenia and borderline personality disorder—for example, a CBT program that targets paranoid delusions (Tai & Turkington, 2009; Wright et al., 2009) and a well-known approach called "dialectical behavior therapy" (DBT) that has been used to help individuals diagnosed with borderline personality disorder change their maladaptive coping patterns (Feigenbaum, 2007). CBT has also been used to help individuals dually diagnosed with mental illness and posttraumatic stress disorder learn to cope with the effects of trauma (Mueser et al., 2008; Lu et al., 2009).

PsyR practitioners can make effective use of CBT techniques even if they are not certified CBT practitioners. They are often used as adjunctive interventions for consumers receiving other types of PsyR services (Corrigan et al., 2008). Consider the following example:

Ashok is a young man who recently moved into his own apartment. He receives services from an assertive community treatment (ACT) team (see Chapter 8). Ashok is lonely and is no longer in touch with his high school friends. His ORG is to make friends in his neighborhood during the next year. He likes to go to the YMCA to exercise and thinks it could be a good place to meet people, but it sometimes gets crowded and noisy. Ashok struggles with both anxiety and paranoid thoughts that can become exacerbated in noisy and crowded environments. Ashok tells one of the ACT team members, Anita, that he thinks some of the YMCA members might be plotting against him. Anita uses Socratic questioning and reality testing exercises to help Ashok examine this belief to help him realize that it is unlikely that anyone at the YMCA wants to harm him. She also teaches Ashok some mindfulness techniques to help reduce his anxiety when at the YMCA and other places.

Many researchers have studied the outcomes of various forms for CBT and there is ample evidence that it can reduce symptoms of many psychiatric disorders. For example, the most recent PORT study paper cited CBT as an evidence-based practice that reduces the symptoms of schizophrenia (Dixon et al., 2010).

GROUP INTERVENTIONS

While many PsyR interventions are provided one-to-one between a PsyR practitioner and an individual consumer, use of group interventions is a long-standing practice in the PsyR field. As you will learn after reading Chapter 7, most of the earliest PsyR programs were day programs that utilized formal and informal group interventions, and many of these programs still exist today. Other PsyR programs may use both one-to-one and group interventions, such as a supported education program (see Chapter 11) that offers a study skills group as part of its service menu. Other examples of group PsyR interventions include social skills training groups (mentioned earlier in this chapter); ADL skills training groups that may focus on topics such as budgeting; illness management and recovery (IMR, described in Chapter 3); support and education groups for individuals with co-occurring disorders (see Chapter 9); and multifamily psychoeducation groups (described in Chapter 14).

Group interventions provided by PsyR practitioners have some commonalities. In contrast to traditional psychotherapy groups that may focus on any issue raised by a group member, PsyR groups usually have a specific purpose and that purpose should be directly related to group members' chosen goals. They also typically follow a structured session plan that includes an orientation to the purpose of the group, interactive exercises, and a concluding segment that allows members to summarize what they gained from the group.

In order to facilitate this type of structured educational and support group, a PsyR practitioner should have a number of knowledge and skill competencies. These include knowledge of group dynamics, strategies for developing group cohesion and group evaluation tools, and skill in group leadership and developing group session plans (United States Psychiatric Rehabilitation Association, 2007). There are many group counseling techniques that are used in both formal and informal PsyR group interventions. Some examples are drawing out quiet members, gently cutting off members who veer off the topic, and linking members through the use of dyads (Jacobs et al., 2012).

CONTROVERSIAL ISSUE
Independence, Dependence, or Interdependence

Independence versus dependence has been an issue in PsyR since deinstitutionalization. Because of their disabilities, many persons who have a severe mental illness require ongoing support to reside successfully in the community. As demonstrated by the effectiveness of case management programs such as ACT (Chapter 8), without effective supports many individuals would be hospitalized more often and for longer periods of time. At the same time, efforts to achieve community integration, self-determination, and empowerment all suggest that independence is an important goal for the individual. Recovery itself is based on the individual deciding what he or she wants in life, something that cannot happen without a degree of independence. Anthony and his colleagues (2002) dealt with the issue of independence versus dependence in their formulation of PsyR principles. One principle states: "Supporting dependency can lead to an eventual increase in the client's independent functioning" (p. 86).

On the first reading, this may seem like a contradiction. It is the same contradiction that has troubled the PsyR community for many years. On further consideration, we can see that in order for a person to gain the benefits of rehabilitation he or she must be willing to go through the process. Hence, the person might follow the lead of (i.e., be somewhat dependent on) the rehabilitation practitioner in order to achieve the eventual goal of acquiring independence.

(Continued)

CONTROVERSIAL ISSUE
Independence, Dependence, or Interdependence—(Continued)

In one way this conception of the independence versus dependence issue may be too simplistic. Who among us is truly independent? In fact, although we all achieve degrees of independence, we all have some areas of dependence. We may be dependent on a spouse or loved one or an institution such as a school or a job or anything else in our life on which we rely. At the same time, these people and institutions may be dependent on us. In fact, the issue is more correctly defined as one of interdependence, which is being simultaneously dependent on others while they are dependent on us. This balance, which is both normalizing and empowering, is often absent in the lives of people with disabilities. To complicate matters further, our degree of interdependence with elements in our environment may go through constant changes. Consider the parents who want to protect their child and help her to grow up and be self-reliant, or the couple that supports each other in their different careers while being dependent on one another. The real goal seems to be much more complicated than simply achieving independence. Instead, we must learn to be simultaneously comfortable with a degree of dependence and a degree of independence.

Evaluating Rehabilitation Progress

The primary importance of establishing specific rehabilitation goals and objectives with a consumer is that these help clarify what she or he is hoping to accomplish, as well as strategies for achieving success. When developing rehabilitation plans, long-range goals are reduced to specific tasks, usually undertaken in sequence, that guide the person through the steps needed to achieve the ORG. An important part of the rehabilitation process is to periodically evaluate progress made on short-term objectives as the person moves closer to the ORG. When this is done, the individual has a sense of his or her own progress and the practitioner can determine if intervention strategies are working. PsyR service providers typically evaluate the progress of consumers on a weekly basis. They may also sit down with the consumer to conduct a thorough review of the entire rehabilitation plan about every three months, to make sure that they are on track and to make any needed updates. It should be noted that the exact length of time between progress evaluations and rehabilitation plan reviews varies and should depend on the individual needs of the consumer as well as agency policies and local government regulations.

Evaluating whether progress is being made is a much simpler task when short-term goals are objective, time-framed, easily quantified, and measurable. Consider the following example:

Tanya's overall rehabilitation goal is to find a part-time job as receptionist within the next six months. Tanya and her practitioner decide that one of the critical skills needed for success in her chosen job is punctuality. Tanya admits that she struggles with this; she says she is often late for doctor's appointments and for her current volunteer job at a community mental health center. They decide that "to improve punctuality" should be one of the short-term goals on her rehabilitation plan. As it stands, this objective is rather nebulous and it would be difficult to assess Tanya's progress. It can be made specific and measurable by stating it this way: Tanya will get to her volunteer job by 9:00 a.m. three days a week. Tanya is required to log in her arrival time each day so it will be easy to keep track of her progress. More importantly, the evaluation results will be unequivocal.

When all the goals and objectives specified on an individual's rehabilitation plan are written in an easily measurable form, determining whether or not progress has been made is easily evaluated, providing clear feedback to the consumer. If a consumer and practitioner have determined that progress has been made toward a goal, the progress should be acknowledged in a positive manner. Once a goal is achieved, a new goal may be set. However, if progress has not been made or is too slow, the crucial task is to determine why. Sometimes practitioners do not ask this question and instead assume that more time is needed to work toward the existing goal. Although this may be the case, one should not jump to such a conclusion until the practitioner and consumer have thoroughly explored possible reasons for lack of progress. It may be that the basis for a particular skill deficit was not clarified to begin with. Getting back to Tanya's plan, her PsyR practitioner might assume that she is often late because she is not used to taking responsibility for being someplace on time. The actual reason could be that Tanya does not own an alarm clock. When practitioners make inaccurate assumptions about the cause of a problem, it is very unlikely that the intervention they devise to solve the problem will be successful. In Tanya's situation, the practitioner's original intervention might have been to give her positive reinforcement. This might consist of praising her as punctuality improved or celebrating progress by treating her to a cup of coffee. However, if the root of the problem is actually the lack of an alarm clock, positive reinforcement may have no discernible effect. The appropriate intervention is helping Tanya purchase an alarm clock, which is an example of an easily achievable resource acquisition.

A lack of progress is often very frustrating for both the individual and the PsyR practitioner. Sometimes it is difficult to determine why progress has not been made. In addition to providing the wrong intervention (as illustrated in Tanya's story), there are many reasons why a person might not be moving toward a goal. The individual may have lost interest in working toward a particular goal because he or she does not understand its relationship to the ORG. Or it could be that the person wants to achieve the goal but is not ready to work on it. This last barrier to goal achievement relates to rehabilitation readiness, discussed earlier in the chapter.

Staff members need to be very thoughtful and empathic when progress is eluding a consumer. Too many staff members automatically associate lack of progress with lack of motivation and then fail to productively address the motivation/readiness issue. Frustrated practitioners tend to place blame on the individual and think, "If she only would try harder she could do it!" The reality is often that practitioners need to make a greater effort to gain a clearer understanding of a person's situation. In some cases, the answer may be to abandon an unrealized goal and return to the initial stage of the service planning process, to help the individual choose a rehabilitation goal that is consistent with her rehabilitation readiness, as well as her hopes and dreams.

Summary

The PsyR process has three stages: the diagnostic stage, the planning stage and the intervention stage. It begins with a consumer choosing a personally meaningful goal. The first task of the PsyR practitioner is often to help the individual understand what the potential choices are and how to make decisions that will be satisfying. However, before rehabilitation planning takes place, an individual's readiness to begin a rehabilitation process may need to be assessed. Increasing rehabilitation readiness can be an important first step for someone who lacks the confidence to identify and work toward a goal.

Once a goal has been established, the PsyR practitioner helps the individual evaluate the skills that will be required and the environmental supports and resources that will support goal achievement. This approach provides the greatest chance for success. This is in contrast to strategies that focus on an individual's deficits without regard to the specific skills needed for success in a specific environment. Instead, only those skills and resources required for success in the environments of the individual choice are addressed. Skill acquisition can be achieved through a number of strategies including direct skills teaching and social skills training. PsyR practitioners should be knowledgeable about the various community resources available that support success in specific roles and environments; they should also have the interpersonal skills needed to obtain these supports. Environmental modifications such as reasonable accommodations in a work environment may also be required. There are a number of counseling strategies that PsyR practitioners may use during the rehabilitation process, including motivational interviewing and CBT techniques. Most importantly, the PsyR process is person-centered, meaning that the practitioner respects the preferences of the individual at each step of the way.

■ ■ ■ ▬▬▬

Class Exercise

This exercise is designed to give you some familiarity with the diagnostic and planning phases of the PsyR process. You will begin by doing a mock functional assessment and then choose critical skills on which to focus. Finally, you will identify appropriate PsyR interventions aimed at the achievement of an overall rehabilitation goal. Start by carefully reading Anne's story and then complete the assigned tasks:

Anne is a 27-year-old woman who has a serious mental illness. She has spent much of the past eight years in and out of psychiatric hospitals. In between hospitalizations, Anne had lived with her parents. However, the last time she was discharged she was placed in a boarding home, where she now resides. Although Anne is currently stable and doing well in her part-time job as a receptionist in a dentist's office, she is unhappy with her living situation. She would like to move to her own apartment.

Anne tells Bill, her PsyR practitioner, that she would like to live on her own in her own place. Bill assists her in the process of researching local housing opportunities that are affordable for Anne. They determine that even with her monthly Social Security check and the salary from her part-time job, it will be difficult to afford a one-bedroom apartment. However, they are able to place her on a waiting list for a federally subsidized housing complex. A few months later Anne gets a call. An efficiency apartment will become available in three months! Anne is both excited and apprehensive, because she is not totally sure she is prepared to live successfully on her own. She is particularly concerned about money, because she has very limited experience managing her own finances. At the same time she knows that she has some important strengths, such as being able to keep the place clean, do food shopping, and prepare meals. It does concern her that she is unfamiliar with the location of the apartment complex. She has grown comfortable with the neighborhood her boarding home is in, in part because she can catch a bus on the corner that takes her to her job and the mental health center.

Anne sits down with Bill to plan for the move. They begin by writing an overall rehabilitation goal: "Anne will move into an efficiency apartment at the Cedar Hill Apartments by November, 2014." Their next steps are (1) complete a functional assessment of the independent living skills that Anne will need; (2) choose critical skills to begin working on; (3) determine strategies for helping Anne acquire the skills; and (4) identify any resources she will need.

Task 1

Create a list of "independent living skills" that you think are critical to Anne's success in her new apartment. It may be helpful to think about what skills you actually use, if you live independently. However, keep in mind that some of these skills may be necessary for some people to be successful and satisfied in their own home, but are not necessarily critical to Anne's success. Be prepared to discuss the rationale for your choices with the class.

Task 2

Now, rank order your list of skills starting with the ones you think will be most important for Anne to develop. Be able to explain why you think one skill might be more important than another.

Task 3

Consider the two or three skills that you have ranked as most important. What specific strategies would you suggest to help Anne develop those skills?

Task 4

List the resources that Anne already has that will support ORG achievement. Identify any additional resources that you think she will need.

■ ■ ■

Applications of Psychiatric Rehabilitation Principles and Methodology

6

Health and Wellness

Mens sana, corpore sano.

A healthy mind in a healthy body.
Juvenal

CHAPTER OUTLINE

Psychiatric Rehabilitation. http://dx.doi.org/10.1016/B978-0-12-387002-5.00006-8

This chapter begins with the story of Ted, a man in his forties who is successfully coping with a severe mental illness, but succumbs to other health problems and dies prematurely. After reading about Ted, you will learn that his tragic story is not unusual. People with serious mental illness tend to have poor overall health due to medication side effects, lifestyle issues, and poverty, often dying 20 to 25 years earlier than others their age. This chapter introduces you to the areas of health promotion and wellness, how they are consistent with the principles of psychiatric rehabilitation (PsyR), and to an evolving set of services and practices to foster better overall health.

This chapter will provide answers to the following questions:

1. *What are the most common, non-psychiatric health problems faced by persons with serious mental illness?*
2. *What are the factors that contribute to these health concerns?*
3. *Which concerns are unique to persons with serious mental illness? Which are shared with the general population?*
4. *What strategies are being used to help people recover from these health conditions?*
5. *How can the principles of psychiatric rehabilitation be applied in this context?*
6. *What more can be done to help individuals with serious mental illness maintain or regain their physical health?*

The Story of Ted

Ted had struggled for many years with a serious mental illness. The onset of what was eventually diagnosed as schizoaffective disorder had significantly disrupted his life. His illness had features of both schizophrenia and bipolar disorder, at times with rapid recurrences. He obtained a bachelor's degree in computer science at the dawn of the world's romance with computers, but his career had been interrupted by difficult to manage symptoms and relapses; he was always either unemployed or under-employed. Now in his forties, he was frustrated that he never lived up to his potential; there were just too many relapses and too many setbacks. He had a supportive family, but at times he resented his dependence on them.

Over the past several years, there seemed to be more reason for hope. One reason, according to Ted, was a new antipsychotic medication, Zyprexa, a so-called second-generation antipsychotic, which, together with several other medications (some for side effects), was doing a good job managing his symptoms. The more important reason was that Ted had found a new career as a peer provider. He returned to school, completed an advanced graduate degree, and had been working for several years at a PsyR program (see Chapter 13 for more on peer providers). Studying to be a peer provider had an interesting side effect: he became very aware of the mental health system and everything it could potentially do for him. So he secured his own case manager, job coach, and supported housing and joked, "Not only am I a service provider, I am one of the best-served people in the state."

Ted's income from his job gave him independence. He met a woman and had a serious love interest for the first time in many years, but all was not rosy. Ted started to gain weight, a lot of weight for him. He was never very active physically, but he felt himself becoming more sedentary. While he still was active enough to work and do household chores, he just didn't have the energy for a regular exercise regimen. In passing, one of his doctors, said, "Be careful, you are showing signs of developing Type II diabetes; you should lose a few pounds." More disturbingly, he was showing signs of shortness of breath, a classic cardiac symptom. His many helpers in his support network noticed that even with no exertion he was sometimes short of breath. Oddly, in retrospect, no one addressed the issue with Ted or made a referral. A few of his helpers said later, "I didn't see it as my place, didn't think of it as my job." His psychiatrist, who had known Ted for a long time, noticed it as well and, like his medical doctor, suggested that Ted lose some weight. Unfortunately, he did nothing further. Frankly, he was focused on the fact that the very difficult course of Ted's psychiatric illness had been successfully managed with psychotropic medications. He was pleased to note in Ted's case record that Ted was experiencing fewer psychiatric symptoms, was functioning well at work, living independently, and happy with his new relationship; as far as his responsibility was concerned, all was successfully handled.

Just shy of his fiftieth birthday, Ted died suddenly from heart failure. Too late, it was found he had both a cardiac illness and respiratory disorder that further aggravated his heart condition.

Ted's story and the broken hearts it left behind in his family, friends, and girlfriend is a tragic one, and you might be wondering what went wrong. Was it just bad luck that he had developed such serious medical conditions in his forties? Why did Ted seem oblivious or unconcerned about his overall health? Why didn't his mental health providers and colleagues realize that Ted was in urgent need of medical care? Unfortunately, Ted's story is not just an individual tragedy; it is an increasingly common tragedy affecting tens of thousands annually in the United States and some other Western nations. A variety of chronic, comorbid medical conditions are worsening the quality of life of persons with serious mental illness and causing many premature deaths. The poor overall health of these individuals is also interfering with the pursuit and maintenance of their rehabilitation goals.

This chapter provides an overview of the many physical health challenges faced by many persons living with serious mental illnesses and explores the factors that contribute to their poor health. An introduction to the variety of innovations and strategies that are being implemented to address the extreme disparities in both health care and health outcomes is provided. Most of these interventions focus on improving accessibility, co-ordination of services, and the integration of psychiatric care, other health care, and health promotion strategies.

Overview of the Problem

In the United States, the life expectancy of the general population continues to grow. In 2010, the Centers for Disease Control estimated it to be about 78 years (http://www.cdc.gov/nchs/fastats/lifexpec.htm). However, the life expectancy of persons with serious mental illness is much lower and there is some evidence it is actually getting shorter. For many years, data has suggested that the average life span of persons with serious mental illness (SMI) was 15 to 20 years less than in the general population (Berren, Hill, Merkile, Gonzalez, & Santiago, 1994). But in the past decade, even more alarming evidence indicates the risk for lost years of life has accelerated to 25 years earlier than in the general population (Parks, Svendesen, Singer, Foti, & Mauer, 2006). According to a multistate mortality study reported by the National Association of State Mental Health Program Directors, the average age at death was 56.8 (range = 48.9–76.7) (Parks, Svendesen, Singer, & Foti, 2006). A man with schizophrenia has a median life expectancy of 52 years; a woman has 57 years. What are the causes of this very troubling disparity? The higher suicide rate and accident rate among persons with SMI is one cause, but it is not the leading factor. Among individuals with schizophrenia, suicide and injury accounted for 30 to 40 percent of early deaths, but 60 percent of early mortality was due to so-called natural causes, including **cardiovascular** disease, **diabetes**, **respiratory** diseases, and blood-borne **infectious diseases**. In this group, individuals die from cardiovascular disease at more than double the rate of the general population and about triple the rate for diabetes, respiratory diseases, and infectious diseases (Parks et al., 2006).

It is also troubling that there are many individuals such as Ted who receive regular psychiatric care and related supports and services but have serious co-occurring medical conditions that go undetected and/or untreated. These **comorbid** medical conditions, including **circulatory disease**, **diabetes**, **obesity**, **hyperlipidemia**, osteoporosis, **chronic pulmonary disease**, **HIV-related illnesses**, **polydipsia**, and **epilepsy** are found to be consistently elevated in individuals with psychiatric illness (Green, Canuso, Brenner, & Wojcik, 2003; Jeste, Gladsjo, Linamer, & Lacro, 1996; Lambert, Velakoulis, & Pantelis, 2003). Among the most common medical comorbidities is the set of disorders known as **metabolic syndrome**, which is a cluster of risk factors that increase an individual's risk for type 2 diabetes and coronary heart disease (Kelly, Boggs, & Conley, 2007). These risk factors include abdominal obesity (a large waist circumference), elevated triglycerides, elevated low-density cholesterol, hypertension, and elevated fasting glucose (Grundy et al., 2005, as cited in Kelly et al., 2007).

> *The metabolic syndrome has been found to be an independent predictor of all-cause mortality. Although each of the individual components may be a risk factor for cardiovascular morbidity, the existence of several of these abnormalities together poses a risk that may be synergistic. (Kelly et al., 2007, p. 460)*

Among the general population in the United States, approximately 22 percent of adults have metabolic syndrome. In comparison, among people with SMI, the prevalence rate of metabolic syndrome ranges from 30 percent to 60 percent. In one large study, the Clinical Antipsychotic Trials of Intervention Effectiveness (CATIE) discussed in Chapter 3, 43 percent of the participants had metabolic syndrome. Among this group, 83 percent received little or no treatment for this very serious condition (Kelly et al., 2007). In addition to being a major contributor to early mortality, the combination of metabolic syndrome and the vast health care disparities and service fragmentation among the mental health and medical service delivery systems results in significantly reduced quality of life and, as we will explore later, poor rehabilitation outcomes.

In addition to the metabolic syndrome and related conditions, there are a number of health problems that are commonly faced by persons with serious mental illness. These include chronic obstructive pulmonary disease, hepatitis, and (to some extent) HIV, the precursor to AIDS. In a sample of about 1000 people from several US states, 3.1 percent were HIV positive, approximately eight times the estimated US population rate (Rosenberg et al., 2001). In an urban setting, the HIV rate was as high as 6 percent (Himelboch et al., 2011). Prevalence rates of hepatitis B (23.4 percent) and hepatitis C (19.6 percent to 26 percent) were approximately 5 and 11 times the rates for the general population, respectively (Rosenberg et al., 2001; Himelhoch et al., 2011).

In 2007, these staggering statistics led SAMHSA (Substance Abuse and Mental Health Services Administration) to inaugurate its 10 in 10 Campaign. The goal of this campaign was to increase the life expectancy of persons with serious mental illness by 10 years in 10 years' time (2017). This was renamed the Wellness Campaign in 2008.

Factors That Contribute to Poor Health

You may be wondering why people with a serious mental illness are prone to serious comorbid medical conditions. There are a number of contributing factors, including medication side effects, consequences of psychiatric symptoms, lack of access to preventative health care, poor nutrition, sedentary lifestyle, and other unhealthy behaviors. Some of these are related to the effects of poverty.

Medication Side Effects

A substantial body of research documents how psychotropic medications prescribed to ameliorate the symptoms of mental illness also may induce serious adverse health issues, including the metabolic syndrome, insulin resistance, diabetes, hyperglycemia, dyslipidemia, obesity, osteoporosis, and sexual dysfunction (Enger et al., 2004; Joukamaa et al., 2006; Meltzer, 2005; Meyer & Nasarallah, 2003; Parks et al., 2006). Results of the CATIE study indicate that these effects may be greater among those taking newer "atypical" antipsychotics (see Chapter 3 for more on psychotropic medication categories). For example, those taking olanzapine (Zyprexa) were at an increased risk for weight gain, abnormal glucose, and lipid metabolism compared to those taking conventional antipsychotics (Liberman et al., 2005). In addition, research suggests that prolonged use of psychotropic medications also causes a range of oral complications and side effects, including tooth decay, periodontal diseases, and dry mouth, known as xerostomia (Barnes et al., 1988; Friedlander & Liberman, 1991; Velasco & Bullon, 1999). Dental and oral hygiene problems are related to both medication side effects, particularly dry mouth (xerostomia), and irregular or poor dental care. Xerostomia leads to gum disease, which leads to the loss of teeth. Infectious diseases have a higher prevalence among persons with serious mental illness. The link between oral health and general health, particularly cardiovascular functioning, has been well established (e.g., the plaque on one's teeth and in one's arteries is correlated) and makes this an additional concern (Almomani, Brown, & Williams, 2006).

Unhealthy Behaviors

Another contributing factor to poor oral health is the lack of personal daily habits—in oral hygiene, failure to brush or floss and infrequent visits or no visits to the dentist because of a lack of accessibility and affordability. Even when dental care is affordable and accessible, some individuals, particularly those with a profile of negative symptom syndromes, infrequently seek regular dental care (Armaiz et al., 2011). There is also evidence people with serious mental illness are less likely to pursue regular medical care and age- and gender-appropriate screenings for cancer and other disorders.

The high incidence of medical comorbidity and increased rates of mortality among people with psychiatric disabilities may be attributed in part to unhealthy, high-risk behaviors. These behaviors include substance abuse, smoking, lack of exercise, and poor diet (Brown, Birtwistle, Roe, & Thompson, 1999). Among individuals with mental illness, estimates are that approximately half also have a substance use disorder, as will be discussed in Chapter 9. Substance use further increases the likelihood that an individual will engage in risky behaviors, including intravenous drug use, needle sharing, and unprotected sex (Davidson et al., 2001). These activities are implicated in elevated rates of HIV and other blood-borne viral infections, such as hepatitis B and C (Rosenberg et al., 2004; Corrigan, Mueser, Bond, Drake, & Solomon, 2008). Although only a small proportion of persons with serious mental illness are very active sexually, even those who are inactive often have had past sexual encounters that are unprotected.

A very high percentage of people with mental illness are nicotine-dependent, primarily through smoking. The reported rates of nicotine dependence range from 60 to 80 percent (Corrigan et al., 2008; Parks et al., 2006). In addition to the high rates of use, people with mental illness tend to be heavier smokers than the average smoker, causing them to experience more toxic exposure (Williams et al., 2010; Parks et al., 2006). Smoking is a known risk factor for cancer, chronic respiratory diseases, and cardiovascular disease and is the single behavior most associated with increased early mortality.

The prevalence of being overweight and having a sedentary lifestyle is also higher among people living with a mental illness as compared to those without a mental illness. Approximately 40 to 60 percent of people with schizophrenia are overweight. According to Dickerson and colleagues (2006), 50 percent of women and 41 percent of men with psychiatric diagnoses studied are obese as compared to 27 percent and 20 percent, respectively, among a comparison group. While individuals with mental illness are often overweight, they generally do not meet the United States Department of Agriculture's (USDA) recommended daily intake for fruits, vegetables, grains, and dairy and often eat fewer than the recommended number of meals per day (Kilbourne et al., 2007; Strassnig et al., 2003). The potential reasons for this increased obesity and poor diet are varied and include restricted meal choice due to congregate living or limited income, side effects of psychotropic medications as already discussed, and poor education related to healthy diets. Sedentary lifestyles may also be a result of medication side effects, unemployment, and lack of financial resources and psychiatric symptomatology.

Psychiatric Symptomatology: Negative Symptoms and Depression

There is some evidence that psychiatric symptoms impact the health status of persons with serious mental illness by contributing to a sedentary lifestyle and to neglect of one's health, including routine care. An interesting example comes from dental care and oral health. Some studies have found that poor oral hygiene and worse dental outcomes are associated with the negative symptoms of psychoses but not the positive symptoms. You will recall from Chapter 2 that negative symptoms include lack of energy, lethargy (anergia), and lack of motivation (avolition), whereas positive symptoms include such things as hallucinations and delusions. People with schizophrenia tend to receive worse dental care and have poorer oral health than the general population (Neilsen et al., 2011). Yet it turns out that positive symptoms are not associated with poor oral health, but negative symptoms are (Arnaiz et al., 2011). This suggests that these specific symptoms of the illnesses themselves are interfering with the motivation to pursue regular care.

It has long been known that depressive symptoms interfere with the pursuit of regular medical care and sometimes with neglect of one's health. Like those with negative symptoms, many individuals with depressed affect are sedentary. The irony is that exercise in itself may have an anti-depressive, affect-lifting effect and has been proposed as a treatment for depression. Of course, the trick is to succeed in encouraging a person who is depressed to want to exercise.

Inadequate Access to Health Care and Discrimination

Individuals with mental illness often receive insufficient preventive services, timely diagnostic care, or high-quality medical treatment. They are less likely to receive primary care services, routine testing, cardiovascular procedures, cancer screenings, and dental care than others (Parks et al., 2006). According to the CATIE study, most individuals who develop complications from psychotropic medications are either not treated for them or treated inadequately (Nasrallah et al., 2006). Rates of nontreatment are 30.2 percent for diabetes, 62.4 percent for hypertension, and 88 percent for dyslipidemia. The explanations for these discrepancies in care include limited financial resources, transportation issues, and prior negative experiences with the health care system. Another factor that may hinder the diagnosis and treatment of medical conditions among people with serious mental illness is a lack of education on the part of medical and mental health care providers. Currently, the education that many medical and mental health care staff receive does not adequately prepare them to work collaboratively with people with mental illness to help them reduce their comorbidities and prevent premature death (Swarbrick, Hutchinson, & Gill, 2008). Consider the following situation:

> Lou had an intestinal blockage that had become infected. It was very painful, and like many people with psychiatric disorders, his psychotic symptoms became aggravated. Lou called 911 saying that he needed help; when asked what for, his responses were incoherent. The police came and brought him to an emergency room of a hospital where he had previous psychiatric admissions. Because of that history, his somewhat incoherent speech, and his growing agitation, he was admitted to the psychiatric ward, where he spent several days complaining of pain. Initially, the staff either did not understand him or were not convinced his abdominal symptoms were real. According to a friend who visited Lou at the hospital, "They were just focused on his psychiatric symptoms. Lou went into the hospital in serious pain, but like a lot of people he had trouble explaining it." Finally, Lou was found on the floor, writhing and crying, by a nurse. He begged for help saying he could not take the pain any longer. He was transferred to a medical-surgical floor, but before the work-ups were complete the infection burst, his intestine ruptured, and he died from sepsis. That Lou's psychiatric symptoms were exacerbated by his physical illness is not at all uncommon. Unfortunately, the tendency for health care professionals to concentrate and treat the psychiatric symptoms first is probably contributing to the negative health outcomes.

Thornicroft and his colleagues (2007) raise a concern they dub "diagnostic overshadowing"; that is, the psychiatric diagnosis overshadows other issues about the whole person, including aspects of the health and other disorders. Some practitioners attribute somatic (bodily) symptoms to one's psychiatric disorders, as mentioned in the previous anecdote. Others may not feel comfortable with people with mental illness and do not explain all the choices for care, thinking they will not understand the options or will not follow through on them. Some may even wish to avoid seeing the person again. Many service recipients report they perceive stigma among health care professionals and feel they get discriminatory treatment. There is evidence that they do receive discriminatory treatment.

Even when people with serious mental illness get services, they are not always the best or "right" services for their condition. For example, people with mental illness are more likely to have a tooth extracted compared to others who might get a restorative procedure for the same dental condition. Those with heart conditions see a general medical practitioner more frequently than others their age, yet when they have specific cardiac complaints, they are less likely to see a cardiologist. When diagnosed with a specific condition, such as blockage of the coronary arteries, they are less likely to receive a cardiac procedure like an angioplasty or bypass surgery (Mitchell & Lawrence, 2011). What is the reason for these treatment disparities?

In the United States, it may be due in part to the lack of insurance or lower quality public sector insurance, but this disparity also seems to exist in other countries where this is not a concern. In part, it may be due to refusal of certain procedures, but this is an incomplete explanation. A very likely explanation is that health care practitioners' stigmatizing beliefs based on fear and misunderstanding result in discriminatory practices (Thornicroft et al., 2007).

A physician colleague of the authors offered a different explanation; he called it a consequence of the "seven-minute office visit." You may have noted that some of your own visits to the doctor are very brief and are completed before you have raised everything you wish to discuss. He said any "complex patient," meaning a person with multiple, serious conditions, gets inadequate attention due to the very brief nature of office visits. He said few of his colleagues have or take the time to consider the multiple interacting conditions of the whole person and focus on what is most salient. This happens not only to "psychiatric patients"; diagnostic overshadowing (a label applied based on the first serious condition diagnosed) takes place with "cardiac patients," "COPD patients," and so on. For example, the back pain of an elderly woman who is "a heart patient" gets thorough screening for a cardiac cause, but osteoporosis, the actual cause, is ignored.

In any case, this raises a number of points. Consistent with principles of overall wellness, the dignity and worth of every individual, and the individualization inherent in person-centered approaches, PsyR practitioners and other health care professionals need to be aware that whatever the cause, persons with serious mental illness are receiving disparate care compared to others. Special efforts may be necessary to overcome prejudices associated with stigma, communication problems, or care coordination challenges.

Poverty Affects Health

As indicated in the previous sections, part of the reason that many individuals with serious mental illnesses have unhealthy diets and lack of access to quality health care is their limited incomes. As noted in Chapter 10, researchers have estimated that at most about 30 percent of this population participates in the workforce (Bazelon Center for Mental Health Law, 2011; Cook, 2006). While some of these individuals may have other financial resources from previous employment or from family members, the logical conclusion is that many of the roughly 70 percent who are unemployed and also some who are employed are living in poverty.

Multiple studies conducted worldwide have concluded people living in poverty are far less healthy than those with better economic resources and, in fact, the lower a person is on the socioeconomic ladder, the shorter his or her life expectancy (Wilkinson & Marmot, 2003). This has led to a growing awareness that health outcomes are greatly affected by a number of factors in the social environment of poor individuals. These factors have been called the social determinants of health (Wilkinson & Marmot, 2003) and they include:

- Stress associated with poverty (e.g., worrying about having enough money for food, rent, or medication)
- Social isolation and social exclusion, particularly among those in extreme poverty, such as people living on the streets
- Unemployment, or lack of steady employment, or low-level jobs (in which people do not have benefits such as health insurance or paid sick days)
- Addiction to alcohol, tobacco, and other substances
- Lack of access to healthy food
- Modes of transportation that lead to sedentary lifestyles and cause pollution

At a quick glance, some of the social determinants of health may not surprise you, for example, that people in extreme poverty may have access to very little food, and may suffer from malnutrition, which is clearly a serious health problem. But examining the situation more closely, you will find that many people on limited incomes in rich countries have plenty of food available, but do not have ready access to affordable, healthy foods. For example, some inner city neighborhoods do not have large grocery stores nearby that sell fresh produce or quality sources of protein such as lean meats and fresh fish. The food that is available is often high in starch and fat, which if consumed over long periods of time, can lead to obesity and health conditions such as metabolic syndrome. You also may not readily associate factors like unemployment, low-level jobs, and social isolation with poor physical health, but experts on social and economic policy have concluded that:

> *Good health involves reducing levels of educational failure, reducing insecurity and unemployment, and improving housing standards. Societies that enable all citizens to play a full and useful role in the social, economic, and cultural life of their society will be healthier than those where people face insecurity, exclusion, and deprivation. (Wilkinson & Marmot, 2003, p. 11)*

CONTROVERSIAL ISSUE
Early death and antipsychotic medication: Is it worth the risk?

Are antipsychotic drugs worth the risk of medical complications and the possibility of early death? Given reports of increased early mortality among people taking second-generation antipsychotic drugs in the United States and the United Kingdom, two Finnish studies addressed this issue and concluded "yes," especially when the comparison is to no psychotropic medication at all.

A Finnish study by Joukamaa and colleagues (2006) raised serious concerns. They found that persons with schizophrenia had a significantly higher likelihood of early death than other persons not using medications. The risk of early mortality among people with schizophrenia was almost three times that of the general population. After adjusting for other illnesses, blood pressure, cholesterol, body mass index, smoking, exercise, alcohol, and education, the risk was still twice that of the general population. Furthermore, they found that the number of antipsychotic medications used was correlated with higher mortality, with each medication doubling the risk of mortality. They concluded there is a need to determine whether high mortality is inherent with the illness or a result of its treatment.

Tiihonen and colleagues (2009) found that among people with psychosis, there is a higher risk of early death among those who take no antipsychotic medication compared to those who do, but the causes of death can be very different. Within the group who do take antipsychotic medication, the risk varies markedly based upon the particular medicine. Ironically, clozapine, which was once removed from the market due to a very serious but rare side effect, is among the safest options, perhaps in part because it is more closely monitored than other medicines.

From 1996 to 2006, the percentage of Finns with schizophrenia taking second-generation antipsychotic medications rose fivefold from 13 percent to 64 percent. Second-generation antipsychotic medicines are known for side effects of increased weight gain and association with diabetes and hypertension. In 1996, Finns with schizophrenia lived 25 years less than those without those disorders. In 2006, the gap was not larger but actually a little narrower, still dying an appalling 22.5 years earlier. However, the highest risk for early death was among those taking a second-generation antipsychotic, quetiapine, commonly known in the United States by the brand name Seroquel. The next highest risk was a first-generation antipsychotic medication, perphenazine (brand name: Trilafon), and the lowest risk was clozapine, an older atypical medication. Importantly, long-term cumulative exposure (7 to 11 years) to any antipsychotic treatment was associated with lower mortality compared to no drug use at all. But among people with one or more prescriptions for any antipsychotic drug, an inverse relation between mortality and duration of cumulative use was noted (i.e., mortality increases with the addition of each drug).

So what do the two studies show us? People with schizophrenia live much shorter lives than their countrymen. The shortening of their life appears to be related to the illness and its consequences. Taking medication is better than not taking it. However, specific medications have higher or lower impacts on mortality and this should be considered. Most second-generation antipsychotic medications are harmful in this regard, first-generation medications are slightly less harmful, and clozapine is best. Also, the addition of more than one antipsychotic medication is particularly harmful to longevity. Of course, adding additional medications may also indicate differences in the severity of the illness that are predictive of early mortality in themselves.

History of Institutionalization and Congregate Living

Institutionalization and other congregate living seem to be associated with a number of risk factors for the problems discussed. Starchy, fatty diets are associated with weight gain and metabolic syndrome. As mentioned above, institutional living is also associated with hepatitis. Those who have been institutionalized are very likely to have respiratory disorders. In one institutional sample, over 31 percent had COPD, 19 percent had interstitial disease—another lung disorder, and 5 percent had tuberculosis (Sanchez-Mora et al., 2007). Pneumonia and COPD are common causes of death in psychiatric hospitals (Copeland et al., 2007). Of course, rampant smoking is a contributing factor. Reduction of smoking and community living will reduce the risks of these disorders. If one acquires them, careful coordination of pulmonary and psychiatric medications is necessary to control multiple and interacting side effects.

Health Problems Interfere with the Attainment of Rehabilitation Goals

Are the physical health problems of persons with SMI relevant to PsyR? The short answer is yes. As you learned in Chapter 4, the overall goals of the PsyR field are recovery, community integration, and improved quality of life. Poor health and a lack of wellness work against recovery. Poor physical health detracts from one's ability to be an active community member. Poor physical health diminishes quality of life in many ways. Consider how your quality of life is diminished when you are not feeling well. Consider how a friend or relative's quality of life is impacted by a chronic disease that causes pain, discomfort, lower energy level, dietary restrictions, mobility challenges, etc.

In addition to the negative consequences of medical comorbidity, poor physical health is a barrier to achieving rehabilitation goals. Psychiatric symptoms can be exacerbated by medical problems with individuals experiencing more severe psychosis, increased depression, and increased suicide attempts (Corrigan et al., 2008). Additionally, functional outcomes—including employment, independent living, utilization of support services, hospitalization rates, and mental health service utilization—are all negatively impacted by the occurrence of serious medical diseases (McIntyre et al., 2006; Sullivan, Han, Moore, & Kotria, 2006). According to Swarbrick and her colleagues (2008), the lack of optimal health is a powerful contributor to the disability, isolation, and lack of community participation people with mental illness often experience.

Melinda is a 42-year-old woman diagnosed with bipolar disorder in her late twenties. Both her manic and depressive episodes sometimes included psychotic symptoms such as grandiose and persecutory delusions. So, in addition to taking antidepressant medications and a mood stabilizer, she has been taking antipsychotic medications for more than a decade. She has steadily gained weight since antipsychotics were added to her medication regimen. She is currently obese, and at 5' 4" she weighs close to 190 lbs., more than 60 lbs. more than she weighed when she became ill. Like many others in her situation, she is currently diagnosed as having metabolic syndrome. The first consequence of Melinda's weight gain was its effect upon her appearance, but now she is more worried about her health. She is also frustrated by the fact that her physical health status has a negative impact on other areas of her life. Her psychiatric symptoms are currently stable, and for the past few years she has felt very hopeful about her recovery. She has been working with a career development counselor who helped her get a job as a part-time administrative assistant for a large corporation. A few months ago, she enrolled in a graduate-level course required for the MBA program she hopes to start in the fall. But Melinda worries that her health problems are getting in the way of her career goals. She says, "My weight causes stress on my joints. Many days I'm in pain and my doctor says I need to have a knee replacement soon, which would require me to take a medical leave from work and might delay my admission to the MBA program. My employer has been asking me to come on full-time, which is great, but if I am gone a few months because of surgery, I fear that I will lose that opportunity, and even worse, they may not want me back at all." Her health also causes low energy, and even on days when the pain isn't so bad it is hard for her to move around easily. She says, "I love being back in college, but it's hard to catch a bus after work and get to class. I used to love to walk, but now it is such a struggle. Some days I feel so exhausted that I can barely move." Melinda concludes, "It has been a hard road learning to cope with bipolar disorder and at times I feel great that I have come so far and I'm finally getting my life back. But other days, I just want to stay home because I feel so crummy. I'm only 42, but I often feel like an old lady! It's discouraging to have worked so hard on my recovery only to be set back by all of my other illnesses."

Strategies for Addressing Comorbid Illnesses

There is an extensive body of literature on demonstration projects seeking to improve both the physical and mental health outcomes of persons living with SMI by integrating their mental health and primary health care; unfortunately, these programs have not yet been widely implemented. The models described in the literature include use of assertive care or special medical care coordinators, co-location of mental health and primary care services, formal affiliations between mental health agencies and primary care providers, adaptations of assertive community treatment (ACT, discussed in Chapter 8), health or medical "homes," and improved illness or disease self-management. Considering the needs of the people being served, the available resources, and characteristics of specific health care systems, no single approach is likely to be suitable for all situations.

Assertive Care Coordination

A promising approach for promoting better overall health care for persons with serious mental illness is the use of a coordinator, sometimes referred to as "counselor" or "care manager," responsible for overseeing integration of services. The World Health Organization (WHO) described such coordinators as "crucial in steering programs around [these] challenges and driving forward the integration process" (WHO, 2008, p. 54). The *Integrating Mental Health and Primary Care: A Global Perspective* report cites examples of countries that have employed coordinators to better serve the mental health and medical care of its citizens, including Argentina, India, Belize, Iran, Saudi Arabia, South Africa, and Australia (WHO, 2008). The Bazelon Center for Mental Health Law, a nonprofit advocacy organization, views health care access for people with disabilities as a critically important issue. In 2004, they published *Get It Together: How to Integrate Physical and Mental Health Care for People with Serious Mental Disorders* in order to highlight US states that are evaluating collaborative models of care that employ counselors or care managers. The report found that some states have made special efforts to address the coordination of primary care and mental health for people with SMI. A common problem noted by the contributors to the Bazelon report during their site visits in several states was the lack of feedback between mental health and primary care providers after making a referral to the other category of provider. The Hogg Foundation for Mental Health has also attempted to identify innovative programs to integrate mental health and medical care around the country. *Connecting Body and Mind: A Resource Guide to Integrated Health Care in Texas and the United States* (Hogg Foundation, 2008) addresses the problems associated with the limited capacity of mental health centers to provide on-site primary care. The report identifies the critical importance of determining ways to improve how referrals to outside primary care providers are made, such as the enhanced referral model. This model employs a nurse who assists consumers with accessing primary medical care, facilitates communication between providers and systems, and helps consumers follow through with medical treatment. The nurse may also provide health education and advocacy to help consumers overcome barriers to accessing primary care.

Druss and his colleagues report on a promising approach (Druss et al., 2010a). Nurse care managers provide communication and advocacy for the individual with medical providers. They also provide health education and support in overcoming system-level fragmentation and barriers to primary medical care. Using this intervention at a one-year follow-up, nearly three times as many preventive services had been provided compared to usual care. Individuals also were more likely to have a primary care provider and to receive evidence-based cardiac and metabolic services, reducing their cardio-vascular risk. They also showed more improvement on mental health status indicators than those without care coordinators.

Co-location of Services

Co-location of mental health and physical health services—literally, offering them at the same location—is a best practice for improving the health status of persons with psychiatric disabilities (Bazelon Center for Mental Health Law, 2004; Corrigan, Mueser, Bond, Drake, & Solomon, 2008; NASMHPD, 2006; Horvitz-Lennon, Kilbourne, & Pincus, 2006). Co-located services improve both access to health care and health outcomes

(Corrigan, Mueser, Bond, Drake, & Solomon, 2008; Druss, Rohrbaugh, Levinson, & Rosenheck, 2001). There are several versions of the co-location approach. The first is primary care embedded in a community mental health center or the placing of a health practitioner such as a nurse or physician assistant at an existing mental health care agency (Bazelon Center for Mental Health Law, 2004). This model has been studied and successfully replicated in Veterans Administration services, the provider of medical care for US veterans of military service (Druss, Rohrbaugh, Levinson, & Rosenheck, 2001; Druss & von Esenwein, 2006).

Druss and his colleagues (2001) compared the provision of overall medical services integrated within a mental health clinic to services delivered the usual way: in two separate clinics, one devoted to psychiatric care, the other clinic specializing in general medical care. Those individuals served in the integrated care clinic had more primary care visits, had more routine preventive screening procedures completed per established clinical guidelines, and had better medical outcomes than those treated the usual way, all at no higher cost (Druss et al., 2001).

Another approach that creatively unifies services integrates a community mental health center (CMHC) and a federally qualified health center (FQHC) (Schuffman, 2008). FQHCs are federally supported local medical clinics in the United States that are low or no cost to people who are lower income or who have no other place to go. This combined CMHC–FQHC approach has several features that address the lack of clinical integration that often contributes to lack of quality and access to health care (Horvitz-Lennon, Kilbourne, & Pincus, 2006). For example, issues of confidentiality are successfully overcome in unified programs, and the use of integrated medical records increases communication between the two types of services. Finally, this model offers a "… *no wrong door* approach to all of health care [which is] more friendly, less stigmatizing, and easier to access" (Bazelon Center for Mental Health Law, 2004, p. 6).

A final model of co-located care entails mental health specialists working within a primary health care site—for example, adding both a master's-level mental health practitioner to coordinate care and an Advanced Practice Nurse (APN) to provide mental health screenings and preventive care (Schuffman, 2008). Mental health practitioners located in primary care settings not only increase access to quality care by diagnosing and treating mental health conditions, but they can also train primary care providers to better understand the needs of persons who have both physical illnesses and psychiatric disorders. The most successful pilot programs have focused on persons with less severe psychiatric disorders, since this model is predicated on persons receiving their mental health services from their primary care practitioners. These settings should have close relationships with community mental health centers (CMHCs) so they can refer persons with more serious mental illnesses for additional supports and services (Bazelon Center for Mental Health Law, 2004).

While co-location has promising results for improved access to care and health outcomes, there are relatively few examples of this model in practice (Horvitz-Lennon, Kilbourne, & Pincus, 2006). Nevertheless, when applied, this model can improve the quality and access of health care for persons with psychiatric disabilities, reduce health disparities, and improve health outcomes and has found positive results in terms of service user satisfaction.

Formal Affiliations

Formal agreements and collaborations for combined mental and physical health care have primarily been between health care centers or individual general practitioners and CMHCs (Horvitz-Lennon et al., 2006). There are also examples of formal affiliations between CMHCs and university medical centers (Schuffman, 2008). Alternately, colleges utilize faculty and students who provide direct care for either mental or physical health conditions (Bazelon Center for Mental Health Law, 2004). Affiliations can also include governmental entities, nonprofit associations representing mental health and substance use services, and programs that provide medical case management for Medicaid enrollees (Overstreet, 2006).

Adapting Assertive Community Treatment

Another approach to integrating mental health and primary health care is the adaptation of Assertive Community Treatment (ACT) teams (see Chapter 8 for a detailed description of ACT). Like others with serious mental illness, people served by ACT teams are often in poor health. Persons receiving ACT services have, on average, three chronic health conditions in addition to the diagnosis of severe mental illness (Ceilley, Cruz, & Denko, 2006). While most ACT teams include nurses, they are not typically utilized to focus on improvement of non-psychiatric health outcomes (Horvitz-Lennon, Kilbourne, & Pincus, 2006). But nurses on ACT teams can be used to provide screening and assessment of health, basic nursing assistance, coordination of services, scheduling of medical visits, and reproductive health education (Morse & McKasson, 2005; Phillips et al., 2001). An experimental model of ACT, called NPACT, compared ACT as usual to an enhanced team, which included an Advanced Practice Nurse (APN) and a peer provider to address modifiable health-promoting behaviors (Kane & Blank, 2004). The persons served found this model satisfying, had a reduction in psychiatric symptoms, and had improved community functioning.

The Promise of Health or Medical Primary Care "Homes"

In recognition of the fact that there are many individuals who have multiple chronic or long-term disorders that require special management and coordination of care, the Affordable Care Act of 2010 in the United States created an optional benefit for US states to establish Health Homes to coordinate care for people who have one or more of these conditions. The health home is not a place, but more a single point of responsibility. These organizations are expected to operate under a "whole-person" philosophy integrating and coordinating all primary, acute, mental health, and long-term services needed to treat the individual. People with severe mental illness are explicitly mentioned in this law, as are chronic conditions including substance abuse, asthma, diabetes, heart disease, obesity, and HIV/AIDS. Comprehensive care management provided by health homes include care coordination, health promotion, comprehensive transitional care/follow-up, patient and family support, and referral to community and social support services. A health home provider can be a physician, a multidisciplinary team of health care professionals, a group practice, a mental health center, a federally qualified health center, a clinic, or a hospital. One can read more about Health Homes at Medicaid.gov (Center for Medicare and Medicaid Services, 2013).

Health homes grew out of the concept of "primary care medical homes," pioneered by Dr. Jeffrey Brenner of Camden, NJ, and others. As recounted in *The New Yorker* magazine, he found that a small but significant proportion of the people living in Camden were accounting for much of its medical expenses, using its emergency response services, emergency rooms, and hospital stays. Literally 1 percent of the people were accounting for one-third of the medical expenses incurred there. While a great deal of money was being spent, their care was very poor and uncoordinated, and was resulting in poor quality of life and premature death. He tried a "primary care medical home" approach that supports individuals in learning to manage their own care and ensures that they and their families are fully informed partners in developing integrated, comprehensive care plans. A team of care providers is wholly accountable for a person's physical and mental health care needs, including prevention and wellness, acute care, and chronic care. This team coordinates care across all elements of the broader health care system, including specialty care, hospitals, home health care, and community services and supports. Patients experience shorter waiting times, enhanced in-person contact, and 24/7 electronic or telephone access and have alternative methods of communication with their health care practitioners available. The home is also dedicated to quality improvement through the use of health information technology shared among all the providers in the city and county. The model has been replicated throughout the United States.

Although it remains untested in many locales, encouraging research is emerging. An evaluation of 46 such medical homes entitled *Benefits of Implementing the Patient-Centered Medical Home: A Review of Cost & Quality Results* (Nielsen et al., 2012) found that program participants demonstrated up to 70 percent reductions in emergency room visits, 40 percent lower hospital readmissions, and hundreds of millions of health care dollars saved. Primary care visits more than doubled, diabetes care improved markedly, yet overall costs dropped.

> … *the findings are clear, consistent, and compelling: Data demonstrates that the "Primary Care Medical Home" improves health outcomes, enhances the patient and provider experience of care, and reduces expensive, unnecessary hospital and emergency department utilization. The results meet the goals of the Institute for Healthcare Improvement's "Triple Aim" for better health outcomes, better care, and lower costs. (Nielsen et al., 2012, p. 2)*

The health or medical home concept holds promise for people with SMI who have comorbid medical disorders.

Promotion of Readiness for Lifestyle Changes

To the extent that lifestyle is contributing to the poor health of persons with SMIs, making changes such as healthier eating or increasing exercise can be very effective in promoting overall health. But as anyone who has struggled to eat healthier foods or implement an exercise regimen knows, actually changing habits is very challenging. Therefore, promoting readiness for change is a recommended principle in health promotion for persons with mental illness (Hutchinson et al., 2006). The construct of readiness comes from Prochaska and DiClemente's *Transtheoretical Model of Behavior Change*, which identifies six stages of change (Archie et al., 2007). Interventions matched to the stages have proven successful in assisting with health changes across different types of health behaviors and multiple behaviors concurrently in the general population and persons with psychiatric disabilities (Rogers et al., 2001). Readiness-based interventions are person-centered and do not require people to be prepared for active change; rather, the opposite is true. For example, someone in the precontemplation stage of healthy lifestyle changes may benefit from **motivational interviewing** (see Chapters 5 and 9 for more on this counseling technique) to elicit personal goals and explore the benefits and drawbacks of changes. Someone in the contemplation stage may benefit from exploring the benefits and costs of changing or staying the same. Someone in the action stage could benefit from learning positive self-reward strategies to reinforce their changes (Archie et al., 2007). A number of effective interventions have been used to target particular unhealthy behaviors. Some of these are described in the sections ahead.

Chronic Disease Self-management: HARP

Disease self-management is a peer-lead approach to dealing with chronic disorders and promoting a healthy lifestyle. Peers—literally, one's equals in terms of a particular characteristic or condition—lead these approaches (Chapter 13 will cover peer and mutual self-help approaches to PsyR). The Health and Recovery Program (HARP) is a specific peer-facilitated approach (Druss et al., 2010b) adapted from the Chronic Disease Self-Management Program (CDSMP) developed by Kate Lorig and her colleagues (Lorig, 2006). Led by two peer educators with chronic medical conditions, any given group typically includes people with a range of long-term conditions such as diabetes and arthritis. Six group sessions address self-management tasks common across different chronic health conditions. The intervention includes action planning and feedback, modeling of behaviors by peers and mutual problem-solving by participants, reinterpretation of symptoms, and education in specific techniques of managing illnesses.

HARP adapts the CDSMP to mental health consumers. Mental health peers, a health educator, and the developer of the CDSMP considered the specific issues faced by persons with serious mental illness in managing their health concerns and developed a manual, taking into account possible cognitive limitations of the participants. It included a tracking system of specific self-management tasks, including medications, upcoming appointments, dietary intake, and physical activity. Each participant was paired with a partner, with the two working together to execute plans and achieve goals. Special materials were added on the mind-body connection and the need to coordinate psychotropic and other medications. Also included was a section on psychiatric advanced directives for when an individual is incapable of making his or her own medical-psychiatric decisions due to severe symptomatology. The diet and exercise sections took into account the limited incomes of the participants, including purchasing healthy foods on a budget and safely exercising in one's own home. Participants in the HARP program had a significant improvement in what is known as "patient activation." Patient activation reflects the person's perception of his or her ability to manage illness and health behaviors and act as the effective manager of their own illness. In addition to general approaches like HARP, there are specific programs dealing with specific health-related problems or behaviors of self-help or mutual self-help.

Smoking Cessation

Smoking and tobacco dependence are serious detriments to good health. Smoking is known to be a major contributor to heart disease, respiratory disorders, and cancer. Williams and colleagues (2010) report that more than 50 percent of individuals with psychiatric illnesses are tobacco dependent (p. 243).

Motivational interviewing, discussed in Chapter 5 and also in Chapter 9, can be an effective strategy. Steinberg and colleagues (2004) reported that individuals with schizophrenia have a much higher prevalence of tobacco smoking, a lower cessation rate, and a higher incidence of tobacco-related diseases than the general population, but even one motivational interviewing session increases the likelihood of pursuit of cessation interventions. Interestingly, motivational interventions have also been successfully used to promote exercise (Beebe et al., 2011).

One program that has been successful in reducing tobacco use among people with serious psychiatric illnesses is called the CHOICES program (Williams et al., 2010). CHOICES stands for Consumers Helping Others Improve their Condition by Ending Smoking. This innovative program is a collaboration among a university, a chapter of the Mental Health Association, and a state mental health agency. CHOICES employs peer counselors to provide education, support, and advocacy. They receive extensive training and provide educational presentations to consumers and providers about the hazards of smoking and the availability of smoking cessation treatments and resources. They meet individually with consumers to identify the effects of smoking on the persons' health and finances and provide a "one-session motivational intervention" meant to encourage the individual to access smoking cessation treatment (Williams et al., 2010, p. 245). As non-smoking former smokers themselves, they also serve as role models. A study of the outcomes of the CHOICES program compared post-intervention data with baseline data from another study with similar participants using the same instruments (Steinberg et al., 2004; reported in Williams et al., 2010). The findings suggest that CHOICES effectively increases the number of smokers who are seriously considering quitting within the next 30 days and those seriously considering quitting within the next six months. Furthermore, at one-month and six-month follow-up points, participants had significantly decreased their tobacco use. Participants also reported at both time periods having discussed quitting smoking with their doctors and mental health providers, having attended tobacco cessation groups, and having used tobacco treatment medications.

Weight Reduction Programs

There is widespread recognition that the use of antipsychotic medication, especially many of the second-generation medications, is associated with significant weight gain. This weight gain is implicated in increases in type II diabetes and cardiovascular and respiratory problems, among others. Strategies to help individuals reduce their weight while taking antipsychotic medications demonstrate small but significant weight loss (Faulkner, Cohn, & Remington, 2010; Alvarez-Jimenez et al., 2006; Brown, Goetz, Van Sciver, Sullivan, & Hamera, 2006). It is unclear whether this weight loss is maintained over time. Typical psychosocial interventions for weight loss include goal setting, nutritional counseling, strategies for self-management (e.g., portion control), self-monitoring (e.g., regular weigh-ins), and lifestyle modifications. While many studies reported modest weight loss, few studies reported positive changes in medical markers such as blood glucose levels and blood pressure, possibly due to lack of follow-up. A review of weight gain studies (Faulkner, Cohn, & Remington, 2010) determined that modest weight loss was achievable. Considering the increasing weight problems for persons in general, it isn't surprising that persons taking medications that can cause extreme weight gain find it difficult to lose weight.

Dealing with Hepatitis

It is recommended that all individuals with SMI be screened for hepatitis and treated if present, because long-term liver disease is painful and fatal. In addition it is infectious, putting others at risk. Rosenberg and his colleagues (Rosenberg et al., 2004; Himelhoch et al., 2011) propose that a public health intervention, known by the acronym STIRR, be used for people with SMIs. STIRR stands for *screen, test, immunize, reduce risk*, and *refer*. It is brief (requiring approximately one hour per client) and is delivered at the site of mental health care by a mobile team of specialists. Clients are provided with risk screening, testing for HIV and hepatitis, immunization for hepatitis A and B, risk-reduction counseling, and treatment referral. They are also provided educational guidance on how to reduce the risk of future infection or, if already infected, how to reduce the risk of infecting others.

Wellness

Beyond reducing the impact of illness, PsyR is about the enhancement of one's quality of life. In other words, it is not just the better health outcomes but also the promotion of a healthy, satisfying lifestyle. This is not just the absence of the disease or the minimization of its impact but the promotion of **wellness**.

> *Wellness is a conscious, deliberate process that requires a person to become aware of and make choices for a more satisfying lifestyle. Creating a lifestyle centered on wellness means continually seeking more information about how we can improve ourselves and realize our full potential in the eight dimensions outlined. (Swarbrick, 2012)*

Eight Dimensions of Wellness

Wellness has been conceptualized as having eight dimensions. These include one's environment, spirituality, occupation, social life, recreation, intellectual life, financial status, and physical health (Swarbrick, 2006). Figure 6.1 provides an overview of these dimensions.

A lack of wellness could be a lack of balance in any of these areas. For example, one might work many hours a week (occupation dimension) and have little or no time to engage in desired social and recreational activities. Another person may be happy with her social life, but unhappy with her physical well-being. A recent retiree may be well set financially and for the first time in his life have ample time to socialize, recreate, and read the classics, yet feel lost without a worthy occupation or a sense of purpose in life. Still another person may be very unhappy in a variety of these areas. Not surprisingly, the dimensions are often interrelated—for example, occupational and financial status. Unfortunately, for many persons with SMI, a lack of physical well-being disrupts the other dimensions of wellness all too frequently.

Consistency with Goals of Psychiatric Rehabilitation

Attending to comorbid issues through the promotion of health and wellness is consistent with the overall goals of the PsyR field: recovery, community integration, and improved quality of life (see Chapter 4). If one's physical health is well managed and one has stamina and feels energetic, the quality of one's life is both objectively and subjectively better. Feeling well makes it easier to engage in social and recreational activities in the community. It also makes it easier to achieve common recovery goals such as working or attending school. In short, helping individuals improve their health and wellness improves the likelihood that their PsyR goals can be accomplished.

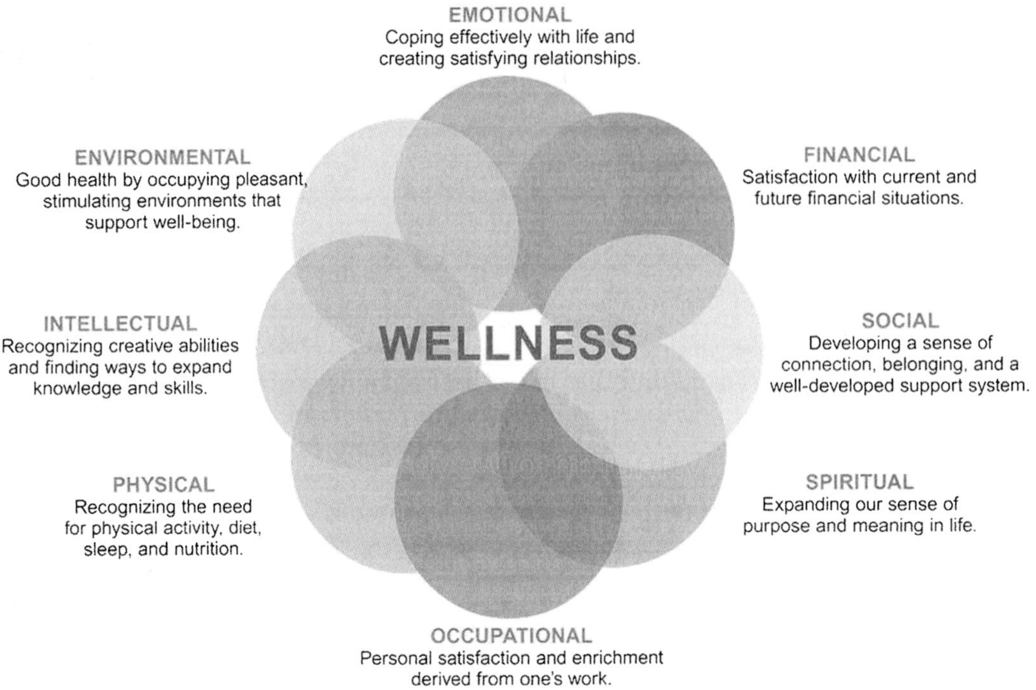

FIGURE 6.1 The eight dimensions of wellness, based upon the illustration by the Substance Abuse and Mental Health Service Administration (http://www.promoteacceptance.samhsa.gov/10by10/dimensions.aspx). © *2011 Collaborative Support Programs of NJ, Inc.*

Wellness Coaching

One intervention that promotes healthier lifestyles and is also a good fit with the goals, values, and principles of PsyR is wellness coaching. Wellness coaching is a growing trend for people with a variety of health and wellness goals. Dr. Peggy Swarbrick has pioneered the application of wellness coaching principles to address the concerns of persons with serious mental illness. Her first application of this strategy was educating peers, persons with serious mental illness themselves, to become wellness coaches. Next, traditional practitioners began to take an interest. Wellness coaching helps the individual identify a self-chosen wellness goal and develop a plan to pursue it and provides the individual with accountability and encouragement to stay on task in pursuit of the goal. While the context of this chapter is the physical health of the individual, wellness coaching can be used to pursue a goal in any of the eight dimensions of wellness. In fact, wellness goals often target multiple interrelated wellness dimensions. Preliminary results of wellness coaching look promising (Swarbrick et al., 2011; Swarbrick, Brice, & Gill, 2013).

Margaret (Peggy) Swarbrick, PhD, OTR, CPRP, FAOTA, is the Director of the Institute for Wellness and Recovery Initiatives, Collaborative Support Programs of New Jersey, and Assistant Professor, Department of Psychiatric Rehabilitation and Counseling Professions, School of Health Related Professions (SHRP), Rutgers University. Peggy worked many years as an occupational therapist in a variety of settings developing health promotion and wellness-focused services. She has published and presented nationally and internationally on wellness, employment, recovery, and peer-delivered service models. She has published over 29 articles in peer-reviewed literature and 10 chapters and contributed to over 18 other publications and manuscripts.

Peggy has devoted her life and career to creating a vision of mental health system reform that includes a holistic eight-dimensional framework of wellness as well as recovery. Her personal life experiences fueled her passion to create services and systems based on health and wellness promotion as a strategy to prevent illness and/or help people better manage their conditions and realize their full potential.

Peggy earned her doctorate in Occupational Therapy from New York University and completed a post-doctoral fellowship, Advanced Training and Research, National Institute on Disability and Rehabilitation Research, at the UMDNJ-SHRP Department of Psychiatric Rehabilitation and Counseling Professions.

What Does a Wellness Coach Do?

A wellness coach helps individuals to identify strengths in the eight dimensions of wellness (spiritual, occupational, intellectual, social, physical, environmental, financial, mental/emotional), and then helps them clarify what they hope to change or improve.

Often there is a specific focus on one or more of the physical health factors previously identified as relevant to persons living with SMI. Typical wellness goals might include reduction in the use of tobacco or alcohol, improved nutrition and dietary monitoring, regular glucose monitoring for diabetes prevention and management, improved oral hygiene/dental health practices, increased physical activity, adherence to an adequate sleep schedule, and regular participation in medical treatments.

Role of a Wellness Coach

Through brainstorming, the coach helps individuals find their own solutions for their health problem(s) and concerns. The coach asks questions that help individuals develop a better understanding of their personal situations and then assists in identifying steps needed to achieve a health and wellness goal. Using a variety of individually tailored methods, the wellness coach provides structure and support in order to promote personal progress and accountability. While wellness is a broad concept involving many facets of life, it is usually best to pursue one narrow or specific wellness goal at a time. This approach is consistent with the PsyR methods described in Chapter 5. Overall rehabilitation goals are very specific, broken down into steps and addressed one at a time.

Integral to the coaching process is setting a SMART goal (Doran, 1981; Swarbrick, 2012). SMART is an acronym that means **s**pecific, **m**easurable, **a**ttainable, **r**ealistic, and **t**ime-*framed*. The components of SMART goals are described as follows:

Specific—Goals should be specific in terms of what exactly a person wants to achieve. Specific goals use action words such as *walk* five days a week for 20 minutes, *quit* smoking, *schedule* an appointment with a doctor, *purchase* fruit and vegetables instead of unhealthy snacks.

Measurable—Measuring progress is established by concrete criteria that indicate attainment of each goal the person sets. For example, how many times per week did the individual walk 20 minutes or more? How many fewer cigarettes did he smoke? How many days did she eat healthy snacks vs. unhealthy ones?

Attainable—The ideal goal requires some effort, but is reachable. The individual should choose a goal believed to be worthy of attainment. Sticking to the long-term commitment required to achieve a goal is more likely if the goal is seen as worthy. For instance, aiming to lose 20 lbs. by the end of the month is unrealistic and unhealthy. Setting a goal to lose 3-4 lbs. over a month-long period and aiming to lose 3-4 lbs. the next month, and so on, is a more achievable goal.

Realistic—This means that it is possible to do. It is not a synonym for "easy." The goal needs to be realistic for the individual at the moment. A goal of never again eating pastries, chips, and chocolate may not be realistic for someone who really enjoys these foods. Reducing the number and portion size of sweet and salty snacks consumed per week may be more realistic.

Time-framed—This means providing clear target dates for completion of work toward the goal. A wellness coach will ask a person, "What will you be doing [in relation to your goal] in one week? In one month? In three months? Six months?" Even if a goal is not achieved in a specific time frame, it should be reviewed and reassessed regularly with new time frames considered.

Although SMART goals are being introduced and discussed in the context of wellness coaching, they are applicable to any approach used to help individuals achieve health and wellness goals.

Once the goal is established, the wellness coach works with the individual on developing a specific plan to pursue it. While a coach cannot be an expert in every health-related area, he or she should have a general knowledge of commonly used approaches and resources. For example, a wellness coach does not have the knowledge and expertise of a nutritionist, but the coach should have knowledge of where those services might be available as well as access to the USDA's information about optimal nutrition. Or, in order to help a person with diabetes who has Medicaid health insurance, the coach may know of the closest endocrinologist at a federally qualified health center. The coach should also know where a diabetes education program is available. If the coach does not have direct, current knowledge about a particular health-related resource, she or he should know strategies for locating such information.

Wellness coaches also help with accountability, checking in with the individual by phone or in person to determine if the individual is sticking to the plan. Is he exercising regularly? Following a prescribed diet plan? Adhering to a smoking reduction or cessation plan? The coach can also help the person develop and utilize self-monitoring tools—for example, a simple calendar for recording the dates that an exercise routine was completed. When an individual fails to adhere to a plan, in part or in whole, the coach helps by encouraging the person to return to the plan. When needed, the coach can help the person identify alternative strategies and supports that promote goal-oriented behavior. In short, the coach provides a structure for helping the person monitor the wellness plan, provides support that encourages adherence, and helps the individual assess progress, periodically reevaluating chosen goals. In addition to providing this accountability and support, the coach can serve as a mentor. Coaches, particularly peer wellness coaches, can consciously and selectively self-disclose about a shared struggle, as long as they are doing it for the benefit of the individual and do not overemphasize their own experience.

Once a wellness goal is achieved, the coach should help the individual make a plan for sustaining change without the coach. This is accomplished by asking the person what he or she will do to stay on track in the pursuit of ongoing health and wellness. What people, places, and things can be used as supports? For example, can a neighbor take regular walks with the person? Has the person made a friend in her Weight Watchers group who will help her stay motivated? If possible, the coach can also periodically check in to support an individual. An overview of the wellness coaching process is provided in Figure 6.2.

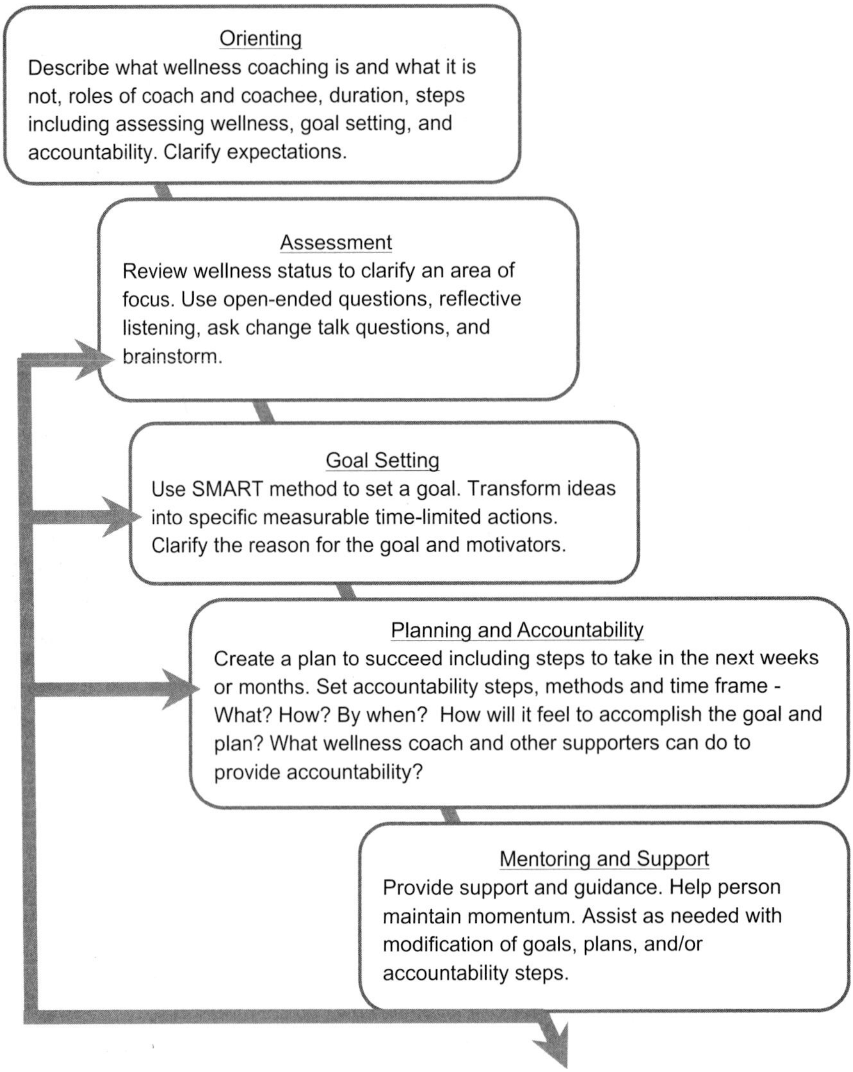

Orienting
Describe what wellness coaching is and what it is not, roles of coach and coachee, duration, steps including assessing wellness, goal setting, and accountability. Clarify expectations.

Assessment
Review wellness status to clarify an area of focus. Use open-ended questions, reflective listening, ask change talk questions, and brainstorm.

Goal Setting
Use SMART method to set a goal. Transform ideas into specific measurable time-limited actions. Clarify the reason for the goal and motivators.

Planning and Accountability
Create a plan to succeed including steps to take in the next weeks or months. Set accountability steps, methods and time frame - What? How? By when? How will it feel to accomplish the goal and plan? What wellness coach and other supporters can do to provide accountability?

Mentoring and Support
Provide support and guidance. Help person maintain momentum. Assist as needed with modification of goals, plans, and/or accountability steps.

FIGURE 6.2 An overview of the entire wellness coaching process *(adapted from Swarbrick, 2012).*

Community-based Group Interventions

There are a number of excellent examples of community-based health and wellness intervention programs for persons with serious mental illness. Two of these are "Wellness for Life" and "In Shape." Wellness for Life (WFL) is a multidisciplinary intervention for persons living with serious mental illness and metabolic syndrome (Zechner, Andersen, & Gill, 2013; Gill, Zechner, & Murphy, 2011). The planned intervention takes place over a period of three to four months, followed by transition to other services to maintain gains. Much of this approach is drawn from chronic disease self-management, diabetes education, and related strategies. The intervention includes educational sessions on topics such as healthy eating, the benefits of physical activity, and the risks of weight gain. Because education by itself is known to be insufficient to bring about a healthier lifestyle and weight loss, nutritional counseling is also provided. This includes individual assessment and planning of each participant's diet, including how to obtain affordable well-balanced meals that include fresh fruits, vegetables, and high-quality meats and fish. Because many individuals enrolled in WFL live sedentary lifestyles, they are unlikely to embark upon a very vigorous exercise program, nor is such a program advisable. To address this issue, WFL includes sessions with physical therapists who conduct individual assessments of each participant's capacity to engage in exercise. Usually a light program of regular exercising "in place" or walking is recommended. The WFL program also includes exercise sessions that are at an appropriate level for the group. Skill development sessions are also part of WFL and focus on skills such as monitoring blood sugar level. Given the poor state of dental health of many people with these disorders, WFL also includes some oral hygiene skill training. Other health and wellness activities can be added to a WFL program, including sessions on smoking reduction and/or cessation. Each participant in the WFL program is assisted in developing an individual wellness plan to support and encourage his or her wellness goals. WFL participants are also assigned a peer wellness coach, described in the previous section.

WFL was developed and initially implemented on a university campus by the faculty and students of an allied health school. Participating departments included psychiatric rehabilitation, nutrition, physical therapy, and dental hygiene. Graduates from the school's peer wellness coaching training program were also involved. WFL has since been offered in community mental health centers in conjunction with day programs (discussed in Chapter 7), as well as the regional health center of a state university. The outcomes of WFL are currently being studied. Initial observations are that the participants learn healthy behaviors and take better care of themselves. Some reduce or quit smoking while others return to medical care or dental care they have been neglecting. At the conclusion of the 10- to 12-week program, positive gains are made by many participants in terms of attainment of their specified goals, weight loss in particular (Gill, Zechner, & Murphy, 2011; Zechner, Andersen, & Gill, 2012).

In Shape, developed in New Hampshire, is another innovative model. A fully community integrated approach, In Shape is potentially replicable anywhere. The In Shape staff are trained to address the symptoms and functional impairment affecting an individual's ability to manage health, wellness, fitness, and nutrition. The staff work in collaboration with the multidisciplinary recovery team to provide health and wellness services to individuals on the various teams. Each consumer works to develop a Health

Action Plan to provide motivation and focus on the desired goal. Services include a health mentor, a certified personal fitness trainer, reduced cost membership to the local YMCA, advice from a nutritionist, materials on exercise and healthy eating, health consultations with nurses, and the opportunity to attend group celebrations. More information is available at the Riverbend CMHC Web site at http://www.riverbendcmhc. org/index.php?option=com_content&view=article&id=82&Itemid=87. Many programs have the potential to offer services such as Wellness for Life and In Shape by coordinating existing resources and creatively reaching out to the local community. Programs can offer health promotion, wellness education, and exercise opportunities or they can access resources available in their community such as the recreational programs of municipalities' and counties' local gyms (often free or low cost). When these resources are more costly, PsyR practitioners seek funding to subsidize participation or negotiate reduced rates at private facilities offering gym equipment, pools, or other resources. The big advantage of In Shape is that it can be implemented in most communities. These programs promote the PsyR goal of community integration, giving individuals with psychiatric disabilities opportunities to recreate and socialize with non-disabled community members.

Throughout our society there is a great interest in promoting health and wellness with many programs and facilities, both public and private, devoted to those purposes. There is no reason persons with serious mental illness should not benefit from their availability as well. Particularly when combined with better access to primary care, health and wellness programs can produce positive outcomes and help to prevent tragedies such as Ted's story (which began this chapter). Consider the much more positive experiences of Gabrielle and Marlena:

Gabrielle and Marlena utilize the services of their local community mental health center, including psychiatric care and a weekly support group for persons living with bipolar disorder. Both in their forties, they are each at least 30 lbs. overweight and concerned about their physical as well as their mental health. One January evening, a guest speaker attends their support group to introduce a new community program co-coordinated by a mental health case manager and the activity coordinator at the local YMCA. Gabrielle and Marlena, who were just discussing their mutual New Year's resolution of cutting back on fried foods and losing at least 20 lbs. by the summer, sign up on the spot. A week later, they join the Y, paying a special affordable membership fee, and begin exercising and attending programs at the facility. Marlena likes using the treadmill and attending the "cooking light" classes. Gabrielle likes walking on the treadmill and is learning to use a few of the weight machines; she particularly enjoys the aerobic dance classes. Both women also enjoy the yoga class offered on Saturday mornings and relaxing in the hot tub afterward. They feel comfortable in the upbeat social atmosphere of the Y and begin to make friends with other members. In May, Marlena goes for an annual physical health exam. Her doctor is impressed that she has lost 18 lbs. and her blood sugar level is lower. Gabrielle is thrilled to find that she has lost 12 lbs. At their CMHC support group, they report that they have stayed motivated because they have found physical activities they enjoy at a place that is fun to go to. Gabrielle adds, "I used to sit home most of the weekend watching TV and eating snacks. I think that lifestyle exacerbated my depression at times. Now I have a place to go be active and be with other people. I really feel better both emotionally and physically." Their testimonials motivated two more group members to join the program.

Summary

There are significant co-occurring medical conditions that negatively impact and shorten the lives of persons living with mental illness. This chapter delineated some specific problems indicative of a true health crisis and described some solutions and strategies that could potentially have a positive impact. The main take-away point from this chapter is that the health problems and dramatically reduced life expectancies of persons with mental illnesses need to be addressed by a community of concerned and committed stakeholders, including PsyR practitioners and other mental health professionals, medical professionals, families, researchers, state- and national-level policy makers, and advocacy organizations. The community can continue to be overwhelmed by the magnitude of this predicament and even seek to ignore it, or they can choose to collectively collaborate on a future course that promotes healthy outcomes and longer lives. The Center for Mental Health Services (CMHS) has set a clear target for this community: within 10 years, eliminate 10 years of the 25-year disparity in lifespan (Manderscheid & DelVecchio, 2008).

The kinds of tragedies described in this chapter are potentially avoidable. Disorders such as diabetes and hypertension are killers if left untreated, but many people with these conditions are living normal life spans because they have the treatment and resources to manage them. They get care and, in many cases, are self-managing these disorders with professional support. Many of the lifestyle factors contributing to the ill health of persons with or without psychiatric disorders are modifiable. For example, nicotine dependence is a terrible addiction, yet many persons with serious mental illness—like people in the general population—can reduce or eliminate their smoking, thereby increasing their average life expectancy. Similarly, people with mental illness can also modify their diets, increase their exercise, and manage their weight. Do they have partial success, outright failure, or relapses in these areas? The answer is yes, just as it is for everyone else struggling with these issues. Yet, also like others, persons with SMI are capable of making these positive changes. Providers, professionals, and paraprofessionals alike can no longer say, "It is not my job to help these people; they have a medical condition, and I am only a mental health worker." Practices must be informed by the fact that physical and mental health conditions impact other dimensions of wellness (emotional, social, mental, intellectual, etc.). Providers should understand how health risk factors impede rehabilitation goals and how health promotion models can foster a wellness lifestyle. People with serious mental illness have the capacity to learn and to grow in their ability to promote their health and maintain their wellness.

■ ■ ■ ━━

Class Exercises

1. Among the service recipients of the PsyR program you work in, a number of people have complained of a great deal of weight gain, lethargy (lack of energy), etc. Many are also smokers. Some have dry mouth and dental problems. Their blood pressures are high as well. Your team is considering a number of steps to take, including:

   • Encouraging service recipients to talk to their psychiatrist or advanced nurse practitioner about the possible medication side effects they are experiencing.
   • Having supervisors raise the medication side effect issue with prescribers if an individual service recipient does not do this on his or her own.
   • Adding a nutritional counseling component to your service with or without input of a dietitian or nutritionist.
   • Ensuring each member of your program has an annual check-up or at least has a primary care physician.
   • Start tracking age-appropriate screenings for cancer and common conditions for each person.
   • Beginning a "smoke enders" group or find this resource in the community.
   • Beginning a light exercise program with the input of a physical therapist or occupational therapist.
   • Occasionally accompanying an anxious person to a doctor or dental visit.
   • Helping service recipients to prepare questions for their health care visits.
   • Developing a series of health literacy lectures on common health topics likely to affect service recipients.
      a) Which, if any, of these strategies should become a regular part of your program? Which might be done in collaboration with other service providers with your organization coordinating the effort?
      b) If multiple strategies are chosen, in what order should the steps be taken? Why did you choose that order?

2. Participants in your program occasionally come to you with a personal resolution to lose weight, quit smoking, or achieve another health-promoting goal. This happens often enough that your organization wants to implement a service to support them. What would your advice be on the nature of the services or supports to be offered?

━━ ■ ■ ■

7

Psychiatric Day Programming

When you get right down to it, what we all need is a place to go.
Takayuki Ikkaku, Arisa Hosaka, and Toshihiro Kawabata

CHAPTER OUTLINE

Psychiatric Rehabilitation. http://dx.doi.org/10.1016/B978-0-12-387002-5.00007-X

Much of the early development of psychiatric rehabilitation took place in community-based settings where groups of consumers gathered during the day for support, recreation, rehabilitation, and treatment. These settings were most effective when their environments were designed to promote improved quality of life, community integration, and the recovery of persons with severe mental illnesses. This chapter will explore the historical roots of these programs in the clubhouse movement and in the partial hospitalization programs set up as part of the Community Mental Health Center initiative. Elements from these two movements contributed to the current conception of psychiatric rehabilitation. Today, many of these programs are falling out of favor with professionals and the people they serve. We will examine some of the reasons these programs may be less effective today and how they may be designed and operated to help facilitate specific rehabilitation outcomes. Finally, we will discuss the potential for improved services inherent in the advent of evidence-based practices and the recovery movement.

This chapter will answer the following questions:

1. *What is psychiatric rehabilitation day programming?*
2. *When did day programming begin and how did it develop?*
3. *What are the common elements that make up a day program?*
4. *How can programs be designed to produce specific outcomes?*
5. *What does the future of these programs look like?*

Introduction

Effective psychiatric rehabilitation (PsyR) day programs rest on the premise that an environment, sometimes referred to as a milieu, can be created to assist in the rehabilitation and recovery of persons with psychiatric disabilities. These programs have their roots in two distinct movements with different philosophies: the clubhouse movement and the partial hospitalization movement. In their initial stages, these program types were quite distinct. For example, partial hospitalization programs, which were essentially a medical model, often had similarities to a ward in a psychiatric hospital. Clubhouse programs, on the other hand, strived to create an accepting, welcoming environment for members while rejecting the idea of treatment, therapy, or medication within the program. Despite these differences, each of these movements shared the belief that by working together in a specialized group setting people can help each other promote rehabilitation.

The clubhouse movement began in the 1940s and 1950s as a natural response to the needs and wants of ex-psychiatric patients living in communities around the country. Facing stigma, rejection, unemployment, and poverty, these individuals began to band together for mutual support and comradeship. As these groups became established, they became recognized community support networks for persons with mental illness. This chapter will describe the development of one of the first clubhouses, Fountain House in New York City. From that modest beginning, a worldwide network of clubhouses was established. The individuals attending these programs are known as members rather than patients and have a real say in how the clubhouse is operated.

As the deinstitutionalization movement in the United States grew in the late 1960s and 1970s, the treatment of many persons with severe and persistent mental illness shifted from hospitals to community mental health center (CMHC) programs called "partial hospitals." Indeed, it was mandated that each CMHC offer this service. The partial hospital label reflects these programs' initial similarity to inpatient psychiatric hospitals. At a typical partial hospitalization program, groups of patients received various types of services or therapies such as group and recreational therapy, socialization, medication monitoring, and activities of daily living skills training. At their inception, both of these community-based program models represented important treatment innovations for persons with severe and persistent mental illness. Much of the early development of PsyR took place in these settings. This chapter covers the history and development of these day programs.

Partial Hospitalization

Ironically, the first published reports on the principal treatment strategy employed for the massive deinstitutionalization of persons in the United States came from Stalinist Russia, a regime known for its forced institutionalization of political enemies (Dzhagarov, 1937). During the 1930s, after a revolution followed by a bitter civil war, there were too few psychiatric beds in Moscow to meet demand. Out of necessity, Dzhagarov, the director of a psychiatric hospital, had some of the patients attend the hospital during the day but return to their own homes at night. Dzhagarov reported that his half-hospital served more than 1200 patients and achieved results equivalent to those produced by full-time hospitalization. Necessity, often the mother of invention, led to an important innovation in psychiatric treatment and rehabilitation.

Shortly after World War II, similar programs emerged in Canada (Cameron, 1947) and the United Kingdom (Bierer, 1948). Cameron, who established a program at the Allen Memorial Institute of Psychiatry in Montreal in 1946, is generally credited with introducing the term "day hospital" to describe this emerging treatment modality (Luber, 1979). In the United States, programs were reported at the Yale University Clinic and the Menninger Clinic as early as 1948. Many of these early programs were organized from a psychoanalytic perspective, emphasizing individual and group therapy as well as expressive therapies such as art and dance. These pre-deinstitutionalization programs provided services to patients who were generally less symptomatic and less disabled than those relegated to continued institutionalization. Possibly, these "healthier" patients were deemed more appropriate for an insight-oriented therapeutic approach.

By 1963, according to a National Institute of Mental Health (NIMH) report, there were 168 operating day treatment programs in the United States (Taube, 1973). With the passage of the 1963 Community Mental Health Act, the number of programs would grow by more than 700 percent in ten years. By 1973, there were 1280 programs in operation serving some 186,000 individuals. This phenomenal growth helped make community treatment available to thousands of people who were deinstitutionalized. At the same time, the meteoric development of this new treatment modality presented some very real challenges and problems. No one was completely sure how these programs should operate, who should staff them, or what kinds of services they should offer the patients. Because there was no clear definition of what a day hospital or day treatment program was, many programs began formulating their own strategies for the community treatment of persons with severe and persistent mental illness.

The Development of Partial Hospitalization Programs

The Community Mental Health Centers Construction Act (PL 88-164), passed in 1963, designated partial hospitalization as one of the five essential service modalities each CMHC must provide to be eligible for funding. The requirement that each CMHC offer partial hospitalization was responsible for the tremendous increase in the number of these services around the country. The partial hospital programs were intended to be the main community-based treatment element for persons deinstitutionalized from state psychiatric hospitals.

This initiative represented a major change in policy regarding responsibility for persons with major mental illness. Until that time, each state had responsibility for providing treatment for this population through their institutions and asylums. With this act, the federal government was providing the states with some of the resources required to move the treatment of persons with severe mental illness from state hospitals into the community. This initiative was also supported on the federal level with the passage of the government-funded health insurance programs Medicaid and Medicare. These programs, especially Medicaid, helped to pay for services for a large proportion of this population.

Given finite resources to foster the development of CMHCs around the country, these centers were placed on eight-year funding cycles. The plan was that in eight years with the help of state and local resources combined with Medicaid and Medicare these centers would become financially self-sufficient. During the first two years of their existence, CMHCs were federally funded at 100 percent of their cost for providing services. From the third year to the eighth year, funding was reduced until the ninth year when the CMHC would receive nothing from the federal government. The federal money that was saved as funding was reduced was earmarked for the funding of new CMHCs in identified areas of need around the country. This highly logical funding plan only worked for a time. The cost of the Vietnam War, rising medical costs, and the failure of many states to supply adequate financial resources helped to scuttle the plan financially (Torrey, 2006). Under President Ronald Reagan (1981–1989), federal support was shifted from these direct grants to block grants to the states.

In the CMHCs themselves, many staff and administrators focused their efforts on "higher functioning" clients with less serious disorders (Torrey, 2006). In some of these centers, people with severe mental illnesses were either ignored or assigned to poorly funded treatment programs operated by staff with little or no training. In short, in many centers the mission of treating people with severe mental illnesses was abandoned in favor of working with what some called the "worried well."

These early partial hospitals were essentially medical model programs. To bill Medicaid, Medicare, or other sources, program participants had to have a psychiatric diagnosis (ICD or DSM as discussed in Chapter 1) conferred by a licensed psychiatrist. By government regulation, psychiatrists also had to supervise or prescribe many of the treatments provided. Medication, medication monitoring, and group, individual, and expressive therapies were emphasized, as well as recreation and socialization.

Components of a Psychiatric Day Program

The following are general components or characteristics of almost any psychiatric day program: service recipients (e.g., clients, consumers, and members), staff, space, program ingredients (e.g., group, recreation, and skills training), and scheduling. Understanding these will help you understand the core elements of these programs. As you read their descriptions, notice that there is room for a good deal of variability within each element. This variability and a lack of universally agreed-upon principles of psychiatric day programming created a situation where no two programs were truly alike. Many professionals regarded the idiosyncratic nature of day programs as a major strength. These different program types were seen as the laboratories where new PsyR strategies were developed and refined. Others pointed out that program differences create nearly insurmountable problems for program evaluation and research. If no two programs are alike, how can we determine which are superior or even which program elements are effective?

Service Recipients

Service recipients should be diagnosed with a condition sufficient to warrant participation in such a program. This relates to the principle of least restrictive setting. This principle states that all consumers of mental health services should be treated in the least restrictive setting that can provide effective services for them. For example, people should not be hospitalized if they are not a danger to themselves or others and they can receive comparable treatment in the community.

Service recipients of a program should have a history of either long or repeated hospitalization or have repeatedly had serious challenges functioning successfully in the community without substantial structure and/or support. People who do well in the community should not be referred to such a program in most cases, despite symptoms or diagnosis. Service recipients of a program should not be a danger to themselves or others. Such persons are better served in a hospital setting where their behavior can be closely monitored. Service recipients of a program should be able to tolerate involvement in the milieu. The milieu of a day program, no matter how it is designed, can be a stressful place for some people.

Staff

The staff at a day program typically includes the following:

Director—The program director's role is critical, setting both the philosophical and administrative tone for the program. The specific tasks of the director may include setting the program design, supervising the daily operations of the program, and recruiting and supervising staff. Program directors usually have years of experience in PsyR and at least a master's degree in rehabilitation, social work, psychology, or a related human service field.

Supervisory-level staff—These staff members typically have responsibility for specific program staff, program elements (e.g., vocational units or intake), or consumer caseloads. These staff members often hold master's degrees in an appropriate field. Supervisory-level staff may also be direct service workers such as case managers, team leaders, clinical supervisors, or unit leaders.

Counselors/case managers—These workers, sometimes referred to as line staff, spend most of their time working directly with consumers. Their academic training may range from a high school education to a master's degree. These workers typically make up staff teams supervised by more experienced staff.

Mental health aides or paraprofessionals—These workers typically have little relevant education or experience in the field. There are numerous tasks that aides can carry out effectively. These staff often work in prevocational units helping out with activities, drive vans to transport program members, and conduct outreach to name just some of their roles.

Auxiliary and support staff—A number of other staff are critical for the operation of a successful PsyR program. Auxiliary staff often includes medical staff such as psychiatrists and nurses, specialized therapists such as art and dance therapists, or other specialized professionals. Support staff includes secretaries, file clerks, accountants, and so forth.

Space

The program should have enough square footage to allow staff and members to function in groups and carry out different kinds of activities. It is usually necessary for there to be at least one space big enough for the entire program to meet. The program area should be safe and clean. It should be well-lit, have proper ventilation (including heating and cooling), and have the necessary equipment and furnishings to carry out designated functions. There should also be appropriate auxiliary facilities such as toilets, washrooms, and kitchens. Last, but most important, the program should be located in a normalized environment and have reasonably easy access by public transportation. A program located on the locked ward of a hospital, for example, would not be in a normalized environment, even if the clients returned home every afternoon.

Program Ingredients

Program ingredients refer to the kinds of activities that take place during the program day. Some typical program ingredients include recreation; socialization; skills training—including social skills, activities of daily living skills, and prevocational skills; education—including basic remedial education and symptoms, illness management, and medication education; medication monitoring; case management; and vocational services such as transitional employment. Sadly, despite years of progress, programs still exist where one might observe clients doing simple arts and crafts or playing Bingo when they are not in individual or group therapy. Better programs have a rational mix of skills training, vocational activities, support, and recreation depending on the individual needs of the program members. These programs also conduct periodic or ongoing needs assessments to ensure that their efforts are in line with the needs and preferences of the members.

Scheduling

Scheduling refers to issues such as what time the program opens, when activities take place, and whether members have to be on time. Programs frequently have evening hours for recreation, graduates, or consumers who work. What happens during the hours the program is operating is a matter of scheduling consumers and staff. Scheduling may reflect a regular work environment or the looseness of a social club. A program's scheduling should be in line with its philosophy, goals, and ingredients. For example, a program that actively encourages its members to volunteer or take part-time jobs may be designed to provide members with very flexible schedules to accommodate time off on different days and at different times. Lastly, how schedules are set and who sets them can be an important empowerment issue. Figure 7.1 shows a sample weekly schedule.

The Development of Clubhouse Programs

During the late 1940s, a group of ex-patients from Rockland Psychiatric Center in New York State formed a support group called WANA (We Are Not Alone), which met on the steps of the New York City Public Library in Manhattan. A private social welfare group, the National Council of Jewish Women, became aware of WANA and began supporting their cause. In 1948, with the help of Elizabeth Schermerhorn, a building on West 47th Street in New York City was purchased as a clubhouse for WANA (Dincin, 1975; Flannery & Glickman, 1996; Propst, 1992a). Because it had a small fountain in the backyard, the group named it Fountain House. Fountain House, initially staffed and operated solely by its members and volunteers, was designed to provide social supports and serve as a meeting place for ex-psychiatric patients. People who joined Fountain House were called members rather than patients and, like a club, they could remain members for as long as they wished. As Fountain House grew, the members decided to hire professional, nonconsumer staff to operate the program. The first nonconsumer mental health staff members were recruited in 1955. Even with the addition of professionally trained staff,

COMPLETE IN PENCIL ONLY

Name: _____   **Date:** _____

TIME	MON	TUE	WED	THU	FRI	SAT
8:00 AM						
8:30 AM	←·······		Breakfast (Optional)		·······→	
9:00 AM	←·······		Unit Meetings		·······→	
9:30 AM	←····· Fresh Start (MICA Members Only) ·····→ ←······· Unit Activities ·······→					
10:00 AM	Unit Activities ←···· (Cont'd.) ····→		Clubhouse Committee	Voice of Prospect House	Unit Activities (Cont'd.)	SOCIAL
10:30 AM	←··· Coffee Break ···→		↓	↓		(OPTIONAL)
11:00 AM	MICA Education		Member Reps. Meeting		MICA Relapse Prevention	10:00 AM
11:30 AM	←······· ↓		Unit Activities		·······→ ↓	TO
12:00 PM	←·······		Lunch		·······→	4:00 PM
12:30 PM	←·······		Community Meeting		·······→	
1:00 PM	Continuing Education					
1:30 PM	↓	←······· Unit Activities (Cont'd.) ·······→				
2:00 PM	Case Mgmt.	←··· Unit Activities ···→			Unit Activities	
2:30 PM	↓			Case Mgmt.		
3:00-7:00 PM			Social (Optional)		Social (Optional)	

Assigned Unit: _____   **Days in Program:** _____

SPECIAL GROUPS:

☐ MICA	☐ Continuing Education	☐ Member Reps	☐ Voice of PH
☐ TE	☐ Coping Groups	☐ Fresh Start	☐ Clubhouse Committee
☐ SE	☐ Other	☐ Clerical Research	☐ Food Services
☐ House Services	☐ Member Services	☐ Seniors	

FIGURE 7.1 Example of a weekly schedule.

Fountain House retained its clubhouse atmosphere and philosophy. After trying out several directors with unsatisfactory results, a social worker named John Beard was hired. Beard helped to change Fountain House from what was essentially a social club into a truly comprehensive psychiatric rehabilitation facility, which became the model for the clubhouse movement (Beard, Propst, & Malamud, 1982).

The clubhouse exists primarily to improve the quality of life of its members. They began as places where members gathered to socialize and to give and receive support. As such, nothing designated as medical treatment took place there. Members were accepted without regard to their symptoms and did not have to "improve" in order to continue their member status. This focus on quality-of-life issues led to an emphasis on members' basic needs: housing, work, socialization, and recreation. Length of stay, the time an individual is in a program, is a good example of the difference in how a clubhouse operates in contrast to a partial hospitalization program. Clubhouse members can stay as long as they wish regardless of their clinical state; they are considered members for life. By contrast, many partial hospitalization programs had prescribed lengths of stay and their clients were discharged if their clinical state improved.

Probably the most important difference between clubhouses and early partial hospitalization was the emphasis on work (Jackson, 1992; Vorspan, 1992). Clubhouse philosophy, embodied in the "work-ordered day," stresses the importance of work for providing a sense of meaning in life and a sense of belonging to a community. Performing meaningful work endows the worker with purpose. For clubhouse members, work begins with the day-to-day operation of the clubhouse itself, from custodial tasks and record keeping to paying bills, making meals, and hiring new staff. The clubhouse emphasizes work, through both its work-ordered day and its transitional employment (TE) service. TE, clubhouse-controlled jobs in real work settings outside the clubhouse, offer time-limited employment experiences for members. This work experience leads to several other important outcomes such as member empowerment, the development of a sense of self-efficacy, increased confidence, and self-esteem. Perhaps most importantly, it is intended to lead to competitive employment outside the clubhouse.

Clubhouse Standards

In 1988, the Robert Wood Johnson Foundation, Pew Charitable Trusts, and the Public Welfare Foundation funded the National Clubhouse Expansion Program (NCEP). One of the tasks of the NCEP was the development of standards for clubhouse programs. This effort culminated in the establishment of the International Center for Clubhouse Development (ICCD; http://www.iccd.org), now doing business as Clubhouse International. The ICCD initially identified 35 standards that should be adhered to by programs that considered themselves clubhouses (Propst, 1992a, b). The ICCD reviews and amends these standards as needed every two years. The following section discusses a select group of standards that outline some of the aspects of clubhouses that set them apart from the more traditional psychiatric day programs.

BOX 7.1 JOHN H. BEARD

John Beard was the father of the worldwide clubhouse movement. Beard, who earned his master's degree in social work from Wayne State University in Detroit, Michigan, had worked at Wayne County General Hospital in Michigan as a social worker. In 1955, Elizabeth Schermerhorn and the board of directors of Fountain House hired Beard as their executive director. He led Fountain House until his death in 1982.

Beard focused on the members' strengths rather than on their illnesses. An excerpt from a video made in 1978 captures his attitude about working with members:

I had no interest in why he was sick. That was not my job .... I wasn't interested in trying to review his ... psychopathology. I had no interest in it at all. I was terribly interested in how normal we might get him to function. (Flannery & Glickman, 1996, p. 28)

Almost single-handedly at first, Beard's vision and efforts were the guiding force behind the creation of the clubhouse movement. Today, there are over 300 clubhouses worldwide and the number is growing. Each of these programs is, in some small way, a symbol of Beard's caring and efforts. In 1982, he received the Extraordinary Service Award for Exceptional Commitment and Dedication in Serving the Mentally Ill of New York. The award reads as follows:

His leadership has provided:

Dignity where there was shame,
Belonging where there was alienation,
Empowerment where there was helplessness,
Self-respect where there was self-denigration,
Hope and opportunity where once there was only despair.

Some Selected Standards for Clubhouse Programs

Program standards can tell us a great deal about the places they describe. As you read the standards for clubhouse programs listed next, try to imagine what such a place would feel like. You might also consider how these policies might be received in a highly formalized environment such as a hospital. More importantly, consider what attitudes about psychiatric treatment and rehabilitation are reflected by these standards. Finally, although clubhouses reject the notion of providing therapy per se, decide whether you think the clubhouse can be a "therapeutic environment" for its members.

Membership

- Membership is voluntary and without time limits.
- Members choose the way they utilize the clubhouse and the staff with whom they work.
- There are no agreements, behavioral contracts, schedules, or rules intended to enforce participation of members.
- Members, at their choice, are involved in the writing of all records reflecting their participation in the clubhouse. All such records are to be signed by both member and staff.

Relationships

- All clubhouse meetings are open to both members and staff. There are no formal member-only meetings or formal staff-only meetings where program decisions and member issues are discussed.
- Clubhouse staff have generalist roles. All program staff share employment, housing, evening, weekend, and unit responsibilities.
- Clubhouse staff members do not divide their time between the clubhouse and other responsibilities.

Space

- All clubhouse space is member- and staff-accessible. There are no staff-only or member-only spaces.

Work-ordered Day

- The work-ordered day engages members and staff together, side-by-side, in the running of the clubhouse.
- The clubhouse focuses on members' strengths, talents, and abilities; therefore, the work-ordered day is inconsistent with medication clinics, day treatment, or therapy programs within the clubhouse.
- All work in the clubhouse is designed to help members regain self-worth, purpose, and confidence; it is not intended to be job-specific training.

Employment

- The clubhouse enables its members to return to the normal work world through transitional employment and independent employment; therefore, the clubhouse does not provide employment to members through in-house businesses, segregated clubhouse enterprises, or sheltered workshops.

(http://www.iccd.org/images/2012edition_intl_standards_english.pdf)

The Proliferation of Clubhouses

The National Council of Jewish Women played a major role in the development of the clubhouse movement and psychiatric rehabilitation nationwide. Capitalizing on the success of their efforts at Fountain House, during the 1950s this philanthropic group supported and encouraged the development of clubhouses nationwide, including Thresholds (Chicago, Illinois), Hill House (Cleveland, Ohio), Council House (Pittsburgh, Pennsylvania), and Bridge Haven (Louisville, Kentucky) (Dincin, 1975). As awareness of the benefits of clubhouses grew, other centers were developed around the country, including Horizon House (Philadelphia, Pennsylvania), Fellowship House (Miami, Florida), Center Club (Boston, Massachusetts), and the Social Rehabilitation Center (Fairfax, Virginia), to name but a few. Most importantly, using a strategy similar to the mythical Johnny Appleseed, Fountain House and programs like it vigorously trained their staff and then sent them out to develop new clubhouses around the country and the world (Propst, 1992a, b; Vorspan, 1992). Today, literally hundreds of clubhouse programs worldwide can trace their roots back to either Fountain House or one of the other early clubhouse programs.

The Story of Jill, Affinity House Member

A great deal goes on each day in a typical clubhouse. As you read about Jill's day, consider how she carries out her role as a program member and the role staff members play. Is attending the program having a positive effect on Jill? Would she be better off returning to college? The answers to these questions are far from obvious. What is the right plan for someone like Jill? Is the clubhouse the right place for her at this stage?

Jill, 27 years old, has been a member of Affinity House for seven months. Diagnosed with schizophrenia at 17, Jill has been in and out of the hospital numerous times, all the while trying to earn a college degree in English and journalism. Two years ago, still a sophomore, she was hospitalized again for six months. While getting ready for discharge, a liaison worker visiting the hospital suggested that she might try Affinity House, because she would be discharged in the middle of the spring semester and could not return to school till the fall semester some seven months away. While still in the hospital, Jill made a visit to Affinity House and it seemed like a warm place with friendly people, so she decided to give it a try.

Today, Jill is the assistant supervisor of the Clerical Unit, where she is mainly responsible for putting out the weekly Affinity House newsletter, All Things Considered. The members and staff at Affinity House were really excited when Jill told them about her studies in journalism. Even though Jill hadn't always been able to complete her courses, she had learned a great deal about creating effective newsletters. Now she had the chance to put her knowledge to good use. Helping improve the newsletter was exciting and fun. She found that her ideas were well received and really made a difference in the quality of the publication, which grew better and better over the weeks.

The hardest part for Jill was that as more of her ideas were put into practice she became the one responsible for supervising other members working on the newsletter. This responsibility was something she had not experienced before or been trained for. The Clerical Unit supervisor, Emil (also a member of Affinity House), and the staff assigned to the unit were important sources of support for Jill in her new role as newsletter supervisor. Jill found it difficult to supervise people, mainly because her first impulse was not to say anything that would upset anyone. She wanted to be liked, but she also took great pride in the newsletter. She spent some time every week speaking to Emil or a staff member about how to motivate the Clerical Unit members or how, when someone had made a mistake, she could correct the person but be supportive and encouraging at the same time. After several months of supervising the newsletter, Jill was gaining some confidence in her ability to supervise and be a leader.

The first scheduled event at Affinity House each morning is the unit meeting, which starts at 9:30 a.m. sharp. Unit members meet to plan the tasks of the day, see how other unit members and staff are doing, and evaluate how things are going. Unit meetings are also the time when new members who might be trying out the unit as part of their orientation are introduced. When a new member is introduced, Jill always remembers how nervous she was when she first came to the Clerical Unit for her orientation. Today, a new member named Bob was introduced to everyone. Jill suggested that Bob might work with her on the initial layout of the next newsletter.

At 10:00 a.m., the unit work begins. Most unit members are clear about the tasks they have to perform, and Jill and Emil spend most of their time supervising the members and helping out when problems arise. One or two staff members may also be present working alongside of members on clerical projects. The staff members are also available to meet with members who are having problems or need assistance with their individual goals. With the members preparing the newsletter, writing outreach letters, and preparing mailings, the unit generally has a very busy, productive feeling in the morning.

Lunch, prepared by members in the Food Service Unit, is usually from 12:00 to 12:30 p.m. Jill often eats with other members from her unit or with a staff person who she had met several years ago in one of her classes in college. After lunch, several of the members and staff go outside to smoke. In the afternoon, in addition to the units, there are meetings to attend both about program operations and about things of interest to members. Jill attends a 2 p.m. meeting designed to orient members who are planning to get a transitional employment position. Members learn about transitional employment (TE) (see Chapter 10 for more about TE), share some of their past experiences at work, talk about what kind of job they would like, and find out about jobs that may be available. Jill has only attended this meeting once in the last two weeks, so she is still getting to know the members and working up her courage to really talk about her concerns about work. Her work in the unit has built up her confidence in her ability to hold down a regular job. During the meeting, a staff person invites anyone who is interested to attend that evening's TE Support Group. The TE Support Group is for members who are out working in the community. The staff person believes that attending this group will give everyone a better idea of the issues they will face when they get a transitional employment job. Jill isn't sure if she wants to attend the evening group. She is still debating whether she should return to college or try to work, and the idea of going to the group feels too much like ruling out college.

Back in the unit, Jill sees that Bob, the new member on orientation, has left early and not finished cutting out some of the illustrations for pasting up on the next newsletter. Jill enlists another unit member, Herb, and they finish the task together. Other members report that Bob said he was going out for a cigarette but didn't return. At 3:30 p.m., the day is over and members head out to their rides or the van. Jill has made sure the computers are turned off and the supplies locked up for the night. Jill decides not to attend the TE Support Group this evening. It's her favorite TV night and she's tired. Maybe she will attend next month.

Evaluating Psychiatric Day Programs

A Day Program Taxonomy

Several researchers have suggested that partial hospitalization programs and PsyR programs in general are most effective when they are designed to produce a specific outcome for a particular type of service recipient (Astrachan, Flynn, Geller, & Harvey, 1970; Neffinger, 1981; Solomon, 1992). For example, if a program had a primary purpose of helping consumers return to regular community life as quickly as possible, the emphasis might be on skills training and supportive therapy. Alternatively, a program with a primary purpose of helping individuals who are acutely symptomatic stay out of the hospital might emphasize support and medication maintenance. This idea might be summed up by the following question: What type of program is effective for what type of individual?

In 1981, Neffinger proposed a taxonomy of partial hospitalization (PH) programs (see Table 7.1) that identified three different primary purposes or functions for PHs: (1) an alternative to inpatient treatment, which he labeled "day hospital"; (2) a supplement to traditional outpatient treatment and vocational rehabilitation, which he labeled "day treatment"; and (3) functional maintenance in the community, which he labeled "day care." Many programs today can still be classified using this taxonomy, although they would probably employ different terms to describe themselves. For example, today, programs designed to function as an alternative to inpatient treatment are typically called "acute partial hospitals." It is instructive to closely review the details of Neffinger's taxonomy in Table 7.1. Notice that the term "chronic," which is no longer acceptable, is used. Also review the variables or program characteristics Neffinger used to distinguish between program types. These variables are still an important consideration when evaluating programs, but their content has changed somewhat as the field has evolved. For example, intensive psychotherapy has been replaced by supportive psychotherapy. In addition, the characterization of day care patients as older is probably an artifact of the deinstitutionalization movement and is certainly less true today. The original exodus from the hospitals included many middle-aged and elderly patients who had spent the better part of their adult lives in institutions.

Table 7.1 A Schematic Presentation of the Theoretical Spectrum of Partial Hospitalization Programs Subdivided into Three Parallel Continua Representing (A) General Taxonomy, (B) Primary Function, and (C) Differential Characteristics[a]

	Day Hospital	Day Treatment	Day Care
Primary Function	Alternative to inpatient transitional setting	Supplement to traditional outpatient treatment, vocational rehabilitation	Functional maintenance
Differential Characteristics			
Treatment Goal	Stabilize acute episode	Catalyze rapid improvement Minimize subsequent treatment	Prevent further deterioration and rehospitalization
Treatment Modality	Psychopharmacology/supportive therapy	Intensive psychotherapy and structure	Activity therapy and advocacy
Symptom Intensity	Acute	Pre/post acute	Chronic
Age	Mixed	Younger	Older
Staffing Pattern	Medical mental health professionals	Nonmedical mental health professionals	Predominantly paraprofessionals
Patient/Staff Ratio	4	6	15+
Maximum Census	12	20 to 40	50+
Treatment Duration	2 to 4 weeks	3 to 4 months	Indefinite
Organizational Relationships	Closely allied to emergency and/or inpatient unit	Separate from but available to inpatient or emergency unit	No necessary relationship to inpatient or emergency unit

[a]Reprinted with permission from Neffinger, G. G. (1981). Partial hospitalization: An overview. *Journal of Community Psychology. 9*, 263.

State-of-the-Art Psychiatric Rehabilitation Day Programming

One of the most important contributions of organizations such as the United States Psychiatric Rehabilitation Association (USPRA) and publications such as the *Psychiatric Rehabilitation Journal* and the *American Journal of Psychiatric Rehabilitation* is that they bring together professionals, consumers, family members, and others interested in services for persons with psychiatric disabilities. This coming together, which has grown year-by-year, has helped to synthesize the best elements of different program types into what we consider today's state-of-the-art program. PsyR services are still largely idiosyncratic, but the best programs contain many of the same elements, though in differing amounts.

From the clubhouse movement, we get a strong respect for each individual's quality of life and those things that support quality of life: individual choice, employment, housing, social supports, and membership in the community. This translates into many support initiatives that go far beyond treating the mental illness itself.

State-of-the-art programs are instrumental in securing housing for their members, have one or more vocational rehabilitation elements (see Chapter 9), support their members' efforts to further their education (see Chapter 10), and help provide opportunities for building social supports and networks. Clubhouses, for example, tend to be open in the evenings and on weekends because their members' social lives and recreation are important.

As previously stated, the development of a nationwide network of clubhouse programs helped give birth to the psychosocial rehabilitation movement. The clubhouse network was also instrumental in the creation of the International Association of Psychosocial Rehabilitation Services (IAPSRS), now USPRA. Today, some clubhouses belong to both USPRA as organizational members and to the national clubhouse movement, the ICCD.

From the partial hospitalization movement, our state-of-the-art program gets its emphasis on medication, medication management, and symptom and medication education for consumers and their families. This aspect is important because the major mental illnesses are biologically based diseases and many of their symptoms can be controlled with medication. It is also believed that the best long-term outcomes are achieved if psychotic episodes are dealt with effectively and in a timely fashion.

Although it would be wrong to give the impression of universal agreement about how things should be done, PsyR is no longer divided among groups with totally different philosophies and strategies. Rather, the field has matured to the point where there is agreement on most of the goals, values, and principles, with continued debate about the proper mix of these elements to address the needs of service recipients. Consider the idea of empowerment: Many people use this term and many professionals believe it is an important PsyR element. But there is still little agreement as to just what the term "empowerment" means and whether it is a good idea in every situation. Consider the issues spelled out in Box 7.2.

BOX 7.2   EMPOWERMENT: WILL WE KNOW IT IF WE SEE IT?

Empowerment is something that comes from within a person, rather than something that is done to a person. People who are empowered may have a sense that what they think and feel counts, that their wishes are important, and that they have choices to make. The best a program can do is create an environment that encourages empowerment. In a PsyR day program, member empowerment might manifest itself in many ways. There might be a strong consumer committee or governing body, members might hold supervisory positions, and they might help to collect data to evaluate the program. Staff members at some programs try to engender some of these activities, but find that they are rejected by service recipients. Empowerment, like recovery, is a personal and complicated phenomenon.

Can you tell whether a program milieu empowers its members? In many programs, the consumers and staff give a great deal of lip service to the importance of empowerment. In other programs, the issue of empowerment is not discussed unless it is raised by a visitor. Does speaking about empowerment indicate that a program is empowering? Apparently not. An unpublished study of programmatic factors indicating consumer empowerment by students of the first author of this text found an inverse relationship in programs between consumer empowerment and talking about empowerment. In short, programs that said they were empowering tended to be less empowering than programs that didn't mention the term at all.

Some measures have been devised to evaluate the program milieu (Wolfensberger, 1983a; Moos, 1974). These scales do not claim to measure empowerment directly. Instead, they touch on many related issues such as normalization and control. While empowerment is considered an important ingredient of PsyR programming, there is still no agreement on an objective way to measure it. Using a participatory action research approach, which involves researchers working hand-in-hand with consumers, a group of researchers developed an empowerment scale that holds some promise of capturing the essence of this term for individuals diagnosed with severe mental illnesses (Rogers, Chamberlin, Ellison, & Crean, 1997).

The Effectiveness of Day Programs

The first reports of effective day hospitals (Bierer, 1948; Cameron, 1947; Dzhagarov, 1937) stressed the innovative strategy of using these programs in place of inpatient treatment. This strategy had several obvious benefits in addition to the fact that it is much less expensive to provide day treatment than inpatient hospitalization. Day programs allowed patients to stay in the community, allowing individuals to maintain normal contacts and supports. Day programs also eliminated the need for what was often a difficult transition back to the community after a long inpatient stay.

The first evaluations of day programs in the United States focused on the question of how this treatment strategy compared with inpatient hospitalization. This research was nearly unanimous in finding that day hospitalization was both clinically superior and more economical than inpatient hospitalization.

In a 1971 study, Herz, Endicott, Spitzer, and Mesnikoff randomly assigned patients to either inpatient treatment or day hospitalization and found that day treatment was superior on each of their outcome measures. A similar study by Washburn, Vannicelli, Longabaugh, and Scheff (1976) found that initially, day hospitalization was superior to inpatient hospitalization in reducing subjective distress, improving community functioning, and reducing family burden, total hospital cost, and length of stay in the program. As the advantages of day hospitalization became clear, the focus of research moved toward determining which elements of the day hospital were most effective. Neffinger's work is one example of this effort. Probably the most important study in this area to date was done by researchers working for the Veterans Administration (VA). Taking advantage of the large number of day hospitals operated by the VA, Linn, Caffey, Klett, Hogarty, and Lamb (1979) randomly assigned patients from ten different hospitals to receive day treatment plus psychotropic drugs or psychotropic drugs alone. The positive results of day programming were not immediately apparent. At the initial 6-month follow-up, the researchers found no difference between the two groups. But at the 18-month follow-up, they found that the combination of medication plus day treatment was superior to medication alone. Individuals who had received day treatment plus medication had fewer episodes of hospitalization, spent less time in the hospital, and had better social functioning. Day treatment plus medication was found to be clearly superior on almost every outcome measure. Interestingly, they also found that the overall treatment cost of day treatment plus medication was not higher than the treatment cost of medication alone. This might be considered a surprising result, since the recipients of day treatment with better outcomes were receiving more services than those receiving medication alone. The lower cost of their treatment was due to the fact that they used fewer inpatient services, spending fewer days hospitalized. Hospital services are very costly. Analyzing the results further, the researchers found that six of the day hospitals produced positive outcomes, while the other four day hospitals produced outcomes no better than medication alone. Studying which program factors were associated with both positive and negative outcomes, they determined: "High patient turnover and brief but more intensive treatment, particularly in terms of psychotherapeutic counseling by professionals, may lead to relapse for some schizophrenic patients" (Linn et al., 1979, p. 1061). In short, group psychotherapy, which costs more because it requires more professionally trained and higher paid staff, also produced poorer outcomes. This evidence supports a more practical, supportive, skills training approach—one of the hallmarks of PsyR—in contrast to more traditional therapy.

Beigel and Feder (1970) had similar results, finding that persons with more persistent conditions do poorly in programs designed to provide treatment more appropriate for individuals experiencing acute symptoms. This indicates that certain types of programs may be effective for persons in some phases of their illness and ineffective or even harmful during other phases.

Achieving Employment Outcomes: Clubhouses versus ACT

The clubhouse movement has pioneered employment strategies for persons with psychiatric disabilities. Having developed transitional employment early on, many clubhouses have also begun to provide supported employment (SE) as well (see Chapter 10 for descriptions of these programs). An early comparison of outcomes achieved by assertive community treatment programs (see Chapter 8) and clubhouse programs conducted by Stein, Barry, Van Dien, Hollingsworth, and Sweeney (1999) found strong similarities between the two approaches on measures of vocational activity, social relationships, social networks, and community integration. More recent studies (Schonebaum, Boyd, & Dudek, 2006; Macias et al., 2006) found that using SE, clubhouses, and ACT programs were able to produce similar employment outcomes. The Macias et al. study (2006) reported on a long-term experimental comparison of the employment results of a vocationally integrated assertive community treatment program (ACT) and an ICCD-certified clubhouse. They found that both the clubhouse and the ACT programs were able to achieve results similar to high-functioning SE programs. Similarly, Schonebaum and his colleagues found that the clubhouse and PACT (Program for Assertive Community Treatment) team they compared produced similarly high employment levels, with a slight edge to the clubhouse for earning higher wages and spending more weeks on the job.

Day Programming vs. Supported Services

Initially, many psychiatric day programs, especially partial hospitalization programs, saw their mission as preventing recidivism. Rather than helping the individual return to work, school, or the community environment of choice, preventing rehospitalization was the primary goal. Many programs effectively prevented recidivism but at the expense of keeping their clients dependent on the program. Some consumers label such programs as "day wasting programs." Dr. Gary Bond's statement "pre-voc is no voc" sums up a basic criticism of the long-term use of these programs: individuals become habituated to them and tend to lose motivation to move on. In addition, these programs were and are "clinic based," meaning that the service recipients had to go to the program or clinic for services. This is in sharp contrast with many of the newer supported (sometimes referred to as supportive) services, such as supported employment, supported education, supported housing, and ACT, which operate in the community in the environment of the individual's choice. These supported services reinforce community integration and actively assist the individual in achieving recovery goals that result in less dependence on the service system. As individuals learn more about these newer supported services, the idea of an extended stay in a psychiatric day treatment facility becomes less and less appealing.

Day Programming and Evidence-based Practice

When carried out effectively, psychiatric rehabilitation day programs are complex entities providing a host of different services designed to meet the needs of individual consumers. For example, a program might provide its members with assertive case management services for advocacy and supports (see Chapter 8), skills training, medication evaluation and monitoring, illness management and recovery (IMR) training (see Chapter 3), family psychoeducation (see Chapter 14), supported employment services (see Chapter 10), supported education (see Chapter 11), and integrated services for persons with substance abuse problems (see Chapter 9). Each of these services, if carried out correctly, is either an evidence-based practice or a promising practice being tested as a possible evidence-based practice. In fact, the ideal psychiatric rehabilitation day program would consist of a large set of high-fidelity, evidence-based practices that could be offered to consumers on an as-needed and as-requested basis.

While the current state of PsyR day programming is very far from such an ideal, the advent of evidence-based practice in combination with the recovery movement may hasten change in this direction. System-wide and individual program change processes based on securing the positive and predictable outcomes obtainable with high-fidelity evidence-based practices have a high potential for success. Chances for positive change may also increase if consumers and consumer advocates demand that programs provide services with proven effectiveness (i.e., evidence-based practices) based on consumer choice. Because an effective PsyR day program is necessarily composed of a constellation of evidence-based practices, as previously described, PsyR day programming itself will not be an evidence-based practice. The advantage of one program providing all of these services is very clear. Coordination of services is carried out more effectively and efficiently. The need for consumers to "negotiate" the system is greatly reduced, which minimizes the stress often experienced when trying to access needed services. Some may see a possible disadvantage since opportunities for community integration created by moving from service to service may be lost. In fact, good services work to connect people to natural community supports as much as possible.

Acute Partial Hospitalization

In many cases, the use of partial hospitalization rather than inpatient hospitalization remains the more normalized and less stigmatizing choice. While there is general agreement that acute partial hospitalization is a viable and often preferable alternative to inpatient hospitalization (see Chapter 15), there are no recent studies or controlled clinical trials comparing outcomes between acute partial hospitals and inpatient treatment. Issues such as which individuals would achieve the greatest benefits from this option and the economic savings of using the partial hospital lack empirical evidence. Still, acute partial hospitalization is a widely recognized modality that is assumed to be beneficial when employed correctly.

CONTROVERSIAL ISSUE
Close Day Programs or Retool Them as Recovery Centers?

If these programs are closed, what will replace them? If they are still open, what good are they doing? Which strategies will produce the best outcomes?

With the advent of supported services such as supported employment, supported education, and supported housing that provide services in the individuals' environments of choice, clinic-based psychiatric day programs have fallen out of favor. With long lengths of stay, resemblance to hospital environments, and lack of community integration psychiatric day programs have been criticized by advocates, funders, and service recipients. Some states continue using day programs as a primary service modality. For example, as of 2011, 12,000+ persons in New Jersey were served in psychiatric day programs, while only approximately 2500 were served in assertive community treatment (http://www.state.nj.us/treasury/omb/publications/13budget/index.shtml; p. D165).

(Continued)

> CONTROVERSIAL ISSUE
> *Close Day Programs or Retool Them as Recovery Centers?—(Continued)*
>
> While these programs continue to be funded, increasing numbers of service recipients simply refuse to attend them, literally voting with their feet.
>
> Several US states, such as Pennsylvania, New Hampshire, and Rhode Island, have successfully closed their day programs, offering supported employment to everyone and a combination of case management and outpatient services without increased negative effects on those served (e.g., Becker et al. 2001; Evans et al., 2012). Other alternative strategies exist, such as creating peer- or consumer-operated drop-in or self-help centers that supply the social support that is lost when psychiatric day programs are closed. In some places, day programs are being replaced by "intensive outpatient" programs, consisting of a few weekly visits of a few hours each. This may be simply an abbreviated version of psychiatric day treatment.
>
> Still, some program members and their families continue to oppose their closing. Individuals who have "found a home" at a psychiatric day program are often reticent to, for example, leave the program to obtain employment (see Bond et al., 1995). Additionally, some families may not feel comfortable about their loved ones functioning more independently in the community with supports provided on an as-needed basis.
>
> Reports in the literature of converting partial hospital programs into platforms for the provision of supported services began with Becker's report on Rhode Island conversions mentioned earlier. More recently, Evans and his colleagues (2012) reported on the conversion of partial hospital programs in Pennsylvania into Community Integrated Recovery Centers. These Centers incorporate consumer choice and supported services with the goal of assisting service recipients to achieve their recovery goals. Other programs may evolve their partial hospital services by adding evidence-based strategies like Illness Management and Recovery (IMR), Family Psychoeducation, and Integrated Dual Diagnosis Treatment (IDDT), as well as wellness approaches. These partial hospital programs may also be set in agencies that offer supported services (i.e., supported education, supported employment, and supported housing) that assist program members to achieve recovery goals and community integration while keeping the service recipients connected to the agency.

Summary

Psychiatric rehabilitation day programming has roots in the clubhouse and partial hospitalization movements. These programs were the principal treatment facilities for many of the people deinstitutionalized during the 1960s, 1970s, and 1980s. When effective, these programs are characterized by the belief that service recipients and service providers together can create an environment that is conducive to treatment, rehabilitation, and recovery. Research has demonstrated that some program designs (e.g., a focus on the here-and-now or less formal therapy) produce outcomes that are superior to medications alone (Linn et al., 1979). Research has also demonstrated that these programs are economically efficient. Today's effective programs are a combination of elements of the partial hospitalization movement (e.g., emphasis on medication or treatment) and the clubhouse movement (e.g., emphasis on quality of life or consumer empowerment). Some of these programs have grown into large multiservice agencies that attempt to provide for most if not all of the needs of individuals diagnosed with severe mental illnesses. While these programs are falling out of favor with many professionals and consumers, the advent of evidence-based practices and the recovery movement may supply the impetus and the standards necessary for effective reform.

Class Exercises

Exercise 1

Psychiatric Rehabilitation Day Program Design Activity

This exercise can be done individually or with groups of students working together, imagining they are assigned to a committee to redesign a day program. In either case, think about the philosophy or approach you wish to implement. Then decide what your choices would be on the following nine variables that will determine how your program functions:

1. **Member/Staff Ratio**—This may range from very low (e.g., 4 members/1 staff) to high (e.g., 16 members/1 staff) depending on the type and philosophy of the program.
2. **Program Size**—May vary from a small (e.g., 25 members) to a very large (hundreds of members) program.
3. **Staffing**—May vary from being predominantly paraprofessional staff (less than a college degree) to predominantly professional (graduate degree).
4. **Staffing Pattern**—May vary from being a generalist pattern where staff carry out multiple roles with little regard for academic or professional credentials to a specialist staffing pattern in which staff carry out specified organizational or professional roles.
5. **Attendance Requirements**—May vary from laissez-faire (consumers attend when they wish) to strict and mandatory (similar to a regular work environment).
6. **Scheduled Program Time**—May be loose, varied, and flexible or may approximate a typical work environment.
7. **Treatment Focus**—May vary from no treatment other than concrete feedback about the task at hand to intensive and frequent group and individual therapy.
8. **Program Ingredients**—May offer differing amounts (from none to all day) of recreation, socialization, supportive individual and/or group therapy, expressive therapies (e.g., art or dance), pre-vocational skills training, specific skills training, work units, and transitional or supported employment. These ingredients should be offered in an internally consistent pattern with respect to program type and philosophy.
9. **Empowerment**—Programs range from being run by consumers to being totally controlled by the staff. Clues to the degree of empowerment in a particular program might be the degree of authority wielded by a member government, the presence of members in important meetings, and the ability of members to shape both their individual treatment plans and the program in ways important to them.

Table 7.2   Program Type by Program Variables Matrix

Program Variables	Program Type		
	Maintenance	Movement	Acute
Member/staff ratio			
Program size			
Staffing			
Staffing pattern			
Attendance requirements			
Scheduled program time			
Treatment focus			
Program ingredients			
Empowerment			

Instructions

Based on Neffinger's taxonomy of partial hospitalization programs, using the program type by program variables matrix shown in Table 7.2, fill in the value of each variable (e.g., member/staff ratio=low, staffing pattern=general, empowerment=high) under each program type. You should have a clear rationale for each decision.

Exercise 2

Assume that the mental health administration of a mid-sized city has determined that the three partial hospitalization programs it operates will be closed within two years. Each of these three programs serves about 20 persons per day. Combined, they have a total census of active participants of approximately 180. Taking cost into consideration as well as the likely needs and recovery goals of the people being served, outline a set of alternative services that can be used as an alternative to these partial hospitalization programs. Provide the likely strengths and weaknesses of each of the elements you are proposing. Write these up as an initial draft proposal to the mental health administration.

8

Assertive Community Treatment and Case Management

I am not a case and I don't need to be managed.
Anonymous

I love them. The team is warm and welcoming just being there. They've been there for me. I've been going through some tragedies. And they're just there to listen and to help me throughout. And that's something that I always wanted, somebody to be there helping.
An ACT participant from an anonymous survey

CHAPTER OUTLINE

Psychiatric Rehabilitation. http://dx.doi.org/10.1016/B978-0-12-387002-5.00008-1

Psychiatric rehabilitation (PsyR) responds to the variety of needs of persons living with serious mental illness. Given the multifaceted nature of the challenges caused by these illnesses and fragmented systems of care, it is necessary to coordinate both services and resources. This co-ordination is generally known as case management and it is an essential ingredient of many psychiatric rehabilitation programs. At the same time, some people with psychiatric illnesses who need a variety of services and resources may not receive them unless they are sought out and contacted in the communities where they live. The most effective strategy for accomplishing this is known as "assertive community treatment" (ACT).

This chapter will answer the following questions:

1. *Why do psychiatric rehabilitation services require so much coordination?*
2. *What are case management, outreach, and assertive community treatment?*
3. *Why are these approaches essential to psychiatric rehabilitation?*
4. *How do assertive community treatment and case management differ?*
5. *What is the evidence that these approaches are effective?*
6. *How is ACT employed to address other unique issues within PsyR?*

Introduction

Deinstitutionalization, the policy of discharging to the community people who had been institutionalized for long periods of time, began in earnest during the early 1970s in the United States and then spread to other countries. Moving the site of treatment from large, long-term institutions to the community was an important milestone for persons living with severe mental illness. In a five-year period between 1970 and 1975, more than 100,000 individuals were discharged into the community for treatment. By 1985, the number of individuals in state and county psychiatric hospitals around the country had been reduced by 450,000 (Geller, 2000).

As deinstitutionalization proceeded, many problems with the community treatment of persons who were formerly institutionalized emerged. One critical report questioned a policy that "releases mentally ill individuals into community facilities that don't exist" (Santiestevan, 1975). In 1986, *Newsweek* magazine wrote an exposé on the effects of deinstitutionalization; titled "Abandoned," the article pointed out that despite the good intentions of the deinstitutionalization reforms, thousands of people with mental illness were left to fend for themselves on the street (*Newsweek*, January 6, 1986, pp. 14–15).

As they deinstitutionalized their populations, psychiatric hospitals also began to reduce the length of stay of newly admitted individuals. Unlike the previous era, when long-term hospitalization was the rule, psychiatric hospitals began discharging individuals after very short stays. Sadly, many of those discharged returned to the hospital after equally short stays in the community. This created a new set of problems for these people and the psychiatric treatment system that was supposed to serve them.

The problem of individuals returning to the hospital, a phenomenon known as **recidivism**, was new. This cycle of frequent discharge and readmission to the hospital became known as the "revolving door" syndrome. While warehousing individuals in large psychiatric institutions was, in large part, a thing of the past, community treatment still had a long way to go to meet the needs of people with psychiatric disabilities. This revolving door issue is still present today.

> *Todd had his first psychotic episode at age 20, after a prep school career marked by brilliance in science, baseball, and the piano. His family spent his college tuition on private psychiatric care and when their savings were exhausted they transferred him to a state mental institution. In and out of the hospital for years, Todd, now 37, recently was released to a boarding home in Worcester, Massachusetts. Three weeks later, he was mugged, an event that precipitated yet another psychotic breakdown. "He tried so hard to make it," his mother says. "They all try so hard, and they fail because they receive no care. It's torture for the families to watch that. These people are too sick to be let out into the community without any help. It's a national disgrace."* (Newsweek, *January 6, 1986, pp. 14–15*)

Some have characterized the deinstitutionalization movement as essentially an overambitious, unrealistic plan driven by rhetoric, myth, and good intentions, but lacking any real planning (e.g., Aviram & Segal, 1973; Kirk & Therrien, 1975; Klerman, 1977; Kohen & Paul, 1976). Planners had underestimated the difficulties of recently released individuals. In fact, people with serious mental illnesses were often "ghettoized," or socially excluded (Aviram & Segal, 1973). One consumer wrote that the conditions she saw in the community were often worse than those in the hospital and that it was a myth that one treatment setting (i.e., the community) was better than another (i.e., the hospital) (Allen, 1974). In fact, for many of the people who were deinstitutionalized, the movement that was heralded as bringing important legal rights to individuals with psychoses was actually a major catastrophe in terms of the quality of life of many people with serious mental illness.

These problems persist today; the coordination of care in the community is often fragmented and is in need of significant repair (President's New Freedom Commission, 2003). One of the authors of this text recently (2012) spoke with the parents of a young man with a serious mental illness and co-occurring disorder who has been hospitalized 20 times in the past 18 months! This is an extreme—but unfortunately not unique—example.

The Need for Continuity of Care

As with any broadly disabling condition, the person coping with major mental illness often requires a wide scope of services. These include basic needs such as food, shelter, and clothing. Various types of treatments and rehabilitation are also required. Ideally, these services are best delivered in an uninterrupted flow over time until the disability is corrected or compensated for. This concept of receiving all the services necessary for the length of time they are required and across all settings is called **continuity of care**. The continuity of care issues for people with psychiatric disabilities are critically important and, given the nature of the disability, often difficult to solve. Hospital environments were designed to meet all the basic needs of patients with serious mental illnesses. Major continuity of care problems first arose as individuals moved from the centralized institutional environment of the psychiatric hospital to the decentralized multiagency environment of the community. Some researchers believed that meeting the continuity of care needs of individuals was an important hospital benefit inadvertently lost with the rush to deinstitutionalize (Kirk & Therrien, 1975). The hospitals usually included medical staff, housekeeping staff, and recreation workers, all integrated within one large institution. In contrast, community services are usually provided by different agencies and programs that often communicate poorly with one another.

On returning to the community, a typical consumer might find herself attending a partial care program or clubhouse during the day, receiving her medication from a private physician, and living in a private boarding home. Previously, the hospital staff had orchestrated even the smallest details of her life. Now, in the community, she has to deal with three or more separate organizations. In the hospital, her modest economic needs for food, clothing, and shelter were met. Outside the hospital, she has concerns about maintaining her income through disability or welfare payments. In addition, she now needs medical benefits, from Medicaid or a similar program, in order to pay for her physician, medication, and treatment services. Worse still, if she failed in any of these community settings she might find herself on the street, out of medication, or back in the hospital. At the very moment she is trying to reestablish herself in the community, her opportunities for failure have been multiplied and the potential sources of stress in her life, which might aggravate her illness, have greatly increased. Paradoxically, improvements in her life might prove to be troublesome as well. In countries like the United States, a large reduction in symptoms or obtaining regular employment might make her ineligible for her disability benefits and perhaps medical coverage. A number of recent improvements in this area are reviewed in Chapter 10, but such concerns still persist.

In the early years of deinstitutionalization, the community services available for discharged individuals were new and often uncoordinated. With different agencies or programs responsible for different aspects of an individual's treatment, a "diffusion of responsibility" problem arose. Diffusion of responsibility refers to a situation in which shared responsibility for an issue or problem allows each of the responsible parties to assume that another party will take care of it, often with the result that no one takes care of the situation (Daley & Latane, 1968). This social psychological phenomenon can be observed in large cities where bystanders have been known to literally step over someone lying on the sidewalk or drivers may pass a broken-down car by the side of the road, assuming that someone else has already called for help. In the context of community services for persons with severe and persistent mental illness, while every service or program had some degree of responsibility for some aspect of an individual's treatment and care, no one was responsible for the whole person. Staff at one agency might assume some other agency or person should be taking care of issues that their agency was not designed or funded to deal with. This increased jeopardy created a situation by which consumers fell through the cracks of the service delivery system. These consumers would often return to the hospital, end up living on the streets, or become homebound recluses.

In addition to the difficulty of connecting with needed community services, the newly discharged person often found that certain services simply did not exist (Test, 1979). Partly because of a lack of affordable housing, in some places individuals were given bus tickets and literally discharged into the streets. Vocational programs were also in very short supply during the early stages of deinstitutionalization. In these situations, continuity of care could not be achieved due to a lack of available services.

To appreciate the vast scope of this problem, we must multiply the plight of each individual consumer by the hundreds of thousands of deinstitutionalized individuals. The increased stress associated with dealing with a complex, often disorganized, and unconnected treatment delivery system contributed to the high rates of recidivism experienced by this population.

A Nonsystem System

In the United States, the responsibility for many of the services and resources that can potentially comprise a system of care are administered at the federal, state, county, and municipality level. Occasionally, different levels of government collaborate. Within levels of government, multiple departments may administer each type of funding or service. In some cases, quasi-governmental, public authorities deliver services. PsyR and other mental health and rehabilitation services are overwhelmingly delivered by non-governmental entities, nonprofit (and sometimes for-profit) organizations primarily financially dependent on government funding and to a lesser extent on private insurance and self-payment. In this mélange of circumscribed and overlapping responsibility, is there a single point where the buck stops? Usually, the answer is no.

One father attempted to diagram the system, or rather nonsystem, of care his family needed to navigate to help his son. This diagram is shown in Figure 8.1.

This diagram of the service system speaks for itself. It is difficult to follow the connections, difficult to understand, even difficult to read its individual components. It is

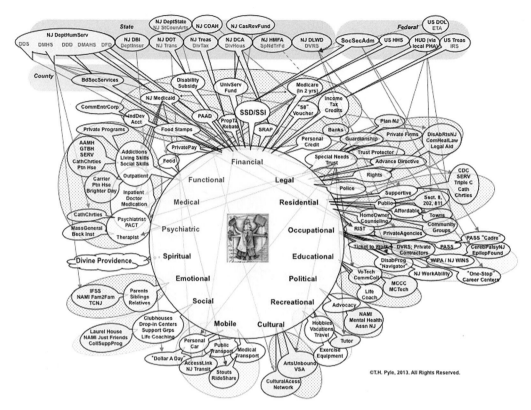

FIGURE 8.1 "The System": A complex web of needs, services, providers, and funders for those afflicted with mental illness in New Jersey. From the perspective of a family entwined in the system. *By T.H. Pyle, April 13, 2013.*

a metaphor for people seeking service, their families, and the service providers who are trying to help them.

Risk of Rehospitalization

The risk of rehospitalization is highest during the first six months after a person is discharged from the hospital. People are hospitalized during the acute phase of their illness and this instability may extend past their discharge. An important contributor to recidivism is failure to connect with needed services and supports in the community. Everyone is aware of the difficulties and frustrations involved in dealing with large, impersonal bureaucratic systems. Many are living under very adverse circumstances and, partly in response to these circumstances and their symptoms, abuse both legal and illegal substances. Some have other sorts of health concerns which they find challenging to manage. Unstable housing and unemployment contribute further to the risk of hospitalization. It is little wonder that persons often relapse during the months directly after discharge.

Awareness of the Need for Care Coordination at the National Level

As the negative effects of massive deinstitutionalization in the United States became obvious, the need for coordination of care in the community for persons with serious mental illness became apparent. The US Congress passed PL 99-660 (1973), the Comprehensive Mental Health Services Act, which required each state to develop a plan for providing community-based services for persons suffering from severe and persistent mental illness. This act required each state to include case management services as an element of their plan.

Case Management

The term "case management" can mean widely different things to PsyR professionals. Despite the varied treatment procedures these differences usually represent, there is fairly good agreement about the goals of a case management system. Case management refers to any "process or method for insuring that the consumer is provided needed services in a coordinated, effective, and efficient manner" (Baker & Intagliata, 1992, p. 215).

The use of the term "case management" has also become an issue for consumers, some of whom state that they are not a "case" and they do not need to be "managed." The United States Psychiatric Rehabilitation Association, for example, cautions against the use of terms such as "case study." Some people have even suggested that the term "care management" be used to replace "case management." In this book, we have decided to continue to use "case management" since it is a useful way to refer to all the issues surrounding individuals' treatment and rehabilitation. In addition, the term is widely understood and is used in the many informative articles that are referenced in this chapter. Clearly, "case" is not an appropriate term for the person served but rather for the circumstances and conditions influencing the individual's life. Much of this chapter focuses on models of service provision described in the PsyR literature and the research that has been done to examine their efficacy.

Baker and Intagliata (1992) have done extensive research on case management. They define four basic service objectives that are common to successful case management services. These programs ensure the following:

1. **Continuity of care**—The individual receives comprehensive services over an appropriate period of time.
2. **Accessibility**—The person can enter and use the services he or she needs.
3. **Accountability**—The system accepts responsibility for the services provided.
4. **Efficiency**—Services are provided in an economical fashion.

Providing consumers with needed services in a coordinated, effective, and efficient manner actually requires many distinct case management functions. Agranoff (1977) suggested that a good case management system should carry out five basic functions for its clients:

1. **Assessing**—identifying the client's needs
2. **Planning**—developing a comprehensive service plan for the client
3. **Linking**—connecting the client with services to be delivered
4. **Monitoring**—ensuring that the services are actually delivered to the client
5. **Evaluating**—assessing the client's response to services and providing follow-up

Furthermore, Baker and Intagliata (1992) suggest that a good case management system may also reach out to clients who are "service-resistant," advocate for clients so that they receive services at other agencies and programs, and provide direct services to clients.

Of course, a case management program's ability to help consumers get their needs met depends in part on the resources available in a given community. An ideal community support system (CSS) offers a wide array of supports and services. The concept of a comprehensive CSS came out of NIMH's Community Support Program demonstration projects in the late 1970s and was used to help states plan their mental health systems. Although the funding for these services has largely disappeared, many US states have adopted these practices. Consumers, family members, practitioners, and mental health administrators all helped to identify the components of an ideal CSS, which include the following:

- Identification of and outreach for those in need of service
- Mental health treatments
- Rehabilitation services
- Crises response services
- Housing
- Health and dental care
- Protection and advocacy
- Peer support
- Family and community support
- Income support and entitlements

Case management is seen as essential to coordinate an effective CSS. It has been described as the glue that holds a CSS together, ensuring that consumers get access to everything they need to live successfully in the community (Stroul, 1989).

The Case Manager

The case manager is both a PsyR Jack of all trades and the single point of responsibility at the core of the case management service. Potentially this practitioner could be an:

> … *Integrator, expeditor, broker, ombudsman, advocate, primary therapist, individual representative, personal program coordinator, systems agent, and continuity agent. (Baker & Intagliata, 1992, p. 217)*

At its best, case management is the epitome of individualized service. Each consumer is met on his or her own ground and is served individually. The first task of the case manager is to comprehend the needs and aspirations of the individual. To accomplish this, the case manager must form a close working relationship with the consumer, based on trust. With this assessment also comes a clear understanding of the aspects of the psychiatric disability that must be addressed through the case management process to achieve the consumer's goals. Working together, the next step for the consumer and case manager is the development of a comprehensive plan. The plan should take into account strengths and weaknesses as well as environmental contingencies, which will help the individual reach his or her desired goals. Consumer input at this planning stage is critical for future success. The consumer will not achieve goals that are not "owned" by the consumer. This concept of service planning is explained in greater detail in Chapter 5.

The next step is for the case manager to help the consumer link up with the agencies, services, or organizations necessary for achieving the goals of the plan. This phase might be carried out by the case manager or by the consumer depending on the types of services needed and the ability of the consumer. Regardless of who makes the initial contact, it is important for the case manager to form and maintain an ongoing professional relationship with each of the services the consumer is utilizing. This will allow the case manager to perform other functions such as monitoring, advocating, and evaluating if they are needed. Some level of monitoring should take place even if no problems exist. If carried out unobtrusively, this process can have important benefits. The consumer may be reassured that someone is watching out for his or her interests. The agency or service will be reminded that the case manager is an available resource and can provide support if the need arises.

One of the most difficult tasks for the case manager is evaluating the consumer's progress toward his or her goal(s). Working with the consumer, the case manager needs to help assess progress and develop priorities for services and goals. Premature advancement to the next phase of a plan can be as much of a threat as failure to advance to the next step when the consumer is ready. Because of the difficulties inherent in assessing others and in being evaluated, the level of trust established in the working relationship between the consumer and the case manager is often tested at this stage of the process.

Finally, achieving goals may not signal the end of the process. Often, new needs and aspirations emerge as goals are achieved. An effective case management process is prepared to provide support for the consumer indefinitely.

Models of Case Management

There are a large number of case management programs composed of service elements and philosophies based on different service provision models. In addition to programs that are specifically designed to provide case management services, many PsyR programs provide case management services as one part of an array of comprehensive services. For example, residential counselors in a program that describes itself as a supported housing program (see Chapter 12 for a description of supported housing) may spend much of their time carrying out the case management functions described above. Despite the diversity of ways that case management services are provided, a number of identifiably unique models of case management exist and can be defined. Historically, six models have been identified (Mueser et al., 1998; Corrigan et al., 2008):

- Broker model
- Clinical case management model
- Rehabilitation model
- Strengths-based model
- Assertive community treatment
- Intensive case management

Mueser and his colleagues (1998) summarized the features of these models as in Table 8.1.

These models have many common characteristics, which are discussed in the following sections. In practice, program administrators and staff often combine one or more elements of these approaches or choose to not include a particular element. Of these six models, assertive community treatment (ACT) or a program of assertive community treatment (PACT) is the most thoroughly researched practice. It was formerly known as the full-support model and is the only model that is an evidence-based practice.

Broker Case Management

Programs that utilize the broker model, also called the generalist model, depend on making referrals to other agencies and services in the community for most of the basic services provided to their clients. This traditional case management model uses its staff primarily for assessment, planning, linking, and advocating. In general, the staff of the expanded broker model program acts as an agent for their client rather than a service provider. Staff members become resource persons who steer their clients to different agencies or services to meet specific needs. Staff members also function as liaisons, advocates, and troubleshooters for their clients. For example, if a consumer is experiencing problems at his or her boarding home, the case manager might meet with the boarding home manager to discuss the problem and arrange for additional services, such as personal skills training (e.g., personal hygiene or clothes washing). It should be obvious from this example that for the staff member using the expanded broker model, direct experience with existing community services (including knowing key staff persons, program rules and hours, and so on) is a must.

While its influence on the quality and emphasis of services provided is necessarily reduced, this model has the advantage of allowing for much larger caseloads than the other three models described here. Obviously, the effectiveness of the expanded broker model depends on the comprehensiveness and effectiveness of a community support system. In other words, this model has difficulty making up for a lack of available services because it can only link to what is currently available. The case management task in such

Table 8.1 Features of Different Case Management Models

Program Feature	Brokered Case Management	Clinical Case Management	Community Care Model		Assertive Community Treatment	Intensive Case Management
			Strengths Model	Rehabilitation Model		
Staff : patient ratio	1 : 50?	1 : 30+	1 : 20–30	1 : 20–30	1 : 10	1 : 10
Outreach to patients	Low	Low	Moderate	Moderate	High	High
Shared caseload	No	No	No	No	Yes	No
24-hour coverage	No	No	No	No	Often	Often
Consumer input	No	Low	High	High	Low	Low
Emphasis on skills training	No	Low	Moderate	High	Moderate?	Moderate?
Frequency of patient contacts	Low	Moderate	Moderate	Moderate	High	High
Locus of contacts	Clinic	Clinic	Community	Clinic/Community	Community	Community
Integration of treatment	Low	Moderate	Low?	Low?	High	High?
Direct service provision	Low	Moderate	Moderate	Moderate	High	High
Target population	SMI	SMI	SMI	SMI	SMI high service utilizers	SMI high service utilizers

From Mueser, Bond, Drake, and Resnick, 1998. Models of community care for severe mental illness: A review of research on case management. *Schizophrenia Bulletin, 24*(1), 40.

an environment becomes one of ensuring that the consumer takes advantage of the services that are available.

Clinical Case Management

Clinical case management resembles the broker model just described, particularly in the coordination of resources and services. However, in addition, some services are provided directly by the case manager. These may include time-limited and intermittent individual counseling, skills training, and psychoeducation. Some monitoring of the individual and crisis services are provided. Generally, the term has come to mean the broker model of case management with supportive counseling.

Rehabilitation Case Management

The rehabilitation model follows a traditional rehabilitation approach. Its emphasis is on helping clients achieve success in the environments of their choice. Clients chose an overall rehabilitation goal and complete a functional assessment from which a rehabilitation plan is developed. Under this model, the case manager focuses on skill development until the client establishes a support network (Goering, Wasylenki, Farkas, Lancee, & Ballantyne, 1988). The rehabilitation model is case management within the context of the overall PsyR approach (Hodge & Draine, 1993). Chapter 5 provides a detailed overview of the PsyR assessment, service planning, and intervention process. It is an intriguing approach because of its heavy emphasis on PsyR values, but it has not been widely researched.

Strengths Case Management

The strengths model is based on two assumptions (Rapp & Goscha, 2006; Modrcin, Rapp, & Chamberlin, 1985). The first assumption is that to be a successful person, regardless of whether you have a serious mental illness or not, you must be able to use, develop, and access your own potential and have the resources to do this. The second assumption is that a person's behavior is dependent of the resources he or she has available. A focus on the individual's strengths, as opposed to his or her pathology, defects, and symptoms, is the defining element of this model, making it consistent with PsyR principles.

In this model, the case manager acts as a mentor who assists the client in problem solving and resource development (Hodge & Draine, 1993). Unlike many traditional approaches, the strengths and interests of the individual are the primary emphasis. Rather than emphasizing problems such as a lack of punctuality or poor personal appearance, interventions are focused on helping persons use their strengths to succeed in natural environments of their choice and their places within those environments, known as niches. Through assertive outreach to the individual and to gain support and resources, the case manager facilitates the person's pursuit of interests and opportunities of his or her choice in the community. Thus, with the strengths approach, individual strengths are emphasized over psychopathology and deficits, both of which have usually been over-emphasized in most of the lives of people served. Its major principles are:

- People can learn, grow, and change.
- The case manager's relationship with the service recipient is essential.
- Interventions are based on self-determination.
- Assertive outreach will be used when necessary.
- The community is seen as a treasure trove of resources, not as a barrier.

This approach is very consistent with the vales and principles of psychiatric rehabilitation. Unfortunately, there is not much controlled research on the strengths model.

Assertive Community Treatment

In addition to providing the five basic case management functions, the assertive community treatment (ACT) model directly provides most or all of the necessary services needed by persons living with serious mental illness. Thus, there is little or no emphasis on referring clients to other services. In other words, ACT treatment team members provide basic case management services plus a variety of rehabilitative and treatment services. People are served as a shared caseload; that is, the entire team (not just one case manager) serves each individual. This team is composed of specialists from different service areas employed to ensure that clients have everything they need to make a good adjustment in the community. The multidisciplinary team typically includes a psychiatrist, nurse, rehabilitation counselor, substance abuse counselor, social worker, and perhaps a peer case manager. One member serves as team leader. This is the most widely researched model of case management and has the most extensive empirical support behind it (Dietrich, Irving, Park, & Marshall, 2011).

Intensive Case Management

Intensive case management is a general approach with a relatively low caseload and relatively few clients per staff person; it has many features of ACT but lacks some of its critical components, such as a multidisciplinary team or team-shared caseload. In some instances, this approach grew out of an existing broker or clinical case management program that saw the inadequacy of just coordinating care and responded to the need to provide coordinated care from a single point of responsibility. All services are delivered in the community and assertive outreach is seen as essential. It might be viewed as "ACT-light" by some experts, and others might not consider it a model or approach because it is not clearly defined or is defined differently in various locales (Corrigan et al., 2008).

Do Effective Case Management Programs Share Similar Characteristics?

Rapp and Goscha (2004) reviewed the relevant research literature on all forms of case management. They began by evaluating the quality of the research represented by each study. Applying very stringent criteria, they selected 22 research papers on case management and identified several important principles or active ingredients across effective case management approaches. These are:

• Case managers should deliver as much of the help as possible themselves rather than refer to other providers.
• Case managers should have primary responsibility for a person's services.
• Natural community supports (including people not paid to help the consumer) are the primary partners of the team.
• Case management work is done primarily in the community as opposed to in an office or program site.
• Caseloads should be small enough to allow frequent contact.
• Services should be time-unlimited, if needed.
• The availability of familiar people 24/7 is helpful to consumers.
• Case managers should facilitate informed choice by the consumers they serve.

The Story of Micky

The situation described in this story is a good example of the day-to-day challenges that face a PsyR professional providing case management services. As you read, consider the strategies represented by the different models of case management.

1. What services did the members of the case management team employ to help Micky?
2. What do you think they could have done differently?
3. What could they have done that might have been more effective?
4. What model of case management does this team most resemble and how can you tell?

At 23 years old, Micky had been hospitalized six times since her 19th birthday. A bright student who got only average grades, Micky had spent most of high school writing poetry and smoking marijuana. She had her first major psychotic episode a month after graduation and was hospitalized the next year with a diagnosis of schizophrenia, undifferentiated type.

The episodes of her illness followed a predictable pattern. After being stabilized on medication, Micky would be discharged. Initially, she would exhibit a high level of functioning and low level of symptomatology. For several months, she would make excellent progress toward her educational or vocational goals. Micky would then stop taking her medication because she was free from any symptoms, had accomplished a great deal, and believed that she no longer needed mental health treatment. After several weeks, her symptoms would return. She would begin to experience paranoid delusions, blame her family for all her problems, drop out of her job or school, and run away. When she was found, she was often in bad shape and required long-term hospitalization. Her doctors had tried long-acting, injectable medication but this did not break Micky's cycle of recurring acute episodes of schizophrenia. At times, she would also attend individual psychotherapy sessions after discharge and demonstrated "good insight" about her illness. Nevertheless, the pattern would repeat itself again and again.

Now, being discharged for the sixth time in four years, Micky was being referred to a case management team. She first met two of the team members in the hospital. They had talked to her about where she wanted to live and what she wanted to do when she left the hospital. Before discharge, one of the team members drove her to a garden apartment complex to meet a woman named Sylvia whom she might share an apartment with there. Micky and Sylvia got along fine. Sylvia had been hospitalized once, two years ago. Since then, she had completed her education and worked for a small company scanning and storing electronic documents. The case management team had served Sylvia since her discharge.

Micky had decided to go to work after discharge rather than go back to school. One member of the team helped Micky get a job as a billing clerk in a local heating oil company. The same team member visited Micky on the job for several weeks until she was sure that everything was going well. After discussing it with her case manager, she decided to tell some of her coworkers that she had been in the hospital. She was nervous about admitting her mental illness but pleased when she found that they were accepting rather than rejecting. Several days after telling the others about her mental illness, one of the other clerks called Micky aside. Swearing her to secrecy, she told her that she had been to a psychiatrist after her divorce and that he had given her pills to take. Micky felt accepted. At home, she also got along well with Sylvia. Team members visited the apartment frequently when she first moved in. They helped arrange for her bank accounts and a low-cost mobile phone. They set up meetings so she and Sylvia could devise ways of sharing the household bills. They divided the household chores between them. At the end of each week, a team member would visit and ask how things were going, if there were any problems, and if there was anything special coming up during the following week. Micky and Sylvia became friends.

As the members of the case management team knew, rapid initial success after discharge was Micky's typical pattern. Their goal was to identify signs of increased symptoms, often referred to as decompensation, and intervene as quickly as possible. They informed Micky and Sylvia about this plan. They told Micky that if and when she began to decompensate they would arrange for her to see the team psychiatrist for evaluation and a possible increase or change in medication. They also told her they had a respite bed available if she needed more support than she had at the apartment. They stressed to her that she had a biological disease like diabetes or arthritis and that one of the characteristics of her illness was periodic psychotic relapses. Her job was to recognize when she was becoming ill and to inform the team so that they could help her get more treatment.

Eight months after moving in with Sylvia, Micky decided to stop taking her medication. After a week, Sylvia noticed that Micky's medication had not been touched and asked her about it. Micky got very angry at first, but Sylvia reminded her of what the team had said about her recurrences of symptoms. She said it wasn't her fault but that she needed to get more help. Micky called a team member and told them what had happened. Within an hour, a team member was at the apartment. After evaluating her and consulting with the psychiatrists by phone, her prescription was changed, adding something to help her sleep better. He asked her to come and see him the next day at the office to see how the new medications where doing. When the team members left, Micky thanked Sylvia.

Micky continued to get worse for several days. She experienced paranoid ideation, had several arguments with Sylvia, and got into a dispute with a coworker. One evening, she even felt so agitated that she asked to sleep at the respite bed where there was a 24-hour nurse for the night. During this crisis period, a team member visited the apartment every evening to see how things were going and monitor Micky's progress. A week and a half after she had seen the psychiatrist, she began to feel better. She felt the same way she had each time she had been discharged from the hospital. But this time she hadn't been in the hospital; she still had her job and her apartment and Sylvia was still talking to her.

Development of Assertive Community Treatment: A Practical Innovation

In the early 1970s, staff working at the Mendota Mental Health Institute in Madison, Wisconsin, began developing strategies to solve the "revolving door" problem at their hospital. Just as with other fields, many of the innovations in psychiatric rehabilitation emerge from seemingly casual observations and the initiatives of regular staff members doing what they see as practical and necessary.

In the fall of 1970, soon after Arnold Marx had assumed leadership of the Special Treatment Unit (STU), a research unit of the Mendota Mental Health Institute, and after his colleague, Mary Ann Test, had been at the STU for two of what had become rather standard six-month-long studies, a critical event happened at the traditional staff party held to celebrate the end of each study and to generate ideas about what type of study to do next. Few staff came. Those present pulled their chairs into a circle and began to discuss why others did not show up. Some staff did not come, it was observed, because their morale was low. They were discouraged because, despite their energetic efforts to create innovative inpatient treatments enabling discharge (Mendota was a Wisconsin state psychiatric hospital), recently discharged patients kept coming back to the hospital.

In this discussion, one aide observed that when a social worker, Barb, followed patients into the community and provided aftercare, these patients tended not to come back to the hospital. As the evening wore on, they talked about how Barb did this. Someone suggested that the STU should do what Barb did and abandon the inpatient interventions. Eventually, it was agreed that this is what they would do, and the STU leadership, Drs. Marx and Test, stuck to this decision the next morning and thereafter. The next STU study was to be one about caring for persons with severe mental illness in the community (Greenley, 1995).

Marx, Test, and their colleagues, including Leonard Stein, a psychiatrist, set out to reduce recidivism rates by supporting their patients in the community so effectively after discharge that they would not need to be continually readmitted for individual treatment. They started with the assumption that high readmission rates came about because the individual needs of people with serious mental illness were not being met in the community (Test & Stein, 1978). From their experience, they knew that discharged hospital patients had the following needs that had to be met for them to be able to remain in the community:

- Material resources, including food, shelter, clothing, medical care, recreation, and so forth
- Coping skills to meet the demands of community life
- Motivation to persevere and remain involved with life
- Freedom from pathological dependent relationships
- A supportive system that assertively helps the individual with the preceding four requirements

The original model they developed was called Training in Community Living (TCL). They implemented it in a program where they could conduct ongoing research, which eventually became known as the Program for Assertive Community Treatment. TCL introduced an important innovation to PsyR: a support system that takes an assertive stance in helping consumers to stay out of the hospital. TCL staff visited clients in the community, wherever and whenever they needed assistance, rather than asking them to come to a particular site. This approach has been referred to as "a hospital without walls" (Harron, 1993) because it was designed as an alternative to inpatient treatment.

Test (1992) reported that the Madison TCL program team consisted of 13 staff providing services for 115 persons diagnosed with schizophrenic disorders. The team's main goal was to meet the needs necessary to maintain people in the community. To accomplish this, the team developed individualized service plans for each individual. Whenever possible, the team also carried out most aspects of the treatment plan. The interdisciplinary team, which was made up of specialists such as mental health technicians, nurses, and vocational rehabilitation counselors, worked together in a generalist mode to meet each client's needs. A generalist staffing pattern implies that each staff person can and sometimes does do each task. A psychiatrist was also a part-time member of the team.

TCL services were provided in the community, at the individual's home, recreation, or job site. This is sometimes referred to as *in vivo*, or in the client's real-life environment. This approach has many advantages; for example, teaching a client a skill in the location where it will be used is a highly effective intervention (see Chapter 5 for more on this concept). Perhaps most importantly, staff used an assertive outreach strategy to ensure that services were provided when and where they were needed. For example, if a client had difficulty remembering to take the correct dosage of medications, the team might visit him at home once or twice a day to deliver and monitor the medications. When appropriate, the TCL team also worked with families, community agencies, landlords, or whoever was involved in a client's support system.

Providing services to consumers in the community ensures that the services are individualized rather than watered down to meet the needs of a large group. The team provides consumers with symptom management in the form of medication monitoring and education, around-the-clock on-call assistance for crisis intervention, and brief hospitalization if necessary. The team also helps consumers obtain and maintain the basic needs of food and shelter and also social supports and assistance with family relations. Finally, the team helps consumers secure and maintain regular employment positions in the community. Initially, TCL was designed as a time-limited program. But they found that many consumers regressed when the program supports were removed. Rather than being time-limited, the current program is designed to provide services indefinitely or on an as-needed basis.

The process of readmitting consumers for short-term hospitalizations and then returning them to the community for aftercare services, sometimes referred to as "the revolving door syndrome," was both ineffective and very costly. Perhaps it would be better for the individual, and less costly for the system, to provide intensive case management services and keep the individual in the community. Research study results (Stein & Test, 1985; Test, 1992) supported this belief, and TCL was soon replicated in other parts of Wisconsin and eventually in other states and countries as well. When implemented in different locations, some agencies began to modify the TCL model in order to address the unique needs of their client population or in order to compensate for limited resources. For example, a program serving a high percentage of individuals with co-occurring diagnoses (e.g., severe mental illness and substance abuse) might require several team members to be substance abuse specialists.

Did Training in Community Living Work?

As the success of TCL became apparent, Test and Stein (1978) conducted research to test the effectiveness of their program compared with the traditional services offered in Madison. Their research design consisted of randomly assigning individuals newly admitted via hospital intakes to either the TCL program or traditional treatment. Traditional or "usual" treatment consisted of hospitalization and referral to a community agency. By the end of the first year, 130 individuals evenly divided between TCL and traditional treatment were included in their study. Of the 65 individuals assigned to TCL, 12 were rehospitalized compared to 58 of the 65 individuals rehospitalized among those served in the traditional treatment. In addition, TCL participants spent an average of 11 days in the hospital compared with the control group's average of 37 days in the hospital.

Evolution into ACT

Over the years, TCL has evolved into ACT with its critical ingredients and principles for implementation outlined in numerous studies (e.g., Phillips et al., 2001; Bond, Drake, Mueser, & Latimer, 2001). ACT employs a multidisciplinary team approach with the capacity to provide services 24 hours per day, 7 days per week when needed. The team approach ensures that someone with knowledge of each individual receiving services is always available if needed. In addition, caseload sizes are kept small (approximate ratio of one ACT team member to ten consumers), allowing a multi-disciplinary team of six to serve a caseload of 60. The team, including a part-time psychiatrist, nurse, case manager, substance abuse counselor, vocational specialist, and sometimes a peer/consumer provider, provides all treatment and rehabilitation services. The team meets frequently (often daily) and is led by a team leader who is also a "front-line" practicing clinician. The team provides all the services the person may need, including counseling or psychotherapy, medication, integrated substance abuse services, vocational rehabilitation, crisis intervention, and coordination with a housing provider.

As discussed earlier, all services are provided to consumers in the community rather than at clinics. All services are provided assertively; that is, individuals who do not respond or may initially refuse treatment are repeatedly contacted and offered the service. Service recipients are met or contacted wherever they can be found: at their homes, public places, and even in the streets. In ACT, there is no fixed length of stay and generally a "no close" policy; individuals can be served for as long as they wish. Services are offered intensively, if needed, with contact between staff and clients averaging four times weekly, but at least two hours per week. Generally, ACT teams control, in part or whole, the screening and evaluation for any needed psychiatric hospitalizations. They participate on hospital treatment teams and facilitate discharge planning. In jurisdictions where permitted by law, ACT teams will collaborate with probation and parole officials.

An additional feature of many ACT programs is the inclusion of peer providers. Peer providers are persons who are themselves recovering from mental illness who serve as team members. Peer providers have been found to be as effective in some ways as non-providers. Added to teams, they bring unique strengths and sometimes produce better outcomes (Craig et al., 2004). The addition of a consumer or peer to an ACT or case management team successfully engages more consumers (see Chapter 13). A recent study has examined whether employing mental health consumers as consumer providers or peer providers in ACT teams can enhance outcomes for clients with severe mental illness (Van Vugt et al., 2012). Twenty ACT teams serving over 530 people were assessed over a two-year period. Teams with peer providers were better at meeting their service recipients' needs in relation to their recovery and the number of days homeless was reduced, as were the number of days hospitalized. A review of 16 studies of consumer/peer providers on case management teams, including ACT by Wright-Berryman, McGuire, and Salyers (2011), found evidence supporting improved engagement but limited support for reduced hospitalizations and no support for some other outcomes. They conclude that including a consumer provider on an ACT team can enhance its outreach capability and improve engagement. The features and ingredients of ACT are shown in Box 8.1.

BOX 8.1   PRINCIPLES OF ASSERTIVE COMMUNITY TREATMENT

- Services are targeted to a specified group of individuals with severe mental illness, usually those at high risk for hospitalization, rehospitalization, or relapse.
- Services are provided to consumers in the community. Interventions are carried out at the locations where problems occur and support is needed, *in vivo* (in real life), rather than in hospital or clinic settings.
- Rather than brokering services, all treatment and rehabilitation services are provided directly by the assertive community treatment team, including counseling, addiction services, employment services, and close collaboration with housing providers.
- Team members share responsibility for all the individuals served by a multidisciplinary team, including a psychiatrist, nurse, social worker or other case manager, substance abuse specialist, vocational specialist, and—increasingly—peer provider. This team meets four or five times weekly.
- The staff-to-consumer ratio is small (approximately one-to-ten or less).
- The range of treatment and services is comprehensive, flexible, and individualized.
- Services are not time-limited, with no fixed or arbitrary length of stay and a "no close" policy.
- The team is assertive in engaging individuals in treatment and monitoring their progress.
- Supports are provided around the clock, including the availability of 24-hour crisis intervention.
- Services are offered fairly intensely with contact between staff and clients averaging four times weekly, at least two hours per week.
- Services emphasize medication management and practical everyday issues.
- ACT controls, in part, the screening and evaluation for any needed psychiatric hospitalizations, participates on hospital treatment teams, and facilitates discharge planning.

(Based on Teague et al., 1998; Phillips et al., 2001; Corrigan et al., 2008).

When Is a Program Actually ACT?

How do you know an ACT program when you see it? A widely used "fidelity scale," the Dartmouth Assertive Community Treatment Scale (DACTS; Teague et al., 1998), has been well validated. Fidelity, as introduced in Chapter 1, is about "faithfulness" to a particular treatment or rehabilitation model. DACTS has been used to assess fidelity of programs to the ACT model (Bond et al., 2001). Recently, a second fidelity instrument has been introduced, the Tool for the Measurement of ACT (TMACT) (Monroe-DeVita, Teague, & Moser, 2011; Stein, 2012), but it is not yet widely accepted and has some limitations (see McGrew, 2011).

Specific protocols exist to check whether a program is faithful to the ACT model. The program includes two or more trained raters assessing whether the principles listed in Box 8.1 are being implemented. Interviews with the staff and team leader are conducted.

BOX 8.2   GARY BOND, PHD

The research and writing of Gary Bond, PhD, retired Chancellor's Professor of Psychology at Indiana University–Purdue University Indianapolis, Research Fellow at Dartmouth University, have contributed to the field of psychiatric rehabilitation since 1979. Since entering the field as director of research at Thresholds, a large PsyR agency in Chicago, he has worked to understand how services can be more effective and to train professionals to work in the field. When he went to Thresholds for the first time, Dr. Bond found that the practical and egalitarian orientation appealed to him, as did the real-world relevance of the research questions. Does psychiatric rehabilitation help people get jobs? Does it help them to live independently? His interest in the answers to such questions has a personal side as well. Inspired by his sister's determination in coping with symptoms of schizophrenia, Dr. Bond is convinced that people with psychiatric disabilities can and should achieve full community integration.

Dr. Bond's research has focused on evidence-based practices, including studies of supported employment, assertive community treatment, and assessment of fidelity of implementation of evidence-based practices. Gary Bond's work is some of the most frequently cited research in the psychiatric rehabilitation literature.

Often, twenty or more charts of individual client records are reviewed. Questions addressed include appropriateness of the service recipients, quality and skill level of the staff, and the services provided in the community and coordination with hospitals. Frequency of team meetings and other organizational questions are also addressed.

One factor that has a large negative influence on fidelity is staff turnover. A five-year study found a staff turnover rate averaging 30 percent annually; that is, three out of ten members of the team leave the job each year! While too high, especially in terms of maintaining an ongoing working alliance with service recipients, it is comparable to the

---

BOX 8.3   ASSERTIVE COMMUNITY TREATMENT: AN EVIDENCE-BASED PRACTICE

Assertive community treatment is one of the most widely studied and utilized evidence-based practices (EBP). As this chapter has pointed out, ACT has many positive characteristics for both the consumer and the service delivery system. Essentially, comprehensive services including medication, counseling, case management, rehabilitation, substance abuse services, and other specialized supports are provided to the consumer in the environments of his or her choice.

ACT is a highly normalized service. The stigma attached in attending a mental health center or a psychiatrist's office is eliminated, although some argue that having one or more professionals arriving at your home or job might be somewhat stigmatizing and intrusive. At the same time, supports are provided on an as-needed basis to help the consumer achieve success in different settings such as school, work, and the community. Although ACT is a fairly high-cost community-based service, this increased cost is more than offset by the reduction in hospital utilization that is achieved. In fact, some states have employed ACT to help reduce the census of state psychiatric hospitals, allowing for reductions in the number of needed hospital beds and the closing of some hospitals.

Random controlled clinical trials have consistently demonstrated that ACT is effective at reducing the number of hospital days (time spent in the hospital). ACT programs have also demonstrated an increase in housing stability for their clients. Results on improved quality of life and increased client satisfaction with services have been mixed (Dixon et al., 2010; Dietrich et al., 2011).

---

wider community mental health field. Not surprisingly, high employee turnover is associated with low fidelity (Rollins, Salyers, Tsai, & Lydick, 2010). Does fidelity matter? Later in this chapter we will find out.

ACT and Other Aspects of Health

Because of the frequent contact of ACT teams with their service recipients, is it an effective intervention to monitor all of the body's systems and health concerns beyond mental health? Shattell and her colleagues (2011) found that ACT teams often recognize serious and chronic health problems and take on a variety of roles to address physical health problems. They face challenges in the integration of primary health care and mental health care and have not yet adopted promising practices in this area. This topic is discussed in more detail in Chapter 6 of this book.

Outcomes of ACT

Participants in ACT programs have more contact with their treatment team than people served in other approaches (Dixon et al., 2010). People in ACT are twice as likely as those in other types of services to maintain contact with their treatment providers. They are also more satisfied with their treatment, as are their family members, compared to their peers

CONTROVERSIAL ISSUE
Is Assertive Community Treatment Too Assertive?

The evidence-based practice assertive community treatment (ACT) has consistently proven effective at reducing hospital utilization and increasing housing stability (Bond et al., 2001; Marshall & Lockwood, 2004). The fact that staff members actively seek out individuals in the community to ensure that they are receiving the services they need is considered an important ingredient in the success of this strategy.

This "assertive" approach on the part of staff has several important benefits. Frequent staff member visits may help remedy the lack of insight experienced by some individuals with severe mental illness. Xavier Amador, in his book *I Am Not Sick: I Don't Need Help*, defines this lack of awareness as "anosognosia," a term referring to impaired awareness or ignorance of illness (Amador & Johanson, 2000). This was discussed in Chapter 2 of this text. In short, the individual is sometimes unaware of the symptoms or presence of the illness. It is not uncommon that a person in a floridly psychotic states says she feels "fine," experiencing no problems and no illness. In these circumstances, left unchecked, the individual typically continues to deteriorate until hospitalization is necessary. Assertive outreach may also help to identify problems before they become full-blown crises. For example, a problem with the landlord may be dealt with in a timely fashion before it escalates and ends in eviction.

While the benefits of an assertive approach are obvious, some consumers and professionals have raised concerns about the negative impact this can have on individuals (e.g., Ahern & Fisher, 2001; Diamond, 1995). Because of the strong emphasis on medication compliance in ACT services, some have questioned whether ACT is a "medical model" program rather than PsyR. In addition, some individuals have complained that ACT is intrusive and occasionally coercive (Ahern & Fisher, 2001).

Is there any evidence that ACT is too assertive or even intrusive? When, if ever, should the principles of choice and respect for the individual be violated in an effort to help? Should society be paternalistic and intrusive when an individual is not aware that he or she is putting himself or others at risk? Bond and his colleagues (2001) in their study reported that only 11 percent of the consumers enrolled in ACT found it to be intrusive, confining, or fostering dependency. Rosenheck and Neale in two reports (Rosenheck & Neale, 2001a, b) studied 40 ACT teams serving more than 1,500 consumers within the Veterans Affairs (VA) system to determine the extent to which "limit-setting" coercive interventions were offered. Coercive interventions included assigning a representative payee (someone other than the consumer to manage his or her money), the contingent withholding of services or supports until a desired behavior is established, invocation of external authorities such as parole or probation officers, and enforced "voluntary" or involuntary hospitalization. These coercive interventions were used with 10 percent of the ACT consumers in the VA. The coercive interventions tended to be used with individuals who had a more difficult course of their illness and recovery and were actually associated with poorer outcomes.

In some places, when someone is involuntarily committed to **outpatient** services, they are often enrolled in ACT. While coercive interventions sometimes result in poorer outcomes, an exception may exist when ACT is delivered as part of involuntary outpatient commitment. In a study comparing people voluntarily in ACT to those involuntarily committed, more improvement in outcomes was seen among those involuntarily receiving the service compared

---

CONTROVERSIAL ISSUE
Is Assertive Community Treatment Too Assertive?—(Continued)

to others, even though they were initially less motivated (Kortrijk, Staring, van Baars, & Mulder, 2010).

Participants served by ACT did not usually perceive a great deal of coercion or negative pressure, nor did they feel excluded from treatment-making decisions (Monroe-DeVita et al., 2012). However, when coercion was perceived, it was usually associated with diminished quality of life, less empowerment, and a weaker working alliance with staff. There is evidence that some staff people working on ACT teams resort to coercive or restrictive approaches. Staff self-report of the use of restrictive practices has been studied (Moser & Bond, 2011). Surveying 122 ACT staff people, they found that pessimistic attitudes and a lack of advanced training were associated with a more frequent use of restrictive practices.

---

in other services. Compared to other service recipients, they have superior treatment outcomes in a number of ways:

- Reduced number and length of hospitalization instances, which has been found in at least 11 controlled studies, with hospitalization reduced by 20 percent or more (Dixon et al., 2010). The number of instances of hospitalization is 40 percent less than that of those served in alternate approaches.
- More days in stable community housing and fewer days homeless, found in at least seven controlled studies. ACT clients were twice as likely to be living independently and were four times less likely to become homeless. They also spent fewer days homeless and more days in stable living arrangements (Bond et al., 2001).
- Less use of emergency, crisis intervention, and other services.
- Increased adherence to prescribed medication although less so among persons with co-occurring disorders (Fries & Rosen, 2011; Manuel, Covell, Jackson, & Essock, 2011).

Interestingly, ACT appears to be most successful among service recipients with the highest rate of hospitalization (Dixon et al., 2010).

The degree of fidelity to the ACT model, discussed elsewhere in this chapter, is associated with better outcomes. When implemented with fidelity, ACT programs are very good at promoting employment outcomes. Compared to other service recipients, ACT service recipients are more likely to have any type of paid employment and competitive employment (Dixon et al., 2010). They are also more likely to retain their jobs. ACT programs, in this regard, face many of the same challenges as other services (Waynor & Pratt, 2010) but as a group are more successful in promoting employment than standard care or other case management (Dietrich et al., 2011).

ACT is not perfect; for example, its effects may be limited to implementation in the United States (Killaspy et al., 2009; Dixon et al., 2010). In other countries, compared to alternate community team approaches, its outcomes are not as positive. It does not appear to have any specific effect upon individuals with co-occurring disorders in terms of substance abuse reduction, despite the fact that it generally includes relevant substance abuse services. Nevertheless, ACT is associated with greater housing stability and reduction of hospitalization utilization for the individuals it serves (Dixon et al., 2010; Dietrich et al., 2011). One study found that people served by ACT teams consistently spend fewer days in hospitals than those served by programs using standard case management approaches (Marshall & Lockwood, 2004). The cost of hospital care was consistently less for those in ACT, so the extra expense of the ACT service itself proved cost-effective.

Evaluating Case Management

Numerous research studies have been carried out to evaluate the effectiveness and efficiency of case management. Partly because of the differences between case management programs or lack of clarity about the definition of program models, the results of these studies have been mixed and sometimes contradictory. Nevertheless, there is clear consensus that case management is effective for achieving certain results. The research literature answers specific questions about the effectiveness of specific types of case management programs (Bond, McGrew, & Fekete, 1995; Chamberlin & Rapp, 1991; Mueser, Bond, Drake, & Resnick, 1998; Solomon, 1992).

Some time ago, Mueser et al. (1998) identified 75 controlled studies of case management for review. Most of these 75 studies examined ACT programs or intensive case management (ICM) programs because other models of case management were less well represented in the research literature. The ACT and ICM program models are very similar with respect to design (see Table 8.1). The major difference between them is that a group of ACT program staff share caseloads, whereas ICM program staff do not. This review provided clear evidence that these programs were effective at reducing time spent in the hospital and increasing clients' housing stability in the community.

Mueser et al. (1998) concluded that when case management services were reduced or withdrawn—for example, when programs had a designated length of service—consumers showed reduced levels of functioning. This has very important implications for funding as well as the design of future case management services. Nevertheless, the gradual reduction of ACT services to a lower level of intensity is possible without significant loss of the gains achieved. This is known as a step-down approach and has been found to be successful (Salyers, Masterton, Fekete, Picone, & Bond, 1998).

More recently, 38 controlled trials (n = 7328 participants) were included in a Cochrane review of case management research combining ACT with other ICM approaches (Dietrich et al., 2011). The trials provided data for two sets of comparisons: contrasting ICM with standard care and contrasting ICM to other types of case management. Regarding the contrast of ICM to standard care, 24 studies reported length of hospitalization data with the results favoring ICM. Nine studies found participants in the ICM group were less likely to be lost to contact and more likely to continue participation in services. Measures on a global level of functioning scale showed improvement among those receiving ICM compared to standard care. Consistent with earlier reviews, employment, housing status, and consumer satisfaction were more favorable in ICM.

When compared to other forms of case management, the Cochrane review (Dietrich et al., 2011) found that ICM did not reduce the average length of hospitalization. Nine studies did find ICM to be more advantageous than non-ICM in maintaining contact. However, in terms of other outcome variables, an advantage of ICM over other case management models was not found. This contrasts with earlier reviews in which ACT was found to have better outcomes. This result may have been confounded or lost by merging ACT with ICM approaches.

Fidelity and ACT

This Cochrane review (Dietrich et al., 2011) also examined whether fidelity to ACT was associated with more positive outcomes among those programs classified as ICM. It found that higher ACT fidelity was associated with decreased time in the hospital. How does a program ensure its own fidelity? Monroe-DeVita and her colleagues (2012) looked at 57 different studies on this subject. Four major strategies were identified as helping to ensure the quality (i.e., fidelity) of ACT programs: fidelity-based policy and administrative processes, training and consultation from outside experts, team operations, and program evaluation strategies.

ACT as an Early Intervention Strategy

Increased attention has been directed at the amount of time it takes before someone with psychotic symptoms receives appropriate treatment. The period between when a person becomes psychotic and when he or she first receives treatment for those symptoms has been labeled "duration of untreated psychosis" (DUP). The DUP for some individuals can be quite long. A DUP of about one year is fairly common (McGlashan, 2000). This situation may be partly due to the fact that many of the individuals in question are in their late adolescent or early adult years, periods of significant change in one's development (Holloway & Aitchison, 2003) or because many persons with psychosis are unaware of their condition (Amador & Johanson, 2000).

Being actively psychotic can be very unpleasant, frightening, and stressful, and longer periods without treatment simply compound the situation and therefore have a detrimental effect on an individual's social relationships, job performance, and family life (Drake, Haley, Akhar, & Lewis, 2000; Melle et al., 2004). Longer DUP has also been related to an increase in the negative symptoms of schizophrenia, the persistence of positive symptoms, and additional cognitive deficits (Malla & Norman, 2002). People who have a shorter duration of untreated negative symptoms or a shorter duration of untreated positive symptoms outperformed individuals with a long duration of untreated symptoms on memory tasks and attentional tasks (Cuesta et al., 2012). An early intervention to shorten DUP should improve both memory and attention span.

There is some evidence that persons with untreated psychosis are losing healthy brain neurons in specific areas of the brain (see Chapter 2). Thus, the longer one is acutely ill, the more damage is being done to the number, structure, and function of one's neurons in the frontal lobes, hippocampus, and other limbic structures (Pentilla et al., 2010; Malla, Bodnar, Joober, & Lepage, 2011). There is also some evidence of overall reduction in brain size (Malla, Bodnar, Joober, & Lepage, 2011). Shortening the duration of DUP should reduce brain neurotoxicity and improve long-term adjustment.

What is the best way to provide services to someone experiencing his or her first psychotic episode? The first problem is to identify people who are candidates for early intervention. One approach is to develop systems for detecting emerging cases and then to employ mobile outreach teams to serve them (Malla & Norman, 2002). Some countries, such as the United Kingdom, mandate this service (Holloway & Aitchison, 2003) and address early intervention by using teams of professionals similar to ACT teams.

To be effective, as a first step these teams need to establish working relationships with persons who have recently become ill and their families, who are often still in a state of denial about the illness. Once a relationship is formed, the teams provide education about the illness, medication, and side effects. They also ensure that the treatment is begun and complied with, reducing the DUP. Both denial and anosognosia are typical responses to these illnesses, making ACT an excellent helping strategy. McFarlane and his colleagues (2012) initiated a multisite study of Family-Aided Assertive Community Treatment and other interventions anticipated to significantly increase knowledge of the early phases of psychotic illness and the factors that may cause acute episodes (see Chapter 14 for more on PsyR interventions that involve family members).

ACT and Persons in the Criminal Justice System

The principles of ACT have been applied to serve persons with severe and persistent mental illness involved in the criminal justice system in a service known as forensic ACT. Examples of two nationally recognized models are the Thresholds Jail Program in Chicago, Illinois, and Project Link in Rochester, New York (Lamberti & Weisman, 2004). Both of these programs use ACT to engage clients through assertive outreach in clinical, residential, and social services. The Thresholds Jail Program is a collaboration between Chicago's largest PsyR provider and one of the nation's largest jail systems, Cook County, Illinois. These programs coordinate with the many components of the criminal justice system and provide services 24 hours per day. Both Threshold's Jail Project and Project Link have demonstrated decreased arrest and incarceration rates, lengthened the time individuals spend in the community, and decreased overall costs. This approach has been named "forensic assertive community treatment" (Lamberti et al., 2004). Compared to other types of services, forensic ACT teams do not avoid serving individuals who are more likely to have violent histories, are sex offenders, or have more complex clinical profiles in general (Cuddleback & Morrissey, 2011). Forensic ACT can meet the needs of persons found "not guilty by reason of insanity," reduces criminal recidivism, promotes abstinence from drugs, and improves quality of life (Smith, Jennings, & Cimino, 2010). Many forensic ACT teams collaborate with probation departments overseeing people with mental illness who are given non-custodial (not jail or prison) sentences (Lamberti, Deem, Weissman, & LaDuke, 2011).

Other Case Management Approaches for Jail Diversion Purposes

Unfortunately, new types of case management programs have become necessary because of the high level of involvement of persons with serious mental illnesses with the criminal justice system. Up to one-quarter of the prison population in the United States may have a serious mental illness (Cloyes et al., 2010). Nationally, attention has focused upon persons with serious mental illness becoming recidivists, that is, "repeaters," in terms of arrests, court appearances, and incarceration in local jails and state prisons (Steadman et al., 2011; Rivas-Vazquez et al., 2009). Often, these individuals are also homeless with co-occurring substance abuse disorders. Most of the criminal charges they face are disorderly persons' offenses or other minor, nonviolent offenses. Many stakeholders in the criminal justice and mental health systems, as well as the general public, believe these offenses are a consequence of their psychiatric disorders, not of criminal intent. All those involved (e.g., the people arrested, their families, police, prosecutors, jailers, and the public) would be better served if these individuals were provided with adequate mental health services and supported housing rather than incarceration.

It is not widely known that people with mental illness spend much longer sentences in jail than their peers who have committed the same offenses (Lamberg, 2004). They are also more likely to be reincarcerated in a shorter period of time. Among offenders with mental illness, 50 percent were reincarcerated in just over a year, half the time span of other offenders (Cloyes et al., 2010). Both rates of recidivism are staggeringly high, but the significantly higher rate for persons with mental illness is particularly noteworthy. Inmates with major psychiatric disorders (major depressive disorder, bipolar disorders, schizophrenia, and non-schizophrenic psychotic disorders) had substantially increased risks of multiple incarcerations (Baillargeon et al., 2009). Individuals with bipolar disorder had the highest risk of multiple reincarceration.

A number of jurisdictions are developing programs to divert persons with mental illness from jail and/or prison (Steadman et al., 2011; Steadman & Naples, 2005; Rivas-Vazquez et al., 2009; Rowe et al., 2007). In jail diversion programs (either prior to booking by police or post-booking), mental health programs typically provide psychiatric assessments, monitor symptoms and medications, provide case management and interpersonal support, and sometimes provide supported housing. The outcomes of jail diversion programs have been positive in terms of reducing arrests and days of incarceration. Unfortunately, previous extensive criminal justice involvement, persistent substance abuse, bipolar disorder, and homelessness are all associated with less positive outcomes. Those with schizophrenia and women have relatively better outcomes. Inclusion of co-occurring disorder services, stable housing, peer support, and employment services all enhance the outcomes of these jail diversion programs.

One of the better known programs is in Brooklyn, New York (O'Keefe, 2006). This mental health court is an effort to balance a fair court process with effective, and usually lengthy, treatment mandates. A multisite study of similar programs including over 800 individuals found that about half of the individuals had an arrest in the 12 months following enrollment in a jail diversion program (Steadman et al., 2011). However, this number of arrests compared to that of the previous year dropped significantly, as did the number of days they spent in jail.

In New Jersey, a collaboration between the Union County Prosecutor's Office, a PsyR provider (Bridgeway Inc.), Trinitas (a community hospital), county judges, and the county jail has proved an effective jail diversion program for persons with serious mental illness (Gill & Murphy, 2011). All program participants have a diagnosis of a serious mental illness, with 58 percent of them also having a co-occurring substance abuse disorder. Many individuals had several previous arrests and convictions and had served jail or prison time. In the first year of follow-up, participation in the program significantly reduced time spent in jail or prison compared to the previous twelve months. Sustained gains in the three subsequent years, in terms of reduction of incarcerations and arrests, were seen among those who were completers of the program, who were arrested less often, and, if arrested, had remained in the community longer. The study's findings emphasized the importance of assertive outreach to keep people enrolled in the service (Gill & Murphy, 2011).

ACT Comes of Age as a Program and a Professional Specialty

In addition to being an evidence-based practice, the practice of ACT is a specialty that has come of age with its own professional association, the Assertive Community Treatment Association (ACTA). On its Web site (http://www.ACTassociation.org), one can learn about ACTA annual conferences, training, and program standards. In the United States, special training and technical assistance centers are sponsored by state mental health agencies (e.g., ACT Center of Indiana—http://www.psych.iupui.edu/ACT/index.html— and the Bridgeway PACT Training & Technical Assistance Center, New Jersey—http://www.bridgewayrehab.com/nj-pact.shtml). ACT services are funded in dozens of US states, in European countries, and in Australia, New Zealand, and Japan.

The Future of ACT and Case Management Approaches

What is the future of ACT and related approaches? In 2005, Gary Bond and his colleagues made a number of predictions that to a large extent have proven true, especially in terms of a focus on illness management strategies and employment. They believed the "basic"

ACT model will continue to improve in two ways. First, ACT will systematically incorporate EBPs such as illness management (Chapter 3), motivational interviewing for dual disorders (Chapter 9), supported employment (Chapter 10), and family psycho-education (Chapter 13) into its service package.

Second, ACT will be enhanced by the development of new strategies. For example, another service that may be integrated within ACT teams is supported socialization. Supported socialization employs volunteers or staff members who go on social and recreational outings with clients. The social isolation and loneliness of many persons with severe and persistent mental illness is well known. Bond and colleagues (2005) pointed out that ACT has had very little impact on social functioning. Yet most ACT clients deeply desire friendships and social contact. Peer support services such as drop-in centers or support groups (see Chapter 12) may provide easily accessible social outlets, but other strategies that connect clients to natural supports and socialization opportunities in their communities should also be employed.

Summary

It is not surprising that the use of case management strategies for the community treatment of persons living with severe mental illnesses has steadily increased. Case management has obvious economic and quality-of-life advantages. Although case management, particularly ACT, is sometimes more expensive than traditional community-based services, it is considerably cheaper than psychiatric hospitalization. Planners on the state and national level see increasing evidence that employing case management strategies reduces hospital usage. Numerous jurisdictions have adopted case management strategies in an effort to reduce the use of hospitalization (see Chapter 15). These new strategies have also proven to be effective for reaching those consumers who have "fallen through the cracks" in the system. Whether because of their illness, underlying personality issues, past experiences that have alienated them from the system, or any number of other reasons, a large number of people are unconnected with the mental health system. Today, we know that treatment and psychosocial interventions have a positive effect on the long-term outcomes of these conditions. Assertive community treatment and other intensive case management approaches have proven to be the most effective strategies for reaching out to this group with the treatment and services they need.

Perhaps most importantly, case management models are a more normalized form of treatment delivery than traditional day programs or supervised residences. Such case management strategies allow the consumer to reside and work in the environment of their choice and receive services there. They are not stigmatized by frequently attending a mental health center or vocational workshop. The services provided have a direct relationship to the "here and now" issues involved with coping with their illnesses and succeeding in the community. This consistency with the PsyR value of promoting valued social roles and normalized environments makes case management attractive.

ACT and a variety of case management approaches were developed in response to the high rate of hospital recidivism often caused by substandard, under-funded, uncoordinated, and incomplete community-based services. These models of service delivery are characterized by the fact that services are provided to the consumer in the community where they live, rather than in a mental health center, clinic, or hospital. The role of the case manager may vary according to the model of program where they work. Some case managers act as brokers or agents, arranging services for their clients. Others may be direct service providers who work one to one with their clients in the community to help meet their needs. By either arranging for or directly providing services, case management systems strive to ensure that client needs are met in an appropriate and timely manner. Evaluation of these programs has demonstrated that they are effective at reducing the length of time of hospital stays. They have also been used effectively to reach out to those segments of the population with severe mental illness that are most resistant to treatment. Today, ACT models are also being employed for early intervention and as a strategy for dealing with individuals with legal system involvement.

■ ■ ■ ▬▬▬▬▬▬▬▬▬▬▬▬▬▬▬▬▬▬▬▬▬▬▬▬▬▬▬▬▬▬▬▬▬▬▬▬▬

Class Exercises

Class Exercise 1: Imagine Being on an ACT Team

Imagine that you and a group of your classmates work for an assertive community treatment (ACT) team. Where you work, this team consists of:

- Psychiatrist
- Nurse
- Employment specialist
- Addictions counselor
- Team leader
- Peer provider

Each of you will assume the role of one member of the team. You will take on the viewpoint of one of these specialists and engage in a team discussion about Harry, who is described in the following. Harry is a 47-year-old man with a 30-year history of psychiatric illness with the co-occurring disorders of schizophrenia and poly-substance abuse. He has survived on the street for a number of years. He has worked a number of jobs briefly "off the books." His ACT team wants to see better adherence to medication because he seems to be very bad at taking his medication as prescribed. Also, they would like to seem him abstain from illegal substances. Some team members think that both medication adherence and drug abstinence are likely to reduce his symptoms and to prevent him from becoming homeless in the future. Harry, on the other hand, wants to find a modest apartment, earn more pay through better jobs, and have a "lady friend," as he says.

Take on the role and possible viewpoint of one of the several practitioners listed previously. For this exercise, you are that person. Among the group of "practitioners," have a discussion about Harry's goals, treatment/rehabilitation plan, and future. Present your thoughts from the likely viewpoint of your chosen specialty.

After the discussion, answer the following questions, staying in your role as a specific ACT team member:

- What do you see as Harry's most important short-term and long-term goals?
- What did you emphasize when speaking to your colleagues?
- What did you say in response to them?
- Did a possible conflict or dispute arise within the group?
- Did the group reach consensus? If not, is there a way to reach consensus?

Class Exercise 2: Thinking from the Strengths Perspective

Now look again at Harry's situation. Think about him from the strengths model perspective.

- How is the strengths perspective more or less consistent with the other principles of psychiatric rehabilitation described in Chapter 4?
- What are Harry's strengths?
- Does the strengths model perspective change how you look at Harry and think about the approach to his circumstances?
- Is the strengths model perspective a denial of his historical and significant problems or is it a better approach to his problems?

Class Exercise 3: New Applications of ACT

Should ACT be used for the community treatment and rehabilitation of persons with mental illness in the criminal justice system beginning with their arrest, through their experience in jails and prisons, and after discharge? What might be the effects of such a program?

- In a few states, ACT is used to serve persons who live in the community but have been committed to involuntary treatment in the community. What do you think of this application of ACT?

■ ■ ■

9

Co-occurring Disorders and Integrated Treatment

Your life does not get better by chance, it gets better by change.
Jim Rohn

CHAPTER OUTLINE

This chapter deals with the treatment and rehabilitation of persons who have both a serious mental illness and a substance abuse disorder, commonly referred to as co-occurring disorders. Persons with a severe mental illness have a much greater risk of developing a substance abuse disorder than those without mental illness. The difficulties of having both types of disorders at the same time are multiplied by the fact that they interact, each aggravating or exacerbating the other. In addition, coming from different philosophical and educational backgrounds, the service providers for these different conditions often have conflicting and sometimes contradictory approaches. Services that have been developed to address these problems and other issues involved in helping this dually diagnosed population are discussed.

Psychiatric Rehabilitation. http://dx.doi.org/10.1016/B978-0-12-387002-5.00009-3

This chapter will answer the following questions:

1. *What unique problems are faced when providing services to someone with co-occurring disorders of mental illness and substance abuse?*
2. *Why are such a large proportion of persons with serious mental illness at risk for substance abuse?*
3. *What barriers prevent the effective treatment and rehabilitation of individuals with co-occurring disorders?*
4. *What is the best way to provide services to persons with co-occurring disorders?*

Introduction

During the 1980s, mental health providers witnessed the emergence of a seemingly new population of service recipients, the "young adult chronic patient" (this term is no longer used) (Pepper, Ryglewicz, & Kirshner, 1981). These individuals had not experienced the lengthy hospitalizations that were common prior to the deinstitutionalization movement (Caton, 1981; Drake & Wallach, 2000; Pepper et al., 1981). Instead, having spent most of their lives in the community, they experienced greater exposure and access to alcohol and street drugs. Over time, it became apparent to mental health providers that a large proportion of individuals with severe mental illness were also engaged in substance abuse (Drake & Wallach, 2000). Studies have indicated substance abuse among people with psychiatric illness ranging from 14 to 70 percent, depending on psychiatric diagnosis and the specific populations being studied (Evans & Sullivan, 1990; Cleary, Hunt, Matheson, Siegfried, & Walter, 2010; Regier et al., 1990; Substance Abuse and Mental Health Services Administration, 2012). The Substance Abuse and Mental Health Services Administration (SAMHSA) reported that, in 2010, 25 percent of adults experiencing mental illness also experienced substance dependence or abuse in the course of that year compared to 6 percent of the general population (SAMHSA, 2012). Further, the SAMHSA report indicated that among adults with a substance use disorder, more than 45 percent had a co-occurring mental illness. Frequently, an individual with a co-occurring disorder is a **polysubstance** abuser (using more than one substance). The population of people with these co-occurring disorders is fairly heterogeneous with a variety of combinations of different psychiatric diagnoses and substances of choice (Drake & Wallach, 2000). Nevertheless, an increased incidence of substance use and abuse has been found to be associated with being younger, male, less educated, and unemployed (Drake & Wallach, 1989; SAMHSA, 2012).

Co-occurring disorders have also been referred to as "coexisting disorder," "dual diagnosis disorder," "mentally ill chemical abuser" (MICA), and "mentally ill substance abuser" (MISA), among many others. Regardless of the label, these conditions present serious problems for both the individual and the service system. To begin with, the disorders negatively interact and worsen each other, complicating the clinical, rehabilitative, medical, and social needs of the dually diagnosed person (Drake, Mueser, Brunette, & McHugo, 2004; Drake & Wallach, 1989, 2000; Evans & Sullivan, 1990; Mueser, Noordsy,

Drake, & Fox, 2003a; Regier et al., 1990). Individuals with co-occurring disorders are at greater risk for medication non-adherence, hospitalization, homelessness, suicide, and illness, including HIV infection. They tend to have more family problems and to be more hostile, disruptive, and violent than individuals with a single disorder. Furthermore, the systems designed to provide services for either a substance abuse or psychiatric disorder are often not particularly skillful at assessing or treating the other disorder.

Another important characteristic of persons with both a mental illness and a substance abuse disorder is that they often have greater sensitivity to substances than persons without a mental illness. This factor may reduce the ability to detect a substance abuse problem because practitioners who are unaware of this increased sensitivity may judge self-reported substance use levels as well within the normal range (i.e., similar or less than their own levels of use). For example, the consumer who tells his counselor that he has two beers a night, an amount the counselor thinks is normal and within reasonable limits since he drinks that much as well, may have a substance abuse problem. In fact, the consumer may be several times more sensitive to alcohol than his counselor. This phenomenon, labeled the "super-sensitivity hypothesis" by Mueser, Drake, and Wallach (1998b), makes it difficult for individuals in normal social gatherings to avoid negative consequences related to their substance use. It is also the likely reason for the high proportion of persons with severe mental illness reporting substance abuse problems.

History of Co-occurring Disorders Treatment

People with a psychiatric disorder who abuse substances have not always been thought of as having two co-occurring disorders. Psychiatric symptoms were seen as signs of an illness, but substance abuse was often considered bad behavior (Evans & Sullivan, 1990). Many mental health clinicians believed that their clients would cease abusing substances if they received adequate treatment for the psychiatric disorder. Substance abuse counselors often mistook psychiatric symptoms for evidence of substance abuse because abuse of drugs and alcohol may cause symptoms that mimic those of mental illness (Evans & Sullivan, 1990; Miller, 1997).

Usually both the mental health and substance abuse treatment systems were unsuccessful when treating individuals with dual disorders. The mental health service provider found that the person with co-occurring disorders was difficult to engage and did not respond to typical mental health treatment. Many in the substance abuse treatment system endorsed abstinence and some even considered psychotropic medications to be mood-altering drugs. Service providers in both systems often refused treatment to people until the other disorder was under control. It was not uncommon for mental health clinics to refuse services to an individual exhibiting signs of intoxication or other evidence of abuse, admonishing them to "return when you are sober." Many people with co-occurring disorders found themselves inadequately treated by both systems or in a "Catch-22" situation, receiving no services at all because they needed both mental health and addiction services simultaneously. Because separate systems already existed for serving individuals with these conditions, the first strategies for treating persons with co-occurring disorders consisted of either a sequential approach or parallel service approach.

Sequential Services

With sequential services, a person with a co-occurring disorder first receives treatment for one of the disorders and later for the other. When the first disorder is successfully "under control," the individual is referred for treatment for the subsequent disorder. This method has been found to be largely ineffective since the disorder that is not being treated often undermines the treatment for the disorder being addressed (Drake, Bartels, Teague, Noordsy, & Clark, 1993). See Table 9.1 later in this chapter for a summary of the limitations of sequential services.

Traditionally, mental health treatment consists of psychotropic medication (Chapter 3), individual and/or group counseling, perhaps day program services (Chapter 7), and case management services (Chapter 8), which are typically used for persons with severe and persistent mental illness. Traditional substance abuse treatment often requires abstinence (refraining from all substances), sometimes including abstinence from psychotropic medication as well, attendance at Alcoholics Anonymous (AA) or Narcotics Anonymous (NA) meetings, and working a 12-step process based on AA's 12-step model (Evans & Sullivan, 1990).

A popular misconception on the part of mental health providers has contributed to this method of treatment. Many providers believe that people with mental illness engage in substance use in an attempt to self-medicate. In other words, drugs or alcohol is used to provide relief from their psychiatric symptoms. If this were the case, it follows that adequate treatment of the psychiatric disorder would eliminate the need for the use of substances. Unfortunately, this theory has not proven to be helpful for many people with co-occurring disorders. Studies of motivation for using substances indicate that people with psychiatric disorders use substances for a variety of reasons other than symptom relief, such as to feel relaxed, improve social interactions, be accepted by their peer group, and alleviate boredom (Bellack & DiClemente, 1999; Nishith, Mueser, Srsic, & Beck, 1997; Spencer, Castle, & Michie, 2002). Not surprisingly, it appears that people with mental illness use substances for some of the same reasons as other substance users and abusers.

Treatment for the psychiatric disorder in the absence of treatment for the substance abuse is ineffective for both disorders. People engaged in substance abuse experience resulting impairments that interfere with their ability to engage in rehabilitative activities, manage a medication regimen, or even keep appointments with doctors and other treatment practitioners (Mueser et al., 2003a). It is not difficult to imagine the challenges in monitoring the effect of a medication regimen, the most important agent for symptom control, at the same time someone is engaged in substance abuse. In addition, there is some evidence that substance abusers are more likely than others to increase or decrease usage of their prescribed psychotropic medications at their own discretion (Heyscue, Levin, & Merrick, 1998; Krystal, D'Souza, Madonick, & Petrakis, 1999).

Likewise, substance abuse treatment without mental health treatment is equally ineffective. Besides the obvious problem of untreated psychiatric symptoms, unaddressed functional impairments related to the psychiatric illness will interfere with the ability to address the substance abuse issues.

Parallel Services

With the parallel services approach, different practitioners, often working in different programs or agencies, treat each of the two disorders separately but simultaneously. While this approach addresses some of the problems inherent in the sequential approach, it introduces several additional issues and often results in "fragmented, contradictory, and inadequate care" (Drake et al., 1993, p. 607).

In the absence of specialized knowledge and training, the mental health provider lacks an understanding of the addictive behavior, while the addictions specialist lacks an understanding of mental illness. Furthermore, the traditional treatments used in each of these approaches tend to contradict each other. Mental health treatment often emphasizes empathy toward the individual and the development of a trusting working relationship. This empathic counseling is used to assist the person to gain insight and to pursue goals. Substance abuse treatment tends to take a more confrontational, nononsense stance toward the client.

An individual's failure to follow through on substance abuse treatment is typically seen as a lack of commitment from the perspective of practitioners. Traditionally, it results in confrontation by the counselor or group members. This approach is in stark contrast to mental health services, which employ active outreach to engage clients in services when they might drop out of treatment. The person with co-occurring disorders in parallel treatment finds himself or herself dealing with systems that may be quite different from each other in terms of philosophies, goals, and strategies. The parallel service strategy forces the individual him- or herself to attempt to integrate these often contradictory treatment approaches (Mueser et al., 2003a).

In some cases, these contradictions cause problems for the treatment systems as well. Confusion may arise concerning who is responsible for advocating for the individual, assisting with housing or social services and other outside services and supports. For example, a traditional addiction treatment model might wait to let a person reach "rock bottom," that is, lose everything as a consequence of the addiction, so he or she might be motivated to get treatment. Mental health staff may be intervening in an opposite manner to prevent just such a scenario. A substance abuse professional might label this "enabling" a person to continue to use substances without negative consequences, while mental health staff will call it case management or crisis intervention.

Contradictions due to differences between these two service systems may emerge at many levels. Although these are not insurmountable, the lack of coordination of services and mutual awareness of these problems make them difficult to overcome for the individual with co-occurring disorders. Treatment plan goals and interventions may conflict with each other with the individual receiving mixed or contradictory messages. Such situations make successful outcomes less likely. See Table 9.1 for summary of the limitations of parallel treatment.

Integrated Services

The integrated approach was developed to overcome the shortcomings of the sequential and parallel approaches. Research literature surveys supported the notion that parallel or sequential services are less effective than an integrated approach (e.g., Ridgely, Goldman, & Willenbring, 1990). With integrated services, the person with both a substance abuse disorder and a psychiatric illness receives treatment for both disorders in the same place, at the same time, by the same practitioners. These practitioners are knowledgeable about both disorders as well as about the complications resulting from co-occurring disorders.

Early efforts at integrating mental health and substance abuse services added substance abuse groups into mental health day treatment programs. These groups often followed the 12-step model adhering to features such as confrontation and the focus on abstinence. Still, practitioners often found that some group members were at different stages with regard to their readiness to recover and were not ready to make a commitment to changing their behavior (Corrigan, Mueser, Bond, Drake, & Solomon, 2008; Drake et al., 2004; Drake, Mercer-McFadden, Mueser, McHugo, & Bond, 1998). Today's integrated service model for co-occurring disorders, an evidence-based practice (EBP), will be described in detail later in this chapter.

Table 9.1   Disadvantages of Traditional Sequential and Parallel Treatment Approaches to Co-occurring Disorders

Sequential Treatment

- The untreated disorder worsens the treated disorder, making it impossible to stabilize one disorder without attending to the other.
- There is a lack of agreement as to which disorder should be treated first.
- It is unclear or impossible to know when one disorder has been "successfully" treated because both disorders may need long-term, perhaps lifelong, attention and/or treatment. Therefore, the second treatment may never commence. The client is never referred for further treatment.

Parallel Treatment

- Mental health and substance abuse treatments are not integrated into a cohesive treatment package.
- Treatment providers fail to communicate with each other.
- The burden of integration falls on the client.
- Funding and eligibility barriers to participating in both treatments simultaneously exist.
- Different treatment providers have incompatible treatment philosophies.
- A client slips through the cracks and receives no services, due to the failure of either treatment provider to accept final responsibility for the client.
- Providers lack a common language and treatment philosophy.

Based on Mueser, Noordsy, Drake, and Fox (2003).

Fundamental Strategies for Providing Integrated Co-occurring Disorders Treatment (ICDT)

Early efforts at substance abuse treatment for persons with co-occurring disorders often consisted of demanding abstinence and teaching consumers about the many dangers of drug and alcohol abuse. While some people responded to this approach, for many, if not most, it was a failure. This approach was ineffective for those who did not want to stop using substances or saw no negative consequences of their substance use. Clearly, another approach was needed.

Stages of Treatment

Working in the area of addictions treatment, Prochaska, Norcross, and DiClemente (1994) developed the **transtheoretical model of behavior** change. They identified five stages through which one progresses in making life changes:

1. Precontemplation
2. Contemplation
3. Preparation
4. Action
5. Maintenance

According to Prochaska and colleagues (1994), in each of the five stages the individual is concerned with different tasks. To be effective, services designed to assist people to make changes (e.g., to reduce or eliminate substance use) must be relevant to the stage the person is in. We now take a look at descriptions of these five stages.

Precontemplation stage—In the precontemplation stage, people do not believe they have a problem and they are therefore not even considering change. They may not be aware of the negative consequences of their behavior (e.g., substance use) or they may be demoralized by their circumstances and unable to envision alternatives. People with dual disorders in the precontemplation stage are likely to deny that their substance use causes problems. Conflict within their personal relationships, inability to meet obligations, poor health, and other consequences are blamed on others or circumstances beyond their control.

The treatment task with a person at this stage is to raise doubts within the individual and help the individual to become aware of the problems associated with his or her use of substances. This may best be accomplished by using a technique called **motivational interviewing**, which will be addressed later in this chapter.

Contemplation stage—In the contemplation stage, people are experiencing ambivalence about their problem and are beginning to think about change. They are aware that there are costs associated with continuing with their problem behavior, but these costs are still outweighed by perceived benefits. They are not ready to take action to change. Individuals with co-occurring disorders may, for example, begin to recognize that their substance use is interfering with their sleep, which in turn is exacerbating their psychiatric symptoms. However, they are also convinced that substance use is an important part of their social interaction with friends.

In this stage, individuals are weighing the benefits and costs of their behavior against the benefits and costs of change. They will move toward change when they perceive that the benefits of changing outweigh the costs of change or the costs associated with their behavior outweigh its benefits. Thus, the treatment task at this stage is to help the individual understand that the benefits of change outweigh the benefits of continued substance abuse. Reinforcing or increasing the benefits of change—for example, by getting a job or acquiring new friends—may also accomplish this.

Preparation stage—In the preparation stage, people recognize the need to change. They have decided to make changes in the near future and are ready to take small steps toward that change. They still experience a certain amount of ambivalence, but most of the time they can see that the benefits of change outweigh the costs of change. A program or practitioner who mandates abstinence will be unsuccessful with these persons. The more successful approach consists of helping to identify the steps to take and supportive counseling to sort through the continued feelings of ambivalence and the difficulties of taking even small steps.

Action stage—In the action stage, people are taking definite steps to change problem behavior and are acquiring new behaviors. Although their commitment to change is strong, some level of ambivalence continues and supportive strategies that help individuals remember their reasons for change are useful. The person with co-occurring disorders in this stage might be learning new avenues for social interaction, taking on new responsibilities, or accessing educational or employment opportunities.

Maintenance stage—In the maintenance stage, people have sustained change for a while and are working toward preventing relapse. Besides supports, effective maintenance depends on realistic expectations of the possibility of relapse and continual reinforcement of the motivational factors that encouraged the change.

Prochaska and his colleagues (1994) have found that at any given time, fewer than 20 percent of people expressing a desire to change (contemplation stage) are ready to take action toward making the change. Practitioners should take this into account and not become unduly frustrated when they hear from individuals that they wish to change their substance abuse, but then see little progress. Furthermore, they also need to understand that interventions designed for a stage different from the one the client is currently at will be unsuccessful. For example, as you read about the stages of change in the following section, you will see that services that mandate abstinence as a condition of receiving treatment will not work for individuals in the precontemplation or contemplation stages. These individuals are not ready to take action.

Prochaska and his colleagues (1994) found that although the amount of time spent in each stage may vary for different people, the process, sequence, and tasks of each stage do not change.

Stages of Change: Applying Motivational Interviewing

If an individual's treatment process consists of passing through stages, the psychiatric rehabilitation professional's task becomes helping the individual move from one treatment stage to the next. In short, the professional helps the individual accomplish the tasks of the stage he or she is currently in and encourages movement to the next stage. A specific strategy to accomplish this, **Motivational Interviewing**, has been developed by Miller and Rollnick (2002).

Defined as "a client-centered, directive method for enhancing intrinsic motivation to change by exploring and resolving ambivalence" (Miller & Rollnick, 2002, p. 25), motivational interviewing is an empathic communication method. Rather than imposing change, the practitioner using motivational interviewing is nurturing the individual's intrinsic motivation to change by assisting the person to see discrepancies between her behavior and her personal goals.

Effective motivational interviewing is based on four principles: (1) express empathy, (2) develop discrepancy, (3) roll with resistance, and (4) support self-efficacy (Miller & Rollnick, 2002, p. 36). In expressing empathy, the practitioner is communicating acceptance and an understanding of the individual's behavior from her perspective. First, the practitioner assists the person in identifying his own goals and values. Then, the practitioner helps the individual examine whether there is any discrepancy between his goals and his behavior. The practitioner does not argue for change when met with resistance but rather accepts ambivalence as natural and assists the person in recognizing the discrepancy between his stated goals and behavior. The practitioner expresses belief in the person's ability to change.

Motivational interviewing is an especially good fit with the values and principles of PsyR. It can be an effective strategy for helping individuals in nearly every aspect of PsyR, from adhering to their medication regimen to getting a job. Some of the EBPs described in this text call for practitioners to employ motivational interviewing with their clients.

Consider John, who has been working with his counselor and has identified obtaining employment as his most important goal. In reviewing John's work history, his counselor learns that John has attempted several jobs in the past and has lost each of them because he missed too many days of work. His missed days always followed nights out drinking with his friends. John's counselor asks him if he thinks his drinking is an obstacle to reaching his goal of employment. John does not think so, but admits it sometimes gets him into trouble. Rather than confronting John's perspective (e.g., "It seems to me that your drinking is a problem. You've lost several jobs because of it and you've been arrested twice for public intoxication. I don't see how you can hold a job until you get control of your drinking problem."), the counselor uses motivational interviewing to engage John in a review of past work experiences and an exploration of what would need to be different in order to make his next employment attempt successful. The counselor might ask John to list the benefits and costs of using alcohol. In this way, the counselor could help John find alternative ways of getting the benefits (e.g., socializing with friends and feeling relaxed) while also examining the costs (e.g., missing work and other appointments, feeling ill, and losing money) and could help John to see the discrepancy between his goals and his behavior.

Principles of Treatment for People with Co-occurring Disorders

As integrated treatment programs have evolved, much has been learned about effective program components. In 2004, based on clinical research findings, Drake and his colleagues articulated nine principles that they believe to be critical for effective treatment (Drake et al., 2004). More recently, Drake and his colleagues reduced these to five principles in which the four interventions are subsumed under "Stagewise Treatments" (Corrigan et al., 2008).

1. **Integrated treatment**—Mental health and substance abuse services are provided concurrently by the same clinician or clinical team. The clinician is knowledgeable about both disorders and their interaction. The services are modified to address the specific needs of the individual and characteristics of their dual disorders.
2. **Stagewise treatments**—Services are relevant to the person's stage of change, similar to the work of Prochaska and colleagues (1994) described earlier. Drake and colleagues (2004, p. 368) describe the stages as engagement, persuasion or motivation, active treatment, and relapse prevention.
   a. **Engagement interventions (precontemplation and contemplation)**—Services use strategies that increase the likelihood of engagement in treatment for this group of people who typically have difficulty engaging and sustaining participation. Examples of these strategies include active outreach, motivational interviewing (also known as motivational counseling), flexibility, practical assistance, and culturally competent services (Drake et al., 2004, p. 368).
   b. **Motivational counseling interventions (preparation phase)**—Services use counseling techniques that develop readiness for movement toward individual goals. These interventions are primarily based on the work of Miller and Rollnick (2002) described earlier.
   c. **Active treatment intervention (active phase)**—Services include interventions such as motivational counseling, cognitive-behavioral counseling, or family interventions that are meant to assist individuals to manage their own illnesses by helping them to develop the needed skills and supports (Drake et al., 2004, p. 369).
   d. **Relapse prevention interventions (maintenance)**—It is well known that there is an increased danger of substance abuse relapse for people with dual disorders. Some experts assert that relapse is almost inevitable. Services that assist the individual in planning strategies to address relapse are recommended.
3. **Long-term perspective**—Services are designed to promote retention (provide active outreach, be flexible enough to tolerate periods of relapse, etc.), recognizing that recovery is a long-term process.

4. **Comprehensive services**—Services address the individual's needs in all life areas. As stated earlier in this chapter, people with co-occurring disorders are at greater risk for hospitalization, homelessness, illness, and incarceration.
5. **Interventions for treatment of non-responders**—Services include specialized or modified options based on the unique needs of the individual. Some of these may include residential treatment, family interventions, trauma interventions, and money management.

Group Treatment of Co-occurring Disorders

Several models of group treatment for people with co-occurring disorders have emerged either within day treatment services for people with psychiatric illness or as stand-alone programs. These models may incorporate a combination of elements, including a 12-step recovery approach based on AA, stages of treatment as developed by Prochaska and colleagues (1994), motivational interviewing strategies developed by Miller and Rollnick (2002), social skills training, cognitive-behavioral interventions, and relapse prevention strategies (Mueser & Noordsy, 1996).

The **12-step models** are modifications of AA's 12-step model, incorporating the principles and philosophy of AA with mental health care. The groups are generally run by professionals, some of whom have personal experience with addictions. Although it is not required, group members are also encouraged to attend self-help groups in the community. **Professionally assisted pre-AA groups** prepare group members for attendance at community AA groups. These groups address education and motivation while adhering to the concepts of AA (working the 12 steps, facing denial, overcoming rationalization, surrendering to a higher power, etc.) (Mueser & Noordsy, 1996, p. 34).

Broad-based educational support groups are based on the belief that people with co-occurring disorders lack the information needed about the effects of substance use and lack the social support needed for sobriety. These groups provide information in a supportive environment and are time-unlimited.

Social skills training groups for people with co-occurring disorders teach group members the skills needed to maintain a substance-free lifestyle (e.g., skills to refuse substances or manage conflict). See Chapter 5 for a detailed description of social skills training methods.

Stagewise treatment groups provide interventions relevant to the different stages of recovery from substance abuse: engagement, persuasion, active treatment, and relapse prevention. Typically, clients in the engagement stage do not attend these groups, although they may attend the persuasion groups. The persuasion groups use education and motivational interviewing to increase awareness of the consequences of substance use and to examine the discrepancy between behaviors and personal goals. People in the active treatment and relapse prevention stages attend active treatment groups. These groups include mutual support, skill building including social skills, relapse prevention strategies, and encouragement to use community self-help programs (Mueser & Noordsy, 1996).

CONTROVERSIAL ISSUE
Total Abstinence vs. Harm Reduction

The notion that substance abuse is a disease and that state and federal governments should provide for its treatment and rehabilitation is a relatively new idea. Today, it seems clear that different people have different levels of tolerance for substance use, some are more prone to addiction than others, and substance abuse has a number of related physiological manifestations. Recognition of the physiological, social, and spiritual damage caused by substance abuse is worldwide. Still, a good deal of controversy surrounds whether the goal of services for substance abusers should be total abstinence or harm reduction.

One of the most successful models for dealing with substance abuse, Alcoholics Anonymous, was begun in 1935 in Akron, Ohio, by a New York City stockbroker, Bill W., and an Ohio surgeon, Dr. Bob (http://www.alcoholics-anonymous.org). Based on self-help in the form of mutual support and a 12-step process, the goal of AA is total abstinence from alcohol. In fact, the first step of the process is to admit that one is powerless over alcohol. The AA Web site reports having more than 2,000,000 members attending 100,000 AA groups worldwide. AA has helped virtually millions of people with alcohol addiction.

Today, many substances besides alcohol, both legal and illegal, are abused. In the 1950s, a similar organization based on the principles of AA, Narcotics Anonymous, emerged (http://www.na.org). NA simply substituted the word "addiction" for "alcohol" in the first step of the 12-step process: One is powerless over the addiction. The NA Web site reports that by 2012 there were 61,800 weekly meetings being held in 129 countries. Recognition that one is powerless over either alcohol or drugs implies that abstinence is the best solution for achieving and maintaining sobriety. Not everyone is in agreement with this position.

Reducing the negative consequences, or harm reduction, is the idea that the goal of treatment or rehabilitation should be to reduce the harm caused by the substance abuse rather than to require total abstinence (Marlatt, Blume, & Parks, 2001). The harm reduction strategy, which fits well with motivational interviewing and Prochaska and colleagues' stages of change, has the advantage of meeting people where they are with respect to their substance abuse problem. It is no secret that many substance abusers have no intention of quitting (Marlatt, 1998). In fact, the drug rehab adage that people have to "hit bottom" before they can start to recover from their addiction is based on just this recognition. The idea seems to be that not until someone hits bottom will he or she decide that the costs of using substances outweigh the benefits.

Interestingly, harm reduction is not as uncommon as one might first suspect. Methadone maintenance, the provision of free methadone to heroin addicts, is a successful harm reduction program. Needle exchange programs to reduce the spread of HIV are another harm reduction strategy. Even ensuring that an intoxicated person does not drive is a harm reduction strategy. In the area of alcohol addiction, one self-help group, Moderation Management, uses a nine-step program to help people modify and manage their drinking (http://www.moderation.org). Starting in the 1980s in Rotterdam, the Netherlands, harm reduction was a natural outgrowth of liberalized drug laws that allowed drug users to organize publicly. This organization, Junkiebond, began advocating for harm reduction strategies for drug users and was able to establish the first needle exchange program in 1984 (Saladin & Santa Ana, 2004).

(Continued)

CONTROVERSIAL ISSUE
Total Abstinence vs. Harm Reduction—(Continued)

The research on harm reduction appears to show that while some people benefit (e.g., suffer fewer negative consequences), others do not and would be better served by adopting the goal of total abstinence. The question may be how to best engage individuals in rehabilitation and then help them to decide whether they should have a goal of harm reduction or total abstinence. As Rusty Foster (personal communication, October, 2005), an experienced professional in this area, puts it:

"The problem for [people with severe mental illness] is their sensitivity to even small amounts of a substance. Though it is important to recognize that most consumers begin reducing substance use gradually rather than moving right to abstinence, it is important to recognize and reward these changes. In the long run, the treatment goal usually is abstinence. But here the movement to abstinence is seen as a process, not an event."

Integrated Services: An Evidence-based Practice

As discussed throughout this text, an EBP is a treatment practice that has been shown to have positive consumer outcomes through controlled clinical trials across a variety of treatment sites. When someone has two simultaneous disorders such as substance abuse and mental illness, the integration of treatments for both disorders has been shown to have better treatment outcomes than traditional treatment. Specifically, this integration refers to the concurrent treatment of both conditions by the same clinicians trained in both disorders. While developed primarily for co-occurring mental illness and substance abuse problems, service integration is generally considered the preferred strategy when faced with other co-occurring disorders (e.g., mental illness and developmental disability). In general, evidence leans toward the integration of all services regardless of the presence of an additional disorder (e.g., simultaneously providing psychiatric treatment and supported employment).

Elements of an Evidence-based Practice: Integrated Treatment for Co-occurring Disorders

Since integrated treatment is associated with positive outcomes, programs that are carried out according to the integrated treatment model are predicted to produce better outcomes for the consumers they serve. To determine how faithful or how well a program resembles the integrated model, the Integrated Treatment Fidelity Scale (formerly IDDT) was developed. (This scale can be downloaded from the Substance Abuse and Mental Health Services Administration Web site at http://store.samhsa.gov/shin/content//SMA08-4367/EvaluatingYourProgram-ITC.pdf.) Some of the items on the Integrated Treatment Fidelity Scale are:

1. **Motivational interventions**—Strategies for engaging the client with co-occurring disorders will be more effective if they are based on the motivational interviewing strategies described by Miller and Rollnick (2002). This approach takes into account

how the client feels about her condition and her readiness to address it. This also incorporates the concept of stages of change put forth by Prochaska and colleagues (1994). Agencies that do not apply this approach tend to find that only a segment of their client population is responsive to their services.

2. **Stagewise interventions**—The services offered are consistent with and relevant to the stage of change the person is in, as discussed earlier in this chapter.

3. **Outreach**—Actively seeking out clients in their own environments, outreach is an element of many of the EBPs. Given the propensity of individuals with either mental illness or substance abuse disorders to drop out of treatment, outreach is often necessary to maintain contact.

4. **Access to comprehensive services**—This is the idea that all of the related issues in a client's life need to be dealt with simultaneously. Clients often need to make fundamental changes in many aspects of their lives as they move through the recovery process. For example, it has long been recognized that a recovering substance abuser may need to change his habits, including the places he frequents, the friends he hangs around with, and how he spends his time. Successfully addressing the addiction may require changes in all of these areas. To assist consumers in making such global changes, a wide array of services must be available, such as residential programs (see Chapter 12), supported employment (Chapter 10), and illness management and recovery (Chapter 3).

5. **Group treatment for co-occurring disorders**—This refers to groups in which both issues related to substance abuse and issues related to mental illness are addressed.

Outcomes of the Evidence-based Practice

Integrated approaches for co-occurring mental illness and substance abuse problems have been found to be superior to nonintegrated approaches. Studies have demonstrated positive outcomes such as reduced substance abuse, reduction of psychiatric symptoms, increased housing stability, reduced hospitalizations, fewer arrests, improved functional status, and improved quality of life (Drake et al., 2002). While the integrated approach is not a panacea with respect to the conditions it is designed to address, it has been shown to be superior to either the sequential or parallel service models described earlier in this chapter (Mueser et al., 2003a).

Limitations on the Research Evidence

Though the evidence cited in the literature has tended to support the effectiveness of integrated treatment for co-occurring disorders, questions have been raised about the research studies. Some of these are discussed later. Clearly, more rigorous studies in this area are warranted.

In a systematic review of the literature, Drake and colleagues (2008) examined 45 controlled studies (experimental and quasi-experimental) of services to people with

BOX 9.1   KIM T. MUESER

Kim T. Mueser, PhD, is a licensed clinical psychologist, executive director of the Center for Psychiatric Rehabilitation, and professor of occupational therapy, psychology, and psychiatry at Boston University, who through his extensive research, writing, and mentoring has added immeasurably to the psychiatric rehabilitation knowledge base. Dr. Mueser effectively combines keen insights from his clinical practice with an ability to design and carry out highly relevant research. A prolific scholar, he has published books and articles on a wide range of topics within psychiatric rehabilitation, some of which include social skills training, co-occurring (mental illness and substance abuse) disorders, family psychoeducation, illness management and recovery, trauma and PTSD, and cognitive behavioral therapy for psychosis. Dr. Mueser is also a highly sought-after speaker for gatherings of psychiatric rehabilitation professionals worldwide.

Dr. Mueser has actively participated in the identification, development, and dissemination of EBPs in psychiatric rehabilitation. He continues to work with state systems and professional groups to ensure that consumers reap the benefits of these advances. He has conducted numerous studies regarding the integrated treatment of persons with co-occurring disorders and is an outspoken advocate in this area.

co-occurring disorders. These studies covered a variety of interventions, including individual counseling, group counseling, family interventions, case management, residential treatment, intensive outpatient rehabilitation, contingency management, and legal interventions. The review examined substance use outcomes, mental health outcomes, and other outcomes and found mixed results. Some interventions (e.g., group counseling) consistently showed improvements in substance use and other outcomes. No interventions consistently showed improvements in mental health outcomes. The authors identified several problems in the comparability of the studies, including "… lack of standardization, absence of fidelity assessment, diversity of participants, varying lengths of intervention, diversity of outcomes, and inconsistency of measures …" (p. 134).

In their 2009 report, the Schizophrenia Patient Outcomes Research Team (PORT; Dixon et al., 2010) examined studies of substance abuse services to people with schizophrenia (and other diagnoses) conducted over the previous 30 years. They found mixed results generally favoring integrated services over parallel services. However, they observe that the comparison has become a "moot point" (p. 57), since integrated services have become the standard of care and studies conducted in the past decade have compared interventions provided in integrated settings. Another important source that has questioned the validity of the research comes from the Cochrane review.

BOX 9.2   COCHRANE REVIEWS

First becoming widespread in the 1990s, Cochrane reviews focus on specific medical specialties or subspecialties, systematically gathering all relevant data generated from controlled clinical trials. Named for one of the earliest proponents of this idea, Professor Archibald L. Cochrane, the reviews are commissioned by the Cochrane Collaboration (http://www.cochrane.org). Formed in 1993, the collaboration is based in Oxford, England, and currently has 10,000 collaborators from more than 80 countries around the world. A number of Cochrane reviews have focused on treatment and rehabilitation services for severe mental illness, including the issue of integrated treatment for persons with severe mental illness who are substance abusers.

A Cochrane review conducted by Cleary, Hunt, Matheson, Siegfried, and Walter (2010) reviewed 25 studies they deemed relevant to the issue. They reported that the design quality of the studies was not high and there was inconsistency across studies in areas such as the fidelity of implementation, outcomes measured, and settings. They found no clear evidence supporting one strategy of providing care over another. In short, they concluded that the current trend toward integrated programming is not based on good evidence. This challenges the basis of an integrated treatment strategy for persons with co-occurring disorders and, indeed, calls into question whether it can be considered a true EBP.

Roger's Story

Roger's story has some similarities with many of the homeless persons you might encounter on the streets of big cities. With a mental illness and co-occurring substance abuse problems, Roger has had a lifetime of difficulty understanding his conditions and trying to fit into society. While some people seem to "get all the breaks," others, like Roger, seem born under a dark cloud. As you read about Roger, you should consider the following questions:

1. What might the outcome have been if Roger had received more attention for his problems when he was in school?
2. What were the system problems that made Roger's first attempts at treatment difficult and how might they have been corrected?
3. What were the important practitioner and system characteristics of the last program that successfully engaged Roger in treatment? Why were they effective?
4. Finally, based on what you know about Roger and the treatment he is receiving, what would you guess his future holds?

Roger is a 45-year-old man with a dual diagnosis of bipolar disorder and substance abuse disorder. He jokes that he's recovering from substance abuse and "the system," meaning the school system, the foster care system, and the legal system. As a child, he moved from one foster home to another. Roger's school performance was generally mediocre. He occasionally did well on tests or assignments, but more often barely passed. Most of the time in school he seemed gloomy and withdrawn. When he did emerge from this withdrawn state, he was animated and loud, arguing with his foster parents, teachers, and fellow students. During these arguments, he frequently became physically aggressive, slamming doors, plates, and textbooks and punching or kicking holes in walls. He hardly slept at all during these periods. His classmates thought he was weird and dangerous. His teachers routinely kicked him out of the classroom for his behavior until finally he ended up in a special school for kids who are emotionally disturbed. Here, he found other kids he thought were "even weirder" than he was. He learned how to cope with his mood swings: cocaine when he needed to perk up, pot when he needed to calm down, and alcohol when he couldn't get anything else. Roger's first arrest was for shoplifting a six-pack of beer. He had no trouble convincing the judge that it was a teenage prank. The third time he was arrested, the judge decided to keep him in jail overnight. The school refused to be involved since Roger had dropped out a few months earlier when he turned 16. In the jail cell, Roger went wild: screaming, cursing, punching his fists, and finally slamming his body into the cell wall over and over again. Roger only vaguely remembers what happened next—the restraints with belts, the ambulance, and the injection. He woke up in the psychiatric ward of the local hospital. He was discharged a week later with a diagnosis of conduct disorder and a bottle of pills that he had no intention of taking. It was not until his second hospitalization following a suicide attempt that he was diagnosed with bipolar disorder.

Roger was mandated to mental health treatment and sent to the local day treatment center. He had almost forgotten about his appointment with the intake worker the night before while he got high with his friends. He awoke feeling tired and groggy, not wanting to go to the mental health center, but not wanting to go back to the hospital or to jail either. He arrived only ten minutes late. While he waited in the front hallway, he could see the people who went to this place. A few looked happy, talking and joking with each other. Many more looked like "zombies" to him, sitting and staring. Almost no one looked like they were even near his age. The intake worker took Roger to an office. She was quiet and calm and seemed nice enough. She did not seem upset that his clothes were a mess and he looked like he had just rolled out of bed. She asked him a lot of questions. He was surprised that she asked so much about drugs and alcohol and even more surprised when she said he had a substance abuse problem. He was not disappointed when she told him he could not get services from them until he stopped using. She would give him the name of a drug and alcohol treatment program. Roger felt great. The social worker from the hospital assured him he was not off the hook and that he would have to go to the drug and alcohol treatment program. She set up an intake for him. The one thing Roger was most sure of was that he did not have a substance abuse problem. He used stuff when he wanted to have fun or relax, but it was social. As if to prove it, he went to bed early the night before the second intake having had only one marijuana joint. The man at the substance abuse treatment program who did the intake was mostly friendly, a little bit gruff. He asked Roger why his clothes were dirty and when he had last had a shower. He also asked a lot of the same questions about his use of drugs and alcohol and a lot more questions too. This time, Roger was more careful with his answers. He said he occasionally smoked pot but only for fun. Despite this, the intake worker said Roger should plan to start the program next Monday when he would do a drug screening, which would take place every so often afterward. He was warned that if he used any drugs he would be kicked out of the program, and if he was kicked out he would be going back to the hospital. Over the weekend, Roger could feel himself getting anxious. He could not sleep. He could barely sit still. He knew he could calm down if he could score some pot. He wondered if it would show up in the drug screening he was led to believe he would have to go through on Monday. He did not want to go back to the hospital. Feeling somewhat desperate, Roger decided to try one of the pills they'd given him when he left the hospital. He popped one. An hour later when he did not feel any different, he angrily tossed the pills in the garbage. Monday morning, he arrived at the program. They were expecting him. He met with a counselor who asked if he was "on" anything. Roger said "no." The counselor sent him to the men's room for a urine sample and then to the group room to attend what he called a 12-step group. Later, the counselor called Roger into his office.

"I thought you said you weren't using."

"What do you mean?" Roger asked.

"You know what I mean. What did you take?"

"Oh," Roger remembered, "I took a pill they gave me at the hospital."

"Listen," the counselor told him, "substance-free. This is a substance-free environment. You want to come here, you can't use."

Roger thought, "Who said I want to come here!" Instead, he said, "Who cares, I threw the pills away yesterday."

The counselor wanted him to attend 30 groups in 30 days. He could barely sit through the one group the first day. He was up all night, pacing around his room at the boarding home, walking the streets. He showed up at the program the next morning.

"You look like hell," the group leader said.

"I didn't sleep last night."

"Your eyes are bloodshot," said one of the group members.

"I told you!" Roger shouted, "I didn't sleep!"

"Yeah?" responded the group member. "Well, it looks like you've been using."

Roger jumped up, knocking over his chair. Heading right for the loudmouthed "know it all" guy, he thought better of it and smashed his fist into the wall. Back in the counselor's office, Roger was told he was out of control. His erratic behavior was interpreted as a sign to the counselor that he had been using. He was suspended for three days. He was told to return next Monday.

The final note in Roger's chart read "Lost to contact." Roger slipped away. Over the subsequent few years, he lived on the street, in shelters, and occasionally spent brief periods in jail. He picked up odd jobs when he could and worked long enough to get money for drugs. He moved back and forth between sullen isolation and angry, aggressive outbursts. One cold winter night during a period of isolation while trying to warm himself in a doorway, Roger was approached by a guy named Henry. Henry was carrying two cups of coffee and offered one to Roger. "Hey man, you must be cold. Here, have some coffee." Roger was startled. Most people passed him on the street as if he were invisible. Henry declined Roger's request for money. Roger declined Henry's offer of food.

Roger was happy to be left alone, but Henry came back night after night, always with a cup of coffee and, after that first night, also with a sandwich. Roger kept pretty much to himself but Henry talked plenty, mostly about himself. He told outlandish stories about things he did during his "drinking days" and some stories about months in the "loony bin" after he tried to kill himself. Depression, he called it. After a while, Roger started to let his guard down and told some of his own tales. Talking this way with Henry reminded Roger of his two best friends from junior high school. They did not get along any better with their fathers than Roger had with his, but they all thought things would be different when they grew up. They talked about it, about what their lives would be like. Roger joked with Henry about how different it had all worked out.

Eventually, they got around to the whole point of Henry's nightly visits.

"So, Roger, is this really the way you want to spend your life?"
"Oh God, what are you? Some kind of social worker?"
"No, not exactly. Well, in a way. And if you want your life back, I think I can help."
Roger shook his head no.
"You don't have to make any promises," Henry told him. "Here's my address. I'm there every day. Just come to my office and meet some other guys a lot like you and see what goes on there."

A few days went by. Henry didn't come back. Roger kept thinking about his question, "Is this the way you want to spend your life?" "Maybe," he thought, "at least nobody's telling me what I can and can't do."

"Oh, what the hell." Roger decided to stop in at Henry's place. Henry invited Roger to sit in on a meeting he was about to start. One guy in the meeting said he was beginning to feel really down, had no energy, and was afraid he was going to start using again. Henry said, "So, that's pretty scary when you feel yourself slipping and you're afraid you'll lose control." They went on to talk about depression, the guy's meds, seeing his psychiatrist, and the people he could call if he was thinking about using and needed support. In a private meeting, Henry and Roger talked about bipolar disorder, what it is, what the meds he was given were supposed to do. They talked about addiction, about what Roger liked about using, about the downside of using. They talked about Roger's future.

Roger's been coming to this program for a year now. He's been taking lithium and that's helped, although he was hospitalized once for a week because of depression. Stopping using has been tough. He's tried repeatedly and has succeeded for brief periods. Right now, he's been clean for 90 days. That's the longest he has gone and he feels pretty hopeful. Henry hooked him up with a GED prep course and a supported employment program. Henry says it's all Roger's doing, but Roger remembers what Henry told him that cold night when he was still living on the street. "If you want your life back, I think I can help."

He did not have to lie about his drug use. In fact, other people seemed to understand the reasons he used drugs and drank. Gradually, his counselors and peers made him doubt he was doing the right thing with his life. The program found him a safe place to live. They introduced him to a psychiatrist who said if he controlled his drug use, he could take medication that would control his mood swings, and he began to try to do this. When he did take this medication, he did feel better, less down and moody. Before Roger realized it, over a number of months, he was actually on the road to recovery.

Discussion of Roger's Story

Roger apparently went through much of his adult life with little or no insight into his many problems. Sadly, this is quite common for persons with co-occurring disorders. One might effectively argue that in some ways Roger exhibited personal strength, and some might still call it ego strength. Not believing he was sick, when the system was going to hospitalize him he left and began a life on the streets. Yet, while he was resourceful enough to survive on the street, that "strength" relegated him to the life of a reclusive outsider living alone and in poverty. Many people have experienced the same problems Roger did on their first encounters with the treatment system. Initially, a mental health system of credentialed professionals generally funded based on medical diagnoses, and an emerging substance abuse system mostly staffed by ex-alcoholics and addicts and funded by grants and private donations represented two very separate worlds. Recognition of the increasing number of individuals with co-occurring disorders has spurred the integration of these two services to provide effective treatment for people like Roger. The services he needed probably did not exist when he was in school and may not have existed the first time he was hospitalized. They do exist today and it is hoped that they will soon be available to everyone, like Roger, who needs them.

Summary

Recognition that persons with severe mental illness are also highly vulnerable to substance abuse did not come about until after the deinstitutionalization movement. For a period of time, there were few, if any, services for persons with co-occurring disorders of substance abuse and severe mental illness. The programs initially developed to address this issue were either sequential, requiring treatment of one condition before the other was addressed, or parallel, treating both conditions using different staff and often different agencies. For a host of reasons, neither of these initial strategies was particularly effective.

Integrated treatment for persons with co-occurring disorders, providing simultaneous treatment for both conditions using the same professionals working in the same program, is the preferred service and is considered by some to be an EBP. Employing staged treatment and motivational interviewing techniques, integrated treatment for individuals living with both a mental illness and a substance abuse disorder deals with the individual's attitudes regarding these conditions and assists his or her progress toward recovery. Our current understanding of the treatment and rehabilitation of these difficult conditions suggests that much more research is needed in this area.

■ ■ ■ ▬▬▬▬▬▬▬▬▬▬▬▬▬▬▬▬▬▬▬▬▬▬▬▬▬▬▬▬

Class Exercise

For this exercise, one or more students will play the role of addictions counselors and others will play the role of mental health practitioners. Students should read the following vignette, select what they believe is the best response from the perspective of the role they are playing, and be prepared to explain their reasoning behind the selection.

William, a 38-year-old white male, has lived in a residence for persons with co-occurring disorders for two months. He has a history of extensive opiate and alcohol abuse as well as a diagnosis of schizophrenia. He is currently maintained on injectable antipsychotic medication twice a month and has not required other medication. William, who has some college education, has been working in the clerical unit of a psychiatric day treatment program and is reported to be doing well there. He attends the Double Trouble group (a 12-step group for people with co-occurring disorders) and other substance abuse–related groups at the day program. William has fit in very well at his residence, forming friendships with other residents and staff members. In general, his adjustment seems to be very good. Usually he presents no problems at the residence or the day program and has been drug- and alcohol-free as well as free from psychiatric symptoms. During the last week, the staff noticed alcohol on William's breath. When confronted about this, he denied drinking. A staff person from the day program called the residence to report that William had been making vague excuses and leaving the program early. They also reported that he has become more withdrawn and may be responding to voices. When confronted by staff members of the day program, he denied hearing voices. Several other residents reported that they had seen William leaving a local liquor store with a brown bag. When asked about this, William responded that he knows that they want him to go back to the hospital and refuses to discuss it further.

1. What is the best response to this problem? Read all of the options below and discuss their benefits and drawbacks. For the purposes of this exercise, choose only one option and be prepared to discuss your rationale.
   - **Option A**—William is obviously using alcohol again. If he refuses to admit he is using he should have a blood test to settle the issue. If he tests positive he should be denied privileges. If he refuses to comply he should be sent back to the hospital.
   - **Option B**—Even though he is on injectable medication, William is probably getting sick again. He should be evaluated by a psychiatrist to see if he needs an increase or change of medication. Confrontation about his drinking should be postponed until after the evaluation.
   - **Option C**—William should be confronted about his drinking at a house meeting with the other residents and the staff present. Peer and staff support will probably help him to open up. Once he admits that he is drinking again, the problem can be dealt with openly.
2. After considering your choice, reexamine the other two responses. Can you craft a better plan consistent with the principles of treatment presented in this chapter? What do you propose?

▬▬▬▬▬▬▬▬▬▬▬▬▬▬▬▬▬▬▬▬▬▬▬▬▬▬ ■ ■ ■

*If working makes people with mental illness sick, what do unemployment,
poverty, and social isolation cause?*
Marrone & Golowka, 2005

CHAPTER OUTLINE

Psychiatric Rehabilitation. http://dx.doi.org/10.1016/B978-0-12-387002-5.00010-X

Many people respond to questions about "who they are" by talking about their job, position, or profession. Whatever people do that is productive or meaningful greatly contributes to their sense of identity. Such information often conveys the individual's interests, values, aspirations, and socioeconomic status. Persons who have a severe mental illness but no job or profession are often relegated to the devalued role of mental patient. This chapter outlines some of the problems associated with helping persons achieve their vocational goals and some of the strategies that have proven to be effective. Persons with severe mental illness can complete school, be effective workers, and have a profession. When they accomplish these goals, their psychiatric condition becomes something that they have overcome rather than the definition of who they are.

This chapter will answer the following questions:

1. *What are the barriers to employment for people with a psychiatric **disability**?*
2. *What skills, resources, or experiences are related to vocational success?*
3. *What constitutes quality vocational services?*
4. *What kinds of vocational services have been developed?*

Introduction

Employment is an essential part of citizenship. If we are fortunate, the work we choose to do reflects our interests, skills, and talents. Working, especially working and earning a paycheck, promotes self-confidence, self-esteem, status in the community, and economic well-being. Because of all these obvious advantages, our culture puts great value on the role of wage earner. In addition, the role of wage earner provides access to other valued social roles, including that of friend, spouse, parent, homeowner, neighbor, customer, and taxpayer (Carling, 1995). For most adults, having a job or profession is an essential element in defining who they are, achieving a positive quality of life, and contributing to society.

Does work have some additional benefits for people with mental illness? It seems logical that successful employment would have a positive impact on other areas such as symptom reduction, community integration, and improved functioning. The results of a number of studies suggest this may be true (Arns & Linney, 1993; Bell, Milstein, & Lysaker, 1993; Bond et al., 2001; Drake, McHugo, Becker, Anthony, & Clark, 1996; Krupa, 2004; Lysaker & Bell, 1995; Siu, Tsang, & Bond, 2010). One study that specifically looked at this issue was conducted by Mueser and his colleagues in 1997. In this study, the researchers examined the relationship between competitive employment and non-vocational domains. The results indicated that:

> *… formerly unemployed psychiatric patients who obtained competitive employment while participating in a vocational program tended to have lower symptoms, better overall functioning, higher self-esteem, and higher satisfaction with vocational services and finances. (p. 423)*

In contrast, a subsequent study by some of the same researchers (Torrey, Mueser, McHugo, & Drake, 2000) failed to find a relationship between employment status and self-esteem. In response, Casper and Fishbein (2002) examined the contribution of job satisfaction and success as moderators of self-esteem. Their findings suggested that employment status is related to self-esteem when job satisfaction and success are taken into account. That is, self-esteem was not improved by simply having a job, but was improved when individuals reported feeling satisfied and successful in their jobs. More studies on this topic are needed to confirm and further illuminate these findings.

The negative effects of unemployment are also important to consider. Studies have found that unemployment, particularly long-term unemployment, results in deterioration of physical, emotional, and psychiatric well-being as well as deterioration in functioning (Kroll & Lampert, 2011; McKee-Ryan, Song, Wanberg, & Kinicki, 2005; Murphy & Athanason, 1999; Turner, 1995). Unemployed persons, with or without a disability, tend to experience more health problems, more symptoms of psychological distress and/or mental illness, and reduced coping skills. These negative effects persist over time (Wadsworth, Montgomery, & Bartley, 1999) and are worse among those with low internal (i.e., self) or external (i.e., others) expectations of employment or reemployment and low social support (Kroll et al., 2011; McKee-Ryan et al., 2005). Clearly, practitioners' attitudes about the possibility of employment for the people they serve are not a trivial matter.

Persons with severe mental illness, however, rarely get to experience the positive effects of having a regular job. Employment rates for people with a psychiatric disability are very low, typically found to be around 30 percent (Anthony, Cohen, & Farkas, 2002; Bazelon Center for Mental Health Law, 2011; Cook, 2006). Many factors contribute to the high unemployment rate among people with severe mental illness.

Barriers to Employment

Prejudice and Discrimination

One of the greatest barriers to employment for people with a psychiatric disability is prejudice. Prejudice refers to the negative reactions to or beliefs about a specific characteristic. In this case we are referring to the uninformed beliefs about mental illness and about the potential for employment of people with a psychiatric disability. Prejudice about people with psychiatric disabilities stems from the stigma associated with psychiatric illness (stigma is discussed thoroughly in Chapter 1 and elsewhere in the textbook). When people hold negative attitudes about a person or group of people and act on those beliefs, the result is discrimination. In the area of employment, discrimination can exist among practitioners who withhold needed services as well as employers whose hiring and personnel practices treat workers with psychiatric disabilities differently.

Prejudice about people with psychiatric illnesses has several sources. The most obvious source, which we have all experienced, is the frequent, negative characterization of people with mental illness by the mass media. This is reflected in many of the attitudes about mental illness held by the community at large as well as the business community. Media reports often leave the false impression that people with mental illness are frequently unstable, irrational, and dangerous.

Workplace discrimination toward people with psychiatric illnesses occurs in all areas of employment: obtaining employment, maintaining a job, and career advancement (Cook, 2006; Russinova, Griffin, Bloch, Wewiorski, & Rosoklija, 2011). People with psychiatric disabilities report that workplace discrimination has a damaging effect, whether experienced first-hand, observed in the treatment of a coworker, or expected due to past experience with the organization or industry (Russinova et al., 2011).

A more subtle example of prejudice is reflected in the beliefs (both conscious and unconscious) of professionals regarding the ability of people with psychiatric disability to work or to work in any but the most menial jobs. These beliefs are reflected in some of the vocational services and choices made available for persons with major mental illnesses (Brice, 2011).

One of the most insidious effects of prejudice is often seen in the beliefs of people with mental illness themselves, sometimes called "self-stigma." When society reduces access to good jobs and mental health professionals give subtle or overt messages of doubt about a person's ability to perform on the job, these negative beliefs can be internalized (Bandura, 1986; Lent, Brown, & Hackett, 1994; *Rehab Brief*, 1993). This self-stigma may be the hardest form of stigma to detect and is often the most difficult form of stigma to overcome (Ritsher, Otilingam, & Grajales, 2003; Ritsher & Phelan, 2004).

Misguided Services

Uninformed beliefs on the part of professionals about the abilities, desires, and needs of people with psychiatric disabilities have resulted in both unnecessarily delayed access to vocational services and unnecessarily limited vocational options (Bond, Dietzen, McGrew, & Miller, 1995; Cook, 2006; *Rehab Brief*, 1993). Concerns about stress, symptomatology, medication compliance, and rehospitalization have caused providers to withhold access to vocational services until an individual has demonstrated successful participation in a setting such as a day program that is segregated from the regular community. These policies persist even though research over the last several decades has found that functioning in one setting is not predictive of functioning in other settings (Anthony & Jansen, 1984). Additionally, studies suggest that direct entry into competitive employment does not result in increased symptoms, rehospitalization, or homelessness, as has often been feared (Bond et al., 2001; McFarlane et al., 2000; Torrey, Becker, & Drake, 1995). Instead, direct entry may result in "increased involvement in other community activities ... increased general supports and ... increased independence of consumers" (Torrey et al., 1995, p. 72). Similarly, Bond and Dincin (1986) and Bond et al. (1995) found increased rates of full-time competitive employment as a result of "accelerated entry into community jobs" (Bond et al., 1995, p. 106). In this latter study, Bond and his colleagues also found that delayed entry into employment because of participation in pre-vocational (often shortened to "pre-voc") activities, including sheltered work, decreased one's likelihood of ever entering competitive employment and lowered the participant's self-expectations (see Box 10.1). Pre-voc activities include the basic skills one needs for work such as punctuality, following directions, focusing on the task at hand, communicating with coworkers, and so forth. In a similar vein, Blankertz and Robinson (1996) point out that although wages are an important motivator, many programs expect people to demonstrate motivation prior to actually accessing paid employment opportunities. Many of the employment options offered by providers are restricted to low-skill jobs with little or no chance of advancement, even when the worker has advanced academic degrees, a strong work history, or simply greater aspirations.

The case for pre-vocational training is very straightforward. Many of the first vocational services, which were set up in response to the deinstitutionalization movement, focused on teaching pre-vocational skills. These programs were designed to help individuals entering the community after years of psychiatric institutionalization. Members of this institutionalized population had spent much of their adult lives in settings where even the simplest decisions were made for them. Program staff could readily identify and work with the pre-vocational skill deficits of their clients, but had scant information about the more specific job skills they might need at particular jobs. A subtle, but possibly no less important, reason for the emphasis on pre-vocational training is how services have been reimbursed. In many places, programs could not bill for offsite services. That meant that any work the staff might do outside the center in the community would not be reimbursable. This created a barrier to the staff to doing realistic kinds of skill training, **job development**, and follow-up support. Instead, given very realistic financial concerns, many administrators and staff members focused on what they felt they could do best, pre-vocational skills training.

Since the advent of **supported employment** (SE), the idea of forgoing pre-vocational training in favor of direct placement and the provision of support services on the job has received increasing research support. As previously mentioned in this chapter, a number of studies (Bond & Dincin, 1986; Bond et al., 1995; Torrey et al., 1995) have found that direct placement is superior to pre-vocational training with respect to vocational

---

BOX 10.1   IS "PRE-VOC" REALLY NO VOC?

A week after an interesting class discussion about the future of vocational services in psychiatric rehabilitation (PsyR), one of our graduate students (with many years of PsyR experience) reported having an interesting dispute at work. It seems that during a staff meeting at the psychiatric day treatment program (Chapter 7) where he worked, he had questioned whether it was really helpful to work on pre-vocational (pre-voc) skills with the clients if the goal was to prepare them for regular jobs. Instead, he had suggested that maybe "pre-voc is really no voc." He was very surprised by how upset some of the staff became by his remark. Yet, today there is a growing body of research suggesting that he was correct.

outcomes. In their 1995 study, Bond and his colleagues suggested that during the time the client spends in pre-vocational training he or she may become dependent on the program, develop a support network that he or she does not want to leave, and lose some of the motivation to work a regular job. This makes sense if we consider the recovery theories put forth by Pat Deegan (1988) and William Anthony (1993b), which are discussed in detail in Chapter 4. These theories suggest that recovery involves creating a new self-image that incorporates the fact of the mental illness. Consider the development of this new self-image after spending a year at pre-vocational training versus spending a year at a regular job.

Some opponents of direct placement SE still argue that this strategy causes higher stress and higher hospitalization rates. Research has not supported these claims. Clearly, this represents an area of PsyR where our knowledge may be moving faster than the attitudes of many staff and administrators about what constitutes good service.

Lack of Vocational Experience

Another barrier to employment for many people with a psychiatric disability is their limited experience and understanding of themselves as workers and of the world of work (Danley & Anthony, 1987). Early experiences in employment provide us with important information about our skills, preferences, interests, and aspirations. These experiences also help us learn about the expectations and opportunities in the world of work (Bandura, 1986; Lent et al., 1994). Over time, multiple employment experiences contribute to our ability to make appropriate career choices and, ultimately, to be successful in a career. For people who experience a psychiatric disability, these employment experiences and the crucial vocational information they contain have often been missed (Danley & Anthony, 1987; Russert & Frey, 1991; *Rehab Brief*, 1993). People entering vocational services after long periods of psychiatric disability often have considerably less knowledge of their own skills, interests, and preferences than would be expected from comparable persons their own age. Typically, vocational service programs are evaluated by how many persons they place in jobs and how long the people hold these jobs. Because of this, they are usually neither willing nor able to provide the multiple employment experiences that may be needed to provide someone with the knowledge necessary to select a vocational direction that is appropriate for that person and provides advancement opportunities.

Lack of Education

In the same way that someone's psychiatric illness may have interfered with early work experiences, it may also have interfered with the completion of high school or college. The absence of education reduces the quantity and quality of jobs available whether an individual has a disability or not (Baron & Salzer, 2002; Gao, Gill, Schmidt, & Pratt, 2010). Strategies for providing support to help individuals complete their education are discussed in Chapter 11.

Psychiatric Disability

Other barriers to employment may be the result of the mental illness itself: the impact of the mental illness on thought and affect as well as the episodic and cyclical nature of the disability (Russert & Frey, 1991; Rutman, 1994; *Rehab Brief,* 1993). This means that many people with serious mental illness experience difficulties with memory, concentration, organization, or even interpersonal interactions at least some of the time. Some effects of the mental illness may be what Jansen (1988) called "psychological problems," such as a lack of self-esteem and self-confidence, fear of failure, anxiety, and difficulty getting along with others (p. 36). Finally, the obvious physical side effects of medications can be severe and pose a significant barrier to employment (Braitman et al., 1995; Rutman, 1994).

Health and Wellness Concerns

As discussed in Chapter 6 and elsewhere in this text, the health and wellness of persons with serious mental illness are significant quality of life concerns and may present a barrier, or at least a challenge, to employment. Many people do not feel well enough to work or to travel to work, or they may have medical concerns that require numerous doctors' appointments, potentially leading to absenteeism difficulties.

Possible Loss of Benefits

For individuals in the United States who receive Supplemental Security Income (SSI) or Social Security Disability Insurance (SSDI), the Social Security Administration (SSA) regulations regarding the effect of earned income on benefits are often perceived as posing a substantial barrier to employment. Persons with SSI or SSDI typically are also eligible for Medicaid or Medicare, which pays for medications that can be very costly. Most people with mental illness are aware that their illness may flare up at any time. In the event of a relapse, the individual may have to reapply for Social Security as their only source of income and health insurance. The fear of losing one's benefits, coupled with the fear that one may not be able to sustain employment, increases the perceived risk of attempting employment (Baron & Salzer, 2002; Cook, 2006; Ford, 1995). In fact, the perceived risk is often much greater than the actual risk. In recent years, SSA has implemented policies and practices that can reduce the risk of lost benefits. Additionally, some states have made it possible for workers with disabilities to purchase Medicaid health benefits in certain circumstances. SSA regulations regarding earned income and work incentives are discussed in Box 10.2. Paradoxically, these work incentives have, in many cases, served as disincentives. Cook (2006) reports that people with disabilities who are aware of the regulations often adjust their work involvement to safeguard their benefits (for the reasons stated above). This results in underemployment. Additionally, earned income also affects other kinds of benefits such as housing subsidies and food stamps.

In spite of what may seem like an overwhelming list of potential barriers to employment, people with psychiatric disabilities do complete post-secondary education/training,

BOX 10.2 SOCIAL SECURITY BENEFITS AND EARNED INCOME

In 1999, President Clinton signed the **Ticket to Work and Work Incentive Improvement Act (TWWIIA)** into law. This law was designed to reduce the disincentives to employment for which the previous regulations were notorious. Following are general descriptions of the current SSI and SSDI regulations regarding earned income and the provisions of the TWWIIA that address the most common concerns of people considering employment.

The regulations for SSI employ a formula for determining specific reductions in cash benefits as a result of earned income. The person's cash benefit will be reduced by $1 for every $2 the person earns in excess of any exclusions to which the person is entitled. Those exclusions may include an **earned income exclusion** and a **general income exclusion**. These exclusions ($20 and $65, respectively) are earnings that the SSA allows without affecting benefits.

The SSDI recipient is entitled to a nine-month **trial work period** (TWP) during which his or her SSDI cash benefit is protected even though the person is earning wages. This period is followed by a 36-month **extended period of eligibility** during which time the person's entitlement to the cash benefit will depend on whether or not the person's earnings exceed the amount that is considered to be **substantial gainful activity**. There is no formula to reduce the SSDI amount. Instead, it is an all-or-nothing proposition; the person either receives the SSDI cash benefit or does not.

Both of these programs include work incentives that can be used to reduce the person's countable earned income and maintain some or all of the cash benefit at least for a time.

PROVISIONS OF TWWIIA

Ticket to Work

The **Ticket to Work** is a voluntary initiative. Each eligible SSI and SSDI recipient is issued a document called a "ticket to work." The ticket holder can use the ticket to obtain employment services from any approved employment service provider known as an **employment network (EN)**. An EN may be a public or private service provider, a state organization such as VR (see Box 10.3), or **One-Stop Centers**, schools, employers, or others (Jensen & Silverstein, 2000; Roessler, 2002). In principle, the ticket holder gains a measure of control and choice in selecting services because he or she can withdraw the ticket and reassign it to another EN if he or she is dissatisfied with the services being provided. An additional benefit to the ticket holder is that while using a ticket he or she will not be subject to continuing disability reviews by Social Security.

Medical Insurance

For most recipients of Social Security benefits, the greater fear is the loss of medical coverage. SSI recipients are covered by Medicaid and may continue to be covered until their earnings reach a particular amount, even after their earnings have resulted in the cessation of their cash benefit. TWWIIA made it possible for states to allow working individuals with incomes greater than 250 percent of the federal poverty rate to purchase Medicaid coverage if it is needed to cover medical costs. SSDI recipients are eligible for Medicare. TWWIIA extended the period of Medicare coverage to 93 months after the trial work period (Jensen & Silverstein, 2000; Roessler, 2002). This results in a total period of 102 months during which time an SSDI recipient can be working and still be covered by Medicare.

(Continued)

BOX 10.2   SOCIAL SECURITY BENEFITS AND EARNED INCOME—Continued

To ensure that the regulations and work incentives are widely understood and administered in a consistent way, SSA established **Community Work Incentives Coordinators** (**CWICs**; originally called employment support specialists) to train local SSA claims representatives and to provide outreach about work incentives. Further, TWWIIA provided funding for the establishment of the **Work Incentives Planning and Assistance Program** (**WIPA**; originally Benefits Planning, Assistance, and Outreach projects). The **CWICs** provide individual consultation on benefits planning and assist the newly established Program Manager for Recruitment and Outreach (PMRO) to coordinate and provide Work Incentives Seminars (WISE) for information dissemination and access to WIPA (www.worksupport.com).

Expedited Reinstatement of Benefits

A major concern for people with psychiatric disabilities in becoming employed is the fear of losing benefits and then being unable to sustain employment. TWWIIA addressed this concern by establishing an expedited reinstatement of benefits process. If individuals become unemployed for reasons related to their disability within 60 months of termination of their benefits, they can request an expedited reinstatement of benefits. That is, they do not have to go through a new application process. During the period that SSA is reviewing their request, individuals may receive temporary benefits, including health care coverage. If SSA determines them to be ineligible for benefits, the temporary benefits will not have to be repaid.

Additional information can be found at the SSA Web site: https://www.socialsecurity.gov/redbook.

BOX 10.3   VOCATIONAL REHABILITATION: THE FEDERAL INITIATIVE IN THE UNITED STATES

In 1918, the federal government established the Office of Vocational Rehabilitation to assist returning World War I veterans to find employment. The scope of vocational rehabilitation to assist veterans has been expanded several times since. In 1920, Congress decided that civilians with physical disabilities should also be eligible for vocational rehabilitation services. In 1943, services were expanded again to include persons with mental retardation and mental illness (Ledbetter & Field, 1978; Neff, 1988; Roberts, 1996). During the Great Society instituted by President Johnson in the 1960s, services were expanded to recipients of SSDI (Social Security Disability Insurance) and later to "the disadvantaged or socially and culturally deprived" (Ledbetter and Field, 1978, p. 36).

Prior to the 1970s, vocational rehabilitation services were not readily accessible to people with a psychiatric disability (Anthony & Blanch, 1987). In 1973, Congress overrode a presidential veto and passed the Rehabilitation Act. This act established the Rehabilitation Services Administration (RSA) and authorized it to do several things, including providing vocational rehabilitation services to people with the most severe disabilities, to those people who had been underserved in the past, and to "develop new and innovative methods" to achieve vocational rehabilitation (PL 93-112, p. 3) (Ledbetter & Field, 1978; McGurrin, 1994; Roberts, 1996). This new emphasis on serving people with the most severe disabilities helped to make services more

(Continued)

BOX 10.3   VOCATIONAL REHABILITATION: THE FEDERAL INITIATIVE IN THE UNITED STATES—
Continued

accessible to people with a psychiatric disability. The Rehabilitation Act also allowed for funding to be allocated to states to provide vocational rehabilitation services. This funding is based on the *per capita* income of the state (PL 93-112). Each state has a state agency that corresponds to the federal RSA. This agency, named different things in different states (Division of Vocational Rehabilitation, Office of Vocational Rehabilitation, etc.), employs vocational rehabilitation counselors in local offices.

In addition, the 1973 act established the **Individual Written Rehabilitation Plan** (IWRP) (Ledbetter & Field, 1978). The IWRP (later changed to **IPE, Individual Plan for Employment**) identified the desired rehabilitation outcome and the services and activities that will be provided to achieve it. Each VR client is required to be actively involved in the development of his or her rehabilitation plan to ensure that it reflects the desires of the individual. The VR counselor works with individuals with disabilities to establish the IPE and then to access the needed services. In some states the VR agency provides those services and in other states the services are purchased from authorized VR vendors such as psychiatric rehabilitation agencies. These services include assessments of the worker's capacity, skills, and interests; work adjustment, such as attendance, grooming, and productivity; education or training; and job acquisition and initial support. Once a VR client is employed and stable on the job, VR will continue to be involved for a brief period of time (currently 90 days) and then will close the person's case.

Access to services was further improved in the 1970s when the National Institute of Mental Health (NIMH) established the **Community Support Program** (CSP) initiative. The CSP stressed VR services as an important element of support for deinstitutionalized psychiatric patients. In 1978, partly based on the CSP initiative, NIMH entered into a collaborative agreement with RSA, establishing two rehabilitation research and training centers focused on psychiatric disability (Anthony & Blanch, 1987; McGurrin, 1994).

In 1980, NIMH, RSA, the National Institute on Handicapped Research, and the Council of State Administrators of Vocational Rehabilitation entered into a cooperative agreement that led to the development of a work group focused on improving services for people with a psychiatric disability. This work group was instrumental in bringing about the 1986 Amendments to the Rehabilitation Act (Anthony & Blanch, 1987). In response to strong advocacy efforts, the 1986 Amendments to the Rehabilitation Act defined SE—a newly emerging vocational service of great promise, established a category of funds to pay for SE (Title VI(C)), and made it possible for vocational rehabilitation counselors to use regular case service funds to pay for SE (Roberts, 1996).

In 1992, the Rehabilitation Act was amended again. In response to testimony from people with disabilities and advocates, the 1992 Amendments to the Rehabilitation Act modified the definition of SE increased the emphasis on consumer choice, and mandated "a 'presumption of employability' for all people" (Roberts, 1996, p. 19).

In August 1998, the **Workforce Investment Act (WIA)** was signed into law (PL 105-220). The law established a one-stop workforce development system that brought together employment, education, and training programs for adults, dislocated workers, youth, veterans, and others. Specifically, Title IV of the WIA contains the amended Rehabilitation Act (Skiba, 2001; http://www.doleta.gov/usworkforce/wia).

(Continued)

> **BOX 10.3   VOCATIONAL REHABILITATION: THE FEDERAL INITIATIVE IN THE UNITED STATES—** Continued
>
> Title IV of the WIA extended appropriations for SE until 2003 and specified that vocational rehabilitation is a component of the one-stop system and that people with disabilities should have access to all one-stop services. The WIA expired in 2003, although funds continue to be appropriated to carry out the goals and activities specified, and reauthorization bills have been proposed in Congress (http://democrats.edworkforce.house.gov/bill/workforce-investment-act-wia-2012).

get jobs, build careers, and achieve successful and satisfying lives. The quality of the services provided is often a crucial factor. The most effective services are provided by practitioners who understand that barriers are support needs that can be ameliorated.

Developing Vocational Services

Features of Effective Vocational Services

Several researchers have attempted to guide effective vocational services by identifying the characteristics, circumstances, or experiences related to or predictive of vocational success. Early efforts proved to be a difficult task. In an extensive review of the literature, Anthony and Jansen (1984) concluded that past work experience is the best predictor of employment success. They also found that, counter to what is often believed, factors such as diagnosis and level of symptomatology were unrelated to vocational success. This finding makes sense based on our previous discussion of how persons tend to prepare for making vocational choices. Employment success is influenced by learning from past experience. In a later review of the literature, Anthony (1994) found that past work history, number and length of hospitalizations, marital status, race, and previous occupational level were found to be related to vocational outcome. In addition, work adjustment skills (i.e., work readiness, attitudes, and quality of interpersonal relations) were associated with positive outcomes. Diagnosis, symptomatology, and functioning in other life domains did not correlate with vocational outcome, with a few exceptions. Anthony, Rogers, Cohen, and Davies (1995) did find negative correlations between symptoms and work skills. People with severe mental illness who became employed had lower symptom scores and higher work skills than those who never became employed. Nevertheless, participation in rehabilitation programs appeared to have a positive effect on symptoms and work skills.

A slightly different picture was revealed by a Boston University Center for Psychiatric Rehabilitation study in which all subjects were individuals who had identified a vocational goal. They found the predictors of vocational outcome to be symptomatology, criminal justice involvement, and marital status. Anthony suggested that the fact that the subjects had selected a vocational goal and were receiving a vocational intervention may distinguish this group from previous research groups (1994). Furthermore, in at least a few studies, diagnosis has been found to be related to vocational outcome (Anthony, 1994; Mowbray, Bybee, Harris, & McCrohan, 1995). McGurk, Mueser, Harvey, LaPuglia, and Marder (2003) found higher levels of positive symptoms to be related to more frequent use of job site supports. Some studies suggest a possible relationship between medication and work performance, finding that medication appears to impair work performance.

Blankertz and Robinson (1996) examined the integration of vocational rehabilitation services with typical mental health services, suggesting that predictors of positive vocational outcomes are not characteristics of individuals but characteristics of programs. These authors asserted that "vocational rehabilitation should be an integral part of the mental health rehabilitation process" (p. 1222). Gowdy, Carlson, and Rapp (2004) agreed. In a study comparing high-performance with low-performance employment programs, they found ten organizational characteristics that differentiated the two groups. In high-performing programs, directors, supervisors, and staff were more likely to hold different viewpoints and engage in specific practices. Ten features of these programs are summarized in Table 10.1. Additionally, Macias, DeCarlo, Wang, Frey, and Barreira (2001) found that a significant proportion of people who initially expressed no interest in employment became employed if vocational services were provided.

A growing number of studies have found that the specific model of service provided is an important contributor to employment success. SE has consistently been shown to produce better employment outcomes than other vocational services and is now considered an **evidence-based practice** (Becker, Smith, Tanzman, Drake, & Tremblay, 2001; Bond, Drake, & Becker, 2008; Bond et al., 2007; Bond, 2004; Bond et al., 2001; Campbell, Bond, Drake, McHugo, & Xie, 2010; Drake & Bond, 2008; Drake et al., 1996, 1999). SE will be discussed later in this chapter.

Table 10.1   High-performing Employment Program Characteristics

Beliefs and Viewpoints

1. Emphasize the possibility and the value of work.
2. Do not view societal stigma as a major barrier to program performance.
3. View consumers as wanting to work and motivated to work.
4. The potential loss of benefits is seen as a need for information and negotiation rather than as a major barrier.

Practices

1. Employ strengths-based practices.
2. Use employment outcome data to improve services.
3. Share stories that reflect a belief in consumers' ability to succeed.
4. Conduct frequent and regular meetings between vocational and case management staff.
5. Case managers are proactive in their support of employment goals and efforts.
6. Therapists are supportive of employment goals.

Source: Based on Gowdy, Carlson, and Rapp (2004).

BOX 10.4   AMERICANS WITH DISABILITIES ACT

The Americans with Disabilities Act (ADA) passed by the US Congress in 1990 is designed to protect people with disabilities from discrimination in five areas: employment, transportation, telecommunication, public accommodation, and the business of local and state government (Mancuso, 1990; National Alliance of Business, 1991; Roberts, 1996). The ADA is not the first law to prohibit discrimination in employment against people with disabilities nor to refer to **reasonable accommodations**. The Rehabilitation Act of 1973 prohibits discrimination by federal agencies or employers who receive federal funds. Additionally, all but a few states have laws protecting people with disabilities from discrimination, as does the District of Columbia (Lee, n.d.).

In the area of employment, the ADA prohibits discrimination against any qualified person because of his or her disability in all areas of employment, including hiring, firing, advancement, compensation, and training. The ADA requires that employers consider whether a qualified applicant is able to perform the "essential functions" of the job with or without accommodations. A "qualified applicant" is one who has the experience or credentials required for the job. For example, if a job requires that the worker have a certain number of years of experience or a particular academic degree or training and the applicant does not have the qualifications, the employer does not have to consider that applicant because the person is not qualified. The "essential functions" are tasks that are integral to the job. In deciding which tasks are integral, employers usually consider whether the job exists to perform those tasks, how many people are available to perform those tasks, or what the result would be if the tasks were not performed. Employers are required to make reasonable accommodations for applicants or employees with disabilities. An accommodation is considered "reasonable" if it is not an "undue burden"—that is, if the cost is not excessive given the business's resources and if the accommodation does not change the nature of the work performed (Jones, 1993; Lee, n.d.; National Alliance of Business, 1991; Roberts, 1996). The ADA holds employers to a higher standard than previous laws regarding the definition of "undue burden." According to Lee (n.d.), the ADA "required the employer to prove that an accommodation would be significantly difficult or expensive" (p. 3).

In 2008, Congress passed the **ADA Amendments Act** (sometimes referred to as the ADA Restoration Act) in response to the eroding of protections due to decisions of the Supreme Court in specific cases. The Act was intended to "restore the intent and protections of the Americans with Disabilities Act of 1990." These amendments "clarify and reiterate who is covered by the law's civil rights protections ... revises the definition of disability [i.e., broadens the definition to include impairments that substantially limit a major life activity] ... states that mitigating measures [i.e., use of accommodations, medications, etc.] ... have no bearing in determining whether a disability qualifies under the law." These amendments went into effect on January 1, 2009 (www.access-board.gov/about/laws/ada-amendments.htm).

Supported Employment

Supported employment is really part of a social movement. It represents inclusion [of people with disabilities] into the fabric of community settings.

(DiLeo in Roberts, 1996, p. 12)

With the advent of SE people with the most severe disabilities, who were thought to have no vocational potential and were therefore denied access to vocational services, were finally given a chance in the workplace. Initially designed for people with severe developmental disabilities, SE emerged in the early 1980s as a response to unsatisfactory employment opportunities (Anthony & Blanch, 1987; Bond, Drake, Mueser, & Becker, 1997). A small number of university-based projects demonstrated that even people with the most severe disabilities could work successfully in community settings if they were placed in jobs and provided with the necessary training and support (Ford, 1995; Roberts, 1996). These project outcomes contributed to the 1986 amendments to the federal Rehabilitation Act which, among other things, included a definition of supported employment.

This new place–train approach reversed the traditional train–place approach whereby clients would attend day programs or simulated work settings that were segregated from the regular community to prepare for employment (Anthony & Blanch, 1987; Danley & Anthony, 1987). Although the vocational and skill deficits produced by severe psychiatric disability made the train–place strategy seem logical, it resulted in very little actual employment and tended to screen out people with the most severe disabilities who were considered too low functioning to be successful in the workplace (Ford, 1995).

SE gained a great deal of attention in the field of psychiatric rehabilitation as well. In 1987, Danley and Anthony articulated the Choose-Get-Keep model of supported employment for people with a psychiatric disability (see Box 10.5). They asserted that, rather than being placed in a job, people with a psychiatric disability needed to be involved in the process of achieving employment outcomes and that the process needed to include choosing a job, that matched an individual's interests, preferences, and skills.

Reviewing studies of supported employment, Bond and his colleagues (1997) found that when workers were in jobs that matched their preferences, they stayed twice as long as when the job did not match the worker's preferences. This combination of choice and support available either on or off the jobsite for the duration of the person's employment tenure has become the hallmark of quality SE for all people with disabilities (Carling, 1995; Corrigan, Mueser, Bond, Drake, & Solomon, 2008; Roberts, 1996; *Rehab Brief*, 1993). A critical feature of SE is the underlying philosophy that given adequate supports everyone is capable of competitive employment (Anthony & Blanch, 1987; Ford, 1995; Roberts, 1996).

The Role of the Employment Specialist

The employee's primary support person is the employment specialist. In the early days of SE, this position was called "job coach." Reflecting the complex nature of the task, the job coach title has undergone some changes. Titles such as employment specialist, employment consultant, and human resource consultant reflect the sophistication and professional nature of the job and the person doing that job. In the early days of SE, the job coach typically

---

BOX 10.5   KAREN S. DANLEY, PHD

Karen Danley, PhD, was one of the founding members of the Center for Psychiatric Rehabilitation at Sargent College of Health and Rehabilitation Sciences, Boston University. Focusing on vocational rehabilitation, Dr. Danley was largely responsible for the development of the Choose-Get-Keep model of SE, which set the tone and standard for this service for PsyR and ultimately the entire field of SE. As the first director of Career Achievement Services, she established many new program initiatives for the Center for Psychiatric Rehabilitation as well as many innovations for the field. An experienced and successful grant writer, Dr. Danley's efforts helped to fund much of the important research and training carried out at the center. Her work included outreach to the inner-city youth of Boston who experience serious mental illness and using the Choose-Get-Keep strategy with veterans who have psychiatric disabilities.

Sadly, Karen Danley passed away in April 1998, a great loss for psychiatric rehabilitation. Perhaps her most important legacy is all the individuals she has helped to achieve vocational and educational success.

---

arranged for the worker to be placed in a job and then provided training and support to the worker at the job site. Today, providing supports away from the job site is more common. Previously, the job coach may have educated the employer about disabilities and effective ways to teach the new employee and encouraged developing relationships between the new worker and his or her coworkers. Today, employment specialists do not disclose the disability status of the worker unless directed by the person him- or herself to do so. Employment specialists continue to assist the supported employee with interpersonal relationships on the job, health and wellness goals, career planning, disclosure decision making, money management, transportation, planning for the effect of earned income on Social Security, and other information.

The role of employment specialist is highly professionalized. Usually working without direct supervision, the employment specialist must successfully accomplish many different tasks. With the emphasis on career choice, the employment specialist has to know about career planning and development. Taking a broad view of potential careers, the employment specialist has to know about marketing, **job development**, and effectively interacting with the business community. The employment specialist has to understand the needs of the business community in general and the needs and work culture of specific work settings. Today, the Internet is an important tool in job development. The employment specialist needs to know how to use company Web sites and social media in the job development process.

In some cases, the employment specialist will teach the skills of job acquisition and the job seeker will carry out the tasks. Many people prefer not to disclose their disabilities to potential employers and so prefer to do their own job development. In other cases, job seekers need more direct support and the employment specialist will be more directly involved in contacting the employer, presenting the candidate's qualifications, and perhaps even accompanying the person to the job interview. The employment specialist also assists in the other tasks of job acquisition such as resume preparation and practice interviewing. According to Becker and Drake (1994), job development strategies include getting to know the particular operations, needs, and hiring practices of potential employers; tapping into personal networks for job leads; and even creating jobs where a task and setting match the skills and interests of a client but the job doesn't currently exist. This is sometimes referred to as **job carving** (DiLeo & Langton, 1993) and is a strategy often used when the severity of a person's disability prohibits the individual from performing all of the duties associated with existing jobs. This technique has led to the recent creation of an SE approach in which this "carving" technique is the preeminent tool used, entitled Customized Employment (Inge, 2006).

Gervey and Kowal (1995) reported that it takes an average of 42 job development contacts to generate one job offer. Obviously, the employment specialist has to be persistent. The employment specialist interacts with family members, community members, doctors, and other service providers in assisting the supported employee to access needed supports. Perhaps the most important characteristic of an employment specialist is flexibility. An active employment specialist may have to provide these services in an executive office, on a loading dock, and in a restaurant kitchen all on the same day.

Supported Employment in Practice

SE is a highly individualized practice rooted in a set of principles. These are zero exclusion of potential participants, integration with clinical services, benefits counseling, following client preferences, rapid job search, follow-along supports after someone is employed, and team-based services (Corrigan et al., 2008, p. 197).

The SE approaches for people with mental illness are the **Individual Placement and Support** approach (IPS) articulated by the New Hampshire-Dartmouth Psychiatric Research Center (Becker & Drake, 1994, 2003) and the Choose-Get-Keep approach articulated by Boston University Center for Psychiatric Rehabilitation (Danley & Anthony, 1987; Danley, Sciarappa, & MacDonald-Wilson, 1992; MacDonald-Wilson, Mancuso, Danley, & Anthony, 1989). Both of these approaches emphasize competitive employment based on the preferences of the individual and the importance of ongoing support. The IPS approach further emphasizes rapid job search and the integration of vocational and clinical services, whereas the Choose-Get-Keep approach provides skill development in career planning activities. Although the two approaches have many similarities, research has consistently found the IPS approach to be superior in achieving employment outcomes (Bond, 2004; Bond et al., 2008; Drake & Bond, 2011).

Both IPS and Choose-Get-Keep engage the client and the significant people in the client's life in identifying the person's skills, preferences, interests, resources, and support needs and then match these to a work setting. In the Choose-Get-Keep approach, this is done in the choose phase. By examining past experiences, the person is helped to identify and objectify those personal values and skills that will have an impact on the person's success and satisfaction in employment. Clients are helped to identify the skills they have developed through previous experiences and also their reactions to those experiences to illuminate their likes and dislikes, preferences, interests, and support needs. This leads to the development of a career goal and a plan for developing or acquiring the skills and resources necessary for success. In some cases, the chosen career requires additional credentials or training. Supported education, a strategy to provide people with the educational background they need, is discussed in Chapter 11. Job development, which also occurs in the choose phase, is based on the skills and values of the individual. Significant people in the client's life are engaged in supporting the goal that the client has articulated (MacDonald-Wilson et al., 1989).

In the IPS approach, these tasks are accomplished in the engagement and vocational assessment stages. This approach emphasizes rapid entry into employment and the need for continual assessment after the client has gotten the first job, using each job to gain new information about skills, preferences, and personal style. In both the get phase of the Choose-Get-Keep approach and the obtaining employment stage of the IPS approach, the client is given the support needed to obtain a job.

The keep phase of the Choose-Get-Keep approach and the job support stage of the IPS approach involve activities that identify and ensure access to adequate and ongoing support to promote successful and satisfying employment. Some supports may be in the area of learning new skills, learning to use skills in a new setting, accessing needed services, or arranging for environmental modifications. Supports are available on or off the job site and may address meeting the requirements of the new job, adjusting to the workplace, and coaching and support in the area of interpersonal interactions. In some cases, the employment specialist accompanies the new worker to the job for a period of time. In this case, the employment specialist may be providing support in mastering the job, negotiating accommodations, and also in fitting into the workplace and developing relationships with coworkers.

If the employment specialist provides some of the job training for the worker, it is usually because the worker requires more training than the employer typically provides. It is less stigmatizing for the supported employee to access the typical training available to all workers in that setting. Often the support is provided off the job site. This may include supportive counseling, problem solving, and even role-playing of difficult interactions. Support provided is not limited to work issues but will include any area of the person's life that affects successful employment. For example, an employment specialist may assist a supported employee in negotiating a different appointment schedule with one's psychiatrist if the current one conflicts with his or her work schedule.

Ideally, the employment specialist is not the sole means of support, but has worked with the employee to identify and develop a support network. The network may include family, friends, counselors, coworkers, or anyone the worker chooses. Recently, there has been greater emphasis placed on applying the PsyR principle of using **natural supports**—that is, those people or things that are naturally present in the setting. Not only is this usually less stigmatizing, it is also frequently more effective. For example, it is almost always better to assist a worker in arranging to carpool with a coworker (for a fee), than to have the employment specialist, agency van, or para-transit system provide transportation. Additionally, most workplaces and workers in that setting have developed ways of supporting each other. In some workplaces, for example, the amount of work to be done varies at different times of the day or days of the week. In some settings, it's common for coworkers to pitch in and help each other when one person's workload is excessive. The supported employee should be assisted in accessing those supports and in contributing support to others. It is important that the supported employee hold a valued role as a participant and contributor in the work setting. Furthermore, a good match between workplace characteristics and employee support needs contributes greatly to successful employment. It is better, for example, for a worker who needs frequent breaks (whether they have a disability or not) to work in a job that is self-regulated or measured by tasks accomplished rather than by time on task. The level, type, and frequency of support needed by the employee may change over time and the support provided should change accordingly.

The IPS approach emphasizes the integration of vocational services and clinical services. This means that the vocational counselor or employment specialist collaborates with the clinical team. In this approach, the clinical team then becomes an important part of the supported employees' support network. In fact, studies show that this vocational/clinical integration is one of the critical factors in positive employment outcomes (Drake, Becker, Bond, & Mueser, 2003).

A decade ago, the Choose-Get-Keep approach was changed to the Choose-Get-Keep-Leave approach, recognizing the importance of assisting people in leaving a job in a way that contributes to future successes.

Supported Employment in Other Modalities

In addition to stand-alone SE programs, SE has been implemented in other service modalities. These include **Assertive Community Treatment** (Russert & Frey, 1991), residential programs (Gao, Waynor, & O'Donnell, 2009), and peer-delivered services (Swarbrick, Bates, & Roberts 2009). These models of service delivery are described in Chapters 8, 12, and 13.

Supported Employment: An Evidence-based Practice

A growing number of studies comparing SE with other vocational services has provided substantial evidence of the superiority of SE in achieving competitive employment outcomes (Bond, 2004; Bond, Drake, & Becker, 2008; Bond et al., 2001; Campbell, Bond, & Drake, 2011; Drake & Bond, 2011; Twamley, Jeste, & Lehman, 2003). These studies have also contributed to identifying the critical principles and practices of SE, which make up the individual placement and support (IPS) model described earlier. SE has been studied in comparison to day treatment services (Bond, 2004; Drake et al., 1994; Lehman et al., 2002; Mueser et al., 2004), conventional or enhanced vocational services (Bond, 2004; Bond et al., 1995; Burns et al., 2007; Drake et al., 1996, 1999; Killackey, Jackson, & McGorry, 2008; Latimer et al., 2006; McFarlane et al., 2000; Mueser et al., 2004; Twamley, Narvaez, Becker, Bartels, & Jeste, 2008; Wong, Chiu, Tang, Mak, Liu, & Chiu, 2008), and other mental health services (Chandler, Meisel, Hu, McGowen, & Madison, 1997). In each case, SE has achieved significantly better employment-related outcomes. That is, persons receiving SE services were significantly more likely to become competitively employed, work more hours, and earn better wages (Bond et al., 2008; Bond, 2004; Drake & Bond, 2011). These superior outcomes have been consistent regardless of geographical characteristics (i.e., rural or urban areas) (Haslett, Drake, Bond, Becker, & McHugo, 2011), demographic background (Bond, 2004; Campbell et al., 2011), prior criminal justice involvement (Frounfelker, Teachout, Bond, & Drake, 2011), or presence of a co-occurring disorder (Founfelker, Wilkniss, Bond, Devitt, & Drake, 2011). As with other evidence-based practices, fidelity to the model is significantly related to better outcomes (Bond et al., 2008; Becker et al., 2001; Drake et al., 1996, 1999; Lehman et al., 2002; McGrew & Griss, 2005; Mueser et al., 2004). The following lists summarize the critical ingredients and service outcomes of SE.

Critical Ingredients of Supported Employment

- Services are focused on competitive employment
- Nonexclusionary criteria
- Rapid job search
- Integration of vocational and mental health services
- Focus on consumer preferences
- Time-unlimited, individualized supports
- Benefits counseling

Service Outcomes of Supported Employment

- Competitive employment
- Higher number of hours worked
- Higher wages earned

SE services, particularly those that adhere faithfully to these principles and practices, are far more successful than other services at achieving competitive employment outcomes. These programs have been shown to achieve 50 to 70 percent employment rates. Still, there is a sizeable proportion of people receiving SE services who do not become employed (Roberts & Pratt, 2007) and many of those who do work part-time, have limited job tenure, and obtain unskilled or low-skilled jobs with little or no chance of advancement (Baron & Salzer, 2002; Murphy, Mullen, & Spagnolo, 2005). Undoubtedly, there are many factors that contribute to these outcomes. Some of these factors appear to include the person's own perceptions of the possibility and benefits of successful employment (Roberts & Pratt, 2010), the absence of education needed to qualify for better jobs and careers (Baron & Salzer, 2002; Gao et al., 2010), and the absence of a social network for job connections and natural supports (Kroll et al., 2011; Murphy et al., 2005; Roberts et al., 2010). There are still many unanswered questions. What are the other factors that inhibit successful employment? What services or supports will improve job retention? What is the role of non-SE providers in promoting and supporting employment goals? How can we assist people to get jobs that promote economic independence? Are there other models that create better outcomes for people in employment other than what has been researched already? What strategies can be used to encourage more people to seek employment and economic engagement? Many more studies are needed to address these issues. As SE evolves, it will undoubtedly expand to include services and supports to address these barriers and many others.

History of Attempts to Promote Employment

Prior to the emergence of supported employment as the evidence-based practice of employment services to persons with serious mental illness, a variety of other approaches were developed. None had the empirical support that SE would gather.

Transitional Employment: Forerunner to SE

Perhaps the first PsyR community services that included work as an integral component took place at Fountain House in New York City, one of the original **clubhouses** (Fountain House is also discussed in Chapter 7 of this text) founded in the 1950s. Arguably, the greatest contribution Fountain House has made to the development of employment services for people with psychiatric disabilities is **transitional employment (TE)**. TE provides program members with experiences at real jobs, in real employment settings, earning competitive wages. A TE job is acquired from the employer by the vocational services agency. The agency takes full responsibility for the job, which is initially managed by agency staff. Once the staff members have learned the job, they are ready to place program members in the job and to provide them with the training and support they need to succeed. A program member works the job for a time-limited period (usually three to nine months, but this varies) before being replaced by another program member. The agency continues to be responsible for the job at all times. In fact, if the program member is unable to work on a certain day, it is the staff member's responsibility to take his or her place on the job. Obviously, the staff members are very motivated to thoroughly train and provide all necessary supports so that the program member can do the job successfully. TE jobs are typically part-time and require minimal skills so that they can accommodate a variety of members with a wide range of skill levels. Members have the opportunity to develop real work skills, gain regular work experience, and earn a paycheck. The employer is assured that the job will be continuously filled with trained workers (or by staff members). Program members may go through a series of TE jobs. In fact, the Fountain House philosophy is that members will experience as many transitional employment jobs as needed to eventually achieve permanent employment in jobs of their own (Beard, Propst, & Malamud, 1994). TE has been an important forerunner to SE.

Carl's Story

Carl first attempts to get into the workforce are representative of some of the problems people face in pursuit of their working goals. His story also illustrates some of the differences between transitional employment and supported employment. As you read his story, consider the following questions:

1. Why did Carl's first attempts at employment fail?
2. What were the differences between Carl's TE and SE experiences?
3. Is SE the best strategy for every person like Carl?
4. What will be required for Carl to continue to succeed as he moves on to college and more demanding jobs?

Carl is a 32-year-old who has been diagnosed with schizophrenia. He experienced his first psychiatric hospitalization at age 18, during his senior year in high school. The first symptoms he was aware of were hearing voices and feeling depressed. Carl's involvement in school activities had been minimal, but his grades were good and he was expecting to go to college. After being discharged from the hospital, he had to really struggle to finish high school, but did manage to graduate with his class.

A month after graduation, Carl was hospitalized again. This time, the voices were more persistent and his depression was more pervasive. When Carl returned home, he still felt confused, unmotivated, and lethargic and spent a great deal of time either sleeping or watching television. His dream of going to college and becoming an art teacher seemed remote. His friends from high school had stopped calling; they were busy getting ready for college. During the next four years, Carl was hospitalized five times. At his mother's urging, he attempted to take an art class offered by the local YMCA on Saturday mornings, but he felt too groggy in the morning and ended up missing most of the classes.

After Carl's seventh hospitalization, and in response to his parents' complaints that all he did was hang out at home, Carl's psychiatrist recommended that he attend the local day treatment program, but the program did not seem right for Carl. He was usually late in the mornings and only participated minimally in the pre-vocational units and recreational activities. He thought he would like the arts and crafts group, but complained that the projects were too childish.

When a position opened for the program's transitional employment job at the local Kmart, Carl's counselor asked him if he would like to try working. Carl lasted for one week at the Kmart. He was almost always late, the voices were making it hard for him to concentrate, and he was reprimanded by his supervisor when he failed to hear a customer ask for help. Carl's counselor said Carl would get another chance to try TE but first he needed to improve his punctuality within the program and learn to accept feedback from his supervisor.

Six months later, Carl was given another TE job. This time, Carl worked as a dishwasher in the cafeteria at the local high school. Carl's counselor thought this would be a good job for him because his punctuality had not improved and he would not have to be at this job until 11 a.m. The counselor also thought that because Carl knew people at the school he would feel less stress. This had been Carl's high school. In reality, Carl felt defeated by ending up back at his school as a dishwasher. He worked there for two weeks before he ran into his former art teacher. Her surprise at seeing him working in the cafeteria highlighted his own feelings of disappointment and failure, and he quit the job.

Carl's program received funding for a new employment strategy, supported employment (SE). Shortly after the program started, Sharon, the SE specialist, found Carl outside her office reading the program description on the bulletin board. When she asked Carl if he was interested in work, he told her that he was not able to work because he couldn't get to most jobs on time, couldn't get along with people, and couldn't concentrate on even the simplest things like stocking shelves. Undaunted, Sharon said she was willing to give it a try if he was, and they agreed to meet the next day.

Sharon started by asking Carl to describe his ideal job, and Carl talked about being an art teacher. He described his love for art and how important his high school art teacher had been to him. He talked about the lost opportunity for college and his present inability to succeed at anything. They researched the necessary credentials to be an art teacher and talked about the possibility of college. Carl insisted that he did not have the concentration necessary to pass college courses right now and he was not even confident about his artistic abilities anymore.

Sharon and Carl examined his past experiences. They discovered many examples of Carl's ability to help others use their artistic abilities both in high school, where he worked with younger students, and at the program, where he helped other members in the arts and crafts group. They saw that even when he had to meet deadlines for his art projects, Carl didn't experience the same kind of stress that made him lose concentration when doing simple tasks. They looked at his work history to figure out why he wasn't successful on his jobs and what kinds of supports might have helped him at the time.

Sharon suggested that they contact Carl's high school art teacher because he liked and trusted her and he had worked for her informally by helping other students when he was in school. Sharon thought the art teacher could give them some ideas about jobs that were related to art but that didn't require a college degree. Carl was a little embarrassed and nervous, but agreed to let Sharon set up the meeting.

The art teacher met with Carl and Sharon and told them that the after-school program at the elementary school was looking for someone to work part-time. She thought that Carl would be allowed to start an art program for the kids and she would be willing to help him plan it. She also agreed to talk to the program director and recommend Carl.

For the first time in a long time, Carl felt hopeful. He knew the morning grogginess from his medication would not interfere because this job started late in the day. He was excited about being involved in art again and felt confident that he could do it. Sharon helped Carl prepare for the interview and select pieces of Carl's artwork that he could show the program director. They reviewed bus schedules and figured out what bus Carl should take. At the interview, Carl told the program director that he hadn't worked for a while and was hoping someone would be nearby at first in case he felt overwhelmed. Carl and Sharon had agreed that knowing who to go to for help might keep Carl from feeling like he had to quit if he was feeling stressed. They also agreed that at first Sharon would drive Carl to work and stay outside in the car in case he needed her.

Sharon drove Carl to work for the first three days. At the end of his third day, Carl told Sharon that he'd take the bus the next day and that he'd call her if he needed help or at the end of the day if he managed OK. During the first month, Carl called Sharon several times to talk through his nervousness about work. He never missed a day. When the school year ended, the program director offered Carl a job working in the summer recreation program. Sharon was surprised when Carl reported that he was thinking of turning it down. He told her he wanted to talk to her about going to college.

Other Vocational Services

Other models of vocational services which have developed over time persist today, even though many are inconsistent with principles of psychiatric rehabilitation and lack evidence of efficacy.

Fairweather Lodges

A very different approach to employment services, Fairweather Lodges, was developed by George Fairweather in 1963 (http://theccl.org/Fairweather.htm). Fairweather Lodges are programs where people with a mental illness live and work together operating a member-run business. The lodge community was organized around a set of principles that addressed issues such as the importance of meaningful work, autonomy, advancement, tolerance, support, and similarity to the larger society (Fairweather, 1980). The lodge community offers its members the opportunity to access valued societal roles in a mutually supportive, albeit segregated, environment. Members of the lodge occupy positions of responsibility within the business. The amount of responsibility one assumes is commensurate with one's ability at the time. Experts, such as accountants, are hired from outside the lodge when needed on a temporary basis (Ford, 1995; Onaga, 1994; Toms-Barker, 1994). Fairweather Lodges are described in more detail in Chapter 12.

Hospital-based Work Programs

Onsite vocational opportunities have been developed at some hospitals, giving patients the chance to do work for pay within the hospital setting during periods of hospitalization. These programs have been less successful than anticipated in improving post-discharge employment outcomes for patients. In fact, there is evidence that such programs result in the development of dependency in some patients and a desire to stay in the hospital (Bond & Boyer, 1988). According to Bond and Boyer, "Most reviewers have concluded that there is no relationship between successful adjustment to work programs within the hospital and post-hospital employment" (p. 235).

Job Clubs

A job club provides structure and resources to assist participants to conduct their own job search. The club provides training and resources, such as instruction in job-seeking skills (resume writing, interviewing, etc.), access to telephones to call employers, and clerical support (McGurrin, 1994). An important feature that the job club supplies its members is peer support. This approach to job development may be less successful for many people with severe mental illness. Many individuals need a greater level of support in accomplishing the tasks of job acquisition (Bond et al., 1997).

Sheltered Workshops

Sheltered workshops solicit manufacturing jobs from local business and industry and provide support and supervision to people with disabilities in a factory-like setting owned or operated by the agency. Workers in the shop are usually paid a piece rate based on their productivity. This piece rate is based on the number of pieces that a worker without a disability could produce in a given period of time. For some, sheltered work is expected to be a step toward competitive employment, whereas others see it as permanent placement (Bond & Boyer, 1988). According to Bond and Boyer, even when sheltered employment is expected to be short-term, "there is a tendency for clients to remain indefinitely" (p. 241). Sheltered workshops have come under much criticism in recent years as their ineffectiveness has been widely demonstrated in empirical studies. They are rarely used any more as an employment service.

Affirmative Industries

Affirmative Industries represent another way agencies offer supervised employment opportunities to clients or members. These businesses are owned, managed, and operated by the agency. Affirmative Industries, which can range from commercial cleaning or landscape crews to bakeries and caterers, provide goods and services to the community at large. The mental health agency secures contracts with local citizens and businesses to provide products or services. The workers are clients who are supervised by agency staff and are paid by the agency. This strategy provides members with a mix of support and a regular work experience. There are, however, a number of disadvantages to this approach. Consumer choice is quite limited. Clients must work in the business the agency runs. People with disabilities, working as a group or "crew," tend to generate stigma. This may be particularly true if the work crew is used as an employment opportunity for people with severe and more obvious disabilities. Finally, crew members' wages tend to be very low (Marrone, 1993). Similar to Affirmative Industries are client-employing businesses (Marrone, 1993). These businesses employ workers without disabilities as well as people with psychiatric disabilities and may be profit-generating.

CONTROVERSIAL ISSUE
Working: A Choice or a Responsibility of Citizenship?

Recently, a colleague was making a presentation to a gathering of people with the lived experience of psychiatric illness. Our colleague, herself a person with a diagnosis of psychiatric illness, stated that people with psychiatric illness not only can work but should work. The reaction of her audience was strong and angry. "How dare you tell me I have to work!" was a common sentiment.

In our society there is an unspoken expectation that adults will work, thus providing for their own well-being, sharing their skills and talents to the benefit of society, and contributing to the general financial welfare of the community. How is it, then, that the adults in this audience would express such outrage at this common societal expectation being applied to them? In fact, this rejection of employment as an expectation of people with psychiatric illness is expressed often by consumers as well as service providers.

The benefits of working are many and well known. Working provides financial and social resources, access to relationships, better healthcare, and better health. The health benefits of working and the detriments of not working are experienced in all areas: physical, emotional, and mental health. Perhaps more importantly, society benefits from the skills, talents, and toil of its members. Almost everything that is done in a community is done by workers. Not surprisingly, the workers in our society gain status. They have earned what the community has to offer because they have contributed to the creation, maintenance, and financial support of those resources. As Marrone and Golowka (2005) and others have pointed out, working is a responsibility of citizenship; it is more than a contribution to the self, it is a contribution to society.

(Continued)

CONTROVERSIAL ISSUE
Working: A Choice or a Responsibility of Citizenship?—(Continued)

How is it, then, that reasonable people can be outraged at the expectation that adults with psychiatric illnesses will work? The goals of psychiatric rehabilitation are recovery, community integration, and quality of life. Employment is essential to each of these. Nevertheless, for someone to be willing to move from unemployed to employed, he or she has to believe it's possible to succeed and that it will be personally beneficial. Many forces have combined to thwart these beliefs among people with psychiatric illness. Long-term unemployment results in decreased physical, emotional, and mental health. Not feeling well makes it hard to take on the burdens of a job. Long-term participation in clinical and/or day treatment services develops a dependence on others and a deterioration in decision-making skills: in effect, an "illness identity." Messages from professionals, family members, and others that one is not well enough to work, not capable of handling stress, or not able to handle the demands of a job, coupled with warnings that the stress of work will bring on an episode of illness, leave the individual doubting that he or she has the capability to work and fearing that an attempt to work will have a negative outcome. Those who do muster the courage to try are often greeted by a work world that stigmatizes and discriminates. Often, their education has been interrupted by the onset of the illness and therefore they lack the credentials necessary to obtain a job that pays enough to raise them out of poverty or provide essential health care benefits. Access to career services such as SE and supported education, which for many people are crucial to success, is extremely limited.

Would simply having the expectation that people will work solve this problem? If the community (including the business community) expected people with psychiatric illness to work, accommodations for these workers would be seen as another form of flexibility afforded to employees. If mental health professionals, family members, and others expected people to work the discussion would be about support mechanisms and coping strategies (as it is for everyone). If people with psychiatric illnesses expected to work, they may demand the services they need to make this happen. If the mental health funding system expected people with psychiatric disabilities to work (i.e., were recovery-oriented) career services would be well funded and employment outcomes would be widely measured. But this is not the current situation. In the absence of a welcoming work world, access to essential support services, and the optimism of professionals, family members, and other supporters, is it surprising that so many people with psychiatric illness consider the risk too great?

Summary

The barriers to employment for people with mental illness include prejudice, the experience of the symptoms of mental illness, the disabilities brought about by the illness and its consequences, and concerns about the loss of government benefits.

Engendered by stigma, prejudice reduces community acceptance of people with mental illness and results in discrimination. The prejudice that exists among mental health professionals results in reduced quality services and fewer options offered to service recipients. An individual's internalized self-stigma reduces the individual's belief in his or her potential and may be the hardest stigma to overcome.

Many people with mental illness have missed out on important vocational experiences. The illnesses themselves affect many areas such as memory, concentration, interpersonal interactions, self-esteem, and anxiety. Medication may have overt physical side effects and less obvious social side effects. There is strong evidence that past work history is the best predictor of vocational or educational success, a research finding that begs for individuals to begin to get some type of vocational experience as young adults.

Innovative vocational services were developed for people with psychiatric disabilities as early as the 1950s. Fountain House, one of the original clubhouses, introduced TE, a program of real jobs in community settings. As discussed earlier, TE is thought by some to be a forerunner of SE.

In the 1980s, SE was introduced for people with severe developmental disabilities and was adopted in the field of psychiatric rehabilitation. SE assists individuals to become employed in jobs that match their skills, interests, and preferences and provides whatever supports are needed to ensure success and satisfaction. Research studies have found SE to be superior in achieving employment outcomes and it is considered an evidence-based practice. A focus on competitive employment, non-exclusionary criteria, rapid job search, integration of vocational and mental health services, focus on consumer preference, time-unlimited supports, and benefits counseling are the critical ingredients of SE.

Services such as Fairweather Lodges, sheltered workshops, and mobile work crews generally lack empirical support for their efficacy. They are also more segregated and therefore more stigmatizing then regular community employment. They are not competitive employment with all its expectations or all its benefits in terms of salary, skill development, and community integration.

In the United States, the Rehabilitation Act of 1973 and subsequent amendments established the Rehabilitation Services Administration, provided federal funding for vocational rehabilitation services, defined supported employment, and emphasized consumer choice and a presumption of employability for all people with disabilities. In 1998, the Workforce Investment Act (WIA) established a one-stop workforce development system and the Rehabilitation Act is subsumed under the WIA. The Americans with Disabilities Act, passed in 1990, along with antidiscrimination laws in many states, protects people with disabilities from discrimination in a number of areas including employment. This act is a far-reaching statement about the right and ability of citizens with disabilities to be fully included in all aspects of community life.

■ ■ ■ ▬▬▬▬▬▬▬▬▬▬▬▬▬▬▬▬▬▬▬▬▬▬▬▬▬▬▬▬▬▬▬▬▬▬▬

Class Exercises

Exercise 1

The clubhouse program where you have been a staff member for three years has just been notified that funding to develop supported employment (SE) services is going to be available soon. The director would like to apply for this funding and has brought together the staff members who are primarily responsible for the transitional employment (TE) program to design the SE program. It becomes evident immediately that there are many different opinions about how to structure the new SE program.

Some think that SE should be completely separate from the rest of the program so that members who want to can access SE without being involved or associated with the clubhouse aspects of the program. Others want to use SE as the next step after TE. Their reasoning is that people have to demonstrate commitment, motivation, and good work behavior before you can convince an employer to hire them. Still others want to develop a multistep program, in which members spend eight weeks in a work unit demonstrating attendance, punctuality, good grooming, adequate productivity, ability to work as a team member, and ability to accept feedback from a supervisor. At the same time, members will attend a work-readiness group where they will discuss reasons for wanting to work. This will be followed by three months on a TE placement and then the individual can go into an SE job.

1. Considering what you have read about predictors of vocational success and quality vocational services, evaluate the options presented.
2. Describe a SE program design that incorporates what you have learned about vocational issues and quality services.

Exercise 2

Your residential program runs a cleaning crew service. The crew employs residents of the program who, under the supervision of a counselor, clean the group homes. The crew members are paid a small stipend. Originally the cleaning service was conceived of as a step toward jobs in the community, but almost no crew members have gone on to other employment.

1. In what ways is this cleaning service different from SE?
2. What are some likely reasons that the crew members rarely go on to regular employment?
3. What would need to be done to change the cleaning service to an SE program?

I'm excited about (school), meeting new people, and I can say I'm a student and not a client at a mental health program.
(Knis-Matthews et al., 2007, p. 110)

CHAPTER OUTLINE

Successful educational achievements such as completion of an academic degree or a technical training program help many people achieve their long-term vocational goals and improve the quality of their lives. A psychiatric rehabilitation approach known as supported education is designed to help individuals coping with a psychiatric disability to complete their education and training. This chapter will explore the challenges encountered by these students, the strategies employed by supported education, and the benefits people with psychiatric disabilities gain from these services.

Psychiatric Rehabilitation. http://dx.doi.org/10.1016/B978-0-12-387002-5.00011-1

This chapter will answer the following questions:

1. *Can people with severe and persistent mental illnesses successfully pursue postsecondary education?*
2. *What are the special needs of students with psychiatric disabilities?*
3. *What does higher education offer persons with severe and persistent mental illnesses?*
4. *What types of special services and supports can be provided?*
5. *Are there supported education strategies that have been proven effective?*
6. *What is the future of supported education as a psychiatric rehabilitation service?*

Introduction

The interruption of postsecondary educational pursuits is a common consequence of schizophrenia and other severe mental illnesses (Anthony & Unger, 1991; Unger, 1990). In Chapter 1, Paul had his first acute episode of schizophrenia during his freshman year at college. Many adolescents and young adults have had similar experiences; it has been estimated that nearly five million people would have completed their college education had they not faced an early-onset psychiatric disorder (Kessler, Foster, Saunders, & Stang, 1995). The inability to achieve an important personal goal such as successful completion of a college semester often results in feelings of failure, shame, and disappointment. In addition, many individuals are told by misinformed mental health professionals that they will probably never be able to return to school and should settle for less stressful pursuits. Countless people diagnosed with severe mental illnesses have had their dreams shattered, believing that college degrees and professional careers were out of their reach.

In addition to the psychological impact of an interrupted education, in this day and age it is important to consider the socioeconomic implications of not acquiring advanced education or training. Without further education, many people have limited employment opportunities and are relegated to work jobs at the lower end of the pay scale (Kessler et al., 1995; Megivern, Pellerito, & Mowbray 2003; Stodden & Conway, 2003).

Benefits of Supported Education

College education or advanced technical education has become a critical ingredient of success for persons seeking professional and semiprofessional employment. Most readers will be familiar with the potential benefits of a higher education, including more opportunities for upward mobility, higher salaries, and increased career satisfaction (Corrigan, Barr, Driscoll, & Boyle, 2008; Megivern et al., 2003; Mowbray, 1999, 2004a; Moxley, Mowbray, & Brown, 1993). In the field of Economics, this is referred to as human capital. College campuses are also an important setting for developing social networks and business contacts (Murphy, Mullen, & Spagnolo, 2005). For people without disabilities these benefits are rarely questioned, but they are just as essential for persons with disabilities (Gao, Schmidt, Gill, & Pratt, 2011).

There are also additional benefits to higher education for persons coping with severe mental illnesses. Mowbray (1997) identified five key benefits of supported education (SEd) for people with psychiatric disabilities:

1. **New identity**—Moving from the role of psychiatric patient or mental health consumer to the socially valued role of student. In the early days of SEd, this transition was often the norm. Now, it is just as likely that the person using SEd services experienced the onset of illness while in the role of student.
2. **New and normalized environment**—Moving from a psychiatric hospital or day treatment program to a classroom on a college campus.
3. **Structure**—Academic studies and other campus activities provide meaningful and productive ways to spend time.
4. **A clean slate**—Often in a bind when a potential employer asks what they have been doing in recent years, persons with psychiatric disabilities who are attending college classes can honestly say that they decided to pursue a new career and took time off to continue their education.
5. **Hope**—Enrollment in college classes and progress toward a degree are major steps toward the realization of goals and dreams that may have seemed impossible prior to involvement in supported education (pp. 67–68).

For many people SEd is an important step on their road to recovery. The following quotes, taken from various first-person accounts, emphasize the important benefits of postsecondary education for people who are recovering from severe mental illnesses.

[Education] means life to me …. I want to be the one to choose what I want …. I don't want somebody to support me; I don't want [others] to run my life. (Knis-Matthews et al., 2007, p. 110)

In my current recovery process, I am doing better in my life than I have ever done before. My personal life has gotten better. I have married since being in this program. I am feeling more hopeful about what I can achieve for myself in life. I am having fun while learning and meeting new and interesting people. (Spencer-Watts, 2002, p. 100)

I know that I have great potential and the Michigan Supported Education Program has given me back the confidence to believe in myself again as well as triggering in me courage, persistence, and determination to continue to pursue my dreams and aspirations. They have alerted me of the fact that, although college is difficult, it is possible. (Ishmael, 2002, p. 32)

While I was attending [the supported education program and college classes]—I was not manic. I was not homeless. I was not a mental patient or an ex-mental patient. I was a STUDENT! And it felt great! (Cloutier, 1997, p. 66)

Barriers to Education

If SEd has the capacity to greatly enrich the lives of people with psychiatric disabilities, why are there still relatively few individuals pursuing educational goals?

The barriers to higher education are the same as those for people without disabilities, particularly persons in the lower socioeconomic classes. For many, a growing barrier to education is **economic instability**. People who are struggling to pay housing and grocery bills are hard pressed to consider managing the rising costs of college tuition. Certainly, financial aid can help; nevertheless, costs such as books, computers, supplies, and fees can make a college education unaffordable for many. Lack of affordable and accessible **transportation** is another major issue for people with limited incomes. In one study, transportation was cited as the number one barrier to attending college (Shearman, Hart-Katuin, & Hicks, 2002).

Many college students, particularly older students who are returning to school, struggle with **balancing schoolwork with other responsibilities**, such as jobs, children, and household chores. Many students, especially those returning to school after some years, may have diminished academic skills. People on limited incomes often have fewer resources available to address these challenges, such as lack of funds to pay for child care. Among the general population, fewer than 50 percent of high school seniors entering college go on to complete a bachelor's degree and overall community college dropout rates also exceed 50 percent. Clearly, postsecondary education can be a daunting task for many people, regardless of illness or disability (Adelman, 2004; Mowbray, 1999).

Unique Challenges for Persons with Psychiatric Disabilities

In addition to these barriers encountered by many college students, people with psychiatric disabilities face a number of unique challenges. One study found that on average these individuals faced five "substantial" barriers (Atkinson, Bramley, & Schneider, 2009). Perhaps the most obvious challenge is the mental illness itself. The case of Paul, explored in Chapter 1, clearly illustrates how acute *psychiatric symptoms* such as hallucinations and delusions can interfere with one's ability to focus on course material or sometimes even get to class. Atkinson and her colleagues (2009) found that the greatest barrier individuals faced was fluctuating illness. However, even when symptoms are in remission, many people continue to struggle with residual symptoms such as reduced ability to concentrate or process information and other executive functioning skills. **Functional deficits** can also interfere with ability to perform well in academic settings. For example, a student who lacks appropriate social skills may monopolize class discussions or repeatedly ask the professor irrelevant questions while at the same time being unaware that his behavior is disrupting the flow of the class. As university professors, however, we can attest that this deficit is not unique to persons with psychiatric illnesses. In addition, **side effects of psychotropic medications** can cause difficulties such as slowed movements and inability to stay alert in class due to sleepiness (Cooper, 1993; Dougherty et al., 1996; Frankie et al., 1996; Megivern et al., 2003; Mowbray, Moxley, & Brown, 1993).

The **stress** associated with final exams or major class projects is a challenge for most students. For those with a severe mental illness, stress may contribute to the recurrence or exacerbation of symptoms (see the discussion of the stress/vulnerability/coping competence model in Chapter 2). At times, either because of stress-induced relapse or simply due to the episodic nature of a severe mental illness, **hospitalizations** occur that can interrupt a student's course of study. Not surprisingly, many students who have psychiatric disabilities become discouraged after even a brief hospital stay due to missed classes and work that needs to be made up. For some, the fear of recurring symptoms or hospitalizations alone creates a barrier to the completion of educational goals.

Systems navigation is another challenge faced by people with psychiatric disabilities trying to return to school. Many people have already been frustrated trying to navigate the complex mental health, vocational rehabilitation, and Social Security Administration systems. Taking on yet another bureaucracy such as a large university with its own complicated systems of admission, financial aid, and registration may be overwhelming. Some students give up before they start because the application process alone is so complex. Managing these systems often requires tenacity, creativity, flexibility, and support (Kiuhara & Huefner, 2008; Cooper, 1993; Dougherty et al., 1996, Frankie et al., 1996). Many schools fail to provide adequate services for students with disabilities and are particularly ill equipped to serve students with psychiatric disabilities. At the same time, many students with psychiatric disabilities do not avail themselves of existing services (Salzer, Wick, & Rogers, 2008; Eisenberg, Golberstein, & Gollust, 2007). These students may not be using services due to a combination of a lack of knowledge of their existence and how to access them and fear of stigma. Lack of coordination between campus-based student support services and community-based mental health services is another systems management failure that, if addressed, could help to rectify this situation (Megivern & Pellerito, 2002; Mowbray, Megivern, & Holter, 2003b).

In addition to the above-mentioned challenges, many people with psychiatric disabilities face **negative attitudes and stigma** while attempting to pursue an education (Mowbray, 1999; Unger, 1994). Sometimes, these come from otherwise well-meaning family members and friends who firmly believe that their loved one is too fragile to cope with the pressures of being in school. Unfortunately, many people are also discouraged by mental health and rehabilitation professionals who hold antiquated beliefs about the capabilities of persons who have severe mental illnesses and are thus reluctant to support them in achieving their educational goals or to refer them to supported education programs (Cook & Solomon, 1993; Frankie et al., 1996; Mowbray et al., 1993). Although many current practitioners do embrace the concepts of recovery and empowerment, too many others still convey disheartening messages such as: "College and competitive employment are not in your future. If you want to stay out of the hospital you should participate in less stressful activities."

Negative attitudes and misconceptions about people with psychiatric disabilities are also commonly held by the faculty, administrators, and staff of many postsecondary educational institutions (Becker, Martin, Wajeeh, Ward, & Shern, 2002; Mowbray, 1999;

Unger, 1994). Most know very little about severe mental illnesses and how these illnesses may affect students in the classroom and in other areas of college life. Many academic personnel express concern that students who experience psychiatric symptoms will be disruptive, violent, dangerous, or unable to meet academic standards (Frankie et al., 1996; Housel & Hickey, 1993; Jasper, 2002; Unger, 1998). This situation has been exacerbated by a number of shooting incidents (e.g., Newtown, Connecticut, 2012; Aurora, Colorado, 2012; Virginia Tech, 2007; etc.) by persons either diagnosed or assumed to have mental illnesses.

In fact, until the passage of the Americans with Disabilities Act in 1990, some colleges and universities had dismissal polices for those who were diagnosed with a severe mental illness, even if there was no evidence of poor academic performance or dangerous behaviors (Mowbray, 1999). Despite the fact that there is now evidence that many people with psychiatric disabilities can successfully complete degree requirements and that laws are in place that protect their right to do so, attitudes on many campuses have been slow to change. Mowbray (1999) reported that in her experience academic administrators are often reluctant to spend time discussing SEd strategies and are sometimes more interested in talking about keeping people with psychiatric disabilities out of the classroom.

Given all these issues, students with psychiatric disabilities who do attempt further education have a very high dropout rate. In 1995, it was estimated that 86 percent of persons with psychiatric disabilities dropped out of college before completing their degree (Kessler et al., 1995). Strategies designed to address this issue have included using motivational interviewing (Manthey, 2011) and increasing resilience (Hartley, 2010). Increased availability of SEd services in general, which are expressly designed to increase retention, will help to address this issue.

As you will see later in this chapter, there are many supports and resources that can help students with psychiatric disabilities overcome what may seem like insurmountable barriers to education. However, sometimes the biggest challenge is the student's own belief that he or she will be unable to manage both a mental illness and a postsecondary education. Many people with a psychiatric disability have expressed fears of failure, discrimination, and isolation in academic settings (Cooper, 1993; Dougherty et al., 1996; Mowbray et al., 1993). In addition, being labeled with a psychiatric diagnosis, failing at attempts to achieve personal goals, and experiencing the stigmatizing attitudes of others can all contribute to the low self-esteem experienced by many people with psychiatric disabilities. This type of low self-esteem has been labeled **self-stigma** and may be the most daunting barrier to overcome.

History of the Supported Education Model

Services to help people with psychiatric disabilities access educational opportunities and overcome the many barriers to education addressed in the preceding section began to emerge in many places around the country in the 1980s. In 1981, the term **supported education** (SEd) was first used by PsyR pioneers, such as Karen Unger at the Boston

University (BU) Center for Psychiatric Rehabilitation. She recognized the importance of postsecondary education for enhancing quality of life, social mobility, career options, career advancement, and self-improvement, while also identifying the critical supports necessary for persons with psychiatric disability to gain these advantages (Anthony, 1993a; Cook & Solomon, 1993; Dougherty, Hastie, Bernard, Broadhurst, & Marcus, 1992; Mowbray et al., 2003b; Unger, 1990, 1993; Wells-Moran & Gilmur, 2002). However, before the concept of SEd became widely known and implementation began, a number of related developments occurred that influenced mental health service systems.

Some of the initial efforts to support people with psychiatric disabilities in their pursuit of educational goals were not necessarily focused on postsecondary education. In the early 1980s, clubhouse model programs such as Fountain House in New York City and Thresholds in Chicago as well as many partial hospitalization programs began offering classes and tutoring aimed at helping members obtain their high school equivalency certificate (i.e., GED) or pursue personal enrichment through subjects such as creative writing (Dougherty et al., 1992; Engelstein, Horowitz, & Romano, 2002; Kerouac & McCoy, 2002).

Also during the 1980s, many providers began to notice a shift in the demographics and characteristics of people receiving community-based services (Unger, 1998). In the early years of deinstitutionalization, many of the people being discharged were middle-aged and older adults who had spent a substantial portion of their lives in psychiatric hospitals. Due to this experience, many of them were passive and dependent and seemed accustomed to a marginalized existence, living in supervised group homes or boarding houses and spending their days in highly structured day treatment programs or sheltered workshops. Many providers serving this population were unprepared to deal with the younger cohort of consumers that followed. This new population between the ages of 18 and 35 had spent very little time in the hospital. Finding them resistant to available services, some frustrated providers labeled them "young adult chronics" (this term is no longer used) (Pepper, Ryglewicz, & Kirshner, 1981). These younger individuals tended to be dissatisfied with the services designed for the needs of the deinstitutionalized population, rejecting participation with older members in stigmatizing treatment programs that suggested a bleak future. Instead, they wanted to live, learn, work, and socialize in the same places as their healthy peers (Unger, 1998). In order to achieve their goals, they needed supports and services that most mental health systems did not yet provide (Corrigan et al., 2008; Anthony, 1993a; Unger, 1993).

To address the needs of this younger population, programs were developed to foster the social, vocational, and independent living skills needed to function successfully in normalized community environments. Some of the more innovative programs were offered in nonstigmatizing settings such as an adult education center at a high school or on a community college campus. These settings were more attractive to young people than mental health clinics and offered opportunities to interact with the community at large. These programs were the precursors of today's SEd programs (Unger, 1998).

The Continuing Education Program, operated by the BU Center for Psychiatric Rehabilitation during the early 1980s, is probably the best known example of these early educational programs. Students attended classes on the BU campus, which helped them develop a positive self-image. Students were assisted in identifying short- and long-term educational and vocational goals and then learned the skills they would need to achieve these goals. They were also encouraged to utilize resources at BU such as the student center and the athletic facilities. The program ran several hours per day over four semesters. Graduates had the opportunity to receive ongoing support from BU center staff as they pursued educational and vocational goals (Sullivan-Soydan, 2004; Unger, 1998).

By the early 1990s, the emerging recovery vision (see Chapter 4) encouraged both consumers and providers to expand their notions of what it was possible to achieve. Enlightened rehabilitation professionals no longer dissuaded people from pursuing ambitious goals and dreams. These new ideas were the catalyst for the development of new services that addressed the skills, supports, and resources needed by persons who wanted to pursue postsecondary educational goals (Anthony, 1993b; Sullivan-Soydan, 2002). Programs such as Thresholds' Community Scholars Programs (Kerouac, 1997; Kerouac & McCoy, 2002) and the Michigan Supported Education Project (Carey, Duff, & Robertson-Kean, 2002; Collins, Bybee, & Mowbray, 1998; Mowbray, 1999; Mowbray, Collins, & Bybee, 1999) served as models for the development of SEd programs in many areas of the United States.

The Federal Response

It is also important to note that the advent of SEd programs beginning in the late 1980s was encouraged in part by the adoption of several federal laws intended to eliminate discrimination in educational settings against people with disabilities and mandate the development of services to help them succeed in school. Four landmark pieces of legislation were passed between the early 1970s and 1990:

1. Section 504 of the Rehabilitation Act of 1973 mandated that people with disabilities have equal access to institutions such as colleges and universities that receive federal funding.
2. The Carl Perkins Vocational Education Act of 1984 provided funding for the establishment of offices on college campuses that provide special services for students with disabilities (Brown, 2002). For example, the staff of a disability services office might assist students in obtaining reasonable accommodations from their professors. The act was reauthorized as the Carl D. Perkins Career and Technical Education Improvement Act of 2006, emphasizing career and technical education over vocational education and including support for the integrated career pathways program.
3. The Individuals with Disabilities Education Act (IDEA) of 1990, which was reauthorized in 1997 and again in 2004, mandated that children with disabilities

receive a free, appropriate public education designed to meet their unique needs and prepare them for employment and independent living. This includes the provision of transition services, which continue until the age of 21, and for some students includes assistance with the move from high school to a postsecondary education or training setting. While children with developmental disabilities most commonly have access to transition services, children and teenagers who have psychiatric disorders should also receive transition services to help them to maximize their chances for success in college and beyond.

4. The Americans with Disabilities Act (ADA) of 1990 and amended in 2008 both expanded the scope and clarified the intent of Section 504 of the Rehabilitation Act. According to Unger (1998), the intent of both Section 504 and the ADA was to make it illegal to deny admission to college programs and services to students with disabilities if they are otherwise qualified.

To summarize, the legislation described in the preceding list intends to ensure that all schools have nondiscriminatory admission policies and provide services, supports, and accommodations for students with disabilities. It is also important to note that the laws described here would not exist without the relentless advocacy efforts of people with disabilities. One such advocate was Ed Roberts, who was motivated by his strong desire to attend college despite a severe physical disability. He pushed for the development of the very first program to support students with disabilities at the University of California at Berkeley in 1970. He went on to become a leader in the disability rights movement and fought for legislation such as the ADA until his death in 1995 (Independent Life USA, 2004).

Definition and Models of Supported Education

Unger (1990) defined SEd as:

> *Education in integrated settings for people with severe psychiatric disabilities for whom postsecondary education has not traditionally occurred or for people for whom postsecondary education has been interrupted or intermittent as a result of a severe psychiatric disability and who, because of their handicap, need ongoing support services to be successful in the educational environment. (p. 10)*

In 2005, Collins and Mowbray defined SEd as:

> *A specific type of intervention that provides supports and other assistance for persons with psychiatric disabilities for access, enrollment, retention, and success in postsecondary education. (as reported in Rogers, 2009)*

Actual SEd services have taken many forms. Some programs are located on college campuses, which are integrated settings. Others are based in PsyR programs or community mental health centers. Some models emphasize peer support groups or classes specifically for people with disabilities, while other models focus on quickly integrating students into campus life and providing supports to assist retention. Some provide time-limited services, whereas others offer long-term supports.

Unger's Three Models of Supported Education

Unger (1998) identified three distinct models of SEd:

1. The self-contained classroom model
2. The onsite support model
3. The mobile support model

In the **self-contained classroom model**, classes of students, all of whom have a psychiatric disability, take a prescribed curriculum. The BU Continuing Education Program mentioned earlier is one example of this model. Another example is Thresholds' Community Scholars Program (CSP). Thresholds, located in Chicago, is a comprehensive PsyR agency that began as one of the early clubhouse programs (for more on clubhouses, see Chapter 7). CSP offers a number of college preparatory classes at the clubhouse—for example, a class on study skills and another on research and writing skills. One-on-one educational counseling and tutoring are available and the use of peer (fellow consumers) tutors is encouraged. Members currently enrolled in a post-secondary school can attend a weekly school support group and some may receive tuition scholarships from Thresholds. CSP also provides training to college faculty in the Chicago area to help them work more effectively with students who have psychiatric disabilities (Kerouac & McCoy, 2002). While the self-contained classroom is the least integrated model of SEd, this approach is thought to provide an essential "confidence-building" step for individuals who do not feel ready to attend regular college classes. The Thresholds Community Scholars Program won a Lilly Reintegration Award in 2005; these awards are given to innovative programs and people that help persons with psychiatric disabilities reintegrate with society (http://www.reintegration.com/preview/index.asp?pid=170).

The **onsite support model** assists students on a college campus and helps them to access resources that already exist within the college community. For example, the SEd staff may work to make regular campus resources such as Disabled Student Services or Student Counseling Services more relevant and accessible for students with psychiatric disabilities (Mowbray et al., 1993; Unger, 1990). A variety of supports and services can be provided on campus such as individual educational counseling, negotiating reasonable accommodations with a professor, and referrals to an academic tutor or a mental health agency. Another important service provided by campus-based SEd staff is assistance in documenting a disability so that a student becomes eligible to receive supports and accommodations. Note that in order to receive academic accommodations, students need to disclose their disability to someone in the school's Disabled Student Services office. Professors and other college personnel may need to be aware that the student has a disability and thus needs accommodations, but they do not need to be given details such as a specific diagnosis (Chmielewski, 2002).

The **mobile support model** provides individualized SEd services. In this model, SEd staff members, sometimes called **mobile education support workers** (Cook et al., 1993), provide support on campus and/or off campus as needed by the student (Cook, Yamaguchi, & Solomon, 1993; Mowbray et al., 1993; Unger, 1990). While much of the SEd literature reflects Unger's classification system, in practice, many programs modify or combine features of these models. For example, the Michigan Supported Education Program, a federally funded demonstration project, piloted approaches to providing supported education services. They labeled one of their most promising approaches the **group model**. Individuals assigned to this approach met in groups that were located on a college campus. Two support staff facilitated each group, one of which was a consumer-provider. Group members were empowered to create their own agenda and explore their academic and career goals via self-directed study projects (Carey et al., 2002).

Other Models of Supported Education

In 2003, Mowbray and her colleagues offered an updated classification system based on their survey of more than 100 SEd programs in the United States. The new classification system includes four models of SEd:

1. Full clubhouse model
2. Partial clubhouse model
3. Onsite model
4. Freestanding model

The majority (66 percent) of the SEd programs surveyed by Mowbray et al. (2003b) were located in clubhouses. To meet the criteria for the **full clubhouse model**, the program must have an educational unit in the clubhouse, commit at least half of a staff member's time to supporting members in their efforts to achieve postsecondary educational goals, and offer individual educational counseling. In addition, at least two other SEd services must be provided, such as tutoring, scholarships, peer support, academic skill refresher classes, and liaisons with the faculty and staff of local colleges. Programs that have an educational unit in the clubhouse and also provide SEd services outside the facility, such as mobile support on a college campus, also meet the criteria for the full clubhouse model (Mowbray et al., 2003b).

The term **partial clubhouse model** refers to clubhouse-based SEd programs that assist members in pursuing postsecondary educational goals but do not meet all of the criteria for the full clubhouse model (Mowbray et al., 2003b). Such a program may have a staff member who spends about one full day a week providing educational counseling and coordinating a peer-run tutoring program. College catalogs and computer resources might also be available in the clubhouse to assist members who are thinking about enrolling in college.

The **onsite model**, which was also identified in the earlier classification system articulated by Unger, refers to SEd programs that are located on a college campus. Sometimes a program will have offices at several schools in a community. This type of SEd program may be located within a college counseling center, in a disability services office, or in its own space on campus. If the program shares an office that provides other student services, it should have at least one staff member who specializes in working with people who have psychiatric disabilities and it should provide at least one service that is specifically geared toward students with psychiatric disabilities—for example, a weekly support group (Mowbray et al., 2003b).

SEd programs that utilize the **freestanding model** can offer a variety of services by affiliating with one or more colleges and campuses. A freestanding SEd program might be part of a PsyR agency or part of a vocational rehabilitation agency that offers both employment and educational services. At the time of their survey, Mowbray and her colleagues noted that a relatively small group of programs followed this freestanding model. This is the most innovative and comprehensive SEd model, but unfortunately it may also be the most expensive to implement. Freestanding programs offer an eclectic mix of services. For example, at a program's main office, service recipients might have access to individual educational counseling, study skill seminars, and a weekly peer support group. Groups designed to help people determine their readiness to return to school might also be offered at PsyR programs in the community. In addition, individualized SEd services would be provided on one or more college campuses by program staff with well-established relationships with key members of the college faculty and staff (e.g., staff in the disability services office). SEd program staff might also provide seminars to college faculty and staff designed to reduce stigmatizing attitudes and help faculty learn about reasonable accommodations that might be needed by students with psychiatric disabilities.

LEARN Programs of NJ offer a good example of this model enhanced by the innovation of integrating SEd with supported employment (described in Chapter 10). All staff of LEARN are cross-trained in supported employment and SEd services. This means that an individual who has received SEd services to complete his or her education can then access supports in the employment arena. Likewise, an individual receiving supported employment who needs additional credentials to develop his or her career of choice can receive SEd services to accomplish this.

An Individual Placement and Support/Choose-Get-Keep-Leave Framework

The strategies used for supported employment, individual placement and support, and Choose-Get-Keep-Leave described in Chapter 10 are also utilized when providing SEd services (Nuechterlein et al., 2008; Russell & Strauss, 2004; Sullivan, Nicolellis, Danley, & MacDonald-Wilson, 1993; Sullivan-Soydan, 2004). This approach can be thought of as a framework for conceptualizing the stages a person goes through when pursuing educational goals. People with a psychiatric disability need to access relevant information in order to make an informed choice about going to school. Then they need to develop or refresh the skills and secure the supports necessary to be admitted to school and maintain enrollment. This framework for providing services can be applied within any of the SEd models described earlier.

A PsyR provider who works in an SEd program may also be thought of as an education coach, in that his or her approach is very similar to that of a job coach in a supported employment program. During the initial phase, or the Choose phase of the SEd process, a person works with his or her education coach to select the educational setting, in other words, deciding what type of academic or trade school program to pursue. A critical first component of the *Choose* phase is the identification of a vocational goal. The educational pursuit is a step toward achieving this goal. Visiting schools, looking at catalogs, and conducting informational interviews with students and/or professors are examples of some useful activities during this phase.

Next, during the *Get* phase of the process, the education coach assists in locating and applying to a specific school, applying for financial aid, or accessing a tuition stipend through the state's office of vocational rehabilitation services.

Once the person starts school, the task is to focus on the skills and resource development necessary to help the person succeed. During the *Keep* phase, skills that may need to be developed include time and task management, maintaining concentration, taking notes, writing papers, and asking for assistance (Murphy et al., 2005). It is important for the supported education coach to be knowledgeable about the effect of psychiatric illness on academic and executive function skills. To address resource development, a visit to the school's office for students with disabilities is often a good idea. As mentioned earlier, federal law ensures access to a variety of reasonable classroom accommodations, also known as academic adjustments. However, students may need assistance in determining which accommodations are most useful in different situations. Some examples of accommodations include note-takers, modified testing environments, books on tape, and use of assistive technologies such as computer programs that help students with learning disabilities compose papers (Murphy et al., 2005).

SEd services should be offered for as long as the person is in school to ensure that the person has the supports needed to successfully complete (*Leave*) the program. Often, the SEd services provided each semester incorporate all of the phases mentioned. The education coach assists the student in selecting courses (*Choose*), registering (*Get*), meeting the requirements (*Keep*), and, if needed, dropping courses (*Leave*) so the person does not jeopardize his or her academic standing or future access to financial aid.

As in supported employment, it is also important to help students with disabilities gain access to **natural supports**. Examples of these include use of existing resources on campus (such as tutors or study skills seminars) and establishing relationships with classmates for emotional support, friendship, note sharing, and study groups. Some SEd programs also help facilitate ongoing peer support groups so that students with disabilities who have educational goals, as well as those who are currently enrolled in classes, can provide each other with support, encouragement, and relevant information.

Jose's Story

The experiences of a person receiving services from an SEd program are described next. When reading about Jose's experiences, think about the following questions:

1. What events led to the first episode of Jose's illness?
2. Why did his early experiences at college make it so difficult for him to return to school?
3. What features of the SEd program described were most helpful to Jose?

Jose is a 36-year-old man who has struggled with bipolar disorder for more than ten years. After graduating from high school, Jose got a job selling office supplies and attended a community college at night. He obtained a certificate in computer programming that helped him to get a better job at a computer software company. After a few years in this job, Jose realized that if he wanted to move up the career ladder he would need more education. He decided to pursue a bachelor's degree in computer science. Jose found the ordeal of dealing with admissions, registering for classes, and securing financial aid to be frustrating and annoying, but no more so than the other students did. However, attending classes at night after working all day was very difficult. Jose had trouble falling asleep at night, which meant he was tired the next day. He found himself making mistakes at work and he started to feel extremely anxious. He was not aware that these were "prodromal" signs of serious mental illness (see Chapters 2 and 3). Soon, it became almost impossible to concentrate on what his teachers were saying in class. Jose began to think he wasn't smart enough to go to college and that he'd be stuck in this dead end job forever.

One night after class when he knew he wasn't going to be able to fall asleep, Jose decided to go to the library to study. But it was after eleven o'clock and the library was closed. Jose was so frustrated that he started pounding on the library door. He pounded harder and harder until his fist broke through the glass. The alarm brought the police, who found Jose lying on the ground bleeding and sobbing uncontrollably. Jose was admitted to the psychiatric hospital where he stayed for a month. He lost his job and dropped out of school. During the next ten years, he held several jobs and made three unsuccessful attempts to return to school, each of which was closely followed by a hospitalization.

Three years ago, after his most recent hospitalization, Jose was referred to a supported housing program where he met Luke, a case manager. After getting to know Luke, Jose began to talk about his dream of finishing college and having a good job with a future. To Jose's surprise, Luke didn't laugh or point out all of Jose's failed attempts as so many others had. Instead, Luke talked to Jose about a supported education program, North Shore Scholars, based on the freestanding model of SEd. Luke explained that the SEd program had education specialists who helped people deal with the stresses of school and helped to get accommodations if they were needed. Jose was interested but a little apprehensive.

He doubted that any school would even accept him after failing so many times and he just couldn't forget that every attempt at school had ended with a stay in the hospital. Luke understood Jose's ambivalence and suggested that he talk to the program's education specialist and possibly attend a four-session readiness group for people who are considering school but are not sure. Jose agreed to give it a try.

At the first group meeting, Jose met Beth, an SEd specialist, and five other people who were thinking about going back to school. Group members spoke openly about their fears and concerns. Over the four weeks, Jose talked about his past failures, his difficulty concentrating, and the overwhelming anxiety he feels when he has to write a paper or take a test. He could really relate to some of the things the other group members described, like the young woman in the group who said, "I'm afraid that the other students will find out that I have a mental illness and will look at me like I'm a scary freak." Beth told the group members about some possible accommodations in the classroom for students who have psychiatric disabilities and described tutoring and study skill seminars that are available to all community college students. She also reassured members that if they chose to disclose to the college disabilities office that they have a mental illness (in order to receive accommodations), the nature of their disability would be kept confidential and would not be shared with faculty members, students, or other college personnel.

During the last group session, a man who had been receiving services from the North Shore Scholars for about two years spoke to the group. He told the members about the challenges he had faced returning to school and how supported education services had helped him achieve success. Afterward, Jose approached Beth and said, "I'm still not sure that I'm ready, but I'm going to give it a try. Can you help me get registered for the fall semester?" Beth seemed pleased and Jose felt hopeful for the first time in a long time. Beth helped Jose prepare for an appointment with an admissions counselor at Middlefield Community College. She also helped him complete his financial aid forms, and together they figured out how Jose would cover the tuition, books, and associated fees.

Jose was admitted to the school and assigned a regular advisor, but he checked in with Beth to get her perspective before registering for two computer science courses. Beth suggested that he consider taking one computer science course to begin with and a pass/fail course called "Reentry Seminar" offered to all beginning students over the age of 25. The seminar course focused on study skills and time management and also helped students become familiar with college resources such as the library and computer lab. Beth told him that it was also a good place to meet other students his age who were probably also anxious about returning to school. Jose decided to follow Beth's advice.

Once the semester began, he met with Beth once a week to talk about his progress and he sometimes checked in with her by phone as well—for example, on the day before an exam. Beth helped Jose think of some specific ways to apply the study skills and time management skills he was learning about in the Reentry Seminar. Jose also found it helpful to talk with Beth when he felt anxious about things like upcoming assignments or approaching his computer science professor who intimidated him. When he decided he wanted to ask for an accommodation for his computer science class, she helped him get registered at the Office of

Disabled Students Services. She explained that his professor would receive written notice that Jose required an alternate testing site for his exams, but that Jose might need to talk to the professor about the logistics. Beth offered to accompany him to meet with his professor, but Jose decided that he would do it himself. To prepare, they role-played the meeting and this helped reduce Jose's anxiety.

While studying for his final exam, Jose told Beth that he thought he was experiencing some early signs of a manic episode. Beth enlisted Luke's help in getting an emergency appointment for Jose with his psychiatrist. The doctor prescribed a slight increase in one of Jose's medications, which was enough to get him through the last few weeks of the semester. Jose got a C on the final exam and a B in the course. He had a very positive experience in the Reentry Seminar and befriended two students in the class with whom he started to socialize outside of school. When Jose received his grade report in the mail, he was flooded with a mixture of feelings. He was certainly relieved and proud of his accomplishment and grateful to Beth for her support, but also a little apprehensive about what his parents' reaction would be. For once he had tried and not failed, but it was a far cry from their expectations of him so many years ago. A few days after Christmas, Jose called Beth to tell her that he showed his grade report to his parents on Christmas day. He told her, "My parents were so proud of me! My father hugged me and looked at me the way he used to before I got sick. It felt so good!"

Applying Psychiatric Rehabilitation Principles to Supported Education

There are some key values and principles that should be inherent in all SEd programs. Note that these SEd principles correspond to the values and principles of PsyR outlined in Chapter 4:

- **Self-determination**—The educational goals, learning environments, and supports are selected by the student (Sullivan et al., 1993; Unger, 1990).
- **Person-centered**—The supports and services provided are designed to meet the unique needs of each student (Sullivan et al., 1993; Unger, 1990).
- **Normal environments**—The services are integrated and "consistent with the routines of the setting" (Unger, 1990, p. 13). Attention is given to achieving a good match between the student and the setting (Sullivan et al., 1993)—for example, providing SEd services at a campus-based Office of Disabled Students rather than at a mental health center.
- **Ongoing support**—Support is available indefinitely and is flexible to match the changing needs of the student (Unger, 1990).
- **Dignity**—Supports and services are provided in a manner that protects the privacy and dignity of the individual (Unger, 1990).
- **Optimism**—There is obvious belief in the capability of the individual to grow and achieve academic and vocational goals (Unger, 1990).

Mowbray (2004b) expanded on these principles and developed specific criteria for implementing them in SEd programs. Her work in this area is summarized in Table 11.1.

Table 11.1 PsyR Principles Relevant to SEd and Associated Criteria

PsyR Principle	Criteria for SEd
1. Normalization	1-1: Supported education programs conduct comprehensive, individualized assessments of participants (including academic needs and skills, personal goals and preferences, and recovery/wellness plans) and help students establish vocational/career objectives.
	1-2: SEd programs utilize a campus setting for at least some of the services provided.
	1-3: SEd services are provided in a manner and in an environment that protects privacy, enhances personal dignity, and respects cultural diversity.
	1-4: SEd services are evaluated on an ongoing basis so they can be revised as needed to keep them responsive to students' needs.
2. Self-determination	2-1: SEd programs provide knowledge of the postsecondary educational environment (demands and resources) and skills training and practice to survive in postsecondary education, including brushing up or acquiring needed academic skills or coping and adaptation methods (e.g., how to access available resources).
	2-2: SEd programs assist students to use their knowledge and skills to set their own educational goals and objectives.
	2-3: In SEd programs, choice is fundamental. Choices are offered in terms of teaching strategies and learning topics, the amount and type of support provided, how services are provided (in terms of modality: group, individual, face to face, mail, phone, etc.), frequency, and intensity. Students can make choices about service provision based on individual needs and preferences.
3. Support and relationships	3-1: SEd programs invest staff resources in outreach to and engagement of potential program participants, making presentations and/or having an ongoing presence at settings in which these individuals are likely to hear the message such as self-help groups, consumer-operated programs, and clubhouses.
	3-2: SEd services have continuing availability; they can be accessed on an as-needed basis for as long as students want or need them.
	3-3: SEd staff establish individualized and personal relationships with students. One-on-one educational counseling is available as needed.
	3-4: Students are encouraged and given skills or assistance in establishing their own support networks to continue beyond the SEd program.
	3-5: Resources are available as needed to assist with overcoming individual barriers to educational involvement, e.g., needs for transportation or child care expenses, scholarship and loan information, resolving prior educational debt, or applying to loan forgiveness/repayment programs.
4. Hope and recovery	4-1: The SEd program philosophy and service delivery methods emphasize participant strengths, encourage possibilities, foster hope, and promote rehabilitation.
	4-2: Exclusion based on participant diagnoses or mental health history is not appropriate because it contradicts SEd values and principles. However, inclusion criteria may specify needed basic academic skill and survival levels.

(Continued)

Table 11.1   PsyR Principles Relevant to SEd and Associated Criteria—*(Continued)*

PsyR Principle	Criteria for SEd
	4-3: SEd programs have a rehabilitation and recovery philosophy, rather than focusing on mental health treatment or clinical services.
	4-4: SEd programs involve students in all aspects of operations, including paid staff positions, so that role modeling and examples of success are available.
	4-5: SEd programs facilitate participants in transforming their perceived identity from the stigmatized role of psychiatric patient to the valued and culturally acceptable role of college student.
5. Systems change	5-1: SEd programs incorporate **personal empowerment** strategies such as promoting and teaching self-advocacy, providing shared access to valued resources, and promoting nonhierarchical thinking and open communication.
	5-2: SEd programs promote and model *group empowerment*, whereby the group advocates on behalf of the generic needs of its members.
	5-3: SEd programs cultivate and maintain stakeholder involvement and incorporate stakeholder perspectives, needs, and demands into their programming. Resources of an educational setting and the community are brought together to work for the benefit of the students.
	5-4: SEd programs have a structure and mechanisms to address systemic barriers to full inclusion of students with psychiatric disabilities. These should include formal involvement with mental health agencies and higher education institutions.

Source: From Mowbray, C. T. (2004, pp. 355–356).

CONTROVERSIAL ISSUE
Do Some SEd Models Adhere to PsyR Values and Principles More Than Others?

Collectively, supported employment, supported housing, and supported education have been referred to as "supported approaches" or "community-integrated services." They share common characteristics and philosophy and strongly emphasize normalization and full inclusion in the community. Full inclusion means that people with disabilities should have the same opportunities to live, learn, and work in their communities as people without disabilities. The role of community-integrated service providers is to ensure that individualized supports are available to people with disabilities in the environments where they are living, learning, and working.

The self-contained classroom provides a supportive environment that helps students with psychiatric disabilities build self-esteem and develop academic skills. Many of the SEd programs described in the literature emphasize using the self-contained classroom where students diagnosed with severe mental illnesses spend one or more semesters together attending noncredit classes either at a psychiatric rehabilitation program or on a college campus (Hain & Gioia, 2004; Gilbert, Heximer, Jaxon, & Bellamy, 2004; Unger, 1998; Weiss, Maddox, Vanderwaerden, & Szilvagyi, 2004). These classes typically focus on academic skill development and the development of career goals. They operate on the premise that many people with psychiatric disabilities interested in returning to college are hesitant to enroll because there are too many barriers to overcome. For example, they believe that psychiatric symptoms such as poor concentration will get in the way, or they are wary of dealing with college students and faculty with stigmatizing attitudes.

(Continued)

CONTROVERSIAL ISSUE
Do Some SEd Models Adhere to PsyR Values and Principles More Than Others?—(Continued)

For these individuals, the self-contained classroom provides a supportive environment where it is hoped they can gradually develop academic skills and get used to the role of student while still having daily access to professionals who can assist in coping with stress, symptoms, and other concerns. Although many self-contained classroom programs are located in normalized settings such as community college campuses, participants in these programs spend most of their time with other "students" who have a mental illness and "teachers" who are trained mental health professionals. Additionally, there is no empirical evidence that such programs improve educational outcomes. To summarize, these programs provide education, skills training, and group support to people with disabilities in a segregated classroom. The goal of the classes, which program members typically take over a period of months or even years, is to prepare people to enroll in regular college classes or pursue other rehabilitation goals such as employment.

The self-contained classroom, essentially a "train and place" model, is in contrast to SEd interventions that focus on rapid enrollment in normalized postsecondary college classes. Similar to pre-vocational programs, long periods of preparation in pre-college programs may inhibit successful transition into integrated educational settings. Such programs that emphasize training persons first, such as pre-vocational psychiatric day treatment programs and transitional group homes, spend time and effort preparing people to move on to independent jobs and apartments that never seem to materialize. In contrast, programs emphasizing a "place and train" approach start by rapidly mainstreaming people into integrated employment or housing settings, and then provide needed skills training or supports in the place where the person is actually living or working. This strategy helps people to quickly begin working or living independently while accessing the supports needed to be successful. (See Chapters 10 and 12 for a thorough review of literature on this topic.)

An SEd program resembling best practice in supported employment or supported housing would emphasize individualized educational counseling. In such a program, an educational specialist would begin by helping individuals clarify their educational goals and would then assist them in enrolling in the school of their choice. Needed supports are then provided where and when a person requires them to maximize academic success.

Research on Supported Education

There are more students with psychiatric disabilities on campus than ever before, yet there is very little empirical research on educational interventions to help them succeed and graduate. SEd was developed to serve individuals with psychiatric conditions who, due to their disability, required specialized supports in order to maintain matriculation in postsecondary environments (Unger, 1990). To date, there is little empirical evidence to support the SEd model as more effective than typical campus services offered by Offices of Students with Disabilities.

A 2009 review of the SEd literature by Rogers and her colleagues found "very few well-controlled studies of supported education and numerous studies with minimal evaluation data and less rigorous designs." Their assessment was that, given the lack of rigorous research in this area, there is insufficient evidence that SEd increases the overall educational achievements of persons with psychiatric disabilities. These results found only a slight improvement over the 2002 Mowbray and Collins review of the SEd literature between 1991 and 1998. They found that the studies varied in methodology and that only one study met the criteria for a true experimental design.

The Department of Psychiatric Rehabilitation and Counseling Professions in the Rutgers School of Health Related Professions is conducting a study, "The Effectiveness of Educational Supports on Retention of Postsecondary Students with Psychiatric Disabilities," which is a multisite, randomized controlled trial funded by the National Institute of Disability Rehabilitation Research (NIDRR). This study is evaluating the effectiveness of the community-based, mobile model of SEd versus an educational support service that is modeled after a typical disability service office on a college campus. The SEd model is expected to promote student retention in higher education and result in the completion of more courses and degrees. Little is known about the services that assist students to maintain matriculation. This study will identify the frequency, duration, and types of services that are effective in assisting college students with a serious mental illness, which in turn will help inform SEd programs about specific interventions resulting in better educational outcomes.

In a second NIDRR study, Michelle Mullen and her colleagues at the Rutgers School of Health Related Professions are studying the impact of cognitive remediation strategies in a 13-week intervention aimed at improving attention, concentration, and memory in order to compensate for the effects of their psychiatric conditions.

Supported Education: An Emerging Evidence-based Practice?

Clearly, the number of research studies examining SEd outcomes is limited. Nevertheless, the US Substance Abuse and Mental Health Administration (SAMSHA) has endorsed Supported Education as a Promising Practice and produced a Supported Education Tool Kit (SAMHSA: SMA11-4654CD-ROM). Moving a service approach from an "exemplary" or promising practice to one that meets the stricter criteria of being an evidence-based practice can be a long journey. Carol Mowbray, a researcher who was at the University of Michigan School of Social Work and who is profiled in this chapter (see Box 11.1), and her colleagues have provided the foundation for this effort (Mowbray, Collins, Bellamy, Megivern, Bybee, & Szilvagyi, 2005). To demonstrate that a PsyR service consistently produces positive outcomes for consumers, researchers must first identify a set of essential ingredients that describe the model. These ingredients are known as **fidelity criteria** (Mowbray, Holter, Teague, & Bybee, 2003a). Establishing fidelity criteria for SEd is a particularly challenging task because a number of diverse SEd models have been identified in the literature as being effective. To address the challenge, Mowbray based her SEd criteria on principles of psychiatric rehabilitation that should be present regardless of a program's approach to providing services. So, for example, based on the

BOX 11.1   CAROL MOWBRAY

Carol Mowbray's career was devoted to reducing stigma and removing barriers to full community integration. Dr. Mowbray, who had a PhD in developmental psychology from the University of Michigan, was one of the most highly respected researchers in the field of psychiatric rehabilitation. She began her career as a research analyst for the Michigan Department of Mental Health and eventually moved into an administrative position. Mid-career she shifted into academia as an associate professor of social work at Wayne State University, and later as a professor at the University of Michigan. She also directed the Center for Research on Poverty, Risk, and Mental Health at the University of Michigan, School of Social Work.

An ongoing theme in all of Dr. Mowbray's studies is the involvement of people with psychiatric disabilities in their own recovery. She has done research on a number of important issues such as women's mental health and consumer-provider services, but is probably best known in the United States and abroad for her work on SEd for persons with psychiatric disabilities. She conducted the first evaluation of an SEd program using a randomized controlled trial, which led to the funding of the Michigan Supported Education Program and other model SEd programs in Michigan. Dr. Mowbray and her colleagues also hosted the first National Conference on Supported Education in 2002. She received much recognition for her efforts, including the prestigious Armin Loeb award given annually by the US Psychiatric Rehabilitation Association (USPRA, formerly known as IAPSRS) to an individual who has done significant research in the field of psychiatric rehabilitation.

Dr. Mowbray's prolific research, writing, and consultation efforts helped to define SEd and promote its dissemination worldwide. Sadly, Carol Mowbray passed away in August 2005. Her passing was a great loss for the field of psychiatric rehabilitation. Her outstanding contributions to the body of research will serve as an inspiration for researchers and practitioners for many years to come. In recognition of her contributions, USPRA has renamed its Early Career Research Award the Carol T. Mowbray Award.

PsyR principle of self-determination, she identified one SEd criterion as "SEd programs assist students to use their knowledge and skills to set their own educational goals and objectives." Addressing PsyR's emphasis on hope and recovery, she arrived at the SEd criteria "SEd programs have a rehabilitation and recovery philosophy, rather than focusing on mental health treatment or clinical services." The complete set of SEd criteria developed by Mowbray is presented in Table 11.1.

Of course, there is still much work to be done from this initial starting point, including determining how to operationalize SEd fidelity criteria. Dr. Mowbray (2004b) urged researchers to conduct effectiveness studies to answer the question: "What works for whom, under what circumstances, and in which settings?" (p. 360). This work has to be carried out in the form of controlled clinical trials conducted by different researchers at different sites, and that will be just the start. Will some form of SEd eventually become an evidence-based practice? Much work remains to be done to determine the answer.

Dissemination of Supported Education

Despite the importance that education plays in helping people with psychiatric disabilities realize their hopes and dreams and the promise that SEd programs provide for helping people achieve their career goals, dissemination of SEd programs remains fairly limited. In 2001, Mowbray, Bellamy, Megivern, and Szilvagi found there were fewer than 30 SEd programs in North America. The majority of these programs was in just six states. A few years later, a national survey with broader acceptance criteria identified more than 100 SEd programs (Mowbray et al., 2003b). Nearly two-thirds of these programs were located in clubhouses (described in Chapter 7). Although this number is more encouraging than what has been previously reported in the literature, it is clear that we have a long way to go before most people with psychiatric disabilities have ready access to educational supports. It is disappointing that such a promising model, which has been in existence for more than 30 years, is still a novelty in many parts of the United States.

Lack of funding has been a key barrier to SEd dissemination. Federal and state legislation ensures that some funding is available to provide mental health and vocational rehabilitation services, but there are no external mandates to promote the development of SEd services (Mowbray et al., 1993). In fact, historically, neither the vocational rehabilitation nor mental health systems have recognized educational attainment as an important outcome for people with psychiatric disabilities (Anthony, Furlong-Norman, & Koehler, 2002; Mowbray, Verdejo, & Levine, 2002; Unger, 1994). Too many programs that provide employment services have not fully embraced the recovery movement. They tend to steer consumers toward low-skill jobs, with little opportunity to move up a career ladder. These programs and staff members do not recognize the potential that people have to pursue career goals that require higher education. Clearly, attitudes and priorities need to change for widespread dissemination of SEd programs to occur.

Future Directions in Supported Education

SEd is an important component of PsyR services that is still not readily available to people with psychiatric disabilities in many parts of the United States. To address this gap in services, resources to support the continuation and expansion of current programs as well as develop new programs need to be secured. Mowbray (2004b) suggested that programs seek funding from diverse sources such as state mental health and vocational rehabilitation offices, Medicaid, and postsecondary institutions. Research that provides mental health and vocational rehabilitation system administrators with a clearer sense of which models are most successful in helping people return to school and eventually to work is also likely to increase dissemination of this important service. As opportunities to develop additional programs present themselves, the authors hope the following challenges for SEd are addressed.

Challenge 1: To Better Meet the Needs of Young Adults

Currently, most SEd programs primarily serve adults who are at least in their late twenties, and have been out of school for many years (Megivern & Pellerito, 2002; Mowbray, 2004b). Early intervention services also need to be provided to help young people in the early stages of their illness stay in school or return to school quickly. Traditional college-age students who have a mental illness are a subgroup of consumers who face unique challenges and require individualized supports. SEd programs that target this population are probably best situated on college campuses and need to be proactive in educating students, faculty, and college administrators about the early signs of mental illness and the benefits of receiving treatment and supportive services as soon as possible (Megivern & Pellerito, 2002; Mowbray, 1999, 2004b). Many treatment and rehabilitation service providers also need to be better informed about the importance of SEd services for the young adult population. Individuals who are struggling with the early stages of mental illness often do not see the relevance of day programs and clubhouses. They feel more comfortable in normalized settings for people their age, such as a college campus (Anthony & Unger, 1991).

Because mental health systems and postsecondary educational institutions both struggle with the issue of adequately serving young adults with psychiatric disabilities, the opportunity for collaboration is rich with possibilities. For example, shared staffing and a cross-referral arrangement between a PsyR program and a campus-based office for students with disabilities could both assist PsyR program members with access to educational opportunities and help college students experiencing their first episode of mental illness get adequate treatment and rehabilitation services. The important topic of early intervention is also addressed in Chapters 8 and 15.

Challenge 2: Fostering More Freestanding Supported Education Programs

Currently, a large majority of SEd programs most closely resemble the clubhouse or partial clubhouse model described by Mowbray et al. (2003b). While clubhouses are certainly an important access point for consumers with educational goals, additional dissemination of the other SEd models is needed in order to reach the many people who are not clubhouse members. As mentioned earlier, campus-based services that follow the onsite SEd model are particularly important for reaching young adults. Additionally, the freestanding model of SEd is a very promising approach. Freestanding programs, which offer a variety of educational support services both at a number of schools in the community and at community-based mental health and PsyR programs, are flexible enough to meet the needs of people who are at different ages and stages of their illness (Mowbray et al., 2003b).

Challenge 3: Integrating the Pursuit of Educational and Career Goals

More programs should be developed that provide career development services combining SEd and supported employment services, since these approaches complement each other. Despite their similarities, these programs have historically been implemented separately (Egnew, 1993). Individuals who only have access to SEd services may lack resources for the additional training and education needed to advance from entry-level, low-paying jobs. Programs that integrate SEd and supported employment emphasize the concept of **career development**, as opposed to just job acquisition, and are essential to the recovery of many people striving to attain meaningful and productive roles in their communities (Murphy et al., 2005).

Russell and Strauss (2004) describe such an integrated program: Career Advancement Resources (CAR), located in Boston, Massachusetts. The program, which is part of the statewide Supported Employment and Education initiative, focuses on career exploration, assistance in gaining access to necessary education and training opportunities, ongoing support to maximize success in the classroom, and a variety of support services that assist in the transition from school to work.

Murphy and her colleagues (2005) proposed an enhanced individual placement and support model of supported employment utilizing SEd services and natural supports. They hypothesize that this combination of services would help individuals find meaningful work and would ultimately increase job tenure. Widespread dissemination of PsyR programs that emphasize career development would go a long way toward helping people with psychiatric disabilities realize the goals of recovery, true community integration, and improved quality of life.

Summary

For many people education is an essential step toward the achievement of career goals. People with psychiatric disabilities have the same dreams as everyone else, but often have their education interrupted by their illness and face additional challenges when trying to return to school. A number of historical developments, including improved understanding of the service and support needs of people with psychiatric disabilities, led to the emergence of SEd programs. Currently, several diverse approaches are used to provide SEd. Critical ingredients consistent with the principles and values of PsyR may provide a basis for synthesizing these approaches into a common strategy. Mental health and vocational rehabilitation systems need to recognize the critically important role that education can play in recovery and assist people to achieve their educational goals.

Additional research also needs to be conducted to improve our understanding of which SEd models produce the best outcomes for persons who are coping with severe mental illnesses.

■ ■ ■ ━━

Class Exercise

Read the two scenarios that follow and then answer the questions given below them.

Scenario 1

Jean is a 29-year-old woman who has a diagnosis of schizophrenia. Jean completed two semesters of college prior to the onset of her illness and is now returning to school after a decade-long interruption. She is taking a single psychology course. She is very anxious about being back in school, but also very enthusiastic. Jean sometimes has difficulty focusing in class due to her thought disorder. There are times when her thoughts begin to wander and she suddenly feels lost in class. Her current response is to interrupt the class when this occurs and ask the teacher questions. Sometimes this happens several times during a class. Jean is beginning to feel that the teacher and other students are annoyed with her for being disruptive.

Scenario 2

Sam is a 25-year-old man who is in his second semester at a community college. He is currently enrolled in three courses. He has done pretty well on all his midterms and written assignments so far (his grades have been B's and C's). The semester ends in three weeks, and Sam is beginning to experience symptoms of a major depressive episode. He is having difficulty getting out of bed to get to his morning classes, and if he does get there he has trouble concentrating. Sam's psychiatrist wants to hospitalize him to try out a new medication. Sam thinks that if this happens he will fail his classes. He is already struggling to pay for tuition and books and worries that he cannot afford to retake the classes. Worrying about school is exacerbating Sam's symptoms.

1. Can you identify some reasonable accommodations (also known as "academic adjustments") that could be provided by the professor or the disability services office that may help these students?
2. Can you identify an individualized and nonstigmatizing support strategy that an educational support specialist could provide for these students?

━━━

12

Residential Services and Independent Living

… there's no place like home.
John Howard Payne

CHAPTER OUTLINE

Helping people with psychiatric disabilities to choose and maintain safe and affordable housing is an important goal of psychiatric rehabilitation practitioners and one of its toughest challenges. Where we live is an integral part of our lives. Having a satisfactory home that we are generally content with and where we feel safe and secure has a positive impact on the quality of our lives. Residing in a place where we are uncomfortable and where our safety and security may be threatened is very stressful and has a negative impact on our sense of well-being and quality of life.

    Many individuals who have serious mental illnesses reside in environments that are not of their own choosing. Some reside in supervised residential programs that have restrictive policies such as curfews or mandatory attendance at day programs. Another source of discomfort may be

Psychiatric Rehabilitation. http://dx.doi.org/10.1016/B978-0-12-387002-5.00012-3
Copyright © 2014 Elsevier Inc. All rights reserved.

sharing their living space with others who they do not know well and may not like. Many consumers do live independently, but because so many people with psychiatric disabilities live below the poverty line they may live in substandard housing in neighborhoods that have high crime rates. In addition, a sizable percentage of people who have a severe mental illness are homeless for some period of their lives (Carling, 1994; Torrey, 2006; O'Hara, 2003). These and other difficult living arrangements are endured by a substantial number of consumers who may not have access to other options.

This chapter will answer the following questions:

1. *Where did ex-psychiatric patients go once the era of deinstitutionalization began?*
2. *What are the current models of residential service provision?*
3. *How can people with psychiatric disabilities achieve the goal of independent living?*
4. *Why is it such a struggle for consumers to find a decent place to live in their communities?*

Introduction

While many people with serious mental illnesses reside in their own homes or with family members, others struggle with finding and maintaining stable housing. When a person is hospitalized, discharge planning often revolves around the question of where the person will live after leaving the hospital. If a person has a home to return to the answer may be easy, but if not, the choices are often limited and less than ideal. In addition, many persons with serious mental illnesses are homeless or are at high risk for homelessness. Persons with disabilities, many with serious mental illnesses or co-occurring disorders, make up a significant proportion of the homeless population in the United States and are more likely to have numerous and long-term periods of homelessness than those without disabilities (O'Hara, 2003). In fact, the US Department of Housing and Urban Development (HUD) now uses the term "chronic homelessness" to describe this specific population (O'Hara, 2003; US Department of Housing and Urban Development, 2007) and has made it a federal priority to reduce their numbers.

We will begin by exploring the early residential options that were developed for persons deinstitutionalized in the United States, who were often discharged after very long hospital stays. Then we will look at how residential services evolved from a continuum of care model to a supportive independent housing model. This latter approach is grounded in some important PsyR values such as self-determination and normalization. It is also consistent with US federal laws aimed at reducing discrimination, promoting community integration, and protecting the civil rights of people with disabilities. We will also look at the research done on supported housing thus far and explore how the dissemination of the supported housing model has been hampered by barriers such as lack of affordable housing and discrimination.

History of Residential Services

From the mid-1950s to the mid-1970s, several hundred thousand people were discharged from psychiatric institutions throughout the United States (Torrey, 2006).

Where did these people go after they were discharged? Unfortunately, there were no clear plans and little money allocated to housing after discharge. Some people went back to their families (see Chapter 14), many went to live in boarding houses or single room occupancy (SRO) hotels, and others were transferred to nursing homes. Increases in the numbers of homeless people have also been associated with deinstitutionalization (Torrey, 2006).

Some residential service models with a rehabilitation focus were developed during this first phase of deinstitutionalization, but implementation was scattered and reached only a small percentage of people. There was little agreement among service providers on what ideal residential services should be, and "the mental health system did not develop a coherent and widely accepted model for residential services in the first few decades of deinstitutionalization" (Ridgway & Zipple, 1990, p. 12). Still, it is informative to examine some of these early residential options because many of them are still utilized today.

Boarding Homes and Single Room Occupancy Residences

A study done by Goldman, Gattozzi, and Taube in 1981 estimated that at that time in the United States, 300,000 to 400,000 persons with severe mental illness were living in boarding homes, or what are also called "board and care facilities." Boarding homes have existed in this country as a residential option for many kinds of people for hundreds of years. They generally involve provision of a room, meals, and other services such as laundry and housekeeping for a weekly or monthly fee. They are typically used by people on the lower levels of the socioeconomic scale and those living a transient lifestyle. Some boarding home operators rent out a few rooms in their own homes; others own one or more large facilities each housing dozens of people.

It is no accident that entrepreneurs throughout the United States responded to deinstitutionalization by opening boarding homes catering exclusively to persons discharged from psychiatric institutions. Some converted old hotels or apartment buildings into SROs that housed 100 or more people. The financial incentive for these residences was established by the 1963 federal Aid to the Disabled (ATD) act that provided a monthly check to persons with disabilities ineligible for Social Security Disability (SSD) benefits due to lack of a substantial work history. ATD is now called Supplemental Security Income, or SSI. Often, boarding home operators are able to establish themselves as payees for the people residing in their facilities. They are allowed to keep most of the money as payment for room and board, and give the remainder to residents in what amounts to a small monthly allowance, typically barely enough to buy coffee and cigarettes or a few personal items. While some boarding home operators viewed deinstitutionalization as an opportunity to provide residents with a caring, homelike environment while making a living, others focused solely on maximizing their profits. Scandalous stories abound of residents subsisting on cold cereal and bologna sandwiches, sharing cramped quarters, living in filthy conditions, and dealing with physical and verbal abuse at the hands of operators, staff, and roommates.

Many boarding homes are located in dangerous inner-city neighborhoods, where large old homes could be purchased inexpensively. It was not unusual, particularly for residents discharged directly to a boarding home after a lengthy hospital stay of ten years or more, to rarely venture out into unfamiliar crime-ridden neighborhoods. The result was a sort of **transinstitutionalization** (Carling, 1995, p. 33), since being discharged to what some referred to as "psychiatric ghettos" in no way resembled normalized community existence. For many consumers, life in a boarding home was not much better than—and in some cases, worse than—hospital life, particularly in terms of issues such as privacy and safety. In a 1982 study done by Lehman, Ward, and Linn, boarding home residents described a quality of life that was significantly less satisfying than the general population's and somewhat less satisfying than that of other socially disadvantaged groups.

Access to psychiatric treatment and rehabilitation varies for boarding home residents. Some sites become licensed residential health care facilities, requiring them to provide some level of medical and psychiatric treatment. In some situations, operators contract with psychiatrists and other mental health professionals to provide services and group activities "in house," making these facilities even more like mini-institutions. Other operators establish a relationship with local community mental health centers or PsyR programs. These situations typically involve sending residents, often "by the van load," to programs on a regular basis. In fact, sometimes boarding home operators require residents to attend psychiatric day treatment programs or to be away from the facility for significant portions of the day.

Family Foster Care

In some parts of the United States, programs were developed that placed one or more consumers with a family other than their own. **Family foster care** in the United States has its roots in Geel, Belgium, where people with psychiatric disabilities have been cared for in private homes for centuries (Lamb, 1982; Linn et al., 1980). This approach was also probably influenced by foster care programs that target other disadvantaged populations, such as those that serve children and elderly adults.

In the early 1980s, it was estimated that the Veterans Administration, probably the largest utilizer of foster care for adults with disabilities, had approximately 11,000 ex-psychiatric patients in family foster care at any one time (Linn et al., 1980). Typically, families received payment and some level of professional support. The arrangement could either be transitional or long term. Ideally, family foster care seeks to incorporate consumers in all aspects of family and community life. For those who desire an active family life but are estranged from their own family, this may be a viable residential option, if a mutually satisfying match is established with the foster family. Research suggests individuals may function better in foster families that care for fewer consumers, are smaller in terms of total number of people residing in the home, and have more children living at home (Linn et al., 1980).

While Carling (1994) cautions that many foster care settings provide only minimal supports and do not foster community integration, he cites the development of creative ways to utilize family foster care—for example, using foster care as a short-term alternative to inpatient hospitalization. Such an arrangement is temporary, allowing an individual to stabilize during a crisis period. Family foster care has also been used as a transition from the hospital to independent living. Such programs can "provide a caring home on a short-term basis for individuals who are leaving a hospital and who are trying to establish roots in a particular community" (Carling, 1994, p. 92).

Fairweather Lodges

During the early years of deinstitutionalization, a social scientist named George Fairweather recognized the difficulties people were having with community adjustment. In response, he designed an experimental program to provide a long-term supportive residential environment that addressed individuals' social and vocational needs. What began as a research study evolved into a distinct PsyR approach known as the **Fairweather Lodge** model. Fairweather began his research at a California Veterans Administration Hospital in the mid-1960s (Onaga, 1994; Onaga & Smith, 2000). Initially, he established small problem-solving groups of patients preparing for discharge. Despite some success, recidivism rates did not improve. H. Richard Lamb (1982) described the development of the Fairweather model:

> *The crucial factor in remaining in the community was found to be the amount of support the patient received from the people with whom he or she lived. When these facts became clear, Fairweather's group decided to move these problem-solving patient groups as units from the hospital to the community. The new phase of the program involved setting up the Community Lodge program: a dormitory for patients and a sheltered workshop situation; a janitorial service owned and operated by the ex-patients themselves. (p. 50)*

Professional staff acted as consultants to the lodge, initially providing a high level of support and assistance in dealing with both work and daily living issues. Eventually, the consultation needs of the lodge members decreased and they were able to maintain the lodge and the business with minimal staff assistance. The original Fairweather Lodge was a resounding success in terms of recidivism rates, vocational outcomes (e.g., all of the lodge members were employed), and increases in self-esteem. The model was soon replicated in other parts of the United States, as well as in foreign countries (Lamb, 1982).

Onaga (1994) noted the similarity of Fairweather Lodge principles (Fairweather et al., 1969) to some of the basic PsyR values and principles—for example:

1. Lodge members must have meaningful roles in the lodge/business and be given as much autonomy as possible (compatible with the PsyR values of normalization and self-determination).

2. Lodge members should have upward mobility within the lodge community (adheres to the PsyR value that people have the capacity to learn and grow).

3. The role of professional staff associated with Fairweather Lodges is that of a consultant who bases his or her level of involvement on the current needs and abilities of lodge members. Staff must be available to lodge members when they are having difficulties, yet be ready to step back when members are able to solve their own problems (echoes the principles of being person-centered and having a partnership with the consumer).

As PsyR models moved toward more integrated community living, the original Fairweather Lodge approach became increasingly problematic. Essentially, the original lodges were sub-societies in which members spent most of their time living, working, and socializing with other people with psychiatric disabilities. Today, we recognize that if given opportunities and continued support, community integration including regular employment is possible and a right of people with psychiatric disabilities. In response to these changes, Onaga and Smith (2000) described how lodges in Minnesota reinvented themselves to address the wishes of some lodge members for full-time integrated employment. This change necessitated lodge members working in regular settings rather than the lodge business. Members also had to accommodate eight-hour workdays. This change eventually led to the creation of a full-time workers lodge, since regular lodge members were on different schedules, which the eight-hour workers found disrupting. The evolution of the Fairweather Lodge model may be instructive for understanding many early PsyR programmatic innovations. An effective innovation at the time it was developed, the lodge model had to evolve in response to environmental changes and changes in peoples' aspirations. As of 2009, ninety lodges were operating in ten US states (Coalition for Community Living, 2012).

Residential Treatment Facilities

While boarding homes, SROs, and family foster care are typically nonprofessional ventures, a variety of residential programs run by mental health professionals emerged in the 1960s and 1970s during the early years of deinstitutionalization that still exist today. Unlike Fairweather Lodges, most of these programs were not based on a clearly articulated model of service provision, but they did have a number of similarities. During this era, the most prolific approaches to residential service provision involved the use of segregated, congregate care facilities (Carling, 1994).

These programs utilize various names, most commonly group homes and halfway houses. Like the partial care programs discussed in Chapter 7, most residential treatment facilities seek to establish a therapeutic milieu: in other words, an environment carefully crafted to encourage clinical and functional improvements (Ridgway & Zipple, 1990). Some of these programs have rehabilitation goals, striving to provide residents with independent living skills so that individuals can eventually move on to a less protected setting or into their own homes. Other programs focus on long-term care in a small, homelike environment rather than a large institutional setting.

The number of consumers residing in a group home may vary. Many utilize typical single-family homes housing three to eight individuals. Some professionally run programs house large numbers of residents and resemble SROs, and some accommodate just a few individuals and resemble foster care settings. In most programs, staff members are present, or readily available, 24 hours a day. Typical program activities may include staff-assisted group menu planning and meal preparation; individual or small group activity of daily living (ADL) skills training (e.g., budgeting, hygiene, and laundry); social and recreational activities; assistance in utilization of local transportation and other community resources; community meetings; individual and group counseling; and symptoms and medication education. In some programs, residents spend weekdays outside of the residential facility at day programs, workshops, school, or jobs. Other programs have onsite treatment and rehabilitation groups.

When an agency provides both treatment and rehabilitation and residential services, housing problems may arise if treatment recommendations are not followed. In such situations, there is often an explicit link between continuation in a residential setting and compliance with a treatment plan (Mize, Paolo-Calabrese, Williams, & Margolin, 1998). Sometimes such links are implicit but not articulated. An individual not following treatment recommendations, for example, might be deemed inappropriate for a particular residence. Although this practice has been correctly labeled "coercive" (Chamberlin, 1978), it is not an uncommon policy of residential treatment facilities.

Mize and colleagues (1998) suggest a collaborative approach for developing a non-coercive situation. The collaborative approach addresses this problem by clearly separating the individuals' "tenant" and "consumer" roles and the provider's "landlord" and "worker" roles. This separation of roles is reinforced if the individual holds the lease to his or her living situation rather than the agency. They suggest that in a successful congregate setting, tenants must chose to live together, set their own rules, and be able to hold one another accountable for their actions. This separation of roles will be examined further in the section on supported housing that follows.

Stigma and Residential Treatment Programs

Many residential treatment programs are located in urban and suburban residential neighborhoods. Ideally, program residents become an integral part of local community life (e.g., developing friendly relationships with neighbors, attending block parties, and joining religious congregations). However, sometimes there is community opposition to living near mental health consumers, commonly referred to as NIMBY, which means "Not in my backyard!" When community residents learn that a residential treatment facility has opened or is being planned, they may have an overt negative reaction. A typical concern, aggravated by the common myth portrayed in the media that mental illness equates with dangerousness, is for the safety of their children, family members, and themselves. Another common concern is that the presence of people with psychiatric disabilities will lower real estate values. Even though research suggests this is an unfounded assumption (Carling, 1995; Cook, 1997), it has been known to fuel organized efforts to rid a neighborhood of unwanted individuals.

NIMBY creates barriers to true community integration and can be hurtful in many ways. Negative actions taken by resistant community members include lawsuits, exclusion from community activities, and verbal and physical harassment. Housing advocates have cited examples of extreme reactions such as group homes that were burned to the ground, allegedly by angry neighbors. These actions clearly convey to people with psychiatric disabilities that they are unwanted and undesirable.

In most situations, community opposition to group homes for people with disabilities is a violation of the US Fair Housing Act. This legislation was initially enacted in 1968 to prohibit discrimination based on race or ethnicity in the sale or rental of housing. In 1988, the US Congress amended the Fair Housing Act to add protections against discrimination for persons with disabilities and families with children. The act prohibits the use of local ordinances or zoning laws that discriminate against protected persons, such as people with disabilities. However, it is not unusual for municipalities to attempt to challenge the Fair Housing Act based on local ordinances that limit the number of unrelated individuals who can live together in single-family homes. While residential programs that have good legal representation will eventually win such cases, the establishment of many programs has been delayed by community opposition.

When establishing a new facility, a key issue is whether or not to notify neighbors about the new group home. Some programs approach the issue collaboratively, notifying neighbors early on in an attempt to establish positive relationships. Sometimes this approach backfires and helps fuel community opposition (Zippay, 1997). Other programs refrain from notifying neighbors in an effort to protect consumers' civil rights and avoid a stigmatizing confrontation. This strategy has been criticized since it can create resentment and mistrust when neighbors realize the group home exists (Zippay, 1997). A third approach is to publicly announce intentions to open a residential facility and then be prepared to act offensively and threaten to sue the community if necessary (Carling, 1995). How would you feel if a group home for people with severe mental illness opened in your neighborhood? If you were a consumer living in a group home, would you want neighbors to be notified before you moved in?

Carling (1995) suggests that community members who oppose the presence of a residential facility aren't automatically "the bad guys." Mental health professionals and consumer advocates must be sensitive to community members' concerns about having a group home in their neighborhood. Sometimes these concerns are based on lack of accurate information. However, one cannot ignore the fact that sometimes residential programs do alter the character of a neighborhood. In some cases, neighbors cite practical concerns such as parking and increased traffic problems (Cook, 1997). Carling states that, in his experience, "… even most mental health professionals do not want a group home or other treatment program sited next to their own homes" (Carling, 1995, p. 116).

Despite numerous instances of community opposition to the establishment of residential treatment facilities, this is not the whole story. There are many communities where group homes and single- or multiple-family residences coexist peacefully. In some instances, a substantial percentage of neighbors were not even aware that a group home for people with disabilities was in their neighborhood (Cook, 1997). Presumably this occurs most often when program staff and residents make an effort to keep a low profile. In other communities, positive relationships have developed between group home residents and their neighbors. One study found that neighbors cited the benefits associated with living near a group home (e.g., learning more about disabilities) about as often as they cited problems and concerns (Cook, 1997).

Emergence of the Linear Continuum Paradigm

Many residential treatment programs were established to provide housing for persons being discharged during the first decades of deinstitutionalization. These individuals had spent considerable time in psychiatric hospitals and often had developed an **institutionalization syndrome** characterized by extreme dependence. Partly in response to the needs of this emerging population and to create an effective transition from the hospital to the community, many of these early programs devised a continuum of residential settings. This continuum was conceptualized as a series of residential steps to accomplish the transition between a long-term psychiatric hospitalization and independent community living (Carling, 1994; O'Hara & Day, 2001). In essence, the first step consisted of a living arrangement similar to an inpatient setting: congregate living, high amounts of structure and rules, 24-hour staff supervision, and few privileges. Subsequent steps, which usually involved moving to another residence, brought increasingly less structure, staff supervision, and rules. At the last step, the individual was "transitioned" into the community at large. This approach to residential treatment has been called the **linear continuum paradigm** (Ridgway & Zipple, 1990), or more simply, the "continuum model" (O'Hara & Day, 2001). In short, this model consisted of different housing situations, each offering varying amounts of staff support, structure, and supervision. One model consisted of quarter-way houses, typically located on the hospital grounds (Carling, 1994), three-quarter-way houses without 24-hour staff supervision (Campbell, 1981), and supervised apartments, semi-supervised apartments, and other residential options that represented independent living. Some residential continua also include crisis alternative residences, also called "respite care," designed to help individuals who are acutely symptomatic avoid a hospitalization (Carling, 1994). Throughout the 1980s and into the 1990s, in many places the linear continuum paradigm dominated the field of residential services (Ridgway & Zipple, 1990). Although this conceptual framework is no longer endorsed by most mental health system administrators, the idea of transitional housing is still in evidence.

It is important to examine how a linear continuum approach affects the consumers' adjustment to community living. Exactly what is offered along a particular residential continuum varies, as do the names given to the different types of programming. It is therefore difficult to compare these residential approaches, and a clear idea of the ideal continuum has never emerged (Ridgway & Zipple, 1990). However, some basic assumptions characterize programs that adhere to the linear continuum paradigm (Ridgway & Zipple, 1990):

1. Several residential settings are available that offer different levels of service provision, staff supervision, and restrictiveness.
2. Program participants are expected to move, in an orderly fashion, from a more restrictive level to a less restrictive level.
3. Participants in each setting are similar in terms of clinical stability and functional ability. They are expected to make progress before graduating to another level on the continuum.
4. If a program participant decompensates and returns to the hospital, he or she often reenters the continuum at the most restrictive level (i.e., he or she has to start over again at the bottom).
5. The ultimate goal is to move on to independent living and no longer require services from the program.

Research conducted on the efficacy of the residential continuum model is scant and inconclusive. As indicated earlier, it is hard to study an approach in which the nomenclature varies and uniform intervention strategies do not exist. In addition, most of the studies that have been done did not use rigorous experimental methods and thus are not very useful. The literature that is available on transitional residential treatment suggests that the approach is not particularly successful in helping people to achieve the PsyR goal of community integration (Carling, 1994). It is also important to keep in mind that publicly funded residential programs of this type only served a small percentage of the people in need. In the early 1990s, the housing resources available in local mental health systems (such as money earmarked to buy houses, rent apartments, and staff residential continuum programs) provided services for fewer than 5 percent of the people with psychiatric disabilities (Carling, 1994).

While the linear continuum approach may have seemed a logical system to help deinstitutionalized individuals gradually reintegrate into the community, there is no longer a large population of persons with long hospital stays and institutional syndrome. Additionally, the stress of moving from one residence to another makes such a system illogical for persons with stress-related diseases. Next, consider some of the issues raised by Joanna's story.

The Story of Joanna

Joanna is a 39-year-old woman who has never had a home of her own as an adult. She was diagnosed with a severe mental illness in her senior year of high school. She spent the next 15+ years shuffling back and forth between psychiatric hospitals and her parents' home.

When Joanna was 37, residing at a state institution and ready for discharge, her parents informed her and the hospital staff that they could not take her back home. They were in the process of selling their house and moving to a retirement community and felt it was an appropriate time for Joanna to become less dependent on them. Joanna was put on a waiting list for a residential program that ran three types of facilities: group homes (with staff supervision 24 hours a day), a supervised apartment complex, and semi-supervised scattered site apartments.

Six months later, Joanna moved into a group home where she was one of six residents and where she shared a bedroom with another woman. She liked the program better than being at the hospital, although she missed the privacy of her own room at her parents' home. She grew quite attached to some of the program staff who were supportive and seemed to truly care about her. However, her relationship with her roommate was not so good. They had little in common and some of the roommate's behaviors, such as pacing back and forth in the middle of the night, made Joanna uneasy. After ten months in the group home, the staff told Joanna she was ready to move to the next level in the agency's housing continuum: the supervised apartment complex where staff members were usually on site just a few hours a day. An opening was expected within a few months. Joanna had ambivalent feelings about the impending move. On the one hand, she was happy that the staff thought she had made progress and she liked the idea of having her own room. On the other hand, she wasn't convinced she was ready to live more independently. She had learned to contribute to shopping and cooking for six people, although the staff was always on hand should something go wrong. Besides, in the new place she would be living with two other people. She wasn't sure if she would be cooking for herself or sharing meal preparation with roommates. What if she didn't like the roommates or got into an argument? The staff wouldn't be as available to intervene. She had many other concerns as well, such as house cleaning routines, sticking to a budget, using public transportation instead of the agency van, and getting used to a new neighborhood. She also felt uneasy about the fact that her stay in the new apartment would also be temporary. She knew that one of the group home graduates, who lived for less than a year at the apartment complex where Joanna would be living, was already being pressured to move on to the semi-supervised apartments.

As the weeks went by and she came closer to her moving date, Joanna began to spend more and more time worrying about the impending changes. She began to get symptomatic again, but did not tell the staff because she feared they would be disappointed in her. One week before moving, Joanna ended up back in the hospital. When a staff person from the group home visited with her several weeks later, Joanna said she was feeling better and would like to discuss some of her concerns about the new apartment. The staff told her not to worry about it. Another group home resident had been moved into her place. When she was ready for discharge, she could come back to the group home again and work on her ADL (activities of daily living) skills so that she could be better prepared for the apartment the next time. Joanna felt both relieved and disappointed. She was back to square one again, as if the progress she had made in the group home had never happened.

The Case against the Linear Continuum Approach

Joanna's story illustrates a number of reasons why the linear continuum approach to residential treatment has been criticized in recent years. One inherent flaw in this approach is the requirement that consumers make frequent changes in their living situation. For most people, moving from one home to another is a stressful event. It means abandoning routines and settings that have become comfortable and getting used to a whole new place. Such changes are often hard to deal with for people without psychiatric disabilities. For people who have a severe mental illness, the stress involved with such a change can create real problems.

Think back to what you learned in Chapter 2. Mental illness is episodic in nature, and stressful life events can exacerbate symptoms. Considering these facts, mental health professionals should not be surprised when people like Joanna end up back in the hospital just as they are about to make a major life transition. In this sense, the linear continuum model and severe mental illness are not a good fit. Even if individuals are able to make it through all the levels of programming and graduate to independent living, they are often short changed by the program structure. With the linear continuum model, independent living typically means that consumers will have less access to program supports at a time when they may need them most. It is not uncommon for persons who have finally achieved their long sought-after goal of obtaining their own apartment to lose it when faced with a crisis situation because the needed supports were no longer available. Another reason why the linear continuum approach may be ineffective was addressed in Chapter 5. Skills needed to function successfully in living, learning, working, and social environments are best learned in the specific settings where they will be used. It is hard for people to generalize what they have learned in one setting (e.g., meal planning and preparation for the eight residents of a group home) to another setting (e.g., meal planning and preparation for oneself in an efficiency apartment). Thus, Joanna's concerns about how prepared she was to make a move may have been quite realistic.

Probably the best reason to question the linear continuum model, or any approach that utilizes facility-based congregate care settings, is that it does not provide the type of housing that most people want. While people with psychiatric disabilities may not always know what treatment is best for their illness, they certainly know where they feel comfortable residing! In a society that places high value on personal freedom, everyone should have the right to pursue a home life of his or her own choosing, and as will be discussed later in this chapter, federal legislation in the United States upholds this civil right.

While prior to the mid-1980s the idea of asking consumers what kind of housing they wanted was rare, studies done in the 1990s examined consumers' housing preferences (Goldfinger & Schutt, 1996; Tanzman, 1993). A literature review of 26 such studies found that the majority of the people surveyed preferred living independently in either a house or an apartment. Not surprisingly, only a very small percentage of respondents in most of the studies had a preference for living in a residential treatment facility (Tanzman, 1993).

Similar results were found in subsequent studies (Collaborative Support Programs of New Jersey, 1996; Yeich et al., 1994).

Some housing preference studies have explored the question of preferred housemates. In the preceding story, one of the things Joanna liked least about the group home was her roommate. Wondering who she would be "placed with" in the supervised apartment was one of her major concerns. Most of us can appreciate Joanna's apprehension about living with strangers. Imagine a living situation in which the only thing you know about your roommates is that they were all recently discharged from a psychiatric hospital. Even if you are an open-minded person who rejects stigmatizing myths about mental illness, you would probably have concerns about living with a person you had never met. Many consumers have these same concerns. Some find it hard to have to deal with both their own illness and the symptoms and problems experienced by roommates (Carling, 1994). When given a choice, most consumers would rather live by themselves or with a spouse, friend, or family member (Tanzman, 1993). This is not a surprising finding. The vast majority of persons without disabilities would probably identify similar preferences.

Finally, continuum model programs, as well most of the other residential service options used in the first few decades of deinstitutionalization, were not a good fit with many of the goals, values, and principles of PsyR (described in Chapter 4). These approaches rarely led to true community integration and did not provide many consumers with the quality of life they were seeking. They also failed to empower individuals to choose their own housing, promote valued social roles such as neighbor and home-owner, or promote normalized environments.

Supported Housing: A Better Approach to Residential Services

In 1987, a policy statement issued by the National Association of State Mental Health Program Directors (NASMHPD) recommended that states begin to move toward a more normalized model of residential services—which by the early 1990s was widely referred to as **supported housing** (Carling, 1990; Knisley & Fleming, 1993). This approach is sometimes referred to as "support*ive*" housing. Sometimes these very similar terms are used interchangeably, but in other cases supportive housing has been used to describe program models that may include congregate care settings or short-term residential placements, while support*ed* housing program descriptions emphasize access to permanent, independent housing (Tabol, Drebing, & Rosenheck, 2010). We will use the term **supported housing** (SH) in this chapter, unless reporting on scholarly works that use the alternate term.

The essence of SH is that people reside in independent living situations of their choice in the community and receive support services to help them maintain those situations. This model was inspired by the independent living movement for people with developmental and physical disabilities described in Box 12.1.

BOX 12.1   THE INDEPENDENT LIVING MOVEMENT

The shift from the linear continuum to a SH approach was inspired in part by the efforts of people with physical disabilities to find innovative ways to leave institutions and live independently. Deegan (1992) describes the Independent Living (IL) movement as three interrelated activities, the first being a grassroots advocacy movement led by people with physical disabilities who demanded civil rights and opportunities to live, work, and socialize in their communities. These efforts culminated in the Americans with Disabilities Act (ADA). The second is an IL philosophy developed and lived by individuals with physical disabilities. Some key principles of the IL philosophy are:

1. It is not something internal such as a spinal cord injury that prevents people with disabilities from living independently, although certainly these internal factors can make the day-to-day experience of living challenging. Rather, it is external barriers such as stairs, curbs, and stigmatizing attitudes that prevent people from getting places that they want to go.

2. People with disabilities have a right to self-determination. They also have a right to make mistakes and choices that others may identify as risky. Deegan (1992) described a young man with a spinal cord injury and his adjustment to independent living. In the early days, he repeatedly tried to do things in his apartment that caused him to fall from a wheelchair and lie on the floor for hours until someone arrived to help. Many professionals would cite these incidents as proof that he could not live by himself. Eventually, he learned his own limits and found the accommodations and supports to live more comfortably. Think about the many mistakes made, and risks taken, by people without disabilities as they first move away from the parental home. They may be criticized by their loved ones, but rarely are they threatened with professional interventions aimed at reducing their control over their lives.

3. "Integral to the philosophy of IL is the notion that people with disabilities can become experts in their own self-care. To live independently means to de-medicalize our lives by learning self-care techniques that minimize the medical presence in our daily lives" (Deegan, 1992, p. 16).

The third IL piece is the existence of independent living centers that provide service delivery, coordinate advocacy efforts, and bring people with disabilities together to tackle mutual concerns. IL centers are primarily run by people with physical disabilities. Deegan (1992) describes her efforts to develop an IL center designed to meet the needs of people with psychiatric disabilities. She emphasizes the importance of establishing both a grassroots movement and a philosophy that are "similar in spirit to what people with physical disabilities discovered for themselves" (p. 17). She is cautious, however, about determining what services IL centers should provide. She does not recommend trying to duplicate what other disability groups have done, nor does she favor a peer-run version of what is offered by the mental health system. Instead, she envisions a new service approach that "will grow out of our emerging sense of what it is we need to regain control over our lives" (p. 17). Deegan's concept of IL centers is similar to what happens at many of the self-help centers that are described in the following chapter on self-help and peer-delivered services (Chapter 13).

(Continued)

BOX 12.1 THE INDEPENDENT LIVING MOVEMENT—Continued

When evaluating whether a person with a psychiatric disability is capable of living in an unsupervised setting, it is important to remember that independent living does not necessarily mean living without supports or services. In the words of the late disabilities advocate Howie the Harp:

Independence involves freedom to choose, to choose whom to be independent with, for what purpose, and to what extent. Independence is one of this country's founding principles, and it should not be surprising that living independently is a goal of many disabled Americans. Inherent in their definition of independent living is the availability of support services. (Howie the Harp, 1993, p. 413)

Some researchers have tied the genesis of SH to three converging developments: the failure of the linear continuum approach; the growing problem of long-term homelessness among persons diagnosed with psychiatric disabilities; and emerging evidence from ACT research that this population can live successfully in regular community settings when provided with *in vivo* supports and services (Tabol et al., 2010; Wong & Solomon, 2002; Wong, Filoromo, & Tennille, 2007). As you will see, SH is closely aligned to many PsyR values such as self-determination and empowerment, as well as PsyR principles such as person-centered treatment and services. Studies show that while most consumers prefer to live independently or with loved ones, many also want supports to help them maintain their living situations (Tanzman, 1993; Yeich et al., 1994). The SH model provides the very things that most consumers want in their living environments.

The Substance Abuse and Mental Health Services Administration (SAMHSA) defines permanent supported housing as "Decent, safe, and affordable community-based housing that provides tenants with the rights of tenancy under state and local landlord tenant laws and is linked to voluntary and flexible support and services designed to meet tenants' needs and preferences" (2010). Borrowing the Choose-Get-Keep framework used by the other "supported" service models (SE and SEd), SH is a way of helping individuals choose a place to live and then acquire the resources and skills needed to obtain and maintain a home in the community (Tabol et al., 2010). While there are different SH models, there is overall agreement on the key elements that define the approach (Carling, 1990; Ogilvie, 1997; Rog, 2004; SAMHSA, 2010; Tabol et al., 2010; Wong, Filoromo, & Tennille, 2007; Wong & Solomon, 2002). These key elements fall into five categories (Tabol et al., 2010):

1. Access to safe, affordable, and normalized housing options
2. Consumer choice of where to live and whom to live with
3. Immediate placement in regular housing
4. Ongoing and flexible provision of individualized support services that are desired by the consumer
5. Functional separation of housing and support services

The first three are pretty straightforward. SH programs assist consumers in finding regular apartments or houses. This is sometimes called "scattered site housing," meaning that the homes where consumers live are scattered around the community among other community members who do not have a psychiatric disability. In addition, individual preferences in terms of neighborhood, type of apartment (e.g., efficiency apartment or three-bedroom house shared with roommates), and whom they share their living space with (if anyone) should be honored. The third feature emphasizes one of the big differences between SH and the continuum of care model. SH programs help a person find housing of his or her choice right away. Often this means that an individual goes straight from the hospital or the streets into his or her own apartment. There is no required preparation for independent living.

The fourth element addresses the various types of supports and services that SH programs provide. As discussed throughout this book, persons living with serious mental illnesses are a heterogeneous group and therefore all PsyR services should be tailored to individual needs. Thus, most SH programs provide a wide range of services. According to the literature, the most frequently mentioned supports include availability of staff by phone 24 hours a day, 7 days a week for assistance in coping with crises; financial resources; assistance in budgeting money; and house furnishings and supplies (Tanzman, 1993; Yeich et al., 1994). It is also important to note that many people with psychiatric disabilities, particularly those who are living independently for the first time, need assistance in developing and maintaining independent living, or ADL, skills. In general, skill development occurs most productively when it is specific to the environment in which the person plans to operate on a long-term basis. This is certainly true of ADL skills, and it is important to understand that the skills developed in an environment such as a group home may be of little use to someone planning to live independently (Carling & Ridgway, 1991). PsyR practitioners who work in supported housing programs should therefore be familiar with the functional assessment and skills training strategies described in Chapter 5, as helping people to develop ADL skills is one of the critical interventions that they provide.

The fifth SH feature specifies that a person's housing and support services should be separated. In practice, not all programs that identify as SH programs operate this way, but there are a number of good reasons for this recommendation. From a practical stance, it allows individuals to access a broader range of affordable housing options, rather than just the sites owned or leased by a residential service provider. Note that in most cases, in order for housing to be affordable it needs to be subsidized, often by government-funded housing vouchers, which will be described later. Separation of housing and services also eliminates some of the conflicts that can occur when the same agency is the landlord and the support service provider. The primary responsibility of a mental health service provider is the health and well-being of the individuals served. If the provider is also the landlord and property manager, it is also responsible for protecting its property and assuming liability for any damages that occur. Imagine a situation in which a support worker discovers that a resident using street drugs has invited drug dealers and prostitutes into his home. The support worker's primary concern is that the consumer has relapsed and his safety may be compromised, but when she reports the situation to her supervisor, who then reports it to the agency administrator, liability issues and complaints by neighbors may become even more pressing concerns.

The separation of housing and services also empowers consumers by ensuring true "ownership" of their homes, with their rights as tenants or homeowners the same as everyone else's. The right to privacy is particularly important. When consumers reside in residential treatment settings, privacy is often limited by the fact that staff work in the same places where consumers live and set rules such as who is allowed to visit, what kind of décor is allowed, and so forth. By contrast, SH staff members are careful to respect individual privacy by calling before each visit and recognizing that people have the right to cancel a visit or deny entry to their homes. Support workers also have no jurisdiction over the apartment's appearance or who visits. To appreciate this SH principle, consider your own privacy and how you would feel if someone came into your home and told you how to live. This isn't to say that SH support workers would not intervene when they believe an individual's behavior is creating a danger of eviction. In such a situation, the support worker can remind the person of the landlord's rules and the consequences of breaking them.

Wong, Filoromo, and Tennille's (2007) conceptualization of SH includes a set of core principles and two types of operational domains, those related to housing and tenancy and those related to mental health support. Their description of the model should help further clarify what makes SH a distinct approach and a good fit with the goals, values, and principles of PsyR. Their ideas are summarized in Figure 12.1.

Housing First

Perhaps the best articulated SH approach is **Housing First**, a model developed in the early 1990s by an agency called Pathways to Housing in New York City (Tsemberis, 2010). In line with PsyR values, the Housing First philosophy emphasizes self-determination and empowerment; optimism that everyone has the capacity to recover, learn, and grow; and the promotion of valued social roles and normalized environments. As with the SE approach (see Chapter 10), individuals in Housing First programs are first assisted in getting into housing of their choice, without having to first overcome unrelated prerequisites or obstacles.

Housing First programs target individuals who are homeless and diagnosed with a mental illness. As mentioned earlier, these individuals often experience repeated episodes of homelessness and may spend long periods of time living on the streets. Many of those served by Housing First also have co-occurring substance abuse disorders, so this approach stresses the concepts of **harm reduction** and stages of change (described in Chapter 9). For example, unlike many other residential services, Housing First does not require persons with co-occurring disorders (a dual diagnosis of mental illness and substance abuse disorder) to be substance-free before obtaining housing. Instead, housing is obtained as soon as possible and then services are provided to help individuals

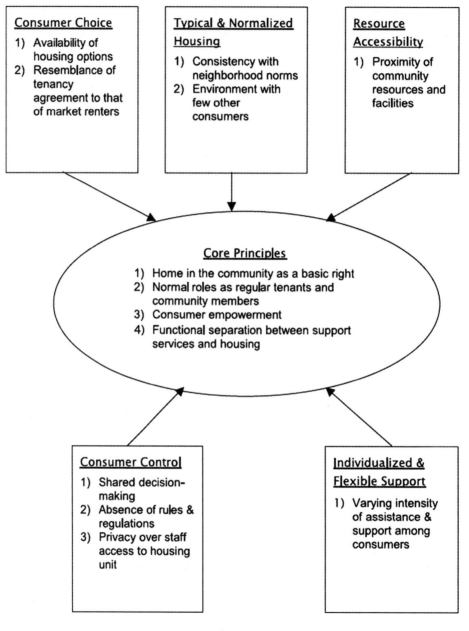

FIGURE 12.1 Principles and operational domains of supported housing. (*From Wong, Filoromo, & Tennille, 2007.*)

cope with their mental illness and substance abuse. The support and treatment services provided by Housing First programs are comprehensive and intensive. In fact, many Housing First programs provide services consistent with the ACT model (see Chapter 8), including psychiatric treatment, nursing care, supported employment, substance abuse counseling, and case management. Similar to ACT, staff teams have a low consumer to staff ratio, allowing for frequent visits; they are also available for 24/7 crisis coverage. Other Housing First programs provide services that are somewhat less comprehensive, more closely resembling the intensive case management approach. These programs—which typically serve consumers who have less severe illnesses than those served by ACT teams—broker out some of the services, are not organized in teams, and have somewhat higher consumer to staff ratios (Tsemberis, 2010).

Providing individuals with access to their own apartments in the early stages of their recovery from co-occurring disorders was initially thought of as a radical approach. But by 2004, Housing First was endorsed by the President's New Freedom Commission as an important strategy for addressing homelessness in the United States. Today, the approach is widely accepted and has been replicated throughout the United States, as well as in other parts of the world (Stanhope & Dunn, 2011). The founder of the model, Sam Tsemberis, is profiled in Box 12.2. Tsemberis (2010) refers to the original Housing First model as Pathway's Housing First, to distinguish it from other programs that do not share all of the essential ingredients, such as scattered site housing or the strong emphasis its service philosophy places on consumer choice. Pathway's Housing First is also a well-researched model. In 2007, Pathway's Housing First program was added to SAMHSA's National Registry of Evidence-based Programs and Practices (SAMHSA's National Registry of Evidence-based Programs and Practices, 2007).

Impact of the *Olmstead v. L.C.* Decision on Residential Service Models

A landmark 1999 US Supreme Court decision set the stage for greater acceptance of the SH approach by government agencies administering mental health systems. It began with two women from Georgia who lived in a state institution for many years despite a medical determination that they were able to live in the community. Their legal advocates filed a complaint against the state of Georgia, citing civil rights violations. The case, *Olmstead v. L.C.*, made it all the way to the US Supreme Court, which found in favor of the plaintiffs, a major victory for the disability community. The judgment upheld Title II of the Americans with Disabilities Act, which prohibits the segregation of persons with disabilities (see Chapter 10 for an overview of the ADA). There were two key aspects of the judgment. The first was that the institutionalization of individuals who can live in the community and benefit from that environment "perpetuates the unwarranted assumptions that persons so isolated are incapable or unworthy of participating in community life" and is a form of discrimination. The second important point was that long-term confinement of persons who are able to live outside of an institution has a profoundly

BOX 12.2   SAM J. TSEMBERIS, PHD

As a young psychologist, Sam Tsemberis worked for years on the streets of New York City as an outreach worker trying to help those homeless with psychiatric disabilities. The prevailing practice was to take these "clients" to the hospital or place them in transitional housing to receive treatment and become "housing-ready." Most clinicians believed that people with severe mental health problems were unable to function without around-the-clock supervision and were not competent to make decisions for themselves. In the late 1980s, after years of trying and failing to help people fit into this "housing-ready system," Sam began collaborating with William Anthony and Mikal Cohen at Boston University. In an NIMH-funded study entitled "Taking Psych Rehab to the Streets," they found that people who were homeless and diagnosed with severe psychiatric problems were also capable of articulating their needs and wishes. They wanted, first and foremost, a place to live. The problem was that there were no existing housing providers willing to take the leap and offer a person living on the streets an apartment of his or her own.

So, in 1992, Sam founded Pathways to Housing, a not-for-profit organization whose clinical approach was guided by PsyR principles emphasizing consumer choice and based on the belief that housing is a basic human right: people do not have to earn their housing by complying first with treatment or sobriety or any requirement other than the terms of a standard lease. This "Housing First" program proved highly effective at engaging, housing, and keeping housed people who had remained homeless for years. There was little association between diagnosis and ability to function; people with lots of symptoms moved in and kept very decent homes. In addition to removing the barriers to housing, the program uses a scattered site approach where people live in regular apartments fully integrated into their buildings and neighborhoods. Tenants receive supports from offsite clinical teams that make home visits. Today, Pathways has programs in New York, Washington, DC, Philadelphia, and Vermont and provides training and technical assistance to organizations operating Housing First programs across the United States, Canada, Europe, and Australia. Housing First programs worldwide have ended homelessness for tens of thousands of people with psychiatric disabilities.

Dr. Tsemberis is a clinical-community psychologist, trained at New York University, currently on the faculty in the Department of Psychiatry at Columbia University Medical Center. He conducts research and has published numerous articles. A renowned expert on the topics of homelessness, mental illness, and addiction, Sam has published widely and directed pivotal research studies on the efficacy of Housing First and other models. His most recent book, *Housing First: The Pathways Model to End Homelessness*, was published by Hazelden Press in 2010.

negative effect on all aspects of their lives, such as relationships, social and cultural activities, and work and educational opportunities (O'Hara & Day, 2001; US Department of Justice, 2011).

As a result of the Olmstead ruling, states are required to provide physical and mental health care services in the community. They are not required to close institutions or immediately discharge everyone able to live in the community, but they have to create a plan to modify their policies and practices and discharge those who are ready as soon as possible. The decision does not specifically use the term SH, but the intent is that states provide the least restrictive community placements possible, which in effect means the development of more SH programs. Many states responded by developing plans, but were slow to implement them. Additional lawsuits were filed in some states to force them to take action. The US Department of Justice is charged with monitoring state *Olmstead* plans. Their 2011 report stated that after more than a decade, the *Olmstead v. L.C.* decision's integration mandate has not yet been fully realized; many individuals who could live in regular community housing are still confined to psychiatric hospitals, nursing homes, and group homes. But many states have made progress and housing advocates are convinced that expansion of supported housing initiatives will play a major role in meeting the Supreme Court's community integration mandate (Corporation for Supported Housing, 2012). For example, in New Jersey, a lawsuit was settled in 2009 to force a clear implementation plan. Since that time, the New Jersey Division of Mental Health and Addictions Services has added a number of SH units. While group homes for people with disabilities still exist in New Jersey, new ones are no longer being funded. In addition, New Jersey closed down a state psychiatric hospital in 2012, and some of the savings have been redirected to fund their *Olmstead* plan to develop additional SH units and other community-based services.

Implementing the Supported Housing Approach

The residential services paradigm shift from a stepwise continuum of care approach to an SH approach is an ongoing process in many mental health systems. Besides changes in the types of services, it requires changes in staff competencies and how financial resources are accessed and structured.

Key changes in service provision include a shift in staff responsibilities requiring different skill sets and attitudes. With the linear continuum approach, staff members provide treatment and supervision in residential facilities in an effort to move residents to the next level of housing. SH staff members work in the community providing individualized, as-needed supports, teaching skills to individuals in their homes, and assisting people to acquire resources and utilize natural supports. SH staff need to be flexible and creative in determining the most effective way to help each person get what he or she needs to live as independently as possible.

Consider the following vignette:

Lisa used to live in a group home with a great deal of staff supervision. They watched her take her medication twice a day. They were always present when it was her turn to cook dinner and they reminded her (repeatedly, if she procrastinated) to clean her room every Saturday morning. Group home staff also provided mental health treatment. A psychiatric nurse met with her regularly to assess her current symptoms and monitor medications. Her case manager, a clinical social worker, met with her once a week to discuss any problems she was having.

Now Lisa has her own efficiency apartment and receives services from an SH program. Initially, she asked the support workers for a great deal of help in getting settled and learning new routines. For example, her laundry was building up because she wasn't sure how to get it to the laundromat and what to do once she got there, so Tanya, a staff member, came over and showed her how to get her laundry done. Then Tanya helped her to write down a step-by-step procedure so Lisa could do it on her own. Tanya also showed her how to fill a weekly medication dispenser and assisted her in establishing a routine for remembering to take her medication. Tanya also helped Lisa learn about social and recreational activities in the community that match her interests and helped her learn to take public transportation to get to these events.

Lisa has now been in her apartment for six months and is doing well. Tanya and other support staff check in with her regularly by phone, but only come over a few times a month, when she asks them to. However, she likes knowing that she can reach someone 24 hours a day, if needed. Lisa sees a psychiatrist once a month, and goes to a weekly support group at a local mental health center. She likes the fact that these treatment services are kept separate from her private home life.

Notice that in the example provided, Lisa has much more control over the services she receives from the SH program. As mentioned earlier, SH promotes personal choice not only in terms of where people live but also in terms of what, when, and how supports are provided. Consider a typical day at a facility-based residential treatment program that requires all residents to be up and out of the house by 9:00 a.m., involved in a PsyR day treatment program, or otherwise productively engaged, and home by 4:00 p.m. to help cook dinner and attend a community meeting. Contrast that picture with an SH program in which service recipients are not required to be accountable to support staff about how they spend their day, and where an individual's preference for when staff visit is respected. Notice that in order for an SH program to be successful, staff members must truly internalize the PsyR value of self-determination and empowerment. For many practitioners, this involves a shift from thinking that staff members know what is best for the people they serve to building real partnerships with people (Pyke & Lowe, 1996).

A number of SH programs have employed consumers in a variety of staff positions, including involvement in the provision of direct services and supports (Basto, Pratt, Gill, & Barrett, 2000; Besio & Mahler, 1993; Butler, 1993). Using consumers as staff, or **peer providers**, has a number of benefits including a strong ability to empathize with the day-to-day concerns of other consumers. Peer providers have also been found to be highly skilled in obtaining necessary resources and advocacy (Besio & Mahler, 1993). Because of their own experiences, consumer-providers may be better attuned to what consumers need in order to accomplish independent living goals. They may also champion attitudes and behaviors that are respectful of consumers' right to privacy and need to be in control of their own home environment. More information about the use of peers as service providers can be found in Chapter 13.

Accessing and Financing Supported Housing

Among the greatest challenges to the implementation of the SH model are accessing and financing enough affordable housing that matches individual preferences, helping people to acquire rental or mortgage assistance, and creating partnerships between housing and service agencies to ensure that both affordable housing and support services are available. Some state and local service systems have made significant progress in addressing these challenges, while others have been slower to develop an adequate number of SH programs.

The housing challenges faced by persons with psychiatric disabilities are directly related to the amount of income they have to pay for housing. Access to affordable housing is a challenge for many people in the United States with low incomes. There is a growing shortage of affordable housing. Part of the decline in low-income housing is due to the gentrification of many inner-city neighborhoods and expanding suburbs, with single professionals and couples with high incomes replacing individuals with lower incomes. The second factor reducing housing availability is a decrease in funding for federally assisted low-income housing (Carling, 1993; Cooper, Herb, & O'Hara, 2003). Both of these factors have been aggravated by the 2008 housing crash and economic downturn. Many persons with psychiatric disabilities rely on entitlements as their sole income, keeping them well below the poverty level and unable to afford most housing options. A study conducted by advocacy groups, *Priced Out in 2010* (Cooper, O'Hara, & Zovistoski, 2011), found that as the average rent for a one-bedroom apartment was 112 percent of disability benefits such as SSI, SSI recipients were unable to afford even modest rents anywhere in the nation. Even the rent for a studio apartment costs 99 percent of average SSI monthly income. For individuals receiving SSI or other disability benefits, rental subsidies or other government-funded housing opportunities are the only way they can afford to live in their own homes or apartments.

Resources to fund housing for persons with psychiatric disabilities can come from a number of places. Even though the costs of operating SH programs can be lower than facility-based residential programs, there are simply not enough dollars available to provide both mental health support services and housing in state and county mental health budgets. This problem may help SH programs to separate the roles of the landlord/property manager and support service provider. This role separation not only creates better conditions for a non-coercive partnership between consumer and provider, but as you will see it also offers additional strategies for financing the housing. So while some residential service providers carry out both these roles, newer approaches to SH unbundle (i.e., separate) housing and support services. To do this, they rely on creative partnerships between state and local housing agencies and health and human service agencies (O'Hara & Day, 2001).

Two SH models that have been successful in this approach are scattered site housing and mixed tenancy housing. Scattered site SH programs help individuals locate apartments through the local community rental market and private landlords. They also help individuals apply for public housing or obtain government-funded housing subsidies, such as tenant-based Section 8 Housing Choice Vouchers, or Shelter Plus Care vouchers so they can afford these apartments. Service dollars are obtained from state or federal grants or from billing Medicaid if a state has a Medicaid program that will pay for community-based rehabilitation and support services. The Housing First programs mentioned earlier typically use this model. In mixed tenancy SH programs, a publicly funded affordable income housing project dedicates a certain percentage of the units for low-income individuals with disabilities, while the other units are occupied by non-disabled tenants who meet income eligibility requirements. Support services in such programs are available as needed to the tenants who have a disability. A mixed tenancy SH program is typically a collaboration between a housing agency and a mental health agency; working together they may be able to access both state and federal dollars to support the project (Corporation for Supported Housing, 2012; Korman, 2006). One example is an innovative collaboration in North Carolina between the state's Housing Finance Agency and their Department of Health and Human Services (DHHS). In order to receive federal Low-Income Housing Tax Credits (LIHTCs), local housing developers agree to rent 10 percent of their units to individuals with physical, developmental, or psychiatric disabilities, including some who are homeless. A state-funded rental assistance program helps to make the rent affordable and DHHS contracts out the support services needed by the various disability groups. Between 2002 and 2006, this program created roughly 900 units of quality independent housing for individuals living with disabilities (Korman, 2006).

Another model that is quickly influencing housing policy at the federal level and in numerous states comes from Louisiana in response to the devastation caused by hurricanes Katrina and Rita. Within five months of Katrina's landfall, the Louisiana Recovery Authority formally adopted the goal of creating 3000 new Permanent Supportive Housing (PSH) opportunities for the hurricane's most vulnerable victims. This initiative brought together state policy makers, homeless and disability advocates, and philanthropic organizations to create the nation's first large scale cross-disability integrated permanent supportive housing initiative. Rather than simply create 3000 PSH units, Louisiana set out to create the nation's first comprehensive PSH system that would help the state achieve several important policy objectives, including addressing chronic homelessness; reducing the unnecessary confinement of people with serious disabilities in nursing homes and other high-cost restrictive settings; and improving the state's fragile behavioral health system through the implementation of evidence-based models of housing and services (O'Hara, 2010).

Discrimination: A Barrier to Independent Living

In addition to the availability and financial problems mentioned above, discrimination can be a barrier to supported housing. Because of the stigma associated with mental illness, landlords may refuse to rent to people with a known history of mental illness. Consider Ellen's experience:

> *After losing an apartment because her building was condemned to make way for a mini-mall, Ellen finally located an apartment she could afford: a third-floor walk-up in a building where the landlord also resided. Ellen made a good impression during her initial meeting with the landlord. He noticed she was a smoker, which wasn't a problem because he smoked cigarettes as well. However, when the landlord called one of her references and discovered her psychiatric history, he became wary. He discussed the situation with his wife, who was quite blunt in her assessment: "I don't want some crazy woman who smokes cigarettes in our building; she'll be sure to burn the place down!" When Ellen stopped by the next day, she was told the apartment was already rented.*

Discriminatory rental practices based on a person's disability are a violation of the US Fair Housing Act discussed previously when addressing NIMBY and group homes. Regardless, such violations often go unreported and may be difficult to prove if a landlord claims that a unit has already been rented to someone else.

Another factor that exacerbates stigma/discrimination problems is that, often due to their illness, some persons with severe mental illness have criminal records. According to a 1999 US Department of Justice report, 16 percent of adult inmates of the US prison system have a mental illness. The President's New Freedom Commission on Mental Health found that a staggering 80 percent of youths entering the juvenile justice system have mental disorders (Honberg, 2004). A criminal record can have a very negative effect on a person's ability to obtain housing. In some areas, landlords require criminal background checks before renting apartments. A criminal record can prohibit someone from obtaining a rental subsidy from the state or federal government, such as a Section 8 Housing Choice Voucher from the US Department of Housing and Urban Development. Landlords may also require a credit check, which can be a barrier for consumers who have spent many years living in poverty. In response to this crisis, a nationwide advocacy group, the Bazelon Center for Mental Health Law, "is committed to reducing the criminalization of people with mental illnesses" (http:// www.bazelon.org).

Outcomes of the Supported Housing Approach

SH studies have been reported on in the literature since the 1990s. Early studies reported mostly on demonstration projects in several states and found outcomes such as increased housing stability, level of functioning, and quality of life as well as decreased hospital usage (Brown, Ridgway, Anthony, & Rogers,1991; Curtis, McCabe, Fleming, & Carling,

1993; Livingston, Gordon, King, & Srebnik, 1991; Texas Department of Mental Health and Mental Retardation, 1994).

Perhaps the most rigorous of the early studies was conducted by the Veterans Administration in 1992. A 2007 paper by Cheng and colleagues reanalyzed data from this randomized clinical trial of 460 homeless veterans with co-occurring disorders who were assigned to one of three conditions. The first condition, dubbed HUD-VASH, was a combination of housing vouchers and intensive case management services that was a joint venture between HUD and Veterans Administration–supported housing providers (VASH). The second group received the intensive case management services but no housing vouchers, and the third condition was standard VA outpatient psychiatric care. The initial study reported on by Rosenheck and colleagues in 2003 found that the HUD-VASH group had greater housing stability than the other two groups. The 2007 reanalysis found that the HUD-VASH group also spent fewer days in the hospital and had significantly better substance abuse outcomes. The authors concluded that their re-analysis provided the best evidence to date that SH programs that combine subsidized housing and intensive case management services can improve both housing stability and clinical outcomes such as reduction in substance abuse.

A 1997 review of the SH literature by Ogilvie concluded that there are still too few outcome studies on SH to draw firm conclusions about the efficacy of the approach. A subsequent 2004 review by Debra Rog found that the evidence on SH was still insufficient. For example, Rog identified only five studies that used "rigorous" scientific designs. However, her review found convincing evidence that SH residents were less likely to become homeless, less likely to be hospitalized, and fared better than similar residents in other settings. The findings of three of these studies (Dickey et al., 1996; Dickey, Latimer, Powers, Gonzalez, & Goldfinger, 1997; Goldfinger et al., 1999) suggest that housing stability is increased by providing supports rather than by a specific program model.

A 2006 Cochrane Review of the SH literature sought to compare the outcomes of single site versus scattered site supported housing programs. A second objective was to compare SH to treatment as usual. The authors searched for all relevant randomized control trials or quasi-randomized studies that met their standards. After doing multiple searches, they found a total of 139 citations; however, none of them met their rigorous criteria (Chilvers, Macdonald, & Hayes, 2006). They concluded that well-designed experimental studies still need to be conducted in order to determine which types of SH interventions produce the best outcomes.

In 2008, a review of the SH literature was conducted by researchers at the Boston University Center for Psychiatric Rehabilitation (Rogers, Kash, & Olschewski, 2008). Part of their rationale for doing the review was their belief that studies on SH that employed acceptable research methods, even if they were not randomized controlled trials, needed to be synthesized for the benefit of mental health system stakeholders. They rated 155 studies based on the quality of their research methods and ended up synthesizing the results of 68 studies. Their results suggested that SH can improve residential stability and reduce rehospitalization rates, but they did not find consistent evidence of reduction in psychiatric symptoms. They concluded that SH programs that use intensive case management interventions have better outcomes. They also found SH to be cost-effective and to lead to higher satisfaction with residents' living environment and improved quality of life.

The most recent review of the literature by Tabol, Drebing, and Rosenheck (2010) sought to clarify the exact nature of the SH model and how adherence to its principles and practices are measured. They looked at 50 articles published between 1987 and 2008 that provided either program descriptions or outcomes studies of supported or supportive housing. While they found agreement on basic principles, they did not find evidence of a well-defined model or consistent strategies for measuring fidelity to specific elements of the model. They also recommended that work be done on refining the one existing SH fidelity tool reported in the literature.

As mentioned earlier, Pathways Housing First (PHF) is the best articulated model of supported housing. Because PHF decided to integrate research into their service delivery model early on, they have been able to demonstrate that their approach produced a number of positive outcomes (Stanhope & Dunn, 2011). In a controlled trial, researchers tested the PHF model by randomly assigning 225 persons with a dual diagnosis to either receive continuum of care housing contingent on prerequisites (e.g., sobriety) or receive housing without prerequisites in a PHF program (Greenwood, Schaefer-McDaniel, Winkel, & Tsemberis, 2005; Gulcer et al., 2003; Tsemberis & Eisenberg, 2000; Tsemberis, Gulcur, & Nakae, 2004; Tsemberis et al., 2003). They found that the addition of the supports of an assertive community treatment (ACT) team nearly doubled the rate of housing stability compared to typical residential treatment (Tsemberis & Eisenberg, 2000). Another paper published on this study (Tsemberis, Gulcur, & Nakae, 2004) found that after two years there were no differences in level of substance abuse between the two groups. Not surprisingly, the PHF group without prerequisites obtained housing much more quickly and, being there longer, demonstrated greater housing stability. The group given prerequisites for housing did have higher substance abuse treatment utilization rates, but apparently did not benefit from the increased level of service. These results strongly suggest that individuals respond favorably to harm reduction strategies and policies that respect and reinforce their rights as individual members of society. As the authors (Tsemberis et al., 2004) point out: "Consumers are allowed to make choices—to use alcohol or not, to take medication or not—and regardless of their choices they are not treated adversely, their housing status is not threatened, and help continues to be available to them" (p. 653). In addition to demonstrating that PHF consumers achieve superior housing stability, this study showed that PHF services can be provided at a lower cost; PHF consumers also reported more choices in terms of their housing, treatment options, and daily activities (SAMHSA's National Registry of Evidence-based Programs and Practices, 2007).

In an effort to confirm PHF outcomes and explore implementation outside of the usual inner-city environment, Stefancic and Tsemberis (2007) studied individuals diagnosed with a serious mental illness with histories of using suburban homeless shelters. Subjects were randomly assigned to a PHF program or a treatment as usual control group. At a 20-month follow-up, more than 80 percent of the PHF participants remained in stable housing, while few control group members had obtained permanent housing. Unfortunately, many control group members either dropped out or were lost to contact. After four years, 68 percent of the PHF group were still living in permanent housing.

The research studies done to date on PHF demonstrate that this model improves housing stability and can end long histories of homelessness for the majority of individuals served. Reductions in the use of hospitals and emergency rooms have also been demonstrated, as have reductions in the cost of providing services. Studies of the PHF model also demonstrate increased consumer choice and improved quality of life (Tsemberis, 2010).

BOX 12.3   IS SUPPORTED HOUSING AN EVIDENCE-BASED PRACTICE?

In 2010, SAMHSA added supportive permanent housing to its list of evidence-based practices and released a toolkit for agencies to use when implementing this approach. The SAMHSA toolkit includes an extensive list of articles that have been published on SH and related residential models. While informative, the bibliography does not distinguish between descriptive studies and studies that used rigorous scientific method. The SAMSHA toolkit also includes a fidelity scale that contains both process measures to ensure that a program is staying true to the principles and practices of the model and outcome measures that allow providers to measure the impact of their services. At the time that this chapter was written, use of this fidelity scale has not yet been reported on in published literature. The SAMHSA toolkit can be found on their Web site (http://store.samhsa.gov/product/Permanent-Supportive-Housing-Evidence-Based-Practices-EBP-KIT/SMA10-4510). SAMHSA has also listed a specific SH model, Pathways to Housing, in its National Registry of Evidence-based Programs and Practices (2007). That report contains a list of rigorously conducted studies and includes a report on the quality of the research, which was done by a team of external reviewers.

As summarized elsewhere in this chapter, some researchers question the evidence produced so far on the SH model. For example, Rog (2004) concluded that more research needed to be done to determine the outcomes of SH services and considered it to be a promising practice rather than an EBP. In 2010, Tabol, Drebing, and Rosenheck concluded that there is still a lack of clarity on the principles and practices of SH, which continues to hinder efforts to evaluate its outcomes. Clearly, arriving at a clearer definition of the elements of SH is a necessary step for defining an EBP.

Hopefully additional research will help identify the critical elements of SH. In the meantime, despite the lack of a clear definition, many providers, researchers, and advocates see SH as the preferred approach to providing residential services because it promotes the PsyR goal of community integration (Bond et al., 2004b; Wong & Solomon, 2002) and is in sync with many other PsyR goals, values, and principles. Helping individuals find and maintain decent affordable housing in the community is not just a form of "treatment," it is a basic human right that profoundly affects the quality of a person's life (Wong, Filoromo, & Tennille, 2007). In the United States, individuals with disabilities also have the legal right to live in the least restrictive setting possible and to participate fully in community life (Korman, 2006; O'Hara & Day, 2001; US Department of Justice, 2011).

CONTROVERSIAL ISSUE
Is Supported Housing the Right Model for Everyone?

Despite the paradigm shift outlined in this chapter, the evidence that consumers prefer to live as most people do, in houses or apartments with friends and family (Tanzman, 1993; Yeich et al., 1994), and the *Olmstead* decision's community integration mandate, many people still reside in segregated facilities such as group homes. In addition, some mental health providers question whether they are able to provide SH to individuals who have multiple diagnoses and criminal justice involvement or who present with challenging behaviors. Does the SH approach have the capacity to support all people with psychiatric disabilities who are deemed able to live outside of an institution? Or should it be conceptualized as one option among a wider range of community-based residential programs?

SH is a flexible, individualized model that many housing advocates believe can be adapted to everyone's needs. It has been used effectively by persons with varying levels of disability and challenging behavior, but it is important to keep in mind that "the more severely disabled the client, the more critical the need for an individualized approach" (Carling & Ridgway, 1991, p. 71). Advocates in the field of developmental disabilities have held this view for quite some time. They maintain that we must move beyond an era of deinstitutionalization to an era of full community membership for all individuals with disabilities (Bradley, 1994). This approach stresses that community membership is everyone's right, not just a privilege reserved for people who are capable of a particular level of functioning. Keep in mind that some people with developmental disabilities have profound cognitive deficits and/or severe physical limitations. Nonetheless, local service systems have had real success in shifting from a residential treatment model to "supportive living," which is conceptually and practically similar to the SH approach (Carmody, 1994; O'Brien & O'Brien, 1994). For example, in Illinois, a project dubbed SPICE (Supported Placements in Integrated Community Environments) was created to help a group of people with severe cognitive and/or mobility impairments move from a nursing home into regular community housing (Carmody, 1994). The participants in the SPICE project were specifically selected because of the fact that they had severe and multiple disabilities, as the project sought to demonstrate that community integration could be a reality for even the most disabled. From the very beginning of the project, the participants' input and involvement were sought. Some of them chose to live with families, others chose to live alone, still others opted for a roommate who was another project participant (such a decision had to be mutual). Participants helped interview and hire personal care assistants and other support staff. They were also assisted in accessing existing community resources and natural supports (e.g., churches, community colleges, etc.). Outcome study results showed a significant gain in community living skills and a tremendous increase in satisfaction with their living arrangement. The project demonstrated "that anyone with disabilities can live in the community and that the community has the capacity to meet the needs of anyone, including people for whom nursing facilities had been thought the only 'appropriate' residential option" (Carmody, 1994, p. 479). In other words, SH should be made available to everyone because all of us deserve the right to live in a place that is truly a home.

(Continued)

CONTROVERSIAL ISSUE
Is Supported Housing the Right Model for Everyone?—(Continued)

While projects such as SPICE show that it is certainly possible to provide SH to even the most disabled individuals, there are instances when SH does not seem to be the most feasible, affordable, or even desired option. Some people with psychiatric disabilities report that they are either not ready to live independently or prefer congregate living arrangements (Tanzman, 1993). For example, people who have spent many years in an institution are accustomed to being extremely dependent on hospital staff and may be reluctant to leave an institutionalized setting. Others may find independent SH so stressful that they end up back in the hospital. For these individuals, a small, homelike congregate care setting staffed around-the-clock by people who are familiar with their needs may ease the stress of moving from an institution to the community.

Some individuals who have multiple physical and psychiatric disabilities and require extensive nursing and personal care services, or those with persistent psychotic symptoms that interfere markedly with their ability to care for themselves, may also benefit from the accessibility of supports and services available in small, congregate care settings. While the SPICE project shows that it may be possible for such individuals to live independently, in some systems it may be cost-prohibitive to provide 24/7 support to individuals. Serving them in specialized residential treatment programs may be the least restrictive option available.

Residential providers have cited other examples of persons who are very difficult to serve in SH programs, such as individuals being discharged from psychiatric institutions with serious criminal histories (e.g., sex offenders). One way to meet this challenge is to rebalance the use of the system's current residential options. In other words, use existing group homes for the small percentage of individuals for whom the SH model has not worked or for those for whom it is not currently practical, and then expand SH options for the rest of the population. An alternative view is that the SH model needs to evolve in order to find solutions to these challenging problems. Some of these problems may require resources that are expensive or difficult to access. But mental health systems that are truly committed to realizing the dream of community integration for everyone able to reside safely in the community need to keep looking for ways to meet these challenges.

Summary

From the mid-19th century to the 1960s, most people with severe mental illness spent a good part of their lives in psychiatric institutions. Once deinstitutionalization began, a key question was "Where should these patients live?" Some individuals returned to their families, who were often ill-prepared for their service and support needs. Others were placed in boarding homes, nursing homes, and SROs where their quality of life was sometimes worse than what they had experienced in the hospitals. A relatively small percentage of individuals were given residential treatment. Most of these housing options resulted in transinstitutionalization (Carling, 1995, p. 33), meaning that true community integration was not realized.

By the 1980s, the preferred model of residential treatment was the linear continuum, which moved individuals through a series of placements that became progressively less supervised and restrictive. The goal of this approach was graduation to independent living, typically without any ongoing support. Eventually, it became clear that this model was not meeting the needs and preferences of most people.

PsyR now embraces SH as the preferred residential services model that is most consistent with the PsyR goal of community integration. The SH approach emphasizes integrated, long-term housing options and flexible, individualized services and supports so that persons living with psychiatric disabilities can live in the same places as non-disabled community members. The philosophy and principles of the SH approach were informed by the values and principles articulated by the Independent Living Movement begun by people who have physical disabilities. PsyR practitioners who work in SH programs do not provide treatment, which is available elsewhere in the mental health system. Nor do they provide supervision, which is not wanted or needed by the vast majority of people with psychiatric disabilities. Instead, SH assists consumers in developing skills and obtaining the resources and supports that they want and need in their particular living situation. SH is philosophically and practically similar to supported employment and supported education (see Chapters 10 and 11, respectively, for more on these approaches). In some places, efforts to implement and expand access to SH programs have been hampered by barriers such as lack of affordable housing stock, limited government funding, and discrimination.

The success of evidence-based models of SH, such as Pathway's Housing First, suggests that SH can help individuals achieve outcomes such as residential stability and reduced use of hospitals and emergency rooms. Additional research needs to be conducted to examine other SH approaches in order to clarify the essential features of effective SH programs. Nonetheless, even without rigorous research studies, we know that many persons who have psychiatric disabilities want and need a safe and affordable place to live in the community and SH programs help them achieve that. The 1999 US Supreme Court *Olmstead* decision made it clear that individuals with disabilities deemed able to reside in the community have the right to live, learn, work, and socialize in the same ways as nondisabled members of the community.

■ ■ ■ ▬▬▬▬▬▬▬▬▬▬▬▬▬▬▬▬▬▬▬▬▬▬▬▬▬▬▬▬▬▬▬▬

Class Exercises

1. Review the following principles of SH, which are adapted from those articulated by Wong, Filoromo, and Tennille (2007):
   - A home in the community should be a basic right for persons with psychiatric disabilities.
   - Persons served by supported housing programs should be helped to become regular tenants and community members.

- Residents and SH staff have a relationship characterized by trust and residents' choices are respected (e.g., what services they need, when staff visit, etc.).
- There is functional separation between housing and support services, so an individual's housing arrangement is not dependent on his or her acceptance of mental health treatment.

Now go back and review the list of PsyR goals, values. and principles in Chapter 4. Match the SH principles above with one or more of the concepts in the Chapter 4 list. Then describe how they are connected.

2. **Designing an Ideal Residential Services Program**—Imagine that you serve on a newly formed board of directors for a new residential services program. Your target population is adults who have a long history of a severe mental illness and are currently at high risk for psychiatric hospitalization and/or homelessness. Some of the individuals also have chronic physical illnesses such as type II diabetes; others still struggle with substance abuse and/or criminal justice involvement. You can assume that most of the people you will be providing services for have had a great deal of difficulty residing in the community because they are sometimes psychiatrically unstable, have severe functional deficits (e.g., lack many ADL skills), have other issues such as problems maintaining sobriety, or most likely some combination of these. Your task is to determine what types of residential services you want to provide and provide a clear rationale for your choices. Consider the following questions:
   a. Do you want to use a scattered site supported housing model? Develop a semi-supervised apartment complex? Utilize a congregate care setting? Or use some combination of these?
   b. If you choose to use utilize facility-based (congregate care) housing, will it be transitional (i.e., residents must move on after a specified time period) or long-term?
   c. What types of services will the staff provide? How often will they be present in residents' living environments (e.g., 24-hour coverage, as-needed visits, etc.)?

13

Self-help and Peer-delivered Services

Nothing about us, without us.
Nihil de nobis, sine nobis.
A motto of the consumer movement; also an ancient Latin expression

CHAPTER OUTLINE

Psychiatric Rehabilitation. http://dx.doi.org/10.1016/B978-0-12-387002-5.00013-5

This chapter outlines the important contributions people diagnosed with a severe mental illness make to their own rehabilitation and the rehabilitation of others. Like the fields of alcohol and drug addiction treatment, there is a long tradition of mutual self-help among persons living with mental illness. Today, these individuals are designing and delivering services and moving into psychiatric rehabilitation service provider positions in larger numbers. They are involved in operating peer support agencies, participating on boards of directors, educating and training practitioners and service recipients, and conducting research.

This chapter will answer the following questions:

1. *How have self-help groups and the self-advocacy movement influenced PsyR?*
2. *What types of support and PsyR services are provided by people in recovery?*
3. *What are some of the important issues related to peer-provided services?*
4. *What are some of the benefits and challenges of peer-provided services?*
5. *Should a practitioner who has a mental illness diagnosis disclose his or her condition to other professionals?*

Introduction

Persons diagnosed with severe mental illnesses have a long tradition of participating in formal and informal **self-help** and mutual support initiatives. Despite the stigma associated with these illnesses, a growing number of persons living with severe mental illness are moving into professional service provider roles, in some cases operating service agencies themselves. The issues they face as they take on these new challenges are complex and exciting. Research on peer support and peer-delivered services suggests that they often achieve results similar to traditional services. These trends represent real empowerment and affirm the principles of psychiatric rehabilitation described in Chapter 4.

This chapter will explore the concepts of self-help and peer-provided services, describe the various roles that are filled by peer employees and volunteers, review research regarding these services, and examine how the peer provider or consumer provider role affects one's own recovery, including the positive gains and the challenges that must be faced.

Defining Mutual Self-help and Peer Support

Persons who have severe mental illnesses can help themselves and assist others in coping with the symptoms and challenges of severe mental illnesses.

Self-help is an attempt by people with a mutual problem to take control over the circumstances of their lives. Founded on the principle that people who share a disability have something to offer each other that professionals cannot provide, self-help efforts take many forms. (Segal, Silverman, & Temkin, 1993, p. 705)

Most forms of self-help emphasize the benefits of mutual support for people dealing with similar concerns; the essence of self-help in this context is "mutual support within a group" (Swarbrick, Schmidt, & Gill, 2010, p. 4).

Today, self-help based on mutual support is an accepted strategy for dealing with all kinds of issues. Consider some well-known examples: Alcoholics Anonymous, Gamblers Anonymous, and Weight Watchers, as well as some pertaining specifically to serious mental illnesses. Self-help groups can provide some of the same benefits as traditional therapy groups, such as the experience of commonality (i.e., recognizing that you are not the only one experiencing difficulties), a sense of belonging, sharing of ideas and resources, opportunities to develop social skills, and increased opportunities to receive constructive feedback (Jacobs, Masson, & Harvill, 2005). Self-help groups provide unique benefits that traditional services either may not offer or may discourage such as the promotion of empowerment or a chance to establish ongoing friendships (Lieberman, 1990). Many people who have a mental illness participate in self-help groups in part because they feel they can be more open and honest with their peers than with professionals. As Swarbrick and Schmidt (2010) point out, these groups "offer a low-risk point of entry for people considering ways to cope with a mental health" (p. 4). Direct exposure to role models who are managing their illnesses and leading satisfying lives may also be an important benefit (Davidson et al., 1999; Deegan, 1993).

Peer support is a term commonly used in the PsyR literature to describe self-help initiatives. Mead, Hilton, and Curtis (2001) offer an insightful definition of peer support:

Peer support is a system of giving and receiving help founded on key principles of respect, shared responsibility, and mutual agreement about what is helpful. Peer support is not based on psychiatric models and diagnostic criteria. It is about understanding another's situation empathically through the shared experience of emotional and psychological pain. When people identify with others who they feel are "like" them, they feel a connection. This connection, or affiliation, is a deep, holistic understanding based on mutual experience where people are able to "be" with each other without the constraints of traditional (expert/patient) relationships. Further, as trust in the relationship builds, both people are able to respectfully challenge each other when they find themselves in conflict. This allows members of the peer community to try out new behaviors with one another and move beyond previously held self-concepts built on disability and diagnosis. (p. 135)

Copeland and Mead (2004) distinguish peer support from other self-help initiatives: "Instead of talking of each other and thinking of each other as 'sick,' in Peer Support we build a sense of family and community that is mutually responsible and focused on recovery" (p. 10). These definitions explain how peer support can assist the recovery process for many individuals trying to reestablish a positive self-concept while struggling with a mental illness.

The History of the Self-help Movement

Many instances of self-help and mutual support among persons with severe mental illnesses predate the establishment of PsyR as a distinct practice. For example, the group of ex-psychiatric patients described in Chapter 7, who dubbed themselves WANA (We Are Not Alone) in the 1940s and then went on to establish Fountain House, were essentially a self-help group. In fact, some scholars trace the roots of this movement to the Alleged Lunatics' Friend Society established by ex-patients in England in 1845 (Bassman, 2010).

In 1952, a psychiatrist named Abraham Low established Recovery Inc. based on a treatment method he began in the 1930s that was similar to what is now called cognitive-behavioral therapy. His technique, described in *Mental Health Through Will-Training* (Low, 1950), involved teaching persons strategies for controlling their symptoms and taking responsibility for their lives. Today, the organization offers member-operated groups worldwide and is known as Recovery International. It is the second oldest continually operating self-help organization in the United States (the oldest is Alcoholics Anonymous (AA), founded in 1935). Meetings consist of members sharing examples of applying Recovery International principles in everyday life situations. They share their stories in four steps, starting with (1) summarizing situations that trigger emotional distress, (2) describing the symptoms that they experienced, and (3) relabeling diagnoses, symptoms, and stressful situations using Recovery International terminology. For example, a person diagnosed with bipolar disorder might stop referring to himself as a "manic-depressive" and instead say, "I am an average nervous person." This part of the process helps members to cognitively reframe symptoms and situations that they previously experienced as devastating into manageable aspects of their day-to-day functioning. The last step (4) involves speculating on how they would have handled the situation before they learned self-help techniques (Ackerman, 1997). Recovery International is an important resource for people who are recovering from a variety of mental illnesses (Lee, 1995). Visit their Web site at http://www.lowselfhelpsystems.org/.

A number of successful self-help initiatives have developed outside of the United States. In 1957, a mutual support organization dubbed GROW (not an acronym) was established in Australia by Father Cornelius B. Keogh and a group of ex-patients (Swarbrick, Madara, White, & Schmidt, 2010). GROW groups are similar to Recovery International and AA groups in that they are highly structured, offer members a strong sense of community, encourage the sharing of personal stories, and utilize materials developed by the members of the organization. GROW, Inc., like AA, has a Blue Book that helps members apply personal growth and problem-solving strategies. There are now more than 300 mutual support groups operated by GROW in Australia, and more than 200 GROW groups in other countries, including the United States (Finn & Bishop, 2001). Other well-known self-help initiatives include Schizophrenics Anonymous, which has been in existence for more than 25 years and includes at least 150 groups in the United States and Canada (http://www.schizophrenia.com/help/Schizanon.html) and the

Depressive and Bipolar Support Alliance (DBSA), whose peer-run support groups and chapters serve over 70,000 persons each year (http://www.dbsalliance.org).

In the mid-1970s, peer support initiatives got a boost when the National Institute of Mental Health (NIMH) sponsored a conference focused on the identification of essential supports and services needed by people being discharged from psychiatric hospitals. This was one of the first times that consumers of mental health services were invited to the table to discuss mental health systems. At the conference, and in subsequent publications, peer support was identified as one of the ten essential ingredients of an ideal community support system (Stroul, 1989, 1993; Turner, 1977). Community support systems are described in more detail in Chapter 8.

Throughout the 1980s, federal funding supported the expansion of self-help initiatives throughout the United States. The Substance Abuse and Mental Health Services Administration's Center for Mental Health Services' (SAMHSA/CMHS) Community Support Program provided technical assistance to a number of consumer-run programs and also funded various demonstration projects in order to promote the development of self-help groups and other innovative peer support programs (Brown & Parrish, 1995; Schmidt, 2005; Van Tosh & Del Vecchio, 2000). State mental health authorities also began to support the development of self-help initiatives. For example, in the early 1980s, the New Jersey Division of Mental Health Services provided funding needed to open and operate drop-in centers, now called **self-help centers**, throughout the state (Barrett, Pratt, Basto, & Gill, 2000). Self-help centers are alternative programs that offer a variety of mutual support, social, and advocacy activities. Based on the original drop-in center model, these initiatives now have an expanded focus on wellness, recovery, and employment (Swarbrick, 2005). We will look more closely at self-help centers later in the chapter.

Today, peer support initiatives are prominent components of many US state mental health systems. A 2010 report from the National Association of Mental Health Program Directors (NASMHPD) found that the growing involvement of persons with mental illness has had a positive effect on services, the administration of services, and public policy. In an effort to further this trend, the NASMHPD report emphasized strategies for integrating peer providers into the service delivery work force. Two earlier federal reports, *Mental Health: A Report of the Surgeon General* (US Department of Health and Human Services, 1999) and the final report of the President's New Freedom Commission on Mental Health (2003), recommend the use of peer support to promote recovery-oriented services.

Self-help for Persons with Co-occurring Disorders

Participating in self-help groups may be even more important for people dealing with the co-occurring diagnoses of both a mental illness and a substance abuse disorder. Historically, individuals with these dual disorders were the first to be referred to self-help groups focused on recovery from substance abuse. Sadly, these referrals were more often caused by an inability or unwillingness of mental health professionals to deal with the substance abuse problem than by an appreciation of the benefits of self-help. Still, professionals were aware that attendance at these substance abuse–related self-help groups was often helpful in the recovery process. For many professionals, this knowledge led to an appreciation of the contributions self-help could make for persons with psychiatric disabilities.

Individuals who have both a mental illness and a substance abuse disorder are still the consumers most likely to be referred to self-help groups. As discussed in Chapter 8, people with co-occurring diagnoses require specialized programs and supports. These individuals are often encouraged by their caseworkers to utilize self-help groups to supplement the professional supports and services that they receive. Alcoholics Anonymous and Narcotics Anonymous (NA) are the most commonly utilized mutual support groups for persons recovering from alcoholism and other substance abuse disorders. Unfortunately, some people do not feel welcome in these groups when they disclose they have a diagnosis of mental illness and take medication. Apparently, the stigma associated with severe mental illness exists even within groups such as AA and NA. In addition, AA and NA groups often discourage the use of psychotropic medications because they are viewed as obstacles to recovery from addiction. Partly in response to this resistance, many consumers have been receiving help in mutual support groups known as "Double Trouble" or **dual recovery** groups (Vogel, Knight, Laudet, & Magura, 1998). Note that the term Double Trouble was used for many years, but dual recovery, a more hopeful term, has become preferred (Magura et al., 2003). Dual recovery groups are specifically geared to meet the needs of individuals who are coping with the symptoms and challenges of both a mental illness and a substance abuse disorder. Even so, they are very similar to AA and NA groups. Like AA and NA groups, these groups utilize a 12-step process of recovery and are run by persons who have substance abuse problems themselves (Alcoholics Anonymous World Services, 1981). In contrast, dual recovery groups have two important differences from AA and NA groups: (1) acceptance of the importance of psychiatric medications and (2) a high tolerance of psychiatric symptomatology (Magura et al., 2003).

Sometimes circumstances arise that require a variation of the traditional self-help model. For example, in certain inpatient settings or community-based agencies where regulations or insurance requirements necessitated staff involvement, consumer-run dual recovery groups have been developed that include the presence of professional staff at meetings or in proximity. Another variation of the dual recovery support group has been used in situations where acute symptoms interfered with group leadership. In this version, staff members who have received training and information from an experienced dual recovery group member provide interim leadership (Caldwell & White, 1991).

Individualized Self-help Strategies

Some self-directed programs can be completed individually, without any interaction with others, using workbooks, audiotapes, or videotapes. Mary Ellen Copeland's Wellness and Recovery Action Plan (WRAP) is probably the best known example of this type of self-help

approach (Copeland Center for Wellness and Recovery, n.d.; http://www.copelandcenter
.com/whatiswrap.html):

> *WRAP is a self-management and recovery system developed by a group of people who*
> *had mental health difficulties and who were struggling to incorporate wellness tools*
> *and strategies into their lives. WRAP is designed to:*
>
> - *Decrease and prevent intrusive or troubling feelings and behaviors*
> - *Increase personal empowerment*
> - *Improve quality of life*
> - *Assist people in achieving their own life goals and dreams*

The WRAP process begins with the development of a daily plan of activities that
promote wellness. Identification of circumstances that trigger symptoms, being aware
of early warning signs of symptoms, and developing a plan to deal with personal
crises are also essential parts of WRAP. While WRAP can be a completely self-directed
process, individuals can choose to have family members, friends, and professionals
assist them (Copeland, 1997). Copeland has also proposed that combining WRAP
and peer support groups is a very effective way to promote recovery (Copeland &
Mead, 2004).

Self-advocacy: Another Form of Self-help

When an individual or group stands up to defend personal or civil rights, including
the right to receive high-quality treatment and rehabilitation services, it is a form of
self-advocacy. The history of self-advocacy among people with severe mental illness
dates back to the formation of the Alleged Lunatic's Friend Society in mid-19th-
century England, the first known organization to protest deplorable conditions in
psychiatric institutions. Two decades later in the United States, a woman named
Elizabeth Packard established the Anti-Insane Asylum Society to protest her forced
commitment (Chamberlin, 1990; Frese & Davis, 1997; Van Tosh, Ralph, & Campbell,
2000).

At the beginning of the 20th century, Clifford Beers was hospitalized for mental
illness treatment and was so dissatisfied with his care that he became a lifelong
advocate for mental health system reform. In 1909, he helped to establish the National
Committee on Mental Hygiene. Known today as Mental Health America (previously
known as the National Mental Health Association), it is still one of the leading
advocacy organizations in the United States (Beers, 1923; Schmidt, 2005; Van Tosh
et al., 2000).

The civil rights movements of the 1960s helped encourage the concepts of consumerism and empowerment for persons diagnosed with a mental illness. Many deinstitutionalized people released after long hospital stays found that the services offered in
outpatient settings were not meeting their needs. Problems such as over-medication,

stigmatizing attitudes of mental health professionals, diagnoses that became negative labels, and limited treatment options effectively undermined efforts to adjust to the community and lead successful, satisfying lives. Increasing numbers of ex-patients began to search for alternatives; by the early 1970s the **ex-patient movement**, also referred to as the **survivor movement**, had begun (Rogers, 1996). Some of the names of these early groups—the Mental Patients' Liberation Front, the Alliance for the Liberation of Mental Patients, and the Network against Psychiatric Assault (Chamberlin, 1984)—provide a clear sense of members' attitudes toward the mental health system and their desire to regain control over their lives.

In contrast to the ex-patient groups adamantly opposed to existing mental health systems, some self-help and self-advocacy organizations developed with support from mental health professionals and administrators. Some peer-run initiatives operated groups in conjunction with traditional mental health services sharing space, resources, and referrals. Still, a segment of the ex-patient movement continued to maintain that separation from the mental health system was essential. The late Judi Chamberlin, an activist for more than 40 years, stated: "Many of us in the ex-patient movement believe that it is only outside the mental health system that self-help and mutual support can flourish" (1984, p. 56).

In her book, *On Our Own*, Chamberlin (1988) describes her personal experiences as a psychiatric inpatient and her involvement in some of these early self-advocacy initiatives. She describes "consciousness-raising" groups, not unlike those inspired by the women's movement, helping people labeled as mentally ill to recognize the negative effects the mental health system had on their self-image. Such groups helped ex-patients rebuild their self-esteem and inspired action such as the development and publication of a patients' rights handbook. These efforts encouraged the development of peer-run drop-in centers, communal residences, and projects focused on publicizing the deplorable conditions in mental institutions.

Today, many mutual support/self-help initiatives and self-advocacy organizations, which started independently, have formed close alliances with one another. With increased funding and partnerships, the ex-patient movement has involved itself in the provision of a wide array of services and supports (Chamberlin, 1990; Chamberlin, Rogers, & Ellison, 1996). These initiatives often combine mutual support activities and peer-provided services with advocacy activities. Individuals are strengthening their own personal support systems, assisting their peers, and also helping to improve mental health systems by advocating for additional resources, rehabilitation and recovery-oriented services, and the protection of civil rights. Recent advocacy issues have included opposition to involuntary treatment and outpatient commitment, eliminating restraints and seclusion in psychiatric hospitals, and ending housing and employment discrimination. The motto "nothing about us, without us" is often used by members of the consumer/survivor movement to emphasize the importance of consumer involvement with decision making (i.e., empowerment) (Campbell, 2005).

Mental Health Mutual Support Groups

The number of mental health mutual support groups, commonly called "peer support groups" or programs, has been steadily increasing. A 2009 report on findings from studies in 2005 and 2008 by the Substance Abuse and Mental Health Services Administration (SAMHSA) indicated that, on average, 2.4 million US adults aged 18 or older with mental health issues are assisted by self-help groups each year. Two-thirds of these individuals also received traditional mental health services. A previous survey identified 3315 mutual support groups, 3019 self-help organizations, and 1133 consumer-operated services operating in the United States (Goldstrom et al., 2006). Interestingly, the authors note that there were only 4546 traditional mental health service provider organizations in the United States at that time. The peer groups and organizations served well over one and a half million people in 2002.

Some people involved with self-help have difficulty accessing or interacting with a traditional face-to-face group. This may occur for a number of reasons, including lack of transportation, residency in a rural area with few resources, or because a person is uncomfortable sharing his or her experiences in a face-to-face situation. Fortunately, a number of options are available for these individuals. Some peer support programs offer assistance via the telephone. This service is sometimes referred to as **warm lines**—in contrast to "hotlines," which are used to respond to crisis situations (Solomon, 2004). A warm line directory is available on the Internet (http://www.warmline.org/). A number of Internet online support groups have also been established in recent years. Many Internet support groups are specific to symptoms or diagnoses (e.g., depression, bipolar disorder, etc.); for example, the Depression and Bipolar Support Alliance (DBSA) offers online peer support. Some groups meet each week using a live chat format, which can be reached at http://www.dbsalliance.org/. With the growing trend toward communication online via e-mail, Skype, ooVoo, chat rooms, bulletin boards, and instant messaging, it should not be surprising that some individuals prefer the convenience and anonymity of Internet support groups (Perron, 2002; Solomon, 2004). Interestingly, in a controlled clinical trial of Internet use involving 300 persons with schizophrenia or bipolar disorder, Internet users, who generally reported positive experiences on the Internet, also reported higher levels of stress than those individuals randomized into a no-Internet-use condition (Kaplan, Salzer, Solomon, Brusilovskiy, & Cousounis, 2011).

Numerous organizations throughout the United States provide information, referrals, and easy access to existing groups that offer support to people with a variety of psychiatric and medical disorders as well as other problems and issues. For example, the New Jersey Self-help Clearinghouse is publishing the 26th Edition of their Self-help Support Group Directory (http://www.njgroups.org). The National Mental Health Consumers' Self-help Clearinghouse is a noteworthy organization that provides up-to-date information and resources relevant to peer support and advocacy initiatives, such as technical assistance to help people organize coalitions and establish self-help groups and other peer-run programs (http://www.mhselfhelp.org/).

Beyond Self-help: The Emergence of Peer-provided Services

Self-help groups are just one way that persons with severe mental illnesses help others who are coping with similar challenges. Within the traditional mental health delivery system, there are services provided by individuals who identify themselves as having a mental illness who are specifically employed to help other consumers (Swarbrick et al., 2010; Solomon, 2004; Solomon & Draine, 2001). Almost from its inception, the field of substance abuse counseling recognized the benefits of utilizing individuals recovering from alcoholism and other substance abuse disorders as regular service providers (Moxley & Mowbray, 1997). An obvious benefit of this strategy is the ability of an individual who is in recovery—a peer—to truly empathize with the experiences of the service recipient. Providers who share the experience of coping with a similar illness or disability may also have an advantage over other professional providers in the length of time it takes to establish trusting relationships with service recipients. Possibly because of the stigma attached to mental illness, the field of mental health has been much slower to recognize these benefits. It is interesting to note that in some substance abuse treatment settings counselors who are in recovery have a higher status than those who have not struggled with an addiction. By contrast, in the mental health field, peer providers have frequently been given job titles such as "peer advocate" that indicate their consumer status and are often relegated to lower-level paraprofessional or counselor aide roles. A recent review of the peer-provided services literature determined that peer services have great potential for promoting system changes toward a recovery philosophy but face many challenges in areas like training and supervision (Repper & Carter, 2011).

History of the Consumer/Peer Provider Movement

The ex-patient's movement has continued to provide people with support and service options separate from the professionally driven mental health system. Even as self-help groups flourished, alternative programs such as drop-in centers and peer-run residential programs were difficult to start up and maintain without reliable funding sources. In many places, "mental health departments were highly skeptical of the ability of ex-patients to run their own projects" (Chamberlin, 1990, p. 326). In states whose mental health departments became interested in funding these services, state funding became a controversial issue for many ex-patient groups. Some people objected in principle to establishing relationships with traditional funding sources because of the associated accountability and the possibility of being co-opted by the state system. Another concern was the creation of salaried staff positions in peer-run organizations where previously members had all shared the same status as peer volunteers. By the early 1980s, however, people involved in the ex-patient movement began to establish greater credibility as presenters at national conferences, articulate participants in legislative hearings, and as members of key boards and committees throughout the United States. Gradually, funding opportunities such as Community

Support Program grants from the National Institute of Mental Health (NIMH) and later from the Center for Mental Health Services (CMHS) for demonstration projects as well as funding from state mental health or vocational rehabilitation departments became available. Thirty years later, some states are just beginning to engage in these peer-operated initiatives.

Today, several prominent consumer-run organizations in the United States are supported by CMHS funding—for example, the National Empowerment Center (http://www .Power2u.org). Their mission is to spread a message of recovery, empowerment, hope, and healing to persons with psychiatric disabilities, their friends and family members, professionals, and the general public.

These organizations and others are involved in advocacy efforts locally and nationally, providing consumers with information and access to peer support and peer support initiatives. They also organize the annual Alternatives Conference, which has been bringing together consumers from around the United States since 1985. The Alternatives Conference provides people involved in a variety of peer support initiatives a chance to network and share innovative ideas.

Categories of Peer-delivered Services

Three distinct categories of peer-delivered services were identified by Solomon (2004):

1. Peer-run or -operated services (also referred to in the literature as consumer-run, consumer-operated, or consumer-delivered services)
2. Peer partnerships
3. Peer employees

More recently, Swarbrick and her colleagues (2010) refined peer employees by differentiating between peer employees in peer-designated roles and those in traditional professional roles. We will look closely at each of these categories in the following subsections, as well as some illustrative examples of peer-delivered service programs. Note that the types of PsyR services and supports that these programs provide are quite varied. Persons who have severe mental illnesses are involved in the implementation of the full range of PsyR models described in this textbook, including employment services, residential programs, case management, and assertive community treatment.

Peer-operated Services

A **peer-operated** service initiative is developed, controlled, and operated by individuals who identify themselves as having a diagnosis of a mental illness. Nonconsumers may also be employed to contribute to service delivery and/or the administration of the program, but a majority of consumers clearly direct the entire service delivery process, including planning, policy development, direct service provision, and program evaluation. Often, their boards of directors consist of 51 to 100 percent of people in recovery themselves. These programs, which often address the basic social and emotional needs of consumers (e.g., housing, employment, etc.), are considered both a complement and an alternative to traditional mental health services (Chamberlin, 1990; Davidson et al., 1999; Petr, Holtquist, & Martin, 2000; Salzer & Shear, 2002; Solomon, 2004; Solomon & Draine, 2001; Van Tosh & del Vecchio, 2000; Zinman, Harp, & Budd, 1987). Peer-operated initiatives come in all shapes and sizes. There are relatively small programs such as self-help centers, as well as large peer-operated agencies that run a variety of programs such as Collaborative Support Programs of New Jersey (CSP-NJ), described in Box 13.1. Such services might include self-help centers, clubhouses, supported employment, housing or education programs, and crisis programs such as warm lines.

BOX 13.1   A PEER-OPERATED AGENCY: COLLABORATIVE SUPPORT PROGRAMS OF NEW JERSEY

Collaborative Support Programs of New Jersey (CSP-NJ) is a good example of the kinds of peer-delivered supports and services that PsyR agencies can offer. In terms of Solomon's categories of peer-provided services, CSP-NJ would be considered to be a peer-operated agency. CSP-NJ started as a grassroots agency in 1985 with a budget of $65,000 and by 2012 was operating with a budget of over $12 million. The agency is directed and managed by a board of directors, two-thirds of whom are peers, and a large staff, of whom over 52 percent are past or current recipients of mental health services.

The development and provision of supported housing are two of CSP-NJ's key missions. Staff members assist individuals in obtaining decent, safe, and affordable housing in apartments and homes. They provide supports to the residents of this housing on an as-needed basis, including a strong focus on financial service, encouraging financial literacy, and economic self-sufficiency. The agency has a subsidiary organization, Community Enterprise Corporation, which helps with the physical maintenance of the homes.

Another key CSP-NJ activity is the development and support of peer-operated self-help centers. CSP-NJ has developed 26 self-help centers throughout the state. CSP-NJ provides a number of technical assistance services to its own self-help centers. The Institute for Wellness and Recovery Initiatives provides training, education, and technical assistance to mental health providers, agencies, and peers nationwide, including the well-attended annual Wellness Conference. The Institute developed the eight-dimensional model of wellness that is now endorsed by SAMHSA. Another innovative project, the Recovery Network, provided peer facilitators at the state psychiatric hospitals to conduct weekly wellness and recovery groups (Swarbrick & Brice, 2006). The Institute has focused on promoting physical health and wellness through the creation of a peer wellness coach training developed through collaboration between CSPNJ and Rutgers-SHRP (Swarbrick, Murphy, Zechner, Spagnolo, & Gill, 2011). Additionally, the Institute operates a supported employment program and partnered with Rutgers Integrated Employment Institute to develop the peer employment support model (Swarbrick, Bates, & Roberts, 2010) CSP-NJ encourages and supports the professional development of all of its staff members, and has encouraged many consumers to prepare for the Certified Psychiatric Rehabilitation Practitioner (CPRP) examination (see Chapter 1 for details on this credential) and to pursue psychiatric rehabilitation education at all academic levels.

Peer Partnerships

In a **peer partnership** program, peers collaborate with non-peer providers to operate a program that emphasizes peer-delivered services. In a peer partnership, the direct services providers are people who identify themselves as peers, and peers also have substantial input into the operation of the program, but the program is closely affiliated with a traditional (i.e., non-peer) human service agency that provides administrative support. For example, a large comprehensive PsyR provider offering a full range of services and supports including case management, vocational, and residential services may operate a peer-provided supported education program. The director of the peer-provided program and the service providers are individuals who identify themselves as peers, but the fiscal management of the program and some of the administrative responsibilities are handled by the agency.

PsyR providers and mental health administrators refer people to peer support services and collaborate with peers in developing such services for two important reasons: (1) They recognize that supports outside the mental health system are essential to the recovery process, and (2) they see it as a cost-effective way to provide people with additional supports, particularly during an era of dwindling mental health dollars (Kaufman, Freund, & Wilson, 1989).

According to Joseph A. Rogers (1996), executive director of the National Mental Health Consumers' Self-Help Clearinghouse, "Consumer-run services are perfectly positioned to fill the service gap .... If consumers are educated and supported in their efforts to expand existing consumer-run projects, launch new ones, and test new models" (p. 22). However, there is a danger in promoting peer-delivered services primarily for cost-cutting purposes. If consumers are providing the same types of services as other professionals, they should receive comparable compensation for their efforts (Lundin, 2005; Solomon, 2004).

An innovative peer partnership program of the US Veterans Administration in Connecticut, Vet-to-Vet, is an excellent example of a peer–professional partnership (Resnick, Armstrong, Sperrazza, Harkness, & Rosenheck, 2004; Resnick & Rosenheck, 2008). The Vet-to-Vet model allows peer providers (in this case, veterans) to remain outside the formal mental health system while receiving supervision and guidance from professionals. To accomplish this, the peer partners are paid by a non-profit agency under contract with the VA.

Another example is the Howie the Harp Center, which is a peer-operated program to train peer providers of services that operates within a large comprehensive non-profit known as Community Access, which provides a wide range of services (Zinman, 1995).

In both peer-operated programs and peer partnerships, the peers who are delivering supports and services may be either paid employees or volunteers. Often, programs utilize both types of resources—for example, a large self-help center may hire several individuals in part-time or full-time positions to take responsibility for the overall operation of the center. Other functions, such as facilitating social events or providing outreach to local mental health agencies, may be carried out by volunteers.

Peer Employees

Growing numbers of PsyR and mental health agencies purposefully employ individuals who have experienced a severe and persistent mental illness (Swarbrick et al., 2010; Davidson et al., 1999; Moxley & Mowbray, 1997; Salzer et al., 2002; Solomon, 2004). Some of these individuals act as service providers in peer-operated initiatives and peer partnerships. They are also hired to provide a wide range of psychiatric rehabilitation and mental health services in the traditional mental health delivery system. There are a number of reasons why this is a positive trend:

- Inclusion of consumers as mental health workers can increase the sensitivity of programs and services about recipients.
- Peers can serve as effective role models for service recipients.
- The inclusion of peers is an expression of affirmative action and is consistent with contemporary civil and disability rights policies (Mowbray et al., 1996, p. 48).

Designated Peer Providers

Some agencies have designated peer employee positions that are meant to be an adjunct to professionally provided services. For example, an assertive community treatment team that consists primarily of professionals with degrees and credentials may include peer employees entitled "peer advocates." Positions that are specifically developed for peer providers have been given a number of job titles, including peer counselor, peer specialist, and consumer case manager (Solomon, 2004), and more recently, peer whole health coach or peer wellness coach (Swarbrick et al., 2011). For these employees, their "peer" status and their willingness to disclose it to others is an important requirement or criterion for obtaining their position. In many cases, these designated peer providers do not hold academic credentials on par with their non-peer colleagues. This raises interesting questions about the ability for these individuals to advance in their careers or to leave their peer-related positions.

Peers in Traditional Professional Roles

There are some individuals who identify themselves as having a mental illness working in traditional roles on staff teams. Rehabilitation counselors, social workers, nurses, psychologists, psychiatrists, and other credentialed PsyR and mental health service providers may also be consumers of mental health services, though most do not formally disclose this experience. Occasionally, they do. Noteworthy examples include the psychiatrist Kay Redfield Jamison and dialectical behavior therapy specialist Marsha Linehan.

WHY SHOULD PEER-OPERATED PROGRAMS WORK AT ALL?

The emergence of self-help and peer-provided services has spurred interest in their benefits and limitations and the source of their effectiveness. PsyR researchers (e.g., Salzer et al., 2002; Solomon, 2004) have identified a number of theories that may account for the unique benefits of peer support, including:

- **Social learning theory** (Bandura, 1977), which emphasizes the importance of modeling of desirable actions
- **Social comparison theory** (Festinger, 1954), which says that people like to develop relationships with those who have had similar experiences
- **Experiential knowledge** (Borkman, 1999), which states that learning from personal experience adds a level of understanding beyond what can be gained from observation and research
- **Helper therapy principle** (Reissman, 1965; Skovholt, 1974), which discusses the benefits to the helper attained through helping others
- **Social support theory** (Sarason, Levine, Basham, & Sarason, 1983), which focuses on the various types of supports that people rely on, including emotional, instrumental, and informational, and companionship and validation.

Research on the Effectiveness of Self-help and Peer-delivered Services

Research examining the feasibility and outcomes of peer support initiatives has increased as the movement has grown. More than 15 years ago, Chamberlin and colleagues (1996) reviewed 64 programs that were administratively operated by consumers. They found a wide array of services being provided, including social/recreational activities, individual and system level advocacy, assistance with housing and employment, transportation, and assistance with activities of daily living. This study also found that the majority of people who utilized these programs were very involved, spending an average of 15.3 hours a week at the program (Chamberlin et al., 1996). The programs studied also received very positive ratings on a variety of program satisfaction measures. Most of the service recipients surveyed also utilized some type of professional mental health service in addition to utilizing peer-delivered services.

A 2006 study by Goldstrom, Campbell, Rogers, and colleagues assessed the utilization of self-help groups by persons with severe mental illness. Based on a 2002 national survey, they estimated that 1,600,000 persons attended 3315 mutual support groups, 3019 self-help organizations, and 1133 consumer-operated organizations. The authors found that self-help and collaboration had taken root in the mental health delivery system, leading to a new conception of services that includes persons with the lived experience of severe mental illness as full participants in their treatment and rehabilitation as well as service providers.

Much of the initial research in this area focused on two specific self-help models: Recovery International and GROW (e.g., Davidson et al., 1999; Rappaport et al., 1985; Van Tosh et al., 2000). These early studies suggested that consumers with longer involvement in mutual support groups have lower levels of symptomatology (Davidson et al., 1999; Finn & Bishop, 2001; Galanter, 1988; Luke, 1989). Studies also found that the duration of hospital stays was reduced for active GROW members (Davidson et al., 1999; Finn & Bishop, 2001; Kennedy, 1989; Rappaport, 1993; Rappaport et al., 1985). In addition, self-help may improve both daily functioning and a person's ability to manage his or her illness (Powell, Yeaton, Hill, & Silk, 2001). A study of Recovery International (Pickett, Phillips, & Kraus, 2011) found strong effects of peer-provided services, including improved symptoms management, increased hopefulness and self-esteem, and enhanced mental health recovery.

Not surprisingly, long-term participants in self-help groups have larger social networks and are more likely to pursue educational and employment opportunities (Carpinello, Knight, & Janis, 1991; Davidson et al., 1999). GROW members showed improvements in psychological well-being such as increased autonomy and personal growth (Finn & Bishop, 2001). Both the length and level of involvement with a self-help group were positively correlated with improved outcomes. These findings were corroborated by Swarbrick (2005, 2009) in a state-wide study of consumer-operated self-help centers, which found higher levels of satisfaction and empowerment were positively related to greater involvement of the center's members.

A multiyear study of a Veteran's Administration Vet-to-Vet peer partnership program (Resnik & Rosenheck, 2008) compared veterans who received peer support with veterans who did not. Veterans with peer support exhibited higher levels of empowerment and self-confidence, higher levels of functioning, and lower levels of alcohol use. In general, the authors believe that participating in the Vet-to-Vet program increased the individual's sense of personal well-being.

Peer-provided Services: Feasibility and Perceived Benefits

Numerous studies have provided evidence that peer-provided services are feasible and enhance the provision of supports and services (Davidson et al., 1999; Schmidt, 2005; Solomon & Draine, 2001; Van Tosh & Del Vecchio, 2000). In the late 1980s and early 1990s, a number of descriptive studies were conducted that explored the feasibility of employing peers as service providers and reported on some of the potential benefits of offering peer-provided services (Kaufman, Ward-Colasante, & Farmer, 1993; Lyons, Cook, Ruth, Karver, & Slagg, 1996; Mowbray, Chamberlain, Jennings, & Reed, 1988; Mowbray & Tan, 1993; Mowbray et al., 1996; Segal et al., 1993; Sherman & Porter, 1991; Van Tosh & Del Vecchio, 2000). These studies suggested that consumers provide services differently than non-consumers while performing their jobs competently (Davidson et al., 1999). Schmidt

(2005) concluded that the early feasibility studies also suggested that consumer and nonconsumer providers can work well together.

In addition to the lived experience of severe mental illness, peer providers bring unique strengths to their work. Among these are life experience, including "street survival" skills, the development of successful coping techniques, and familiarity with successful resource acquisition strategies (Paulson, 1991; Van Tosh, Finkle, Hartman, Lewis, Plumlee, & Susko, 1993). Peer specialists can also help with communication—for example, as members of an intensive case management team they developed a distinct liaison role, representing the client's perspective in discussions with case managers about clients' problems and needs (Felton et al., 1995). Consumer providers may be especially effective in programs that emphasize mobile outreach (e.g., ACT) and in providing services directly to consumers in the community (Lyons et al., 1996). Peer providers are frequently perceived as more credible on medication adherence issues, particularly when they share their own experiences. Along the same lines, they can be particularly helpful in helping consumers recognize signs or symptoms that precede acute episodes of mental illness (Paulson, 1991). As advocates, they are able to provide important information about rights and alternative treatment approaches, providing consumers with a wider array of options than is usually offered by nonconsumer providers (Mowbray & Moxley, 1997a). Other reports found the peer providers are more likely to appreciate the strengths of consumers, to understand and respond to consumers' needs, and to promote independence (Davidson et al., 1999; Mowbray & Moxley, 1997a).

Perhaps the best reason for including peer providers in PsyR service provision is their ability to serve as role models. Their presence powerfully conveys the message that people with severe mental illnesses can succeed in competitive employment. They display competence and demonstrate regaining control over their lives to consumers who may have lost hope of ever moving beyond the "mental patient" role (Mowbray, 1997a; Mowbray et al., 1996; Nikkel, Smith, & Edwards, 1992). Peer providers also deliver a concrete message about empowerment:

> *Through the symbol and the reality of consumers who provide services, empowerment is actualized. Power is given (away) to those with a disability label, power to take control over their own outcomes and over systems' operations. (Mowbray, 1997a, p. 47)*

The Issue of Disclosure

Should an individual working in a PsyR professional role disclose to other staff or supervisors that he or she is also a recipient of mental health services? While many peer providers are hired, in part, because of their experiences as mental health service recipients, others are hired based solely on past work or educational experiences. This latter group may struggle with the issue of whether or not to disclose their experiences as a person living with a psychiatric disability. Past experiences with stigmatizing attitudes of mental health professionals leave some peer providers determined to avoid self-disclosure at all costs. Some are concerned that their consumer or peer status might diminish their reputation, given the stigma that persists among mental health professionals (Kottsieper, 2010). However, many peer providers report that this is a difficult stance to maintain. What if they should come in contact with a consumer who is familiar with their status as a service recipient? In contrast, Patricia Deegan and others raise the issue that one may diminish his or her efficacy by not disclosing relevant personal experiences to consumers (Deegan & Smoyak, 1996). As mentioned earlier, disclosing one's status as a service recipient also provides an important opportunity to act as a positive role model for both consumers and staff (Roberts et al., 1995).

The choice also involves issues such as who to disclose to, what to disclose, reasons why it is (or is not) important or useful to disclose, when is an appropriate time to disclose, and how to convey what one chooses to share. The values and principles of PsyR may be more generally in line with a policy of disclosure if done for the right reasons, whereas the more traditional therapy disciplines tend to be more conservative regarding this matter (Kottsieper, 2010). Another important consideration is that it is necessary to disclose a disability in order to access the supports and protection of the Americans with Disabilities Act (Fisher, 1994b). Each peer provider must weigh his or her unique circumstances when grappling with the complicated issue of disclosure. However, in all cases, it is essential that the choices be left to the peer provider; disclosure should never be required (Roberts et al., 1995). For more on the issue of disclosure in the workplace, see Chapter 10.

Are Peer Providers as Effective as Other Providers?

Studies have confirmed that peer-delivered services are often as effective as services delivered by nonconsumers and may in some cases be more effective (Davidson et al., 1999; Salzer et al., 2002; Schmidt, Gill, Pratt, & Solomon, 2008; Schmidt, 2005; Solomon, 2004; Solomon & Draine, 2001). For example, peer providers may be more effective in assertively engaging peers (Roe et al., 2007) and serving as effective role models (Curtis, 1999). Studies often find that programs that include peer providers produce outcomes similar to other programs. Solomon and Draine (1995) compared a peer partnership case management program with a traditional non-peer case management program. After two years, both programs were associated with improvements in the lives of the consumers served, but there were no significant differences between programs in terms of symptoms, social adjustment, and quality of life. This study was later replicated in a peer-operated agency with two assertive community treatment teams, one of which employed peer providers. Again, a two-year comparison found no significant differences in clinical or social outcomes or in retention rates (Herinckx, Kinney, Clarke, & Paulson, 1997; Paulson et al., 1999; Solomon & Draine, 2001). Chinman, Rosenheck, Lam, and Davidson (2000) compared case management teams serving homeless clients that used peer providers with those that employed nonconsumer staff and found them to be equally effective. Taken as a group, these studies suggest that peer providers can be as helpful to consumers as non-peer staff.

Between 1998 and 2006, a major, multisite study called the Consumer-Operated Service Program (COSP) Research Initiative was funded by SAMHSA's Center for Mental Health Services. The goal of the COSP study was to compare the utilization of peer-operated services as an adjunct to traditional mental health services with the utilization of traditional mental health services alone. Eight peer-operated programs participated in the study, and consumers were involved with every aspect of the research project including its design. The service recipient outcomes examined included housing, employment, social inclusion, well-being, and empowerment (Campbell, 2002).

One important benefit of conducting the COSP study was the analysis of common ingredients utilized by various types of consumer-operated programs. The sites in the COSP study included drop-in centers, peer mentoring programs, and education/advocacy programs. Despite the wide variety of program models, six domains of common ingredients were identified:

- **Program structure**, emphasizing consumer control, participant responsiveness, and the capacity to link service recipients to other services
- An **environment** that is safe, accessible, informal, and provides reasonable accommodations
- A **belief system** emphasizing the benefits of mutual support, empowerment, choice, recovery, respect for diversity, and spiritual growth
- Formal and informal **peer support strategies**, including opportunities to share personal stories and raise consciousness as well as provide crisis prevention, peer mentoring, and teaching
- **Education** focusing on self-management and problem solving, skills practice, and job readiness
- **Advocacy** (both self-advocacy and peer advocacy)

The identification of common ingredients led to the development of a fidelity instrument, the COSP Fidelity Assessment Common Ingredients Tool, or FACIT (Johnsen, Teague, McDonel, & Herr, 2005).

Consumer-operated Services as an Evidence-based Practice

In 2011, SAMHSA recognized consumer-operated services as an evidence-based practice. Implementation materials, PowerPoint presentations, and a video are available from the SAMHSA Web site: http://store.samhsa.gov/product/Consumer-Operated-Services-Evidence-Based-Practices-EBP-KIT/SMA11-4633CD-DVD.

The SAMHSA report on the evidence for consumer-operated services cites five randomized controlled trials covering treatment outcomes, wellness outcomes, and service costs (Campbell et al., 2006; Dumont & Jones, 2002; Gordon, Edmundson, Bedell, & Goldstein, 1979; Kaufmann, Schulberg, & Schooler, 1994; Kaufmann, 1995). The Center for Evidence-based Medicine (http://www.cebm.net) provides a 1 to 5 scale (1 being the highest) for assessing the quality of the evidence provided by research studies based on their design. Using this method of grading the evidence, the SAMHSA report states that one of these studies achieved an evidence level of 1b, just below the highest level of 1a. The other studies received level 2 designations, quasi-experimental studies. Results from these five studies suggest the following outcomes for consumer-operated services:

1. Fewer instances of hospitalization
2. Lower rates of hospital utilization (i.e., fewer days in the hospital)
3. Reduced number of contacts with the rest of the mental health system
4. Better employment outcomes
5. Lower costs to the mental health system
6. Increased well-being and empowerment of service participants

Benefits to Peer Providers and Mental Health Systems

Peer support appears to provide very positive benefits to the peer providers as well as those receiving the services. Peer providers report positive gains from their work on many levels (e.g., Salzer & Shear, 2002; Basto et al., 2000; Mowbray et al., 1998). Several studies have found increases in self-esteem, confidence, and empowerment (Ratzlaff, McDiarmid, Marty, & Rapp, 2006; Bracke, Christianens, & Verhaeghe, 2008; Salzer & Shear, 2002). Interestingly, while supporting the importance of peer services for recovery, the 2008 Bracke et al. study of 628 participants from 51 vocational and rehabilitation centers in Flanders determined that "the net beneficial effects of receiving support from peers are overestimated" (p. 436), and that based on the measures they used, being a peer provider is more beneficial than receiving peer-provided services.

Many of these studies rely on interviews with peer providers (Solomon, 2004). Sherman and Porter (1991) found that peer providers had fewer hospitalizations after becoming providers. Peer providers have also reported a number of quality-of-life improvements (Armstrong, Korba, & Emard, 1995; Mowbray, Moxley, & Collins, 1998). Salzer and Shear (2002) conducted in-depth interviews with 14 peer providers and reported improved self-esteem, valuable gains in knowledge and skill development, and help in facilitating their own recovery. Increased independence and enhancement of social support networks are also benefits experienced by peer providers (Mowbray, 1997). To better understand the potential benefits of being a peer provider, consider the following story:

> *Laura, a 38-year-old woman who currently works as a peer advocate on an ACT team, was diagnosed with bipolar disorder when she was 24. A college graduate with a degree in English, Laura hoped for a career in publishing. She had some*

success as an assistant editor when she was in her early twenties, but her illness interrupted her career, and by the time she was 30 she wondered if she could even hold a job. After experiencing success as a co-facilitator of a self-help group, Laura decided to apply for the ACT team position. After two years working as a peer provider, she says, "It was one of the best decisions I ever made. For many years my illness got in the way of my career. I felt sorry for myself and thought I was a failure. Now I see that my illness has helped me to become a more compassionate person who can make a difference in other people's lives. My job has done wonders for my self-esteem. I feel like every time I help someone I am taking a step forward in my own recovery."

Peer-provided services can also have a positive effect on the quality and quantity of mental health services. There is evidence that utilization of peer providers has a positive impact on staff attitudes, helping staff to be more sensitive to the experiences and needs of consumers. The inclusion of peer providers is also recognized as a viable strategy for assisting services in adopting a recovery perspective (Gates & Akabas, 2007). Working side-by-side with consumers forces nonconsumer staff to examine their own attitudes and prejudices. The experience enables service providers to get to know individuals with the lived experience of severe mental illness as colleagues who have strengths, skills, and abilities (Dixon, Krauss, & Lehman, 1994; Doherty, Craig, Attafua, Boocock, & Jamieson-Craig, 2004; Mowbray, 1997; Mowbray et al., 1996; Solomon, 2004). This allows staff members to see that the consumers they serve are "people first," rather than solely a manifestation of a psychiatric diagnosis. Mowbray and Moxley (1997a) also suggest that the presence of peer employees helps nonconsumer staff gain a clearer understanding of the recovery process.

Mental health systems that include peer-delivered services increase their ability to provide an expanded array of services. The inclusion of self-help and peer-provided services within a mental health system expands the number of service and support providers available and increases the capacity of the system (Solomon, 2004). In addition, peer providers can reach a segment of the population that is not easily reached by traditional providers. Individuals who have had negative experiences with professional mental health services are more likely to be engaged by a peer-operated program than by traditional services. As mentioned earlier, peer providers are more effective at engaging the high-risk population of individuals who are resistant to accepting services, including persons who are homeless, acutely symptomatic, and abusing substances (Craig et al., 2004).

Challenges for Peer Providers

In their efforts to assist consumers, it is important for peer providers to recognize and utilize their unique strengths. At the same time, they need to be aware of some potential limitations and challenges inherent in their dual role as a consumer provider. One of these limitations is the tendency of some peer providers to generalize their own experiences to the life situations of the individuals they are supporting (Nikkel et al., 1992). They may "fail to fully appreciate the diversity of experiences of persons with major mental illnesses and the individuality of a person's response" (Paulson, 1991, p. 75). For example, a peer provider may make the mistake of thinking that his experience coping with symptoms of depression is typical, whereas it is likely that each person he is helping experiences symptoms somewhat differently. In addition, effective strategies used to relieve symptoms may differ from person to person.

Because mental illnesses are in part stress-related, many peer providers and their employers have concerns about coping with the high stress associated with PsyR service provision. Will they be prone to burn out sooner than other providers? Such concerns may impact peer providers, have a negative impact on job performance, and prevent consumers from considering the peer provider role. Nevertheless, research suggests that the career commitment of peer providers is stronger and job retention longer than that of non-peer staff (Basto, Pratt, Gill, & Barrett, 2000).

Other challenges involve issues of **dual relationships** (having both a professional and personal relationship with another peer), role conflict, and maintaining confidentiality. Peer providers, particularly those who practice in or near an agency where they are receiving services or have received services in the past, may struggle with boundary issues due to prior relationships they have had with both service providers and service recipients (Carlson, Rapp, & McDiarmid, 2001; Mowbray, 1997; Mowbray et al., 1996). Peer providers may struggle with conflicting roles. In terms of fellow service providers, they should now be relating to them as a colleague rather than as a service recipient. At the same time, individuals who used to be acquaintances or friends may now be those for whom they provide services.

Nonconsumer service providers also often have a difficult time relating to a peer or colleague they once served. In terms of confidentiality, access to case records of individuals with whom a peer provider has had a personal relationship raises ethical concerns. In the case of peer providers working at an agency where they have received services in the past, their colleagues might have access to their records, which should be kept confidential. While many individuals establish comfortable relationships more easily with peer providers than non-peer providers, some are wary of receiving help from a person who may be struggling with his or her own mental illness. These concerns can stem from stigmatizing attitudes, since service recipients can be both victims and perpetuators of stigma, or mistrust of peers once they move into a provider role (Mowbray, 1997). Such reactions can frustrate peer providers in their efforts to provide help and cause them to question their own capabilities.

Relationships with Nonconsumer Providers

For many peer providers, the most formidable challenge is establishing positive relationships with the nonconsumer staff (Waynor & Pratt, 2011; MaCauley, 1993; Mowbray, 1997). PsyR staff members who have internalized PsyR values, goals, and

---

BOX 13.2   CHALLENGES IDENTIFIED BY PEER PROVIDERS

1. Taking on dual roles (e.g., service provider and service recipient), which can be difficult to clarify and can sometimes raise conflict.
2. Role transition can affect relationships with other consumers.
3. Relationship boundary issues with service recipients.
4. Feeling isolated, especially if the person is the sole or "token" peer or consumer provider.
5. Confidentiality issues, such as access to case records for peer providers who received or are still receiving services from the agencies where they work.
6. Dealing with difficult memories and emotions elicited by experiences of service recipients that may remind peer providers of their own experiences.
7. Negotiating reasonable accommodations.
8. Stigmatizing job titles (e.g., consumer case manager).
9. Deciding whether to disclose that you have a mental illness, what to disclose, and whom to disclose to.
10. Relationships with nonconsumer providers, who may be uncomfortable with the presence of peer providers and/or treat them like service recipients.
11. Job discrimination (e.g., some peer providers receive lower salaries than nonconsumer providers).

Source: Adapted from Barrett et al., 2000, p. 86.

---

principles should be pleased to work side-by-side with colleagues recovering from a mental illness. Unfortunately, this is not always the case. Peer providers frequently report discrimination and the experience of being stigmatized by coworkers (Waynor et al., 2011). According to Daniel Fisher (1994b), a psychiatrist who is also an activist and self-described "person in recovery from a psychiatric disability":

> *The mental health profession is one of the most discriminating and stigmatizing towards consumers/survivors. Consumers/survivors who work as providers are labeled and objectified in the same fashion as consumers. Their behavior and principles are filtered through their psychiatric disability. (p. 68)*

At times, expressions of anger or frustration may lead colleagues to assume that a peer provider is experiencing symptoms. In these situations, peer providers report being treated differently from the way other staff are treated when they are in a bad mood or are experiencing the common stresses associated with service delivery. For example, when a peer provider expresses too much emotion, the relationship may suddenly shift from collegial to therapeutic. Staff may question the professionalism of peer providers, for example, by expressing resentment when reasonable accommodations are made for staff members who have psychiatric disabilities (Mowbray, 1997). Peer providers have also reported hearing comments from colleagues that are mean-spirited and hurtful (Waynor et al., 2011; Roberts et al., 1995). Stigma may not be the only reason that peer providers are sometimes treated poorly. Non-peer staff may fear being displaced by peer providers and thus exhibit resentful behaviors (Mowbray, 1997).

Happily, negative treatment of peer providers is not always the case. Many peer providers report very positive, supportive working relationships with nonconsumer colleagues. In fact, many consumers cite that a key reason for choosing a career in PsyR is working in an environment that is more supportive and accommodating than other work settings. Peer providers in one study reported a higher level of support from the community mental health organizations that employed them than did their nonconsumer colleagues (Basto et al., 2000).

Training Peer Providers

As the potential contribution of peer providers has become more widely acknowledged, there has been increased emphasis on training peers to effectively fill these roles. Several training strategies have been developed, including Intentional Peer Support (Mead, 2005), Certified Peer Specialists (Sabin & Daniels, 2003), Consumer as Providers Training Program (Ratzlaff, McDiarmid, Marty, & Rapp, 2006), and Peer Employment Training— also known as META. META's Recovery Education Center is licensed as a secondary education institution and provides peer support training in 12 US states and New Zealand. The training consists of 16 modules presented over 70 hours, as a two-, three-, or five-week course. They state that the learning is highly interactive, competency-based, and uses adult learning principles. (http://recoveryinnovations.org). In 2006, META became Recovery Innovations Inc. in order to extend its services outside Arizona.

In 2009, a wide group of stakeholders met at the Carter Center in Atlanta, Georgia, to form Pillars of Peer Support. The group's primary goal was to support and increase peer-provided services nationwide by encouraging individual states in their system transformation efforts. Pillars of Peer Support Services Summits have been held each year for representatives of states providing peer training and certification in mental health and whole health (Daniels et al., 2012). The Pillars of Peer Support initiative has been supported by the Substance Abuse and Mental Health Services Administration (SAMHSA), the Center for Mental Health Services (CMHS), the National Association of State Mental Health Program Directors (NASMHPD), the Depression and Bipolar Support Alliance (DBSA), Wichita State University Center for Community Support and Research, Appalachian Consulting Group (ACG), the Carter Center, OptumHealth, and the Georgia Mental Health Consumer Network.

Supports and Ongoing Professional Development

Given the issues involved, it is important to consider the provision of supports both inside and outside of the work environment and the education and training needs of peer providers. Skilled supervision is essential for peer providers who are dealing with both typical professional growth and development issues and the unique challenges outlined earlier.

BOX 13.3   RECOVERY INNOVATIONS PEER EMPLOYMENT TRAINING PROGRAM CURRICULUM
Content of the Training

- Part I: Personal Development; Knowing Yourself
  - Recovery
  - The Power of Peer Support
  - Developing Self-esteem and Managing Self-talk
  - Community, Culture, and Environment
  - Meaning and Purpose
  - Emotional Intelligence

- Part II: Turning Point; Preparing Yourself for Work
  - Telling Your Personal Story
  - Employment as a Path to Recovery

- Part III: Skill Development
  - Communication Skills
  - Conflict Resolution
  - Recovery from Trauma and Developing Resilience
  - Recovery from Substance Abuse
  - Being with People in Challenging Situations
  - Peer Support in Action; Partnering with Professionals

---

http://www.recoveryinnovations.org/recovery_concepts.html

Also, supervisors working with peer providers may require specialized training (Griffin-Francell, 1997; Mowbray & Moxley, 1997b). Peer provider support groups outside the agency can be helpful because they allow individuals to openly share feelings and concerns that they may not want to share in the workplace. These groups may also allow peer providers who have not chosen to disclose to obtain support (Fishbein, Manos, & Rotteveel, 1995). Peer providers should also have access to reasonable accommodations in the workplace, as required by the Americans with Disabilities Act. Flexible work schedules, environmental modifications to reduce distractions, and training opportunities that are modified to compensate for cognitive deficits are examples of accommodations that might facilitate the productivity of employees who have a disability. Chapters 10 and 11 provide additional information on reasonable accommodations for employees and students.

It is possible that peer providers who move into professional roles, rather than identified peer provider roles, have a number of advantages. They are less likely to be segregated from other staff and do not have to struggle with role-definition issues. They may also encounter less stigma, particularly if their colleagues perceive that their qualifications for the position are similar to their own. To move into these traditional roles, consumers must have access to appropriate training as well as opportunities to obtain academic degrees and required credentials (Brockelman, 2010). The Certified Psychiatric

Rehabilitation Provider (CPRP) credential (discussed in Chapter 1) is an excellent opportunity for peer providers to augment their professional qualifications (Gill, 2010). For example, peer-operated programs in the state of Georgia accord a special status to individuals who have the CPRP. Other peer-operated agencies, such as the Collaborative Support Program of New Jersey (described in Box 13.1), encourage their staff members to obtain the CPRP certification and provide them with resources to do so, such as arranging to have CPRP preparation courses offered onsite.

Without additional education, many peer providers face a "glass ceiling" effect (they can see the more desirable positions, but cannot reach them) and may remain frustrated in peer-designated positions.

Historically, professional degree programs preparing human service practitioners have shown biases against admitting consumers to their programs (Kottsieper, 2010; Paulson, 1991). In some universities, this trend is changing (Barrett et al., 2000; Brockelman, 2010; Gill, Pratt, & Barrett, 1997; Paulson, 1991). Efforts to recruit consumers and integrate them into academic programs with students who are not identified consumers are well-known by the authors, who teach in such programs. Rutgers, the State University of New Jersey offers consumers who want to move into service delivery roles a variety of options, including certificate programs, undergraduate and graduate degree programs (Gill & Barrett, 2009).

It is important to distinguish between integrated professional training programs that are regular academic offerings and those that are designed solely to prepare a consumer provider, such as Recovery Innovations, Kansas' Consumers as Providers, or Howie the Harp Peer Advocacy Center. Whereas the latter programs give consumers an opportunity to enter the helping professions and gain knowledge and skills that are essential for practice, they typically prepare consumers for paraprofessional roles. They also result in peer providers emerging with a different credential than their nonconsumer colleagues, which may promote segregation and discriminatory practices.

While education, training, and supports for peer providers are essential, PsyR agencies also need to create work cultures that reduce segregation and stigma and ensure that peer providers have well-defined and meaningful roles. Some mental health professionals have spent years of practice creating clear boundaries between themselves and the recipients of their services and may now find it difficult to accept peer providers as "full-fledged" team members. Agencies may need to provide team training sessions aimed at changing staff attitudes in order to incorporate peer providers on teams (McCauley, 1993; Waynor & Pratt, 2012). The following text describes an example of a PsyR program that still needs help in this area.

Sara works in a psychiatric day treatment program as a rehabilitation counselor. She possesses educational and experiential qualifications similar to those of her colleagues, but chose to disclose her status as a consumer when applying for the job. Initial reactions to her self-disclosure were positive and she did not experience any overt discrimination. But later, some staff members became uncomfortable around her, particularly when program members were not present. A very unfortunate aspect of the staff culture in this location is that program members are sometimes joked about or imitated during informal staff-only interactions. Sara has noticed people looking at her uncomfortably when this occurs. Sometimes, when she enters a room in which staff were talking and laughing she is met with sudden silence.

CONTROVERSIAL ISSUE
Does the Professionalization of the Peer Provider Role Enhance or Diminish the Potential of the Mental Health System to Become Truly Consumer-directed?

Those peer providers who acquire advanced degrees and professional credentials are in a much better position to move out of designated peer positions and into supervisory and administrative positions that offer them higher status, higher salaries, and more opportunities to make a stronger impact on the mental health service delivery system. These more influential positions allow for opportunities to help transform services and progress to a more consumer-driven and recovery-oriented service system model. Thus, the professionalization of the peer provider work force offers many potential advantages for both individual peer providers and mental health systems.

Another point of view highlights some possible disadvantages in the professionalization of both peer providers and peer-operated service initiatives. Because peer employees are paid by the mainstream mental health system and some obtain degrees and credentials that allow them to move into influential positions in traditional service delivery programs, they may lose the opportunity to bring their unique perspective into the work environment. As the person develops more of a traditional professional identity, he or she may begin to identify less with the consumers served. In addition, service recipients may feel less connected to a peer provider who is viewed as a full-fledged professional than to one who comes across as a true peer and advocate. The sense of shared experience that helps build rapport and trust may be diminished as a peer provider becomes more comfortable with professional jargon and counseling techniques. Some have used the term "co-opted" to describe a phenomenon in which a peer provider enters the world of professional service providers, perhaps begins to adopt the pretensions associated with the profession, and loses touch with the worldview of consumers who are struggling with both psychiatric symptoms and the experience of being treated by a system that emphasizes their illness rather than their personhood. Even programs that are fully consumer-run may struggle with a similar evolution of identity. Davidson and his colleagues (1999) describe the professionalization of consumer-run programs:

> This process involves what have been less formal services, based on such values as flexibility, autonomy, and consumer choice, becoming more structured and more driven by their needs to attract and justify funding. To the degree that such a service comes to resemble a more conventional provider agency, it also begins to lose its unique character and role within a system of care. (p. 180)

It may be that systems need to stay focused on the development of two divergent trends: on the one hand, increased opportunities for individuals diagnosed with severe mental illnesses to move into professional roles and influence the evolution of professionally run programs; on the other hand, the ongoing promotion of alternative peer-run programs that stay true to the principles and values of mutual support.

Other Influential Roles for Peers

In addition to working in a variety of provider roles, peers make other important contributions to the field of PsyR. In recent years, more individuals are being asked to participate in leadership roles such as membership on organization boards of directors or administrative positions in state mental health departments. Peers also participate actively in PsyR professional organizations such as USPRA and its state chapters. Increasingly, peers are also contributing in meaningful ways to program evaluation and research studies. These roles allow individuals to have an impact on practice and policy issues on the agency, state, and national levels. However, this can only occur if peers are afforded true legitimacy. As in their provider roles, it is important that their perspective in these influential positions be acknowledged and that they are not simply functioning as tokens to satisfy agency requirements or to help an organization appear progressive (Swarbrick et al., 2010).

Activists in the ex-patient/consumer/survivor movement have had a meaningful impact on local, state, and national policy issues that relate to the concerns of people identified as mental health consumers. Typically, they achieve their goals by working outside of the mental health system. But to change a system that many people who have severe mental illnesses are dissatisfied with, the consumer perspective needs to be heard inside of the mental health system as well.

In terms of statewide mental health systems, progress is being achieved through the establishment of Offices of Consumer Affairs, which now exist within most state mental health authorities (Van Tosh et al., 2000). These positions were expressly created to insure better consumer input into the service planning process (Swarbrick, 2009).

Progress has been made on the national level as well. In 1995, SAMHSA's Center for Mental Health Services created the Associate Director of Consumer Affairs for the Center for Mental Health Services (CMHS). More recently, in 2011, Paolo del Vecchio—who was the Associate Director for Consumer Affairs at CMHS, Substance Abuse and Mental Health Services Administration (SAMHSA), in the US Department of Human Services— was appointed Acting Director of the CMHS. Other examples of consumer involvement on the national level included the appointment of activist Daniel Fisher to the President's New Freedom Commission on Mental Health, which issued its final report, *Achieving the Promise: Transforming Mental Health Care in America,* in 2003.

Consumer involvement on local mental health and PsyR organization boards is essential to the planning and implementation of consumer-centered services. A board of directors that has a substantial percentage of consumers filling meaningful roles is an excellent example of empowerment. It is important to realize that nonprofit agency administrators must answer to their board of directors. The board has the power to hire and fire administrators, develop and refine the agency's mission and goals, and create policies that govern day-to-day service provision. Consumers serving on these boards also have a chance to combat stigma by serving as role models in their communities. For example, residential programs often have to deal with resistant community members when opening new group homes or apartments. Board representatives who are also self-identified consumers can help ease fears and misconceptions by speaking to neighbors and community representatives.

PsyR professional organizations are another place where consumer involvement is essential. Consumer participation on the boards and subcommittees of these organizations provides an excellent opportunity for collaboration between consumers and professionals that can positively influence both local and national service systems. Consumer involvement at local and national professional conferences as both presenters and attendees is another way in which consumers can share their perspective with PsyR and mental health professionals. In the 1970s, when PsyR professional associations began to emerge, these conferences were opportunities for professionals to talk with each other about their work with persons with psychiatric disabilities. Now, many of these conferences provide opportunities for professionals, peer providers, consumers, and family members to share concerns and strategies for improving services, with consumers often assuming important roles such as keynote speaker.

Finally, program evaluation and research are areas where consumers are making important contributions. Increased collaboration between providers and consumers in evaluating individual program outcomes is increasingly evident. In terms of more rigorous studies, consumers act not only as subjects and survey respondents but also as active partners in research projects and even as independent researchers (Campbell, 2002; Van Tosh et al., 2000). Activist Dan Fisher (1994b) recommended "basing total quality improvement of mental health services on outcome measures designed by survivors and consumers" (p. 915). He cites the formation of the Consumer/Survivor Research and Policy Work Group, an entity that has been supported by SAMHSA's Center for Mental Health Services, as an important example of this goal. Thus, persons who have severe mental illnesses are helping to enhance both our knowledge of best practices and our understanding of recovery through their involvement in planning, designing, conducting, and reporting on important research studies (Van Tosh et al., 2000).

Summary

Peer support is an important component of psychiatric rehabilitation and community support systems. Peer support is offered through both self-help groups and various forms of peer-delivered services. These services include peer-operated programs, and the purposeful inclusions of peer employees in programs operated by non-peers. While the body of research on the outcomes of self-help and peer-provided services has yet to offer conclusive evidence, it seems clear that people with psychiatric disabilities gain some unique benefits from participation in peer support initiatives. Peer providers themselves, and the nonconsumer staff who they work with, also seem to benefit from these programs. However, there are also a number of challenges faced by peer providers and their colleagues, and it is important to address these challenges by providing appropriate supports and training opportunities.

Persons who have severe mental illnesses play other important roles in mental health systems as well. They act as policy makers, advocates, researchers, and board members. Their input into how PsyR services are provided is essential to the development of a truly consumer-driven mental health system. Such input helps to insure consumer satisfaction and contributes to the protection of the rights and dignity of people with disabilities. It is essential for psychiatric rehabilitation providers who are not diagnosed with a mental illness to learn to work in conjunction with the various types of peer providers, activists, and policy makers and to recognize all of the valuable roles that they can play in transforming mental health systems.

■ ■ ■ ▬▬▬▬▬▬▬▬▬▬▬▬▬▬▬▬▬▬▬▬▬▬▬▬▬▬▬▬▬▬▬▬▬▬▬▬

Class Exercises

Exercise 1: Establishing a Self-help Group

Imagine that you are part of a group of people who have psychiatric disabilities and want to start a self-help group.

1. How would you begin the process?
2. What resources would you need to achieve your goal?
3. Would the group be open to:
   • Anyone with a psychiatric disability?
   • People who had certain issues (e.g., diagnosis) in common?
   • Only your own circle of acquaintances?

What are the advantages and disadvantages of each membership approach?

4. How would you deal with the issue of leadership? Some options are voting on a single leader or co-leaders, shared leadership among all group members, or rotating leadership.
5. Now that you have discussed your hypothetical self-help group in some detail, how would you define the mission and goals of your group?

Exercise 2: Promoting Peer Support

Imagine that you are working in a PsyR program that is primarily operated by nonconsumer staff members. From your discussions with some program participants, you conclude that many of them would enjoy or profit from participation in peer support self-help activities, such as those offered at a nearby self-help center. You suggest this to a few consumers, but they say that they are not familiar with the self-help center and don't pursue the idea. You don't want to push the idea too strongly because it is contrary to the philosophy of such services, yet you feel many individuals would find self-help to be a beneficial adjunct to the PsyR services they are currently receiving. What other strategies might you pursue to foster their involvement in peer support activities?

Exercise 3: Hiring Peer Providers

Imagine that you are a staff member of a large multiservice psychiatric rehabilitation center that has no peer providers on staff, either in designated peer provider roles or as individuals who have disclosed their lived experience. After visiting another program with many peer providers and speaking to the staff and program members, you become convinced that adding peer providers to your agency will improve services and help people with their recovery. Finding that some other staff members share your opinion, you decide to work as a group to devise a strategy to convince your agency to adopt a policy of hiring peer providers. Identify the probable barriers to hiring peer providers and, if possible, devise remedies to overcome each of these barriers.

14

The Role of the Family in Psychiatric Rehabilitation

When mental illness strikes, it is a family affair.
The Family Survival Handbook (2009, p. 3)

CHAPTER OUTLINE

Psychiatric Rehabilitation. http://dx.doi.org/10.1016/B978-0-12-387002-5.00014-7

Attitudes towards the role of the family in psychiatric rehabilitation (PsyR) have gone through many changes. Formerly, family influences were viewed by providers as a contributing cause of mental illnesses; today, the family is seen as an important partner in the rehabilitation process. Family interventions focusing on psychoeducation and coping strategies have been proven to be effective and are now an established evidence-based practice.

This chapter will describe how having a member with mental illness affects the family and how families can contribute to the recovery of a person with mental illness. It will review the development of family advocacy organizations like the National Alliance on Mental Illness (NAMI), which help to keep state legislatures, administrative offices, and public policy forums aware of the needs of people with mental illness.

This chapter will answer the following questions:

1. *What is the effect on the family of having a member with a major mental illness?*
2. *How does living with the family affect the adjustment and recovery of a person with major mental illness?*
3. *What kinds of family interventions have been shown to be effective for family members with mental illness?*
4. *How does the family fit into the concept of recovery?*
5. *What is the role of NAMI in supporting people with mental illness?*

Introduction

The onset of mental illness strikes not only the individual but also the entire family, creating an undue burden on them (Hatfield, 1987a). As one family member was quoted, "We are all surviving schizophrenia" (Marsh et al., 1996, p. 11). The role of the family in recovery from mental illness has become increasingly important as community integration has become more of a reality. Many of the first community-based psychiatric rehabilitation services of the 1950s, 1960s, and 1970s were designed for single, deinstitutionalized adults, many of whom were completely estranged from their families. Today, shorter hospital stays often mean that acutely ill individuals return home to their family for continuing care in the community. With long-term hospitalization the exception rather than the rule, families are often the primary agents of care by default (Hatfield, 1987a). Today, people with mental illness are more likely to stay involved with their family of origin, including parents and siblings. They are also more likely to marry or stay in other long-term relationships and to have children. At the same time, community-based care has also increased the burden that family members must bear, both subjectively and objectively.

A long-overdue paradigm shift has taken place with respect to families. In the past, providers assumed families to be dysfunctional "systems" causing psychiatric illness. They had been inaccurately identified as etiological agents, literally causing serious mental illness. Mothers often bore the brunt of these assertions (e.g., "the schizophrenogenic mother"; Fromm-Reichmann, 1948). In contrast, today, family members are increasingly viewed as making important contributions to the recovery process (Mannion, 1996). Indeed, family interventions are among the most successful categories of psychosocial treatment and rehabilitation, actually reducing the frequency and length of psychotic relapse (Dixon & Lehman, 1995; Dixon et al., 2001; Hogarty, 1993; McFarlane, Dixon, Lukens, & Lucksted, 2003). These services, typically labeled "family psychoeducation," combine elements of education about the illness, support, problem solving, coping strategies, and crisis intervention. A body of data shows that the decompensation and/or hospital recidivism of persons with mental illness who reside with their families can be reduced by this type of intervention in combination with psychotropic medication more effectively than with just medication alone (Lehman & Steinwachs, 1998; Pharaoh, Mari, & Streiner, 2004).

While it is clear that families are not the cause of serious mental illnesses (see Chapter 2), in some cases familial psychosocial factors, such as stress caused from an environment high in criticism, hostility, and emotional over-involvement may contribute to relapses (Butzlaff & Hooley, 1998; Anderson, Reiss, & Hogarty, 1986). This type of environment has been termed high in **expressed emotion (EE)**. Nevertheless, most family households with members who have mental illness are not high EE environments (Lefley, 1989). Indeed, high EE environments can also be found outside family settings such as other residential settings and some clinics (Solomon, Alexander, & Uhl, 2010; Hogarty, 1993).

Individuals whose families manifested high EE as demonstrated by criticism, hostility, and levels of emotional overinvolvement were at higher risk for relapse (sometimes 50 percent or more over a nine-month period), compared to individuals residing in low EE families (13 to 15 percent relapse rate). If consumers had frequent contact (more than 35 hours per week) with a high EE relative, the increased relapse rate occurred even if they were compliant with their regimen of antipsychotic medications. A high EE environment apparently serves as a trigger for relapse. This negative high EE effect seems to be most relevant for unmarried men living in their parental homes (Harding & Zahniser, 1994).

The importance of EE has not been embraced by all PsyR professionals. Possible negative and stigmatizing effects of rating families as "high" or "low" EE, just when the importance of supporting the family was being recognized, were pointed out by Hatfield, Spaniol, and Zipple (1987).

Working with Families and Psychiatric Rehabilitation Principles

Like many members of our society who have outdated ideas about the causes of mental illness, some mental health professionals let fear and blame dominate their interactions with the families of persons who have a mental illness (Lundwall, 1996). All professionals, including psychiatric rehabilitation (PsyR) practitioners, need to create better options and resources for families and their members. Family involvement in treatment, rehabilitation, and support has been recognized for some time as an important element of a person's rehabilitation (Cook & Hoffschmidt, 1993). For example, more than 20 years ago it was recognized that the psychoeducation of families and consumers helps ensure that they have reasonable expectations regarding the disease, its treatment, and rehabilitation (Hatfield, 1990).

Indeed, a guiding principle of PsyR is that the involvement and partnership of persons receiving services with their family members is essential to effective rehabilitation and recovery (see Chapter 4; USPRA, 2012).

Because psychiatric rehabilitation is about community-based services, integrated settings, and natural supports, the involvement of family members (parents, spouses, children, and others) is essential in order to provide normalized services. Some individuals may need treatment and support for their entire lives. To this end, when adequately trained and supported, family members are potentially the best partners in the long-term process of recovery (Cook & Hoffschmidt, 1993).

The Family as a "Caring Agent"

With today's short hospital stays, many families have had to become primary care providers. Since the early 1980s, more than half of all persons leaving state hospitals have returned to live with their families. Among short-stay patients, as many as four out of five individuals return to their families for care (Hatfield, 1987b). Lefley (1989) notes that families must cope with both the positive and negative symptoms of severe mental illness (see Chapter 2). The obvious losses associated with negative symptoms often have the most devastating effect on both the individual and the family. Impaired levels of functioning are related to loss of old skills and the failure to acquire new ones, negatively affecting the individual's productivity, self-concept, and potential for positive change.

This, in turn, often increases the family burden, perpetuating the individual's dependence socially and economically.

Dual Diagnosis and the Family

The impact on the family unit of a member with a co-occurring substance abuse disorder can be even more complex (the co-occurrence of mental illness and substance abuse is discussed in detail in Chapter 9). Depending on the severity and duration of both the mental illness and the addiction, the family may expend considerable emotional and financial resources in coping with the situation. All areas of family functioning may be affected by the presence of dual diagnosis in a family member, including the general atmosphere, the ways family members communicate with each other, and the relationships, roles, and responsibilities that family members assume or are assigned (Daley, Moss, & Campbell, 1993). Likewise, in the case of a dually diagnosed loved one, the compound problems of the dual diagnosis can be especially problematic for the family. In their attempts to "control the uncontrollable," some family members may become overinvolved or "enmeshed." Others become completely shut off or "disengaged" from their family member with a disability (Evans & Sullivan, 1990). In the case of a substance abuse disorder, sometimes well-intentioned behavior on the part of caring family members has the unintended effect of enabling the person to continue to abuse substances. For example, money given to the individual for living expenses or rent may actually be spent on alcohol or drugs (Evans & Sullivan, 1990).

Nevertheless, families have often developed skills and strategies for coping with even such extremely difficult situations, and services to families should build on those strengths. Evans and Sullivan (1990) address the need for families dealing with substance abuse and mental illness to enter a recovery process of their own. Education about chemical dependence and psychiatric disability, support groups such as Al-Anon, the 12-step program for families, and skill development in problem solving, negotiation, and communication are all services that are helpful to families in recovery (Evans & Sullivan, 1990). The concept of family recovery is addressed in more detail later in this chapter.

Burden and Stigma

When a family member has a mental illness, it clearly places a burden on the family as a whole. Family members often experience a profound loss and sense of chronic sorrow (Eakes, Burke, & Hainsworth, 1998), complicated by additional feelings of anger, shame, and guilt (Jones, 2004). In one study, half of the parents and spouses of persons hospitalized for a mental disorder reported concealing the hospitalization to some degree (Phelan, Bromet, & Link, 1998). Indeed, a significant portion of family members (16 percent) reported that they believed other people were avoiding them, suggesting a strong awareness of stigma by family members. Marsh and colleagues (1996) collected comments regarding familial burden. The burden the family bears has been described as suffering, very sad, draining, and lonely. Family members speak of the care of their loved one as being a full-time job. Some report the abandonment of their own jobs and careers. Often, they feel as if they have not done enough. Some report permanent distraction. Others report anger toward their spouses or other family members. For example, parents of adults may be angry with the siblings of the person who is ill for their lack of support and involvement and sometimes their lack of acknowledgment of the existence of the disabled family member to other people. Many family members experience a sense of unending grief (Atkinson, 1994).

To understand family burden, researchers interviewed over 600 caregivers of participants in the CATIE (Clinical Antipsychotic Trials of Intervention Effectiveness) study (Perlick, Rosenheck, Kaczynski, Swartz, Canive, & Lieberman, 2006). Four factors explained almost all the sources of family burden: (1) problem behaviors, (2) resource demands and disruption, (3) impairment in activities of daily living (i.e., personal hygiene, cooking, etc.), and (4) perceived helpfulness or reciprocity (i.e., how much the individual with mental illness helps around the house, etc.). The authors suggested that providing the family with continued skills training would be an effective strategy to address these issues and reduce family burden. A study carried out in Lahore, Pakistan, comparing family psychoeducation and medication with medication alone supported this idea (Nasr & Kausar, 2009). Using a simple pre-post design, the study found that the main factor in reducing family burden was family training in coping and problem solving.

A study carried out in Hong Kong found that the main sources of family burden were stigma and lack of mental health service resources (Tsang, Tam, Chan, & Chang, 2003). Lefley (1989) reported that families often fear that the behavior of a relative with mental illness will diminish their reputation as individuals and as a family, jeopardizing their relationships with friends and neighbors. Because of this stigma, some family members may try to distance themselves from their ill relative, but often feel guilt if they do so.

Families coping with any chronic medical condition, mental illness or otherwise, attempt to adjust. Under conditions of constant strain, regardless of the diagnostic category, family members see the illness as cycles or patterns of exacerbation with contrasting periods of remission—they experience cycles of hope and disappointment.

Families experience a variety of stresses, both tangible, such as the economic burden of high health care costs, and intangible, such as fear, anxiety, and fatigue. The stress on the family has been categorized into two broad areas: objective burden and subjective burden. Both types of burdens will be discussed next.

The Objective Burden

Objective burden deals with specifically identifiable, observable, tangible, or material problems associated with the person's mental illness. The objective burdens of families in which a member has a chronic developmental, mental, or physical disability have a degree of commonality. Objective burden includes financial hardships due to medical bills, the cost of the consumer's economic dependence, disruptions in household functioning, restriction of social activities, and altered relationships because of the demands of caregiving. There is often a significant time commitment to the individual's needs at the expense of other family activities. Individual members of the family, particularly the primary caregiver, may often need to change their role in the family, often at the expense of their own careers.

The Subjective Burden

Subjective burden refers to the psychological or emotional distress borne by family members. Subjective burden is related to objective burden, but not always directly. A caregiver, for example, the wife of the identified consumer, may carry the highest objective burden in the family, yet because she has accommodated herself to it, she may feel a relatively lower subjective burden than other family members. Other family members who are not regular caregivers might bear less objective burden but feel stressed because of episodic abrupt disruptions in their routine. Besides the long-term burdens families face, there can also be acute crises involving interactions with emergency services and the police. In addition, involuntary commitment procedures can pit family members against one another in an adversarial manner that is often poorly understood and causes resentment in a loved one and dread and angst in family members. Consider the following situation:

> *Gina, a 28-year-old woman with four children, had become very distressed. Her husband, Mike, had stopped seeing his psychiatrist. He had not bathed in months and had literally stopped speaking. He was not working and remained in the house. For weeks, she had begged him to get help. When he became completely mute, she finally called crisis services and filed a complaint to commit him. He was hospitalized, received medication, improved markedly, and went back to work. But he was very resentful. Years later, Gina's father-in-law, Ralph, who was normally supportive and mild mannered, said, "Do you realize she had Mike COMMITTED! I will never forgive her for that!" When other relatives pointed out it was the only option she had left to get Mike help, Ralph refused to listen.*

A study of the effects of outpatient commitment on caregivers found that while the objective burden did not change, caregivers reported that the subjective burden was significantly reduced (Groff et al., 2004). In some places, outpatient commitment involves placing conditions for participation in treatment on individuals being discharged from public psychiatric hospitals or as an alternative to involuntary hospitalization. If the conditions are not met, the individual may be returned to the hospital. A complete discussion of the controversy surrounding involuntary outpatient commitment is presented in Chapter 4.

The Anguish of the Individual

Lefley (1987a, b) suggests that the most devastating stressor for family members may be learning to cope with the person's own anguish over an impoverished life—that is, the individual's acute awareness of what is being missed and will be missed in the future.

Both the individual with mental illness and the family mourn changes in personality, lost skills, and diminished strengths secondary to the illness.

Troublesome Actions That Contribute to Burden

In describing family life with a person with severe and persistent mental illness, Lefley noted a variety of behaviors of some persons with serious mental illness that contribute to the burden borne by their family members (Lefley, 1987a, b, 1989):

- Hostile, abusive, or assaultive behaviors (even if rare)
- Mood swings or other unpredictable behavior
- Socially offensive or embarrassing behavior
- Poor motivation or apparent malingering (often due to negative symptoms)
- Apparently self-destructive actions such as poor handling of money, deteriorated personal hygiene, and neglect or damage of property

Another source of burden labeled the "control attribution" takes place when family members believe that the ill individual can control his or her symptoms but chooses not to do so (Greenberg, Kim, & Greenly, 1997). This misunderstanding, which often indicates a lack of knowledge about the illness, can be addressed through family psychoeducation.

The burden that family members must bear can include abusive and assaultive behaviors during acute phases of illness. While there is very little research in this area, Solomon and colleagues (2005) reported estimates that 10 to 40 percent of families have experienced some form of domestic violence. In a California study, 11 percent of families reported that their mentally ill family member had physically assaulted other family members in the two weeks preceding hospital admission (Torrey, 2008). While infrequent or even based on a single instance, these incidents often become indelible within a family's memory, recounted and dwelled upon for years to come. Also, there are a variety of other troublesome behaviors that are particularly upsetting, including symptoms such as paranoid ideation about loved ones and negative symptoms that may lead to poor self-care, chronic depression, and lack of engagement.

As if these problems were not enough, parents also worry about what will happen to their adult child "when I am gone." That is, they worry about who will provide care if they themselves become disabled or after their own deaths. In some areas, resources are available to help parents with estate planning that will help care for their children, a practice begun for parents of persons with developmental disabilities. An organization called the National PLAN Alliance (http://www.nationalplanalliance.org/) is dedicated to helping to meet the planning needs of families with disabled offspring, including those with psychiatric disabilities. For instance, they help families set up trusts so that their child will be financially protected after they are gone.

Independence/Dependence: The Dilemma of Functional Expectancy

Hatfield (1992) defines the central dilemma facing adults with serious mental illness and their families as the issue of dependence vs. independence. In most cultures, the independence of young adults or even adolescents is seen as an important developmental goal. For many adults with psychiatric disabilities, continued dependence on others is a virtual necessity. This requirement of continuing dependence often causes extreme tension among family members. This is particularly true for parents who see fostering independence in their adult offspring as an important goal of parenting, as well as desiring more independence for themselves in their golden years.

"Functional expectancy," or the familial and societal expectations of how one should function in society, is an aspect of the dependence vs. independence dilemma. Failure to meet these expectations can be a burden for the person with mental illness. Living with one's family, especially one's family of origin, presents constant reminders of disabilities and unfulfilled plans and aspirations that may be stressful—for example, being confronted daily with the fact that one is not making normal, expected contributions to family life. Having to depend on one's family for basic needs is a constant reminder of failing to achieve a degree of independence. This situation tends to lower one's self-esteem, further adding to the burden.

The "dilemma of functional expectancy" describes a unique problem (Lefley, 1987a, p. 114). Often the family member with mental illness cannot meet the expectations of functioning in the family. For example, parents may expect their grown son to maintain his own apartment. If he fails, the parents may then decide it was too much to expect and lower their expectations for the future. In turn, the son may then live up to these low expectations and cease striving to achieve the original goal. Regardless, the degree of burden experienced by the parents is directly related to how dependent the individual is on the parents. Today's family psychoeducation and support interventions, by involving family members very extensively, succeed in promoting a degree of independence and reducing family burden (McFarlane et al., 2003; Pharaoh et al., 2004). This evidence is discussed in more detail later in this chapter.

In contrast to the negative context of family burden, Corrigan, Mueser, Bond, Drake, and Solomon (2008) suggest that caring for a family member is not always perceived as a burden by families. Families, in fact, can be "quite resilient" and are strengthened by the challenges they face (p. 239). For some, caring for an ill family member provides a degree of gratification. For these families, assisting their loved one strengthens the family bond and may hasten the recovery of the individual as well as the family.

Family Dissatisfaction with Services

Given the numerous burdens families must deal with, one would hope that the mental health system would be simple to navigate. Unfortunately, the complexity and confusion of the system of available services and supports systems can be daunting to family members as well as to service recipients (see Figure 8.1 in Chapter 8).

Families are often very unhappy with the way their relatives are served. They express general dissatisfaction with the service delivery system and often with mental health professionals themselves. Families have frequently been subjected to irrelevant, conflicting, confusing, and insufficient treatment models that do not meet their expressed needs or respect their concerns and experience. The expectations offered to family members by professionals are often too low, too high, or absent altogether. Whether for reasons of confidentiality, workload stresses, or insufficient training, often professionals do not provide relevant information or guidance in managing difficult behaviors. Kim and Salyers (2008) surveyed over 450 clinicians in Indiana and confirmed that family services were lacking, partly due to a lack of staff training about these issues.

Consider the lot of the mother of a person with a serious mental illness who is living at home after hospital discharge:

> She is suffering the pain of her child's illness, the stigmatization of having caused it, the burden of overseeing a treatment plan that may be unrealistic . . . at the same time, she is trying to balance conflicting advice. . . . (Lefley, 1989, p. 557)

For example, on the one hand, a mother might to be told that in the past she has been neglectful or rejecting and, on the other, that she must now encourage independence. Then, if she does not take the paradoxical advice of the professional, she will be accused of sabotaging treatment (Lefley, 1989).

Too often professionals have been disapproving in the messages they give family members. Their overt or covert disapproval evokes defensive reactions on the part of the family members, thus fulfilling the self-confirming bias of clinicians that the family is "too defensive." Given these communication problems, family members may become alienated and resentful. Other families may become overly submissive, inordinately deferring to the professionals. Some families, following instructions from mental health professionals, have disengaged from or abandoned their family member with mental illness.

Who Is a Family Member?

The definition of family is changing, sometimes becoming whoever is in the household even if there is no relationship "by blood" or marriage. The US Centers for Disease Control and Prevention (http://www.cdc.gov/nchs/fastats/unmarry.htm) reported that in 2009 the number of children born to unmarried parents aged 15 to 44 exceeded 50 percent of all US births. Same-sex marriages are now recognized by at least nine states and many other states recognize civil unions. This evolution of the family unit is increasingly an issue perplexing to service providers who need to determine which "significant others" to include in family services or psychoeducation. Certainly, the consumer's preferences about who should be included must be primary. Addressing this issue is necessary for family interventions to be effective (Solomon, Molinaro, Mannion, & Cantwell, 2012).

Three Levels of Family (or Significant Other) Involvement

The burdens experienced by family members and significant others vary based on their level of involvement with the ill individual. Terkelson (1987a) proposed three tiers of involvement. In the immediate family, one individual usually assumes the **first-tier** role of **principal caregiver**. Often (but not always) this is a woman: the mother, wife, sister, or daughter of the person with mental illness. Much of her daily life becomes a series of illness-related occupations and preoccupations. She acknowledges the illness more than others and also suffers its impact more than others in this family. Terkelson describes this sort of caregiver as living a life that is a stream of nursing activities. Other activities include attempting to keep the illness from disrupting the rest of the family members' lives. Free time is often filled with worrying or at least thinking about the person.

Second-tier relatives/persons may live with or near the person with mental illness, but are less intimately exposed to the "ups" and "downs" of the person's life. Thanks to the primary caregiver or first-tier relatives, as well as their own efforts, these second-tier relatives experience less frequent intrusions on their lives. However, occasionally they experience a noticeable disruption when some troublesome aspect of the illness inserts itself into their lives. For example, while their daily routine is not burdened by the care of a relative with a disability, their lives may be abruptly disrupted in the midst of an exacerbation of that person's symptoms. They may come to dread both the illness and interaction and avoid involvement whenever possible. Sometimes to avoid indirect involvement with the individual, they avoid involvement with the primary caregiver. Thus, a husband may become estranged from a wife, siblings from each other, a child from a parent, and so forth.

Third-tier relatives/persons are not in the immediate household but still share a common interest in the well-being of the consumer. At times, these individuals may play down or deny the presence of the illness and associated disability. Sometimes they regard the person with the illness as faking or lazy. Occasionally, they may blame the primary caregiver or under-involved second-tier relatives for the person's mental illness. As you can see by Terkelson's very insightful description of the situation, the objective and subjective burdens of each group vary markedly.

Confidentiality: An Important Barrier to Family Services

As a result of federal and state legislation, especially the Health Insurance Portability and Accountability Act of 1996 (HIPAA) that expanded the confidentiality rights of all health care receivers, the importance of maintaining an individual's right to confidentiality is stressed during education and training and by service provider organizations. Confidentiality is an ethical responsibility of providers and the legal right of service recipients (Solomon et al., 2012). Additionally, assurance of confidentiality is a fundamental part of an effective working relationship between a provider and service recipient. Unfortunately, issues of confidentiality often get in the way of family involvement and many service providers are unclear of just what the boundaries of confidentiality are (Solomon et al., 2012). For example, in a study of 640 staff members, administrators, and students in Pennsylvania, contrary to specific permissions in confidentiality regulations, over 40 percent believed that they could not provide even general information about services offered to callers who identified themselves as family or significant others. This study and others highlight the need for additional training on confidentiality (Solomon et al., 2012). Also, many professionals do not understand that for purposes of coordination of care, a specific consent to release information is often not necessary.

Consider the following situation:

Bob is a semi-retired man in his early 60s. Almost every day, he drives his son, Craig, who is 30, to the local psychiatric rehabilitation day program. He drops him off at about 9 a.m. and picks him up about 3 p.m. One day, Bob decides to talk things over with the staff at the center because Craig is sleeping poorly and often paces all night. He decides to call the center after he arrives at his part-time job. Bob asks for Craig's case manager, who gets on the phone. When Bob starts talking about Craig, the case manager stops him claiming confidentiality, saying "I cannot even say whether your son is served here or not." In fact, the case manager is upholding the agency's policy of not revealing information about the people they serve to anyone, unless the client expressly consents to the disclosure. Enraged at this "snippy" attitude and the rejection of his attempts to share information for his son's benefit, Bob responds: "I know damn well he is there. I drive him there every day and pick him up, so don't give me that nonsense. Besides, you call my wife and me when it suits you—we have spoken before!"

The Unique Burdens of Spouses

Spouses of persons with severe mental illness bear a unique burden. Mannion (1996) estimated that 35 to 40 percent of people hospitalized for psychiatric disabilities are discharged to live with their spouses. Mannion reported that the great majority of spouses surveyed reported a process of adaptation and recovery. Nevertheless, the burden of spouses includes these problems:

- Marital dissatisfaction and disruption
- Financial problems
- Socialization difficulties
- Personal experience of emotional and mood symptoms
- Separations and divorce

Clearly, when one's spouse has a major mental illness it puts a great deal of stress on the marriage. Despite this, because of issues of confidentiality and lack of auxiliary services such as marriage counseling, it is often difficult for the well spouse to receive help to keep the marriage together. A reciprocal flow of information between spouses and professional caregivers would improve the quality of care and effectively reduce relapse, but unfortunately, this is all too rare.

Siblings and Children

Siblings of people with mental illness also experience significant levels of stress (Kinsella, Anderson, & Anderson, 1996). Young family members, both siblings and children of people with the disorders, share a special vulnerability to the familial experience of mental illness

(Marsh et al., 1993). For example, one grown child of a mother with mental illness reported, "The mental illness shaped my life . . . it revolved around her problems." An interesting paper titled "You'd think this roller coaster was never going to stop" (Foster, 2010) describes a narrative research study of children of parents with schizophrenia. The study identified four common themes running through the narratives: (1) being uncertain, (2) struggling to connect with the ill parent, (3) being responsible (taking on the adult role), and (4) seeking balance (in the family). Adults who dealt with the mental illness of a relative during their own childhood reported a variety of difficulties, including subjective burden in the form of feelings of grief and loss, empathy for the suffering of other family members, stigma of the individual and family, and objective burden in needing to deal with symptomatic behavior and illness-related crises. Specific problems include the following:

- Absence of a model of normal development
- Difficulty determining which experiences were "normal" and which were not normal
- Altered roles, for example, "parentification," a child having to care for the sick parent
- Their own mental health problems
- Strain in relationships outside family (e.g., at school)
- Fear of developing mental illness themselves

In adulthood, these individuals attribute impaired self-esteem, poor self-concept, and fear of rejection to their childhood experience (Marsh et al., 1993).

People with Mental Illness as Parents

Parenting is a normal adult role that many people with mental illness fulfill or wish to pursue. Like other roles, it requires skills and resources, possibly the assistance of professionals, but also natural supports such as family, neighbors, and friends. Of course, there are the unique challenges that are added by parenthood and children. There is evidence that the better the parent's understanding of his or her own illness, the better the adjustment of his or her child (Mullick et al., 2001).

Parents with mental illness face the same challenges as other parents, but they are often exacerbated by their mental illness, poverty, and social isolation. For example, people with mental illness can face serious economic challenges, particularly if they are dependent on public benefits barely adequate for their own support, let alone those of dependent children. Many individuals, because of the nature of the course of their illness, have had the development of parenting skills and household management skills disrupted. In addition, they often have inadequate social networks with few others available to support them in their role as parents.

Single parents with mental illness often bear a special burden. Much of the research to date on this topic is about mothers with mental illness because in society in general they are more likely than the father to be the custodial parent. A 2010 study of 17,830 mothers of children up to age 17 receiving Medicaid or insurance coverage from a State Children's Health Insurance Program (CHIP) found that mothers with mental illness tended to be single and poorer with lower levels of education, fewer supports, and greater difficulty coping with parenting than their peers. Possibly because of eligibility for Medicaid and/or CHIP, the children of these mothers with mental illness still received comparable levels of pediatric care (Cullen, Matejkowski, Marcus, & Solomon, 2010).

The timing of the onset of mental illness is associated with the course and recovery of women who are mothers. Those whose illness began well after the birth of a child had the best adaptation to the role of mother. Those whose onset of illness was before the birth of their child had the second best adaptation, and those with the worst adaptation to motherhood were women whose onset of the illness coincided with the birth of one of her children (Mowbray, Bybee, Oyserman, & MacFarlane, 2005). These women tended to be younger at the birth of their first child and have more children. This is an alarming finding considering the relatively high incidence of postpartum mental illnesses.

The number of single fathers rearing a child is increasing (Styron, Pruett, McMahon, & Davidson, 2002) and in many ways they face the same issues as single mothers with a mental illness (Nicholson, Nason, Calabresi, & Yando, 1999). Single fathers are very likely to be impoverished, fairly isolated, and often unskilled as a parent. A fairly large number of men with serious mental illness are fathers (20 to 33 percent), and among these fathers a majority wish to be involved with their children even if they do not have custody (Styron et al., 2002).

Issues of Parental Custody

Some studies have found a small but significant relationship between parents with mental illness and child neglect or abuse (Walsh, MacMillan, & Jamieson, 2002). It is generally agreed that the children of parents with a mental illness also face a greater likelihood of experiencing developmental and/or behavioral problems (Friesen, Nicholson, Kaplan, & Solomon, 2009). Given these problems, it's not surprising that many of these families temporarily or permanently lose custody of their children (Mowbray, Oyserman, Baybee, MacFarlane, & Rueda-Riedle, 2001).

In the United States, the Adoption and Safe Families Act (ASFA) of 1997 attempted to address both the welfare of children and the rights of parents. The act requires the states to make a reasonable effort to keep families together, which includes returning children to families of parents with a mental illness when possible. When required, reasonable efforts might include the state providing available and accessible services to these families. But ASFA also allows states to determine circumstances under which it is not reasonable to keep a family intact. In fact, it is now becoming apparent that state restrictions on the custody rights of parents with mental illness are becoming stricter, causing parents with mental illness to be singled out. Many states are deciding a mental illness is sufficient reason not to make the reasonable efforts to preserve a family unit (Scott, 2008).

Friesen and colleagues (2009) found four main issues that put parents with mental illness at risk of losing custody of their children: (1) the challenges that the symptoms of mental illness present in themselves, (2) the lack of available and accessible community services, (3) poorly informed professionals, including child welfare workers, and (4) state laws, regulations, and procedures. These issues highlight the effects of stigma, prejudice, and discrimination aimed at parents with mental illness and the importance of increased knowledge and education.

Successful Coping Strategies

Like many others, people with mental illness consider their role as a parent to be the most important one of their life, more important than being a citizen, a student, or a worker. There are a number of interventions and supports available to assist parents with a mental illness to pursue their role successfully. These have been summarized by Temple University's Rehabilitation Research and Training Center on Community Integration in their publications, which are available through their Web site: http://www.tucollaborative .org/. Applicable publications include *Parenting with a Mental Illness: Positive Parenting & Child Resilience* (2005a) and *Parenting with a Mental Illness: Child Welfare & Custody Issues* (2005b).

Some of the most important strategies include the following:

1. **Development of natural supports for both parent and child**—persons with mental illness who become parents and/or are considering becoming parents need a social support network to help with daily coping, provide emotional support, and assist during periods of stress and crisis. Similarly, children need and benefit from the support of family, friends, classmates, and participation in school and community activities. Parents need to make the effort to connect children with supports outside the home.
2. **Parenting skills**—parenting is a complicated role that includes complex cognitive and emotional tasks. This unique form of skill development is virtually nonexistent in psychiatric rehabilitation services. Like other parents facing the challenges of disciplining children, parents who have a mental illness could benefit greatly from a parenting skills training program. A number of behaviorally based models are available.
3. **The necessity of a relapse plan**—all persons with a serious mental illness should have a relapse plan for the management of their own illness and the maintenance of their jobs, homes, and other aspects of their lives. For persons with children, a plan to manage relapse is particularly critical for many reasons, particularly the safety and well-being of their children for time periods when they may not be able to care for them. This is essential not only for the child's health and emotional well-being but also to establish that the children are not endangered and the parent can retain legal custody.
4. **Normal interests outside the home**—it is important that both child and parent have normal interests outside the home. These interests are a source of natural supports as alluded to earlier but also provide relief from each other. While parents and

children are capable of providing mutual support, it is also important that each has interests and supports other than their all-important first-tier relative. When a parent or child is the only support available to the other, a great deal of pressure on each can result. In fact, expectations of high levels of support from their child/children can be a predictor of maternal behavior that puts a child at risk for abuse, neglect, or other maltreatment (Mullick, Miller, & Jacobsen, 2001).

5. **Awareness of legal rights**—parents need to be aware of their legal rights and responsibilities in terms of maintaining custody and legal recourse for regaining child custody. There is often a great deal of pressure to relinquish custody. In contrast, understanding about alternatives such as adoption, including open adoption (i.e., adoption where the biological and adoptive parents know each other's identity), is important, as is understanding the limitations and problems associated with foster care.

6. **Professional supports**—maintaining regular contact with mental health professionals to continue to receive appropriate medication and psychosocial interventions is essential. Sometimes, children are also in need of these professional supports.

7. **Age-appropriate education of children regarding mental illness**—parents, in collaboration with professionals, should educate their children regarding mental illness with accurate information the child can assimilate, with its complexity increasing as the child becomes older. In this way, unnecessary stigma is avoided and as an adolescent and adult, the child can later support his or her parent in managing the illness.

Family Interventions

Clearly, families are a primary support system for many individuals with psychiatric disabilities. Providing families with assistance and the tools that they need is one of the most effective strategies for helping individuals manage their illnesses and achieve their recovery goals. Professionals as well as family advocacy organizations such as the National Alliance on Mental Illness (NAMI) have developed initiatives for family education and support.

Goals for Helping Families

The family–professional relationship should be one of collaboration that avoids blaming or pathologizing family members. Coursey and colleagues outlined principles for working with families (Coursey et al., 2000).

A competent practitioner:

- Understands the unique issues facing family members of persons with mental illness
- Becomes knowledgeable about family support resources and intervention strategies

- Addresses the expressed needs of individual families
- Engages families in the treatment and rehabilitation process when appropriate and desired

Professional Interventions: Family Psychoeducation

As the negative conception of the family as etiological agent has faded, positive strategies to assist families as caregivers have emerged. These approaches are in sharp contrast to the traditional family therapies based on etiological theories that assert the family and/or its communication patterns are a major causative factor of the illness. These new family interventions have been delivered in a variety of formats, settings, and methods (Hatfield, 1990; McFarlane, 1994; Dixon, 2001).

Family psychoeducation approaches are among the best methods of promoting better outcomes among people with severe and persistent mental illness (Lucksted et al., 2012; Dixon et al., 2001; Lehman & Steinwachs, 1998). If family members can be engaged, these interventions are among the most effective social techniques that can be employed to improve the course and outcome of illnesses such as schizophrenia (Hogarty, 1993).

Specifically, psychoeducational approaches that include the person in recovery in the family intervention appear to be superior. Multiple family groups working together are particularly effective, perhaps because of the mutual emotional support and practical advice they can share with each other (McFarlane et al., 2003).

Some Early Empirical Evidence for Family Psychoeducation

Many studies of family interventions began as assessments of aftercare programs following discharge from a psychiatric hospital. Early on, Goldstein, Rodnick, Evans, May, and Steinberg (1978) found that even as few as six weekly sessions focusing on education, building acceptance, and planning for the future result in a significantly lower number of relapses.

Some family interventions were initially developed as explicit efforts to change high EE family environments, although as mentioned earlier, most families who have persons with mental illness do not exhibit the high EE style. Nevertheless, Falloon and his colleagues (1982, 1985) studied families with members diagnosed with schizophrenia predicted to be at high risk for relapse because they were living with high EE relatives. His treatment group included behavioral family therapy, problem solving, and communication skills designed to promote a low EE style. This family intervention approach was compared to supportive individual psychotherapy and brief family counseling. Measured at nine months and two years, the comprehensive family intervention produced significantly fewer relapses, increased patient functioning, reduced family burden, and lowered overall treatment costs.

Hogarty and colleagues (1986, 1991) developed a family-centered approach that sought to empower families by promoting useful skills, knowledge, and attitudes. The strategy focused on building an alliance with the family, providing concrete information and management suggestions, building a support network, and providing skills in individual family therapy with the patient included. One of the most compelling findings from Hogarty's random assignment studies was that after two years only 25 to 29 percent of the individuals who received the family treatment relapsed, compared to relapse rates as high as 62 percent for individuals who received social skills training or day treatment alone.

Expanding on Hogarty's approach, McFarlane and his colleagues conducted studies of a psychoeducational family intervention delivered in a multi-family group format (McFarlane, 1994; McFarlane et al., 1995; McFarlane et al., 2003). They compared multi-family groups and single families receiving psychoeducation with a multi-family group that did not receive the psychoeducational component. Based on a high relapse rate of the multi-family group without psychoeducation, this condition was discontinued after one year. At the two- and four-year follow-ups, the multi-family group with psycho-education had significantly lower relapse rates than the single-family psychoeducation condition. McFarlane replicated this study using 172 families at six sites throughout New York State (McFarlane et al., 1995). The multi-family group condition again proved superior to the single-family condition. A number of studies with related findings support the efficacy of educational interventions with families and consumers (McFarlane, 1994).

Core Characteristics of Family Psychoeducation

Now established as an evidence-based practice, professional interventions known as Family Psychoeducation (FPE) produce positive outcomes for both individuals with mental illness and families. Lucksted and her colleagues (Lucksted, McFarlane, Downing, Dixon, & Adams, 2012) describe FPE as "designed to engage, inform, and educate family members, so they can assist the person with SMI [sic] in managing their illness" (p. 101). In their recent review of the literature on FPE, they identified eight common components of family psychoeducation:

1. Assumes that most involved family members of individuals with mental illness need information, assistance, and support to best assist their ill family member and cope with the challenges posed to the family system
2. Assumes that the way in which relatives behave toward and with the person(s) with mental illness can have important effects on that person's well-being and clinical outcomes
3. Combines informational, cognitive, behavioral, problem-solving, emotional, coping, and consultation therapeutic elements
4. Is created and led by mental health professionals
5. Is offered as part of a clinical treatment plan for a specific consumer
6. Focuses primarily on benefitting consumer outcomes, but family member outcomes (e.g., reducing stress) are also important
7. Includes content about illness, medication, and treatment management; service coordination; attention to all parties' expectations, emotional reactions, and distress; assistance with improving family communication; structured problem-solving

BOX 10.1   WILLIAM R. MCFARLANE

William R. McFarlane, MD, is a Professor of Psychiatry at Tufts University School of Medicine and Director of the Center for Psychiatric Research at Maine Medical Center. He has been working with families of the mentally ill, especially in multiple family groups, since training at Albert Einstein College of Medicine in Social and Community Psychiatry, from 1970 to 1975. Dr. McFarlane's research and writing have helped provided the critical knowledge based for the establishment of family psychoeducation as an evidence-based practice. He developed, tested, and disseminated worldwide the psychoeducational multifamily group model for the treatment of schizophrenia, severe mood disorders, and early intervention in psychosis.

He is presently testing a comprehensive community prevention system involving early identification of youth in the prodromal phase of schizophrenia and other psychotic disorders. This strategy, Portland Identification and Early Referral (PIER), the only one of its kind in the United States, trains educators, mental health clinicians, and physicians in the early signs of psychosis, prior to onset. The treatment provided, Family-aided Assertive Community Treatment (FACT), offers intensive support and guidance to family members, support for the young person's education and employment, and low-dose medication for severe symptoms. It is now being tested in a multisite replication and dissemination project funded by the Robert Wood Johnson Foundation at six sites representing a wide spectrum of the population of the United States.

Dr. McFarlane edited and contributed to Family Therapy in Schizophrenia (1983) and Multifamily Groups in the Treatment of Severe Psychiatric Disorders (2002). He has published more than 80 articles and book chapters and was an Associate Editor of Family Process and Families, Systems and Health. In 2003, he was awarded the Distinguished Contribution to Family Systems Research Award by the American Family Therapy Academy; in 2004, the Warren Williams Award by the American Psychiatric Association; and in 2007 the Alexander Gralnick Award for Schizophrenia Research by the American Psychiatric Association and the American Psychiatric Foundation.

instruction; expanding social support networks; and explicit crisis planning with professional involvement

8. Are generally diagnosis-specific, although cross-diagnosis models are being developed (Lucksted, McFarlane, Downing, Dixon, & Adams, 2012, p. 102)

Psychoeducation with high fidelity to these components results in reductions in the number of relapses, fewer and shorter hospitalizations, and increased family knowledge of mental illness, medications and their side effects, and the services available. Additionally, family psychoeducation may improve family problem solving, may reduce family stress, and is theorized to assist with family "recovery."

Ten years ago, McFarlane et al. (2003) summarized the state of the empirical evidence on family interventions:

> *Family psychoeducation has emerged as a treatment of choice for schizophrenia, bipolar disorder, major depression, and other disorders. More than 30 randomized clinical trials have demonstrated reduced relapse rates, improved recovery of patients, and improved family well-being among participants. Interventions common to effective family psychoeducation programs have been developed, including empathic engagement, education, ongoing support, and clinical resources during periods of crisis, social network enhancement, and problem-solving and communication skills. (p. 223)*

Unfortunately, this evidence has not been broadly incorporated into general practice:

> *Application of family psychoeducation in routine settings where patients having these disorders are usually treated has been limited, reflecting attitudinal, knowledge, practical, and systemic implementation obstacles. (p. 223)*

McFarlane et al. (2003) continued to say that in order for it to be implemented, there needs to be "consensus among patient and family advocacy organizations, clinician training, and ongoing technical consultation and supervision." While FPE strategies continue to be carried out differently in different settings, they appear to have one common goal: to provide the family with the knowledge and skills they need to assist the recovery of their ill family member (Jewell, Downing, & McFarlane, 2009).

Family Psychoeducation for Different Diagnostic Categories

Symptoms, course of illness, and long-term prognosis can differ depending on an individual's diagnosis and even with diagnostic categories (see Chapters 2 and 3). Therefore, FPE strategies are designed to provide families with the knowledge and skills necessary for addressing the specific diagnosis of their family member.

FPE for Schizophrenia

Considerable attention has been given to FPE for schizophrenia (Dixon et al., 2009; Jewell et al., 2009; Taylor et al., 2009). The Cochrane Collaboration, which collects and combines well-executed research studies (i.e., randomized controlled trials) on a specific topic, published a review of Psychoeducation for Schizophrenia (Xia, Merinder, & Belgamwar, 2011). They selected only the best designed and executed studies for review. This review looked at 44 randomized controlled clinical trials comprising over 5000 participants and concluded that psychoeducation is a promising approach that "seems to reduce relapse and readmission and encourage medication compliance, as well as reduce the length of hospital stay" (p. 2). Interestingly, while studies consistently report the positive outcomes listed above, some well-designed studies have found that FPE does not reduce family burden (McDonell, Short, Berry, & Dyck, 2003; Mueser et al., 2001).

FPE for Bipolar Disorder

Unlike FPE for schizophrenia, the research base for FPE interventions with bipolar disorder is much less extensive with considerably fewer studies. The Cochrane Collaboration reviewed seven controlled clinical trials of family interventions for bipolar disorder comprising nearly 400 participants and determined that while there was a small body of evidence that these strategies are effective, it was not yet possible to draw a definite conclusion of the efficacy of this strategy (Justo, Soares, & Calil, 2009).

FPE for Other Disorders

Lucksted and her colleagues (2012) report on the use of FPE for eating disorders, obsessive–compulsive disorder, dual diagnoses, posttraumatic stress disorder, and traumatic brain injury. While results are frequently positive, there is still insufficient evidence for the effectiveness of the FPE strategy for these conditions. They do point out common elements in each of these strategies: information, skill building, problem solving, social support, and reducing social isolation. Given the diversity of conditions FPE is being used to address, one conclusion they reach is that "… FPE implementation must be tailored to each situation" (p. 114).

Family Psychoeducation: An Evidence-based Practice

Family psychoeducation is one of the six evidence-based practices that were identified by the 1998 Robert Wood Johnson Foundation–sponsored panel of psychiatric rehabilitation experts (Drake et al., 2001).

Critical Ingredients of Family Psychoeducation

The elements critical for effective family psychoeducation consist of the following:

- **Mental illness education**—this consists of providing the family with information about the probable etiology, course, and treatment of the mental illness in question. Additional information about medications, medication side effects, treatment options, and psychiatric rehabilitation services is also provided.

- **Problem solving**—families are taught problem-solving strategies that they role-play and practice on a regular basis. Besides improving the family's response to crisis, this training helps to improve family morale and confidence. An important aspect of family psychoeducation is that it provides support to the caregivers as well as the consumer.
- **Stress reduction**—family members and the consumer are taught stress reduction techniques. In combination with problem solving, this helps to improve morale, reinforce caregiving, and sometimes forestall crisis.
- **Long-term duration**—supports are provided as long as they are needed. This is similar to other evidence-based practices. Families are different, they exist in different circumstances, and their ill members are different. The family psychoeducation services are tailored to the needs of the individual family.
- **Family and consumer involvement**—family psychoeducation training is conducted with the consumer present as an integrated member of the family.

Outcomes of Family Psychoeducation

High-fidelity FPE produces the following results:

1. Reduced relapse rates
2. Reduced hospitalizations and hospital utilization (i.e., length of stay)
3. Improved family knowledge of mental illness, symptoms, medications, therapeutic effects, and side effects
4. May improve family problem solving*
5. May reduce family stress*
6. May assist family recovery *

* The research evidence for these outcomes remains preliminary.

Family to Family Initiatives

There is a long and varied tradition of families functioning in a mutual self-help mode to assist each other with the burden of mental illness. The primary goals of these efforts are to help families deal with the issues related to the mental illness, assist in their understanding the illness, and provide support as well as information and advice about the mental health delivery system.

Family meetings, with or without the member with mental illness present, might consist of sharing knowledge about the illness, problem solving specific situations, sharing knowledge about resources, and encouraging each other through role modeling. Typically, experienced families who have successfully handled issues help and encourage less experienced families who are just learning about these issues.

Some of these groups have adopted specific curricula and strategies; NAMI's Family to Family (FTF) Education program is a good example of families as peers helping other families. Below is a brief synopsis of the history of NAMI, followed by a discussion of their very successful FTF approach.

History of NAMI

As caregivers for persons with mental illness, many family members also assume an organized advocacy role to bring about changes in public policy. The largest and most successful American group is the National Alliance for the Mentally Ill (NAMI), renamed the National Alliance on Mental Illness in 2005. NAMI's major activities include providing family members and consumers with mutual support, sharing information, educating the public, and advocating for improved public policy and legislation.

The organization was founded in 1979, in Madison, Wisconsin, by family members who wanted to help both their relatives with mental illness and themselves. Emanating from the grassroots formation of state and local family member organizations, notably Parents of Adult Schizophrenics founded by Eve Oliphant in San Mateo, CA, in 1972 (Cadigan & Murray, 2009), the first national meeting of NAMI included about 250 people who spent an emotional and memorable weekend together. Although professionals were in attendance, family members who founded this organization were determined to have it governed by and for families and consumers (NAMI, 1996, 1998). Within the year, NAMI was incorporated, achieved nonprofit status, and elected a board of directors. Early efforts centered on making connections with existing family support groups throughout the United States, holding an annual conference, and publishing a newsletter. By 1982, NAMI opened an office in Washington, DC, and began the work of advocating for improved mental health services.

NAMI describes itself as "the nation's largest grassroots mental health organization dedicated to building better lives for the millions of Americans affected by mental illness" (2012). Most NAMI members are parents of people with mental illness. They have a firsthand understanding of the social stigma their son or daughter has experienced. NAMI families come together to advocate for needed change in both public attitudes and public policy. They have been supportive of research demonstrating the biochemical basis of major mental illnesses, which are now often referred to as "brain diseases." There are over 1000 state, county, and local NAMI affiliates throughout the United States (see their Web site at www.nami.org). They are very active public advocates for mental illness awareness. For example, in 2011, over 135,000 people walked in 84 NAMI Walks events across the country (NAMI Web site, December, 2012).

NAMI has been an effective advocacy organization. For example, working with federal and state legislators, NAMI helped introduce and pass laws to have serious mental illness covered by health insurance like any other serious medical disorder. According to Dausey (2004), there is empirical evidence that the likelihood and speed of passing an insurance parity bill are directly correlated with the extent of NAMI advocacy and the size of its membership in a particular state. They were also instrumental in seeing that the evidence-based practice ACT (assertive community treatment), was implemented in almost every US state (see Chapter 8). NAMI's current emphasis is on mental illness awareness and education.

Thanks in large part to the efforts of NAMI, there is an increased emphasis on alliances between professionals and families. These alliances result in family representation on the advisory and governance boards of mental health services, as well as family and consumer input in treatment, rehabilitation, and research. Family groups, NAMI in particular, have been very active in advocating, sponsoring, and raising funds for mental illness research.

Families Helping Each Other

One of NAMI's efforts is the FTF education program course where family members teach other families about mental illness free of charge. Conceived and developed by Dr. Joyce Burland (Burland, 1998), in over 20 years NAMI's FTF has educated over 100,000 family members. During intensive weekend trainings organized by NAMI state chapters, family members are trained as teachers and facilitators to provide education and support to other families. Provided by two members over a 12-week period, FTF covers the following topics as listed in the FTF teaching manuals:

- Learning about feelings, learning about facts
- Introduction to schizophrenia (e.g., diagnosis, crucial periods, etc.)
- Introduction to depression
- Basics about the brain
- Problem-solving skills workshop
- Medication review
- "What Is It Like to Be Mentally Ill?" empathy workshop
- Relative groups and self-care
- Communication skills
- Rehabilitation
- Advocacy (fighting stigma)
- Certification and celebration

The FTF education program has been researched in a controlled study, examining the course's effectiveness (Dixon et al., 2011). Family members were randomly assigned to either participate in FTF immediately or to be on a waiting list of at least three months. In the interim, they had unrestricted access to any other community or professional supports they desired. Participants were interviewed at study enrollment and after 12 weeks regarding problem solving and emotion-focused coping, subjective illness burden, and distress. After only three months, FTF participants improved in their problem-focused coping as indicated by greater self-report of empowerment and knowledge of mental illnesses compared to those on the waiting list. FTF participants also had improved emotionally focused coping and increased acceptance of their family member's illness, as well as reduced distress. Subjective illness burden did not change. This study provides evidence that NAMI's widely implemented, real-world FTF intervention is effective for enhancing coping and empowerment of families of persons with mental illness (Dixon et al., 2011).

Self-help Texts for Families

Apart from NAMI's FTF education program, there are numerous other independent resources, including books expressly designed to assist families dealing with mental illness, particularly schizophrenia. First published in 1983, E. Fuller Torrey's book *Surviving Schizophrenia: A Manual for Families, Patients, and Providers* (2006) is now in its fifth edition. This book provides historical background explaining many issues that affected the development of the current service system in the United States since deinstitutionalization. Kim Mueser and Susan Gingerich authored a comprehensive text, *The Complete Family Guide to Schizophrenia: Helping Your Loved One Get the Most out of Life* (2006). Their book provides information about schizophrenia, the issues facing different family members, and strategies to prevent relapse and improve the quality of life.

The Concept of Family Recovery

In our efforts to help consumers and their families, it might be helpful to recognize that, similar to the recovery process of an individual with mental illness, families may also go

---

CONTROVERSIAL ISSUE
Supervision vs. Self-determination

Some years ago, a state legislator proposed a bill stipulating that all state-licensed residences serving people with mental illness provide 24-hour supervision for their residents. This bill would even cover those programs that intentionally have minimal staff intervention because they are designed to promote independence. Not surprisingly, this bill received a very mixed review from different groups. Some of the family advocate groups in the state praised the legislator for her vision, while other family advocates were uncomfortable with such a sweeping proposal. Some particularly vocal consumer advocates vigorously opposed the measure, while some other consumers preferred staff in the homes at all times.

What psychiatric rehabilitation principles were at stake here? Why were some of the family member advocates and consumer advocates on opposing sides? Basically, they share the same concerns: the well-being of mental health consumers. One family advocate said he is for promoting quality of life and the 24-hour supervision would ensure good medication compliance and prompt crisis intervention. A consumer advocate said he was seeking a better quality of life by opposing the measure for his constituents, which he said would only hinder community integration, consumer choice, and self-determination.

One wise observer commented, "I guess where you stand on this issue depends on where you sit." That is, some of the family advocates simply wanted their family member cared for, while some consumer advocates wanted to promote independence.

through a process of recovery. Spaniol (2009) characterizes family recovery as a multi-dimensional (emotional, physical, social, vocational, and spiritual) process of accepting the disease (consolidation) and adjusting to it (transformation). Spaniol and Zipple (1994) described family recovery as an essential goal for helping people with mental illness and their families. Their conception of family recovery parallels the concept of recovery for individuals discussed throughout this text. They identified four stages in a family's recovery from serious and persistent mental illness: (1) discovery/denial, (2) recognition/acceptance, (3) coping/competence, and (4) personal/political advocacy. These four stages are discussed next.

Stage 1: Discovery/Denial

Family members' initial response to severe and persistent mental illness may range from minimizing the importance of the condition ("it's not so serious") to active denial ("it's just a phase" or "he is experimenting with drugs"). A lack of information and inadequate communication with professionals about what is happening can aggravate this situation. The fear of stigma is also a major factor. Sometimes, the best way to characterize this stage is as a state of disbelief.

Stage 2: Recognition/Acceptance

As they become aware of the seriousness of the illness, family members may experience feelings of guilt, embarrassment, and self-blame. As they accept the reality of the illness, they experience a deep sense of loss. This sense of loss is often made more difficult by the cyclical nature of the illness, especially the periods of improvement that can cause a roller coaster of repeated hope followed by disappointment.

Stage 3: Coping/Competence

With increased understanding born of experience and possibly a sense of resignation and acceptance, most families marshal their resources and begin to cope with the illness. Coping strategies may be effective or ineffective, informed by so-called expert opinion, or devised on their own. As outlined earlier in this chapter, a variety of effective approaches are available to help families cope better and become competent in their crisis intervention, problem solving, and understanding of mental illness.

Stage 4: Personal/Political Advocacy

Finally, having learned to accept and cope with mental illness, many families are propelled by the passion of their personal experiences to the stage of personal/political advocacy. This stage is characterized by efforts to influence how the mental health system responds to the needs of the family member with mental illness and other individuals in the same predicament. These advocacy efforts often involve attempts to influence public policy through groups such as NAMI and its local affiliates.

Familial Strengths and Resilience

As discussed in Chapter 2, the available evidence suggests that schizophrenia and other major mental illnesses can be exacerbated by stress. We are all aware that family life can cause stress, which may trigger relapse or an increase of symptoms. Still, family stress is not a cause of serious mental illness. This discussion of the role of stress in the etiology of schizophrenia and other disorders is not to deny that some people with serious mental illness have had traumatic or difficult family experiences (as have many people who do not have serious mental illnesses). Nor is it to deny that many individuals with serious mental illness live under adverse familial circumstances as adults.

Equally undeniable is the evidence of the resilience and strength of some families despite the objective and subjective burdens they face. Resilience has been described as the ability to "bounce back" from adversity (Smith, Dalen, Wiggins, Tooley, Christopher, & Bernard, 2008). Mannion (1996) sees family resilience as ". . . a process of constructive change and growth in response to a serious psychiatric disorder in a loved one" (p. 4).

Family members faced with the adversity of severe mental illness may be less concerned with issues of resiliency than the solutions to the immediate crises they face. Since families constitute a primary support system for persons with severe mental illness, focusing on fostering resiliency has obvious long-term payoffs for the family as well as the individual with mental illness. We have known for some time that family members can be effective problem solvers, intervene in crises, and promote recovery for their relative with mental illness (Lehman & Steinwachs, 1998). Helping families to "bounce back" will benefit everyone involved.

Summary

Families are a primary support system for persons with severe mental illness. The PsyR practitioner can greatly enhance the recovery prospects of consumers they serve by encouraging strong partnerships with family members. If mental health consumers desire family involvement and if family members can be successfully engaged, they are among the most important partners in the processes of rehabilitation and recovery.

The influence of family life on the lives of persons with mental illness can be profound. The individual and the family each bear a burden, but at the same time, many families prove to be resourceful and resilient. Some families, those with high levels of EE (expressed emotion), may present specific stresses to the individual with mental illness that produce negative outcomes. Studies suggest that these families may be capable of changing this style of interaction to promote coping, competence, and recovery.

Family psychoeducation, designated an evidence-based practice, can reduce the frequency of relapse, the number of rehospitalizations, and the length of hospital stays by providing families with knowledge, support, and coping skills. These psychoeducation and skills training initiatives appear to be more effective when they are diagnosis-specific.

Families go through their own process of recovering and adapting, incorporating mental illness into their self-image as a family. They can be a great source of support to not only their own members, but also other families. In the face of serious mental illness, many families are found to be ultimately capable and resilient. Some also go on to be quite effective advocates for the interests of persons with serious mental illness.

■ ■ ■ ▬▬▬▬▬▬▬▬▬▬▬▬▬▬▬▬▬▬▬▬▬▬▬▬▬▬▬▬▬▬▬▬▬▬▬▬▬

Class Exercise

Designing a Family Intervention and Support Program

Question 1

It is clear that family interventions that are primarily psychoeducational have been found to be very effective, especially if started when the relative with psychiatric illness is in the acute phase of his or her illness. In this exercise, the task is to generate the variety of possible reasons that FPE can lead to a reduction in both the frequency and length of relapses. For example, how do knowledge and skills translate into a lower likelihood of relapse? Remember, this effect can take place in both high EE and low EE families. Also, consider the following questions about what these interventions actually accomplish for the family. Do they help families to (1) be better observers, (2) intervene sooner when relapse is coming, or (3) be better symptom management agents?

Based on the information in this chapter, generate a list of possible reasons why these psychoeducational family interventions have positive effects for a person with mental illness. Provide the rationale for each reason on your list.

Question 2

Those family interventions that include people with mental illness directly in the training or group result in better outcomes. Is this fact consistent with PsyR principles? If so, which principles does it relate to and why?

Question 3

Mowbray, Bybee, Harris, and McCrohan (1995) found that high family contact on the part of the individual with mental illness was associated with poorer vocational outcomes, while less contact was associated with better outcomes. Alternatively, McFarlane's group (1995) found that families can help to promote vocational outcomes. Are these two sets of findings inconsistent? If they are reconcilable, what do they imply about the role of families in the vocational rehabilitation of people with severe and persistent mental illness?

▬▬▬▬▬▬▬▬▬▬▬▬▬▬▬▬▬▬▬▬▬▬▬▬▬▬▬▬▬▬▬▬▬▬ ■ ■ ■

Psychiatric Rehabilitation in Acute Care and Hospital Settings

I come to present the strong claims of suffering humanity. I come to place before the Legislature of Massachusetts the condition of the miserable, the desolate, the outcast. I come as the advocate of helpless, forgotten, insane, and idiotic men and women, of beings sunk to a condition from which the most unconcerned would start with real horror, of beings wretched in our prisons, and more wretched in our almshouses.

Dorothea Dix (1843)

CHAPTER OUTLINE

Psychiatric Rehabilitation. http://dx.doi.org/10.1016/B978-0-12-387002-5.00015-9

Most of the chapters of this book are devoted to the implementation of the guiding principles of psychiatric rehabilitation (PsyR) in community settings in the pursuit of recovery, community integration, and improved quality of life. Can these goals be pursued when people are acutely ill? Are there acute care interventions that are based on the principles of PsyR that can be used to promote recovery and reintegration in the community? Historically, hospitals have been the settings for managing these disorders. Are the principles of PsyR applicable to hospital settings? As this chapter will explain, barriers to the pursuit of these goals in a hospital setting are often formidable. The treatment values and assumptions within hospitals are very different from those of community settings. Traditionally, there have been significant restrictions on the freedom of choice of persons in psychiatric hospitals. An individual's stay often begins involuntarily. By design and definition, they are rarely integrated with the community. Yet, in many places, psychiatric hospitals remain a critical part of the mental health service system. The people served in psychiatric hospitals are very often the same individuals who are served by PsyR in the community. Alternatives to hospitalization, more consistent with the values of psychiatric rehabilitation, are discussed in detail in this chapter.

This chapter will answer the following questions:

1. *Can the principles of psychiatric rehabilitation be applied in hospitals?*
2. *Are psychiatric hospitals an impediment, or can they help foster community integration?*
3. *Can recovery and quality of life be fostered by hospitalization experiences?*
4. *What are the common barriers to both the application of PsyR principles and the pursuit of PsyR goals in hospitals?*
5. *What alternatives to hospitals are available for the management of acute care?*

Introduction

Large psychiatric hospitals around the nation have been plagued by well-documented reports of patient neglect or abuse (e.g., Geller, 2000). In addition, there are many reports of deteriorating, unhealthy, and unsanitary living conditions. There is also strong evidence that the psychiatric care in some of these institutions is quite inadequate, with even basic guidelines for the prescription of medications not being followed. At the same time, the mission of psychiatric hospitals is evolving and requires reexamination and redefinition (Glick, Sharfstein, & Schwartz, 2011; Smith & Bartholomew, 2006).

Many of the so-called reform movements aimed at improving these hospitals have focused primarily on improving the physical plant, reducing the size of institutions, building smaller wards with private or semiprivate bedrooms, and generally reducing the buildings' resemblance to prisons. Given the reports of neglect, abuse, and the negative effects of institutional treatment, can these hospitals where involuntary care is the norm possibly promote recovery, enhance quality of life, and promote community integration?

Experts disagree. Two of these experts, E. Fuller Torrey (2003) and Patrick Corrigan (2003), offer a "yes." Other experts assert that psychiatric patients would be better off without these institutions. While neither Corrigan nor Torrey reports being pleased with the overall quality of care offered, each sheds light on how hospitalization can play a positive role. Torrey suggests that the relative lack of availability of hospitalization, the difficulties of getting into a hospital, and the short, inadequate lengths of stay in hospitals all inhibit the recovery of persons with mental illness, detracting from their integration in the community and harming their quality of life. Corrigan indicates that hospitals can, in fact, be one of the settings, like other types of residential programs (described in Chapter 12), where successful rehabilitation interventions can be implemented. Strategies such as goal setting, skills training, and cognitive rehabilitation can all be initiated in the hospital. Reduced symptoms, improved skills, and increased supports can also be achieved in hospital settings.

Other experts say hospitals need significant restructuring to meet today's needs (Glick, Sharfstein, & Schwartz, 2011) and are in many ways a long way off from implementing PsyR principles to promote recovery (Bartholomew & Smith, 2006) and wellness (Swarbrick, 2009). Hospital policies and rules rarely promote key values of PsyR such as empowerment and choice. There is little emphasis on skills training in the hospital environment. Finally, community and family coordination is typically postponed until the individual is close to being discharged, if at all. If hospital administrators and staff members adhere to PsyR values, is it possible to promote recovery, improve quality of life, and foster community reintegration? In short, can hospitals be organized to deliver PsyR? If not, what are the alternative services to reduce the number of hospitals required?

A 19th-century Institution in the 21st Century

To understand both the barriers to implementing PsyR in hospitals and the potential for its success, it may be instructive to briefly review the history of these institutions. In the United States, large public psychiatric hospitals are operated by most state governments, the Veterans Administration, lower levels of government such as county or city governments, and occasionally by charities. They exist in some other countries as well and are often state-run. They are, in large part, 19th-century institutions struggling to adapt to the demands and conditions of the 21st century. Most of these institutions grew out of faith in the potential for large, orderly institutions, to promote the safety of society, and to provide peaceful sanctuary for those disturbed by troubling mental disorders. In the United States, the large institution–asylum concept also grew out of a concern for the inhumane treatment and the neglect of persons with mental illness who were often jailed in poorhouses as debtors, were homeless, or were living under extremely restrictive and inadequate conditions (Rothman, 2002).

The movement to develop these institutions peaked in the mid-19th century. Many are still in existence today. These institutions were clearly meant to be a mechanism for reform to provide an orderly environment that helped individuals manage the chaos of their illness through participation in a self-sustaining community that kept individuals occupied by useful activity (Rothman, 2002). This movement coincided with the development of a variety of other large institutions with a significant moral or ethical purpose, such as state penitentiaries directed toward moral reform of criminals and large state schools that taught practical skills to people who were blind (Rothman, 2002).

Before the development of state institutions, private charities—rather than governments—were the primary helpers of persons with mental illness. There were some rare exceptions, such as Eastern State Hospital founded in 1773 and operated by the city of Williamsburg, Virginia. Eastern State actually sought out psychiatric patients by making an appeal to their friends and loved ones.

National reform took place in the United States in the mid-19th century, led by the social activist Dorothea Dix (1802-1885). This movement was part of a paradigm shift in which larger units of government accepted greater accountability for societal problems. In the United States, the states themselves—as opposed to cities or towns—began to take on the responsibility of opening and operating these institutions. The other issue addressed by the development of this type of facility was the thinking that such institutions could have some curative, indeed, rehabilitative, impact (Rothman, 2002). Dorothea Dix left quite a mark, contributing to the founding of 32 psychiatric hospitals (a hospital named after Dix in North Carolina closed in 2010), 12 facilities for persons with intellectual disabilities, a school for people who are blind, and several nursing schools. She lived for six years at Trenton (New Jersey) Psychiatric Hospital, which she helped found in 1878, and her contributions are documented in a small museum there.

Comparison and Contrast with Today's Hospitals

In some ways, the 19th-century state hospital bears little resemblance to today's hospitals. The locations are often similar, usually remote settings and often self-sustaining communities. Many had large working farms, produced crops, and raised livestock. Most of the support services needed—hardware, blacksmiths, and central heating or power plants—were on the grounds. Some had their own factories. Until the 1950s, everyone associated with such a hospital—staff, nurses, and doctors—lived on the grounds near the patients.

At the peak of what was known as the "moral treatment era," the precursors of two intervention strategies that later became prominent in PsyR were initiated in these hospitals. While the exact phrases were not employed, early attempts at **milieu therapy** and the work-ordered day (discussed in Chapter 6) were pioneered at these institutions. There was a strong belief, for example, that (as in milieu therapy) the environment was the treatment. In addition (when feasible), the work-ordered day, later utilized by the clubhouse movement (see Chapter 7), was seen as beneficial for persons who had uncontrolled psychotic symptoms.

Many hospitals were based on the model developed by Thomas Kirkbride (1809-1883) described by Osborn (2009) in *On the Construction, Organization, and General Arrangements of Hospitals for the Insane,* which outlined the components of an asylum. Ideally, a hospital was built on the outskirts of a moderately sized town, accessible by railroad, and with land for farming and gardens. These institutions literally maintained themselves with the goods, services, and products they required to have a functioning community (Rothman, 2002). They were their own worlds, or at least their own separate communities. The hospitals would have symmetrical wings coming off a central administrative building with at least eight wards per wing. The wings were designed for good ventilation and lighting. Large windows and solariums were provided, especially in areas where patients spent their days. However, there were bars on the windows to prevent patients from escaping. The symptomatic and violent people lived in the wards farthest from the central administrative building, the "back wards" (a phrase still in use today) so as not to upset calmer patients. Thomas Kirkbride, who served as a hospital superintendent, instituted therapeutic beauty, including gardens, fountains, trails, and a grandiose architecture. He thought the hospital should look as attractive and impressive as possible to reassure and calm the patients, while bolstering support of family members who committed their loved ones. Kirkbride believed that architecture and landscape could help cure insanity. He also paid a great deal of attention to security, ensuring the durability of the hospital to withstand wear and tear by the patients.

He founded his masterpiece, Greystone Park Psychiatric Hospital, Morris Plains, NJ, in 1876. At its peak, the campus covered a square mile. Its 43 buildings once housed more than 6000 patients as well as about the same number of staff. The buildings themselves offer a remarkable record of 19th- and 20th-century institutional and residential architecture. From 1876 to 1943, the main administration and treatment building, the Kirkbride Building, was the largest structure on a single foundation in the United States (Preservation New Jersey, 2003). In its history, the hospital saw the introduction of a number of positive developments, including occupational therapy, antipsychotic medication, and the use of small cottage residences organized around PsyR principles. However, other earlier treatment approaches actually proved to be harmful to many patients, such as psychosurgery, the long-discredited severing of nerve fibers in the brain's frontal lobes referred to as lobotomy.

Greystone has been consolidated mostly into a new single building finished in 2008 that, from its exterior, bears a resemblance to a prison. It now has fewer than 600 patients at any given time, half of whom are awaiting placement in the community. The hospital had been scheduled for a downsizing by a further 250 beds, accompanied by a significant expansion in community services.

State hospitals have other continuing legacies besides their architecture and physical plant. In some places, large dormitory-style housing without privacy for the patients still exists. Other elements of the legacy include separation from the rest of the world, including both a physical and psychological distance from most communities. In many hospital settings, there is another vestige from an earlier time: the belief that recovery of any sort from a serious mental illness is not a likely outcome (Birkmann, Sperduto, Smith, & Gill, 2006; Dhillon & Dollieslager, 2000).

One of the greatest barriers to implementing PsyR in hospitals may be an attitudinal one, embedded in the culture and practices of the institutions (Dhillon & Dollieslager, 2000; Birkmann et al., 2006). Many staff members in these institutions simply do not believe that persons with severe and persistent mental illness can actually recover to any meaningful extent. In part, this may be a consequence of the fact that hospital staff sees patients in the acute phase of their illness (Cohen & Cohen, 1984) rather than when they are not symptomatic, coping well in the community, and living independently. This is a version of what Harding and Zahniser (1994) refer to as the "clinician's mistake based on experience". Cohen and Cohen (1984) refer to it as the "clinician's illusion". Hospital staffs literally see people at their worst in the acute stages of their illness. They rarely see patients at their best. As a result, their conception of persons with these disorders is based on their experiences of the patients as they are in the hospital rather than on how they function in the community.

The economic crisis that began in 2008 spurred an increased number of US state psychiatric hospital closures. Despite significant growth in population, there has been a long-term trend in decreasing state psychiatric hospital censuses since the 1950s (Geller, 2000). Recently (2008-2012), the trend has reaccelerated because states, starved of their usual level of tax revenues, have been cutting their expenditures. State hospitals remain expensive; closing them appears to save a lot of dollars, at least in the short-term. Still, if recidivism or the number of persons with unmanageable illness increases, this trend may reverse itself.

In many places, public hospital closures have resulted in reinvestment of funds for community services. In some US states, Italy, and other countries, legislation provides that resources saved by the closing of public hospitals must be reinvested in community-based mental health programs, including PsyR services such as assertive community treatment, co-occurring disorders programs, supported housing, and supported employment. It makes sense that to live in the community, people who were formerly hospitalized need enhanced services. Hospital utilization (i.e., number of hospital days) by these individuals can be greatly reduced by such services. Sadly, with today's economic downturn, the closure of hospitals is resulting in the reinvestment of only 25 percent or less of their operating expenses for community-based services.

The *Olmstead* Decision

Another important development in this area was the US Supreme Court's 1999 *Olmstead v. L.C.* decision. Two women, dually diagnosed with a serious mental illness and a developmental disability, sued the State of Georgia, citing the Americans with Disabilities Act. Their lawyers' argument was that they were illegally segregated because of their disability rather than for medical or treatment purposes. The State of Georgia argued they did not have the funds to move L.C. and E.W. to the community, although they admitted that is where they belonged. The Supreme Court ruled in favor of both ladies and said each state, even if they did not have the resources or funding at the moment, had to have a plan to move all people back into the community.

The states have been very slow to implement the decision as outlined in the Bazelon Center's report *Still Waiting: The Unfulfilled Promise of Olmstead* (2009). Since 1999, there has been a steady stream of lawsuits against states by advocates for persons who are institutionalized to force them to implement the *Olmstead* decision. Although often long in coming, people who are unnecessarily institutionalized plaintiffs win these suits. Many states are in the position now of finding appropriate community living for persons who have been institutionalized. Some of the people leaving the hospitals under these so-called *Olmstead* decisions face multiple challenges upon discharge. Often, the reason for their long length of stay is multiple needs: dual diagnoses, co-morbid medical conditions, legal problems, and other concerns that make it difficult to find a good place to live and the right services. Some, due to their long length of stay, exhibit the institutionalized behavior mentioned in Chapter 1. In all, they present a new challenge for psychiatric rehabilitation services to meet their many needs and many skill deficits.

The Many Meanings of the "Shame of the States"

As mentioned earlier, Dorothea Dix devoted her life to developing psychiatric hospitals and advocating for their establishment in various states in the mid-19th century. After World War II, Deutsch (1948) referred to some of the conditions of these hospitals as the "shame of the states," because they did little or nothing for persons with mental illnesses except house them in facilities that were deteriorating. This phrase continued to be relevant in the years that followed. In the 1960s and 1970s, the shame of the states remained the hospitals themselves, rocked with scandals about inhumane conditions and lack of treatment (Geller, 2000).

Unfortunately, the scandalous conditions that preceded deinstitutionalization continue today. Some state psychiatric hospitals in the United States have been placed under federal supervision by the US Department of Justice because of evidence of violations of civil rights. Concerns about treatment and conditions have led other states to eliminate or curtail the number, size, and census of their state hospitals. Several state mental health departments have instituted major projects in collaboration with universities and community providers to improve the conditions at their institutions, including the introduction of evidence-based practices such as illness management and recovery, staff development, treatment malls, and academic programs (Birkmann et al., 2006; Smith & Bartholomew, 2006).

At the same time, the insufficient availability of hospital beds or alternate forms of providing acute and intermediate psychiatric care are equally shameful. E. Fuller Torrey (2003) points out that we may have turned the clock back further than the mid-19th century. In many places, there are more persons with mental illness in state prisons and county jails than in hospitals operated by states and counties. In fact, in the United States, the most populous institutions housing the most persons with mental illness are the following county or city jails: Los Angeles, California; Cook County, Illinois; and Rikers Island, New York (Torrey, 2003).

Functions of State Psychiatric Hospitals

State psychiatric hospitals formerly served the primary functions of the physical maintenance and long-term, sometimes lifelong, care of persons with psychotic disorders. A number of important developments since the 1950s have changed this situation:

1. *The advent of psychotropic medications, first introduced in the late 1950s,* did a great deal to provide symptom relief and promote some level of recovery. For many individuals, these medications eliminated the necessity of lifelong confinement.
2. *Changes in the US Social Security laws in 1965 and 1966* provided income support and medical coverage that permitted persons with disabilities in all states to be maintained outside institutions.
3. *A series of US Supreme Court cases in the 1960s and 1970s* affirmed the civil rights of patients. These included *Wyatt v. Stickney* and *Donaldson v. O'Connor*, which found that state psychiatric hospitals often deprived individuals of basic civil rights (Geller, 2000).

These US Supreme Court rulings resulted in changes in the involuntary commitment laws, limiting who could be confined against their will (i.e., only those who pose an imminent risk to themselves, other people, and sometimes property due to a mental illness). In addition, one could no longer be committed without being offered active treatment. "Active Treatment" refers to the requirement that individuals who are committed to state institutions cannot be deprived of liberty for public safety purposes alone. Rather, during their confinement, individuals who are committed must also receive an active program of care to address the symptoms and deficits associated with their psychiatric illness. More than 40 years later, many hospitals are still trying to achieve these standards (Dhillon & Dollieslager, 2000; Geller, 2000).

According to Leona Bachrach (1999), today's state psychiatric hospitals serve a number of functions, including care of persons who require one of the following:

- **Short stays (less than one month)**—used for the rapid management and reduction of acute symptoms.

- **Extended stays**—providing time to stabilize symptoms. For some individuals, longer stays (several weeks to months) are required for stabilization as compared to the very short stays that are typically provided in the psychiatric units of general hospitals.
- **Long stays (several months to many years)**—for those to whom the hospital provides both residential and case-management services (care coordination) in addition to their psychiatric services.

In addition, many state hospitals also serve the following functions:

- **Forensic care**—hospitals serve a heterogeneous population of persons with legal involvement, including those who are not guilty by reason of insanity, are on other types of court retainers for criminal charges, or are sexual offenders who have been civilly committed under special sexual predator laws. After serving a jail sentence for sexual offenses, in many states, these individuals are committed to a hospital stay based on the premise that they are a danger to others.
- **Geriatric care**—this type of care is provided for people who are elderly and have numerous medical concerns but have nowhere to go in the community to have their multiple health care needs served.

Most state psychiatric hospitals provide care primarily to individuals under court-ordered involuntary commitment. Because of this, they are likely to admit individuals in the acute phase of their illness, individuals who are not responding to treatment for one reason or another, and persons who are potentially harmful to themselves or others. Thus, these hospitals face great challenges.

A variety of factors have contributed to this multiplicity of demands on state psychiatric hospitals; however, the primary problem is that these hospitals are often the "last stop" or a state's only alternative to providing care when other parts of the system are uninterested, unwilling, or incapable.

In some places, public psychiatric hospitals provide acute care services because local community hospitals have no psychiatric units. Due to changes in insurance practices and managed care policies, many hospitals have very short lengths of stay of seven to ten days or less. This persists despite the fact that it takes four to six weeks for antipsychotic medication to develop its full therapeutic effect. A lack of hospitals to provide intermediate or long stays often necessitates the transfer of individuals to state hospitals.

Length of Hospital Stay and Rehabilitation Outcome

Evidence has accumulated that neither very short nor very long hospital stays are helpful for recovery. Very long stays are associated with iatrogenic effects, referred to in Chapter 1 as "institutionalization syndrome." These include extreme dependence and passivity. In addition, the coercive aspects of hospital stays are associated with the experience of trauma (Reddy & Spaulding, 2010). Very short stays allow insufficient time to manage and reduce symptoms. Is there an optimal length of hospital stay for recovery from severe and persistent mental illnesses?

The lengths of hospital stays have been dramatically reduced during the past 40 years, although not in all US locations, nor all other countries, notably Japan (Tsuchiya & Takei, 2004). In the past couple of decades, this has been primarily for economic reasons, not clinical ones (Glick, 2011). Some argue that this reduction has led to a pattern of revolving door admissions and worsening mental health outcomes despite apparent cost savings (Talbott, 2004). In contrast, others suggest longer stays may be more harmful in the long term by fostering dependence on institutions. Alwan, Johnstone, and Zolese (2008) completed a review of the studies examining lengths of hospital stays for people with serious mental illness. Short stays varied from one week to three to four weeks and, in all the studies reviewed, ranged from an average of 11 to 25 days. In these studies, those randomly assigned to short stays received treatments such as medication, crisis resolution, and discharge planning. These short-stay studies focused on short length of stay by state hospital standards, but not by today's community hospital standards. Antipsychotic drugs were the main treatment for participants and most studies reported similar use of these medications in both long- and short-stay participants. Persons assigned to planned short stays experienced no more readmissions, were not more difficult to follow up, and were more successfully discharged compared to those who received long stays, an average of 28 to 94 days (Alwan, Johnstone, & Zolese, 2008). The short-stay patients had a greater chance of becoming employed. These findings suggest that a planned short-stay policy does not, in itself, encourage a "revolving door" pattern of admission or a lack of continuity of care and may foster community integration (Alwan, Johnstone, & Zolese, 2008). Unfortunately, the research on this topic was completed over 30 years ago and may have limited generalizability today. Nevertheless, many experts (e.g., Capdevielle & Ritchie, 2008) have questioned the ongoing shortening of hospital stays for people with psychosis. Decisions about the duration of hospitalizations are driven more by economic than clinical considerations.

Population Served by State Psychiatric Hospitals

In large part, the persons served in state psychiatric hospitals are the same individuals described throughout this text who receive PsyR services. The two vignettes that follow illustrate common profiles of persons currently residing in state hospitals. When reading their stories, consider the following questions: In addition to a psychiatric disorder, what other challenges are they facing? Are other factors contributing to the lengthening of their hospitalization? Does the hospital environment foster their recovery?

Stan's Story

Consider Stan's story, which describes the lifestyle of a wanderer not fully aware of his illness, a pattern of revolving door admissions, and some unnecessarily long lengths of stay in hospitals.

Stan is now in his early sixties. He remembers an incident from his early twenties that resulted in his having a psychiatric evaluation performed in an emergency room (ER). "My girlfriend kicked me out of her house and called the police. I was calm and cool with the cops, but they didn't know what to do with me." He remembers talking to a counselor and a psychiatrist in the ER and being informed that he had "delusions" and that they were going to prescribe medication that would help alleviate this problem. "They gave me the prescription, which I filled, and the number of some sort of clinic to follow up with . . . but I was ready to move on, even though I had a pretty good job." For a period of a few years, he traveled around the East Coast looking for work and living in various unsafe situations, including on the street. During this period, he is sure that he had no treatment and took no medication.

"Looking back, I can't quite believe that I stayed alive. I was extremely confused. I believed at one point that I was a famous Hollywood actor starring in a movie that was my life. It led to one really bad decision." After conferring with some acquaintances from his boarding home, Stan attempted to rob a gas station and was immediately apprehended. The court-appointed attorney recommended that he plead "not guilty by reason of insanity" with the promise that he would be out of the hospital in six months. He accepted this advice and was admitted to a state psychiatric hospital. The six-month stay, according to Stan, was "good news and bad news."

"It was good that I was in the hospital and realized that I've got this illness, that it's real, it is probably not going away, and that I need to take medicine. The bad news is that six months became three years." At the end of six months, he was recommitted because of "erratic behavior." He also continued to be on the state list of those patients who had criminal charges pending a disposition from the justice system. Somewhere in the second year of his hospitalization, his social worker began to emphasize plans for discharge. "This was very good news for me. I felt ready to leave and that I had done my time, so to speak. The problem was that my plans and the social worker's were not the same." Stan was looking forward to living on his own, and his social worker felt that he needed to live in a group home for people with psychiatric diagnoses. Stan went to a series of interviews and visits with residential providers.

"They seemed more interested in whether my beard was trimmed than anything else and whether I was ever going to rob a gas station again. I finally ended up on a waiting list. I was at the point where I would go anywhere to get out, but no one would take me." After three-and-a-half years in a state hospital, he was discharged to a group home in a nearby suburb. He lived in the group home and attended a day program for nine months but says, "I never really felt at home, I wanted to work, maybe get off disability and find a place on my own. The staff always told me to wait for the right time. I sort of went along with it and finally just left."

For the next three years, he repeated the earlier pattern of intermittent work, marginal housing, and no psychiatric or support services. While traveling through a small city, he was questioned by police and evaluated once again in an ER. He had an untreated wound on his leg from a construction work accident and also recounted his history of hospitalization and psychiatric services. He was readmitted to the same state hospital. He was stabilized on medication, and within six months was determined to be ready for discharge. Once again, he cited his preference for independent living, but he had to repeat the process of interviewing for group homes. The main concern now was his "elopement" from the previous group home. A series of failed interviews resulted in his transfer from a unit that had high expectations for discharge to a unit that had minimal expectations. He then found himself on a list of patients who do not meet criteria for commitment but for whom no residential program is available.

"I have tried to get my social worker and the team to work with me on this. I know I need help when I get out there. I've brought up going to the city where I have family and I know there are programs. They won't go for it." After four years, Stan was discharged again. He lives a fairly quiet life in the community; occasionally, his symptoms get worse. He knows of a crisis residence in his area. Now if he feels signs of his illness getting worse, or if someone tells him he or she thinks he is not doing well, he voluntarily goes to the residence. Usually, after a few days, he feels better and leaves.

Stan's story resembles that of many people served by state hospitals. His struggle with mental illness is long term. When it began, he was not even aware it was an illness. His poor judgment, poorly thought-out plans, and symptoms led to encounters with law enforcement. He spent much of the time in the hospital not for a medical or psychiatric reason but simply because no community placement was available for him.

Julie's Story

Now consider Julie's story. Like Stan, she faces multiple challenges in addition to her mental illness, but there are also a number of differences.

Julie is a 43-year-old single woman who was admitted to the state hospital in 1996 at age 35 and has been hospitalized there on and off through 2011. Her IQ is 55, putting her in the range for mental retardation. Before being hospitalized, she was living with her sister. On the day of her admission, she felt depressed when her sister left the house. She called the police, threatening to harm herself. Previously, she had been hospitalized twice at the Elm Foundation Hospital. She was exhibiting self-mutilating behaviors, depression, and suicidal ideation. She was diagnosed as suffering from impulse control disorder and returned to live with her sister. Julie has numerous medical problems, including diabetes, obesity, anemia, and ovarian cysts. She lived with her parents until her father died in 1995. Then, she went to live with her sister. Julie has several close relatives who are mentally ill and/or mentally retarded and has a daughter who is around 17 years old, who lives with her sister. She has exhibited so-called behavioral problems without much improvement since the time she was admitted. These problems have included banging walls and doors, verbal and physical threats and assaults, blocking doorways, swallowing inedible objects, and attempting to escape. She has difficulty trusting others and hears voices. She has been depressed occasionally.

Julie also has a good sense of humor, can be playful, and teases other people. She has earned the highest level of hospital privileges in the past and was conditionally released to her sister's care in May 1997, but remained in the community for only two months and was returned because she refused to take her medications and became self-destructive.

At a special case conference, Julie complained of hearing her father's voice often (he had died six years previously). She also stated that he was coming to get her. The treatment team requested she be transferred to another ward where she would be with other "higher functioning" patients who could be good role models for her. Unfortunately, she continued her disruptive behaviors and was transferred to the state's forensic hospital.

She improved significantly at the forensic hospital and was returned to the previous ward. She has remained in the same ward since her transfer. She has been prescribed many different medications, including antipsychotics, mood stabilizers, antidepressants, and benzodiazepines. Team members report no significant improvement except when Clozaril was prescribed. Unfortunately, she refused to comply with required blood tests and the medication was withdrawn. Julie has a behavioral plan, but the team members report that it has been difficult to implement throughout the three work shifts of the day because of staff changes.

She has maintained contact with her sister and her daughter only by phone. Julie had a boyfriend, Bob, at the hospital and liked to talk about the relationship. She was proud of the bracelet he had given her. They broke up on a day she was not feeling well. She didn't go out for the smoke break and she did not want to talk with Bob when he called the unit later that day. When informed of the latter, Bob told another patient who answered the phone to "tell Julie we're through." When Julie was informed of this, she initially was sad, but later would smile when staff kidded her that "men do dumb things sometimes."

After several days, Julie's mood became increasingly depressed and she was constantly crying. She would sit on the floor with tears streaming down her face. She described feeling depressed and frightened that she was "losing her mind." When asked why, she said she was hearing the voices of "some men" who were telling her to "scratch and cut" herself. She said the voices woke her up at 2 a.m. She also said the voices made it difficult for her to focus.

After a time, she was no longer crying and she looked less depressed, but she was relatively nonverbal and extremely self-abusive. As a result, she was repeatedly placed in restraints. She would scream that she wanted her restraints loosened only to use this little bit of freedom to scratch her face or arms. On one occasion, she rubbed the side of her hand on the metal bedside. She was rubbing so hard that she was removing her skin. When a staff person said it was better to talk about her feelings than to hurt herself, she stared at him, as if infuriated, and rubbed her hand harder and more rapidly.

Several weeks later, Julie was talking about her medication and she said she needed something to make her feel better, but she didn't want the medicine that made her "so sleepy." She noted that she even fell asleep while going to the bathroom. Later, she discussed with her doctor how Haldol had helped her in the past. Although initially dismissed by some staff, her doctor decided to try it and her symptoms significantly subsided.

There have been many attempts to match Julie to an appropriate community residence. As a result of a lawsuit by state public advocates under the Olmstead *decision, she was put on a list on people who were on priority for discharge, but community providers say they do not have the resources to serve her effectively. Developmental disabilities agencies say her mental illness would be difficult to manage. Mental health providers say they are not prepared to manage her developmental disability.*

Like many people in state hospital, Julie has at least two diagnoses, in her case a developmental disability and a mental illness. She also has many other health problems. Her psychiatric diagnosis is in question as well. Which severe and persistent mental illness does she have? After all these years, there is no consensus among the professionals. It is not an academic question, because if an accurate diagnosis were known it would imply a specific treatment. The hospital setting does not seem to be conducive to her recovery, yet no community option is available for her.

Also implied in Julie's story is how "abnormal" or "un-normalized" Julie's life is in the hospital. Indeed, she must bear additional stresses that most people do not experience. She only knows about her teenage daughter's life through the phone or by mail. She does not get to experience the normal rewards and challenges that being the mother of a young girl involves. Also note that Julie's boyfriend lived in another hospital unit. To carry on that relationship, other patients had to pass personal messages through a ward telephone shared by all who live there. How does one carry on a relationship with such indirect and non-private circumstances? The circumstances of Julie's life in the hospital are very different from the lives of other women her age who are living in the community.

Challenges in the Hospital Environment

Many large psychiatric institutions have been plagued by well-documented reports of patient neglect or abuse and reports of deteriorating, unhealthy, and unsanitary living conditions. Also, there is growing evidence that the psychiatric care in these institutions is inadequate. Basic guidelines for the prescription of medications are not always followed. Medical model thinking often prevails over rehabilitative approaches.

Violence and Its Causes in the Hospital

Anecdotal evidence, that is, first-person accounts, have long suggested that violent incidents in hospitals are not primarily the result of symptoms but due in large part to interactions with staff that escalate into an incident in which a patient becomes violent. It turns out there is a good deal of evidence to support this assertion. In reviewing the results of 71 studies, Papadopoulos and colleagues (2012) found that staff–patient interactions, including limiting patients' freedoms, placing restrictions on the freedom of the patient, or denial of a request, were the most common precursors of incidents. This review underscores the influence that staff have in making inpatient psychiatric wards safe and efficacious environments. Respectful communication and non-punitive interactions are less likely to provoke violence.

Seclusion and Restraint: Definitely Not Psychiatric Rehabilitation

One traditional feature of many psychiatric hospitals has been seclusion and restraint. **Seclusion** is being segregated from others in a supposedly quiet and low-stimulation environment. **Restraint** is restricting the physical movement of the individual, including binding individuals to beds by the arms and legs for hours, days, and even longer periods of time. These techniques have been traditionally used to restrict the movement of individuals acutely distressed and displaying aggressive behavior. However, there was never any evidence that it succeeded in doing anything to the individual other than humiliating and exhausting the person. Often restraint took place when other approaches had failed and sometimes when staff had contributed to the escalation of the person's distress. In any case, restraints have been primarily used for staff safety as opposed to the care of persons with mental illness. In many countries and in some US states, seclusion and restraints have been completely eliminated. In other places, their use has been severely reduced. Busch (2005) wrote:

> Seclusion *and* restraint *are increasingly controversial, and with good reason.* Seclusion *and* restraint *can be deadly. However, no medical literature guides as to which methods are safer and under which circumstances. Patients have described these experiences as negative at best, and as traumatic at worst. Of further concern,* seclusion *and* restraint *are not applied uniformly—numerous studies have shown considerable variation in their frequency and duration. Nonclinical factors, such as patients' ethnicity and level of staff experience, are known to be associated with the use of* seclusion *and* restraint. *(p. 1104)*

Medication used for solely sedative purposes and not for symptom management is another form of physical restraint, sometimes called chemical restraint (Donat, 2005). A number of treatment improvement programs aimed at reducing seclusion and restraint have proven successful, without increased risk to patients or staff (Busch, 2005; Curie, 2005; Donat, 2005; Smith et al., 2005). These techniques generally involved improved communication. Staff learn to become more sensitive to the cues of escalating aggression, engaging in speech and making comments that are deescalating, as opposed to being antagonistic. Behavioral interventions, such as consistent use of rewards for positive coping and ignoring negative behaviors, although not a PsyR approach per se, may be helpful in decreasing the need for seclusion and restraint as well as for helping staff not to escalate crisis situations. Sometimes individuals are rewarded through point systems or tokens in exchange for privileges. This has the advantage of employing learning principles, primarily positive reinforcement, but also helps staff to be consistent and less emotional in their approach to potentially troublesome behaviors (Dixon et al., 2010). In addition, they learn to reward the individual for nonaggressive acts. Another technique is reducing unnecessary stimulation by allowing the individual to retreat to a quiet but non-secluded area. The individual may utilize or leave it at will and it is not locked away from the rest of the hospital.

The coercion of being involuntarily committed to treatment, the observation of violence or being the subject of violence when hospitalized, and the experience of being secluded or, worse, restrained, are all often associated with trauma.

Reddy and Spaulding (2010) pointed out that psychiatric hospitals are meant to be places of treatment and sanctuary; indeed, the original meaning of the word *asylum* is a place of retreat and security. Often, however, iatrogenic events in the hospital may prevent the development of this sort of environment. Reddy and Spaulding found that 98 percent of participants had experienced at least one negative event in the psychiatric hospital. A history of being abused as a child was also significantly related to the number of reported negative hospital events. People with a history of being abused reported experiencing more negative events in the hospital and a higher level of subjective distress. Thus, care in the hospitals must be "trauma-informed" to avoid retriggering traumatic experiences.

Beyond Eliminating Restraints: Is Psychiatric Rehabilitation Possible in the Hospital Setting?

Given the context and history of psychiatric hospitalization, can hospitals be organized to deliver PsyR? Consider the following analysis of how the goals, values, and guiding principles of PsyR introduced in Chapter 4 may relate to psychiatric hospitalization.

Psychiatric Rehabilitation Goals

The goals of PsyR as introduced in Chapter 4 include the following.

- **Recovery**—potentially, hospitals can provide the best setting for the resolution of acute symptomatology through the use of psychotropic medication. There is ample opportunity to titrate or "adjust" dosages and observe the individual's responsiveness to medication. Thus, the portion of recovery that involves symptom amelioration can be very well managed if quality psychiatric care is provided. Unfortunately, there is evidence that the medication management services need improvement to be closer to existing psychopharmacology practice guidelines (Glick et al., 2011). Unnecessary and potentially harmful **polypharmacy** (i.e., prescribing numerous medications) is too frequent. In any case, symptom reduction is only one component of recovery. Recovery is further enhanced through community integration.
- **Community integration**—to promote community integration, close coordination with community providers is necessary. If community agency staff have access to hospital treatment team meetings, participate in hospital treatment teams, work on discharge planning, and meet with the consumer before they leave, community reintegration can be promoted (Glick et al., 2011). Visits by the consumer to the community before discharge are often helpful.

- **Quality of life**—a reasonable quality of life is more likely to be ensured if the concerns of symptom amelioration and reintegration in the community are addressed. Yet as illustrated earlier in Julie's story, normal privacy, an important component of quality of life, can be impossible to achieve in a state hospital setting.

Values of Psychiatric Rehabilitation

The values of PsyR were also introduced in Chapter 4. A great challenge to the implementation of PsyR in hospital settings is the fact that the values of PsyR clash directly with those of the medically oriented asylum.

- *Self-determination and empowerment* are not always possible, certainly under conditions of involuntary commitment for psychiatric care. Yet, subsequent treatment planning and interventions can be used to engage the consumer and promote self-determination. Treatment plans should be person-centered and have the real input of people who are inpatients. Stan's story illustrates the importance of this value. Stan was dismayed when he was not included in his treatment and discharge planning; if he had been, a successful life in the community would have been more likely. In Julie's story, she finally got some relief from her symptoms when hospital staff listened to her input and responded to her description of which medicines had helped her in the past. Giving each individual input on his or her goals and interventions is an example of what can be done within the hospital to promote self-determination (Starkey & Leadholm, 1997). Being able to choose activities, such as in the treatment mall approach described later in this chapter, is another example (Bopp, Ribble, Cassidy, & Markoff, 1996).
- *Recognizing the dignity and worth of every individual* is difficult in hospitals that are overcrowded and focused primarily on custodial maintenance care. Indeed, decades of scandal suggest that many hospitals definitely do not treat individuals with dignity. However, it is certainly possible for hospital staff to communicate respect. Communication skills training has been found to be effective in this regard (Smith, 1998). More respectful communication is also associated with less violence and a reduced need for restraints in hospitals (Smith, 1998).
- *Promoting optimism and hopefulness* is also needed, but not typically emphasized in psychiatric hospitals. Learning about the findings of longitudinal studies (as discussed in Chapters 1, 2, and 3 of this text) and meeting with consumers who have left the hospital and are doing well are among strategies that help staff become more optimistic and promote this optimism.
- The *capacity of every individual to learn and grow* should be nourished. Although some hospitals do little more than provide custodial care, they can develop a wide range of programming, services, and activities that appeal to people of different abilities and interests (Bopp et al., 1996; Tsang, Liberman, Hilty, & Drake, 2002). This can include skills training activities, career exploration, and opportunities to pursue hobbies and other interests.

- Many hospitals struggle with the issue of sensitivity to cultural diversity. Too often, cultural activities within the hospital actually reflect cultural preferences of the dominant staff culture. Staff should attend to the cultural interests of the patient population and plan activities consistent with the interests and backgrounds of the people they serve.

Guiding Principles of Psychiatric Rehabilitation

Equally challenging is the implementation of the guiding principles of PsyR.

- **Person-centered orientation**—hospitals are geared toward serving groups, sometimes very large groups in a similar, apparently efficient manner. This works against the individualization of all services. Mall programs are an example of how programming can be individualized by having a choice of group activities (Bopp et al., 1996). Psychiatry should follow the example of the rest of medicine, which increasingly is adopting an individualized approach.
- **Partnership between service provider and recipient**—in the acute phase of the illnesses, maximum involvement by the patient is difficult, because symptoms often interfere. Nevertheless, as symptoms subside, more opportunities for participation arise if staff members are open to patient involvement. Participation in treatment planning, choosing of activities, and contributing to discharge preferences can allow for the partial implementation of this principle (Glick et al., 2011). An example is the use of recovery-oriented action plans or advanced directives by which consumers can express their treatment preferences prior to the onset of an acute episode.
- **Strengths focus**—by their nature, hospitals and their staff focus on patient deficits and weaknesses. However, hospital staff could focus on patients' skills (i.e., strengths) in recovering from acute episodes in the past. Their attention can also be focused on different services that can potentially engage and interest these individuals by having a variety of activities available that permit the individual to demonstrate his or her potential. This thinking can extend to discharge planning by choosing placements and services that capitalize on individuals' prior successes in the community (Smith & Bartholomew, 2006; Swarbrick, 2009).
- **Wellness approach**—a wellness approach should be the goal of every psychiatric hospital (Swarbrick, 2009). Unfortunately, many hospitals focus only on symptom management, sometimes at the expense of the whole individual. This is unfortunate since most hospitals have a variety of professionals and resources available. If the treatment/rehabilitation team offers services collaboratively, an integrated, holistic program of care can be provided. A holistic approach includes attention to the eight domains of wellness as described in Chapter 6, so that the hospital is not only a site of managing crisis and acute symptoms, but one of promoting overall well-being (Swarbrick, 2009).
- **Ongoing, accessible, coordinated services**—these types of services are possible in hospital settings, but large bureaucracies characterized by overlapping multiple

reporting lines among the staff and narrow divisions of responsibilities create many barriers to the coordination of services. Ongoing coordination with community providers to make services accessible is equally challenging. Hospitals need to explore simplified reporting lines, work on team functioning by including all relevant staff in discussions, and coordinate with community providers whenever possible. Community providers should respond in kind.

- **Skills training**—skills training is a favorite intervention in certain hospital settings. However, to promote ongoing recovery, provision must be made for the transferability or generalization of skills to the community. This is a difficult task, especially since behaviors tend to be situation-specific and difficult to generalize to other settings.
- **Environmental modifications**—hospital staff and administration typically resist modifying the environments of their institutions to accommodate individual patient preferences. But care should be taken to make ward environments less noisy or overstimulating. Environments may also need to be modified to accommodate the cultural preferences of the patients. In recent years, there has been too little attention paid to the actual physical environments of hospitals (Geller, 2000; Glick et al., 2011; Osborn, 2009).
- **Partnership with the family**—when family members are involved or their involvement can be solicited, their full participation with the treatment team and in discharge planning is critical (Glick et al., 2011). Involvement in the treatment team, support groups on hospital grounds, and a family advisory group are all possible steps to encourage this. Planning of treatment while hospitalized, discharge planning, and, ultimately, community reintegration can be enhanced by family member involvement.
- **Vocational focus**—a vocational focus has been a part of hospitals, but success in a hospital work program does not readily translate to the community (see Chapter 10). Any vocational work should focus on clarification of the individual's employment preferences and the pursuit of opportunities in the individual's home community.

Are Hospital Staff Members Open to Learning Psychiatric Rehabilitation?

The quick answer is "yes, to some extent." Staff's orientation to rehabilitation and recovery principles is measurable (Salyers, Tsai, & Stultz, 2007). Different interventions for organizations have been described in the literature, including traditional classes, in-service training, and hospital-wide, multidisciplinary forums to share key information and to develop an institution-wide vision (Birkmann et al., 2006; Pollard, Gelbard, Levy, & Gelkopf, 2008). When exposed to the content of PsyR courses, staff develop a better understanding of the goals, principles, attitudes, and practices of the field. In fact, increased exposure to PsyR courses is associated with a more complete understanding of PsyR knowledge (Gill, Murphy, & Birkmann, 2005). Also, there is evidence that staff can develop specialized skills in new evidence-based practices, such as illness management and recovery (Bartholomew & Kensler, 2010). Preliminary findings suggest that these skills and knowledge result in better outcomes, including lower hospital **recidivism** (Bartholomew & Zechner, 2013).

Psychiatric Rehabilitation Models within Hospitals

There are, in fact, some examples of PsyR program models within psychiatric hospitals. These include the social and independent living skills (SILS) model, a skills training approach that focuses on social learning principles and was promoted initially by Liberman and his colleagues (Wallace, Liberman, MacKain, Blackwell, & Eckman, 1992); the PsyR integrated service model (PRISM) (Starkey & Leadholm, 1997), a comprehensive PsyR approach; and the treatment mall model, which incorporates changes in the physical plant with programming changes (Bopp et al., 1996). These three models are discussed in more detail in the following subsections.

Social and Independent Living Skills (SILS) Model

The SILS approach provides step-by-step training activities for patients to learn the skills they will need outside the hospital (Wallace et al., 1992). SILS has been used effectively in both community-based and hospital settings. Modules focus on these broad areas:

- Social skills
- Symptom management skills
- Medication management skills
- Community reentry skills

The modules consist of an overview and explanation of the relevant skill, demonstration of the skill by staff, group member participation in practicing the skill, and "homework" assignments to practice skills between sessions. In addition, the groups include suggestions on how to apply the skills outside the groups. A number of hospitals have been very successful implementing these skills training modules (e.g., Smith, 1998).

Psychiatric Rehabilitation Integrated Service Model (PRISM)

The PRISM approach, described by Starkey and Leadholm (1997), is far more comprehensive than the SILS approach. The goal of PRISM is to increase patients' participation in their own treatment through these means:

- Patient participation in treatment planning meetings
- Treatment plans with a rehabilitation focus that emphasize goals, skill development, and development of external supports

- Problem reconceptualization as obstacles that need to be overcome to reach independent living goals
- True patient participation in treatment team meetings, with the patient identified as a **member** of the team
- Involvement of family members (with consent of the patient) and community providers directly in the treatment team

PRISM also focuses on improving the ward atmosphere and promoting patient involvement there. These improvements require significant restructuring of ward activities, including the following:

- Community meetings co-led by patients and staff
- The development of patient committees on each unit to advise unit staff leaders regarding patient concerns
- Meetings of patient representatives or advisors from each ward with hospital staff and administrators

The PRISM approach requires extensive staff training, particularly emphasizing interaction with the patients and promotion of patient choice (Starkey & Leadholm, 1997).

Treatment Mall

The "treatment mall" is another PsyR approach. With this approach, most daily programming is conducted off the ward in a central location, where a variety of programming options are available to people attending the activities. Wards are solely used as dormitories or living space. The mall, often located in a separate building, offers a variety of activities both occupational and recreational. The patients choose to attend the activities they prefer. It differs from some traditional hospitals where only one activity at a time is offered in the same location as one's main living space. The mall model is a strategy to increase normalization (leaving one's sleeping space) that offers some degree of consumer choice by offering an array of activity options (Bopp, 1996). Currently, there are efforts under way to measure the specific components of malls and to determine the fidelity of specific malls to these characteristics (Bartholomew & Cook, 2013).

Case Study of a Hospital Implementing Individualized Psychiatric Rehabilitation

Dhillon and Dollieslager (2000) described turning around a troubled state psychiatric hospital by adopting a PsyR treatment philosophy. The story of Eastern State Hospital in Virginia and the problems it has faced are similar to the situations faced by many state psychiatric hospitals. This hospital, like many others, has been under the supervision of both the US Department of Justice and the US Health Care Financing Administration (HCFA, now the Center for Medicare and Medicaid Services, CMS). The deteriorating physical plant of the hospital, insufficient staffing, and inadequately credentialed staff all contributed to their inability to provide active treatment. They obtained external consultation and a hospital-wide mandate for psychiatric rehabilitation services to be developed.

Recognizing and overcoming obstacles to incorporating the principles and practices of PsyR were essential to their success. Here are some of the barriers they had to overcome:

- Many staff members believed that television watching and naps during most of the normal waking hours were acceptable for most patients most of the time.
- Team members often expressed the belief that acutely ill patients were generally unable to participate in activities. This prevailing attitude is a barrier in many hospitals.
- Staff members viewed psychosocial treatment as being solely in the realm of occupational, recreational, and activity therapists, not doctors, nurses, and social workers.

Like most hospitals, Eastern State also had:

- A history of emphasizing biological treatment, primarily medication
- A necessary emphasis on maintaining a safe environment for staff and patients
- A lack of treatment team ownership of responsibility for individual patients
- Numerous patients with chemical or substance dependency
- Programming that was not individualized to the patient's unique needs

These sorts of barriers, attitudinal and otherwise, seem prevalent in state hospital settings. For example, Birkmann and colleagues (2006) reported similar attitudes among staff.

Implementing Psychiatric Rehabilitation Innovations

An essential component of the intervention at Eastern State Hospital in Virginia was the use of **coaches**, who were assigned to each team to encourage an interdisciplinary focus that included an emphasis on PsyR. Corrigan and McCracken (1995) suggested a similar strategy, proposing that champions of the cause of PsyR be identified to help design and initiate the implementation of PsyR principles.

For Eastern State, adopting PsyR meant the following:

- Clarify each person's goals, promote his or her freedom of choice, enhance privacy and dignity, and increase time with friends and family while still in the hospital.
- Educate each individual about the nature of his or her illness and how medications work to restore self-control (illness management).
- Teach about medication and its side effects, self-monitoring, and communicating with the psychiatrist and other members of the treatment team.
- Connect with the family or other natural supports in the community.

- Enable the patient to make appropriate aftercare plans for residential and continuing treatment needs post-discharge.

Dhillon and Dollieslager viewed treatment and rehabilitation as complementary, that is, as components of the same holistic approach. They integrated psychiatric rehabilitation into more traditional methods of treatment that blended rehabilitation programming with medication interventions, efforts to improve the supervision of staff, and efforts to promote safety.

What Keeps People from Having to Return to the Hospital?

Assuming one has a fairly successful stay in a hospital, what predicts an individual's having to return or not? Can successful adaptation to the community be explained and can particular services provided during or after a hospital stay lead to a good community adjustment?

Schmuette, Dunn, and Sledge (2010) sought to determine what individual characteristics predicted readmission within 12 months. As expected, the number of previous admissions was a predictor of shorter time to readmission. This is not surprising, given that about half of the people with repeated hospitalizations are readmitted within a year. The level of psychotic symptoms and substance abuse were not strong predictors. Those with a stable housing arrangement were less likely to be hospitalized. A somewhat unexpected finding was that unemployment was a very strong predictor of who would be hospitalized in the near future. The results suggested that readmission is more influenced by residential and employment status than by severe mental illness, strong evidence in favor of the utility of PsyR interventions (see Chapters 10 and 12). Evidence is also emerging that illness management and recovery (IMR) teaches self-management skills that help prevent relapses and the need for rehospitalization (Bartholomew & Zechner, 2013).

Are There Alternatives to Hospitals?

Any large-scale changes or reconfigurations of mental health delivery systems focused on deinstitutionalization should include consideration and exploration of alternatives to hospitalization. The goal should be to make the use of a large, public psychiatric institution either unnecessary or minimally necessary. At present, the best evidence is that nonhospital alternatives are available for most of the services and functions provided within the institutions such as crisis residences and early intervention teams. The alternatives, which are described next, are generally more consistent with PsyR principles than hospitalization in large psychiatric institutions. Some of the alternatives described here rely on the availability of hospital beds in local community hospitals, sometimes subsidized by the state mental health authority.

Approaches That May Be More Consistent with Psychiatric Rehabilitation

Are there ways to handle acute episodes in a manner more consistent with the principles of PsyR than hospitalization? Yes, but these are not yet available in all locations. Alternatives include crisis or respite residences (both peer-run and traditional practitioners), acute care partial hospital or day programs, in-home crisis or respite support, and mobile early intervention teams. All of these methods have the limitation that they are not very secure for helping persons who have already become a risk to themselves or others. Nevertheless, they all do have the virtue of having research evidence showing that they reduce the likelihood of someone becoming such a risk, thereby promoting a speedier recovery; they reduce the need for expensive hospital stays in the future, which are often restrictive and unpleasant, interfering with the person's quality of life; and they are far less disruptive than a hospital stay in terms of a person's integration in his or her community.

Crisis Residential Care

Crisis residences that offer 24/7 acute care are another alternative to inpatient hospitalization (Rakfeldt et al., 1997). These well-staffed programs provide residential and psychiatric care around-the-clock in a setting with a very small census, and often have medical staff for prescribing medication. In many ways, they look more like a group home than a hospital and are usually located in a regular house in the community. Some geographic areas in the United States, including parts of California and other states, have turned over a large portion of acute care to this type of setting, reserving inpatient care solely to those requiring the very severe restriction of locked wards. Crisis residences are unlocked, truly voluntary, so an individual can leave if he or she wishes. They provide a safe, low-stimulation environment.

Peer-delivered Crisis Services

Some of these crisis residences are peer-run, such as Rose House in New York. Located in a suburban community in the Hudson Valley, it is a small, homelike, four-bedroom residential program that assists individuals in coping with acute psychological distress. Specially trained peers who provide case management and crisis intervention services to persons experiencing acute distress staff it 24/7. They work collaboratively with non-consumer-run mental health services to coordinate treatment. Residents, known as guests, develop their own treatment plans in collaboration with consumer staff, based on their own assessment of what services will be helpful. Guests can self-refer, but they are also often referred by a psychiatric crisis center located in a local hospital. Peer staff members are available to the crisis center. An evaluation comparing Rose House to a traditional inpatient setting (Bologna & Pulice, undated) found that Rose House was more person-centered and less restrictive than an inpatient unit. Rose House staff were also more respectful than hospital staff and the residents felt less stigma, higher life satisfaction, and greater social involvement than hospital patients. Crisis residences have very positive outcomes in general, indeed, more positive than locked hospital wards. Those who attend enjoy a better quality of life, stay more integrated in the community, and return to their normal activities faster than those hospitalized (Greenfield et al., 2008).

Crisis residences are, however, only one of the peer-run alternatives to hospitals. The National Empowerment Center (NEC) maintains a current listing of mental health peer-operated crisis residential programs on its Web site at http://www.power2u.org/peer-run-crisis-services.html. This listing details program descriptions and contact information but does not present outcome data. Dan Fisher, who directs the NEC states,

These programs to date have been practice-based evidence. They have received so little funding, they have not had the opportunity for adequate research and evaluation. However, they work, and the descriptions section attests to that. (personal communication, November 2, 2009)

In-home Crisis Intervention and Psychosis Management

A number of strategies are used to manage psychotic disorders in the home through crisis intervention approaches, the use of personal assistants, and intensive familial support where appropriate. Toprac and colleagues (1996) reported on a demonstration project of eight alternative treatments comprising two main program components. These components included brief hospitalization (up to 72 hours of inpatient care) and then transfer to the experimental alternative and respite care provided either in the service user's home or in a crisis apartment. Respite care was defined as 24-hour, one-on-one care by para-professionals (mental health peer providers or non-peer providers). The eight groups were a combination of the following: brief hospitalization before respite care, respite care in the home or crisis apartment, and respite care provided by consumer or non-consumer staff. The full report can be viewed at http://www.power2u.org/downloads/Crisis_Alternative_Project_Texas.pdf. In terms of symptom remission and functional ability, there were no significant differences across all treatment groups. That is, respite care in home or in crisis apartments resulted in clinical outcomes similar to those of inpatient hospitalization.

Greenfield and colleagues (2008) reported on the first "experimental, prospective evaluation of an important form of consumer-managed service: crisis residential programs for psychiatrically disabled adults facing civil commitment" (p. 135). The experimental condition was a community-based crisis residential program (CRP) run by consumers of mental health services who had previously been trained in a community college case management curriculum designed for peer providers. The CRP could accommodate six individuals in an unlocked residence. The control condition was a locked, inpatient facility. The inpatient facility utilized a traditional medical model approach and was staffed by non-consumer professionals. The experimental condition also provided assertive community outreach to individuals after discharge from the program while the hospital control did not. The sample was representative of indigent individuals with serious mental illnesses, facing civil commitment. Of note are two criteria that excluded individuals from participation: having a serious co-occurring medical condition and meeting criteria for "danger to others." Individuals who were a danger to themselves were included. Individuals were assessed at baseline and at 30 days, six months, and one year post-admission. The outcomes indicate that individuals in the consumer-run, crisis respite services demonstrated greater improvement or comparable outcomes to those in the inpatient condition. Participants in the CRP had greater gains in social activity, a higher rate of improvement on the interviewer-rated symptom scale, and greater improvement on the self-report symptom subscales of psychoticism, depression, and anxiety. Additionally, satisfaction with services was higher for individuals in the CRP condition.

In a review of alternative service models conducted by Lloyd-Evans and colleagues (2009), they found evidence that community-based residential alternatives are less expensive and their service recipients are more satisfied than people served in standard inpatient wards. Community-based residential crisis services provide a feasible and acceptable alternative to hospital admission.

Similarly, a hospital diversion program that consists of short-term respite care, clinical monitoring, connection or reconnection to other mental health services, and peer support may be sufficient (Burns-Lynch & Salzer, 2001). Sometimes, individuals are heading for a hospitalization for reasons other than a recurrence of symptoms, or their symptoms have just begun to recur and early intervention might help. Policymakers and service providers recognized a need for a short-term respite program that focuses on connecting or reconnecting people who are seeking psychiatric emergency services with other community-based services. CONNECTIONS was developed to meet this need and was open all night. These overnight hours were viewed as necessary because other resources available to persons in crisis generally operate on a daytime schedule with limited after-hours support. Each shift was staffed by peer support counselors, a master's degree–level mental health specialist, and clerical support staff. Almost everyone received clinical monitoring and peer support, which were the basic services provided by program staff. Two services were provided that are not usually available in crisis emergency room settings: meals and overnight respite (i.e., a safe place to sleep and be observed). Referrals and transportation were also frequently provided. One of the most frequent combinations of referrals was to a housing or shelter placement and referral to drug/alcohol treatment. The program also served an important function of reconnecting the person with his or her case manager or other service provider. Burns-Lynch and Salzer (2001) recommend the development of alternative crisis services as a necessary component of a system of care and that these alternative crisis services receive the full support and integration of all participants across the service system.

Acute Partial Hospitals/Day Hospitals

There is a very large body of evidence that acute partial hospitalization is an excellent alternative to inpatient care with equal or better efficacy than inpatient care, yet without some of its deleterious side effects (Horvitz-Lennon, Normand, Gaccione, & Frank, 2001). Generally, programming is available 7 days per week for 6 to 12 hours per day, with a maximum length of stay of 4 to 8 weeks. More than 30 years of research supports the efficacy of these programs.

Day hospitals or acute partial hospitals have a long history and have fallen out of practice in many places and become intermediate- or long-term support, similar to the day programs described in Chapter 6. The evidence of their usefulness as long-term services is limited. However, as short-term programs to shorten or prevent the need for hospitalization, they have had a great deal of success (Marshall et al., 2011). The day hospital has been defined as an outpatient service that provides "diagnostic and treatment services for acutely ill individuals who would otherwise be treated in psychiatric inpatient units." The acute psychiatric day hospital is distinguished from other types of "partial hospitalization" or "day care," such as transitional care for those leaving the hospital or long-term outpatient care (day treatment programs).

Usually, people attend daily and receive close attention and medication monitoring. Best of all, they get to stay in their own homes. If they fail to attend, they are assertively outreached. There is a large body of evidence that these programs prevent future hospitalizations and shorten them if they have to take place (Marshall et al., 2011). People treated at day hospitals had the same level of treatment satisfaction and quality of life as those cared for in inpatient units and are no more likely to be readmitted to day or full-time hospitalization than persons discharged from inpatient units. Thus, day hospitals are a less restrictive, effective alternative to inpatient admission. The effectiveness and costs of care in a day hospital providing acute treatment were studied in a controlled trial in which 206 voluntarily admitted patients were allocated to either day hospital or conventional inpatient services wards (Priebe et al., 2006). Day hospital patients showed significantly more favorable changes in symptoms at discharge. They also reported higher treatment satisfaction at discharge. There were no differences in being readmitted over the next year.

Early Intervention Teams

Another alternative is comprehensive multidisciplinary treatment and rehabilitation teams that resemble ACT but may be employed even before a person's diagnosis as severely and persistently mentally ill is confirmed. Comprehensive integrated early intervention teams intervene at the time of the first psychotic episode and continue to follow the person as long as needed. This strategy has been found to help reduce persistent symptomatology, the revolving door effect (cycling in and out of the system), and the (unnecessary) deterioration in functioning that often takes place before the person receives effective care. Where used, these teams have significantly reduced the need for public psychiatric hospital care (Abas et al., 2003; Thornicraft & Tansella, 2004).

Early intervention teams are similar to ACT teams, discussed in Chapter 8. Multidisciplinary in nature, these teams visit and assertively outreach people who are showing signs of psychotic symptoms. They assess symptoms and substance abuse and monitor medication. People can continue their normal activities since the team, or some of its members, only visit part of the day. At a minimum, they include physician, nurse, and case managers. These teams are in wide use in a number of countries with government-funded national health systems such as Canada, Denmark, and Australia. The reasons for their popularity are quite clear. They effectively prevent expensive hospitalizations that the government bears the expense for, so it is better to intervene earlier at a lower cost. (In the United States, historically, the ineffective but prevalent strategy tends toward delaying hospitalization in state hospitals so that private insurance bears more of the cost in community or private hospitals.) With early intervention teams, hospitalization is less often needed. Early intervention teams are also discussed in Chapter 10.

Combination of One or More of These Approaches

Using the approaches outlined previously in combination is another viable alternative. For example, there is strong empirical evidence that partial hospitalization and crisis residence programs can work effectively in tandem to provide 24-hour acute care (Budson, 1994).

Intermediate- and Long-Term Care Needs without Large Institutions

For individuals who might require and/or prefer 24-hour care, long-term residences in the community have been developed. Typically, these long-term residences consist of several individuals living in a group setting with onsite staff present 24 hours per day. These facilities usually have indefinite lengths of stay.

Employing such residences can reduce the need for state hospital care. For example, in Pennsylvania it was found that 300 to 400 percent more residential placements were needed than the number of state hospital beds eliminated (Kamis-Gould et al., 1999; Rothbard, Kuno, Schinnar, Hadley, & Turk, 1999; Rothbard, Schinnar, Hadley, Foley, & Kuno, 1998). That is, to reduce a hospital census by 300 beds, for example, required additional enhanced services for 900 to 1200 adults residing in the community. This increase in the number of residential placements seems to be the rule. In the Netherlands, for instance, a fivefold increase in community-based services was needed. Why is this? In the hospital, in the course of a year, three or four different individuals fill each bed. Therefore, to eliminate the need for one bed, at least three hospitalizations must be prevented.

CONTROVERSIAL ISSUE
Large Public Psychiatric Hospitals: Should They All Be Closed?

Are large psychiatric hospitals necessary or useful? To many consumer advocates and PsyR practitioners, large public psychiatric hospitals are a waste of money and, perhaps worse than that, a potentially harmful form of care. In many US states and in some other countries, state hospitals account for more than 50 percent of the state's mental health budget. Often, much of this expense goes to maintaining an outdated physical plant that provides for very unpleasant congregate (group) living.

Others argue that these hospitals are a "necessary evil," and some say they are clearly beneficial, preventing even more negative outcomes. On the whole, deinstitutionalization is judged to have been good for those individuals actually deinstitutionalized. But that may not be the whole story. What about those individuals who formerly would have entered these institutions, but now must stay in the community? There is evidence that some of these individuals are served poorly and are at risk for many difficulties (Shepherd, 1998).

The "necessary evil" argument proceeds as follows. There are individuals who are so symptomatic (either on a long- or short-term basis) that local community hospitals and outpatient programs cannot serve them. Community living is not an option for them, and community providers are either not equipped or are unwilling to help them. Therefore, large psychiatric hospitals are needed as the last stop or last resort. Following this line of thinking, hospitalization actually prevents homelessness, unnecessary victimization, and incarceration in jail or prison (Perez, Leifman, & Estrada, 2003; Talbott, 2004).

As previously discussed, there are numerous alternatives to the provision of inpatient psychiatric care in large institutions, although many places do not have these alternatives in place. Some of the alternatives rely on the availability of hospital beds in local community hospitals, sometimes subsidized by the state mental health authority. Others do not. As discussed in this chapter, these alternatives include acute partial hospitalization, crisis residential care, in-home illness management, and a combination of these approaches. Indeed, with very comprehensive crisis services and long-term community services, large public psychiatric hospitals have been eliminated without negative outcomes in places such as parts of Italy (Ruggieri et al., 2004).

What is the best way to view these large psychiatric hospitals? It depends on a number of factors, primarily the quality of the hospitals involved and their level of integration with the community system. To what extent does a particular hospital provide best practices that foster recovery? Are the staff members there unprepared to offer these? Does the living environment provide for some dignity or privacy, or is it a setting without any of the comforts of home where individuals are ignored and sometimes abused (Miller, 2005)? Does the hospital foster community reintegration by working closely with community providers?

Some jurisdictions, such as the US states of Vermont and California, have sought to eliminate psychiatric hospitals altogether only to find it was not possible. For example, Vermont had to continue its hospital, at least for persons with mental illness who are elderly with forensic or legal issues. There is also the issue that the acute phases of the illness, as discussed in both Chapters 2 and 3, need to be adequately managed. Italy, with a fair amount of success, has spent more than 30 years trying to fully implement its 1978 law to close all its psychiatric hospitals. Most of it was effectively implemented within 20 years (Burti, 2001). Its success, however, was dependent upon replacing the hospitals with an array of acute, rehabilitative, and residential services.

Summary

Public psychiatric hospitals remain a part of the mental health system in many places, despite the fact that a body of evidence has emerged indicating that their closure and planned deinstitutionalization result in better outcomes for persons formerly hospitalized and that comprehensive community services can fill the needs met by state hospitals. The implementation of deinstitutionalization becomes difficult when community providers are reluctant to serve persons with very challenging needs. Given that in many areas hospitals remain a large part of the system of care, inpatient stays, if needed, must provide for continuity with community life and not be disruptive to rehabilitation efforts and the person's individual recovery.

Psychiatric hospital stays that are long enough to provide for stabilization of symptoms, usually a period of several weeks, can be conducive to recovery. At the same time, very long stays work against recovery by promoting passivity and contributing to a deterioration of community living skills. Treatment programming in the hospital should be offered according to PsyR principles and be based on known evidence-based practices. In addition, during the course of a hospital stay, a sustained effort should be made to coordinate the hospital and community-based services on the part of both hospital and community staff in order to facilitate reintegration.

There are a number of alternatives to hospitalization available in some places. These include crisis residences, in-home care, acute partial hospitals, and early intervention teams. Indeed, there is also the research to support their usefulness. Many of these alternatives are more consistent with the goals, values, and principles of PsyR than inpatient care, given they are much less restrictive and help individuals to stay more integrated with their home community.

■ ■ ■ ▬▬▬▬▬▬▬▬▬▬▬▬▬▬▬▬▬▬▬▬▬▬▬▬▬▬▬▬

Class Exercise

The following exercise can be done as an individual or in small groups.

You and some of your colleagues, who have been studying the acute care of persons with serious mental illness, have been assigned to a task force to redesign the acute care system of a county near where you live. Your committee is charged with the task of proposing one inpatient and one community-based model for managing the acute care of persons with serious mental illness.

1. Propose two approaches consistent with promoting recovery and quality of life.
2. One approach must be an inpatient hospital model.
   - What are the components and main features of this service? Describe them.
   - What are its goals?
   - To promote community integration, who should be on the treatment team?
   - What will be the role of seclusion and restraints (if any) in this unit?
   - How should staff be trained?

3. Also, choose one community-based approach.
  • What are the components and main features of this service? Describe them.
  • What are its goals?
  • Who should be on the treatment team?
  • Who should staff the program?
  • How should they be trained?

Glossary

action stage: At this stage of change, the individual is actively changing his or her behavior.

acute (active) phase: The phase of an illness in which the most severe symptoms are experienced.

acute care: In the context of psychiatric hospital stays, a service intended to manage the acute phase of a psychiatric illness, lasting from a few days to several weeks in length.

ADA Amendments Act: A law passed by the US Congress in 2008 amending the 1990 Americans with Disabilities Act. These amendments were intended to improve the protections of people with disabilities by more specifically defining the terms of the original act.

addiction: The persistent voluntary and/or involuntary use of chemicals, including alcohol and other drugs, to the detriment of one's physical and mental health.

affect: The experience of feeling or emotion.

algorithm: A process or set of rules for problem solving—for example, the rules being developed for the titration (adjustment) of psychotropic medications based on symptoms, responsiveness, side effects, and other factors.

amygdala: A subcortical (below the cortex) brain structure.

anhedonia: An inability to experience pleasure.

anosognosia: Literally, not knowing what you do not know; the lack of awareness that a psychotic symptom is actually a symptom.

antidepressant: A medication that reduces or eliminates one or more symptoms of depression.

antimanic: A medication that reduces or eliminates one or more or the symptoms of mania.

antipsychotic: A medication that reduces or eliminates one or more the symptoms of psychosis.

assertive community treatment (ACT): A full support approach to the provision of case management, rehabilitative, and treatment services. ACT programs utilize assertive outreach and in vivo service provision techniques.

assisted outpatient treatment: A term used by mental health advocates who support involuntary outpatient treatment laws; it implies a combination of a court order and access to an enhanced package of treatment services.

behaviorism: A theory of human and animal behavior, initially developed by psychologist B. F. Skinner, that focuses on the use of rewards and punishments to reinforce or extinguish behaviors.

benzodiazepines: A form of minor tranquilizer, used to relieve anxiety or induce sleep; chemically similar to and cross-tolerant with alcohol.

biological treatment: Also known as somatic treatment; the biological treatment of choice for severe mental illness is medication (e.g., antipsychotic medications, antidepressant medications, or mood stabilizers).

burnout: Reaction by some psychiatric rehabilitation practitioners who have experienced frustration and a sense of failure in their work with people who have severe mental illness, often characterized by lethargy and a lack of motivation.

career development: Persons diagnosed with psychiatric disabilities need assistance in building a career that matches their interests and abilities, rather than being steered toward low-skill, low-paying jobs. Psychiatric rehabilitation programs that integrate supported education and supported employment strategies emphasize this concept.

cardiovascular: To do with the heart and its blood vessels.

chronic: Meaning "over time," from the Greek *Kronos*, father of the gods, father of time. This term, no longer in fashion, was used to describe the long-term course of severe mental illness.

chronically mentally ill: Refers to persons with long-lasting mental illness who may suffer repeated relapses. Recently, the term "chronic," which carries a negative connotation, has been replaced by "severe and persistent."

chronic obstructive pulmonary disease: Emphysema and related conditions in which airway passages are blocked in the lungs.

circulatory illness: Diseases of the heart, blood, or blood vessels.

clubhouse: A model of psychiatric rehabilitation day programming, also known as the Fountain House model. Clubhouses are places to congregate for social support and recreation and to address community living needs and problems. Consumers who go to clubhouses are referred to as members and are involved in all aspects of the program's operation.

cognition: Thinking and problem-solving processes, or the study of thinking and problem solving.

cognitive–behavioral therapy: Interventions designed to assist persons to solve problems and think about and deal with symptoms in alternative ways that are less distressing.

cognitive remediation: A set of behavioral intervention strategies, sometimes referred to as "cognitive rehabilitation," that help improve cognitive functioning through the use of repetitive exercises and positive reinforcers.

community integration: The practice of ensuring that persons living with mental illness have opportunities to live, work, attend school, socialize, and otherwise participate in their communities like everyone else.

community support program: A nationwide demonstration project instituted by the National Institute of Mental Health in the 1970s to encourage effective community support systems (case management).

community support system: A comprehensive community-based, case management system designed to ensure that the most comprehensive supports and services are available to consumers.

community work incentive coordinators (CWICS): Benefits planning specialists (formerly employment support representatives) who provide individual consultation to Social Security and Supplemental Security Income recipients on benefits planning to assist people in the use of SSA work incentives.

comorbid: A term used to describe the co-occurrence of a psychiatric and a medical condition—for example, a person diagnosed with schizophrenia and diabetes.

congregate care: Any community-based residential environment in which groups of people with psychiatric disabilities live together and receive services.

contemplation stage: At this stage of change, the individual is seriously considering making a change.

continuity of care: The provision of services, both according to need and over time.

controlled clinical trial: A research design typically involving randomized experimental and control groups with assessors "blind" to participants' group memberships.

co-occurring disorder: The simultaneous presence of two distinct psychiatric conditions within one individual; that is, two DSM-IV diagnoses usually a psychiatric disorder and an addiction or substance use disorder.

cortex: The outside or "bark" of the brain, divided into two halves (hemispheres), each of which has four lobes: frontal, temporal, parietal, and occipital.

course: The natural history or sequence of events throughout the length of an illness. For persons experiencing severe mental illness, the course can be lifelong, marked by a risk of recurrence of severe symptoms.

crisis residences: Community-based alternatives to psychiatric hospitals, usually small homes designed to provide acute care in a safe, low-stimulation environment.

critical skills: The specific skills that a person needs to function effectively in a chosen role or environment.

culturally competent: Being knowledgeable and skilled in a domain of PsyR practice that focuses on the cultural identity of each consumer, as well as the importance of being sensitive to and respectful of diverse cultural groups.

decompensation: Failure to maintain a stable, relatively symptom-free status.

deinstitutionalization: The movement away from treating and housing people with mental illness in large mental hospitals, accomplished by discharging individuals to live in the community.

delusions: False beliefs that an individual maintains despite an absence of supporting evidence or despite evidence to the contrary.

depressive episode: Episode characterized by feelings of extreme sadness or emptiness lasting most of the day, every day, for a period of two or more weeks.

diabetes: A disease in which blood glucose, or sugar levels are too high.

diathesis–stress model: An etiological theory that proposes that stress can trigger symptoms in individuals with a biological predisposition to severe mental illness.

direct skills teaching: An individualized skill development and acquisition method developed at the Boston University Center of Psychiatric Rehabilitation that emphasizes a combination of telling, showing, and doing.

disability: A functional loss due to the symptoms of mental illness.

dual diagnosis: The simultaneous presence of two distinct psychiatric conditions within one individual; that is, two DSM-IV diagnoses.

dual recovery groups: Groups that offer a 12-step program to people who have both a mental illness and a substance abuse disorder; also known as "Double Trouble" groups.

early intervention team: A multidisciplinary team that provides treatment and sometimes rehabilitative services at the early signs of an acute phase or early in the course of a mental illness; a team that visits persons and provides care at the first sign of their illness.

earned income exclusion: Earnings that are excluded from the Social Security Administration's calculation of countable earned income.

emotion: Feelings or the state of reaction to events; how someone feels.

employment network (EN): An employment service provider that has been approved to provide services to a holder of a Ticket to Work (i.e., SSI or SSDI recipient). An EN may be a public or private service provider, a state organization such as VR or a One-Stop Center, schools, employers, or others.

empowerment: A term frequently used in conjunction with the psychiatric rehabilitation value of self-determination. It is often addressed in psychiatric rehabilitation programs via involvement strategies such as sharing knowledge, power, and economic resources with consumers, and it has been recently defined in the literature as being composed of three elements: self-esteem and self-efficacy combined with optimism and a sense of control over the future; possession of actual power; and righteous anger and community activism.

environmental modifications: A type of PsyR intervention that focuses on ensuring that persons' environments are conducive to goal achievement. For example, an individual who becomes easily distracted may perform better if he or she has a quiet workplace.

epilepsy: One of several brain disorders that cause people to have recurring seizures, episodes of disturbed brain activity.

etiology: The cause or origin of a disorder.

evidence-based practice (EBP): A practice that is well defined with specific interventions that have been tested through rigorous research design, preferably randomized controlled trial experiments. Findings need to be replicated or repeated by more than one independent research group.

exacerbate: To aggravate or worsen.

ex-patient/consumer/survivor movement: Organized efforts by persons with a history of psychiatric illness to advocate for civil rights and humane treatment approaches. The movement has also provided access to a variety of self-help and alternative treatment opportunities.

expressed emotion (EE): Familial psychosocial factors, such as an environment high in criticism, hostility, and levels of emotional over-involvement that may contribute to relapse in some cases.

extended period of eligibility: A period of time following a trial work period during which the worker's eligibility for SSDI cash benefit depends on their earned income. As of 2013, the EPE lasts for 36 consecutive months.

extrapyramidal: A class of motor (movement) side effects caused by antipsychotic medication.

Fairweather Lodge: A residential service model developed by George Fairweather and characterized by groups of people with psychiatric disabilities living and working together on a long-term basis.

family foster care: A situation in which one or more consumers reside with, and are supported by, a family that is not their own.

family psychoeducation: An evidence-based family intervention for improving outcomes and assisting families in caring for their loved ones.

family recovery: The concept that, similar to individual recovery, families can go through a recovery process wherein they set new family aspirations and expectations.

fidelity scale: An instrument designed to assess a particular service's level of agreement with an ideal service model, typically an evidence-based practice.

functional assessment: An evaluation of a person's level of ability in specific life areas such as vocational, self-care, or education.

GABA: A neurotransmitter.

general income exclusion: Income that is excluded from the Social Security Administration's calculation of countable income.

genetic: Inherited, due to the coding on chromosomes.

gentrification: The buying and renovation of homes in deteriorating urban neighborhoods, which may improve property values, but often displaces lower income individuals.

global assessment: An overall assessment of a consumer that does not address ability to function in specific environments.

goals: Desired states or objectives to strive for and achieve.

hallucinations: Sensory perceptions in the absence of appropriate external stimulation, such as hearing voices.

harm reduction: The idea that the important issue in substance abuse treatment is to reduce the harm caused by the substance abuse rather than to require abstinence.

hippocampus: Literally, "sea horse." A sub-cortical brain structure, shaped somewhat like a sea horse, that is involved in important cognitive functions and working memory.

HIV-related illnesses: Very serious disorders caused by human immunodeficiency viruses, the most well known being acquired immunodeficiency syndrome (AIDS).

hyperlipidemia: Several conditions of high levels of fat in the bloodstream including high cholesterol and high triglyceride levels.

Housing First: A supported housing model offering immediate independent housing and intensive support services to homeless individuals who often have co-occurring disorders; sometimes referred to as *Pathways Housing First* to distinguish it from Housing First programs that do not share all of the essential ingredients of Pathways, such as scattered site housing or the emphasis its service philosophy places on consumer choice.

iatrogenic: Refers to the phenomenon of a treatment or environment having unintended negative effects on the persons. "Institutionalized" behavior such as excessive passivity is an example of an iatrogenic effect of long-term hospitalization.

illness management and recovery (IMR): An evidence-based practice that emphasizes psychoeducation, relapse prevention strategies, and social skills training. Also called "wellness management and recovery."

infectious disease: Also known as communicable, diseases comprise clinically evident illness resulting from the infection, presence, and growth of pathogenic biological agents such as bacteria or a virus.

in vivo: Literally "in life"; as opposed to a clinic or service setting, this is the provision of services to clients in the environments where they live, work, and socialize.

Independent Living Movement: The efforts of people with physical disabilities to advocate for civil rights, develop a shared philosophy, and provide peer support in order to recover and maintain control over their lives.

individually written rehabilitation plan (IWRP): The plan written by a vocational rehabilitation counselor and consumer that describes the consumer's vocational goal and the services that will be accessed to reach that goal.

individual placement and support (IPS): The evidence-based supported employment practice. IPS has consistently been shown to achieve superior employment outcomes compared to any other employment-related service.

individual plan for employment (IPE) (formerly IWRP): The plan written by a vocational rehabilitation counselor and consumer that describes the consumer's vocational goal and the services that will be accessed to reach that goal.

institutionalized: The negative behavioral effects of long-term stays in institutions such as state psychiatric hospitals, typically manifested by extreme dependency.

integrated services: Services that address dual disorders simultaneously and are provided by staff who are knowledgeable about both disorders affecting the client.

intermediate care: In the context of psychiatric care, a period of several weeks to several months for the management of extended acute episodes and residual phases of the illness.

job development: The tasks involved in job acquisition. These may include generally developing relationships with the business community, investigating the hiring needs of a specific employer, communicating the program's available services to all customers, or more specifically assisting the consumer with job applications, résumé writing, interview skills, and employer contacts.

length of stay: The period of time when an individual is attending a program, a service, or treatment; also, the number days in residence at a psychiatric hospital.

linear continuum model: A residential service approach in which consumers move from a relatively restrictive congregate care setting to a series of progressively less restrictive living environments and eventually to independent living.

longitudinal study: A research study that follows participants and documents relevant outcomes for a lengthy period of time (months or years).

long-term care: In the context of psychiatric hospitals, a period of several months or longer for the long-term treatment and management of psychiatric illnesses.

maintenance stage: At this stage, the individual has changed and is actively maintaining the change.

manic episode: Characterized by an elevated mood, in which the person feels excessively "up" or "high," and occasionally excessively irritable, for a period of a week or more.

medical model: An integral element of the medical system or profession; part of medicine.

meta-analysis: A study that combines the findings of previous studies, statistically combining the effects of all studies to determine an average effect.

metabolic syndrome: The name for a group of risk factors, such as high blood glucose and hypertension, that raise your risk for heart disease and other health problems, such as diabetes, heart attacks and stroke.

milieu therapy: Milieu is a French term that literally means "environment." Milieu therapy is a technique based on the idea that every aspect (i.e., physical, social, and cultural) of a treatment setting or environment can be used to help achieve therapeutic or rehabilitation goals or results.

mixed episode: Meets the criteria for both depressive and manic episodes simultaneously.

modeling: A mechanism for leaning social behaviors by observing role models and then replicating their actions.

motivational interviewing: A non-confrontational counseling strategy that focuses on the discrepancy between an individual's stated goals and his or her behavior that attempts to ally itself with the individual's wants, needs, and aspirations rather than confronting the individual about negative behaviors.

multidisciplinary: Literally, "many disciplines"; any approach that involves individuals from more than one profession or educational background, for example, physicians, nurses, social workers, and rehabilitation staff, working together.

natural supports: Supports provided to persons who have a disability by nonprofessionals such as family members, friends, or coworkers.

negative symptoms: Symptoms that reflect a lessening or loss of functioning; essentially, abilities or senses that are lost due to a disease (e.g., restricted emotional expression or reduced productivity of thought) (DSM-IV).

neuroanatomy: The structure of the nerves or neurons composing an individual's brain and nervous system.

neurology: The medical specialty dealing with the nervous system.

neurotransmitter(s): A group of substances produced by the body that function within the central nervous system to facilitate the passing of impulses between nerve cells.

NAMI: National Alliance on Mental Illness.

NIMBY: "Not in my backyard"; an acronym describing community opposition to living near a group home or other residential setting in which people with psychiatric disabilities reside.

normalization: The achievement or acquisition of valued social roles for consumers; normalization is a guiding principle of psychiatric rehabilitation.

normalized: A term used to describe an environment (such as a day program) that is consistent with the psychiatric rehabilitation principle of normalization, which is the creation and maintenance of valued social roles for consumers.

obesity: A medical condition in which excess body fat has accumulated to the degree that it has an adverse effect on health, leading to reduced life expectancy and increased health problems.

objective burden: Specifically identifiable problems associated with a person's mental illness. The objective burdens of families may include financial hardships due to medical bills, the cost of the consumer's economic dependence, disruptions in household functioning, restriction of social activities, and so on.

One-stop Center: Created by WIA, One-stop Centers contain the combined government-funded employment and training services for all workers (with or without disabilities). Often these are literally in one center, but sometimes different services are at different locations.

outcomes: Specific results, the end of a specific course of treatment, or the end result of the course of an entire illness.

parallel services: Services for two or more conditions that are provided at the same time but by different staff members or by different programs, each of which is knowledgeable about only one of the disorders.

partial hospitalization program: Day programs that are essentially based on the medical model. Treatment strategies include medication and medication monitoring; group, individual, and milieu therapies; and recreation and socialization. Some partial hospitals also incorporate psychiatric rehabilitation intervention strategies.

participatory action research: Research carried out by professional researchers working together with the subjects of the research. In psychiatric rehabilitation, studies are carried out with persons with severe mental illness participating at all levels of the research process.

peer partnership: An initiative in which consumers collaborate with nonconsumer providers to operate a program that emphasizes peer-delivered services.

peer provider: A psychiatric rehabilitation service provider who has a history of severe mental illness; these individuals have also been called peer counselors, peer advocates, peer specialists, consumer providers, consumer case managers, and prosumers.

peer support: A term commonly used to describe self-help and other peer-delivered service initiatives in which individuals who are diagnosed with a mental illness assist other consumers.

peer-delivered services: Rehabilitation and support services provided by individuals who identify themselves as having a mental illness. These services encompass peer-operated programs, peer partnership programs, and traditional mental health programs that utilize peer employees.

peer-operated services: Programs that are developed, controlled, and operated by individuals who identify themselves as having a diagnosis of a mental illness. Non-consumers may also be employed to contribute to service delivery and/or the administration of the program, but consumers clearly direct the entire service delivery process.

personal criteria: Features of living, learning, working, and social environments that are most valued by an individual; assisting a person in identifying his or her most highly valued personal criteria is an important aspect of setting an overall rehabilitation goal.

person-centered: Also known as person-directed, this term emphasizes the critical importance of incorporating a service user's input, needs, and preferences into the provision of PsyR services.

person-first language: Intentionally putting the person first in a statement about the individual, for example, saying "a person with schizophrenia" as opposed to saying "a schizophrenic."

pharmacology: The study of medications or chemical compounds used to treat disease.

physiological: To do with the body; physical.

polydipsia: Excessive drinking or water or other fluids, when not from a physical cause, can lead to water intoxication with such symptoms as confusion, lethargy, psychosis, and seizures or death.

polysubstance abuser: An individual who is abusing more than one substance—for example, alcohol and marijuana.

positive symptoms: Indicators or signs of illness that are significant because of the presence (positive status) of something normally not present; hallucinations and delusions are examples.

precontemplation stage: At this stage, the individual is not considering making a change.

premorbid: The period of time before a psychiatric illness developed.

preparation stage: At this stage, the individual is preparing to make a change.

principles: Specific dictums designed to promulgate values and goals by providing guidelines for addressing specific situations or behaviors.

prodromal phase: "Before the full syndrome"; a period before the full onset of the illness that is characterized by deterioration in functioning and increasing positive and negative symptoms.

prognosis: The probable course or outcome of a disorder.

prosumers: A term used to describe identified consumers of mental health services who are also mental health professionals.

psychiatric rehabilitation diagnosis: This has three main components: the overall rehabilitation goal, the functional assessment, and the resource assessment. In some situations, a readiness assessment is also part of the PsyR diagnosis.

psychoanalytic: A therapeutic approach based on psychological theories proposed by Sigmund Freud; psychoanalytic techniques emphasize the exploration of intra-psychic processes and their relationship to past events.

psychodynamic: A theory that psychopathology arises from conflicts within the psyche or mind of the individual. These conflicts may be rooted in past events.

psychodynamic therapy: An insight-oriented approach that focuses on the interpretation of unconscious material and therapeutic transference. In the treatment of serious mental illnesses, this form of psychotherapy has been found to be generally ineffective.

psychoeducation: A psychiatric rehabilitation intervention that involves connecting with family members by focusing on their current concerns; providing basic information regarding schizophrenia or other major mental illnesses; teaching crisis intervention techniques; and providing other resources that aid families in becoming effective partners in the treatment and rehabilitation process.

psychopharmacology: The study of medication or chemical compounds to relieve psychiatric symptoms.

psychosis: Incorrect evaluation of reality.

psychosocial treatment: Any approach that attempts to effect change through the manipulation of social or psychological factors.

quality of life: A person's subjective evaluation of the aspects of his or her life that he or she deems important.

reasonable accommodations: Modifications made to a job or work setting to enhance the ability of a qualified worker with a disability to perform the job. The Americans with Disabilities Act defines "reasonable" as an accommodation that is not excessively expensive compared to the resources of the business and does not fundamentally change the nature of the work being performed.

recidivism: Returning to the psychiatric hospital after discharge (e.g., relapse).

recovery: For a lifelong mental illness, recovery refers to a reformulation of one's self-image and an eventual adaptation to the disease; recovery is one of the goals of psychiatric rehabilitation.

rehabilitation: Any action intended to reduce the negative effects of the disease on the person's everyday life.

relapse: A recurrence of a past condition or its symptoms; a recurrence of symptoms of a disease after a period of improvement.

remission: A time period when an individual with an illness is essentially symptom-free.

residential treatment facility: Congregate care settings, such as group homes, that are operated by mental health professionals.

residual phase: The period after the acute phase of an illness when symptoms become milder.

resource assessment: An assessment of the persons, places, things, or activities that a person needs to achieve his or her chosen rehabilitation goal.

respiratory disease: Disease to do with the lungs or trachea or other organs involving breathing.

restraint: Prevention of free movement of the individual through physically binding the individual's body, particularly the limbs; can also be achieved through use of medication through sedation (as opposed to symptom relief).

ROPES method: An acronym that describes the important components of direct skills teaching: Review, Overview, Presentation, Exercise, and Summary.

schizoaffective disorder: A psychiatric disorder characterized by both symptoms of schizophrenia and symptoms of affective disorders.

seclusion: Removal of an individual from all social contact to a separate room.

self-advocacy: An individual's efforts to defend his or her own personal or civil rights, including the right to receive quality treatment and rehabilitation services. This term also refers to efforts by an organized group of consumers to rally support for a common cause.

self-contained classroom: A model of supported education in which a group of students, all of whom have a psychiatric disability, take a prescribed curriculum designed to help them achieve post-secondary educational goals.

self-determination: A psychiatric rehabilitation value that is based on the belief that consumers have the right to participate in all decisions that affect their lives; closely related to the concept of empowerment.

self-help: Involvement in nonprofessional activities that provide support and information for oneself and others who share a similar illness or problem.

self-help centers: Alternative programs that offer a variety of mutual support and social and advocacy activities. Sometimes called drop-in centers, many of these initiatives now have an expanded focus on wellness, recovery, and employment.

self-medicate: Use by an individual of non-prescribed substances to deal with the symptoms of his or her psychiatric illness.

sequential services: Services provided by one program to address one disorder, followed by services provided by another program to address another disorder.

shared decision making: A collaborative approach (involving the consumer and practitioner) to making important decisions; may involve the use of decision aids to assist consumers in learning more about treatment and rehabilitation options.

side effects: Unintended, undesired, or harmful effects of a treatment, usually medication; this is in contrast to therapeutic side effects.

situational assessment: An evaluation of the presence or absence of the skills and resources needed for a consumer to function successfully in the environments (i.e., situations) of their choice; this is in contrast to doing a global assessment unrelated to specific client goals.

skill generalization: The ability to use a skill in a variety of other environments. For example, the ability to use social skills learned in a PsyR program at one's workplace.

skills programming: Assisting a person in developing a program of skill use that includes real-world practice opportunities in settings that are relevant to the person's overall rehabilitation goal.

skills training: Skill development and acquisition methods based social learning theory and behavioral therapy approaches. The most well-known PsyR approaches are social skills training (SST) and direct skills teaching (DST).

social learning theory: A theory of human behavior, which postulates that we learn social behaviors mostly through observational learning.

somatic: "Of the body"; biologically based.

subjective burden: The psychological distress, borne by family members, that is engendered by the severe mental illness of a relative.

substantial gainful activity (SGA): An amount of earnings designated by the Social Security Administration as an indication of a worker's ability to be self-supporting.

super-sensitivity hypothesis: Hypothesis that persons with severe mental illness are more sensitive to substances and therefore at greater risk of becoming substance abusers.

supported approaches: Also known as community-integrated services, these are psychiatric rehabilitation models that share a common philosophy and strongly emphasize normalization and full inclusion in the community. Collectively, supported employment, supported housing, and supported education have been referred to as supported approaches.

supported education (SEd): Services and supports that are aimed at helping persons diagnosed with severe mental illnesses achieve their postsecondary educational goals.

supported employment (SE): An individualized approach to assist a consumer to achieve integrated employment. SE emphasizes training and support provided in settings of choice rather than demonstration of skills prior to access to vocational services. Supported employment services provide support to the individual in selecting, obtaining, and maintaining employment. SE is one of the evidence-based practices.

supported housing: Integrated, community-based housing opportunities for people with psychiatric disabilities that emphasize consumer choice and provision of flexible and ongoing supports.

symptoms: Signs or indicators of an illness or disorder.

tardive dyskinesia: Involuntary movements of the mouth and other parts of the body as a consequence of the use of traditional antipsychotics; caused by changes to neurons involving dopamine.

teams: The group of professionals and other staff working together to serve the same consumer.

Ticket to Work: A voucher provided by SSA to SSI and SSDI recipients. This voucher is used to access employment services from an employment network. The Ticket to Work is meant to give the job seeker a measure of control and choice of services.

Ticket to Work and Work Incentive Improvement Act (TWWIIA): A law passed by Congress in 1999 designed to reduce the disincentives to employment for which the previous SSA regulations were notorious. TWWIIA established the Ticket to Work program and modified many of the SSA work incentives.

titrate: To adjust to the right dosage or amount; usually refers to medication, but can be used for any treatment.

transinstitutionalization: Moving from a psychiatric institution to another congregate care setting that limits opportunities to engage in normalized community life.

transition services: Supports and services provided to teenagers who are diagnosed with a disability. They include assistance with the move from high school to a postsecondary education or training setting and should continue until the age of 21.

transitional employment (TE): A program of time-limited jobs in regular work settings for real pay. Agency staff acquire the job from an employer and subsequently provide training and support to consumers in that job. Consumers in TE jobs earn the going rate of pay from the employer and remain in the job for a specified period of time. The job will then be filled by another consumer.

transtheoretical model of behavior change: An approach that emphasizes stages of change and the need to match intervention strategies to particular stages. This model is closely tied to a counseling approach known as motivational interviewing.

treatment: Any action designed to cure a disease or reduce its symptoms; treatment for serious mental illnesses can be broken into two broad categories, biological (somatic) and psychosocial.

trial work period: Nine nonconsecutive months in which an SSDI recipient can earn income while maintaining his or her cash benefit, thus allowing the individual to try working with limited risk.

12-step model: The 12 steps of Alcoholics Anonymous that an alcoholic must complete to remain in recovery, or similar models based on the AA model.

values: Deeply held beliefs that may inform specific behaviors, attitudes, and ideas.

warm lines: Peer support or assistance offered via the telephone.

Wellness and Recovery Action Plan (WRAP): A self-help strategy that utilizes a structured tool to help individuals learn to cope with their illnesses and lead healthy, satisfying lives.

word salad: A fairly rare symptom of severe psychosis, in which language has become so impaired, the person attempts to express himself or herself in what sounds like a jumble or mixture of words, rather than coherent sentences.

Work Incentives Planning and Assistance Program (WIPA): Community-based programs of SSA designed to disseminate information about Social Security work incentives and provide benefit planning consultation to recipients through the efforts of CWICS. WIPA was formerly called Benefits Planning, Assistance, and Outreach (BPAO).

Workforce Investment Act (WIA): The law that established a one-stop workforce development system. It brought together employment, education, and training programs for adults, dislocated workers, youth, veterans, and others. WIA contains the amended Rehabilitation Act.

References

Abas, M., Vanderpyl, J., Prou, T. L., Kydd, R., Emery, B., & Foliaki, S. A. (2003). Psychiatric hospitalization: Reasons for admission and alternatives to admission in South Auckland, New Zealand. *Australian and New Zealand Journal of Psychiatry, 37*(5), 620–625.

Ackerman, L. P. (1997). A Recovery, Inc. group leaders story. In C. T. Mowbray, D. P. Moxley, C. A. Jasper, & L. L. Howell (Eds.), *Consumers as providers*. Columbia, MD: International Association of Psychosocial Rehabilitation Services.

Ackerman, S. J., & Hilsenroth, M. J. (2003). A review of therapist characteristics and techniques positively impacting the therapeutic alliance. *Clinical Psychology Review, 23*, 1–33.

ADA amendments act 2008. (2008). Retrieved August 7, 2012, from http://www.access-board.gov/about/laws/ada-amendments.htm.

Adams, C. E., Fenton, M. K., Quraishi, S., & David, A. S. (2001). Systematic meta-review of depot antipsychotic drugs for people with schizophrenia. *British Journal of Psychiatry, 179*(4), 290–299.

Adams, J. R., & Drake, R. E. (2006). Shared decision making and evidence-based practice. *Community Mental Health Journal, 42*(1), 87–105.

Adams, N., & Grieder, D. M. (2005). *Treatment planning for person-centered care: The road to mental health and addiction recovery*. Burlington, MA: Elsevier.

Adelman, C. (2004). *Principal indicators of student academic histories in postsecondary education, 1972–2000*. Washington, DC: US Department of Education.

Agar-Jacomb, K., & Read, J. (2009). Mental health crisis services: What do service users need when in crisis? *Journal of Mental Health, 18*(2), 99–110.

Agranoff, R. (1977). Services integration. In W. F. Anderson, B. J. Friedad, & M. J. Murphy (Eds.), *Managing human services*. Washington, DC: International City Management Association.

Ahern, L., & Fisher, D. (2001). *PACE: Personal assistance in community existence*. Lawrence, MA: The National Empowerment Center.

Alcohol Anonymous World Services. (1981). *Twelve steps and twelve traditions*. New York: Author.

Algeria, M., Canino, G., & Rios, R. (2002). Inequalities in the use of specialty mental health services among Latinos, African-Americans, and non-Latino Whites. *Psychiatric Services, 53*, 1547–1555.

Allen, F. (2012). The DSM 5 Follies as told in its own Words, Huffington Post, February 9, 2012. *Huffington Post*. Retrieved from http://www.huffingtonpost.com/allen-frances/ds"m-5_b_1251448.html.

Allen, M., Carpenter, D., Sheets, J., Miccio, S., & Ross, R. (2003). What do consumers say they want and need during a psychiatric emergency? *Journal of Psychiatric Practice, 9*(1), 39–58.

Allen, P. A. (1974). A consumer's view of California's mental health care system. *Psychiatric Quarterly, 48*, 1–13.

Allison, D. B., & Casey, D. E. (2001). Antipsychotic-induced weight gain: A review of the literature. *Journal of Clinical Psychiatry, 62*(Suppl. 7), 22–31.

Almomani, F., Brown, C., & Williams, K. (2006). The effect of an oral health promotion program for people with psychiatric disabilities. *Psychiatric Rehabilitation Journal, 29*, 274–281.

Alphs, L. D., & Anand, R. (1999). Clozapine: The commitment to patient safety. *Journal of Clinical Psychiatry, 60*(Suppl. 122), 22–31.

Alvarez-Jimenez, M., Gonzalez-Blanch, C., Vazquez-Barquero, J. L., Perez-Iglesias, R., Martinez-Garcia, O., Perez-Pardal, T., Ramirez-Bonilla, M. L., & Crespo-Facorro, B. (2006). Attenuation of antipsychotic-induced weight gain with early behavioral intervention in drug-naive first-episode psychosis patients: A randomized controlled trial. *Journal of Clinical Psychiatry, 67*, 1253–1260.

Alwan, N., Johnstone, P., & Zolese, G. (2008). *Length of hospitalization for people with severe mental illness.* (Publication no. 10.1002/14651858.CD000384.pub2).

Amador, X. F. (2007). *I am not sick: I don't need help!* (2nd ed.). Peconic, NY: Vida Press.

Amador, X. F., & Paul-Odouard, R. (2000). Defending the Unabomber: Anosognosia in schizophrenia. *Psychiatric Quarterly, 71*, 363–371.

American Psychiatric Association (Ed.). (1994). *Diagnostic and statistical manual of mental disorders.*

American Psychiatric Association (Ed.). (2000). *Diagnostic and statistical manual of mental disorders - Text revision* (4th ed.).

American Psychiatric Association (Ed.). (2013). *Diagnostic and statistical manual of mental disorders - V Text revision* (5th ed.).

Anderson, C. M., Reiss, D. J., & Hogarty, G. E. (1986). *Schizophrenia and the family.* New York: The Guilford Press.

Andreasen, N. C. (1984). *The broken brain.* New York: HarperCollins.

Andresen, R., Caputi, P., & Oades, L. G. (2000). Interrater reliability of the Camberwell Assessment of Need Short Appraisal Schedule. *Australian and New Zealand Journal of Psychiatry, 34*(5), 856–861.

Andresen, R., Caputi, P., & Oades, L. G. (2006). The stages of recovery instrument: Development of a measure of recovery from serious mental illness. *Australian and New Zealand Journal of Psychiatry, 40*, 972–980.

Andresen, R., Caputi, P., & Oades, L. G. (2010). Do clinical outcome measures assess consumer-defined recovery? *Psychiatry Research, 177*(3), 309–317.

Andresen, R., Oades, L. G., & Caputi, P. (2003). The experience of recovery from schizophrenia: Towards an empirically-validated stage model. *Australian and New Zealand Journal of Psychiatry, 37*, 586–594.

Angst, J. (2004). Bipolar disorder: A seriously underestimated health burden. *European Archives of Psychiatry and Clinical Neuroscience, 254*, 59–60.

Anthony, W. A. (1979). *The principles of psychiatric rehabilitation.* Baltimore, MD: University Park Press.

Anthony, W. A. (1993). Recovery from mental illness: The guiding vision of the mental health system in the 1990's. *Psychosocial Rehabilitation Journal, 16*(4), 11–23.

Anthony, W. A. (1993b). Editorial. *Psychosocial Rehabilitation Journal, 17*(1), 1.

Anthony, W. A. (1994). Characteristics of people with psychiatric disabilities that are predictive of entry into the rehabilitation process and successful employment. *Psychiatric Rehabilitation Journal, 17*(3), 3–13.

Anthony, W. A. (2000). A recovery-oriented service system: Setting some system level standards. *Psychiatric Rehabilitation Journal, 24*(3), 11–23.

Anthony, W. A., & Blanch, A. (1987). Supported employment for persons who are psychiatrically disabled: An historical and conceptual perspective. *Psychosocial Rehabilitation Journal, 11*(2), 5–23.

Anthony, W. A., Cohen, M. R., Farkas, M. D., & Gagne, C. (2002). *Psychiatric rehabilitation* (2nd ed.). Boston, MA: Center for Psychiatric Rehabilitation, Boston University.

Anthony, W. A., Cohen, M. R., & Vitalo, R. (1978). The measurement of rehabilitation outcome. *Schizophrenia Bulletin, 4*, 365–383.

Anthony, W. A., & Farkas, M. D. (2009). *A primer on the psychiatric rehabilitation process*. Boston, MA: Boston University Center for Psychiatric Rehabilitation.

Anthony, W. A., Furlong-Norman, K., & Koehler, M. (2002). Shifting paradigms in mental health service systems: Supported education within the context of rehabilitation and recovery. In C. T. Mowbray, K. S. Brown, K. Furlong-Nornan, & A. Sullivan-Soydan (Eds.), *Supported education and psychiatric rehabilitation: Models and methods* (pp. 287–294). Linthicum, MD: International Association of Psychosocial Rehabilitation Services.

Anthony, W. A., & Jansen, M. A. (1984). Predicting the vocational capacity of the chronically mentally ill: Research and policy implications. *American Psychologist, 39*, 537–544.

Anthony, W. A., & Liberman, R. P. (1986). The practice of psychiatric rehabilitation: Historical, conceptual and research base. *Schizophrenia Bulletin, 12*(4), 542–559.

Anthony, W. A., & Nemec, P. B. (1983). Psychiatric rehabilitation. In A. S. Bellack (Ed.), *The treatment and care of schizophrenia*. New York: Grune and Stratton.

Anthony, W. A., Rogers, E., Cohen, M., & Davies, R. R. (1995). Relationship between psychiatric symptomatology, work skills, and future vocational performance. *Psychiatric Services, 46*(4), 353–358.

Anthony, W. A., & Unger, K. V. (1991). Supported education: An additional program resource for young adults with long-term mental illness. *Community Mental Health Journal, 27*, 145–156.

Archie, S., Goldberg, J., Akhtar-Danesh, N., Landeen, J., McColl, L., & McNiven, J. (2007). Psychotic disorders, eating habits, and physical activity: Who is ready for lifestyle changes? *Psychiatric Services, 58*(2), 233–239.

Armstrong, M. L., Korba, A. M., & Emard, R. (1995). Mutual benefit: The reciprocal relationship between consumer volunteers and the clients they serve. *Psychiatric Rehabilitation Journal, 19*, 45–49.

Arnaiz, A., Zumárraga, M., Díez Altuna, I., Uriarte Jose, J., Moro, J., & Pérez Ansorena, M. A. (2011). Oral health and the symptoms of schizophrenia. *Psychiatry Research, 188*(1), 24–28.

Arnone, D., Cavanagh, J., Gerber, D., Lawrie, S. M., Ebmeier, K. P., & McIntosh, A. M. (2009). Magnetic resonance imaging studies in bipolar disorder and schizophrenia: Meta-analysis. *British Journal of Psychiatry, 195*(3), 194–201.

Arnow, B. A., & Constantino, M. J. (2003). Effectiveness of psychotherapy and combination treatment for chronic depression. *Journal of Clinical Psychology, 59*(8), 893–905.

Arns, P. (1998). *Update on using the IAPSRS toolkit for measuring psychosocial rehabilitation outcomes*. Orlando, FL: Paper presented at the International Association of Psychosocial Rehabilitation Services Conference.

Arns, P. G., & Linney, J. A. (1993). Work, self, and life satisfaction for persons with severe and persistent mental disorders. *Psychosocial Rehabilitation Journal, 17*(2), 63–79.

Astrachan, B. M., Flynn, H. R., Geller, J. D., & Harvey, H. H. (1970). Systems approach to day hospitalization. *Archives of General Psychiatry, 22*, 550–559.

Atkinson, S. D. (1994). Grieving and loss in parents with a schizophrenic child. *American Journal of Psychiatry, 151*(8), 1137–1139.

Atkinson, S., Bramley, C., & Schneider, J. (2009). Professionals' perceptions of the obstacles to education for people using mental health services. *Psychiatric Rehabilitation Journal, 33*(1), 26–31.

Aviram, U., & Segal, S. P. (1973). Exclusion of the mentally ill: Reflection on an old problem in a new context. *Archives of General Psychiatry, 29*, 126–131.

Bachrach, L. L. (1999). The state of the state mental hospital at the turn of the century. *New Directions for Mental Health Services*, 1999: 7–24.

Baillargeon, J., Penn, J. V., Knight, K., Harzke, A. J., Baillargeon, G., & Becker, E. A. (2009). Risk of reincarceration among prisoners with co-occurring severe mental illness and substance use disorders. *Administrative Policy in Mental Health*. http://dx.doi.org/10.1007/s10488-009-0252-9.

Baker, F., & Intagliata, J. (1992). Case management. In R. P. Liberman (Vol. Ed.). *Handbook of psychiatric rehabilitation*, Vol. 166. Boston: Allyn and Bacon.

Bandura, A. (1977). *Social learning theory*. Englewood Cliffs, NJ: Prentice Hall.

Bandura, A. (1986). *Social foundations of thought and action*. Englewood Cliffs, NJ: Prentice Hall.

Bandura, A., Ross, D., & Ross, S. A. (1961). Transmission of aggression through imitation of aggressive models. *Journal of Abnormal and Social Psychology, 63*, 575–582.

Barnes, G. B., Allen, E., Parker, W., Lyon, T., Armentrout, W., & Cole, J. (1988). Dental treatment needs among hospitalized adult mental patients. *Special Care Dentistry, 8*(4), 173–177.

Baron, R. C. (2007). *Promoting community integration for people with serious mental illnesses: A compendium of local implementation strategies*. Philadelphia, PA: University of Pennsylvania Collaborative on Community Integration.

Baron, R. C., & Salzer, M. S. (2002). Accounting for unemployment among people with mental illness. *Behavior Sciences and the Law, 20*, 585–599.

Barrett, N. M., MacDonald-Wilson, K. L., & Nemec, P. B. (2005). Establishing a consortium of psychiatric rehabilitation educators. *American Journal of Psychiatric Rehabilitation, 8*(2), 121–133.

Barrett, N. M., Pratt, C. W., Basto, P., & Gill, K. J. (2000). Integrating consumer providers into a service delivery system: The role of education and credentials. *Psychiatric Rehabilitation Skills, 4*(1), 82–104.

Barrio, C., Yamada, A., Hough, R. L., Hawthorne, W., Garcia, P., & Jeste, D. (2003). Ethnic disparities in use of public mental health case management services among patients with schizophrenia. *Psychiatric Services, 54*, 1264–1270.

Bartholomew, T., & Kensler, D. (2010). Illness Management and Recovery in state psychiatric hospitals. *American Journal of Psychiatric Rehabilitation, 13*(2), 105–125.

Bartholomew, T., & Zechner, M. (2013). Preliminary findings of the impact of illness management and recovery on hospital recidivism: A survival analysis. Manuscript in preparation.

Bartholomew, T. J., & Cook, R. (2013). Toward a fidelity scale for inpatient treatment malls. *American Journal of Psychiatric Rehabilitation*. In press.

Basile, V. S., Masellis, M., Potkin, S. G., & Kennedy, J. L. (2002). Pharmacogenomics in schizophrenia: The quest for individualized therapy. *Human Molecular Genetics, 11*(20), 2417–2530.

Bassman, R. (2010). The evolution from advocacy to self-determination. In M. Swarbrick, L. T. Schmidt, & K. J. Gill (Eds.), *People in recovery as providers of psychiatric rehabilitation: Building on the wisdom of experience* (pp. 2240–2257). Linthicum, MD: USPRA.

Basto, P., Pratt, C. W., Gill, K. J., & Barrett, N. M. (2000). The organizational assimilation of consumer providers. *Psychiatric Rehabilitation Skills, 4*(1), 105–119.

Basu, D. (2004). Quality of life issues in mental health care: Past, present and future. *German Journal of Psychiatry, 7*(3), 35–43.

Baum, A. E., Akula, N., Cabanero, M., Cardona, I., Corona, W., Klemens, B., & McMahon, F. J. (2008). A genome-wide association study implicates diacylglycerol kinase eta (DGKH) and several other genes in the etiology of bipolar disorder. *Molecular Psychiatry, 13*, 197–207. http://dx.doi.org/10.1038/sj. mp.4002012.

Baxter, E. A., & Diehl, S. (1998). Emotional stages: Consumer and family members recovering from the trauma of mental illness. *Psychiatric Rehabilitation Journal, 7*(3), 35–43.

Bazelon Center for Mental Health Law. (1999). *Under court order: What the community integration mandate means for people with mental illness.* Retrieved July 30, 2012, from http://www.bazelon.org/News-Publications.aspx.

Bazelon Center for Mental Health Law (Ed.). (2009). *Still waiting.* Washington, DC: Bazelon Center for Mental Health Law.

Bazelon Center for Mental Health Law. (2004). *Get it together: How to integrate physical and mental health care for people with serious mental disorder.* Retrieved December 2, 2008, from http://www.bazelon.org/issues/mentalhealth/publications/Gettogether/execsumm.htm.

Bazelon Center for Mental Health Law. Employment and unemployment of people with serious mental illness. Retrieved July 19, 2011, from http://bazelon.org.gravitatehosting.com/.

Beard, J. H., Propst, R. N., & Malamud, T. J. (1982). The Fountain House model of psychiatric rehabilitation. *Psychosocial Rehabilitation Journal, 5*(1), 47–53.

Beard, J. H., Propst, R. N., & Malmud, T. J. (1994). The Fountain House model of psychiatric rehabilitation. In L. Spaniol et al. (Eds.), *An introduction to psychiatric rehabilitation* (pp. 45–52). Columbia, MD: IAPSRS.

Beck Institute for Cognitive Behavior Therapy History of Cognitive Behavior Therapy. Retrieved January 10, 2013, from http://www.beckinstitute.org/history-of-cbt/.

Becker, D. R., Bond, G. R., McCarthy, D., Thompson, D., Xie, H., Gregory, G. J., & Drake, R. E. (2001). Converting day treatment centers to supported employment programs in Rhode Island. *Psychiatric Services, 52*(3), 351–357.

Becker, D. R., & Drake, R. E. (1994). Individual placement and support: A community mental health center approach to vocational rehabilitation. *Community Mental Health Journal, 30*(2), 193–206.

Becker, D. R., Smith, J., Tanzman, B., Drake, R. E., & Tremblay, T. (2001). Fidelity of supported employment programs and employment outcomes. *Psychiatric Services, 52*(6), 834–836.

Becker, M., Diamond, R., & Sainfort, F. (1993). A new patient focused index for measuring quality of life in persons with severe and persistent mental illness. *Quality of Life Research, 2*(4), 239–251.

Becker, M., Martin, L., Wajeeh, E., Ward, J., & Shern, D. (2002). Students with mental illnesses in a university setting: Faculty and student attitudes, beliefs, knowledge, and experiences. *Psychiatric Rehabilitation Journal, 25*(4), 359–368.

Beebe, L. H., Smith, K., Burke, R., McIntyre, K., Dessieux, O., Tavakoli, A., Tennison, C., & Velligan, D. (2011). Effect of a motivational intervention on exercise behavior in persons with schizophrenia spectrum disorders. *Community Mental Health Journal, 47*(6), 628–636.

Beers, C. W. (1923). *A mind that found itself.* Garden City, NY: Doubleday.

Beigel, A., & Feder, S. L. (1970). Patterns of utilization in partial hospitalization. *American Journal of Psychiatry, 126*, 1267–1274.

Bell, M. D., Milstein, R. M., & Lysaker, P. H. (1993). Pay and participation in work activity: Clinical benefits for clients with schizophrenia. *Psychosocial Rehabilitation Journal, 17*(2), 173–176.

Bellack, A. S., & DiClemente, C. C. (1999). Treating substance abuse among patients with schizophrenia. *Psychiatric Services, 50*(1), 75–80.

Bellack, A. S., Mueser, K. T., Gingerich, S., & Agresta, J. (2004). *Social skills training for schizophrenia: A step-by-step guide* (2nd ed.). New York: The Guilford Press.

Belmaker, R. H., & Agam, Galila (2008). Mechanisms of disease: Major depressive disorder. *New England Journal of Medicine, 358*, 55–65. http://dx.doi.org/10.1056/NEJMra073096.

Belmaker, R. H. (2004). Medical progress: Bipolar disorder. *New England Journal of Medicine, 351*(5), 476–486.

Benes, Francine M. (2009). Neural circuitry models of schizophrenia: Is it dopamine, GABA, glutamate, or something else? *Biological Psychiatry, 65,* http://dx.doi.org/10.1016/j.biopsych.2009.04.006, 4003–1005.

Berren, M. R., Hill, K. R., Merikle, D., Gonzales, N., & Santiago, J. (1994). Serious mental illness and mortality rates. *Hospital Community Psychiatry, 45,* 604–605.

Besio, S. W., & Mahler, J. (1993). Benefits and challenges of using consumer staff in supported housing services. *Hospital and Community Psychiatry, 44*(5), 490–491.

Bienvenu, O. J., Davydow, D. S., & Kendler, K. S. (2011). Psychiatric 'diseases' versus behavioral disorders and degree of genetic influence. *Psychological Medicine, 41,* 33–40. http://dx.doi.org/10.1017/S003329171000084X.

Bierer, J. (1948). *Therapeutic social clubs.* London: HK Lewis.

Birkmann, J. C., Sperduto, J., Smith, R. C., & Gill, K. J. (2006). A collaborative rehabilitation approach to inpatient treatment. *Psychiatric Rehabilitation Journal, 29*(3), 157–155.

Blankertz, L., & Robinson, S. (1996). Adding a vocational focus to mental health rehabilitation. *Psychiatric Services, 47*(11), 1216–1222.

Bologna, M. J., and Pulice, R. T. (in press). An evaluation of a peer-run hospital diversion program: A descriptive study. *American Journal of Psychosocial Rehabilitation.*

Bond, G. R. (2004). Supported employment: Evidence for an evidence-based practice. *Psychiatric Rehabilitation Journal, 27*(4), 345–359.

Bond, G. R., & Boyer, S. L. (1988). Rehabilitation programs and outcomes. In J. A. Ciardiello, & M. D. Bell (Eds.), *Vocational rehabilitation of persons with prolonged psychiatric disorders* (pp. 231–263). Baltimore, MD: Johns Hopkins University Press.

Bond, G. R., & Dincin, J. (1986). Accelerating entry into transitional employment in a psychosocial rehabilitation agency. *Rehabilitation Psychology, 31,* 143–1555.

Bond, G. R., Dietzen, L. L., McGrew, J. H., & Miller, L. D. (1995). Accelerating entry into supported employment for persons with severe psychiatric disabilities. *Rehabilitation Psychology, 40*(2), 91–111.

Bond, G. R., Drake, R. E., & Becker, D. R. (2008). An update on randomized controlled trials of evidence-based supported employment. *Psychiatric Rehabilitation Journal, 31*(4), 280–290.

Bond, G. R., Drake, R. E., Mueser, K. T., & Becker, D. R. (1997). An update on supported employment for people with severe mental illness. *Psychiatric Services, 48*(3), 335–346.

Bond, G. R., Drake, R. E., Mueser, K. T., & Latimer, E. (2001). Assertive community treatment for people with severe mental illness: Critical ingredients and impact on patients. *Disease Management and Health Outcomes, 9*(3), 141–159.

Bond, G. R., Kim, H.-W., Meyer, P. S., Gibson, P., Tunis, S., Evans, J. D., & Xie, H. (2004). Response to vocational rehabilitation during treatment with first- or second-generation antipsychotics. *Psychiatric Services, 55*(1), 59–66.

Bond, G. R., McGrew, J. H., & Fekete, D. M. (1995). Assertive outreach for frequent users of psychiatric hospitals: A meta analysis. *Journal of Mental Health Administration, 22*(1), 4–16.

Bond, G. R., Resnick, S. R., Drake, R. E., Xie, H., McHugo, G. J., & Bebout, R. R. (2001). Does competitive employment improve nonvocational outcomes for people with severe mental illness? *Journal of Consulting and Clinical Psychology, 69,* 489–501.

Bond, G. R., Salyers, M. P., Dincin, J., Drake, R. E., Becker, D. R., Fraser, V. V., et al. (2007). A randomized controlled trial comparing two vocational models for persons with severe mental illness. *Journal of Consulting and Clinical Psychology, 75,* 968–982.

Bond, G. R., Salyers, M. P., Rollins, A. L., & Moser, L. L. (2005). The future of ACT. In C. L. M. H. Kroon (Ed.), *Assertive community treatment: Evidence-based bemoeizorg voor patiënten met ernstige psychiatrische aandoeningen.* Arnhem, The Netherlands: Cure and Care Publishers.

Bond, G. R., Salyers, M. P., Rollins, A. L., Rapp, C. A., & Zipple, A. M. (2004). How evidence based practices contribute to community integration. *Community Mental Health Journal, 40*(6), 569–588.

Bopp, J., Ribble, D., Cassidy, J., & Markoff, R. (1996). Re-engineering the state hospital to promote rehabilitation and recovery. *Psychiatric Services, 47*(7), 697–698.

Borkman, T. J. (1999). *Understanding self-help/mutual aid: Experiential learning in the commons.* New Brunswick, NJ: Rutgers University Press.

Bottlender, R., Sato, T., Jaeger, M., Wegener, U., Wittmann, J., Strauss, A., et al. (2003). The impact of the duration of untreated psychosis prior to first psychiatric admission on the 15-year outcome in schizophrenia. *Schizophrenia Research, 62*, 37–44.

Bouras, N. (2011). Mental health problems and related issues for people with developmental and intellectual disability. *Current Opinion in Psychiatry, 24*, 365–366.

Boutillier, C. B., Bird, L. M., Davidson, L., Williams, J., & Slade, M. (2011). What does recovery mean in practice? A qualitative analysis of international recovery-oriented practice guidance. *Psychiatric Services, 62*(12), 1470–1476.

Bracke, P., Christiaens, W., & Verhaeghe, M. (2008). Self-esteem, self-efficacy and the balance of peer support among persons with chronic mental health problems. *Journal of Applied Social Psychology, 38*(2), 436–459.

Bradley, V. J. (1994). Evolution of a new service paradigm. In V. J. Bradley, J. W. Ashbaugh, & B. C. Blaney (Eds.), *Creating individual supports for people with developmental disabilities.* Baltimore, MD: Paul H. Brookes Publishing.

Braitman, A., Counts, P., Avenport, R., Zurbinden, B., Rogers, M., Clauss, J., & Montgomery, L. (1995). Comparison barriers to employment for unemployed clients in a case management program: An exploratory study. *Psychiatric Rehabilitation Journal, 19*(1), 3–8.

Brammer, L. M., Shostrom, E. L., & Abrego, P. J. (1989). *Therapeutic psychology: Fundamentals of counseling and psychotherapy* (5th ed.). Englewood Cliffs, NJ: Prentice Hall.

Brice, G. H., Jr. (2011). My journey to work. *Psychiatric Rehabilitation Journal, 34*(2), 409–410.

Brockelman, K. (2010). The role of education for persons in recovery as providers in the mental health field. In M. Swarbrick, L. T. Schmidt, & K. J. Gill (Eds.), *People in recovery as providers of psychiatric rehabilitation: Building on the wisdom of experience.* Linthicum, MD: USPRA.

Brown, A. S. (2012). Epidemiologic studies of exposure to prenatal infection and risk of schizophrenia and autism. *Developmental Neurobiology, 72*, 1272–1276. http://dx.doi.org/10.1002/dneu.22024.

Brown, A. S., & Derkits, E. J. (2010). Prenatal infection and schizophrenia: A review of the epidemiological and translational studies. *American Journal of Psychiatry, 167*, 261–280.

Brown, C., Goetz, J., Van Sciver, A., Sullivan, D., & Hamera, E. (2006). Psychiatric rehabilitation approach to weight loss. *Psychiatric Rehabilitation Journal, 29*, 267–273. http://dx.doi.org/10.2975/29.2006.267.273.

Brown, D. (1997). Excess mortality in schizophrenia: A meta-analysis. *British Journal of Psychiatry, 171*, 502–508.

Brown, K. S. (2002). Antecedents of psychiatric rehabilitation: The road to supported employment programs. In C. T. Mowbray, K. S. Brown, K. Furlong-Norman, & A. Sullivan-Soydan (Eds.), *Supported education and psychiatric rehabilitation: Models and methods* (pp. 13–21). Linthicum, MD: International Association of Psychosocial Rehabilitation Services.

Brown, M. A., Ridgway, P., Anthony, W. A., & Rogers, E. S. (1991). Comparison of outcomes for clients seeking and assigned to supported housing services. *Hospital and Community Psychiatry, 42*(11), 1150–1153.

Brown, N. P., & Parrish, J. (1995). CSP champion of self-help. *California Alliance for the Mentally Ill, 6*(3), 6–7.

Brown, S., Birtwistle, J., Roe, L., & Thompson, C. (1999). The unhealthy lifestyle of people with schizophrenia. *Psychological Medicine, 29,* 697–701.

Brown, S., & Chan, K. (2006). A randomized controlled trial of a brief health promotion intervention in a population with serious mental illness. *Journal of Mental Health, 15,* 543–549.

Buchanan, R. W., & Carpenter, W. T., Jr. (1997). The neuroanatomies of schizophrenia. *Schizophrenia Bulletin, 23*(3), 367–372.

Budson, R. D. (1994). Community residential and partial hospital care: Low-cost alternative systems in the spectrum of care. *Psychiatric Quarterly, 65*(3), 209–220.

Burland, J. F. (1998). Family-to-family: A trauma and recovery model of family education. *New Directions for Mental Health Services, 77,* 179–182.

Burns, T., Catty, J., Becker, T., Drake, R. E., Fioritti, A., Knapp, M., et al. (2007). The effectiveness of supported employment for people with severe mental illness: A randomized controlled trial. *Lancet, 370,* 1146–1152.

Burns, T., Catty, J., Dash, M., Roberts, C., Lockwood, A., & Marshal, M. (2007). Use of intensive case management to reduce time in hospital in people with severe mental illness: systematic review and meta-regression. *BMJ | ONLINE FIRST |.* http://dx.doi.org/10.1136/bmj.39251.599259.55. bmj.com.

Burns-Lynch, W., & Salzer, M. S. (2001). Adopting innovations-lessons learned from a peer-based hospital diversion program. *Community Mental Health Journal, 37*(6), 1–11.

Burti, L. (2001). Italian psychiatric reform 20 plus years after. *Acta Psychiatrica Scandinavica Supplement, 410,* 41–46.

Busch, A. B. (2005). Introduction to the special section. *Psychiatric Services, 56*(9), 1104.

Buschbaum, M. S., & Haier, R. J. (1987). Functional and anatomical brain imaging: Impact on schizophrenia research. *Schizophrenia Bulletin, 13*(1), 115–132.

Business, National Alliance of. (1991). *ADA sourcebook, what you need to know about the Americans with Disabilities Act: A guide for small and medium-sized businesses.* Washington, DC: Author.

Butler, W. (1993). The consumer supported housing model in New Jersey (the cornerstone to a new paradigm). *Innovations and Research, 2*(3), 73–75.

Butzlaff, R. L., & Hooley, J. M. (1998). Expressed emotion and psychiatric relapse. *Archives of General Psychiatry, 55*(6), 547–552.

Cadigan, K., & Murray (Writer), L. (2009). When medicine got it wrong [Documentary Film]: imageReal Pictures, KQED and the Independent Television Service (TVS) with funding by the Corporation for Public Broadcasting.

Caldwell, S., & White, K. K. (1991). Co-creating a self-help recovery movement. *Psychosocial Rehabilitation Journal, 15*(2), 91–95.

Callaway, E. (2012). Fathers bequeath more mutations as they age. *Nature, 488,* 439.

Cameron, D. E. (1947). The day hospital: Experimental forms of hospitalization for patients. *Modern Hospital, 69*(3), 60–62.

Campbell, J. (2002). *Working science: Consumer Operated Service Program. Multi-site research initiative, study overview.* Baltimore, MD: Paper presented at the 12th Annual Conference on State Mental Health Services Agency Research, Program Evaluation and Policy.

Campbell, J. (2005). The historical and philosophical development of peer-run support programs. In S. Clay (Ed.), *On our own together: Peer programs for people with mental illness.* Nashville, TN: Vanderbilt University Press.

Campbell, J., Lichtenstein, C., Teague, G., Johnsen, M., Yates, B., Sonnefeld, et al. (2006) *The Consumer operated service programs (COSP) Multi-site Research Initiative: Final Report.* St. Louis, MO: Coordinating Center at the Missouri Institute of Mental Health.

Campbell, K., Bond, G. R., & Drake, R. E. (2011). Who benefits from supported employment: A meta-analytic study. *Schizophrenia Bulletin, 37*, 370–380.

Campbell, K., Bond, G. R., Drake, R. E., McHugo, G. J., & Xie, H. (2010). Client predictors of employment outcomes in high-fidelity supported employment: A regression analysis. *Journal of Nervous and Mental Disease, 198*(8), 556–563.

Campbell, M. E. (1981). The three-quarterway house: A step beyond halfway house toward independent living. *Hospital and Community Psychiatry, 32*(7), 500–501.

Campinha-Bacote, J. (2003). Many faces: Addressing diversity in health care. *Online Journal of Issues in Nursing, 8*(1). www.nursingworld.org/MainMenuCategories/ANAMarketplace/ANAPeriodicals/OJIN/TableofContents/Volume82003/No1Jan2003/AddressingDiversityinHealthCare.aspx.

Cannon, M., Jones, P. B., & Murray, R. M. (2002). Obstetric complications and schizophrenia: Historical and meta-analytic review. *American Journal of Psychiatry, 159*, 1080–1092.

Capdevielle, D., & Ritchie, K. (2008). The long and the short of it: Are shorter periods of hospitalization beneficial? [References]. *British Journal of Psychiatry, 192*(3), 164–165.

Carey, B. (2012). Father's age linked to autism and schizophrenia. August 22, 2012. *New York Times.*

Carey, M., Duff, S., & Robertson-Kean, L. (2002). Michigan Supported Education Program. In K. S. B. C. T. Mowbray, K. Furlong-Norman, & A. Sullivan-Soydan (Eds.), *Supported education and psychiatric rehabilitation: Models and methods* (pp. 89–98). Linthicum, MD: International Association of Psychosocial Rehabilitation Services.

Carkhuff, R. R. (2009). *The art of helping in the 21st century* (9th ed.). Amherst, MA: Human Resources Development Press, Inc.

Carling, P. (1995). *Return to community.* New York: Guilford Press.

Carling, P. J. (1990). Supported housing: An evaluation agenda. *Psychosocial Rehabilitation Journal, 13*(4), 95–104.

Carling, P. J. (1993). Housing and supports for persons with mental illness: Emerging approaches to research and practice. *Hospital and Community Psychiatry, 44*(5), 439–449.

Carling, P. J. (1994). Supports and rehabilitation for housing and community living. In L. Spaniol, et al. (Eds.), *An introduction to psychiatric rehabilitation* (pp. 45–52). Columbia, MD: IAPSRS.

Carling, P. J., & Ridgway, P. (1991). A psychiatric rehabilitation approach to housing. In M. D. Farkas, & W. A. Anthony (Eds.), *Psychiatric rehabilitation programs: Putting theory into practice.* Baltimore, MD: The Johns Hopkins University Press.

Carlson, L. S., Rapp, C. A., & McDiarmid, D. (2001). Hiring consumer-providers: Barriers and alternative solutions. *Community Mental Health Journal, 37*(3), 199–213.

Carmody, K. (1994). Creating individual supports for people moving out of nursing facilities: supported placements in integrated community environments (SPICE). In J. W. A. Bradley, & B. C. Blaney (Eds.), *Creating individual supports for people with developmental disabilities.* Baltimore, MD: Paul H. Brookes Publishing.

Carpinello, S. E., Knight, E. L., & Janis, L. (1991). *A qualitative study of the perception of the meaning of self-help, self-help groups, processes and outcomes by self-help group leaders, members and significant others.* Albany, NY: New York State Office of Mental Health.

Casper, E. S., & Fishbein, S. (2002). Job satisfaction and job success as moderators on the self-esteem of people with mental illnesses. *Psychiatric Rehabilitation Journal, 26*(1), 33–42.

Caton, C. L. M. (1981). The new chronic patient and the system of community care. *Hospital and Community Psychiatry, 32*, 475–478.

Ceilley, J. W., Cruz, M., & Denko, T. (2006). Active medical conditions among patients on an assertive community treatment team. *Community Mental Health Journal, 42*(2), 205–211.

Center for Medicare and Medicaid Services. (2013). *Health homes.* Accessed at http://www.medicaid.gov/Medicaid-CHIP-Program-Information/By-Topics/Long-Term-Services-and-Support/Integrating-Care/Health-Homes/Health-Homes.html.

Chamberlin, J. (1978). *On our own.* New York: McGraw-Hill.

Chamberlin, J. (1984). Speaking for ourselves: An overview of the ex-psychiatric inmates' movement. *Psychosocial Rehabilitation Journal, 8*(2), 56–64.

Chamberlin, J. (1990). The ex-patient movement: Where we've been and where we're going. *Journal of Mind and Behavior, 11*, 323–336.

Chamberlin, J., Rogers, E. S., & Ellison, M. L. (1996). Self-help programs: A description of their characteristics and their members. *Psychiatric Rehabilitation Journal, 19*(3), 33–42.

Chamberlin, R., & Rapp, C. A. (1991). A decade of case management: A methodological review of outcome research. *Community Mental Health Journal, 27*(3), 171–188.

Chan, W. I., et al. (2009). Duration of illness, morphology, and neurocognitive correlates in schizophrenia. *Annals of the Academy of Medicine Singapore, 38*, 388–395.

Chandler, D., Meisel, J., Hu, T., McGowen, M., & Madison, K. (1997). A capitated model for a cross-section of severely mentally ill clients: Employment outcomes. *Community Mental Health Journal, 33*(6), 501–516.

Charych, E. I., Liu, F., Moss, S. J., & Brandon, N. J. (2009). GABA$_A$ receptors and their associated proteins: Implications in the etiology and treatment of schizophrenia and related disorders. *Neuropharmacology, 57*, 481–495. http://dx.doi.org/10.1016/j.neuropharm.2009.07.027.

Chase, M., Malden, A., Lansbusry, L., Hansen, J., Ambose, A., Thomas, C., Wilson, C., & Costall, A. (2011). In sight, out of mind: The experiences of the compliantly engaged community psychiatric out-patient. *Community Mental Health Journal.* http://dx.doi.org/10.1007/s10597-011-9414-9.

Chen, J., Calhoun, V. D., Pearlson, G. D., Ehrlich, S., Turner, J. A., Ho, B., & Liu, J. (2012). Multifaceted genomic risk for brain function in schizophrenia. *NeuroImage, 61*, 866–875. http://dx.doi.org/10.1016/j.neuroimage.2012.03.022.

Chen, Y. R., Swann, A. C., & Johnson, B. A. (1998). Stability of diagnosis in bipolar disorder. *Journal of Nervous and Mental Disease, 186*(1), 17–23.

Cheng, A., Lin, H., Kasprow, W., & Rosenheck, R. (2007). Impact of supported housing on clinical outcomes: Analysis of a randomized trial using multiple imputation technique. *Journal of Nervous and Mental Disease, 195*(1), 83–88.

Chilvers, R., Macdonald, G., & Hayes, A. (2006). *Supported housing for people with severe mental disorders.* http://onlinelibrary.wiley.com/doi/10.1002/14651858.CD000453.pub2.

Chinman, M. J., Rosenheck, R., Lam, J. A., & Davidson, L. (2000). Comparing consumer and non-consumer provided case management services for homeless persons with serious mental illness. *Journal of Nervous and Mental Disease, 188*(7), 446–453.

Chmielewski, M. (2002). Serving student with psychiatric disabilities through the disability support services office. In C. T. Mowbray, K. S. Brown, K. Furlong-Norman, & A. Sullivan-Soydan (Eds.), *Supported education and psychiatric rehabilitation: Models and methods* (pp. 253–261). Linthicum, MD: International Association of Psychosocial Rehabilitation Services.

Cleary, M., Hunt, G. E., Matheson, S. L., Siegfried, N., & Walter, G. (2010). *Psychosocial interventions for people with both severe mental illness and substance misuse (Review).* The Cochrane Collaboration. John Wiley and Sons, Ltd.

Cloutier, G. (1997). Going sane: One man's battle with schizoaffective disorder. *Journal of the California Alliance for the Mentally Ill, 8*(2), 65–66.

Cloyes, K. G., Wong, B., Latimer, S., & Abarca, J. (2010). Time to prison return for offenders with serious mental illness released from prison. *Criminal Justice and Behavior, 37*(2), 175–187.

Cnaan, R. A., Blankertz, L., Messinger, K. W., & Gardner, J. R. (1988). Psychosocial rehabilitation: Towards a definition. *Psychiatric Rehabilitation Journal, 11*(4), 61–77.

Cnaan, R. A., Blankertz, L., Messinger, K. W., & Gardner, J. R. (1989). Psychosocial rehabilitation: Towards a theoretical base. *Psychiatric Rehabilitation Journal, 13*(1), 33–55.

Cnaan, R. A., Blankertz, L., Messinger, K. W., & Gardner, J. R. (1990). Experts assessment of psychosocial rehabilitation principles. *Psychiatric Rehabilitation Journal, 13*(3), 59–73S.

Coalition for Community Living. *The Fairweather Lodge.* Retrieved August 7, 2012, from http://theccl.org/fairweather.htm.

Cohen, M. R., Farkas, M. D., & Cohen, B. (1992). *Training technology: Assessing readiness for rehabilitation.* Boston, MA: Center for Psychiatric Rehabilitation.

Cohen, M. R., & Forbes, R. (1992). *Training technology: Developing readiness for rehabilitation.* Boston, MA: Center for Psychiatric Rehabilitation.

Cohen, M. R., & Mynks, D. (1993). *Compendium of activities for assessing and developing readiness for rehabilitation services.* Boston, MA: Center for Psychiatric Rehabilitation.

Cohen, P., & Cohen, J. (1984). The clinician's illusion. *Archives of General Psychiatry, 41*(12), 1178–1182. http://dx.doi.org/10.1001/archpsyc.1984.01790230064010.

Coleman, L. M. (Ed.). (1986). *The dilemma of difference.* New York: Plenum Press.

Collaborative Support Programs of New Jersey. (1996). *Boarding home resident survey for Monmouth and Ocean counties.* Freehold, NJ: Author.

Collins, F. (2010). *The language of life.* New York: HarperPerennial.

Collins, M. E., Bybee, D., & Mowbray, C. T. (1998). Effectiveness of supported education for individuals with psychiatric disabilities: Results from an experimental study. *Community Mental Health Journal, 34*(6), 595–613.

Colman, I., & Ataullahjan, A. (2010). Life course perspectives on the epidemiology of depression. *The Canadian Journal of Psychiatry / La Revue canadienne de psychiatrie, 55*(10), 622–632.

Colman, I., Naicker, K., Zeng, Y., Ataullahjan, A., Senthilselvan, A., & Patten, S. B. (2011). Predictors of long-term prognosis of depression. *Canadian Medical Association Journal, 183,* 1969–1976. http://dx.doi.org/10.1503/cmaj.110676.

Colom, F., Vieta, E., Martinez, A., Jorquera, A., & Gasto, C. (1998). What is the role of psychotherapy in the treatment of bipolar disorder? *Psychotherapy and Psychosomatics, 67*(1), 3–9.

Conklin, H. M., & Iacono, W. G. (2002). Schizophrenia: A neurodevelopmental perspective. *Current Directions in Psychological Science, 11,* 33–37.

Conley, R. R., & Buchanan, R. W. (1997). Evaluation of treatment-resistant schizophrenia. *Schizophrenia Bulletin, 23*(4), 663–674.

Cook, J. (2006). Employment barriers for persons with psychiatric disabilities: Update for a report for the president's commission. *Psychiatric Services, 57*(10), 1391–1405.

Cook, J. A., & Hoffschmidt, S. J. (1993). Comprehensive models of psychosocial rehabilitation. In R. W. Flexer, & P. A. Solomon (Eds.), *Psychiatric rehabilitation in practice.* Boston: Andover Medical Publishers.

Cook, J. A., & Solomon, M. L. (1993). The community scholar program: An outcome study of supported education for students with severe mental illness. *Psychosocial Rehabilitation Journal, 17*(1), 83–97.

Cook, J. A., Yamaguchi, J., & Solomon, M. L. (1993). Field-testing a postsecondary faculty in-service training for working with students who have psychiatric disabilities. *Psychosocial Rehabilitation Journal, 17*(1), 157–170.

Cook, J. R. (1997). Neighbors' perceptions of group homes. *Community Mental Health Journal, 33*(4), 287–299.

Cooper, E., O'Hara, A., & Zovistoski, A. (2011). Priced out in 2010: The housing crisis for people with disabilities. A joint publication of The Technical Assistance Collaborative, Boston, MA; and The Consortium for Citizens with Disabilities, Housing Taskforce.

Cooper, E., Herb, M., & O'Hara, A. (2003). Solutions that work: Innovative strategies to meeting the housing needs of people with disabilities. A joint publication of The Technical Assistance Collaborative, Boston, MA; and The Consortium for Citizens with Disabilities.

Cooper, L. (1993). Serving adults with psychiatric disabilities on campus: A mobile support approach. *Psychosocial Rehabilitation Journal, 17*(1), 25–38.

Copeland, L. A., Mortensen, E. M., Zeber, J. E., Pugh, M. J., Restrepo, M. I., & Dalack, G. W. (2007). Pulmonary disease among inpatient decedents: Impact of schizophrenia. *Progress in Neuro-Psychopharmacology and Biological Psychiatry, 31*, 720–726. http://dx.doi.org/10.1016/j.pnpbp.2007.01.008.

Copeland, M. E., & Mead, S. (2004). *Wellness recovery action plan and peer support.* Brattleboro, VT: Peach Press.

Copic, V., Deane, F. P., Crowe, T. P., & Oades, L. G. (2011). Hope, meaning and responsibility across stages of recovery for individuals living with an enduring mental illness. *The Australian Journal of Rehabilitation Counseling, 17*(2), 61–73.

Corporation for Supported Housing. (2012). *Supported housing and Olmstead: Creating opportunities for people with disabilities.* Retrieved January 5, 2013, from http://www.csh.org/resources/supportive-housing-olmstead-creating-opportunities-for-people-with-disabilities/.

Corrigan, P. (2003). Towards an integrated, structural model of psychiatric rehabilitation. *Psychiatric Rehabilitation Journal, 26*(4), 346–358.

Corrigan, P., Mueser, K., Bond, G., Drake, R., & Solomon, P. (2008). Physical health and medical care. In P. Corrigan, et al. (Eds.), *Principles and practice of psychiatric rehabilitation: An empirical approach* (pp. 346–358). New York: The Guilford Press.

Corrigan, P., Thompson, V., Lambert, D., Sangster, Y., Noel, J. G., & Campbell, J. (2003). Perceptions of discrimination among persons with serious mental illness. *Psychiatric Services, 54*, 1105–1110.

Corrigan, P. W., Barr, L., Driscoll, H., & Boyle, M. G. (2008). The educational goals of people with psychiatric disabilities. *Psychiatric Rehabilitation Journal, 32*(1), 67–70.

Corrigan, P. W., Giffort, D., Rashid, F., Leary, M., & Okeke, I. (1999). Recovery as a psychological construct. *Community Mental Health Journal, 35*(3), 231–239.

Corrigan, P. W., Larson, J. E., & Rusch, N. (2009). Self-stigma and the "why try" effect: Impact on life goals and evidence-based practices. *World Psychiatry, 8*(2), 75–81.

Corrigan, P. W., & McCracken, S. G. (1995). Psychiatric rehabilitation and staff development: Educational and organizational models. *Clinical Psychology Review, 15*(8), 699–719.

Corrigan, P. W., & Phelan, S. M. (2004). Social support and recovery in people with serious mental illnesses. *Community Mental Health Journal, 40*(6), 513–523.

Coursey, R., Curtis, L., Marsh, D., Campbell, J., Harding, C., Spaniol, L., et al. (2000). Competencies for direct service staff members who work with adults with severe mental illness in outpatient public mental health managed care systems. *Psychiatric Rehabilitation Journal, 23*, 370–377.

Craig, T., Doherty, I., Jamieson-Craig, R., Boocock, A., & Attafua, G. (2004). The consumer-employee as a member of a mental health assertive outreach team. I. Clinical and social outcomes. *Journal of Mental Health, 13*(1), 59–69.

Craighead, W. E., Craighead, L. W., & Ilardi, S. S. (1998a). Psychosocial treatments for major depression. In P. E. Nathan, & J. M. Gorman (Eds.), *A guide to treatments that work* (pp. 226–239). New York: Oxford University Press.

Craighead, W. E., Craighead, L. W., & Ilardi, S. S. (1998b). Psychosocial treatments for major depression. In P. E. Nathan, & J. M. Gorman (Eds.), *A guide to treatments that work* (pp. 240–248). New York: Oxford University Press.

Cuddeback, G. S., & Morrissey, J. P. (2011). Program planning and staff competencies for forensic assertive community treatment: ACT-eligible versus FACT-eligible consumers. *American Psychiatric Nurses Association, 17*(1), 90–97. http://dx.doi.org/10.1177/1078390310392374.

Cuesta, M. J., García de Jalón, E., Campos, M. S., Ibáñez, B., Sánchez-Torres, A. M., & Peralta, V. (2012). Duration of untreated negative and positive symptoms of psychosis and cognitive impairment in first episode psychosis. *Schizophrenia Research, 141*(2–3), 222–227. http://dx.doi.org/10.1016/j.schres.2012.08.019.

Cuffel, B. J. (Vol. Ed.). (1996). *Comorbid substance abuse disorder: Prevalence, patterns of use and course*, Vol. 70, San Francisco: Jossey-Bass.

Cullen, S. W., Matejkowski, J. C., Marcus, S. C., & Solomon, P. L. (2010). Maternal mental health and pediatric health care use among a national sample of Medicaid and SCHIP insured children. *Journal of Behavioral Health Services and Research, 37*, 443–460.

Cunha, A. B. M., Frey, B., Andreazza, A. C., Goi, J. D., Rsa, A. R., Goncalves, C. A., Santin, A., & Kapczinski, F. (2006). Serum brain-derived neurotrophic factor is decreased in bipolar disorder during depressive and manic episodes. *Neuroscience Letters, 398*, 215–219.

Curie, C. G. (2005). SAMHSA's commitment to eliminating the use of seclusion and restraint. *Psychiatric Services, 56*(9), 1139–1140.

Curtis, L. C. (1999). *Modeling recovery: Consumers as service providers in behavioral healthcare*. Rockville, MD: National Council for Behavioral Healthcare.

Curtis, L. C., McCabe, S. S., Fleming, M., & Carling, P. J. (1993). *Implementing the supported housing approach: An impact evaluation of the Texas supported housing demonstration initiative*. Burlington, VT: Trinity College, Center for Community Change through Housing and Support.

Cusin, C., Serretti, A., Lattuada, E., Mandelli, L., & Smeraldi, E. (2000). Impact of clinical variables on illness time course in mood disorders. *Psychiatry Research, 97*(2-3), 217–227.

Daley, D. C., Moss, H. B., & Campbell, F. (1993). *Dual disorders: Counseling clients with chemical dependency and mental illness* (2nd ed.). Center City, MN: Hazelden Foundation.

Daley, J. M., & Latane, B. (1968). Bystander interventions in emergencies: Diffusion of responsibility. *Journal of Personality and Social Psychology, 8*, 377–383.

Daniels, A. S., Tunner, T. P., Ashenden, P., Bergeson, S., Fricks, L., & Powell, I. (2012). *Pillars of Peer Support – III: Whole health peer support services*. Retrieved January, 2012, from www.pillarsofpeersupport.org.

Danley, K. S., & Anthony, W. A. (1987). The choose get keep approach to supported employment. *American Rehabilitation, 13*(4), 6–9, 27–29.

Danley, K. S., Sciarappa, K., & MacDonald-Wilson, K. (1992). Choose-get-keep: A psychiatric rehabilitation approach to supported employment. In R. P. Liberman (Vol. Ed.). *Effective psychiatric rehabilitation*, Vol. 53, (pp. 87–96). San Francisco: Jossey-Bass.

Davidson, L. (1992). Developing an empirical-phenomenological approach to schizophrenia. *Journal of Phenomenological Psychology, 23*(1), 3–15.

Davidson, L. (2003). *Living outside mental illness: Qualitative studies of recover in schizophrenia*. New York: New York University Press.

Davidson, L., Borg, M., Marin, I., Topor, A., Mezzna, R., & Sells, D. (2005). Recovery in serious mental illness: Findings from a multinational study. *American Journal of Psychiatric Rehabilitation, 8*(3), 177–201.

Davidson, L., Chinman, M., Kloos, B., Weingarten, R., Stayner, D., & Tebes, J. K. (1999). Peer support among individuals with severe mental illness: A review of the evidence. *Clinical Psychology: Science and Practice, 6*(2), 165–187.

Davidson, S., Judd, F., Jolley, D., Hocking, B., Thompson, S., & Hyland, B. (2001). Risk factors for HIV/AIDS and hepatitis C among the chronic mentally ill. *Australian and New Zealand Journal of Psychiatry, 35*, 203–209. http://dx.doi.org/10.1046/j.1440-1614.2001.00867.x.

Davidson, L., & Strauss, J. S. (1992). Sense of self in recovery from severe mental illness. *British Journal of Psychiatry, 65*, 131–145.

Davidson, L., Tondora, J., O'Connell, M. J., Kirk, T., Jr., Rockholz, P., & Evans, A. C. (2007). Creating a recovery-oriented system of behavioral health care: Moving from concept to reality. *Psychiatric Rehabilitation Journal, 31*(1), 23–31. http://dx.doi.org/10.2975/31.1.2007.23.31.

de Almeida, A. M., & Neto, F. L. (2003). Cognitive-behavioral therapy in prevention of depression relapses and recurrences: A review. *Revista Brasileira de Psiquiatria, 25*(4), 239–244.

Deegan, P. E. (1988). Recovery: The lived experience of rehabilitation. *Psychiatric Rehabilitation Journal, 11*(4), 11–19.

Deegan, P. E. (1992). The independent living movement and people with psychiatric disabilities: Taking back control over our own lives. *Psychosocial Rehabilitation Journal, 15*(3), 3–19.

Deegan, P. E. (1993). Recovering our sense of value after being labeled mentally ill. *Journal of Psychosocial Nursing, 15*, 3–19.

Deegan, P. E., & Smoyak, S. A. (1996). Blending two realities into a unique perspective. *Journal of Psychosocial Nursing, 34*(9), 39–46.

Department of Health and Human Services. (2009). *Practice guidelines: Core elements for responding to mental health crises* (Vol. HHS Pub. No. SMA-09-4427). Rockville, MD: Center for Mental Health Services, Substance Abuse and Mental Health Services Administration.

DeSisto, M. J., Harding, C. M., McCormack, R. V., Ashikaga, T., & Brooks, G. W. (1995a). The Maine and Vermont three-decade studies of serious mental illness I. *British Journal of Psychiatry, 167*, 331–337.

DeSisto, M. J., Harding, C. M., McCormack, R. V., Ashikaga, T., & Brooks, G. W. (1995b). The Maine and Vermont three-decade studies of serious mental illness II. *British Journal of Psychiatry, 167*, 338–342.

Deutsch, A. (1948). *The shame of the states*. Oxford, England: Harcourt, Brace.

Dhillon, A. S., & Dollieslager, L. P. (2000). Overcoming barriers to individualized psychosocial rehabilitation in an acute treatment unit of a state hospital. *Psychiatric Services, 51*(3), 313–317.

Dickerson, F., Brown, C., Daumit, G., LiJuan, F., Goldberg, R., Wohlheiter, K., & Dixon, L. (2006). Health status of individuals with serious mental illness. *Schizophrenia Bulletin, 32*(3), 584–589.

Dickey, B., Gonzalez, O., Latimer, E., Powers, K., Schutt, R., & Goldfinger, S. M. (1996). Use of mental health services by formerly homeless adults residing in group and independent housing. *Psychiatric Services, 47*(2), 152–158.

Dickey, B., Latimer, E., Powers, K., Gonzalez, O., & Goldfinger, S. M. (1997). Housing costs for adults who are mentally ill and formerly homeless. *Journal of Mental Health Administration, 24*(3), 291–305.

DiClemente, C. C., & Prochaska, J. O. (1998). Toward a comprehensive, transtheoretical model of change: Stages of change and addictive behaviors. In W. R. M. N. Heather (Ed.), *Treating addictive behaviors* (2nd ed.). (pp. 3–24). New York: Plenum Press.

Dietrich, M., Irving, C. B., Park, B., & Marshall, M. (2011). *Intensive case management for severe mental illness*. (Art. No.: CD007906) (Publication no. 10.1002/14651858.CD007906.pub2).

DiLeo, D., & Langton, D. (1993). *Get the marketing edge*. St. Augustine, FL: Training Resource Network.

Dincin, J. (1975). Psychiatric rehabilitation. *Schizophrenia Bulletin, 13*, 131–147.

Dincin, J. (1990). Speaking out. *Psychosocial Rehabilitation Journal, 14*(2), 83–85.

Dix, Dorothea (1843). *Memorial to the Legislature of Massachusetts.* Boston: Munroe and Francis.

Dixon, L., Krauss, N., & Lehman, A. (1994). Consumers as service providers: The promise and the challenge. *Community Mental Health Journal, 30*, 615–629.

Dixon, L. B., Dickerson, F., Bellack, A. S., Bennett, M., Dickinson, D., Goldberg, R. W., & Kreyenbuhl, J. (2010). The 2009 schizophrenia PORT psychosocial treatment recommendations and summary statements. *Schizophrenia Bulletin, 36*(1), 48–70. http://dx.doi.org/10.1093/schbul/sbp115.

Dixon, L. B., & Lehman, A. F. (1995). Family interventions for schizophrenia. *Schizophrenia Bulletin, 21*(4), 631–644.

Dixon, L. B., Lucksted, A., Medoff, D. R., Burland, J., Stewart, B., Lehman, A. F., & Murray-Swank, A. (2011). Outcomes of a randomized study of a peer-taught family-to-family education program for mental illness. *Psychiatric Services, 62*(6), 591–597.

Dixon, L. B., McFarlane, W. R., Lefley, H., Lucksted, A., Cohen, M., Falloon, I., et al. (2001). Evidence-based practices for services to families of people with psychiatric disabilities. *Psychiatric Services, 52*(7), 903–910.

Doherty, I., Craig, T., Attafua, G., Boocock, A., & Jamieson-Craig, R. (2004). The consumer-employee as a member of a mental health assertive outreach team. II. Impressions of consumer-employees and other team members. *Journal of Mental Health, 30*, 615–629.

Donat, D. C. (2005). Encouraging alternatives to seclusion, restraint, and reliance on PRN drugs in a public psychiatric hospital. *Psychiatric Services, 56*(9), 1105–1108.

Doran, G. T. (1981). There's a S.M.A.R.T. way to write management's goals and objectives. *Management Review, 70*(11), 35–36.

Dougherty, S., Hastie, C., Bernard, J., Broadhurst, S., & Marcus, L. (1992). Supported education: A clubhouse experience. *Psychosocial Rehabilitation Journal, 16*(2), 91–104.

Dougherty, S., Kampana, K., Kontos, R., Flores, M., Lockhart, R., & Shaw, D. (1996). Supported education: A qualitative study of the student experience. *Psychiatric Rehabilitation Journal, 19*(3), 59–70.

Drake, R., & Bond, G. (2011). IPS supported employment: A 20 year update. *American Journal of Psychiatric Rehabilitation, 14*(3), 155–164.

Drake, R. E., & Bond, G. R. (2008). Supported employment: 1998 – 2008. *Psychiatric Rehabilitation Journal, 31*(4), 274–276.

Drake, R. E., & Wallach, M. A. (1989). Substance abuse among the chronic mentally ill. *Hospital and Community Psychiatry, 40*(10), 1041–1045.

Drake, R. E., & Wallach, M. A. (2000). Dual diagnosis: 15 years of progress. *Psychiatric Services, 51*(9), 1126–1129.

Drake, R. E., Bartels, S. J., Teague, G. B., Noordsy, D. L., & Clark, R. E. (1993). Treatment of substance abuse in severely mentally ill patients. *Journal of Nervous and Mental Disease, 181*(10), 606–611.

Drake, R. E., Becker, D. R., Biesanz, J. C., Torrey, W. C., McHugo, G. J., & Wyzik, P. F. (1994). Rehabilitative day treatment vs. supported employment: I, Vocational outcomes. *Community Mental Health Journal, 30*(5), 519–531.

Drake, R. E., Becker, D. R., Bond, G. R., & Mueser, K. T. (2003). A process analysis of integrated and non-integrated approaches to supported employment. *Journal of Vocational Rehabilitation, 18*, 51–58.

Drake, R. E., Deegan, P. E., & Rapp, C. (2010). The promise of shared decision making in mental health. *Psychiatric Rehabilitation Journal, 34*(1), 7–13.

Drake, R. E., Goldman, H. H., Leff, H. S., Lehman, A. F., Dixon, L., Mueser, K. T., et al. (2001). Implementing evidence-based practices in routine mental health service settings. *Psychiatric Services, 52*, 179–182.

Drake, R. E., McHugo, G. J., Bebout, R. R., Becker, D. R., Harris, M., Bond, G. R., et al. (1999). A randomized clinical trial of supported employment for inner-city patients with severe mental illness. *Archives of General Psychiatry, 56,* 627–633.

Drake, R. E., McHugo, G. J., Becker, D. R., Anthony, W. A., & Clark, R. I. (1996). The New Hampshire study of supported employment for people with severe mental illness. *Journal of Consulting and Clinical Psychology, 64*(2), 391–399.

Drake, R. E., McLaughlin, P., Pepper, B., & Minkoff, K. (1991). Dual diagnosis of major mental illness and substance disorder: An overview. *New Directions for Mental Health Services, 50,* 3–12.

Drake, R. E., Mercer-McFadden, C., Mueser, K. T., McHugo, G. J., & Bond, G. R. (1998). Review of integrated mental health and substance abuse treatment for patients with dual disorders. *Schizophrenia Bulletin, 24*(4), 589–608.

Drake, R. E., Mueser, K. T., Brunette, M. F., & McHugo, G. J. (2004). A review of treatments for people with severe mental illnesses and co-occurring substance use disorders. *Psychiatric Rehabilitation Journal, 27*(4), 360–374.

Drake, R. E., Mueser, K. T., Torrey, W. C., Miller, A. L., Lehman, A. F., Bond, G. R., Goldman, H. H., & Leff, H. S. (2000). Evidence-based treatment of schizophrenia. *Current Psychiatry Reports, 2,* 393–397.

Drake, R. E., O'Neal, E. L., & Wallach, M. A. (2008). A systematic review of psychosocial research on psychosocial interventions for people with co-occurring severe mental and substance use disorders. *Journal of Substance Abuse Treatment, 34,* 123–138.

Drake, R. J., Haley, C. J., Akhar, S., & Lewis, S. (2000). Causes and consequences of duration of untreated psychosis in schizophrenia. *Psychiatry, 177,* 511–514.

Drapalski, A. L., Medoff, D., Unick, G. J., Velligan, D. I., Dixon, L. B., & Bellack, A. S. (2012). Assessing recovery of people with serious mental illness: Development of a new scale. *Psychiatric Services, 63*(1), 48–53.

Druss, B., Rohrbaugh, R., Levinson, C., & Rosenheck, R. (2001). Integrated medical care for patients with serious psychiatric illness. *Archives of General Psychiatry, 58*(9), 861–868.

Druss, B., & von Esesnwein, S. (2006). Improving general medical care of persons with mental and addictive disorders: Systematic review. *General Hospital Psychiatry, 28,* 145–153.

Druss, B. G., von Esenwein, S. A., Compton, M. T., Rask, K. J., Zhao, L., & Parker, R. M. (2010a). A randomized trial of medical care management for community mental health settings: The Primary Care Access, Referral, and Evaluation (PCARE) Study. *American Journal of Psychiatry, 167,* 151–159. http://dx.doi.org/10.1176/appi.ajp.2009.09050691.

Druss, B. G., Zhao, L., von Esenwein, S. A., Bona, J. R., Fricks, L., Jenkins-Tucker, S., et al. (2010b). The health and recovery peer (HARP) program: A peer-led intervention to improve medical self-management for persons with serious mental illness. *Schizophrenia Research, 118,* 264–270. http://dx.doi.org/10.1016/j.schres.2010.01.026.

Druss, B. G., Zhao, L., von Esenwein, S. A., Bona, J. R., Fricks, L., Jenkins-Tucker, S., Sterling, E., DiClemente, R., & Lorig, K. (2010). The Health and Recovery Peer (HARP) program: A peer-led intervention to improve medical self-management for persons with serious mental illness. *Schizophrenia Research, 118,* 264–270.

Dumont, J., & Jones, K. (2002). Findings from a consumer/survivor defined alternative to psychiatric hospitalization. *Outlook, a Joint Publication of the Evaluation Center @ HSRI and NASMHPD Research Institute.* Retrieved November 3, 2003, from http://nri.rdmc.org/Outlook3.pdf.

Dzhagarov, M. (1937). Experience in organizing a half hospital for mental patients. *Neuropathologia Psikhatria,*137–147.

Eakes, G., Burke, L., & Hainsworth, M. A. (1998). Middle-range theory of chronic sorrow. *Image: Journal of Nursing Scholarship, 30*(2), 179–184.

Egnew, R. C. (1993). Supported education and employment: An integrated approach. *Psychosocial Rehabilitation Journal, 17*(1), 121–127.

Eisenberg, D., Golberstein, E., & Gollust, S. E. (2007). Help-seeking and access to mental health care in a university student population. *Medical Care, 45*(7), 594–601.

Engelstein, J., Horowitz, G., & Romano, J. (2002). The education mentoring program at Fountain House. In C. T. Mowbray, K. S. Brown, K. Furlong-Norman, & A. Sullivan-Soydan (Eds.), *Supported education and psychiatric rehabilitation: Models and methods* (pp. 129–137). Linthicum, MD: International Association of Psychosocial Rehabilitation Services.

Enger, C., Weatherby, L., Reynolds, R., Glasser, D., & Walker, A. (2004). Cardiovascular disease and schizophrenia serious cardiovascular events and mortality among patients with schizophrenia. *Journal of Nervous and Mental Disease, 192*, 19–27.

Evans, K., & Sullivan, J. M. (1990). *Dual diagnosis: Counseling the mentally ill substance abuser.* New York: The Guilford Press.

Fairweather, G. W. (Ed.). (1980). *The Fairweather Lodge: A twenty-five year retrospective.* San Francisco: Jossey-Bass.

Fairweather, G. W., Saunders, D. H., Maynard, H., & Cressler, D. L. (1969). *Community life for the mentally ill.* Chicago: Aldine.

Falloon, I. R., Boyd, J. L., McGill, C. W., Ranzani, J., Moss, H. B., & Gilderman, A. M. (1982). Family management in the prevention of exacerbation of schizophrenia. *New England Journal of Medicine, 306*, 1437–1440.

Falloon, I. R., & Pedersen, J. (1985). Family management in the prevention of morbidity of schizophrenia: The adjustment family unit. *British Journal of Psychiatry, 147*, 156–163.

Farkas, M., & Anthony, W. A. (2010). Psychiatric rehabilitation interventions: A review. *International Review of Psychiatry, 22*(2), 114–129.

Farkas, M., Cohen, M., & Nemec, P. (1988). Psychiatric rehabilitation programs: Putting concepts into practice. *Community Mental Health Journal, 24*(1), 7–21.

Faulkner, G., Cohn, T., & Remington, G. (2007). Interventions to reduce weight gain in schizophrenia. *Cochrane Database of Systematic Reviews,* (1). http://dx.doi.org/10.1002/14651858.CD005148.pub2.

Feigenbaum, J. (2007). Dialectical behavior therapy: An increasing evidence base. *Journal of Mental Health, 16*(1), 51–68.

Felton, C. J., Stastny, P., Shern, D. L., Blanch, A., Donahue, S. A., Knight, E., et al. (1995). Consumers as peer specialists on intensive case management teams: Impact on client outcomes. *Psychiatric Services, 46*(10), 1037–1044.

Fernandes, B. S., Gama, C. S., Ceresér, K. M., Yatham, L. N., Fries, G. R., Colpo, G., de Lucena, D., Kunz, M., Gomes, F. A., & Kapczinski, F. (2011). Brain-derived neurotrophic factor as a state-marker of mood episodes in bipolar disorders: A systematic review and meta-regression analysis. *Journal of Psychiatric Research, 45*(8), 995–1004.

Festinger, L. A. (1954). A theory of cultural comparison processes. *Human Relations, 7*, 117–140.

Finn, L., & Bishop, B. (2001). *Mutual help, an important gateway to well-being and mental health.* Retrieved January 4, 2006, from http://www.communitybuilders.nsw.gov.au/download/mutual.doc.

Fishbein, S. M., Manos, E., & Rotteveel, J. (1995). Helping the helpers: A unique colleague support system for mental health professionals-consumers. *Journal of Psychosocial Nursing, 33*(11), 41–43.

Fisher, D. B. (1994). A new vision of healing as constructed by people with psychiatric disabilities working as mental health providers. *Psychosocial Rehabilitation Journal, 17*(3), 67–81.

Flannery, M., & Glickman, M. (1996). *Fountain House: Portraits of lives reclaimed from mental illness.* Center City, MN: Hazelden.

Ford, L. H. (1995). *Providing employment support for people with long-term mental illness.* Baltimore, MD: Brookes Publishing Co.

Foster, K. (2010). Patient experiences: 'You'd think this roller coaster was never going to stop': Experiences of adult children of parents with serious mental illness. *Journal of Clinical Nursing, 19,* 3143–3151.

Fox, V. (2000). Empathy: The wonder quality of mental health treatment. *Psychiatric Rehabilitation Journal, 23*(3), 292–293.

Fox, V. (2001). First person account: Schizophrenia, medication, and outpatient commitment. *Schizophrenia Bulletin, 27*(1), 177–178.

Fox, V. (2004a). First person account: Schizophrenia and motherhood. *Schizophrenia Bulletin, 30*(4), 763–765.

Fox, V. (2004b). Medication. *Psychiatric Rehabilitation Journal, 27*(3), 287–289.

Fox, V., & Geller, J. L. (2004). Cresting. *Psychiatric Services, 55*(6), 641–642.

Frankie, P., Levine, P., Mowbray, C. T., Shriner, W., Conklin, C., & Thomas, E. (1996). Supported education for persons with psychiatric disabilities: Implementation in an urban environment. *Journal of Mental Health Administration, 23*(4), 406–417.

Freeman, M. P., & Stoll, A. L. (1998). Mood stabilizer combinations—A review of safety and efficacy. *American Journal of Psychiatry, 155*(1), 12–21.

Frese, F. J., & Davis, W. W. (1997). The consumer-survivor movement, recovery and consumer professionals. *Professional Psychiatry, Research and Practice, 28,* 243–245.

Friedlander, A., & Liberman, R. (1991). Oral health care for the patient with schizophrenia. *Special Care Dentistry, 11*(5), 179–183.

Friedman, M. A., Detweiler-Bedell, J. B., Leventhal, H. E., Horne, R., Keitner, G. I., & Miller, I. W. (2004). Combined psychotherapy and pharmacotherapy for the treatment of major depressive disorder. *Clinical Psychology: Science and Practice, 11*(1), 47–68.

Fries, H. P., & Rosen, M. I. (2011). The efficacy of assertive community treatment to treat substance use. *Journal of the American Psychiatric Nurses Association, 17,* 45–50. http://dx.doi.org/10.1177/1078390310393509.

Friesen, B. J., Nicholson, J., Kaplan, K., & Solomon, P. (2009). Parents with a mental illness and implementation of the Adoption and Safe Families Act. *Intentions and results: A look back at the Adoption and Safe Families Act.* In O. Golden, & J. Macomber (Eds.). Washington, D.C.: Urban Institute, Center for the Study of Social Policy, 2009, 102–114.

Frith, C. D. (1997). Functional brain imaging and the neuropathology of schizophrenia. *Schizophrenia Bulletin, 23*(3), 403–422.

Fromm-Reichmann, F. (1948). Notes on the development of treatment of schizophrenics by psychoanalytic psychotherapy. *Psychiatry, 11,* 263–273. http://www.isps-ch.org/fr/archives/archives%2020historiques/Fromm-Reichmann-Psychiatry1948.pdf.

Frounfelker, R. L., Teachout, A., Bond, G. R., & Drake, R. E. (2011). Criminal justice involvement of individuals with severe mental illness and supported employment outcomes. *Community Mental Health Journal, 47,* 737–741.

Frounfelker, R. L., Wilkniss, S. M., Bond, G. R., Devitt, T. S., & Drake, R. E. (2011). Enrollment in supported employment services for clients with a co-occurring disorder. *Psychiatric Services, 62*(5), 545–547.

Fujita, E., Kato, D., Kuno, E., Suzuki, Y., Uchiyama, S., Watanabe, A., et al. (2010). Implementing the illness management and recovery program in Japan. *Psychiatric Services, 61,* 1157–1161. http://dx.doi.org/10.1176/appi.ps.61.11.1157.

Galanter, M. (1988). Zealous self-help groups as adjuncts to psychiatric treatment: A study of Recovery, Inc. *American Journal of Psychiatry, 145,* 1248–1253.

Gao, N., Gill, K., Schmidt, L. T., & Pratt, C. W. (2010). The application of human capital theory in vocational rehabilitation for individuals with mental illness. *Journal of Vocational Rehabilitation, 32*(1), 25–33.

Gao, N., Schmidt, L. T., Gill, K., & Pratt, C. W. (2011). Building human capital to increase earning power among people living with mental illnesses. *Psychiatric Rehabilitation Journal, 35*(2), 117–124.

Gao, N., Waynor, W. R., & O'Donnell. (2009). Creating commitment to change: Key to consumer employment success in a supportive housing agency. *Journal of Vocational Rehabilitation, 31*(1), 45–50.

Gao, Shang-Feng, & Bao, Ai-Min (2011). Corticotropin-releasing hormone, glutamate, and γ-amino-butyric acid in depression. *Neuroscientist, 17*, 124–144. http://dx.doi.org/10.1177/1073858410361780.

Garber-Epstein, P., Zisman-Ilani, Y., Levine, S., & Roe, D. (2013). Comparative impact of professional background in mental health on ratings on consumer outcome and fidelity in an illness management and recovery intervention. *Psychiatric Rehabilitation Journal*. In press.

Gates, L. B., & Akabas, S. H. (2007). Developing strategies to integrate peer providers into the staff of mental health agencies. Administration and policy IN. *Mental Health and Mental Health Services, 34*, 293–306.

Gawande, A. (2011). The hot spotters: Can we lower medical costs by giving the neediest patients better care? *The New Yorker.* http://www.newyorker.com/reporting/2011/01/24/110124fa_fact_gawande#ixzz2 MOS5CpsX.

Geller, J. L. (2000). The last half-century of psychiatric services as reflected in *Psychiatric Services. Psychiatric Services, 51*, 41–67.

Gervey, R., & Kowal, H. (1995). Job development strategies for placing persons with psychiatric disabilities into supported employment jobs in a large city. *Psychosocial Rehabilitation Journal, 18*(4), 95–113.

Gilbert, R., Heximer, S., Jaxon, D., & Bellamy, C. D. (2004). Redirection through education: Meeting the challenges. *American Journal of Psychiatric Rehabilitation, 7*(3), 329–345.

Gill, K. J. (2001). Editor; special issue on psychiatric rehabilitation education. *Psychiatric Rehabilitation Skills,* (3).

Gill, K. J. (2010). Certified psychiatric rehabilitation practitioner: A viable option for persons in recovery as providers. In M. Swarbrick, L. T. Schmidt, & K. J. Gill (Eds.), *People in recovery as providers of psychiatric rehabilitation: Building on the wisdom of experience*. Linthicum, MD: USPRA.

Gill, K. J. (2011). *Report on Union County Jail Diversion program*. August 2011. Trenton, NJ: Paper presented at the Administrative Office of the Courts.

Gill, K. J., & Barrett, N. (2009). Psychiatric rehabilitation: An emerging academic discipline. *Israeli Journal of Psychiatry, 46*(2), 94–102.

Gill, K. J., & Murphy, A. A. (2011). *Report on Union County Jail Diversion Program 2006-2011 to The Union County Prosecutor's Office*. Scotch Plains, NJ: UMDNJ School of Health-Related Professions.

Gill, K. J., Murphy, A., & Birkmann, J. (2005). Developing an attitude: The role of psychiatric rehabilitation education. *American Journal of Psychiatric Rehabilitation, 8*, 135–149.

Gill, K. J., Pratt, C., & Barrett, N. (1997). Preparing psychiatric rehabilitation specialists through undergraduate education. *Community Mental Health Journal, 33*(4), 323–329.

Gill, K. J., & Pratt, C. W. (1993). Profit sharing in psychiatric rehabilitation: A five-year evaluation. *Psychosocial Rehabilitation Journal, 17*(2), 33–41.

Gill, K. J., & Pratt, C. W. (2005). Clinical decision making and the evidence-based practitioner. In R. E. Drake, M. R. Merrens, & D. W. Lunde (Eds.), *Evidence-based mental health practice*. New York: W.W. Norton and Company.

Gill, K. J., Zechner, M., & Murphy, A. (2011). *Promoting health and wellness: Innovations under development in New Jersey*. Edison, NJ: Paper presented at the NJPRA.

Glick, I., Sharfstein, S., & Schwartz, H. (2011). Inpatient psychiatric care in the 21st century: The need for reform. *Psychiatric Services, 62*, 206–209.

Goering, P., Wasylenki, D., Farkas, M., Lancee, W., & Ballantyne, R. (1988). What difference does case management make? *Hospital and Community Psychiatry, 39*, 272–276.

Goldberg, J. F., & Harrow, M. (2011). A 15-year prospective follow-up of bipolar affective disorders: Comparisons with unipolar nonpsychotic depression. *Bipolar Disorders, 13*, 155–163.

Goldfinger, S. M., & Schutt, R. K. (1996). Comparison of clinicians' housing recommendations and preferences of homeless mentally ill persons. *Psychiatric Services, 47*(4), 413–415.

Goldfinger, S. M., Schutt, R. K., Tolomiczenko, G. S., Seidman, L., Penk, W. E., Turner, W., & Caplan, B. (1999). Housing placement and subsequent days homeless among formerly homeless adults with mental illness. *Psychiatric Services, 50*(5), 674–679.

Goldman, H. H., Gattozzi, A. A., & Taube, C. A. (1981). Defining and counting the chronically mentally ill. *Hospital and Community Psychiatry, 32*(1), 22–27.

Goldstein, M. J., Rodnick, E. H., Evans, J. R., May, P. R., & Steinberg, M. R. (1978). Drug and family therapy in the aftercare of adult schizophrenics. *Archives of General Psychiatry, 35*, 1169–1177.

Goldstrom, I. D., Campbell, J., Rogers, J. A., Lambert, D. B., Blacklow, B., Henderson, M. J., & Manderscheid, R. W. (2006). National estimates for mental health mutual support groups, self-help organizations, and consumer operated services. *Administration and Policy in Mental Health and Mental Health Services Research, 33*(1), 92–103.

Gordon, R. E., Edmunson, E., Bedell, J., & Goldstein, N. (1979). Reducing rehospitalization of state mental patients: Peer management and support. *Journal of the Florida Medical Association, 65*, 927–933.

Gowdy, E. A., Carlson, L. S., & Rapp, C. A. (2004). Organizational factors differentiating high performing from low performing supported employment programs. *Psychiatric Rehabilitation Journal, 28*(2), 150–156.

Gray, R., Wykes, T., & Gournay, K. (2002). From compliance to concordance: A review of the literature on interventions to enhance compliance with antipsychotic medication. *Journal of Psychiatric and Mental Health Nursing, 9*(3), 277–284.

Green, A., Canuso, C., Brenner, M., & Wojcik, J. (2003). Detection and management of co-morbidity in patients with schizophrenia. *Psychiatric Clinics of North America, 26*(1), 115–139.

Greenfield, T. K., Stoneking, B. C., Humphreys, K., Sundby, E., & Bond, J. (2008). A randomized trial of a mental health consumer managed alternative to civil commitment for acute psychiatric crisis. *American Journal of Community Psychology, 42*(1/2), 135–144.

Greenley, J. R. (1995). *Implementation of an innovative service in Madison, Wisconsin: The program of assertive community treatment (PACT) (Research Paper Series 49)*. Madison, WI: Mental Health Research Center.

Greenwood, R. M., Schaefer-McDaniel, N. J., Winkel, G., & Tsemberis, S. J. (2005). Decreasing psychiatric symptoms by increasing choice in services for adults with histories of homelessness. *American Journal of Community Psychology, 36*(3-4), 223–238.

Griffin-Francell, C. (1997). Consumers as providers of psychiatric rehabilitation: Reflections of a family member. In D. P. Moxley, C. T. Mowbray, C. A. Jasper, & L. L. Howell (Eds.), *Consumers as providers*. Columbia, MD: International Association of Psychosocial Rehabilitation Services.

Groff, A., Burns, B., Swanson, J., Swartz, M., Wagner, H. R., & Tompson, M. (2004). Caregiving for persons with mental illness: The impact of outpatient commitment on caregiving strain. *Journal of Nervous and Mental Disease, 192*(8), 554–562.

Grundy, S. M., Cleeman, J. I., Daniels, S. R., Donato, K. A., Eckel, R. H., et al. (2005). Diagnosis and management of the metabolic syndrome. An American Heart Association/National Heart, Lung, and Blood Institute Scientific Statement. *Circulation, 112*, 2735–2752.

Gulcur, L., Tsemberis, S., Stefancic, A., & Greenwood, R. M. (2007). Community integration of adults with psychiatric disabilities and histories of homelessness. *Community Mental Health Journal*.

Gulcur, L., Stefancic, A., Shinn, M., Tsemberis, S., & Fischer, S. N. (2003). Housing, hospitalization, and cost outcomes for homeless individuals with psychiatric disabilities participating in Continuum of Care and Housing First programmes. *Journal of Community and Applied Social Psychology, 13*, 171–186.

Gur, R. E., & Pearlson, G. D. (1993). Neuroimaging in schizophrenia research. *Schizophrenia Bulletin, 19*(2), 163–181.

Hain, R., & Gioia, D. (2004). Supported Education Enhancing Rehabilitation (SEER): A community mental health and community college partnership for access and retention. *American Journal of Psychiatric Rehabilitation, 7*(3), 315–328.

Hall, W., Andrews, G., & Goldstein, G. (1985). The cost of schizophrenia. *Australian and New Zealand Journal of Psychiatry, 19*, 3–5.

Halter, C. A., Bond, G. R., & De Graaf-Kaser, R. (1992). How treatment of persons with serious mental illness is portrayed in undergraduate psychology textbooks. *Community Mental Health Journal, 28*(1), 29–42.

Harding, C. M., Brooks, G. W., Ashikaga, T., Strauss, J. S., & Breier, A. (1987a). The Vermont longitudinal study of persons with severe mental illness, II: Long-term outcome of subjects who retrospectively met DSM-III criteria for schizophrenia. *American Journal of Psychiatry, 144*(6), 727–735.

Harding, C. M., Brooks, G. W., Ashikaga, T., Strauss, J. S., & Breier, A. (1987b). The Vermont longitudinal study of persons with severe mental illness, II: Long-term outcome of subjects who retrospectively met DSM-III criteria for schizophrenia. *American Journal of Psychiatry, 144*(6), 718–726.

Harding, C. M., & Zahniser, J. H. (1994). Empirical correction of seven myths about schizophrenia with implications for treatment. *Acta Psychiatric Scandanavica* (Suppl. 384), 140–146.

Harding, C. M., Zubin, J., & Strauss, J. S. (1992). Chronicity in schizophrenia: Revisited. *British Journal of Psychiatry—Supplement, 18*, 27–37.

Harron, B. (1993). *Hospital without walls [videotape]*. Durham, NC: Duke University Medical Center.

Harrow, M., & Jobe, T. H. (2007). Factors involved in the outcome and recovery of schizophrenia patients not an anti-psychotic medication: A 15 year multi follow-up study. *Journal of Nervous and Mental Disease*, (195), 406–414.

Harrow, M., Jobe, T. H., & Faull, R. N. (2012). Do all schizophrenia patients need antipsychotic treatment continuously throughout their lifetime? A 20-year longitudinal study. *Psychological Medicine, 42*(10), 2145–2155. http://dx.doi.org/10.1017/S0033291712000220.

Hartley, M. T. (2010). Increasing resilience: Strategies for reducing dropout rates for college students with psychiatric disabilities. *American Journal of Psychiatric Rehabilitation, 13*, 295–315.

Haslett, W. R., Drake, R. E., Bond, G. R., Becker, D. R., & McHugo, G. J. (2011). Individual placement and support: Does rurality matter? *American Journal of Psychiatric Rehabilitation, 14*, 237–244.

Hatfield, A. B. (1987a). Families as caregivers: A historical perspective. In A. B. Hatfield, & H. P. Lefley (Eds.), *Families of the mentally ill: Coping and adaptation* (pp. 3–29). New York: The Guilford Press.

Hatfield, A. B. (1987b). Coping and adaptation: A conceptual framework for understanding families. In A. B. Hatfield, & H. P. Lefley (Eds.), *Families of the mentally ill: Coping and adaptation* (pp. 60–84). New York: The Guilford Press.

Hatfield, A. B. (1990). *Family education in mental illness*. New York: The Guilford Press.

Hatfield, A. B. (1992). Leaving home: Separation issues in psychiatric illness. *Psychosocial Rehabilitation Journal, 15*(4), 37–47.

Hatfield, A. B., Spaniol, L., & Zipple, A. M. (1987). Expressed emotion: A family perspective. *Schizophrenia Bulletin, 13*(2), 221–226.

Heckers, S. (1997). Neuropathology of schizophrenia: Cortex, thalamus, basal ganglia, and neurotransmitter projection systems. *Schizophrenia Bulletin, 23*(3), 525–528.

Herinckx, H. A., Kinney, R. F., Clarke, G. N., & Paulson, R. I. (1997). Assertive community treatment versus usual care in engaging and retaining clients with severe mental illness. *Psychiatric Services, 48,* 1297–1306.

Herz, M. I., Endicott, J., Spitzer, R. I., & Mesnikoff, A. (1971). Day versus inpatient hospitalization: A controlled study. *American Journal of Psychiatry, 127,* 1371–1382.

Heyscue, B. E., Levin, G. M., & Merrick, J. P. (1998). Compliance with depot antipsychotic medication by patients attending outpatient clinics. *Psychiatric Services, 49,* 1232–1234.

Himelhoch, S., Goldberg, R., Calmes, C., Medoff, D., Slade, E., Dixon, L., et al. (2011). Screening for and prevalence of HIV and hepatitis C among an outpatient urban sample of people with serious mental illness and co-occurring substance abuse. *Journal of Community Psychology, 39,* 231–239. http://dx.doi.org/10.1002/jcop.20422.

Ho, B. C., Andreasen, N. C., Ziebell, S., Pierson, R., & Magnotta, R. (2011). Long-term antipsychotic treatment and brain volumes: A longitudinal study of first-episode schizophrenia. *Archives of General Psychiatry, 68*(2), 128–137.

Hodge, M., & Draine, J. (1993). Development of support through case management services. In R. W. F. P. L. Solomon (Ed.), *Psychiatric rehabilitation in practice.* Boston: Andover Medical Publishers.

Hogarty, G. E. (1993). The prevention of relapse in chronic schizophrenic patients. *Journal of Clinical Psychiatry, 54,* 18–23.

Hogarty, G. E., Anderson, C. M., Konrblith, S. J., Greenwald, D. P., Javana, C. D., & Moadonia, M. J. (1986). Personal indicators in the course of schizophrenia research group. Family psychoeducation, social skills training, and maintenance chemotherapy in the aftercare treatment of schizophrenia: I. One year effects of a controlled study on relapsed and expressed emotion. *Archives of General Psychiatry, 43,* 633–642.

Hogarty, G. E., Anderson, C. M., Konrblith, S. J., Greenwald, D. P., Ulrich, R. F., & Carster, M. (1991). Family psychoeducation, social skills training, and maintenance chemotherapy in the aftercare treatment of schizophrenia: II. Two year effects of a controlled study on relapse and adjustment. *Archives of General Psychiatry, 48,* 340–347.

Hoge, M. A., & Morris, J. A. (2002). Behavioral health workforce education and training (Special Issue). *Administration and Policy in Mental Health, 29*(4/5).

Hoge, M. A., Morris, J. A., Daniels, G. W., Leighton, Y. H., & Adams, N. (2007). *An action plan on behavioral health workforce development.* From http://www.samhsa.gov/workforce/annapolis/workforceactionsplan.pdf.

Hogg Foundation for Mental Health. (2008). *Connecting body and mind: A resource guide to integrated health care in texas and the united states.* Austin, TX: Division of Diversity and Community Engagement, The University of Texas at Austin.

Holloway, F., & Aitchison, K. (2003). Early intervention in psychosis: From government prescription to clinical practice. *Psychiatric Bulletin, 27,* 243–244.

Holt, G., Hardy, S., & Bouras, N. (2011). *Mental health in intellectual disabilities.* Brighton, UK: Pavilion Publishing.

Honberg, R. (2004). *Advocates praise efforts to address criminalization of people with mental illness.* Campaign for Mental Health Reform press release. Arlington, VA: National Alliance on Mental Illness.

Horvitz-Lennon, M., Kilbourne, A., & Pincus, H. (2006). From silos to bridges: Meeting the general health care needs of adults with severe mental illnesses. *Health Affairs, 25*(3), 659–669.

Housel, D. P., & Hickey, J. S. (1993). Supported education in a community college for students with psychiatric disabilities: The Houston Community College model. *Psychosocial Rehabilitation Journal, 17*(1), 41–50.

Howie the Harp. (1990). Independent living with support services: The goal and future for mental health consumers. *Psychosocial Rehabilitation Journal, 13*(4), 85–89.

Howie the Harp. (1991). *A crazy folks guide to reasonable accommodation and psychiatric disability.* Burlington, VT: Trinity College, Center for Community Change through Housing and Support.

Howie the Harp. (1993). Taking a new approach to independent living. *Hospital and Community Psychiatry, 44*(5), 413.

Hubert, A., Szoke, A., Leboyer, M., & Schurhoff, F. (2011). Influence of paternal age in schizophrenia. *L'Encephale: Revue de psychiatrie clinique biologique et therapeutique, 37,* 199–206. http://dx.doi.org/10.1016/j.encep.2010.12.005.

Hughes, R. (1994). Psychiatric Rehabilitation: An essential health service for people with serious and persistent mental illness. In IAPSRS An Introduction to Psychiatric Rehabilitation Services (1996). Ore Principles of PsyR. Columbia, MD: author.

Hutchinson, D. S., Gagne, C., Bowers, A., Russinova, Z., Skrinar, G. S., & Anthony, W. A. (2006). A framework for health promotion services for people with psychiatric disabilities. *Psychiatric Rehabilitation Journal, 29*(4), 241–250.

Inge, K. J. (2008). Choice and customized employment: A critical component. *Journal of Vocational Rehabilitation, 28*(1), 67–70.

In-Shape. (2013). From http://www.riverbendcmhc.org/index.php?option=com_contentandview=articleandid=82andItemid=87.

Interlandi, J. (2012). A madman in our midst. June 24. *The New York Times Magazine,* 24–29(8), 6–47.

International Association of Psychosocial Rehabilitation Services (IAPSRS). (1994). An introduction to psychiatric rehabilitation. In L. Spaniol, M. A. Brown, L. Blankertz, D. J. Burnham, J. Dincin, et al. (Eds.). Columbia, MD: Publications Committee.

International Association of Psychosocial Rehabilitation Services. (1996). *Core principles of psychiatric rehabilitation.* Columbia, MD: Author.

International Association of Psychosocial Rehabilitation Services. (2001). *Role Delineation of the Psychiatric Rehabilitation Practitioner.* Morrisville, NC: Columbia Assessment Services.

Ishmael, S. (2002). Out of the darkness and into the light. In C. T. Mowbray, K. S. Brown, K. Furlong-Norman, & A. Sullivan-Soydan (Eds.), *Supported education and psychiatric rehabilitation: Models and methods* (pp. 31–32). Linthicum, MD: International Association of Psychosocial Rehabilitation Services.

Jacobs, E., Masson, R., & Harvill, R. (2005). *Group counseling: Strategies and skills* (5th ed.). Belmont, CA: Brooks/Cole.

Jacobs, E., Masson, R., Harvill, R., & Schimmel, C. (2012). *Group counseling: Strategies and skills* (7th ed.). California: Brooks/Cole.

Jacobson, N. (2001). Experiencing recovery: A dimensional analysis of recovery narratives. *Psychiatric Rehabilitation Journal, 24*(3), 248–256.

Jansen, M. A. (1988). The psychological and vocational problems of persons with chronic mental illness. In J. A. Ciardiello, & M. D. Bell (Eds.), *Vocational rehabilitation of persons with prolonged psychiatric disorders* (pp. 35–46). Baltimore, MD: Johns Hopkins University Press.

Jasper, C., & Mowbray, C. T. (2002). Life before supported education: The long journey. In K. S. Brown, K. Furlong-Norman, & A. Sullivan-Soydan (Eds.), *Supported education and psychiatric rehabilitation: models and methods* (pp. 23–30). Linthicum, MD: International Association of Psychosocial Rehabilitation Services.

Jensen, A., and Silverstein. (n.d.). Policy brief. Washington, DC: Center for the Study and Advancement of Disability Policy.

Jeste, D., Gladsjo, J., Linamer, L., & Lacro, J. (1996). Medical co-morbidity in schizophrenia. *Schizophrenia Bulletin, 22,* 413–430.

Jewell, T. C., Downing, D., & McFarlane, W. R. (2009). Partnering with families: Multiple family group psychoeducation for schizophrenia. *Journal of Clinical Psychology, 65*(8), 868–878.

Johnsen, M., Teague, G., McDonel, E., & Herr, E. (2005). Common ingredients as a fidelity measure for peer-run programs. In S. Clay (Ed.), *On our own together: Peer programs for people with mental illness.* Nashville, TN: Vanderbilt University Press.

Jones, D. W. (2004). Families and serious mental illness: Working with loss and ambivalence. *British Journal of Social Work, 34,* 961–979.

Jones, T. L. (1993). *The Americans with Disabilities Act, a review of best practices.* New York: American Management Association.

Joukamaa, M., Heliovaara, M., Knekt, P., Aromaa, A., Raitasalo, R., & Lehtinen, V. (2006). Schizophrenia, neuroleptic medication and mortality. *British Journal of Psychiatry, 188,* 122–127.

Justo, L., Soares, B. G. D. O., & Calil, H. (2009). *Family interventions for bipolar disorder.* (Review) (Publication no. 10.1002/14651858.CD005167.pub2).

Kalachnik, J. E., Leventhal, B. L., James, D. H., Sovner, R., Kastner, T. A., Walsh, K., et al. (1991). Guidelines for the use of psychotropic medication. In S. Reiss, & M. G. Aman (Eds.), *Psychotropic medication and developmental disabilities: The international consensus handbook* (pp. 45–72). Columbus, OH: Nisonger Center for Mental Retardation and Developmental Disabilities.

Kamis-Gould, E., Snyder, F., Hadley, T. R., & Casey, T. (1999). The impact of closing a state psychiatric hospital on the county mental health system and its clients. *Psychiatric Services, 50,* 1297–1302.

Kane, C., & Blank, M. (2004). NPACT: Enhancing programs of Assertive Community Treatment for the seriously mentally ill. *Community Mental Health Journal, 40*(6), 549–559.

Kane, J. M. (2003). Long-term treatment of schizophrenia: Moving from relapse-prevention model to a recovery model. *Journal of Clinical Psychiatry, 64*(11), 1384–1385.

Kaplan, K., Salzer, M. S., Solomon, P., Brusilovskiy, E., & Cousounis, P. (2011). Internet peer support for individuals with psychiatric disabilities: A randomized controlled trial. *Social Science and Medicine, 74,* 54–62.

Kaufman, C. (1995). The self-help employment center: Social outcomes form the first year. *Psychosocial Rehabilitation Journal, 18*(4), 145–162.

Kaufman, C. L., Freund, P. D., & Wilson, J. (1989). Self-help in the mental health system: A model for consumer-provider collaboration. *Psychosocial Rehabilitation Journal, 13*(1), 5–21.

Kaufmann, C. L., Schulberg, H. C., & Schooler, N. R. (1994). Self-help group participation among people with severe mental illness. In F. Lavoies, T. J. Iorkman, & B. Girdon (Eds.), *Self-help and mutual aid groups: International and multicultural perspectives.* Binghamton, NY: Hayworth Press.

Kaufman, C. L., Ward-Colasante, C., & Farmer, J. (1993). Development and evaluation of drop-in centers operated by mental health consumers. *Hospital and Community Psychiatry, 44,* 675–678.

Keck, P. E., & McElroy, S. A. (1998). Pharmacological treatment of bipolar disorders. In P. E. Nathan, & J. M. Gorman (Eds.), *A guide to treatments that work* (pp. 249–269). New York: Oxford University Press.

Kelly, D. L., Boggs, D. L., & Conley, R. R. (2007). Reaching for wellness in schizophrenia. *Psychiatric Clinics of North America, 30,* 453–479.

Kendler, K. S., & Deihl, S. R. (1993). The genetics of schizophrenia: A current genetic-epidemiologic perspective. *Schizophrenia Bulletin, 19*(2), 87–112.

Kendler, K. S., Gruenberg, A. M., & Kinney, D. K. (1994). Independent diagnoses of adoptees and relatives as defined by DSM-III in the provincial and national samples of the Danish Adoption Study of Schizophrenia. *Archives of General Psychiatry, 51*(6), 456–458.

Kendler, K. S., Gruenberg, A. M., & Strauss, J. S. (1981). An independent analysis of the Copenhagen sample of the Danish adoption study of schizophrenia. II. The relationship between schizotypal personality disorder and schizophrenia. *Archives of General Psychiatry, 38*, 982–984.

Kendler, K. S., & Schaffner, K. F. (2011). The dopamine hypothesis of schizophrenia: An historical and philosophical analysis. *Philosophy, Psychiatry, and Psychology, 18*, 41–63. http://dx.doi.org/10.1353/ppp.2011.0005.

Kennedy, M. (1989). *Psychiatric hospitalizations of Growers*. East Lansing, MI: Paper presented at the 2nd biennial conference of Community Research and Action.

Kennedy, N., Abbott, R., & Paykel, E. S. (2003). Remission and recurrence of depression in the maintenance era: Long-term outcome in a Cambridge cohort. *Psychological Medicine, 33*(5), 827–838.

Kerouac, J. W. (1997). Off the road: Supported education for college students with psychiatric disabilities. *Journal of the California Alliance for the Mentally Ill, 8*(2), 41–43.

Kerouac, J. W., & McCoy, M. L. (2002). The Thresholds Community Scholar Program. In C. T. Mowbray, K. S. Brown, K. Furlong-Norman, & A. Sullivan-Soydan (Eds.), *Supported education and psychiatric rehabilitation: Models and methods* (pp. 147–153). Linthicum, MD: International Association of Psychosocial Rehabilitation Services.

Kessing, L. V., Andersen, P. K., Mortensen, P. B., & Bolwig, T. G. (1998). Recurrence in affective disorder: I. Case register study. *British Journal of Psychiatry, 172*, 23–28.

Kessler, R., Foster, C., Saunders, W., & Stang, P. (1995). Social consequences of psychiatric disorders, I: Educational attainment. *American Journal of Psychiatry, 152*(7), 1026–1032.

Kety, S. S., Wender, P. H., Jacobsen, B., Ingraham, L. J., Janson, L., Britta, F., & Kinney, D. K. (1994). Mental illness in the biological and adoptive relatives of schizophrenic adoptees: Replication of the Copenhagen study in the rest of Denmark. *Archives of General Psychiatry, 51*(6), 442–455.

Kilbourne, A. M., Rofey, D. L., McCarthy, J. F., Post, E. P., Welsh, D., & Blow, F. C. (2008). Nutrition and exercise behavior among patients with bipolar disorder. *Bipolar Disorders, 9*, 443–452.

Killackey, E., Jackson, H. J., & McGorry, P. D. (2008). Vocational intervention in first-episode psychosis: Individual placement and support v. treatment as usual. *British Journal of Psychiatry, 193*(2), 114–120.

Killaspy, H., Kingett, S., Bebbington, P., Blizard, R., Johnson, S., Nolan, F., & King, M. (2009). Randomised evaluation of assertive community treatment: 3-year outcomes. *The British Journal of Psychiatry, 195*(1), 81–82. http://dx.doi.org/10.1192/bjp.bp.108.059303.

Kim, H., & Salyers, M. (2008). Attitudes and perceived barriers to working with families of persons with severe mental illness: Mental health professionals' perspectives. *Community Mental Health Journal, 44*, 337–345.

Kinsella, C. B., Anderson, R. R., & Anderson, W. T. (1996). Coping skills, strengths, and needs as perceived by adult offspring and siblings of people with mental illness: A retrospective study. *Psychiatric Rehabilitation Journal, 20*(2), 24–32.

Kirk, S. A., & Therrien, M. G. (1975). Community mental health myths and the fate of former hospitalized individuals. *Psychiatry, 38*, 209–217.

Kisely, S., Campbell, L. A., & Preston, N. (2005). Compulsory community and involuntary outpatient treatment for people with severe mental disorders. *Cochrane Database of Systematic Reviews*, (3). http://dx.doi.org/10.1002/14651858.

Kiuhara, S. A., & Huefner, D. S. (2008). Students with psychiatric disabilities in higher education settings: The Americans with Disabilities Act and beyond. *Journal of Disability Policy Studies, 19*(2), 103–113.

Klerman, G. (1977). Better but not well: Social and ethical issues in the deinstitutionalization of the mentally ill. *Schizophrenia Bulletin, 3*(4), 617–631.

Klinkenberg, W., & Calsyn, R. J. (1996). Predictors of receipt of aftercare and recidivism among persons with severe mental illness: A review. *Psychiatric Services, 47*(5), 487–496.

Knisley, M. B., & Fleming, M. (1993). Implementing supported housing in state and local mental health systems. *Hospital and Community Psychiatry, 44*(5), 456–461.

Knis-Matthews, L., Bokara, J., DeMeo, L., Lepore, N., & Mavus, L. (2007). The meaning of higher education for people diagnosed with a mental illness: Four students share their experiences. *Psychiatric Rehabilitation Journal, 31*(2), 107–114.

Kohen, W., & Paul, G. L. (1976). Current trends and recommended changes in extended care placement of mental individuals: The Illinois system as a case in point. *Schizophrenia Bulletin, 2*, 275–594.

Kopelowicz, A., Liberman, R. P., & Zarate, R. (2006). Recent advances in social skills training for schizophrenia. *Schizophrenia Bulletin, 32*(S1), S12–S23. http://dx.doi.org/10.1093/schbul/sbl023.

Korman, H. (2006). *Best practice principles for achieving civil rights in permanent supportive housing.* Boston, MA: A joint publication of The Technical Assistance Collaborative. The Consortium for Citizens with Disabilities.

Kortrijk, H. E., Staring, A. B. P., van Baars, A. W. B., & Mulder, C. L. (2010). Involuntary admission may support treatment outcome and motivation in patients receiving assertive community treatment. *Social Psychiatry and Psychiatric Epidemiology, 45*, 245–252. http://dx.doi.org/10.1007/s00127.

Kottsieper, P. (2010). Wounded healers need not apply? In M. Swarbrick, L. T. Schmidt, & K. J. Gill (Eds.), *People in recovery as providers of psychiatric rehabilitation: Building on the wisdom of experience.* Linthicum, MD: USPRA.

Krech, D., Crutchfield, R. S., & Livson, N. (1969). *Elements of psychology* (2nd ed.). New York: Alfred A. Knopf.

Kroll, L. E., & Lampert, T. (2011). Unemployment, social support and health problems—results of the GEDA study in Germany 2009. *Dtsch Arztebl Int, 108*(4), 47–52.

Krupa, T. (2004). Employment, recovery, and schizophrenia: Integrating health and disorder at work. *Psychiatric Rehabilitation Journal, 28*(1), 8–14.

Krystal, J. H., D'Souza, D. C., Madonick, S., & Petrakis, I. (1999). Toward a rational pharmacotherapy of comorbid substance abuse in schizophrenic patients. *Schizophrenia Research, 40*(35 (Suppl.), 35–49.

Kupfer, D. J., Kuhl, E. A., & Regier, D. A. (2013). DSM-5—The future arrived. *Journal of the American Medical Association* 1–2. http://dx.doi.org/10.1001/jama.2013.2298.

Kurachi, M. (2003a). Pathogenesis of schizophrenia: Part I. Symptomatology, cognitive characteristics and brain morphology. *Psychiatry and Clinical Neurosciences, 57*, 3–8.

Kurachi, M. (2003b). Pathogenesis of schizophrenia: Part II. Temporo-frontal two-step hypothesis. *Psychiatry and Clinical Neurosciences, 57*, 9–15.

Kurtz, M. M., & Mueser, K. T. (2008). A meta-analysis of controlled research on social skills training for schizophrenia. *Journal of Consulting and Clinical Psychology, 76*(3), 491–504.

Lamb, H. R. (1982). *Treating the long-term mentally Ill.* San Francisco: Jossey-Bass.

Lamb, H. R., & Bachrach, L. L. (2001). Some perspectives on deinstitutionalization. *Psychiatric Services, 52*(8), 1040–1045.

Lamberg, L. (2004). Efforts grow to keep mentally ill out of jails. *Journal of the American Medical Association, 292*(5), 555–556.

Lambert, T., Velakoulis, D., & Pantelis, C. (2003). Medical co-morbidity in schizophrenia. *Medical Journal, 178*, 67–70.

Lamberti, J., & Weisman, R. L. (2004). Persons with severe mental disorders in the criminal justice system: Challenges and opportunities. *Psychiatric Quarterly, 75*(2), 151–164.

Lamberti, J., Weisman, R. L., Schwarzkopf, S. B., Price, N., Ashton, R. M., & Trompeter, J. (2001). The mentally ill in jails and prisons: Towards an integrated model of prevention. *Psychiatric Quarterly, 72*(1), 63–77.

Lamberti, J. S., Deem, A., Weisman, R. L., & LaDuke, C. (2011). The role of probation in forensic assertive community treatment. *Psychiatric Services, 62*, 418–421. http://dx.doi.org/10.1176/appi.ps .62.4.418.

Latimer, E., Lecomte, T., Becker, D., Drake, R., Duclos, I., Piat, M., et al. (2006). Generalizability of the individual placement and support model of supported employment: Results of a Canadian randomized controlled trial. *British Journal of Psychiatry, 189*, 65–73.

Leamy, M., Bird, V., Boutillier, C. L., Williams, J., & Slade, M. (2011). Conceptual framework for personal recovery in mental health: Systematic review and narrative synthesis. *British Journal of Psychiatry, 199*, 445–452.

Ledbetter, J., & Field, T. F. (1978). A brief history of vocational rehabilitation legislation. *Psychosocial Rehabilitation Journal, 2*(3), 35–42.

Lee, B. A. (n.d.). *Reasonable accommodation under the Americans with Disabilities Act.* New Brunswick, NJ: Bureau of Economic Research, Rutgers University.

Lee, D. T. (1995). Professional underutilization of Recovery Inc. *Psychiatric Rehabilitation Journal, 19*(1), 63–70.

Lee, K. L., Woon, P. S., Teo, Y. K., & Sim, K. (2012). Genome wide association studies (GWAS) and copy number variation (CNV) studies of the major psychoses: What have we learnt? *Neuroscience & Biobehavioral Reviews, 36*, 556–571.

Leff, H. S., Campbell, J., Gagne, C., & Woocher, L. S. (1997). Evaluating peer providers. In C. T. Mowbray, D. P. Moxley, C. A. Jasper, & L. L. Howell (Eds.), *Consumers as providers.* Columbia, MD: International Association of Psychosocial Rehabilitation Services.

Lefley, H. P. (1989). Family burden and stigma in major mental illness. *American Psychologist, 44*(3), 556–560.

Lehman, A. F. (1983). The well-being of chronic mental patients: Assessing their quality of life. *Archives of General Psychiatry, 40*, 369–373.

Lehman, A. F. (1988). A quality of life interview for the chronically mentally ill. *Evaluation and Program Planning, 11*(1), 51–62.

Lehman, A. F. (1996). Measures of quality of life among persons with severe and persistent mental disorders. *Social Psychhiatry and Psychiatric Epidemiology, 31*, 78–88.

Lehman, A. F., Goldberg, R., Dixon, L. B., McNary, S., Postrado, L., Hackman, A., et al. (2002). Improving employment outcomes for persons with severe mental illnesses. *Archives of General Psychiatry, 59*(2), 165–172.

Lehman, A. F., Kreyenbuhl, J., Buchanan, R. W., Dickerson, F. B., Dixon, L. B., et al. (2004). The Schizophrenia Patient Outcomes Research Team (PORT): Updated treatment recommendations 2003. *Schizophrenia Bulletin, 30*(2), 193–217.

Lehman, A. F., & Steinwachs, D. M. (1998). At issue: Translating research into practice: The schizophrenia Patient Outcome Research Team (PORT) treatment recommendations. *Schizophrenia Bulletin, 24*, 1–10.

Lehrman, N. S. (1961). Do our hospitals help make acute schizophrenia chronic? *Diseases of the Nervous System, 22*(9), 489–493.

Lent, R. W., Brown, S. D., & Hackett, G. (1994). Toward a unifying social cognitive theory of career and academic interest, choice, and performance. *Journal of Vocational Behavior, 45*, 79–122.

Leucht, S., Barnes, T. R. E., Kissling, W., Engel, R. R., Correll, C., & Kane, J. M. (2003). Relapse prevention in schizophrenia with new-generation antipsychotics: A systematic review and exploratory meta-analysis of randomized, controlled trials. *American Journal of Psychiatry, 160*(7), 1209–1222.

Levitt, A. J., Mueser, K. T., DeGenova, J., Lorenzo, J., Bradford-Watt, D., et al. (2009). Randomized controlled trial of illness management and recovery in multiple-unit supportive housing. *Psychiatric Services, 60*(12), 1629–1636.

Lewis, S., & Lieberman, J. (2008). CATIE and CUTLASS: Can we handle the truth? *British Journal of Psychiatry, 192*, 161–163 http://dx.doi.org/10.1192/bjp.bp.107.037218.

Liberman, R. P., DeRisi, W. J., & Mueser, K. T. (1989). *Social skills training for psychiatric patients.* Elmsford, NY: Pergamon Press.

Liberman, R. P., Massel, H. K., Mosk, M., et al. (1985). Social skills training for chronic mental patients. *Hospital and Community Psychiatry, 36*, 396–403.

Liberman, R. P., Wallace, C. J., Blackwell, G., Eckman, T. A., Vaccaro, J. V., & Kuehnel, T. G. (1993). Innovations in skill training for people with serious mental illness: The UCLA social and independent living skills modules. *Innovations and Research, 2*(2), 46–59.

Licht, R. W. (1998). Drug treatment of mania—A critical review. *Acta Psychiatrica Scandinavica, 97*(6), 387–397.

Lidz, T. (1992). *The relevance of the family to psychoanalytic theory.* Madison, CT: International Universities Press.

Lieberman, J. A., Drake, R. E., Sederer, L. I., Belger, A., Keefe, R., Perkins, D., & Stroup, S. (2008). Science and recovery in schizophrenia. *Psychiatric Services, 59*(5), 487–496.

Lieberman, J. A., Stroup, T. S., McEvoy, J. P., Swartz, M. S., et al. (2005). Effectiveness of antipsychotic drugs in patients with chronic schizophrenia. *New England Journal of Medicine, 353*(12), 1209–1223.

Lieberman, J. A., Stroup, T. S., McEvoy, J. P., Swartz, M. S., Rosenheck, R. A., Perkins, D. O., et al. (2005). Effectiveness of antipsychotic drugs in patients with chronic schizophrenia. *New England Journal of Medicine, 353*(12), 1209–1223.

Lieberman, M. (1990). A group therapist's perspective on self-help groups. *International Journal of Group Psychotherapy, 40*, 251–279.

Linn, M. W., Caffey, E. M., Klett, C. J., Hogarty, C. E., & Lamb, H. R. (1979). Day treatment and psychotropic drugs in the aftercare of schizophrenic patients. *Archives of General Psychiatry, 36*, 1055–1066.

Linn, M. W., Klett, C. J., & Caffey, E. M. (1980). Foster home characteristics and psychiatric patient outcome. *Archives of General Psychiatry, 37*(2), 129–132.

Liu, R. T. (2010). Early life stressors and genetic influences on the development of bipolar disorder: The roles of childhood abuse and brain-derived neurotrophic factor. *Child Abuse & Neglect, 34*, 516–522. http://dx.doi.org/10.1016/j.chiabu.2009.10.009.

Livingston, J. A., Gordon, L. R., King, D. A., & Srebnik, D. S. (1991). *Implementing the supported housing approach: A national evaluation of NIMH supported housing demonstration projects.* Burlington, VT: Trinity College, Center for Community Change through Housing and Support.

Lloyd, C., King, R., & Moore, L. (2010). Subjective and objective indicators of recovery. *International Journal of Social Psychiatry, 29*(1), 48–55.

Lloyd-Evans, B., Slade, M., Jagielska, D., & Johnson, S. (2009). Residential alternatives to acute psychiatric hospital admission: Systematic review. *British Journal of Psychiatry, 195*, 109–117.

Lorig, K. (2006). *Chronic disease self management leader's manual.* Palo Alto, CA: Stanford Patient Education Research Center.

Low, A. A. (1950). *Mental health through will-training* (15th ed.). Boston, MA: Christopher.

Lu, W., Fite, R., Kim, E., Hyer, L., Yanos, P. T., Mueser, K. T., & Rosenberg, S. D. (2009). Cognitive-behavioral treatment of PTSD in severe mental illness: A pilot study replication in an ethnically diverse population. *American Journal of Psychiatric Rehabilitation, 12*(1), 73–91.

Luber, R. F. (1979). The growth and scope of partial hospitalization. In R. F. Luber (Ed.), *Partial hospitalization: A current perspective* (pp. 3–20). New York: Plenum Publishing.

Lucksted, A., McFarlane, W., Downing, D., Dixon, L., & Adams, C. (2012). Recent developments in family psychoeducation as an evidence-based practice. *Journal of Marital and Family Therapy, 28*(1), 101–121.

Luke, D. A. (1989). *The measurement of change in a self-help context.* Unpublished doctoral dissertation. Urbana–Champaign, IL: University of Illinois.

Luke, D. A., Mowbray, C. T., Klump, K., Herman, S. E., & Boots-Miller, B. (1996). Exploring the diversity of dual diagnosis: Utility of cluster analysis for program planning. *Journal of Mental Health Administration, 23*(3), 298–316.

Lundin, R. (2005). Phyllis Solomon speaks on consumer operated services and jail diversion. *American Journal of Psychiatric Rehabilitation, 8*(1), 1–7.

Lundwall, R. R. (1996). How psychoeducational support groups can provide multi-disciplinary services to families of people with mental illness. *Psychiatric Rehabilitation Journal, 20*(2), 64–72.

Lyons, J. S., Cook, J. A., Ruth, A. R., Karver, M., & Slagg, N. B. (1996). Service delivery using consumer staff in a mobile crisis assessment program. *Community Mental Health Journal, 32*(1), 33–40.

Lysaker, P., & Bell, M. (1995). Work rehabilitation and improvements in insight in schizophrenia. *Journal of Nervous and Mental Disease, 183*(2), 103–106.

Lysaker, P. H., Evans, J. D., Kim, H. W., Marks, K. A., Meyer, P. S., Tunis, S. L., et al. (2001). Symptoms and working in performance in schizophrenia. *Schizophrenia Research, 49*, 139.

MaCauley, R. (1993). Professionals need training to accept ex-patients as colleagues. *Resources, 5*(1), 18.

MacDonald-Wilson, K. L., Mancuso, L. L., Danley, K. S., & Anthony, W. A. (1989). Supported employment for people with psychiatric disability. *Journal of Applied Rehabilitation Counseling, 20*(3), 50–57.

MacDonald-Wilson, K., Nemec, P. B., Anthony, W., & Cohen, M. (2001). Assessment in psychiatric rehabilitation. In B. Bolton (Ed.), *Handbook of measurement and evaluation in rehabilitation* (3rd ed.). Gaithersburg, MD: Aspen Publications.

Macias, C., DeCarlo, L. T., Wang, Q., Frey, J., & Barreira, P. (2001). Work interest as a predictor of competitive employment: Policy implications for psychiatric rehabilitation. *Administration and Policy in Mental Health, 28*(4), 279–297.

Macias, C., Rodican, C. F., Hargreaves, W. A., Jones, D. R., Barreira, P. J., & Wang, Q. (2006). Supported employment outcomes of a randomized controlled trial of ACT and Clubhouse models. *Psychiatric Services, 57*(10).

Magura, S., Laudet, A., Mahmood, D., Rosenblum, A., Vogel, H., & Knight, E. (2003). The role of self-help processes on achieving abstinence in dual recovery. *Addictive Behaviors, 28*(3), 399–413.

Maj, M., Pirozzi, R., Magliano, L., & Bartoli, L. (1998). Long term outcome of lithium prophylaxis in bipolar disorder: A 5 year prospective study of 402 patients at a lithium clinic. *American Journal of Psychiatry, 155*(1), 30–35.

Malla, A. K., Bodnar, M., Joober, R., & Lepage, M. (2011). Duration of untreated psychosis is associated with orbital-frontal grey matter volume reductions in first episode psychosis. *Schizophrenia Research, 125*, 13–20. http://dx.doi.org/10.1016/j.schres.2010.09.021.

Malla, A. K., & Norman, R. M. G. (2002). Early intervention in schizophrenia and related disorders: Advantages and pitfalls. *Current Opinion in Psychiatry, 15*, 17–23.

Mancini, M. A., Hardiman, E. R., & Lawson, H. A. (2005). Making sense of it all: Consumer providers' theories about factors facilitating and impeding recovery from psychiatric disabilities. *Psychiatric Rehabilitation Journal, 29*(1), 48–55.

Mancuso, L. L. (1990). Reasonable accommodations for workers with psychiatric disabilities. *Psychosocial Rehabilitation Journal, 14*(2), 3–19.

Manderscheid, R., & Del Vecchio, P. (2008). Moving toward solutions: Responses to the crisis of premature death. *International Journal of Mental Health, 37*(2), 3–7.

Mannion, E. (1996). Resilience and burden in spouses of people with mental illness. *Psychiatric Rehabilitation Journal, 20*(2), 13–23.

Manos, E. (1993). Prosumers. *Psychosocial Rehabilitation Journal, 16*(4), 117–120.

Manthey, T. (2011). Using motivational interviewing to increase retention in supported education. *American Journal of Psychiatric Rehabilitation, 14*, 120–136.

Manuel, J. I., Covell, N. H., Jackson, C. T., & Essock, S. M. (2011). Does assertive community treatment increase medication adherence for people with co-occurring psychotic and substance use disorders? *Journal of the American Psychiatric Nurses Association, 17*, 51–56. http://dx.doi.org/10.1177/1078 390310395586.

Marcus, J., Hans, S. L., Nagler, S., Auerbach, J. G., Mirsky, A. F., & Aubrey, A. (1987). Review of the NIMH Israeli kibbutz-city study and the Jerusalem infant development study. *Schizophrenia Bulletin, 13*(3), 425–437.

Marlatt, G. A. (1998). Basic principles and strategies of harm reduction. In G. A. Marlatt (Ed.), *Harm reduction: Pragmatic approaches to managing high risk behaviors*. New York: Guilford Press.

Marlatt, G. A., Blume, A. W., & Parks, G. A. (2001). Integrating harm reduction therapy and traditional substance abuse treatment. *Journal of Psychoactive Drugs, 33*, 13–21.

Marneros, A., Tottig, S., Wenzel, A. R., & Brieger, P. (2004). Affective and schizoaffective mixed states. *European Archives of Psychiatry and Clinical Neuroscience, 254*(2), 76–81.

Marrone, J. (1993). Creating positive vocational outcomes for people with severe mental illness. *Psychosocial Rehabilitation Journal, 17*(2), 43–62.

Marrone, J., & Golowka, E. (2000). If you think work is bad for people with mental illness, then try poverty, unemployment, and social isolation. *Psychiatric Rehabilitation Journal, 23*(2), 187–193.

Marsh, D. T., Dickens, R. M., Koeske, R. D., Yackovich, N. S., Wilson, J. M., et al. (1993). Troubled journey: Siblings and children of people with mental illness. *Innovations and Research, 2*(2), 13–23.

Marsh, D. T., Lefley, H. P., Evans-Rhodes, D., Ansell, V. I., Doerzbacher, B. M., et al. (1996). The family experience of mental illness: Evidence for resilience. *Psychiatric Rehabilitation Journal, 20*(2), 3–12.

Marshall, M., Crowther, R., Sledge, W. H., Rathbone, J., & Soares-Weiser, K. (2011). Day hospital versus admission for acute psychiatric disorders. *Cochrane Database of Systematic Reviews* (12). http://dx.doi.org/10.1002/14651858.CD004026.pub2.

Marshall, M., & Lockwood, Al (2004). *Assertive community treatment for people with severe mental disorders*. From Wiley Interscience.

Mauch, D. (1991). *Separate paths to a common understanding: Treating the human condition of a disability*. In *The community integration of persons labeled as dually diagnosed: Issues and models, selected conference proceedings*: Cincinnati, OH: University Affiliated Cincinnati Center for Developmental Disorders, 1–14.

Mausbach, B. T., Moore, R., Bowie, C., Cardenas, V., & Patterson, T. L. (2009). A review of instruments for measuring functional recovery in those diagnosed with psychosis. *Schizophrenia Bulletin, 35*(2), 307–318.

McColl, M. A., Davies, D., Carlson, P., Johnston, J., & Minnes, P. (2001). The Community Integration Measure: Development and preliminary validation. *Archives of Physical Medicine and Rehabilitation, 82*(4), 429–434.

McDonell, M. G., Short, R. A., Berry, C. M., & Dyck, D. G. (2003). Burden in schizophrenia caregivers: Impact of family psychoeducation and awareness of patient suicidality. *Family Process, 42*(1), 91–103.

McFarlane, W. R., Cook, W. L., Downing, D., Ruff, A., Lynch, S., Adelsheim, S., et al. (2012). Early detection, intervention, and prevention of psychosis program: Rationale, design, and sample description. *Adolescent Psychiatry, 2*(2), 112–124.

McFarlane, W. R., Dixon, L., Lukens, E., & Lucksted, A. (2003). Family psychoeducation and schizophrenia: A review of the literature. *Journal of Marital and Family Therapy, 29*(2), 223–245.

McFarlane, W. R., Dushay, R. A., Deakins, S. M., Stastny, P., Lukens, E. P., Toran, J., & Link, B. (2000). Employment outcomes in family-aided assertive community treatment. *American Journal of Orthopsychiatry, 70*(2), 203–214.

McFarlane, W. R., Lukens, E., Link, B., Dushay, R., Deakins, S. A., Newmark, M., Dunne, E. J., Horen, B., & Toran, J. (1995). Multiple family group and psychoeducation in the treatment of schizophrenia. *Archives of General Psychiatry, 52*, 679–687.

McGlashan, T. H. (2000). Duration of untreated psychosis in first-episode schizophrenia: Marker or determinant of course. *Biological Psychiatry, 46*, 899–907.

McGrew, J. (2011). Letter to the editor: Evidence based or eminence based. *Journal of the American Psychiatric Nurses Association, 17*(1), 32–33.

McGrew, J., & Griss, M. (2005). Concurrent and predictive validity of two scales to assess the fidelity of implementation of supported employment. *Psychiatric Rehabilitation Journal, 29*(1), 41–47.

McGurk, S. R., Mueser, K. T., Harvey, P. D., LaPuglia, R., & Marder, J. (2003). Cognitive and symptom predictors of work outcomes for clients with schizophrenia in supported employment. *Psychiatric Services, 54*(8), 1129–1135.

McGurrin, M. C. (1994). An overview of the effectiveness of traditional vocational rehabilitation services in the treatment of long-term mental illness. *Psychiatric Rehabilitation Journal, 17*(3), 37–54.

McIntyre, R. S., Konarski, J. Z., Soczynska, J. K., Wilkins, K., Panjwani, G., Bouffard, B., Bottas, A., & Kennedy, S. H. (2006). Medical co-morbidity in bipolar disorder: Implications for functional outcomes and health service utilization. *Psychiatric Services, 57*, 1140–1144.

McKee-Ryan, F. M., Song, Z., Wanberg, C. R., & Kinicki, A. J. (2005). Psychological and physical well-being during unemployment: A meta-analytic study. *Journal of Applied Psychology, 90*(1), 53–76.

Mead, S. (2005). *Intentional peer support: An alternative approach.* Self-published by the author.

Mead, S., Hilton, D., & Curtis, L. (2001). Peer support: A theoretical perspective. *Psychiatric Rehabilitation Journal, 25*(2), 134–141.

Medalia, A., & Choi, J. (2009). Cognitive remediation in schizophrenia. *Neuropsychology Review, 19*, 353–364.

Megivern, D., & Pellerito, S. (2002). Early intervention for students with psychiatric impairments. In C. T. Mowbray, K. S. Brown, K. Furlong-Norman, & A. Sullivan-Soydan (Eds.), *Supported education and psychiatric rehabilitation: Models and methods* (pp. 279–284). Linthicum, MD: International Association of Psychosocial Rehabilitation Services.

Megivern, D., Pellerito, S., & Mowbray, C. (2003). Barriers to higher education for individuals with psychiatric disabilities. *Psychiatric Rehabilitation Journal, 26*(3), 217–231.

Melle, I., Larsen, T. K., Haahr, U., et al. (2004). Reducing the duration of untreated first-episode psychosis. *Archives of General Psychiatry, 61*, 143–150.

Meltzer, H. Y. (2005). Focus on metabolic consequences of long-term treatment with olanzapine, quetiapine and risperidone: Are there differences? *International Journal of Neuropsychopharmacology, 8*(2), 153–156.

Mental Health America. (2012). *Position statement 22: Involuntary mental health treatment.* Retrieved July 11, 2012, from http://www.nmha.org/go/position-statements/p-36.

Mezzina, R., Davidson, L., Borg, M., Marin, I., Topor, A., & Sells, D. (2006). The social nature of recovery: Discussion and implications for practice. *American Journal of Psychiatric Rehabilitation, 9*, 63–80.

Miller, A. L., Hall, C. S., Buchanan, R. W., Buckley, P. F., Chiles, J. A., Conley, R. R., & Tarin-Godoy, B. (2004). The Texas Medication Algorithm Project antipsychotic algorithm for schizophrenia: 2003 update. *Journal of Clinical Psychiatry, 65*(4), 500–508.

Miller, N. S. (1997). Clinical approach to diagnosis of comorbid addictive and psychiatric disorders. *Psychiatric Rehabilitation Skills, 2*(1), 77–90.

Miller, R. (2005). Publicity re: past abuses of patients in mental hospitals. *Australian and New Zealand Journal of Psychiatry, 39*(5), 425–426.

Miller, W. R., & Rollnick, S. (2002). *Motivational interviewing: Preparing people to change addictive behavior* (2nd ed.). New York: The Guilford Press.

Mitchell, A. J., & Lawrence, D. (2011). Revascularisation and mortality rates following acute coronary syndromes in people with severe mental illness: Comparative meta-analysis. *British Journal of Psychiatry, 198*, 434–441. http://dx.doi.org/10.1192/bjp.bp.109.076950.

Mize, T. I., Paolo-Calabrese, M. A., Williams, T. J., & Margolin, H. K. (1998). Managing the landlord role: How can one agency provide both rehabilitation services and housing collaboration. *Psychiatric Rehabilitation Journal, 22*(2), 117–122.

Modrcin, M., Rapp, C., & Chamberlin, R. (1985). *Case management with psychiatrically disabled individuals: Curriculum and training program.* Lawrence, KS: University of Kansas School of Social Welfare.

Monroe-DeVita, M., Morse, G., & Bond, G. R. (2012). Program fidelity and beyond: Multiple strategies and criteria for ensuring quality assertive community treatment. *Psychiatric Services, 63*, 743–750. http://dx.doi.org/10.1176/appi.ps.201100015.

Monroe-DeVita, M., Teague, G. B., & Moser, L. L. (2011). The TMACT: A new tool for measuring fidelity to assertive community treatment. *Journal of the American Psychiatric Nurses Association, 17*, 17–29. http://dx.doi.org/10.1177/1078390310394658.

Moos, R. (1974). *Evaluating treatment environments: A social ecological approach.* New York: John Wiley and Sons.

Morganthau, T., Agrest, S., Greenberg, N. F., Doherty, S., & Raine, G. (1986). Abandoned. *Newsweek, 107*(1), 14–15.

Morse, G., & McKasson, M. (2005). Assertive community treatment. In R. Drake, M. Merrens, & D. Lynde (Eds.), *Evidence-based mental health practice: A textbook* (pp. 317–347). New York: W. W. Norton Company.

Moser, L. L., & Bond, G. R. (2011). Practitioner attributes as predictors of restrictive practices in assertive community treatment. *Journal of the American Psychiatric Nurses Association, 17*, 80–89. http://dx.doi.org/10.1177/1078390310394360.

Mowbray, C. T. (1997). Benefits and issues created by consumer role innovation in psychiatric rehabilitation. In C. T. Mowbray, D. P. Moxley, C. A. Jasper, & L. L. Howell (Eds.), *Consumers as providers.* Columbia, MD: International Association of Psychosocial Rehabilitation Services.

Mowbray, C. T. (1997). The future of supported education. *Journal of the California Alliance for Mental Illness, 8*(2), 67–69.

Mowbray, C. T. (1999). The benefits and challenges of supported education: A personal perspective. *Psychiatric Rehabilitation Journal, 22*(3), 248–254.

Mowbray, C. T. (2004a). Overview of the special issue on supported education. *American Journal of Psychiatric Rehabilitation, 7*(3), 223–226.

Mowbray, C. T. (2004b). Supported education: Diversity, critical ingredients and future directions. *American Journal of Psychiatric Rehabilitation, 7*(3), 347–362.

Mowbray, C. T., Bellamy, C. D., Megivern, D., & Szilvagyi, S. (2001). Raising our sites: Dissemination of supported education. *Journal of Behavioral Health Services and Research, 28*(4), 484–491.

Mowbray, C. T., Bybee, D., Harris, S. N., & McCrohan, N. (1995). Predictors of work status and future work orientation in people with a psychiatric disability. *Psychiatric Rehabilitation Journal, 19*(2), 17–28.

Mowbray, C. T., Bybee, D., Oyserman, D., & MacFarlane, P. (2005). Timing of mental illness onset and motherhood. *Journal of Nervous and Mental Disease, 193*(6), 369–378.

Mowbray, C. T., Chamberlain, P., Jennings, M., & Reed, C. (1988). Consumer-run mental health services: Results from five demonstration projects. *Community Mental Health Journal, 24*, 151–156.

Mowbray, C. T., & Collins, M. E. (2002). The effectiveness of supported education: Current research findings. In C. T. Mowbray, K. S. Brown, K. Furlong-Norman, & A. Sullivan-Soydan (Eds.), *Supported education and psychiatric rehabilitation: Models and methods* (pp. 181–194). Linthicum, MD: International Association of Psychosocial Rehabilitation Services.

Mowbray, C. T., Collins, M., & Bybee, D. (1999). Supported education for individuals with psychiatric disabilities: Long-term outcomes from an experimental study. *Social Work Research, 23*(2), 89–100.

Mowbray, C. T., Collins, M. E., Bellamy, C. D., Megivern, D. A., Bybee, D., & Szilvagyi, S. (2005). Supported education for adults with psychiatric disabilities: An innovation for social work and psychosocial rehabilitation practice. *Social Work, 50*, 7–20.

Mowbray, C. T., Holter, M. C., Teague, G. B., & Bybee, D. (2003a). Fidelity criteria: Development, measurement and validation. *American Journal of Evaluation, 24*(3), 315–340.

Mowbray, C. T., Megivern, D., & Holter, M. (2003b). Supported education programming for adults with psychiatric disabilities: Results from a national survey. *Psychiatric Rehabilitation Journal, 27*(2), 159–167.

Mowbray, C. T., & Moxley, D. P. (1997a). Consumers as providers: Themes and success factors. In C. T. Mowbray, D. P. Moxley, C. A. Jasper, & L. L. Howell (Eds.), *Consumers as providers*. Columbia, MD: International Association of Psychosocial Rehabilitation Services.

Mowbray, C. T., & Moxley, D. P. (1997b). Futures for empowerment of consumer role innovation. In C. T. Mowbray, D. P. Moxley, C. A. Jasper, & L. L. Howell (Eds.), *Consumers as providers*. Columbia, MD: International Association of Psychosocial Rehabilitation Services.

Mowbray, C. T., Moxley, D. P., & Brown, K. S. (1993). A framework for initiating supported education programs. *Psychosocial Rehabilitation Journal, 17*(1), 129–149.

Mowbray, C. T., Moxley, D. P., & Collins, M. (1998). Consumers as mental health providers: First person accounts of benefits and limitations. *Journal of Behavioral Health Services and Research, 25*, 397–411.

Mowbray, C. T., Moxley, D. P., Thrasher, S., Bybee, D., McCrohan, N., Harris, S., & Clover, G. (1996). Consumers as community support providers: Issues created by role innovation. *Community Mental Health Journal, 32*(1), 47–67.

Mowbray, C. T., Oyserman, D., Baybee, D., MacFarlane, P., & Rueda-Riedle, A. (2001). Life circumstances of mothers with serious mental illness. *Psychiatric Rehabilitation Journal, 25*, 114–123.

Mowbray, C. T., & Tan, C. (1993). Consumer-operated drop-in centers: Evaluation of operations and impact. *Journal of Mental Health Administration, 20*, 8–19.

Mowbray, C. T., Verdejo, F., & Levine, P. (2002). The role of community mental health and vocational rehabilitation service systems in enhancing supported education services. In C. T. Mowbray, K. S. Brown, K. Furlong-Norman, & A. Sullivan-Soydan (Eds.), *Supported education and psychiatric rehabilitation: Models and methods* (pp. 199–213). Linthicum, MD: International Association of Psychosocial Rehabilitation Services.

Moxley, D. P., & Mowbray, C. T. (1997). Consumers as providers: Forces and factors legitimizing role innovation in psychiatric rehabilitation. In C. T. Mowbray, D. P. Moxley, C. A. Jasper, & L. L. Howell (Eds.), *Consumers as providers*. Columbia, MD: International Association of Psychosocial Rehabilitation Services.

Moxley, D. P., Mowbray, C. T., & Brown, K. S. (1993). Supported education. In P. W. Flexler, & P. Solomon (Eds.), *Psychiatric rehabilitation in practice* (pp. 137–153). Boston, MA: Andover Medical Publishers.

Mueser, K. T., Bennett, M., & Kushner, M. G. (1995). Epidemiology of substance abuse among persons with chronic mental disorders. In A. F. Lehman, & L. Dixon (Eds.), *Double jeopardy: Chronic mental illness and substance abuse* (pp. 9–25). New York: Harwood Academic.

Mueser, K. T., Bond, G. R., Drake, R. E., & Resnick, S. G. (1998). Models of community care for severe mental illness: A review of research on case management. *Schizophrenia Bulletin, 24*, 37–74.

Mueser, K. T., Clark, R. E., Haines, M., Drake, R. E., McHugo, G. J., Bond, G. R., et al. (2004). The Hartford study of supported employment for persons with severe mental illness. *Journal of Consulting and Clinical Psychology, 72*(3), 479–490.

Mueser, K. T., Corrigan, P. W., Hilton, D. W., Tanzman, B., Schaub, A., Gingerich, S., et al. (2002). Illness management and recovery: A review of the research. *Psychiatric Services, 53*(10), 1272–1284.

Mueser, K. T., Drake, R. E., & Wallach, M. A. (1998). Dual diagnosis: A review of etiological theories. *Addictive Behaviors, 23*, 717–734.

Mueser, K. T., & Gingerich, S. (2006). *The complete family guide to schizophrenia: Helping your loved one get the most out of life*. New York: Guilford Press.

Mueser, K. T., Glynn, S. M., Corrigan, P. W., & Baber, W. (1996). A survey of preferred terms for users of mental health services. *Psychiatric Services, 47*(7), 760–761.

Mueser, K. T., & Noordsy, D. L. (1996). Group treatment for dually diagnosed clients. *New Directions for Mental Health, 70*, 33–51.

Mueser, K. T., Noordsy, D. L., Drake, R. E., & Fox, L. (2003). *Integrated treatment for dual disorders: A guide to effective practice*. New York: The Guilford Press.

Mueser, K. T., Rosenberg, S. R., Xie, H., Jankowski, M. K., Bolton, et al. (2008) A randomized controlled trial of cognitive-behavioral treatment of posttraumatic stress disorder in severe mental illness. *Journal of Consulting and Clinical Psychology, 76*, 259–271.

Mueser, K. T., Sengupta, A., Bellack, A. S., Glick, I. D., Schooler, N. R., Xie, H., et al. (2001). Family treatment and medication dosage reduction in schizophrenia: Effects on patient social functioning, family attitudes and burden. *Journal of Consulting and Clinical Psychology, 69*(1), 3–12.

Mueser, K. T., Torrey, W. C., Lynde, D., Singer, P., & Drake, R. E. (2003). Implementing evidence-based practices for people with severe mental illness. *Behavior Modification, 27*(3), 387–411.

Mullick, M., Miller, L. J., & Jacobsen, T. (2001). Insight into mental illness and child maltreatment risk among mothers with major psychiatric disorders. *Psychiatric Services, 52*(4), 488–492.

Munetz, M. R., & Frese, F. J. (2001). Getting ready for recovery: Reconciling mandatory treatment with the recovery vision. *Psychiatric Rehabilitation Journal, 25*(1), 35–42.

Munetz, M. R., Galon, P. A., & Frese, F. J. (2003). The ethics of mandatory community treatment. *Journal of the American Academy of Psychiatry and the Law, 31*(2), 173–183.

Murphy, A. A., Mullen, M. G., & Spagnolo, A. B. (2005). Enhancing individual placement and support: Promoting job tenure by integrating natural supports and supported education. *American Journal of Psychiatric Rehabilitation, 8,* 37–61.

Murphy, G. C., & Athanason, J. A. (1999). The effect of unemployment on mental health. *Journal of Occupational and Organizational Psychology, 72,* 83–89.

Nasr, T., & Kausar, R. (2009). Psychoeducation and the family burden in schizophrenia: A randomized controlled trial. *Annuls of General Psychiatry, 8*(17).

Nasrallah, H. A., Meyer, J. M., Goff, D. C., McEvoy, J. P., Davis, S. M., Stroup, T., et al. (2006). Low rates of treatment for hypertension, dyslipidemia and diabetes in schizophrenia: Data from the CATIE schizophrenia trial sample at baseline. *Schizophrenia Research, 6*(1-3), 15–22.

Nasrallah, H., Tandon, R., & Keshavan, N. (2011). Beyond the facts in schizophrenia: Closing the gaps in diagnosis, pathophysiology and treatment. *Epidemiology and Psychiatric Sciences, 20,* 317–327.

National Alliance of Business. (1991). *ADA sourcebook, what you need to know about the Americans with Disabilities Act: A guide for small and medium-sized businesses.* Washington, D.C.: Author.

National Alliance on Mental Illness. (1995). *Policy on involuntary commitment and court ordered treatment.*

National Association of Mental Health Program Directors Council (NASMHPD) Medical Directors. (2010). Technical report, consumer involvement with state mental health authorities. In N. J. S. -H. C. (Ed.), *The self-help group directory* (20th ed.). Cedar Knolls, NJ: Saint Clare's Health System.

Neff, W. S. (1988). Vocational rehabilitation in perspective. In J. A. C. M. D. Bell (Ed.), *Vocational rehabilitation of persons with prolonged psychiatric disorders.* Baltimore, MD: Johns Hopkins University Press.

Neffinger, G. G. (1981). Partial hospitalization: An overview. *Journal of Community Psychology, 9,* 262–269.

Nemec, P. B. (2008). *Psychiatric rehabilitation workforce development.* Pohang, South Korea: Paper presented at the Psychiatric rehabilitation workforce development.

Nemec, P. B., McNamara, S., & Walsh, D. (1992). Direct skills teaching. *Psychosocial Rehabilitation Journal, 16*(1), 13–25.

Nemec, P. B., Spaniol, L., & Dell Orto, A. E. (2001). Psychiatric rehabilitation education: Special issue. *Rehabilitation Education, 19*(2).

Nemeroff, C. B., & Schatzberg, A. F. (1998). Pharmacological treatment of unipolar depression. In P. E. Nathan, & J. M. Gorman (Eds.), *A guide to treatments that work* (pp. 212–225).

New Jersey Developmental Disabilities Council. (1997/1998). *Resources directory* (8th ed.). Trenton, NJ: Author.

New Jersey Psychiatric Rehabilitation Association. (2008). *Testimony before the NJ Senate Health and Human Services Committee on S.735: Involuntary outpatient commitment.*

New Jersey, Collaborative Support Programs of New. (1991). *Consumer housing preference survey.* Consumer housing preference survey: Author.

New Jersey, Collaborative Support Programs of New. (1996). *Boarding home resident survey for Monmouth and Ocean counties.* Consumer housing preference survey: Author.

New York Association of Psychiatric Rehabilitation Services. (2005). *Testimony before NYS assembly Codes and Mental Health Committees public hearing on Kendra's Law.*

Nicholson, J., Nason, M. W., Calabresi, A. O., & Yando, R. (1999). Fathers with severe mental illness: Characteristics and comparisons. *American Journal of Orthopsychiatry, 69*(1), 134–141.

Nielsen, M., Langner, B., Zema, C., Hacker, T., & Grundy, P. (2012). *Benefits of implementing the patient-centered medical home: A review of cost and quality results.* Washington, D.C.: Patient-centered primary care collaborative.

Nikkel, R. E., Smith, G., & Edwards, D. (1992). A consumer operated case management project. *Hospital and Community Psychiatry, 43*(6), 577–579.

Nishith, P., Mueser, K. T., Srsic, C. S., & Beck, A. T. (1997). Expectations and motives for alcohol use in a psychiatric outpatient population. *Journal of Nervous and Mental Disease, 185*(10), 622–626.

Norcross, J. C. (Ed.). (2002). *Psychotherapy relationships that work: Therapist contributions and responsiveness to patients.* New York: Oxford University Press.

Nord, M., & Farde, L. (2011). Antipsychotic occupancy of dopamine receptors in schizophrenia. *CNS Neuroscience and Therapeutics, 17*, 97–103. http://dx.doi.org/10.1111/j.1755-5949.2010.00222.x.

Nuechterlein, K. H., Subotnik, K. L., Turner, L. R., Ventura, J., Becker, D. R., & Drake, R. E. (2008). Individual placement and support for individuals with recent-onset schizophrenia: Integrating supported education and supported employment. *Psychiatric Rehabilitation Journal, 31*(4), 340–349.

O'Brien, J., & O'Brien, C. L. (1994). More than just a new address: Images of organization for supported living agencies. In V. J. Bradley, J. W. Ashbaugh, & B. C. Blaney (Eds.), *Creating individual supports for people with developmental disabilities.* Baltimore, MD: Paul H. Brookes Publishing.

O'Connell, M. (2011). *Self-betermination, beneficence, choice, and adherence.* Retrieved June 12, 2012, from www.casd1.org.

O'Hara, A. (2003). *Permanent supported housing: A proven solution to homelessness.* Boston, MA: A joint publication of The Technical Assistance Collaborative and The Consortium for Citizens with Disabilities.

O'Hara, A. (2010). *A katrina success story: Louisiana's 3,000 unit permanent supportive housing initiative.* Boston, MA: The Technical Assistance Collaborative.

O'Hara, A., & Day, S. (2001). Olmstead and supportive housing: A vision for the future. *Consumer Action Series.* Retrieved January 5, 2013, from http://www.tacinc.org/media/13054/Olmstead%20Supportive %20Housing.pdf.

O'Keefe, K. (2006). *The Brooklyn Mental Health Court Evaluation Planning, Implementation, Courtroom Dynamics, and Participant Outcomes.* New York: Center for Court Innovation.

O'Connor, A. M., Bennett, C. L., Stacey, D., Barry, M., Col, N. F., Eden, K. B., et al. (2009). Decision aids for people facing health treatment or screening decisions. *Cochrane Database of Systematic Reviews, 3.* http://dx.doi.org/10.1002/14651858.CD001431.

Ogilvie, R. J. (1997). The state of supported housing for mental health consumers: A literature review. *Psychiatric Rehabilitation Journal, 21*(2), 122–131.

Olmos-Gallo, P. A., Starks, R., Lusczakoski, K. D., Huff, S., & Mock, K. (2012). Seven key strategies that work together to create recovery based transformation. *Community Mental Health Journal, 48*(3), 294–301.

Onaga, E. E. (1994). The Fairweather Lodge as a psychosocial program in the 1990s. In L. Spaniol, et al. (Eds.), *An introduction to psychiatric rehabilitation.* Columbia, MD: IAPSRS.

Onaga, E. E., & Smith, B. A. (2000). Reinvention of the lodge program: A case study of program changes to promote full-time employment. *Psychiatric Rehabilitation Skills, 4*(1), 41–60.

Onken, S. J., Craig, C. M., Ridgway, P., Dorman, D. H., & Ralph, R. O. (2002). *Mental health recovery: What helps and what hinders?* Washington, DC.

Onken, S. J., Craig, C. M., Ridgway, P., Ralph, R. O., & Cook, J. A. (2007). An analysis of the definitions and elements of recovery: A review of the literature. *Psychiatric Rehabilitation Journal, 31*(1), 9–22.

Osborn, L. A. (2009). From beauty to despair: The rise and fall of the american state mental hospital. *Psychiatric Quarterly, 80*, 219–231. http://dx.doi.org/10.1007/s11126-009-9109-3.

Overstreet, J. (2006). North Carolina improves health through a coordinated approach to behavioral and medical care. *National Council News*. Retrieved November 26, 2008, from http://www.thenationalcouncil.org/galleries/NCMagazine-gallery/ncnews_sept06.pdf.

Papadopoulos, C., Ross, J., Stewart, D., Dack, C., James, K., & Bowers, L. (2012). The antecedents of violence and aggression within psychiatric in-patient settings. *Acta Psychiatrica Scandinavica* 1–15. http://dx.doi.org/10.1111/j.1600-0447.2012.01827.x.

Parks, J., Svendsen, D., Singer, P., Foti, M. E., & Mauer, B. (2006). *Morbidity and mortality in people with serious mental illness [Technical Report]*. Retrieved June 12, 2007, from http://www.nasmhpd.org/general_files/publications/med_directors_pubs/Technical%20Report%20on%20Morbidity%20and%20Mortaility%20-%20Final%2011-06.pdf.

Parsons, J. A., May, J. G., Jr., & Menolascino, F. J. (1984). The nature and incidence of mental illness in mentally retarded individuals. In F. J. Menolascino, & J. A. Stark (Eds.), *Handbook of mental illness in the mentally retarded* (pp. 3–43). New York: Plenum Press.

Paulson, R. I. (1991). Professional training for consumers and family members: One road to empowerment. *Psychosocial Rehabilitation Journal, 14*(3), 69–80.

Paulson, R., Herinckx, H., Demmler, J., Clarke, G., Cutler, D., & Birecree, E. (1999). Comparing practice patterns of consumer and non-consumer mental health service providers. *Community Mental Health Journal, 35*(3), 251–269.

Pekkala, E. T., & Merrinder, L. B. (2002). *Psychoeducation for schizophrenia*. (Publication no. 10.1002/14651858.CD002831).

Penttila, M., Jaaskelainen, E., Haapea, M., Tanskanen, P., Veijola, J., Ridler, K., et al. (2010). Association between duration of untreated psychosis and brain morphology in schizophrenia within the Northern Finland 1966 Birth Cohort. *Schizophrenia Research, 123*, 145–152. http://dx.doi.org/10.1016/j.schres.2010.08.016.

Pepper, B., Ryglewicz, H., & Kirshner, M. C. (1981). The young adult chronic patient: Overview of a population. *Hospital and Community Psychiatry, 32*, 463–469.

Perlick, D. A., Rosenheck, R. A., Kaczynski, R., Swartz, M. S., Canive, J. M., & Lieberman, J. A. (2006). Components and correlates of family burden in schizophrenia. *Psychiatric Services, 57*(8), 1117–1125.

Perron, B. (2002). Online support for caregivers of people with a mental illness. *Psychiatric Rehabilitation Journal, 26*(1), 70–77.

Petr, C., Holtquist, S., & Martin, J. (2000). Consumer-run organizations for youth. *Psychiatric Rehabilitation Journal, 24*, 142–148.

Pharoah, F. M., Mari, J. J., & Streiner, D. (2004). Family intervention for schizophrenia. The Cochrane Database of Systematic Reviews. *The Cochrane Collaboration*, (12).

Phelan, J., Bromet, E. J., & Link, B. J. (1998). Psychiatric illness and family stigma. *Schizophrenia Bulletin, 24*, 115–126.

Phelan, J. C., Sinkewicz, M., Castille, D., Huz, S., & Link, B. G. (2010). Effectiveness and outcome of assisted outpatient treatment in New York State. *Psychiatric Services, 61*, 137–143.

Phillips, S. D., Burnes, B. J., Edgar, E. R., Mueser, K. T., Linkins, K. W., Rosenheck, R. A., et al. (2001). Moving assertive community treatment into standard practice. *Psychiatric Services, 52*, 771–779.

Pickett, S., Phillips, H., & Kraus, D. (2011). *Recovery International group meeting evaluation: Final Report*. Chicago, IL: UIC Department of Psychiatry, Center on Mental Health Services Research and Policy.

Pirildar, S., Gonul, A. S., Taneli, F., & Akdeniz, F. (2004). Low serum levels of brain-derived neurotrophic factor in patients with schizophrenia do not elevate after antipsychotic treatment.

Progress in Neuro-Psychopharmacology & Biological Psychiatry, 28, 709–713. http://dx.doi.org/10.1016/j.pnpbp.2004.05.008.

Pitschel-Walz, G., Leucht, S., Bauml, J., Kissling, W., & Engel, R. R. (2001). The effect of family interventions on relapse and rehospitalization in schizophrenia – A meta-analysis. *Schizophrenia Bulletin, 27*(1), 79–92.

Pollard, L., Gelbard, Y., Levy, G., & Gelkopf, M. (2008). *Examining attitudes, beliefs and knowledge of effective practices in psychiatric rehabilitation in a hospital setting preservation new jersey.* From http://www.preservationnj.org/ten_most/ten_most_property_detail.asp?COUNTY=Morris%20Countyand PropID=98.

Popovic, D., Reinares, M., Amann, B., Salamero, M., & Vieta, E. (2011). Number needed to treat analyses of drugs used for maintenance treatment of bipolar disorder. *Psychopharmacology, 213*(4), 657–667. http://dx.doi.org/10.1007/s00213-010-2056-8.

Powell, T., Yeaton, W., Hill, E., & Silk, K. (2001). Predictors of psychosocial outcomes for patients with mood disorders: The effects of self-help group participation. *Psychiatric Rehabilitation Journal, 24*(1), 3–11.

Pratt, C. W. (2005). Editor; special issue on psychiatric rehabilitation education and credentials. *American Journal of Psychiatric Rehabilitation, 8*(2).

Pratt, C. W., & Gill, K. J. (1990). Sharing research knowledge to empower people who are chronically mentally ill. *Psychosocial Rehabilitation Journal, 13*(3), 75–79.

Pratt, C. W., Lu, W., Swarbrick, M., & Murphy, A. (2011). Selective provision of illness management and recovery modules. *American Journal of Psychiatric Rehabilitation, 14,* 245–258. http://dx.doi.org/10.1080/15487768.2011.622133.

Pratt, C. W., Smith, R. C., Kazmi, A., & Ahmed, S. (2011). Introducing psychiatric rehabilitation at a psychiatric facility in Pakistan. *American Journal of Psychiatric Rehabilitation, 14,* 259–271. http://dx.doi.org/10.1080/15487768.2011.622140.

President's New Freedom Commission on Mental Health. (2003). *Achieving the promise: Transforming mental health care in America.* Final report. Rockville, MD: Substance Abuse and Mental Health Services Administration.

Price, J. L., & Drevets, W. C. (2012). Neural circuits underlying the pathophysiology of mood disorders. *Trends in Cognitive Sciences, 16,* 61–71. http://dx.doi.org/10.1016/j.tics.2011.12.011.

Priebe, S., Jones, G., McCabe, R., Briscoe, J., Wright, D., Sleed, M., & Beecham, J. (2006). Effectiveness and costs of acute day hospital treatment compared with conventional in-patient care: Randomized controlled trial. *British Journal of Psychiatry, 188*(3), 243–249.

Prochaska, J. O., Norcross, J. C., & DiClemente, C. C. (1994). *Changing for the good.* New York: Harper Collins.

Propst, R. N. (1992a). Introduction to special issue: The clubhouse model. *Psychosocial Rehabilitation Journal, 16*(2), 25–30.

Propst, R. N. (1992b). Standards for clubhouse programs: Why and how they were developed. *Psychosocial Rehabilitation Journal, 16*(2), 25–30.

Pyke, J., & Lowe, J. (1996). Supporting people, not structures: Changes in the provision of supportive housing. *Psychiatric Rehabilitation Journal, 19*(3), 5–12.

Rakfeldt, J., Tebes, J. K., Steiner, J., Walker, P. L., et al. (1997). Normalizing acute care: A day hospital/crisis residence alternative to inpatient hospitalization. *Journal of Nervous and Mental Disease, 185*(1), 46–52.

Rapp, C. A., & Goscha, R. J. (2004). The principles of effective case management of mental health services. *Psychiatric Rehabilitation Journal, 27,* 345–359.

Rapp, C. A., & Goscha, R. J. (2006). *The strengths model: Case management with people with psychiatric disabilities.* New York: Oxford University Press.

Rappaport, J. (1987). Terms of empowerment/exemplars of prevention: Toward a theory for community psychology. *American Journal of Community Psychology, 15*(2), 121–144.

Rappaport, J. (1993). Narrative studies, personal stories and identity transformation in the mutual help context. *Journal of Applied Behavioral Science, 29*, 239–256.

Rappaport, J., Seidman, E., Toro, P. A., McFadden, L. S., Reischl, T. M., et al. (1985). Collaborative research with a mutual help organization. *Social Policy, 15*, 12–24.

Ratzlaff, S., McDiarmid, D., Marty, D., & Rapp, C. (2006). The Kansas consumer as provider program: Measuring the effects of a supported education initiative. *Psychiatric Rehabilitation Journal, 29*(3), 174–182.

Reddy, L. F., & Spaulding, W. D (2010). Understanding adverse experiences in the psychiatric institution: The importance of child abuse histories in iatrogenic trauma. *Psychological Services, 7*(4), 242–253.

Regier, D. A., Farmer, M. E., Rae, D. S., Locke, B. Z., Keith, S. J., Judd, L. L., et al. (1990). Comorbidity of mental disorders with alcohol and other drug abuse: Results from the epidemiologic catchment area (ECA) study. *Journal of the American Medical Association, 264*(19), 2511–2518.

Rehab Brief: Bringing research into effective focus. (1993). Washington, DC: US Department of Education.

Reissman, F. (1965). The "helper-therapy" principle. *Social Work, 10*, 27–32.

Repper, J., & Carter, T. (2011). A review of the literature on peer support in mental health services. *Journal of Mental Health, 20*(4), 392–411.

Resnick, S. G., Armstrong, M., Sperrazza, M., Harkness, L., & Rosenheck, R. A. (2004). A model of consumer provider partnership: Vet-to-Vet. *Psychiatric Rehabilitation Journal, 28*(2), 185–187.

Resnick, S. G., & Rosenheck, R. A. (2008). Integrating peer-provided services: A quasi-experimental study of recovery orientation, confidence, and empowerment. *Psychiatric Services, 59*(1), 1307–1314.

Ridgely, M. S., Goldman, H. H., & Willenbring. (1990). Barriers to the care of persons with dual diagnoses: Organizational and financing issues. *Schizophrenia Bulletin, 16*, 123–132.

Ridgway, P. (2001). Re-storying psychiatric disability: Learning from first person recovery narratives. *Psychiatric Rehabilitation Journal, 24*(4), 335–343.

Ridgeway, P., & Zipple, A. M. (1990). The paradigm shift in residential services: From the linear continuum to supported housing approaches. *Psychosocial Rehabilitation Journal, 13*(4), 11–31.

Ritsher, J. B., Otilingam, P. G., & Grajales, M. (2003). Internalized stigma of mental illness: Psychometric properties of a new measure. *Psychiatry Research, 121*(1), 31–49.

Ritsher, J. B., & Phelan, J. C. (2004). Internalized stigma predicts erosion of morale among psychiatric outpatients. *Psychiatry Research, 129*(3), 257–265.

Rivas-Vazquez, R. A., Sarria, M., Rey, G., Rivas-Vazquez, A. A., Rodriguez, J., & Jardon, M. E. (2009). A relationship-based care model for jail diversion. *Psychiatric Services, 60*(6), 766–771. http://dx.doi.org/10.1176/appi.ps.60.6.766.

Roberts, M. (Ed.). (1996). *Supported employment training competency-based instructional modules* (3rd ed.). Piscataway, NJ: The University Affiliated Program at UMDNJ-Robert Wood Johnson Medical School.

Roberts, M. M., Murphy, A. A., Dolce, J., Spagnolo, A. B., Gill, K. J., Lu, W., & Librera, L. (2010). A study of the impact of social support development on job acquisition and retention among people with psychiatric disabilities. *Journal of Vocational Rehabilitation, 33*, 203–207.

Roberts, M. M., & Pratt, C. W. (2007). Putative evidence of employment readiness. *Psychiatric Rehabilitation Journal, 30*, 175–181.

Roberts, M. M., & Pratt, C. W. (2010). A construct validity of employment readiness in persons with severe mental illness. *American Journal of Psychiatric Rehabilitation, 13*(1), 40–54.

Roberts, M., Rotteveel, J., & Manos, E. (1995). Mental health consumers as professionals: Disclosure in the workplace. *American Rehabilitation, Spring*, 20–23.

Rodgers, M. L., Norell, D. M., Roll, J. M., & Dyck, D. G. (2007). An overview of mental health recovery. *Primary Psychiatry, 14*(12), 76–85.

Roe, D., Hasson-Ohayon, I., Salyers, M. P., & Kravetz, S. (2009). A one year follow-up of illness management and recovery: Participants' accounts of its impact and uniqueness. *Psychiatric Rehabilitation Journal, 32*, 285–291. http://dx.doi.org/10.2975/32.4.2009.285.291.

Roe, D., Mashiach-Eizenberg, M., & Lysaker, P. H. (2011). The relation between objective and subjective domains of recovery among persons with schizophrenia-related disorders. *Schizophrenia Research, 131*(3), 133–138.

Roe, D., Penn, D., Bortz, L., Hasson-Ohayon, I., Hartwell, K., & Roe, S. (2007). Illness management and recovery: Generic issues in group format implementation. *American Journal of Psychiatric Rehabilitation, 10*, 131–147.

Roe, D., Rudnick, A., & Gill, K. (2007). The concept of "being in recovery." *Psychiatric Rehabilitation Journal, 30*(3), 171–173.

Roessler, R. T. (2002). TWWIIA initiatives and work incentives: Return-to-work implications. *Journal of Rehabilitation, 68*(3), 11–15.

Rog, D. J. (2004). The evidence on supported housing. *Psychiatric Rehabilitation Journal, 27*(4), 334–344.

Rogers, E. S. (2009). *Systematic review of supported education literature 1989 – 2009*. Unpublished report. Center for Psychiatric Rehabilitation with support from the National Institute on Disability and Rehabilitation Research.

Rogers, E. S., Chamberlin, J., Ellison, M. L., & Crean, T. (1997). A consumer-constructed scale to measure empowerment among users of mental health services. *Psychiatric Services, 48*, 1042–1047.

Rogers, E. S., Chamberlin, J., Ellison, M. L., & Crean, T. (1997). A consumer-constructed scale to measure empowerment among users of mental health services. *Psychiatric Services, 48*(8), 1042–1047.

Rogers, E. S., Kash, M., & Olschewski, A. (2008). *Systematic review of supported housing literature 1993-2008*. From http://www.bu.edu/drrk/research-syntheses/psychiatric-disabilities/supported-housing/.

Rogers, E. S., & Palmer-Erbs, V. (1994). Participatory action research: Implications for research and evaluation in psychiatric rehabilitation. *Psychosocial Rehabilitation Journal, 18*(2), 3–12.

Rogers, E. S., Ralph, R. O., & Salzer, M. S. (2010). Validating the empowerment scale with a multisite sample of consumers of mental health services. *Psychiatric Services, 61*(9), 933–936.

Rogers, E. S., Teague, G. B., Lichtenstein, C., Campbell, J., Lyass, A., Chen, R., & Banks, S. (2007). Effects of participation in consumer-oriented service programs on both personal and organizationally mediated empowerment: Results of a multi-site study. *Journal of Rehabilitation Research and Development, 44*(6), 785–800.

Rogers, E., Martin, R., Anthony, W., Massaro, J., Danley, K., Crean, T., & Penk, W. (2001). Assessing readiness for change among persons with severe mental illness. *Community Mental Health Journal, 37*(2), 97–112.

Rogers, J. A. (1996). National clearinghouse serves mental health consumer movement. *Journal of Psychosocial Nursing, 34*(9), 22–25.

Rollins, A. L., Salyers, M. P., Tsai, J., & Lydick, J. M. (2010). Staff turnover in statewide implementation of ACT: Relationship with ACT fidelity and other team characteristics. *Administration and Policy in Mental Health and Mental Health Services Research, 37*, 417–426. http://dx.doi.org/10.1007/s10488-009-0257.

Rosenberg, S., Brunette, M., Oxman, T., Marsh, B., Dietrich, A., Mueser, K., et al. (2004). The STIRR model of best practices for blood-borne diseases among clients with serious mental illness. *Psychiatric Services, 55*, 660–664. http://dx.doi.org/10.1176/appi.ps.55.6.660.

Rosenberg, S. D., Goodman, L. A., Osher, F. C., Swartz, M. S., Essock, S. M., et al. (2001). Prevalence of HIV, hepatitis B, and hepatitis C in people with severe mental illness. *American Journal of Public Health, 91*(1), 31–37.

Rosenheck, R., Kasprow, W., Frisman, L., & Liu-mares, W. (2003). Cost-effectiveness of supported housing for homeless persons with mental illness. *Archives of General Psychiatry, 60*, 940–951.

Rosenheck, R., & Neale, M. S. (2001b). A critique of the effectiveness of assertive community treatment: In reply. *Psychiatric Services, 52*(10), 1395–1396.

Rosenthal, H. (2008). From forcing patients to fixing treatment. *Mental Health Weekly,* 5–6.

Rothbard, A. B., Kuno, E., Schinnar, A. P., Hadley, T. R., & Turk, R. (1999). Service utilization and cost of community care for discharged state hospital patients: A 3-year follow-up study. *American Journal of Psychiatry, 156*(6), 920–927.

Rothbard, A. B., Schinnar, A. P., Hadley, T. P., Foley, K. A., & Kuno, E. (1998). Cost comparison of state hospital and community-based care for seriously mentally ill adults. *American Journal of Psychiatry, 155*(4), 523–529.

Rothman, D. J. (2002). *The discovery of the asylum: Social order and disorder in the New Republic.* New York: Walter de Gruyter.

Rowe, M., Bellamy, C., Baranoski, M., Wieland, M., O'Connell, M. J., Benedict, P., et al. (2007). A peer-support, group intervention to reduce substance use and criminality among persons with severe mental illness. *Psychiatric Services, 58*(7), 955–961. http://dx.doi.org/10.1176/appi.ps.58.7.955.

Ruggeri, M., Leese, M., Slade, M., Bonizzato, P., Fontecedro, L., & Tansella, M. (2004). Demographic, clinical, social and service variables associated with higher needs for care in community psychiatric service patients: The South Verona outcome project 8. *Social Psychiatry and Psychiatric Epidemiology, 39*(1), 860–863.

Russell, A. C., & Strauss, S. (2004). Career Advancement Resources (CAR): Supported education as a career development strategy. *American Journal of Psychiatric Rehabilitation, 7*(3), 249–264.

Russert, M. G., & Frey, J. L. (1991). The PACT vocational model: A step into the future. *Psychosocial Rehabilitation Journal, 14*(4), 7–18.

Russinova, Z., Griffin, S., Bloch, P., Wewiorski, N. J., & Rosoklija, I. (2011). Workplace prejudice and discrimination toward individuals with mental illnesses. *Journal of Vocational Rehabilitation, 35*, 227–241.

Rutman, I. D. (1994). How psychiatric disability expresses itself as a barrier to employment. *Psychosocial Rehabilitation Journal, 17*(3), 15–35.

Rychener, M., Salyers, M. P., Labriola, S., & Little, N. (2009). Thresholds' wellness management and recovery implementation. *American Journal of Psychiatric Rehabilitation, 12*, 172–184. http://dx.doi.org/10.1080/15487760902813186.

Saladin, M. E., & Santa Ana, E. J. (2004). Controlled drinking: More than just a controversy. *Current Opinions in Psychiatry, 17*, 175–187.

Salerno, A., Margolies, P., Cleek, A., Pollock, M., Gopalan, G., & Jackson, C. (2011). Wellness self-management: An adaptation of the Illness Management and Recovery Program in New York State. *Psychiatric Services, 62*, 456–458. http://dx.doi.org/10.1176/appi.ps.62.5.456.

Salyers, M. P., Masterton, T. W., Fekete, D. M., Picone, J. J., & Bond, G. R. (1998). Transferring clients from intensive case management: Impact on client functioning. *American Journal of Orthopsychiatry, 68*(2), 233–245.

Salyers, M. P., Rollins, A. L., Clendenning, D., McGuire, A. B., & Kim, E. (2011). Impact of illness management and recovery programs on hospital and emergency room use by Medicaid enrollees. *Psychiatric Services, 62*, 509–515. http://dx.doi.org/10.1176/appi.ps.62.5.509.

Salyers, M. P., Tsai, J., & Stulz, T. A. (2007). Measuring recovery orientation in a hospital setting. *Psychiatric Rehabilitation Journal, 31*(2), 131–137.

Salzer, M. S. (2002). The Mental Health Association of Southeastern Pennsylvania Best Practices Team. *Psychiatric Rehabilitation Skills, 6*(3), 355–382.

Salzer, M. S. (2006). Introduction. In M. S. Salzer (Ed.), *Psychiatric rehabilitation skills in practice: A CPRP preparation and skills workbook.* Columbia, MD: USPRA.

Salzer, M. S., & Shear, S. L. (2002). Identifying consumer provider benefits in evaluations of consumer-delivered services. *Psychiatric Rehabilitation Journal, 25*(3), 281–288.

Salzer, M. S., Wick, L. C., & Rogers, J. A. (2008). Familiarity with and use of accommodations and supports among postsecondary students with mental illness. *Psychiatric Services, 59*(4), 370–375.

SAMHSA see Substance Abuse and Mental Health Service Administration

Sanchez-Mora, N., Medina, O., Francisconi, B., Meza, N. W., Rossi, N., Colmenares, F., et al. (2007). Risk factors for respiratory disease in chronic psychiatric inpatients. *European Journal of Psychiatry, 21,* 212–219. http://dx.doi.org/10.4321/S0213-61632007000300006.

Santiestevan, H. (1975). *Deinstitutionalization: Out of their beds and into the streets.* Washington, DC: American Federation of State, County and Municipal Employees.

Sarason, I., Levine, H., Basham, R., & Sarason, B. (1983). Assessing social support: The social support questionnaire. *Journal of Personality and Social Psychology, 44,* 127–139.

Satcher, D. (2000). Mental health: A report of the Surgeon General Executive Summary. *Professional Psychology—Research and Practice, 31*(1), 5–13.

Sato, M. (2006). Renaming schizophrenia: A Japanese perspective. *World Psychiatry, 15*(1), 53–55.

Schauer, C., Everett, A., & del Vecchio, P. (2007). Promoting the value and practice of shared decision making in mental health care. *Psychiatric Rehabilitation Journal, 31,* 54–61.

Schmidt, L. T. (2005). *Comparison of service outcomes of case management teams with and without a consumer provider.* Unpublished dissertation.

Schmidt, L. T., Gill, K. J., Pratt, C. W., & Solomon, P. (2008). Comparison of service outcomes of case management teams with and without a consumer provider. *American Journal of Psychiatric Rehabilitation, 11*(4), 310–329.

Schmieding, N. J. (1968). Institutionalization: A conceptual approach. *Perspectives in Psychiatric Care, 6*(5), 205–211.

Schmutte, T., Dunn, C. L., & Sledge, W. H. (2010). Predicting time to readmission in patients with recent histories of recurrent psychiatric hospitalization: A matched-control survival analysis. *Journal of Nervous and Mental Disease, 198*(12), 860–863.

Schonebaum, A. D., Boyd, J. K., & Dudek, K. J. (2006). A comparison of competitive employment outcomes for the Clubhouse and PACT models. *Psychiatric Services, 57*(10), 1416–1420.

Schuffman, D. (2008). *Bringing primary care and behavioral health together: The Missouri Integration Initiative.* Retrieved May 1, 2008, from http://www.openminds.com.

Schulze, K., McDonald, C., Frangou, S., Sham, P., Grech, A., Toulopoulou, T., et al. (2003). Hippocampal volume in familial and nonfamilial schizophrenic probands and their unaffected relatives. *Biological Psychiatry, 53,* 562–570.

Schwartz, D. B. (1992). *Crossing the river: Creating a conceptual revolution in community and disability.* Cambridge, MA: Brookline Books.

Sciacca, K., & Thompson, C. M. (1996). Program development and integrated treatment across systems for dual diagnosis: Mental illness, drug addiction, and alcoholism (MIDAA). *Journal of Mental Health Administration, 23*(3), 288–297.

Scott, J. (2008). *Reunification statute table*. Philadelphia, PA: UPenn Collaborative on Community Integration. Philadelphia: University of Pennsylvania.

Scott, J., & Watkins, E. (2004). Brief psychotherapies for depression: Current status. *Current Opinion in Psychiatry, 17*(1), 3–7.

Segal, S. P., Silverman, C., & Temkin, T. (1993). Empowerment and self-help agency practice for people with mental disabilities. *American Journal of Psychiatric Rehabilitation, 11*, 310–329.

Shadow voices: Finding hope in mental illness. (2005). *Mennonite Media*. http://www.shadowvoices .com/about.asp.

Shattell, M. M., Donnelly, N., Scheyett, A., & Cuddeback, G. S. (2011). Assertive community treatment and the physical health needs of persons with severe mental illness: Issues around integration of mental health and physical health. *Journal of the American Psychiatric Nurses Association, 17*, 57–63. http://dx.doi.org/10.1177/1078390310393737.

Shearman, K., Hart-Katuin, C., & Hicks. (2002, April). *Postsecondary education for persons with mental illness: Exploring needs in Indiana*. Ann Arbor, MI: Paper presented at the Supported Education Conference.

Shepherd, G. (1998). System failure? The problems of reductions in long-stay beds in the UK. *Epidemiologia e Psichiatria Sociale, 7*(2), 127–134.

Sherman, P. S., & Porter, R. (1991). Mental health consumers as case management aides. *Hospital and Community Psychiatry, 42*(5), 494–498.

Silverstone, T., McPherson, H., Hunt, N., & Romans, S. (1998). How effective is lithium in the prevention of relapse in bipolar disorder? A prospective naturalistic follow up study. *Australian and New Zealand Journal of Psychiatry, 32*(1), 61–66.

Siu, P. S. K., Tsang, H. W. H., & Bond, G. R. (2010). Non vocational outcomes for clients with severe mental illness. *Journal of Vocational Rehabilitation, 32*, 15–24.

Skiba, J. A. (2001). Reaching the door to employment: Is it really open? *Journal of Vocational Rehabilitation, 32*(1), 15–35.

Skovholt, T. M. (1974). The client as a helper: A means to promote psychological growth. *Counseling Psychologist, 43*, 58–64.

Slade, M., Amering, M., & Oades, L. (2008). Recovery: An international perspective. *Epidemiologia e Psichiatria Sociale, 17*(2), 128–137.

Smith, B. W., Dalen, J., Wiggins, K., Tooley, E., Christopher, P., & Bernard, J. (2008). The brief resilience scale: Assessing the ability to bounce back. *International Journal of Behavioural Medicine, 15*, 194–200.

Smith, M. K. (2000). Recovery from a severe psychiatric disability: Findings of a qualitative study. *Psychiatric Rehabilitation Journal, 24*(2), 149–158.

Smith, R. (1998). Rehab rounds: Implementing psychosocial rehabilitation with long-term patients in a public psychiatric hospital. *Psychiatric Services, 49*, 593–595.

Smith, R. C., & Bartholomew, T. (2006). Will hospitals recover? The implications of recovery-orientation. *American Journal of Psychiatric Rehabilitation, 9*(2), 85–100.

Smith, R. J., Jennings, J. L., & Cimino, A. (2010). Forensic continuum of care with assertive community treatment (ACT) for persons recovering from co-occurring disabilities: Long-term outcomes: Reply. *Psychiatric Rehabilitation Journal, 34*, 91–92. http://dx.doi.org/10.1037/h0094663.

Solomon, P. (1992). The efficacy of case management services for severely mentally disabled clients. *Community Mental Health Journal, 28*(3), 163–180.

Solomon, P. (2004). Peer support/peer provided services: Underlying processes, benefits and critical ingredients. *Psychiatric Rehabilitation Journal, 27*(4), 392–401.

Solomon, P., Alexander, L., & Uhl, S. (2010). The relationship of case manager's expressed emotion to client's outcomes. *Social Psychiatry and Psychiatric Epidemiology, 45,* 165–174.

Solomon, P., Cavanaugh, M., & Gelles, R. (2005). Family violence among adults with severe mental illness: A neglected area of research. *Trauma, Violence and Abuse, 6,* 40–54.

Solomon, P., & Draine, J. (1995). The efficacy of a consumer case management team: Two-year outcomes of a randomized trial. *Journal of Mental Health Administration, 22*(2), 135–146.

Solomon, P., & Draine, J. (1996). Perspectives concerning consumers as case managers. *Community Mental Health Journal, 32*(1), 41–46.

Solomon, P., & Draine, J. (2001). The state of knowledge of the effectiveness of consumer provided services. *Psychiatric Rehabilitation Journal, 25*(1), 20–27.

Solomon, P., Molinaro, M., Mannion, E., & Cantwell, K. (2012). Confidentiality policies and practices in regard to family involvement: Does training make a difference? *American Journal of Psychiatric Rehabilitation, 15*(1), 97–115.

Spagnolo, A. B., Murphy, A. A., & Librera, L. A. (2008). Reducing stigma by meeting and learning from people with mental illness. *Psychiatric Rehabilitation Journal, 31,* 186–193.

Spaniol, L. (2009). The pain and the possibility: The family recovery process. *Community Mental Health Journal, 46*(5), 482–485.

Spaniol, L., & Zipple, A. M. (1994). The family recovery process. *Journal of the California Alliance of the Mentally Ill, 5*(2), 57–59.

Spencer, C., Castle, D., & Michie, D. T. (2002). Motivations that maintain substance use among individuals with psychotic disorders. *Schizophrenia Bulletin, 28*(2), 233–247.

Spencer-Watts, R. L. (2002). Supported education turned my life around. In C. T. Mowbray, K. S. Brown, K. Furlong-Norman, & A. Sullivan-Soydan (Eds.), *Supported education and psychiatric rehabilitation: Models and methods* (pp. 99–100). Linthicum, MD: International Association of Psychosocial Rehabilitation Services.

Stanhope, V., & Dunn, K. (2011). The curious case of Housing First: The limits of evidence based policy. *International Journal of Law and Psychiatry, 34,* 275–282.

Stanhope, V., Solomon, P., Finley, L., Pernell-Arnold, A., Bourjolly, J. N., & Sands, R. G. (2008). Evaluating the impact of cultural competency trainings form the perspective of people in recovery. *American Journal of Psychiatric Rehabilitation, 11*(4), 356–372.

Stark, J. A., McGee, J. J., Menolascino, F. J., Baker, D. H., & Menousek, P. E. (1984). Treatment strategies in the habilitation of severely mentally retarded–mentally ill adolescents and adults. In F. J. Menolascino, & J. A. Stark (Eds.), *Handbook of mental illness in the mentally retarded* (pp. 189–218). New York: Plenum Press.

Starkey, D., & Leadholm, B. A. (1997). PRISM: The Psychiatric Rehabilitation Integrated Service Model – A public psychiatric hospital model for the 1990's. *Administration and Policy in Mental Health, 24,* 497–508.

Steadman, H. J., & Naples, M. (2005). Assessing the effectiveness of jail diversion programs for persons with serious mental illness and co-occurring substance use disorders. *Behavioral Sciences and the Law, 23*(2), 163–170. http://dx.doi.org/10.1002/bsl.640.

Steadman, H. J., Redlich, A., Callahan, L., Robbins, P. C., & Vesselinov, R. (2010). Effect of mental health courts on arrests and jail days: A multisite study. *Archives of General Psychiatry, 68*(2), 167–172. http://dx.doi.org/10.1001/archgenpsychiatry.2010.134.

Steele, D., Moore, R. L., Swan, N. A., Grant, J. S., & Keltner, N. L. (2012). Biological perspectives: The role of glutamate in schizophrenia and its treatment. *Perspectives in Psychiatric Care, 48,* 125–128. http://dx.doi.org/10.1111/j.1744-6163.2012.00333.x.

Stefancic, A., & Tsemberis, S. (2007). Housing First for long-term shelter dwellers with psychiatric disabilities in a suburban county: A four-year study of housing access and retention. *Journal of Primary Prevention, 28*, 265–279.

Stein, C. H., Rappaport, J., & Seidman, E. (1995). Assessing the social networks of people with psychiatric disability from multiple perspectives. *Community Mental Health Journal, 31*(4), 351–367.

Stein, L. I., & Test, M. A. (1985). The evolution of the training in community living model. *New Directions for Mental Health Services, 26*, 7–16.

Stein, L. I., Barry, K. L., Van Dien, G., Hollingsworth, E. J., & Sweeney, J. K. (1999). Work and social support: A comparison of consumers who have achieved stability in ACT and clubhouse programs. *Community Mental Health Journal, 35*(2), 193–204.

Steinberg, M. L., Ziedonis, D. M., Krejci, J. A., & Brandon, T. H. (2004). Motivational interviewing with personalized feedback: A brief intervention for motivating smokers with schizophrenia to seek treatment for tobacco dependence. *Journal of Consulting and Clinical Psychology, 72*(4), 723–728. http://dx.doi.org/10.1037/0022-006X.72.4.723.

Stern, R., & Minkoff, K. (1979). Paradoxes in programming for chronic patients in a community clinic. *Hospital and Community Psychiatry, 30*(9), 613–617.

Stodden, R. A., & Conway, M. A. (2003). Supporting individuals with disabilities in postsecondary education. *American Rehabilitation, 27*(1), 24–33.

Strassnig, M., Brar, J. S., & Ganguli, R. (2003). Nutritional assessment of patients with schizophrenia: A preliminary study. *Schizophrenia Bulletin, 29*, 393–397.

Stroul, B. (1993). Rehabilitation in community support systems. In R. Flexer, & P. Solomon (Eds.), *Psychiatric rehabilitation in practice*. Boston, MA: Andover Medical Publishers.

Stroul, B. A. (1989). Community support systems for persons with long-term mental illness: A conceptual framework. *Psychosocial Rehabilitation Journal, 12*(3), 9–26.

Styron, T. H., Pruett, M. K., McMahon, Y. J., & Davidson, L. (2002). Fathers with mental illness: A neglected group. *Psychiatric Rehabilitation Journal, 25*(3), 215–222.

Substance Abuse and Mental Health Service Administration. (2006). *SAMHSA issues consensus statement on mental health recovery*. Retrieved August 13, 2012, from http://www.samhsa.gov/news/newsreleases/060215_consumer.htm.

Substance Abuse and Mental Health Service Administration. (2008). *Examples of mental health decision aids*. Retrieved June 27, 2012, from http://www.samhsa.gov/consumersurvivor/pdf/SAMHSA_Decision_Aid_Chart_Jan08.pdf.

Substance Abuse and Mental Health Service Administration's National Registry of Evidence-based Programs and Practices. (2007). *Pathways' Housing First Program*. Retrieved January 18, 2012, from http://www.nrepp.samhsa.gov/ViewIntervention.aspx?id=155.

Substance Abuse and Mental Health Services Administration (Ed.). (2012). *Results from the 2010 national survey on drug use and health: Mental health findings* (HHS Publication No. (SMA) 11-4667 ed.). Rockville, MD: Substance Abuse and Mental Health Services Administration.

Substance Abuse and Mental Health Services Administration. (2010). *Permanent supportive housing: Evaluating your program* (Vol. HHS Pub. No. SMA-10–4509). Rockville, MD: Center for Mental Health Services, Substance Abuse and Mental Health Services Administration, US Department of Health and Human Services.

Substance Abuse and Mental Health Services Administration. (2010). *Permanent supportive housing: The evidence* (Vol. HHS Pub. No. SMA-10–4509). Rockville, MD: Center for Mental Health Services, Substance Abuse and Mental Health Services Administration, US Department of Health and Human Services.

Substance Abuse and Mental Health Services Administration. (2011). *Consumer-operated services: The evidence.* HHS Pub. No. SMA-11-4633. 2011, from http://www.oas.samhsa.gov/2k9/161/161MHSupportGroupHTML.pdf.

Sullivan, A. P., Nicolellis, D. L., Danley, K. S., & Macdonald-Wilson, K. (1993). Choose-Get-Keep: A psychiatric rehabilitation approach to supported education. *Psychosocial Rehabilitation Journal, 17*(1), 55–68.

Sullivan, G., Han, X., Moore, S., & Kotria, K. (2006). Disparities in hospitalization for diabetes among persons with and without co-occurring mental disorders. *Psychiatric Services, 57,* 1126–1131.

Sullivan, P. F., Kendler, K. S., & Nedo, M. C. (2003). Schizophrenia as a complex trait. *Archives of General Psychiatry, 60,* 1187–1192.

Sullivan-Soydan, A. (2002). An overview of supported education. In C. T. Mowbray, K. S. Brown, K. Furlong-Norman, & A. Sullivan-Soydan (Eds.), *Supported education and psychiatric rehabilitation: Models and methods* (pp. 3–10). Linthicum, MD: International Association of Psychosocial Rehabilitation Services.

Sullivan-Soydan, A. (2004). Supported education: A portrait of a psychiatric rehabilitation intervention. *American Journal of Psychiatric Rehabilitation, 7*(3), 227–248.

Swarbrick, M. (2005). *Consumer-operated self-help centers: The relationship between the social environment and its association with empowerment and satisfaction.* Unpublished dissertation.

Swarbrick, M. (2006). A wellness approach. *Psychiatric Rehabilitation Journal, 29*(4), 311–314.

Swarbrick, M. (2009). A wellness and recovery model for state psychiatric hospitals. *Occupational Therapy in Mental Health, 25,* 343–351.

Swarbrick, M. (2010). People in recovery as leaders and innovators. In M. Swarbrick, K. Gill., & L. Schmidt (Eds.), *People in recovery as providers of psychiatric rehabilitation: Building on the wisdom of experience.* Linthicum, MD: USPRA.

Swarbrick, M. (2012). *Introduction to wellness coaching.* Freehold, NJ: Collaborative Support Programs of New Jersey Inc., Institute for Wellness and Recovery Initiatives.

Swarbrick, M., Bates, F., & Roberts, M. (2010). Peer employment support model. In M. M. Swarbrick, L. Schmidt, & K. J. Gill (Eds.), *People in recovery as providers of psychiatric rehabilitation: Building on the wisdom of experience.* Linthicum, MD: USPRA.

Swarbrick, M., & Brice, G. (2006). Sharing the message of hope, wellness and recovery with consumers and staff at psychiatric hospitals. *American Journal of Psychiatric Rehabilitation, 9,* 101–109.

Swarbrick, M., Brice, G. H., & Gill, K. J. (2013). Promoting the wellness of peer providers through coaching. *Journal of Psychosocial Nursing and Mental Health Services.*

Swarbrick, M., Hutchinson, D., & Gill, K. (2008). The quest for optimal health: Can education and training cure what ails us? *International Journal of Mental Health, 37*(2), 69–88.

Swarbrick, M., Madara, E., White, B., & Schmidt, L. (2010). People in recovery as members of self-help groups. In M. Swarbrick, K. Gill., & L. Schmidt (Eds.), *People in recovery as providers of psychiatric rehabilitation. Building on the wisdom of experience.* Linthicum, MD: USPRA.

Swarbrick, M., Pratt, C., & Schmidt, L. (2009). Consumer-operated self-help centers: The impact of the social environment on member empowerment and satisfaction. *Journal of Psychosocial Nursing, 47,* 40–47.

Swarbrick, M., & Roe, D. (2011). Experiences and motives relative to psychiatric medication choice. *Psychiatric Rehabilitation Journal, 35*(1), 45–50.

Swarbrick, M., Schmidt, L., & Gill, K. (2010). *People in recovery as providers of psychiatric rehabilitation services: Building on the wisdom of experience.* Linthicum, MD: USPRA.

Swarbrick, M., Spagnolo, A., Zechner, M., Murphy, A., & Gill, K. (2011). Wellness coaching: A new role for peers. *Psychiatric Rehabilitation Journal, 34,* 328–331.

Swartz, M. S., Perkins, D. O., Stroup, T. S., Davis, S. M., Capuano, G., Rosenheck, R. A., et al. (2007). Effects of antipsychotic medications on psychosocial functioning in patients with chronic schizophrenia: Findings from the NIMH CATIE study. *American Journal of Psychiatry, 164,* 428–436. http://dx.doi.org/10.1176/appi.ajp.164.3.428.

Swartz, M. S., Swanson, J. W., Hiday, V. A., Wagner, R., Burns, B. J., & Borum, R. (2001). A randomized controlled trial of outpatient commitment in North Carolina. *Psychiatric Services, 52*(3). http://dx.doi.org/10.1176/appi.ps.52.3.325.

Szasz, T. S. (2010). *The myth of mental illness: Foundations of a theory of personal conduct.* New York: HarperPerennial.

Szymanski, L. S., King, B., Goldberg, B., Reid, A. H., Tonge, B. J., & Cain, N. (1998). Diagnosis of mental disorders in people with mental retardation. In S. R. M. G. Aman (Ed.), *Psychotropic medication and developmental disabilities: The international consensus handbook* (pp. 3–17). Columbus, OH: Nisonger Center for Mental Retardation and Developmental Disabilities.

Tabol, C., Drebing, C., & Rosenheck, R. (2010). Studies of "supported" and "supportive" housing: A comprehensive review of model descriptions and measurement. *Evaluation and Program Planning, 33,* 446–456.

Tai, S., & Turkington, D. (2009). The evolution of cognitive behavior therapy for schizophrenia: Current practice and recent developments. *Schizophrenia Bulletin, 35*(5), 865–873.

Talbott, J. A. (2004). Deinstitutionalization: Avoiding the disasters of the past. *Psychiatric Services, 55*(10), 1112–1115.

Tanzman, B. (1993). An overview of surveys of mental health consumers' preferences for housing and support services. *Hospital and Community Psychiatry, 44*(5), 450–455.

Taube, C. A. (1973). *Day care services in federally funded community mental health centers (Statistical Note No. 96).* Rockville, MD: Survey and Reports Section, Biometry Branch, National Institute of Mental Health.

Taylor, T. L., Killaspy, H., Wright, C., Turton, P., White, S., Kallert, T. W., et al. (2009). A systematic review of the international published literature relating to quality of institutional care for people with longer term mental health problems. *BMC Psychiatry, 9,* 55–84.

Teague, G. B., Bond, G. R., & Drake, R. E. (1998). Program fidelity in assertive community treatment: Development and use of a measure. *American Journal of Orthopsychiatry, 68,* 216–232.

Terkelson, K. G. (1987). The meaning of mental illness to the family. In A. B. Hatfield, & H. P. Lefley (Eds.), *Families of the mentally ill: Coping and adaptation* (pp. 128–150). New York: The Guilford Press.

Test, M. A. (1979). Continuity of care in community treatment. *New Directions for Mental Health Services, 2,* 15–23.

Test, M. A. (1992). *Training in community living. General Psychology Series: Vol. 166. Handbook of psychiatric rehabilitation.* Boston: Allyn and Bacon.

Test, M. A., & Stein. (1978). Training in community living: Research design and results. In L. I. Stein, & M. A. Test (Eds.), *Alternatives to mental health treatment.* New York: Plenum.

Texas Department of Mental Health and Mental Retardation, Research and Special Projects. (1994, January). *TXMHMR supported housing program evaluation: Year one findings.* Austin, TX: Author.

Thompson, J. L., Kelly, M., Kimhy, D., Harkavy-Friedman, J. M., Khan, S., Messinger, J. W., Schobel, S., Goetz, R., Malaspina, D., & Corcoran, C. (2009). Childhood trauma and prodromal symptoms among individuals at clinical high risk for psychosis. *Schizophrenia Research, 108,* 176–181. http://dx.doi.org/10.1016/j.schres.2008.12.005.

Thompson, J. L., Urban, N., & Abi-Dhargham, A. (2009). How have developments in molecular imaging techniques furthered schizophrenia research. *Imaging Medicine, 1*(2), 135–153.

Thornicroft, G., Rose, D., & Kassam, A. (2007). Discrimination in health care against people with mental illness. *International Review of Psychiatry, 19*(2), 113–122.

Thornicroft, G., & Tansella, M. (2004). Components of a modern mental health service: A pragmatic balance of community and hospital care: Overview of systematic evidence. *British Journal of Psychiatry, 185*(4), 283–290.

Tiihonen, J., Lönnqvist, J., Wahlbeck, K., Klaukka, T., Niskanen, L., Tanskanen, A., & Haukka, J. 11-year follow-up of mortality in patients with schizophrenia: A population-based cohort study (FIN11 study). *The Lancet, 374*(9690), 620–627. http://dx.doi.org/10.1016/S0140-6736(09)60742-X.

Toms-Barker, L. (1994). Community based models of employment services for people with long term mental illness. *Psychosocial Rehabilitation Journal, 17*(3), 55–65.

Toprac, M. G., Sherman, P. S., Holzer, C. E., et al. (1996). *Texas crisis alternatives project: Cost-effectiveness of 9 crisis residential modalities: Final report.* Houston, TX: Texas Department of Mental Health and Mental Retardation.

Torrey, E. F. (1994). *Schizophrenia and manic depressive disorder: The biological roots of mental illness as revealed by the landmark study of identical twins.* New York: Basic Books.

Torrey, E. F. (1997). *Out of the shadows: Confronting America's mental illness crisis.* New York: John Wiley and Sons.

Torrey, E. F. (2003). *Keynote address at the World Association of Psychosocial Rehabilitation Congress.* New York: Paper presented at the World Association of Psychosocial Rehabilitation Congress.

Torrey, E. F. (2006). *Surviving schizophrenia: A manual for families, patients and providers.* New York: HarperCollins.

Torrey, E. F. (2008). *The insanity offense.* New York: W. W. Norton and Co. Inc.

Torrey, W. C., Becker, D. R., & Drake, R. E. (1995). Rehabilitative day treatment vs. supported employment II: Consumer, family and staff reactions to a program change. *Psychosocial Rehabilitation Journal, 18*(3), 67–75.

Torrey, W. C., Mueser, K. T., McHugo, G. H., & Drake, R. E. (1993). Psychiatric care of adults with developmental disabilities and mental illness in the community. *Community Mental Health Journal, 29*(5), 461–473.

Torrey, W. C., Mueser, K. T., McHugo, G. H., & Drake, R. E. (2000). Self-esteem as an outcome measure in studies of vocational rehabilitation for adults with severe mental illness. *Psychiatric Services, 51*(2), 229–233.

Torrey, W. C., Drake, R. E., Dixon, L., Burns, B. J., Flynn, L., Rush, A., et al. (2001). Implementing evidence-based practices for persons with severe mental illnesses. *Psychiatric Services, 52*(1), 45–50.

Treatment Advocacy Center. (2012). *Assisted outpatient treatment - backgrounder.* Retrieved July 30, 2012, from http://www.treatmentadvocacycenter.org/resources/assisted-outpatient-treatment/about-aot/471.

Trivedi, M. H., Rush, A., Crismon, M., et al. (2004). Clinical results for patients with major depressive disorder in the Texas Medication Algorithm Project. *Archives of General Psychiatry, 61*(7), 669–680. http://dx.doi.org/10.1001/archpsyc.61.7.669.

Tsang, H. W. H., Liberman, R. P., Hilty, D. M., & Drake, R. E. (2002). Requirements for multidisciplinary teamwork in psychiatric rehabilitation: Reply. *Psychiatric Services, 53*(6), 768–769.

Tsang, H. W. H., Tam, P. K. C., Chan, F., & Chang, W. M. (2003). Sources of burdens on families of individuals with mental illness. *International Journal of Rehabilitation Research, 26*(2), 123–130.

Tsemberis, S. (2010). *Housing First: The Pathways Model to end homelessness for people with mental illness and addiction manual.* Center City, MN: Hazelden.

Tsemberis, S., & Eisenberg, R. F. (2000). Pathways to housing: Supported housing for street-dwelling homeless individuals with psychiatric disabilities. *Psychiatric Services, 51*(4), 487–493.

Tsemberis, S., Gulcur, L., & Nakae, M. (2004). Housing first, consumer choice, and harm reduction for homeless individuals with a dual diagnosis. *American Journal of Public Health, 94*(4), 651–656.

Tsemberis, S. J., Morn, L., Shinn, M., Asmussen, S. M., & Shern, D. (2003). Consumer preference programs for individuals who are homeless and have psychiatric disabilities: A drop-in center and a supported housing program. *American Journal of Community Psychology, 32*(3-4), 3045–3317.

Tsuchiya, K. J., & Takei, N. (2004). Focus on psychiatry in Japan. *British Journal of Psychiatry, 184*(1), 88–92.

Turner, J. B. (1995). Economic context and the health effects of unemployment. *Journal of Health and Social Behavior, 36*, 213–229.

Turner, J. C. (1977). Comprehensive community support systems for mentally disabled adults: Definitions, components, guiding principles. *Psychosocial Rehabilitation Journal, 1*(13), 39–47.

Twamley, E. W., Jeste, D. V., & Lehman, A. F. (2003). Vocational rehabilitation in schizophrenia and other psychotic disorders: A literature review and meta-analysis of randomized controlled trials. *Journal of Nervous and Mental Disease, 191*(8), 515–523.

Twamley, E. W., Narvaez, J. M., Becker, D. R., Bartels, S. J., & Jeste, D. V. (2008). Supported employment for middle-aged and older people with schizophrenia. *American Journal of Psychiatric Rehabilitation, 11*(1), 76–89.

Unger, K. V. (1990). Supported postsecondary education for people with mental illness. *American Rehabilitation, 14*(10), 10–14, 32–33.

Unger, K. V. (1993). Creating supported education programs utilizing existing community resources. *Psychosocial Rehabilitation Journal, 17*(1), 11–23.

Unger, K. V. (1994). Access to educational programs and its effect on employability. *Psychosocial Rehabilitation Journal, 17*(3), 117–126.

Unger, K. V. (1998). *Handbook on supported education: Providing services for students with psychiatric disabilities*. Baltimore, MD: Paul H. Brookes Publishing.

United States Psychiatric Rehabilitation Association. (2008a). *Principles of multi-cultural psychiatric rehabilitation services: Executive summary*. Retrieved June 28, 2012, from https://uspra.ipower.com/Certification/2008_Multicultural_Principles.pdf.

United States Psychiatric Rehabilitation Association. (2008b). *Principles of multicultural psychiatric rehabilitation services: Background for USPRA multicultural principles*. Retrieved June 28, 2012, from http://uspra.ipower.com/Website/MC_Principles_Background_Document.pdf.

United States Psychiatric Rehabilitation Association. (2012). *Code of ethics for certified psychiatric rehabilitation practitioners*. Retrieved March 1, 2013, from https://uspra.ipower.com/Certification/Practitioner_Code_of_Ethics.pdf.

United States Psychiatric Rehabilitation Association (USPRA), Committee for Persons in Recovery. (2007a). *Position paper on involuntary outpatient commitment*. Retrieved July 11, 2012, from http://uspra.ipower.com/Education/IOC_Position_Paper_2007.pdf.

United States Psychiatric Rehabilitation Association. (2003). *Language guidelines*. From http://www.bu.edu/cpr/prj/langguidelines.pdf.

United States Psychiatric Rehabilitation Association. (2007b). *Certification exam blue print*. Retrieved January 9, 2013, from https://uspra.ipower.com/Certification/CPRP_Exam_Blueprint_2009.pdf.

United States Psychiatric Rehabilitation Association. (2009). *Core principle and values*. Retrieved August 14, 2012, from http://uspra.ipower.com/Board/Governing_Documents/USPRA_CORE_PRINCIPLES2009.pdf.

US Department of Health and Human Services. (1995). *Assessment and treatment of patients with coexisting mental illness and alcohol and other drug abuse.* Washington, DC: Substance Abuse and Mental Health Administration.

US Department of Health and Human Services. (1999). *Mental health: A report of the surgeon general.* Rockville, MD: US Department of Health and Human Services, Substance Abuse and Mental Health Services Administration, Center for Mental Health Services, National Institutes of Health, National Institute of Mental Health.

US Department of Housing and Urban Development. (2007). *Defining chronic homelessness: A technical guide for HUD programs.*

US Department of Justice. (2011). *Statement of Department of Justice on enforcement of the integration mandate of the Title II of the Americans with Disabilities Act and Olmstead v. L.C.* Retrieved January 6, 2013, from http://www.ada.gov/olmstead/olmstead_enforcement.htm.

US Department of Labor Employment and Training Administration Workforce Investment Act. Retrieved August 7, 2012, from http://doleta.gov/usworkforce/wia/wialaw.pdf.

US House of Representatives Committee on Education and the Workforce. Retrieved August 7, 2012, from http://democrats.edworkforce.house.gov/bill/workforce-investment-act-wia-2012.

van Os, J., & Kapur, S. (2009). Schizophrenia. *Lancet, 374,* 635–645.

Van Tosh, L., & del Vecchio, P. (2000). Consumer-operated self-help programs: A technical report. DHHS Publication No. SMA 01-3510. Retrieved November 3, 2003, from http://www.mentalhealth.org/publications/ allpubs/SMA01-3510/SMA01-3510.pdf.

Van Tosh, L., Finkle, M., Hartman, B., Lewis, C., Plumlee, L. A., & Susko, M. A. (1993). *Working for a change: Employment of consumer/survivors in the design and provision of services for persons who are homeless and mentally disabled.* Rockville, MD: Center for Mental Health Services.

Van Tosh, L., Ralph, R. O., & Campbell, J. (2000). The rise of consumerism. *Psychiatric Rehabilitation Skills, 4*(3), 383–409.

Van Vugt, M. D., Kroon, H., Delespaul, P., & Mulder, C. L. (2012). Consumer-providers in assertive community treatment programs: Associations with client outcomes. *Psychiatric Services, 63,* 477–487. http://dx.doi.org/10.1176/appi.ps.201000549.

Van Winkel, R., Stefans, N. C., & Myen-Germys, I. (2008). Psychosocial stress and psychosis: A review of the neurobiological mechanisms and evidence for gene-stress interaction. *Schizophrenia Bulletin, 34*(6), 1095–1105.

Velasco, E., & Bullon, P. (1999). Periodontal status and treatment needs among Spanish hospitalized psychiatric patients. *Special Care Dentistry, 19*(6), 254–258.

Ventura, J., Green, M. F., Shaner, A., & Liberman, R. P. (1993). Training and quality assurance with brief psychiatric rating scale: "The drift busters." *American Journal of Public Health, 3*(4), 221–244.

Viguera, A. C., Baldessarini, R. J., & Friedberg, J. (1998). Discontinuing antidepressant treatment in major depression. *Harvard Review of Psychiatry, 5,* 293–306.

Vogel, H. S., Knight, E., Laudet, A. B., & Magura, S. (1998). Double trouble in recovery: Self-help for the dually-diagnosed. *Psychiatric Rehabilitation Journal, 21*(4), 356–364.

Vorspan, R. (1992). Why work works. *Psychosocial Rehabilitation Journal, 16*(2), 49–54.

Wadsworth, M. E. J., Montgomery, S. M., & Bartley, M. J. (1999). The persisting effect of unemployment on health and social well-being in men early in working life. *Social Science and Medicine, 48,* 1491–1499.

Walker, E., Kestler, L., Bollini, A., & Hochman, K. M. (2004). Schizophrenia: Etiology and course. *Annual Review of Psychology, 55,* 401–430.

Wallace, C. J., Liberman, R. P., MacKain, S. J., Blackwell, G., & Eckman, T. A. (1992). Effectiveness and replicability of modules for teaching social and independent skills to the severely mentally ill. *American Journal of Psychiatry, 149*, 654–658.

Walsh, C., MacMillan, H., & Jamieson, E. (2002). The relationship between parental psychiatric disorder and child physical and sexual abuse: Findings from the ontario health supplement. *Child Abuse and Neglect, 26*(1), 11–22.

Warner, R., Taylor, D., Powers, M., & Hyman, J. (1989). Acceptance of the mental illness label by psychotic patients: Effects on functioning. *American Journal of Orthopsychiatry, 59*(3), 398–409.

Washburn, S., Vannicelli, M., Longabaugh, R., & Scheff, B. J. (1976). A controlled comparison of psychiatric treatment and inpatient hospitalization. *Journal of Consulting and Clinical Psychology, 44*, 665–675.

Waynor, W., & Pratt, C. W. (2012). Assessing mental health and rehabilitation providers' perceptions of consumer-providers. *Occupational Therapy in Mental Health, 28*(2), 160–169.

Waynor, W. R., & Pratt, C. W. (2010). Barriers to achieving employment outcomes: Assessing assertive community treatment staff. *American Journal of Psychiatric Rehabilitation, 13*, 9–21.

Weiss, J., Maddox, D., Vanderwaerden, M., & Szilvagyi, S. (2004). The Tri-County Scholars Program: Bridging the clubhouse and community college. *American Journal of Psychiatric Rehabilitation, 7*(3), 281–300.

Weiss, R. D., Mirin, S. M., & Frances, R. J. (1992). The myth of the typical dual diagnosis patient. *Hospital and Community Psychiatry, 43*(2), 107–108.

Wells-Moran, J., & Gilmur, D. (2002). *Supported education for people with psychiatric disabilities.* Lanham, MD: University Press of America.

Whitaker, R. (2010). *Anatomy of an epidemic: Magic bullets, psychiatric drugs, and the astonishing rise of mental illness in america.* New York: Random House.

Wiersma, D., Nienhuis, F. J., Slooff, C. J., & Giel, R. (1998). Natural course of schizophrenic disorders: A 15 year follow-up of a Dutch incidence cohort. *Schizophrenia Bulletin, 24*(1), 75–85.

Wiersma, D., Wanderling, J., Dragomirecka, E., Ganev, K., Harrison, G., An Der Heiden, W., et al. (2000). Social disability in schizophrenia: Its development and prediction over 15 years in incidence cohorts in six European centres. *Psychological Medicine, 30*(5), 1155–1167.

Wilkinson, R., & Marmot, M. (2003). *Social determinants of health: The solid facts* (2nd ed.). World Health Organization.

Williams, J. M., Dwyer, M., Verna, M., Zimmermann, M. H., Gandhi, K. K., Galazyn, M., Szkodny, N., Molnar, M., Kley, R., & Steinberg, M. L. (2010). Evaluation of the CHOICES program of peer-to-peer tobacco education and advocacy. *Community Mental Health Journal, 47*(3), 243–251.

Williams, J., and Dietrich, A. (n.d.). Integrating mental and physical health care to better identify and treat depression. Retrieved November 30, 2008, from http://www.macfound.org/atf/cf/%7BB0386CE3-8B29-4162-8098-E466FB856794%7D/PRIMARYCARE.PDF

Wisdom, J. P., Bruce, K., Saedi, G. A., Weis, T., & Green, C. A. (2008). Stealing from me: Identity and recovery in personal accounts of mental illness. *Australian and New Zealand Journal of Psychiatry, 42*(6), 489–495.

Wolfensberger, W. (1983). Social role valorization: A proposed new term for the principle of normalization. *Mental Retardation, 21*(6), 235–239.

Wolfensberger, W. (1994). Social role valorization: A proposed new term for the principle of normalization. *Mental Retardation, 18*(2), 75–86.

Wong, K. K., Chiu, R., Tang, B., Mak, D., Liu, J., & Chiu, S. (2008). A randomized controlled trial of a supported employment program for persons with long-term mental illness in Hong Kong. *Psychiatric Services, 59*(1), 84–90.

Wong, Y. I., Filoromo, M., & Tennille, J. (2007). From principles to practice: A study of implementation of supported housing for psychiatric consumers. *Administration and Policy in Mental Health and Mental Health Services Research, 34,* 13–28.

Wong, Y. I., & Solomon, P. L. (2002). Community integration of persons with psychiatric disabilities in supportive independent housing: A conceptual model and methodological considerations. *Mental Health Services Research, 4*(1), 13–28.

World Health Organization (WHO). (2008). *Integrating mental health and primary care: A global perspective.* Singapore: Author.

Wray, N. R., Pergadia, M. L., Blackwood, D. H. R., Penninx, B. W. J. H., Gordon, S. D., Nyholt, D. R., et al. (2012). Genome-wide association study of major depressive disorder: New results, meta-analysis, and lessons learned. *Molecular Psychiatry, 17,* 36–48. http://dx.doi.org/10.1038/mp.2010.109.

Wright, J. H., Turkington, D., Kingdon, D. G., & Basco, M. R. (2009). *Cognitive-behavior therapy for severe mental illness.* Washington, D.C.: American Psychiatric Publishing.

Wright-Berryman, J. L., McGuire, A. B., & Salyers, M. P. (2011). A review of consumer-provided services on assertive community treatment and intensive case management teams: Implications for future research and practice. *Journal of the American Psychiatric Nurses Association, 17,* 37–44. http://dx.doi.org/10.1177/1078390310393283.

Xia, J., Merinder, L. B., & Belgamwar, M. R. (2011). Psychoeducation for schizophrenia. *Cochrane Database of Systemic Reviews, 15*(6). Jun.

Yeich, S., Mowbray, C. T., Bybee, D., & Cohen, E. (1994). The case for a "supported housing" approach: A study of consumer housing and support preferences. *Psychosocial Rehabilitation Journal, 18*(2), 75–86.

Young, S., & Ensing, D. (1999). Exploring recovery from the perspective of people with psychiatric disabilities. *Psychiatric Rehabilitation Journal, 22*(3), 219–231.

Zechner, M., Andersen, E., & Gill, K. (2013). *Evaluation of Wellness for Life (WFL).* In preparation.

Zinman, S. (1995). The legacy of Howie the Harp lives on. *National Empowerment Center Newsletter* 1–9. Spring/Summer.

Zinman, S., Harp, H. T., & Budd, S. (1987). *Reaching across.* Sacramento, CA: California Network of Mental Health Clients.

Zippay, A. (1997). Trends in siting strategies. *Community Mental Health Journal, 33*(4), 301–310.

Index

Note: Page numbers with "f" denote figures; "t" tables; "b" boxes.